EU LAW AFTER LISBON

EU Law After Lisbon

Edited by
ANDREA BIONDI
and
PIET EECKHOUT
with
STEFANIE RIPLEY

OXFORD
UNIVERSITY PRESS

OXFORD
UNIVERSITY PRESS

Great Clarendon Street, Oxford OX2 6DP

Oxford University Press is a department of the University of Oxford.
It furthers the University's objective of excellence in research, scholarship,
and education by publishing worldwide in

Oxford New York

Auckland Cape Town Dar es Salaam Hong Kong Karachi
Kuala Lumpur Madrid Melbourne Mexico City Nairobi
New Delhi Shanghai Taipei Toronto

With offices in

Argentina Austria Brazil Chile Czech Republic France Greece
Guatemala Hungary Italy Japan Poland Portugal Singapore
South Korea Switzerland Thailand Turkey Ukraine Vietnam

Oxford is a registered trade mark of Oxford University Press
in the UK and in certain other countries

Published in the United States
by Oxford University Press Inc., New York

© The several contributors, 2012

The moral rights of the authors have been asserted
Database right Oxford University Press (maker)

Crown copyright material is reproduced under Class Licence
Number C01P0000148 with the permission of OPSI
and the Queen's Printer for Scotland

First published 2012

British Library Cataloguing in Publication Data

Data available

Library of Congress Cataloging in Publication Data

Library of Congress Control Number : 2011943529

Typeset by SPI Publisher Services, Pondicherry, India
Printed in Great Britain
on acid-free paper by
CPI Group (UK) Ltd, Croydon, CR0 4YY

ISBN 978–0–19–964432–2

3 5 7 9 10 8 6 4 2

Preface

The increasing influence of European Union law is all around us. Those daily immersed in EU activities may absorb the terminology and revised Treaty paragraph numbering, become familiar with the dynamics and issues, osmotically. But others need a copy of the two, inter-dependent Treaties fashioned by the Treaty of Lisbon—the Treaty on the European Union (TEU) and the Treaty on the Functioning of the European Union (TFEU)—and, above all, a good commentary.

The present work amply satisfies this latter need. It contains a wide-ranging, well-informed and stimulating set of contributions by expert contributors. Together, they explain the origins and effect of the Treaty of Lisbon, and they bring the story up to date with an account of subsequent developments in law and thinking.

The area covered starts with the replacement of the EC and EU by the single EU with redefined competences, and the consequent (merciful) release from 'three pillar talk'. It goes on to include the relationships between different EU institutions, between the EU and national parliaments and between the EU, the Charter of Fundamental Rights, and the European Convention on Human Rights—including the implications of the EU's potential accession to the Convention. Practitioners will find particular value in the examination of the role and jurisprudence of the Court of Justice, Parliamentarians in the chapter on the evolving relationship of the European and national parliaments. Both will be interested in the discussion of subsidiarity. One notable feature of the Lisbon Treaty has been its stimulus to national parliaments to review and strengthen their own procedures for scrutinizing EU legislative proposals— an area in which even serving members of the Judicial Committee of the House of Lords once had a role, before constitutional purity intervened.

In addition to this wealth of material, there are chapters focusing on a wealth of individual topics. These include EU competence in criminal law—a sensitive field where the Court of Justice produced controversial jurisprudence before the Treaty of Lisbon, bypassing the unanimity rule of the former third pillar in a manner which Treaty subscribers had probably never envisaged; the position is undoubtedly improved under the new Treaties, although the relevant chapter shows there may still, unhappily, be unresolved issues here about the possibility of different bases of EU criminal law competence outside the conventional basis of the provisions on Freedom, Security and Justice. Other important areas addressed include the Common Foreign and Security Policy (CSFP), the Common Commercial Policy, Energy and Competition Policy.

The contributors and editors are to be congratulated on combining to produce so accessible, penetrating and up to date a compilation, which it is a pleasure both to introduce and to commend.

October 2011   Lord Mance

Contents

Table of Cases ix
Table of Treaties and Legislation xviii
List of Abbreviations xxix
List of Contributors xxxi

I. CONSTITUTIONAL FRAMEWORK

1. From Laeken to Lisbon: The Origins and Negotiation
of the Lisbon Treaty 3
Paul Berman

2. The Two (or Three) Treaty Solution: The New Treaty Structure
of the EU 40
Marise Cremona

3. Lawmaking after Lisbon 62
Alexander H Türk

4. Does the Lisbon Treaty Provide a Clearer Separation of Competences
between EU and Member States? 85
Lucia Serena Rossi

5. Treaty Revision Procedures after Lisbon 107
Bruno De Witte

6. 'Don't Mention Divorce at the Wedding, Darling!': EU Accession
and Withdrawal after Lisbon 128
Allan F Tatham

7. The Charter of Fundamental Rights 155
David Anderson and Cian C Murphy

8. Accession to the ECHR 180
Giorgio Gaja

II. INSTITUTIONAL FRAMEWORK

9. The Lisbon Treaty and the Court of Justice 197
Francis G Jacobs

10. Subsidiarity in the Courtroom 213
Andrea Biondi

11. The European Union after the Lisbon Treaty: An Elusive
'Institutional Balance'? 228
Thomas Christiansen

12. The Evolving Roles of the European Parliament and of
National Parliaments 248
Richard Corbett

III. EXTERNAL RELATIONS

13. The EU's Common Foreign and Security Policy after Lisbon:
From Pillar Talk to Constitutionalism   265
Piet Eeckhout

14. The Reform of the Common Commercial Policy   292
Markus Krajewski

15. Towards an EU Policy on Foreign Direct Investment   312
Federico Ortino and Piet Eeckhout

IV. EU POLICIES

16. EU Competence in Criminal Law after Lisbon   331
Ester Herlin-Karnell

17. Writing Straight with Crooked Lines: Competition Policy
and Services of General Economic Interest in the Treaty of Lisbon   347
José Luis Buendia Sierra

18. Energy Policy after Lisbon   367
Leigh Hancher and Francesco Maria Salerno

19. EU Sports Law: The Effect of the Lisbon Treaty   403
Stephen Weatherill

Index   421

Table of Cases

EUROPEAN UNION
Court of Justice of the European Union

Alphabetical List

Albany International (Case C-67/96) [1999] ECR I-5751 418
Altmark (Case C-280/00) [2003] ECR I-7747 363
Akzo Nobel Chemicals (Case C-550/07) (ECJ (Grand Chamber), 14 September 2010) 99
André Rossius v État Belge (Case C-267/10) [2010] C 221/22. 171
Arduino (Case C-35/99) [2002] ECR I-1529 357
Arnold Andre and Swedish Match (Cases C-43/02 and C-210/03) [2004] ECR I-11825 . . . 227
Atlanta v Council and Commission (Case C-104/97 P) [1999] ECR I6983. 78
Bernard (Case C-325/08) [2010] ECR I-2177 . . . . .416, 418
Bertelsmann and Sony Corp of America v Impala (Case C-413/06 P) [2008] ECR I-4951. . . 225
BNIC v Clair (Case 123/83) [1985] ECR. 391 356
Booker Aquaculture v Scottish Minister (Cases C-20/00 and C-64/00) [2003] ECR I-7411 . . 320
Bosman (Case C-415/93) [1995] ECR I-4921 . . . . .404, 405, 406, 407, 410, 417
Brasserie du Pêcheur SA v Germany and R v Secretary of State for Transport ex p Factortame Ltd (Case
    C-48/93) [1996] ECR I-1029. 53
Carpenter (Case C-60/00) [2002] ECR I-6279 . . . . 165, 174, 176
Central-Import Münster (Case 291/86) [1988] ECR 3679. 79
Chemiefarma v Commission (Case 41/69) [1970] ECR 661 78
CIF (Case 198/01) [2003] ECR I-8055. 357
Commission v Austria (Case C-205/06) [2009] ECR I-1301. 396
Commission v Council (AETR) (Case 22/70) [1971] ECR 263 89, 299, 305, 316, 317
Commission v Council (Case 45/86) [1987] ECR 1493 .87
Commission v Council (Case C-300/89) (Titanium oxide) [1991] ECR I-2867. 58, 276, 340, 343
Commission v Council (Case C-170/96) (Airport Transit Visas) [1998] ECR I-2763 270
Commission v Council (Case C-281/01) (Energy Star Agreement) [2002] ECR I-12049 . . . 394
Commission v Council (Case C-94/03) [2006] ECR I-1. . . . . 56, 58
Commission v Council (Case C-176/03) (Environmental Penalties) [2005] ECR I-7879 63,
                                        270, 331, 332, 333, 339, 342, 343, 346
Commission v Council (Case C-91/05) (SALW) [2008] ECR I-3651 . . . . .55, 56,
                                        57, 63, 270, 271, 272, 273, 274, 275
Commission v Council (Case C-440/05) (Shipsource Pollution) [2007] ECR I-9097 63,
                                        87, 270, 333
Commission v Denmark (Case C-467/98) (Open Skies) [2002] ECR I-9519 . . . . 316, 318, 397
Commission v Finland (Case C-118/07) [2009] ECR I-10889. 396
Commission v Germany (Case C-476/98) [2002] ECR I-9855. 397
Commission v Germany (Case C-518/07) [2010] ECR I-1885. 217
Commission v Ireland (Case C-459/03) [2006] ECR I-4635. 189
Commission v Ireland (Case C-507/03) [2007] ECR I-9777. 400
Commission v Parliament and Council (Case C-178/03) [2006] ECR I-107 . . . . . 58, 88, 383
Commission v Parliament and Council (Case C-122/04) [2006] ECR I-2001. 75
Commission v Portugal (Case C-171/08) (ECJ (First Chamber), 8 July 2010) 315
Commission v Scott (Case C-290/07 P) [2010] OJ C 288/6. 225
Commission v Spain (Case C-313/89) [1991] ECR I-5231 109

Commission v Sweden (Case C-249/06) [2009] ECR I-1335 396
Commission v Tetra Laval (Case C-12/03 P) [2005] ECR I-987 225
Common Market Fertilizers v Commission (Case C-443/05) [2007] ECR I-7209 66
Cornelius Kramer (Cases 3, 4 and 6/76) [1976] ECR 1279 88
Costa v ENEL (Case 6/64) [1964] ECR 585 142
Courage v Crehan (Case C-453/99) [2001] ECR I-6297 418
Cullet (Case 231/83) [1985] ECR 307 356
Defrenne v SABENA (Case 43/75) [1976] ECR 480 136
Deliége v Ligue de Judo (Cases C-51/96 and C-191/97) [2000] ECR I-2549 . . . . 405, 406, 410
Demirel (Case 12/86) [1987] ECR 3719 46
Einfuhrstelle v Köster (Case 25/70) [1970] ECR 1161 . . . . 63, 66, 78, 79
ERT (Case C-260/89) [1991] ECR I-2925 164
Fearon (Case 182/83) [1984] ECR 3677 319
Federutility (Case 265/08) [2010] ECR I-3377 . . . . 392, 400, 401
Francovich & Bonifaci v Italy (Cases C-6/90 and C-9/90) [1991] ECR I-5357 53
Germany v Commission (Case C-240/90) [1992] ECR I-5383 . . . . 78, 342
Germany v Council and European Parliament (Case 376/98) [2000] ECR I-8419 . . 56, 216, 227
Germany v European Parliament and Council (Case C-233/94) [1997] ECR I-2405 . 96, 219, 220
Germany v European Parliament (Case C-380/03) (Tobacco Advertising II) [2006]
    ECR I-11573 . . . . 227, 343
GlaxoSmithKline Services Unlimited v Spain (Cases C-501/06 P, C-513/06 P, C-515/06 P
    and C-519/06 P) [2009] ECR I-9291 360
Government of the French Community and Walloon Government (Case C-212/06) [2008]
    ECR I-1683 223
Grad (Case 9/70) [1970] ECR 825 52
Inno v ATAB (Case 13/77) [1977] ECR 2144 356
International Transport Workers' Federation v Viking Line ABP (Case C-438/05) [2007] ECR
    I-10779 . . . . 169, 176, 419
Internationale Handelsgesellschaft (Case 11/70) [1970] ECR 1125 161
Ireland v European Parliament and Council (Case C-301/06) [2009] ECR I-593 . . . . . 334, 340
Johnston (Case 222/84) [1986] ECR 1651 201
Josemans (Case C-137/09) (ECJ (Second Chamber), 16 December 2010) 224
Karlsson (Case C-292/97) [2000] ECR I-2737 164
Karner (Case C-71/02) [2004] ECR I-3025 165
Konle (Case C-302/97) [1999] ECR I-3099 319
Kücükdeveci v Swedex GmbH & Co (Case C-555/07) [2010] ECR I-365 173
LAISA v Council (Cases 31–5/86) [1988] ECR 2285 136
Leclerc v Au Blé Vert (Case 229/83) [1985] ECR 1 356
Lehtonen (Case C-176/96) [2000] ECR I-2681 . . . . 406, 416
Lélos (Cases C-468 to 478/06) [2008] ECR I-7139 360
Lindquist (Case C-101/01) [2003] ECR I-12971 343
Les Verts v European Parliament (Case 294/83) [1986] ECR 1339 281
Meca-Medina and Majcen v Commission (Case C-519/04 P) [2006] ECR I-6991 406,
                                                                            408, 409
Meng (Case C-2/91) [1993] ECR I-5797 357
Meroni v ECSC High Authority (Cases 9, 10/56) [1957/8] ECR Spec Ed 133 63,
                                                                        82, 83, 379, 380
Metallurgiki Halyps AE v Commission (Case 258/81) [1982] ECR 4261 136
Metro v Commission (Case 26/76) [1977] ECR 1875 359
Netherlands v European Parliament and Council (Case C-377/98) [2001] ECR I7079 96,
                                                                            217, 226
Nouvelles Frontiéres (Cases 209 to 213/84) [1986] ECR 1425 356
NS v Secretary of State for the Home Department (Case C-411/10) [2010] OJ C 274/34 . . . 170

Ohra (Case C-245/91) [1993] ECR I-5878 357
Olivier Roujansky v Council (Case C-235/94 P) [1995] ECR I-7 109
Omega (Case C-36/02) [2004] ECR I-9609 224
Ordre des barreaux francophones et germanophone (Case C-305/05) [2007] ECR I-5305 . . . 172
Ospelt v Schlössle Weissenberg Familienstiftung (Case C-452/01) [2003] ECR I-9743 319
Parliament v Council (Case 70/88) [1990] ECR I-12041 103
Parliament v Council (Case C-540/03) [2006] ECR I-5769 . . . . 157, 172
Parliament v Council (Case C-155/07) [2008] ECR I-8103 58
Parliament v Council (Case C-166/07) (International Fund for Ireland) [2009] ECR I-7135. . 276
Parliament v Council (Case C-130/10) 57
Placanica (Cases C-359/04 to C-360/04) [2007] ECR I-1891 224
Portugal v Commission (Case C-88/03) [2006] ECR I-7115. 22
Pupino (Case C-105/03) [2005] ECR I-5285 49
Queen, The v Secretary of State for Health, ex parte British American Tobacco (Investments) Ltd
    and Imperial Tobacco Ltd (Case C-491/01) [2002] I-11453. . . . . .96, 216, 217
Queen, The (on the Application of Alliance for Natural Health and Nutri-link Ltd) v Secretary of
    State for Health and The Queen (on the Application of National Association of Health Stores
    and Health Food Manufacturers Ltd v Secretary of State for Health and National Assembly
    for Wales (Cases C-154/04 and C-155/04) [2005] ECR I-6451 . . . . 96, 380
Queen, The (on the application of Vodafone Ltd) v Secretary of State for Business, Enterprise and
    Regulatory Reform (Case C-58/08) (Opinion of Maduro A-G, 1 October 2009) . . . 218, 219
Queen, The (on the application of Vodafone Ltd) v Secretary of State for Business, Enterprise
    and Regulatory Reform (Case C-58/08) (ECJ (Grand Chamber), 8 June 2010). . .96, 218, 344
R v Kent Kirk (Case 63/83) [1984] ECR 2689 162
Reiff (Case C-185/91) [1993] ECR I-5847 357
Rundfunk (Cases 465/00, C-138/01 and C-139/01) [2003] ECR I-4989. 343
Segi v Council (Case C-355/04 P) [2007] ECR I-1657 . . . . 53, 282, 284
Showa Denko (Case C-289/04 P) [2006] ECR I-5859 351
Simmenthal (Case 106/77) [1978] ECR 629 53
Spain v Council (Case C-350/92) [1995] ECR I-1985. . . . . 319, 320
Spain v Lenzing (Case C-525/04) [2007] ECR I-9947. 225
SPUC v Grogan (Case C-159/90) [1991] ECR I-4685 177
Stauder v City of Ulm (Case 29/69) [1969] ECR 419 161
Swedish Match (Case C-210/03) [2004] ECR I-11893 343
Syfait (Case C-53/03) [2005] ECR I-4609 . . . . 360, 361
Test Claimants in the FII Group Litigation (Case C-446/04) [2006] ECR I-11753 314
TNT Traco (Case C-340/99) [2001] ECR I-4112 172
Tralli v ECB (Case C-301/02) [2005] ECR I-4071 379
UGT-Rioja (Cases C-428/06 to C-434/06) [2008] ECR I-6747 223
United Kingdom v Council (Case C-84/94) [1996] ECR I-5755. 96
United Kingdom v Parliament and Council (Case C-66/04) [2005] ECR I-10553 78
United Kingdom v Parliament and Council (Case C-217/04) [2006] ECR I-3771 379
Unión de Pequenós Agricultores v Council (UPA) (Case C-50/00 P) [2002] ECR I-6677 . 53, 200
Van Eycke (Case 267/86) [1988] ECR 4769 356
Vlaamse Reisbureaus (Case 311/85) [1987] ECR 3801 356
Wachauf (Case 5/88) [1989] ECR 2609 164
Walrave and Koch (Case 36/74) [1974] ECR 1405 . . . . 404, 416, 418
Wouters (Case C-309/99) [2002] ECR I-1577 357
Yasim Abdullah Kadi and Al Barakaat International Foundation v Council and Commission (Case
    C-402/05 P and Case C-415/05 P) [2008] ECR I-6351 . . . . 55, 104, 201, 276, 281, 342
Zambrano v Office national de l'emploi (Case C-34/09) (Opinion of Sharpston A-G,
    30 September 2010) 165, 174, 179
Zuckerfabrik Franken v Hauptzollamt Würzburg (Case 121/83) [1984] ECR 2039 66

Numerical List

Cases 9, 10/56 Meroni v ECSC High Authority [1957/8] ECR Spec Ed 133 . . . . .63, 82,
  83, 379, 380
Case 6/64 Costa v ENEL [1964] ECR 585 142
Case 29/69 Stauder v City of Ulm [1969] ECR 419 161
Case 41/69 Chemiefarma v Commission [1970] ECR 661 78
Case 9/70 Grad [1970] ECR 825 52
Case 11/70 Internationale Handelsgesellschaft [1970] ECR 1125 161
Case 22/70 Commission v Council (AETR) [1971] ECR 263 . . . . . . 89, 299, 305, 316, 317
Case 25/70 Einfuhrstelle v Köster [1970] ECR 1161 . . . . 63, 66, 78, 79
Case 36/74 Walrave and Koch [1974] ECR 1405 . . . . 404, 416, 418
Case 43/75 Defrenne v SABENA [1976] ECR 480 136
Cases 3, 4 and 6/76 Cornelius Kramer [1976] ECR 1279 88
Case 26/76 Metro v Commission [1977] ECR 1875 359
Case 13/77 Inno v ATAB [1977] ECR 2144 356
Case 106/77 Simmenthal [1978] ECR 629 53
Case 258/81 Metallurgiki Halyps AE v Commission [1982] ECR 4261 136
Case 63/83 R v Kent Kirk [1984] ECR 2689 162
Case 121/83 Zuckerfabrik Franken v Hauptzollamt Würzburg [1984] ECR 2039 66
Case 123/83 BNIC v Clair [1985] ECR 391 356
Case 182/83 Fearon [1984] ECR 3677 319
Case 229/83 Leclerc v Au Blé Vert [1985] ECR 1 356
Case 231/83 Cullet [1985] ECR 307 356
Case 294/83 Les Verts v European Parliament [1986] ECR 1339 281
Cases 209 to 213/84 Nouvelles Frontiéres [1986] ECR 1425 356
Case 222/84 Johnston [1986] ECR 1651 201
Cases 311/85 Vlaamse Reisbureaus [1987] ECR 3801 356
Case 12/86 Demirel [1987] ECR 3719 46
Cases 31–5/86 LAISA v Council [1988] ECR 2285 136
Case 45/86 Commission v Council [1987] ECR 1493 87
Case 267/86 Van Eycke [1988] ECR 4769 356
Case 291/86 Central-Import Münster [1988] ECR 3679 79
Case 5/88 Wachauf [1989] ECR 2609 164
Case 70/88 Parliament v Council [1990] ECR I-12041 103
Case C-260/89 ERT [1991] ECR I-2925 164
Case C-300/89 Commission v Council (Titanium oxide) [1991] ECR I-2867 . . . . . . 58, 276,
  340, 343
Case C-313/89 Commission v Spain [1991] ECR I-5231 109
Cases C-6/90 and C-9/90 Francovich & Bonifaci v Italy [1991] ECR I-5357 53
Case C-159/90 SPUC v Grogan [1991] ECR I-4685 177
Case C-240/90 Germany v Commission [1992] ECR I-5383 . . . . 78, 342
Case C-2/91 Meng [1993] ECR I-5797 357
Case C-185/91 Reiff [1993] ECR I-5847 357
Case C-245/91 Ohra [1993] ECR I-5878 357
Case C-350/92 Spain v Council [1995] ECR I-1985 . . . . 319, 320
Case C-48/93 Brasserie du Pêcheur SA v Germany and R v Secretary of State for Transport
  ex p Factortame Ltd [1996] ECR I-1029 53
Case C-415/93 Bosman [1995] ECR I-4921 . . . . 404, 405, 406, 407, 410, 417
Case C-84/94 United Kingdom v Council [1996] ECR I-5755 96
Case C-233/94 Germany v European Parliament and Council [1997] ECR I-2405 . . 96, 219, 220
Case C-235/94 P Olivier Roujansky v Council [1995] ECR I-7 109
Case C-51/96 and C-191/97 Deliége v Ligue de Judo [2000] ECR I-2549 . . . . . 405, 406, 410

Case C-67/96 Albany International [1999] ECR I-5751 418
Case C-170/96 Commission v Council (Airport Transit Visas) [1998] ECR I-2763 270
Case C-176/96 Lehtonen [2000] ECR I-2681 . . . . 406, 416
Case C-104/97 P Atlanta v Council and Commission [1999] ECR I-6983 78
Case C-292/97 Karlsson [2000] ECR I-2737 164
Case C-302/97 Konle [1999] ECR I-3099 319
Case 376/98 Germany v Council and European Parliament [2000] ECR I-8419 . . . 56, 216, 227
Case C-377/98 Netherlands v European Parliament and Council [2001] ECR I-7079 96,
217, 226
Case C-467/98 Commission v Denmark (Open Skies) [2002] ECR I-9519 . . . . . 316, 318, 397
Case C-476/98 Commission v Germany [2002] ECR I-9855 397
Case C-35/99 Arduino [2002] ECR I-1529 357
Case C-309/99 Wouters [2002] ECR I-1577 357
Case C-340/99 TNT Traco [2001] ECR I-4112 172
Case C-453/99 Courage v Crehan [2001] ECR I-6297 418
Cases C-20/00 and C-64/00 Booker Aquaculture v Scottish Minister [2003]
ECR I-7411 320
Case C-50/00 P Unión de Pequenós Agricultores v Council (UPA) [2002] ECR I-6677 . . 53, 200
Case C-60/00 Carpenter [2002] ECR I-6279 . . . . 165, 174, 176
Case C-280/00 Altmark [2003] ECR I-7747 363
Cases 465/00, C-138/01 and C-139/01 Rundfunk [2003] ECR I-4989 343
Case C-101/01 Lindquist [2003] ECR I-12971 343
Case 198/01 CIF [2003] ECR I-8055 357
Case C-281/01 Commission v Council (Energy Star Agreement) [2002] ECR I-12049 394
Case C-452/01 Ospelt v Schlössle Weissenberg Familienstiftung [2003] ECR I-9743 319
Case C-491/01 The Queen v Secretary of State for Health, ex parte British American Tobacco
(Investments) Ltd and Imperial Tobacco Ltd [2002] ECR I-11453 . . . . 96, 216, 217
Case C-36/02 Omega [2004] ECR I-9609 224
Case C-71/02 Karner [2004] ECR I-3025 165
Case C-301/02 Tralli v ECB [2005] ECR I-4071 379
Cases C-43/02 and C-210/03 Arnold Andre and Swedish Match [2004] ECR I-11825 227
Case C-12/03 P Commission v Tetra Laval [2005] ECR I-987 225
Case C-53/03 Syfait [2005] ECR I-4609 . . . . .360, 361
Case C-88/03 Portugal v Commission [2006] ECR I-7115 223
Case C-94/03 Commission v Council [2006] ECR I-1 . . . . 56, 58
Case C-105/03 Pupino [2005] ECR I-5285 49
Case C-176/03 Commission v Council (Environmental Penalties) [2005] ECR I-7879 63,
270, 331, 332, 333, 339, 342, 343, 346
Case C-178/3 Commission v Parliament and Council [2006] ECR I-107 . . . . 58, 88, 383
Case C-210/03 Swedish Match [2004] ECR I-11893 343
Case C-380/03 Germany v European Parliament (Tobacco Advertising II) [2006]
ECR I-11573 . . . . .227, 343
Case C-459/03 Commission v Ireland [2006] ECR I-4635 189
Case C-507/03 Commission v Ireland [2007] ECR I-9777 400
Case C-540/03 Parliament v Council [2006] ECR I-5769 . . . . .157, 172
Case C-66/04 United Kingdom v European Parliament and Council [2005] ECR I-10553 . . . 78
Case C-122/04 Commission v European Parliament and Council [2006] ECR I-2001 75
Cases C-154/04 and C-155/04 The Queen (on the Application of Alliance for Natural Health
and Nutri-link Ltd) v Secretary of State for Health and The Queen (on the Application of
National Association of Health Stores and Health Food Manufacturers Ltd) v Secretary of
State for Health and National Assembly for Wales [2005] ECR I-6451 . . . . 96, 380
Case C-217/04 United Kingdom v Parliament and Council [2006] ECR I-3771 379
Case C-289/04 P Showa Denko [2006] ECR I-5859 351

Case C-355/04 P Segi v Council [2007] ECR II-1657. . . . . 53, 282, 284
Cases C-359/04 to C-360/04 Placanica [2007] ECR I-1891 224
Case C-446/04 Test Claimants in the FII Group Litigation [2006] ECR I-11753. 314
Case C-519/04 P Meca-Medina and Majcen v Commission [2006] ECR I-6991 . . 406, 408, 409
Case C-525/04 Spain v Lenzing [2007] ECR I-9947 225
Case C-91/05 Commission v Council (SALW) [2008] ECR I-3651 . . . . 55, 56, 57,
                                                              63, 270, 271, 272, 273, 274, 275
Case C-438/05 International Transport Workers' Federation v Viking Line ABP [2007]
    ECR I-10779 . . . . 171, 176, 419
Case C-305/05 Ordre des barreaux francophones et germanophone [2007] ECR I-5305. . . . 172
Case C-402/05 P and Case C-415/05 P Yasim Abdullah Kadi and Al Barakaat International
    Foundation v Council and Commission [2008] ECR I-6351 . . . . 55, 104,
                                                              201, 276, 281, 342
Case C-440/05 Commission v Council (Shipsource Pollution) [2007] ECR I-9097 63,
                                                              87, 270, 333
Case C-443/05 Common Market Fertilizers v Commission [2007] ECR I-7209 66
Case C-205/06 Commission v Austria [2009] ECR I-1301 396
Case C-212/06 Government of the French Community and Walloon Government [2008] ECR
    I-1683. 223
Case C-249/06 Commission v Sweden [2009] ECR I-1335 396
Case C-301/06 Ireland v European Parliament and Council [2009] ECR I-593. . . . . . .334, 340
Case C-413/06 P Bertelsmann and Sony Corp of America v Impala [2008] ECR I-4951 . . . 225
Cases C-428/06 to C-434/06 UGT-Rioja [2008] ECR I-6747. 223
Cases C-468 to 478/06 Lélos [2008] ECR I-7139. 360
Cases C-501/06 P, C-513/06 P, C-515/06 P and C-519/06 P GlaxoSmithKline Services
    Unlimited v Spain [2009] ECR I-9291 360
Case C-118/07 Commission v Finland [2009] ECR I-10889 396
Case C-155/07 European Parliament v Council [2008] ECR I-08103 58
Case C-166/07 European Parliament v Council (International Fund for Ireland) [2009]
    ECR I-7135 276
Case C-290/07 P Commission v Scott [2010] OJ C 288/6 225
Case C-518/07 Commission v Germany [2010] ECR I-1885 217
Case C-550/07 Akzo Nobel Chemicals (ECJ (Grand Chamber), 14 September 2010) 99
Case C-555/07 Kücükdeveci v Swedex GmbH & Co [2010] ECR I-365 173
Case C-58/08 The Queen (on the application of Vodafone Ltd) v Secretary of State for
    Business, Enterprise and Regulatory Reform (Opinion of Advocate General Maduro,
    1 October 2009) 218, 219
Case C-58/08 The Queen (on the application of Vodafone Ltd) v Secretary of State for Business,
    Enterprise and Regulatory Reform (ECJ (Grand Chamber), 8 June 2010) 96, 218, 344
Case C-171/08 Commission v Portugal (ECJ (First Chamber), 8 July 2010) 315
Case C-254/08 Futura [2009] ECR I-6995. 398
Case 265/08 Federutility [2010] ECR I-3377. . . . . 392, 400, 401
Case C-325/08 Bernard [2010] ECR I-2177 . . . . .416, 418
Case C-34/09 Zambrano v Office national de l'emploi (Opinion of Sharpston A-G,
    30 September 2010) 165, 174, 179
Case C-137/09 Josemans (ECJ (Second Chamber), 16 December 2010) 224
Case C-130/10 European Parliament v Council (not yet reported) 57
Case C-267/10 André Rossius v État Belge [2010] C 221/22 171
Case C-411/10 NS v Secretary of State for the Home Department [2010] C 274/34 170
Opinion 1/75 Understanding on a Local Costs Standard [1975] ECR 1355 . . . . . . 293, 298,
                                                              305, 319
Opinion 1/76 laying-up fund for inland waterway vessels [1977] ECR 741 . . . 299, 316, 318, 397
Opinion 1/94 WTO [1994] ECR I-5267. 316

Opinion 1/94 WTO [1994] ECR I-5416. . . . . 299, 397
Opinion 2/91 ILO Convention No 170 [1993] ECR I-1061 316
Opinion 2/94 on the Accession by the Community to the ECHR [1996] ECR I-1759 155,
                                                                                 181, 342
Opinion 2/00 Cartegena Protocol [2001] ECR I-9713 394
Opinion 1/03 Lugano Convention [2006] ECR I-1145 316

GENERAL COURT

Alphabetical List

Afrikanische Frucht-Compagnie GmbH v Council and Commission (Cases T-64/01 and T-65/01)
    [2005] ECR II-521. 78
Alpharma v Council (Case T-70/99) [2002] ECR II-3495. 225
Comunidad Autonoma de Galicia v Commission (Case T-520/10) (case pending). 392
Endesa v Commission (Case T-490/10) (case pending) 392
FMC Chemical v EFSA (Case T-311/06) [2008] ECR II-88. 379
Gas Natural v Commission (Case T-484/10) (case pending) 392
Gibraltar v Commission (Case T-221/04) [2008] ECR II-3745 223
Iberola v Commission (Case T-486/10) (case pending) 392
Kadi (Case T-315/01) [2005] ECR II-3649. 55
max.mobil v Commission (Case T-54/99) [2002] ECR II-313. 172
Meca-Medina and Majcen v Commission (Case T-313/02) [2004] ECR II-3291 407
Pfizer Animal Health v Council (Case T-13/99) [2002] ECR II-3305 225
Poland v Commission (Cases T-183/07 and T-263/07) [2009] ECR II-3395. 225
Schräder v Community Plant Variety Office (Case T-187/06) [2008] ECR II-3151. 83
Solvay Pharmaceuticals v Council (Case T-392/02) [2003] ECR II-4555. 235
X v ECB (Case T-333/99) [2001] ECR II-3021. 379

Numerical List

Case T-13/99 Pfizer Animal Health v Council [2002] ECR II-3305 225
Case T-333/99 X v ECB [2001] ECR II-3021 379
Case T-54/99 max.mobil v Commission [2002] ECR II-313. 172
Case T-70/99 Alpharma v Council [2002] ECR II-3495. 225
Cases T-64/01 and T-65/01 Afrikanische Frucht-Compagnie GmbH v Council and
    Commission [2005] ECR II-521 78
Case T-315/01 Kadi [2005] ECR II-3649 55
Case T-313/02 Meca-Medina and Majcen v Commission [2004] ECR II-3291. 407
Case T-392/02 Solvay Pharmaceuticals v Council [2003] ECR II-4555. 235
Case T-221/04 Gibraltar v Commission [2008] ECR II-3745 223
Case T-187/06 Schräder v Community Plant Variety Office [2008] ECR II-3151. 83
Case T-311/06 FMC Chemical v EFSA [2008] ECR II-88 379
Cases T-183/07 and T-263/07 Poland v Commission [2009] ECR II-3395. 225
Case T-484/10 Gas Natural v Commission (case pending). 392
Case T-486/10 Iberola v Commission (case pending) 392
Case T-490/10 Endesa v Commission (case pending) 392
Case T-520/10 Comunidad Autonoma de Galicia v Commission (case pending) 392

COMMISSION DECISIONS

Application of Article 86(2) of the EC Treaty to State aid in the form of public service
  compensation (etc) Commission Decision 2005/842/EC [2005] OJ L312/67 363
Champions League Commission Decision 2003/778/EC [2003] OJ L291/25. 410
Conseil Européen de la Construction d'Appareils Domestiques (CECED) (Case IV.F.1/36.718)
  [2000] OJ L187/47. . . . . .388, 389

COMPETITION CASES

Austria – stranded costs compensation (Case N 34/99) [2002] OJ C 5/2 390
Ireland – public service obligations imposed on the Electricity Supply Board with respect to the
  generation of electricity out of peat (Case N 6/A/2001) [2002] OJ C 77/27 390
Slovenia – electricity tariffs (Case 7/2005) [2007] OJ L 219/9 . . . . .390, 391
Spain – costs of transition to competition (Case NN 49/99) [2001] OJ C 268/7 390
Spain – public service compensation linked to a preferential dispatch mechanism for indigenous
  coal power plants (Case N 178/2010) (unreported). 390, 391, 392

INTERNATIONAL COURTS

European Court of Human Rights

Bosphorus v Ireland (2006) 43 EHRR 1 . . . . 177, 182, 190, 192, 205
Cantoni v France ECHR Reports 1996-V 1614. 192
Cyrprus v Turkey App no 2578/94 (1996) 86-A DR 104 191
Eskelinen v Finland (2007) 45 EHRR 43. 175
Fretté v France (2002) 38 EHRR 438 175
Golder v United Kingdom (1975) Series A No 18. 201
Goodwin v United Kingdom (2002) 35 EHRR 18 175
Guzzardi v Italy (1980) Series A No 39. 192
Hatton v United Kingdom (2002) 34 EHRR1 175
I v United Kingdom (2003) 36 EHRR 53 175,. 176
Kokkelvisserij v The Netherlands App no 13645/05. 188
Le Petit v United Kingdom App no 33574/97 (ECtHR (Fourth Section), 15 June 2004) . . . 177
Martinie v France (2006) 40 EHRR 15. 177
Matthews v United Kingdom ECHR 1999-I 251 .180, 206
Neulinger and Shuruk v Switzerland (ECtHR (Grand Chamber), 6 July 2010) 175
Schalk and Kopf v Austria (ECtHR (First Section), 24 June 2010) 176
Scoppola v Italy (No 2) (ECtHR (Grand Chamber), 17 September 2009) 176, 177
VO v France (2005) 40 EHRR 15 177
X v Germany (1984) 7 EHRR 153. 177
Zaprianov v Bulgaria (ECtHR (First Section), 6 March 2003) 177

European Commission on Human Rights

Confédération Française Démocratique de Travail v European Communities (1978)
  13 DR 231. 180

NATIONAL COURTS

Germany

Brunner v European Union Treaty [1994] CMLR 57 . . . . 7, 32, 148
General Public Prosecution Services v C 1 Ausl (24) 1246/2010 (OLG (Stuttgart)) 171

Ireland

Crotty v An Taoiseach [1987] IESC 4, [1987] IR 713 (Irish SCt) 18

United Kingdom

R (Derwin and others) v Attorney General [2007] QB 305 (CA), [2008] 1 AC 719 (HL) . . . 165
R (NS) v Secretary of State for the Home Department [2010] EWCA Civ 990 . . . . . . 170, 171
R (S) v Secretary of State for the Home Department [2010] EWHC 705 Admin 170, 171
R (Wheeler) v Office of the Prime Minister and the Secretary of State for Foreign and
    Commonwealth Affairs [2008] All ER (D) 333. 31
R (Zagorski) v Secretary of State for Business, Innovation and Skills [2010] EWHC 3110
    (Admin) 165, 170, 171

Table of Treaties and Legislation

EUROPEAN UNION

Acts and Treaties

Act concerning the conditions of accession of the Czech Republic, the Republic of Estonia, the Republic of Cyprus, the Republic of Latvia, the Republic of Lithuania, the Republic of Hungary, the Republic of Malta, the Republic of Poland, the Republic of Slovenia and the Slovak Republic and the adjustments to the Treaties on which the European Union is founded [2003]
OJ L 236/33
Arts 37–39 137
Act concerning the conditions of accession of the Republic of Bulgaria and Romania and the adjustments to the Treaties on which the European Union is founded [2005]
OJ L 157/203
Art 36 137
Art 39 136
Charter of Fundamental Rights of the European Union 117, 127, 155,156, 157, 159, 166, 172, 175, 178, 179, 207–8, 211
Arts 1–50 159
Art 1 . . . . 170, 177
Arts 2–3 161
Art 3 162
Art 4 . . . . 161, 170
Art 6 161
Art 7 162
Art 8 162
Art 9 161
Arts 10–13 161
Art 11 161
Art 13 160
Art 14 161
Art 15 161
Art 16 . . . . 160, 161
Art 17 320
Art 18 . . . . 160, 170
Art 19(2) 170
Art 21 163
Art 21(1) 173

Art 24 . . . . 160, 172
Arts 25–26 162
Art 27 . . . . 162, 166, 169
Art 28 . . . . 166, 169
Art 29 . . . . 162, 169
Art 30 . . . . 162, 166, 169
Arts 31–33 162
Art 33(1) 169
Art 33(2) 162
Art 34 . . . . 162, 166, 169
Art 35 . . . . 166, 169, 171
Art 36 169
Art 37 . . . . 169, 175
Art 41 160
Art 47 206
Art 41(2)(a) 72
Arts 42–44 160
Art 45 160
Art 47 . . . . 170, 177
Art 49 . . . . 162, 176
Art 50 185
Art 51 . . . . 94, 164–5, 170
Art 51(1) 161, 164
Art 51(2) 165
Art 52 . . . . 161, 168, 178
Art 52(1) 72, 163, 173
Art 52(2) 165
Art 52(3) 162, 163, 171, 178
Art 52(5) 161, 168, 169
Art 52(6) 166, 169
Preamble 161
Part II, Title V 169
Title I-VII 160
Title IV. 168
UK-Ireland Protocol 169–70
UK-Poland Protocol 166–9, 170, 171, 178
Art 1(1) 167, 168, 171
Art 1(2) 167, 168, 169
Art 2 169
Merger Treaty 1965 [1967] OJ
13 July. 5, 228
Shengen Agreement 1985 8

Shengen Convention 1990. 8
Single European Act 1986 [1987]
   OJL 169 5–6, 108,
                  129, 231, 248
Treaty amending with regard to Greenland the
   Treaties establishing the European
   Communities 1984 (Greenland Treaty)
   [1985] OJ l29/1 . . . . 146, 147
Treaty Establishing a Constitution for Europe
   2004 (Draft) 14, 16–18,
      19, 21, 22, 26, 29, 40, 41, 51,62,
      71, 130, 131, 142, 158, 175, 181,
      209, 333, 369, 412, 413
   Part I 44
   Part II 18, 44
   Part III 18
   Arts I–3. 26
   Art I.3.2 . . . . .352, 355
   Art I-8 16
   Art I-13. 369
   Art I-14. 371
   Art I-16. 370
   Art I-23(3) 65
   Art I-24(6) 65
   Art I-33. 68
   Arts I-34–I-37. 64
   Art I-34(1)–(2) 64
   Art I-58. 130
   Art I-60. . . . . 16, 148
   Art III-122 363
   Art III-130 . . . . .370, 372
   Art III-131 372
   Art III-152 369
   Art III-157 369
   Art III-163 64
   Art III-365(4) 14
   Art III-396 69
   Art IV-437 108
   Arts IV-443–IV-445. 119
   Art IV-447 . . . . 18, 108
Protocol No 27 on the Internal Market and
   Competition 27
Treaty Establishing the Coal and Steel
   Community 1952 (ECSC) 3, 128,
                 368, 399
   Art 96 146
   Art 97 142
   Art 98 129
Treaty Establishing the European Atomic Energy
   Community (EAEC) 44, 55,
      58, 59, 60, 127, 128, 368, 398, 399
   Art 106a(1)–(2) 59
   Art 106a(3) 59, 60

Art 184 60
Art 187 . . . . .381, 382
Art 204 146
Art 205 129
Treaty Establishing the European Community
   (TEC) 25, 28, 40, 270,
               271, 368, 398
   Art 2 . . . . 45, 46, 86, 351,
                358, 367
   Art 3 . . . . 46, 351
   Art 3(1). 357
   Art 3(1)(g) 351, 353, 356,
             357, 368, 418
   Art 4 . . . . 46, 84, 351, 355
   Art 5(1). 404
   Art 10 . . . . .356, 357
   Art 11 45
   Art 16 . . . . .362, 363
   Art 40(4) 144
   Art 61(a) 45
   Art 61(e) 45
   Arts 67–73 144
   Arts 81-82 . . . . .356, 357
   Art 86(1)-(2) 362
   Art 86(3) 363
   Art 87 362
   Art 95 . . . . .375, 379, 381, 385
   Art 106 144
   Arts 108–109 144
   Arts 131–136 143
   Art 131 143
   Art 131(1) 293, 294, 295
   Art 131(2) 293
   Art 133 . . . . .293, 394
   Art 133(6) 300
   Art 133(7) 301
   Art 134 293
   Art 149(1) 307
   Art 170 382
   Art 175 394
   Art 175(1)-(2). 381
   Art 221 209
   Art 226 144
   Art 227(2) 144, 145
   Art 235 180
   Art 236 146
   Art 237 129
   Art 251 308
   Art 268 45
   Art 284 383
   Art 300 45
   Art 301 45
   Art 308 . . . . 33, 86, 103,109, 123

Art 309 45
Preamble 350
Treaty of Amsterdam 4, 7–8, 87, 129,
        181, 215, 248, 250, 257, 297, 332, 362
Treaty of Athens 125
Treaty of Lisbon. 3, 4, 7, 22–39,
    40, 41, 49, 50, 55, 58, 62, 65, 66, 67, 71,
    79, 85, 86, 87, 97, 99, 102, 103, 107, 114,
    116, 117, 121, 125, 126, 127, 128, 129,
        130, 139, 159, 166, 170, 172, 177,
    197–212, 214, 228, 229–32, 234, 239,
    240, 241, 242, 245, 246, 248, 250, 251,
    252, 253, 256, 257, 261, 265, 266, 272,
    273, 275, 277, 279, 285, 292, 293, 295,
    296, 297, 298, 300, 306, 308, 310, 311,
    312, 320, 327, 331, 332, 333, 338, 346,
    347, 348, 349, 352, 359, 360, 366, 367,
    374, 380, 381, 393, 403, 404, 410, 411,
                413, 416, 418, 419
Preamble 361
Art 4 223
Arts 9–12. 248
Art 14 399
Arts 107–109 399
Art 308 353
Art 352 33
Title V 334
Preamble 361
Protocol 1. . . . . 59, 96, 258, 259
    Art 9 260
Protocol 2. . . . . 96, 214, 220, 221,
                223, 227, 257
    Art 2 221
    Art 5 221
    Art 6 222
    Art 8 . . . . 221, 222, 260
Protocol 3
    Art 1 59
Protocol 6. 59
Protocol 7. 59
Protocol 12 59
Protocol 36 . . . . 59, 337
    Art 10 337
Protocol of Services of General Interest
    (26) 399
    Art 1 364
    Art 2 362
Protocol on the Application of the
    Principles of Subsidiarity and
    Proportionality 352
    Art 2 342
Protocol on the Internal Market and
    Competition (27). 368

Treaty of Maastricht 6–7, 50, 86,
                87, 121, 129, 202, 213,
                214, 248, 250, 257
Treaty of Nice. 4, 8–10, 18,
    26, 38, 63, 98, 110, 121, 157, 181, 209,
        232, 234, 235, 248, 257, 297, 313
Treaty of Rome 1958 3
Treaty on European Union (TEU) 6–7,
    17, 25, 26, 28, 40, 41, 42, 90, 117, 126,
                192, 268, 289, 294, 369, 413
    Arts 1–3 (old) 273
    Art 1 . . . . 42, 44, 55, 58
    Art 1 (old) 269, 273
    Art 1(3). 44
    Art 2 . . . . 42, 45, 46, 91, 129,
                130, 131, 135, 139, 149, 269, 281
    Art 3 . . . . . . .42, 45, 46, 353, 358, 418
    Art 3(1). 91, 92, 93
    Art 3(1)(b) 91
    Art 3(1)(e) 298, 394
    Art 3(2). 92, 398
    Art 3(3). 91, 92, 307, 360, 418
    Art 3(5). 50, 91, 92, 273, 298
    Art 3(6). 90, 93, 354
    Art 4 . . . . 42, 45, 96
    Art 4(1). 93, 305
    Art 4(2). 27, 149, 411
    Art 4(3). 53, 54, 151,
                305, 332, 356, 357, 396
    Art 5 . . .42, 44, 93, 95, 97, 215, 216, 404
    Art 5(1). 48, 93, 305
    Art 5(2). 93, 305
    Art 5(3). 71, 214
    Art 6 . . . . .27, 42,
                59, 117, 120, 158, 166, 183, 281
    Art 6(1). 43, 117, 120,
                159, 160, 163, 165, 183, 204, 206
    Art 6(2). . . .181, 182, 183, 184, 194, 204
    Art 6(3). 163, 168, 178, 194
    Art 7 . . . . 42, 45, 59
    Art 7(2). 48
    Art 7(3). 48
    Art 8 . . . . 42, 46, 47
    Arts 9–12. 280
    Art 9 46
    Art 10(2) 69
    Art 10(3) 280
    Art 11 46
    Art 11(1) –(4). 261
    Art 11(1)(old) 267
    Art 12 257
    Art 12 (old) 277
    Art 12(c) 257

Art 13 93
Art 13(2) 70
Art 13(2)(old) 277
Art 14(1)(old) 277
Art 15(old) 277
Art 15(2) 199
Art 15(6) 37, 230, 253
Art 16(3)–(4) 151
Art 16(8) 261
Art 17(1) 45, 69, 286
Art 17(5) 34, 230
Art 17(6) 250
Art 17(8) 251
Art 18 231
Art 18(2) 286
Art 18(4) 287
Art 19(1) 45, 197
Art 19(2) 209
Art 20(4) 45
Art 21 92, 273, 294, 296,
297, 298, 324
Art 21(1) 46, 47, 50, 92, 297, 298
Art 21(2) 46, 47, 184, 296
Art 21(3) 287, 324
Art 21(2)(c) 275
Art 22 . . . . 92, 278
Art 22(1) 50, 278
Art 22(2) 50, 56, 286
Arts 23–41 294
Art 23 47
Art 24 51
Art 24 286
Art 24(1) 50, 51, 56, 193,
266, 268, 274, 279, 286, 290
Art 24(2) 286
Art 24(3) 53, 54, 286
Art 25 . . . . 277, 278
Art 26 50
Art 26(1) 50, 278
Art 26(2) 50, 51
Art 26(3) 50, 53, 286
Art 27(1) 50, 283, 286
Art 27(3) 287
Art 28 . . . . 50, 278
Art 28(2) 53
Art 29 . . . . 53, 278
Art 30(1) 286
Art 31 51
Art 31(1) 50, 93, 279
Art 31(2) 278
Art 31(3) 123
Art 32 53
Art 33 . . . . 286, 287

Art 34 281
Art 34(1) 287
Art 34(2)(a) 281
Art 34(3) 287
Art 35 . . . . 282, 337
Art 35(1) 282
Art 39 . . . . 49, 53, 58
Art 40 . . . . 48, 50, 51, 54, 55,
56, 57, 204, 272–6, 283, 290
Art 40(2) 104
Art 42(1) 53, 266
Art 42(2) 266
Art 43(1) 266, 287
Art 42(3) 53
Art 43(3) 286
Art 47 . . . . 42, 88, 265, 269
Art 47(old) 269, 270, 271,
272, 275, 290, 331, 340
Art 48 . . . . . .18, 42, 45, 107,108, 111,
113, 118, 119, 120, 121,
122, 196, 254
Art 48(2)–(5) 94, 119
Art 48(3) 259
Art 48(6)–(7) 33, 122
Art 48(6) 47, 94, 124, 125
Art 48(7) 123, 124, 255, 259
Art 49 . . . . . . .42, 125, 129, 130–1,
133, 134, 138, 148, 149, 150, 154
Art 49(1) 130
Art 49(2) 136
Art 50 . . . . 42, 125, 148, 150, 152, 154
Art 51 351
Art 52 . . . . 42, 46
Art 53 47
Art 54 47
Art 55 . . . . 42, 47
Title I 42, 61
Title II 42
Title III 42
Title IV 42
Title V 42, 55
Title VI 42
Preamble 139
Protocol 1 73
Protocol 2
  Art 3 72
  Art 6 72
Protocol on the Internal Market and
  Competition 418
Treaty on the Functioning of the European
  Union (TFEU) 25, 40, 41, 42–4,
90, 117, 126, 192, 266,
268, 269, 290, 413

Art 1 . . . . 55, 90
Art 1(2). 45
Art 2 . . . . 44, 47, 98
Art 2(1). 70, 299, 321
Art 2(2). 54, 100, 268
Art 2(3). 47, 101
Art 2(4). 47, 50, 54, 101, 268
Art 2(5). 101
Art 2(6). 70
Arts 3–6 . . . . 55, 357
Art 3 . . . . 98, 99, 100
Art 3(1). 54
Art 3(1)(b) 354, 357, 360
Art 3(2). 54, 299, 305, 316
Art 4(2). 47, 100
Art 4(2)(a) 317
Art 4(2)(j). 334
Art 4(3). 102
Art 4(4). 102
Art 5 101
Art 5(1). 227
Art 5(1)–(2). 47
Art 6 . . . . 52, 100, 415
Art 6(a). 305
Art 6(e). 414
Art 7 . . . . .46, 48, 93, 388
Arts 8–9 48
Art 10 48
Art 11 . . . . 48, 416
Art 12 . . . . 48, 416
Art 13 48
Art 14 . . . . . 48, 362, 364, 366, 399
Art 15 . . . . . . 48, 49, 59, 164, 198
Art 15(1). 365
Art 15(2)–(3). 52
Art 16 . . . . 48, 49, 58, 164, 198
Art 16(1). 493
Art 17 48
Art 17(1)–(3). 140
Art 19 . . . . 93, 102
Art 19(1). 69
Arts 20–24 46
Art 20(2). 337
Art 21 104
Art 21(2). 267
Art 21(3). 69
Art 22(2). 69
Art 23 69
Art 24 46
Art 25 69
Art 31 70
Art 42 70
Art 43(3). 70

Art 45(3)(d). 70
Art 45(4) 124
Arts 63–66 302
Art 63 316
Art 64 314
Art 64(2) 314, 316, 317
Art 64(3) 69
Art 65(1) 317
Art 66 . . . . 70, 317
Art 67 . . . . 334, 340, 341
Art 69 344
Art 70 . . . . 70, 259
Art 75 . . . . .57, 317, 341
Art 77 . . . . .104, 105
Art 77(3) 69
Art 78(3) 70
Art 79 102
Art 81(2) 70
Art 81(3) 69, 70, 123, 259
Arts 82–83 . . . . 331, 333,
335, 336, 341, 342,
344, 346
Art 82 335
Art 82(2) 335, 336
Art 82(2(d) 335
Art 83 . . . . 332, 334,
335, 336, 339, 340, 341, 343
Art 83(1) 335, 336
Art 83(2) 334, 336, 338, 339, 344
Art 84 102
Art 85 259
Art 86(1) 69
Art 86(4) 123
Art 87(3) 45, 69
Art 88 259
Art 89 69
Art 95(3) 70
Art 98 70
Art 101. . . . . . 348, 349, 356, 357, 358
Art 101(1) 71
Art 101(3) 388, 389
Art 102 . . . . 71, 348, 349, 356, 357, 358
Art 103(1) 69, 70, 71
Art 103(2)(a) 71
Art 105(3) 348
Art 106 . . . . .348, 349, 364, 365
Art 106(1) 362
Art 106(2) 362, 400, 401
Art 106(3) 70, 363
Art 107 . . . . . . 348, 349, 362, 364, 365
Art 107(2)(c) 348
Art 107(3)(a) 348
Art 107(3)(e) 70

Art 108 347	Art 207(1) 294, 295, 296, 297, 299,
Art 108(4) 348	312, 315, 394
Art 109 . . . . 70, 348	Art 207(2)–(3) 300, 308, 309
Art 112 70	Art 207(4) 300, 306, 307, 308
Art 113 . . . . 69, 95	Art 207(6) 98, 303, 304, 305, 306
Art 114 . . . . 217, 333, 334,	Arts 208–211 . . . . .274, 294
340, 342–4, 346,	Art 212 . . . . 57, 294
375, 382, 383	Art 213 . . . . 70, 294
Art 115 69	Art 214 294
Arts 116–117 365	Art 215 . . . . . . .46, 276, 284, 294, 317
Art 119 355	Art 215(3) 52
Arts 120–126 47	Arts 216–219 . . . . 65, 294
Art 121(4) 70	Art 216 . . . . .393, 398
Art 122 . . . . .105, 374	Art 216(1) 299, 393
Art 122(1)–(2) 70	Art 217 46
Art 125(2) 70	Art 218 . . . . 57, 182, 185, 275, 309, 395
Art 126(4) 69	Art 218(3) 150, 275
Art 126(6) 70	Art 218(6) 182, 275, 309
Art 126(14) 70	Art 218(6)(a) 70
Art 127(6) 69	Art 218(6)(a)(ii) 182
Art 128(2) 70	Art 218(6)(v) 70
Art 129(4) 70	Art 218(8) 182
Art 132 70	Art 218(9) 70
Art 138(1) 70	Art 218(10) 250
Art 140(2) –(3) 70	Art 218(11) 183
Arts 145–150 47	Art 220 294
Art 148(2) 70	Art 221 . . . . 51, 286, 292
Art 149 101	Art 222 294
Art 153 101	Art 223(1) 69
Art 153(2) 69	Art 223(2) 70
Art 153(5) 124	Art 222 51
Art 155(2) 70	Art 226 70
Arts 165–166 416	Art 228(4) 70
Art 165 416	Arts 251–281 197
Art 165(2) –(4) 414	Art 252 209
Art 167(4) 45	Art 253(2) 210
Art 182(4) 69	Art 253(4) 210
Art 188 70	Art 255 210
Arts 191–192 333	Art 262 69
Art 192 . . . . .381, 397	Art 263 . . . . 50, 124, 198, 221
Art 192(2) 69, 392	Art 263(2) 199
Art 192(3) 376	Art 263(4) 14, 73
Art 193 45	Art 267 . . . . .202, 338
Art 194 . . . . 368, 373–4,	Art 275 . . . . 51, 193, 204,
375, 381, 382, 383, 393, 397	281, 282, 283
Art 194(2) 374, 382, 384, 390, 392	Art 275(2) 52
Art 194(3) 69	Art 276 203
Art 203 69	Art 281 122
Art 205 . . 47, 91, 275, 294, 296, 297, 324	Art 288 . . . . 51, 277, 279
Arts 206–207 . . . . .293, 314	Art 289 . . . . 51, 74
Art 206 . . . . .294, 295, 303, 312	Art 289(1) 67, 198, 279
Art 207 . . . . . . 299, 300, 301, 302, 303,	Art 289(2) 68, 70, 199, 279
310, 315, 317, 320, 395, 396	Art 289(3) 67, 68, 70, 198, 279

Art 290 . . . . 51, 66, 71,
74, 74–7, 78, 79,
82, 252, 349
Art 290(1) 68, 72, 75
Art 290(2) 68, 72, 75, 76
Art 290(2)(a)–(b) 75
Art 291 . . . .51, 71, 74, 75, 77–9, 82, 252
Art 291(1) 77
Art 291(2) 77
Art 294 . . . . 67, 69, 308
Art 295 65
Art 296(3) 65
Art 300(5) 70
Art 305 70
Art 308(3) 69
Art 311(3) 69
Art 312(2) 69, 123
Art 314 . . . . 65, 93, 254
Art 322(2) 70
Art 325 . . . . .344, 346
Arts 326–334 46
Art 329 . . . . 70, 336
Art 333(2) 69
Art 337 . . . . .383, 384
Art 344 . . . . .188, 189
Art 345 . . . . .303, 319, 320, 376
Art 346(2) 70
Art 349 69
Art 351 . . . . 89, 396
Art 352 . . . . . . 50, 57, 90, 92, 93, 104,
105, 109, 123, 255,
342, 353, 393
Art 352(1) 70
Art 352(4) 50, 51, 56, 104
Art 353 . . . . .104, 123
Art 355 46
Arts 356–8 47
Part I 42
Title I 414
Part III 259, 414
Part IV 43
Part V 43, 294
Part VI 43, 195
Part VII 43
Title I 42
s 5 195
Title II 42, 48
Title V 334
Ch 1 . . . . 335, 340, 341
Ch 4 340
Preamble 360
Protocol 3
Art 64 70

Protocol 4
Art 34 70
Art 41 70
Protocol 8 . . . . .181, 182
Art 1(a) 185
Art 1(b) 187, 190
Art 2 . . . . 183, 184, 189
Art 3 187
Protocol 13
Art 6 70
Protocol 19
Art 5(3)–(4) 70
Protocol 21
Art 4a(2)–(3) 70
Art 5(2)–(3) 70
Protocol 27 99
Protocol 30 215
Protocol 36
Art 10 203
Art 10(4) 70
Protocol 37 70
Art 2 70
Protocol on the Internal Market and
Competition 353, 360, 418

Directives

Commission Directive 55/2004/EC of 20 April
2004 amending Council Directive 66/401
[2004] OJ L 114/18 399
Commission Directive 81/2005/EC of 28
November 2005 amending Directive 80/
723/EEC on the transparency of financial
relationships between Member States and
public undertakings as well as on financial
transparency within certain undertakings
[2005] OJ L 312/47 363
Council Directive 88/361/EEC of 24 June 1988
for the implementation of Article 67 of the
Treaty [1988] OJ L 178/5 314
Council Directive 2000/78/EC of 27 November
2000 establishing a general framework for
equal treatment in employment and
occupation [2000] OJ L 303/16 . . . 173
Council Directive 2003/86/EC of 22 September
2003 on the right to family reunification
[2003] OJ L 251/12 (Family Reunification
Directive) 172
Council Directive 2004/67/EC of 26 April 2004
concerning measures to safeguard the
security of natural gas supply [2004] OJ L
127/92 on gas security and
supply 384, 385, 386, 387

European Parliament and Council Directive 96/
92/EC of 19 December 1996 concerning
common rules for the internal market in
electricity [1997] OJ L 27/20 399
European Parliament and Council Directive 98/
30/EC of 22 June 1998 concerning
communities for the internal market in
natural gas [1998] OJ L 204/1 . . . 399
European Parliament and Council Directive
2003/54/EC of 26 June 2003 concerning
common rules for the internal market in
electricity and repealing Directive 96/92
[2003] OJ L176/37 (Second Electricity
Market Directive)
Art 3(2). 401
Art 11(4) 401
European Parliament and Council Directive
2003/55/EC of 26 June 2003 concerning
common rules for the internal market in
natural gas and repealing Directive 98/30/
EC (Second Gas Directive)
Art 3(2). 400
Art 18 395
European Parliament and Council Directive
2004/54/EC of 29 April 2004 on minimum
safety requirements for tunnels in the
Trans-European Road Network . . . 399
European Parliament and Council Directive
2002/21/EC of 7 March 2002 on a
common regulatory framework for
electronic communications [2002] OJ L
108/33. 378
European Parliament and Council Directive
2003/87/EC of 13 October 2003
establishing a scheme for greenhouse gas
emission allowance trading within the
Community [2004] OJ L 338/18 . . 226
European Parliament and Council Directive
2009/28/EC on the promotion of energy
from renewable sources and amending and
subsequently repealing Directives 2001/77/
EC and 2003/30/EC [2009]
OJ L140/16 (Renewable Energy
Directive) 381
European Parliament and Council Directive
2009/29/EC of 23 April 2009 amending
Directive 2003/87/EC so as to improve
and extend the greenhouse gas emission
allowance trading scheme of the
Community [2009]
OJ L140/63 380
European Parliament and Council Directive
2009/31/EC of 23 April 2009 on the
geological storage of carbon dioxide [2009]
OJ L140/16 380

European Parliament and Council Directive
2009/72/EC of 13 July 2009 concerning
common rules for the internal market in
electricity and repealing Directive 2003/54/
EC [2009] OJ L 211/55 (Third Electricity
Directive)
Art 3 399
Art 3(2). 400
Art 9 . . . . .375, 377
Art 11 . . . . .377, 395
Art 15(4) 390, 401
Art 35(4)–(5) 378
Art 37(4)(d). 378
Art 47 377
Recital 25. 377
Recital 42. 400
European Parliament and Council Directive
2009/73/EC of 13 July 2009 concerning
common rules for the internal market in
natural gas and repealing Directive 2003/
55/EC [2009] OJ L 211/94
Art 3 399
Art 3(2). 400
Art 5 384
Art 6 384
Art 9 . . . . .375, 377
Art 11 . . . . .377, 395
Art 39 378
Art 41(3)(d). 378
Art 52 377
Recital 47. 400
European Parliament and Council Directive
2010/30/EC of 19 May 2010 on the
indication by labelling and standard
product information of the consumption
of energy and other resources by
energy-related products [2010] OJ L 153/1
Art 10 75
European Parliament and Council Directive
2010/40 of 7 July 2010 on the framework
for the deployment of Intelligent Transport
Systems in the field of road transport and
for interfaces with other modes of transport
[2010] OJ L 207/1
Art 7 75
Arts 13–14 76

Regulations

Council Regulation (EEC) 768/92 of 18 June
1992 concerning the creation of a
supplementary protection certificate for
medicinal products [1992] OJ L 182/1
. . . . 319

Council Regulation (EC) 2100/94 of 27 July
1994 on community plant variety rights
[1994] OJ L 227/1
Art 62 . . . . 81, 82
Council Regulation (EC) 1236/2005 of 27 June
2005 concerning trade in certain goods
which could be used for capital punishment,
torture or other cruel, inhuman or
degrading treatment or punishment [2005]
OJ L 200/1 184
Council Regulation (EC) 207/2009 of 26
February 2009 on the Community trade
mark [2009] OJ L 78/1 82
Art 42(5) 81
Council Regulation (EU, Euratom) 617/2010 of
24 June 2010 on notification to the
Commission of investment projects in
energy infrastructure [2010]
OJ L 180/7 384
European Parliament and Council Regulation
(EC) 1049/2001 of 30 May 2001 regarding
public access to European Parliament,
Council and Commission documents
[2001] OJ L 145/43
Art 4(1)(a) 52
European Parliament and Council Regulation
(EC) 1592/2002 of 15 July 2002 on
common rules in the field of civil aviation
and establishing a European Aviation Safety
Agency [2002] OJ L 240/1 82
European Parliament and Council Regulation
(EC) 726/2004 of 3 March 2004 laying
down Community procedures for the
authorisation and supervision of medicinal
products for human and veterinary use and
establishing a European Medicines Agency
[2004] OJ L 136/1 82
European Parliament and Council Regulation
(EC) 717/2007 of 27 June 2007 on
roaming on public mobile telephone
networks within the Community and
amending Directive 2002/21/EC [2007]
OJ L 171/32 218
European Parliament and Council Regulation
(EC) 713/2009 of 13 July 2009 establishing
an Agency for the Cooperation of Energy
Regulators [2009] OJ L 211/1 . . . 375,
379, 399
European Parliament and Council Regulation
(EC) 714/2009 of 13 July 2009 on
conditions for access to the network for
cross-border exchanges in electricity and
repealing Regulation 1228/2003/EC
[2009] OJ L 211/15 . . . . . . 375, 399

European Parliament and Council Regulation
(EC) 715/2009 of 13 July 2009 on
conditions for access to the natural gas
transmission networks and repealing
Regulation 1775/2005/EC [2009] OJ L
211/36 . . . . 375, 399
Art 8(10)(a) 384
European Parliament and Council Regulation
(EU) 994/2010 of 20 October 2010
concerning measures to safeguard security of
gas supply and repealing Council Directive
2004/67/EC [2010] OJ L 295/1 . . . 385
Art 2(2) 387
Arts 3–4 387
Arts 6–7 387
European Parliament and Council Regulation
(EU)182/2011 of 16 February 2011 laying
down the rules and general principles
concerning mechanisms for control by
Member States of the Commission's
exercise of implementing powers [2011] OJ
L 55/13 . . . . 78, 79
Art 5(3) 79
Art 5(4)(2) 79

INTERNATIONAL TREATIES AND AGREEMENTS

American Convention on Human Rights 1969
. . . . 176
Energy Charter Treaty 1994 392
European Convention for the Protection of
Human Rights and Fundamental Freedoms
(ECHR) 155, 161,
180–94, 204–6, 208, 211
Art 1 171
Art 2 177
Art 3 . . . . 162, 177
Art 4(1) 191
Art 4(2)–(3) 192
Art 6 188
Art 6(1) 163, 201, 206
Art 7 177
Arts 8–11 163
Art 8 . . . . 162, 175
Art 8(1) 161
Art 10 161
Art 11(2) 185
Art 12 . . . . 175, 176
Art 13 193
Art 14 163
Art 20 186

Art 22 186
Art 27(2) 186
Art 33 188
Art 35(1) 192
Art 36 191
Art 46 186
Art 55 189
Art 59 . . . . .181, 185
Art 59(2) 185
Art 59(2)(d)–(e) 186
Protocol 1 185
Protocol 4 185
Protocol 6 185
Protocol 7 185
Protocol 12 163
Protocol 14 . . . . 181, 182, 185
General Agreement on Trade in Services
   (GATS) 318
Art XVI 313
Art XVII 313
Art XXI 295
Art XXVIII(d) 313
General Agreement on Tariffs and Trade
   (GATT) 297
Art XXVIII 295
Rome Statute on the International Criminal
   Court 176
Universal Declaration of Human Rights 161
Art 19 161
Vienna Convention on the Law of Treaties
   1969 142
Arts 39–41 108
Art 39 109
Art 62 126

MULTILATERAL AND BILATERAL AGREEMENTS

Australia-Chile Free Trade Agreement 2008
   Preamble 324
Canada-Columbia Free Trade Agreement
   2008 Preamble 324
Canada-EFT Free Trade Agreement 2009
   Preamble 324
Canada-Jordan Foreign Investment Protection
   and Promotion Agreement 2007
   Preamble 324
Economic Partnership Agreement between the
   EC and Cariforum
Art 73 325

Art 184 325
Arts 191–192 325
North American Agreement on Environmental
   Co-operation (NAAEC)
Art 3 325
Art 14 325
North American Free Trade Agreement
   (NAFTA) 325
United States-Oman Free Trade
   Agreement 2006
   Preamble 324
United States-Peru Trade Promotion
   Agreement 2006
   Preamble 324

NATIONAL LEGISLATION

France

Algerian Statute 1947 143
Constitution 1958
   Art 88-5 138
Constitutional Act No 2005-204
   s 2 138
   s 47 138
Décret 62-535 (1962) 143

Germany

Act amending the Act on the Co-operation
   between the Federal Government and the
   Länder on EU matters 33
Act on Co-operation between the Government
   and the Bundestag on EU Matters . . . 33
Act to Implement Amendments to the Basic
   Law for the Ratification of the Lisbon
   Treaty 33
Basic Law (Grundgesetz) 32, 33, 161
Constitution
   Art 80 76
Integration Responsibility Act 33

United Kingdom

European Union (Amendment) Act 2008
   s 5 30
Banking Act 1979 Appeals Procedure (England
   and Wales) Regulations 1979 201

United States

Sherman Act 356

List of Abbreviations

ACER	Agency for the Cooperation of Energy Regulators
AFSJ	Area of Freedom, Security and Justice
BITs	Bilateral Investment Treaties
CAP	Common Agricultural Policy
CCP	Common Commercial Policy
CDDH	Steering Committee for Human Rights
CEECs	Central and Eastern European Countries
CFSP	Common Foreign and Security Policy
CoR	Committee of the Regions
COSAC	Conference of European Affairs Committees
CSDP	Common Security and Defence Policy
CT	Constitutional Treaty
DG	Directorate-General
DSU	Dispute Settlement Understanding
EAEC	European Atomic Energy Community Treaty
ECtHR	European Court of Human Rights
ECJ	European Court of Justice
ECHR	European Convention for the Protection of Human Rights and Fundamental Freedoms
ECSC	European Coal and Steel Community Treaty
ECT	Energy Charter Treaty
EEA	European Economic Area
EEAS	European External Action Service
EMU	Economic and Monetary Union
ENISA	European Network and Information Security Agency
FA	Framework Agreement
FDI	Foreign Direct Investment
FIPA	Foreign Investment Protection and Promotion Agreement
FOU	Full Ownership Unbundling
GCG	Gas Coordination Group
IEA	International Energy Agency
IGA	Intergovernmental Agreement
IGC	Intergovernmental Conference
IMF	International Monetary Fund
ISO	Independent System Operator
ITO	Independent Transmission Operator
JHA	Justice and Home Affairs
MAI	Multilateral Agreement on Investment
NAAEC	North American Agreement on Environmental Cooperation
NAALC	North American Agreement on Labor Cooperation
NAFTA	North American Free Trade Agreement
NAP	National Allocation Plan
NRA	National Regulatory Authority
OCTs	Overseas Countries and Territories
OECD	Organization for Economic Cooperation and Development
OMC	Open Method of Coordination
PJCCM	Police and Judicial Cooperation in Criminal Matters

PSC	Political and Security Committee
QMV	Qualified Majority Voting
RPS	Regulatory Procedure with Scrutiny
SEA	Single European Act
SGEIs	Services of General Economic Interest
TEC	Treaty Establishing the European Community
TEU	Treaty on European Union
TFEU	Treaty on the Functioning of the European Union
TPA	Third Party Access
TRIMs	Agreement on Trade-Related Investment Measures
TSOs	Transmission System Operators
VIU	Vertically Integrated Undertaking
WTO	World Trade Organization

List of Contributors

David Anderson QC practises in the field of EU Law. He has made more than 130 appearances in the European Court of Justice and has argued more than 30 cases before the European Court of Human Rights. In England, he practises before the full range of courts and tribunals with a particular emphasis on Public Law in the High Court and above. David has been appointed as the Government's independent reviewer of terrorism legislation from 2011.

Paul Berman is Director of the Cabinet Office European Law Division. He studied at the Universities of Oxford and Geneva and after qualifying as a barrister joined HM Diplomatic Service in 1991. He has served as Legal Counsellor at the Foreign and Commonwealth Office and the UK's Permanent Representation to the European Union and as the Attorney General's adviser on international and EU law. He was the UK's lead legal representative during the treaty negotiations at successive Intergovernmental Conferences and European summits.

Andrea Biondi is Professor of European Union Law and the Co-Director of the Centre for European Law at King's College London. Professor Biondi is also Visiting Professor at the College of Europe in Warsaw and at Georgetown University. He is an Academic Member of Francis Taylor Building Chambers in London.

José Luis Buendia Sierra is a Partner at Garrigues and leads the Brussels office of the firm. He previously worked at the European Commission (Legal Service, DG Competition, DG Internal Market and Cabinet of Commissioner Oreja) advising and litigating for the Institution in areas such as State aid or Antitrust. He is currently Visiting Professor at King's College London and at Vrije Universiteit Brussels.

Thomas Christiansen is Jean Monnet Professor of European Institutional Politics and Director of Studies for the Research Masters in European Studies at Maastricht University, on which he is also teaching courses on European institutions and EU treaty reform. He is Executive Editor of the Journal of European Integration, co-editor of the 'Europe in Change' series at Manchester University Press and a member of the steering committee of the Standing Group of the European Union of the European Consortium of Political Research.

Richard Corbett is a Special Advisor to Herman Van Rompuy, President of the European Council, on political and institutional questions. From 1996–2009, he was an MEP. He was spokesperson for the Socialist Group on constitutional affairs and was Parliament's rapporteur on both the Constitutional and Lisbon Treaties. He was three times rapporteur for an overhaul of Parliament's Rules of Procedure. He was Deputy Leader of the Labour MEPs. Prior to being an MEP, Richard gained a PhD at Hull University and a BA at Oxford University.

Marise Cremona is Professor of European Law at the European University Institute, Florence, a Director of the Academy of European Law, and currently Head of the Department of Law. Until December 2005 she was Professor of European Commercial Law at the Centre for Commercial Law Studies, Queen Mary University of London. Marise's research interest is in the external relations law of the European Union, including its foreign policy, trade, neighbourhood and development policies.

Bruno De Witte is Professor of European Law at Maastricht University, and part-time Professor at the Robert Schuman Centre of the European University Institute (EUI) in Florence. Previously, from 2000 to February 2010, he was Professor of EU Law at the EUI. His principal interest is the constitutional law of the European Union, with a focus on relations between international, European and national law; the protection of fundamental rights; lawmaking and treaty revision procedures; internal market law and non-market values.

Piet Eeckhout is Professor of European Law and Director of the Centre of European Law, King's College London and Visiting Professor at Católica Global Law School, Lisbon, and at the Universidad Autónoma, Madrid. He is Editor, with Prof T Tridimas, of the *Yearbook of European Law*; and, with David Anderson QC, of the *Oxford EU Law Library*. Associate academic member, Matrix Chambers, London.

Giorgio Gaja is Professor of International Law at the University of Florence. He is also a Member of the International Law Commission, of the Institut de Droit International and of the Advisory Board of the Common Market Law Review.

Leigh Hancher is Professor of European Law at Tilburg University, the Netherlands and Of Counsel, Allen & Overy, Amsterdam. European energy law is an area in which she has worked both as a legal adviser and as an academic for many years. She has published widely on this subject. She is also Director of the European Law and Energy Policy Programme at the Florence School of Regulation, EUI, Florence.

Ester Herlin-Karnell is currently Assistant Professor in EU Law at the Free University of Amsterdam (VU). She holds a DPhil in law from Somerville College, Oxford University as well as an LLM from King's College London and a Jur Kand (LLM) from Stockholm University. She has previously worked as a legal secretary and judge assistant in a Swedish District Court. Her research interests lie within EU (constitutional) law and European criminal law.

Sir Francis G Jacobs KCMG, QC is Professor of Law at King's College London and Jean Monnet Professor. From October 1988 to January 2006 he was an Advocate General at the European Court of Justice. In November 2005 he was appointed to the Privy Council. He is President of the newly formed European Law Institute, and since 2007 President of Missing Children Europe.

Markus Krajewski is Professor of Public and International Law at the University of Erlangen-Nürnberg (Germany). Prior to his current position he taught at the Universities of Bremen and Potsdam and at King's College London. His research focuses on international economic law (WTO and investment law), services of general interest and EU external relations.

Lord Jonathan Mance is a Justice of the Supreme Court of the United Kingdom. He became Lord of Appeal in Ordinary in 2005. He was from 1999 to 2005 a Lord Justice of Appeal and from 1993 to 1999 a Judge of the High Court, Queen's Bench Division.

Cian C Murphy is a Lecturer in Law and Director of Graduate Research Studies at the School of Law at King's College London. He teaches and researches in European public law and has consulted in litigation on EU immigration and counter-terrorism law.

Federico Ortino is Reader in International Economic Law, King's College London; Founding Committee Member, Society of International Economic Law; Editorial Board Member, *Journal of International Economic Law*, *Yearbook of International Investment Law and Policy*; Visiting Professor, IELPO, University of Barcelona. Previously, Director, Investment Treaty Forum, British Institute of International and Comparative Law; Emile Noël Fellow and Fulbright Scholar, New York University; Legal Officer, UNCTAD. He holds an LLB, Florence; LLM, Georgetown; and PhD, EUI.

Stefanie Ripley is a PhD Researcher at the Centre of European Law, King's College London; she is also a Visiting Tutor and Research Assistant at the University. She holds an LLB from the University of East Anglia and an LLM from the University of the Pacific, USA and the University of Salzburg, Austria. Stefanie is a Member of the Bar of England and Wales.

Lucia Serena Rossi is Professor of European Law at the University of Bologna. She is Director of the Centre of European Law at the same University (CIRDE) and Ad Personam Jean Monnet Chair. She is Visiting Professor at King's College London and has lectured in many universities all over the world.

Francesco Maria Salerno is a senior attorney at international law firm Cleary Gottlieb Steen & Hamilton LLP, based in the firm's Brussels office. He has a PhD from the London School of Economics (2009). His practice focuses on competition law and regulation in network industries and he has extensive experience advising clients in the energy sector, in particular with respect to state aid matters.

Allan F Tatham is Assistant Professor, Faculty of Law and Political Sciences, Pázmány Péter Catholic University, Budapest, Hungary and has lectured on EU law throughout central and Eastern Europe. He worked as legal advisor at the Delegation of the European Commission to Hungary and has published extensively on EU enlargement and law harmonization. He is presently lecturing at the Faculty of Law, CEU San Pablo University, Madrid.

Alexander H Türk is Professor of Law at the School of Law, King's College London. He obtained his MA in Augsburg, Germany; an LLM at the College of Europe in Bruges, Belgium; and a PhD from the University of London. Professor Türk is Director of the LLM Programme and the PG Diploma/MA in EU Law (by distance learning). He is General Editor of LexisNexis EU Tracker. He teaches on the London Programmes of the London Law Consortium and Pepperdine University, California. He is an adjunct Professor of Georgetown University, Washington.

Stephen Weatherill is the Jacques Delors Professor of European Law in the University of Oxford. He also serves as Deputy Director for European Law in the Law Faculty's Institute of European and Comparative Law, and is a Fellow of Somerville College.

PART I

CONSTITUTIONAL FRAMEWORK

1

From Laeken to Lisbon: The Origins and Negotiation of the Lisbon Treaty[1]

Paul Berman[2]

I. Introduction

Opinions on the Lisbon Treaty differ widely. For some, the Treaty simply sets out incremental reforms designed to make the EU more accountable and efficient. For others, it represents an important new departure for the EU, particularly on the international stage. Some have attacked it as an assault on national sovereignty: the outcome of an unaccountable process and a further step towards a European super-state. Yet others have criticized it as a victory for a distinctly 'Anglo-Saxon' vision of the EU, reinforcing the Member State as the fundamental building-block of the Union.

But whatever their views on its merits, most commentators would agree that the road leading to the entry into force of the Lisbon Treaty in December 2009 was one of the most troubled of any European Union agreement. It was also one of the longest. The process had its origins in the Nice European Council nine years earlier. It spanned a Convention, two Intergovernmental Conferences (IGCs), the agreement and abandonment of a Constitutional Treaty, six referendums in Member States including three critical 'no' votes, a 'period of reflection', successive fraught negotiations and last-minute deals at European summits, long debates in national Parliaments, and, even after the text had been agreed and signed, the negotiation of two further Protocols and other texts to get the Treaty over the finishing line. By comparison, the process of agreeing even the original treaties appears brief and straightforward—just over two years from the Schuman Declaration to the entry into force of the Treaty Establishing the Coal and Steel Community in 1952 and only a few months longer from the start of the Messina Conference to the entry into force of the Treaty of Rome in 1958.

The successive crises certainly had a material impact on the conduct of EU business and the potential to do lasting damage to the Union. The negotiations on

[1] This chapter is based on lectures given by the author to the UK Association of European Law, the Bar European Group, King's College London and the Foreign and Commonwealth Office. The author would like to express his appreciation to Heather Walker for her assistance.
[2] The views expressed are those of the author and do not necessarily represent those of HM Government.

the Constitutional and Lisbon Treaties may well come to be regarded as a critical point in the process of European integration. But their relevance for those seeking to understand and apply the treaty text may be less evident. For legal practitioners, the history of EU treaty texts is generally of limited interest. Notwithstanding the emphasis placed in public international law on the intentions of the parties to international agreements, the European Court of Justice only rarely has recourse to the *travaux préparatoires* of EU Treaties and to the negotiators' intentions.[3] But it is precisely because it was so complicated and prolonged, that the development of the Lisbon Treaty is important in understanding the Treaty's nature, structure and significance.

Rather than being the outcome of a single, coherent negotiation, the text is the multi-layered product of a succession of negotiations, taking place across several years and involving a number of different participants and negotiating methods, with each stage adding to, or re-writing, previous drafts. Reading the treaty text can be like conducting an archaeological dig or examining a mediaeval palimpsest. Different provisions, and sometimes different parts of the same provision, have their origins in different stages, and reflect the various policy objectives and drafting styles, of the negotiating process. Indeed the very structure of the Treaty, including the precise location of different chapters and articles, can only be understood by reference to the Treaty's chequered history.

In addition, the crises and political debates surrounding the development of the Lisbon Treaty can obscure an assessment of its legal significance. The level of controversy surrounding a treaty may extend beyond the importance of the changes that it actually makes and reflect more general reservations about the nature of European integration, misgivings about the accountability of the negotiating process, competing visions of Europe and wider regional and domestic political issues.

Placing the Lisbon Treaty in its context, and understanding its origins and troubled development is, therefore, important not only for the historian of European Union politics, but also for those seeking to assess the nature of the changes made by the Treaty, and to interpret and apply its provisions.

II. The Run-up to Laeken: Accelerating Treaty Change

The Lisbon Treaty opens by declaring the Contracting Parties' desire 'to complete the process started by the Treaty of Amsterdam and by the Treaty of Nice'.[4] Certainly the Lisbon Treaty must be viewed in the context of an accelerating

---

[3] See P Craig and G De Búrca, *EU Law, Text, Cases and Materials* (4th edn) (Oxford University Press, 2007) 73. For a more general discussion on the use of *travaux préparatoires* see S Schønberg and K Frick, 'Finishing, Refining, Polishing: On the Use of *travaux préparatoires* as an Aid to the Interpretation of Community Legislation' (2003) 28 *ELRev* 149.

[4] Treaty of Lisbon, preamble para 1. For the complete text of the Lisbon Treaty, see Foreign and Commonwealth Office Command Paper 7294. The text can also be found at <http://eur-lex.europa.eu/en/treaties/index.htm>.

process of treaty change and one which started not just with the Amsterdam Treaty but even earlier.

A. The first three decades

For the first three decades, the treaty framework of the then European Communities had remained essentially unchanged. With the exception of modifications to streamline the institutional framework in the 1960s,[5] and to provide for successive waves of enlargement from 1973 onwards,[6] the three founding Treaties establishing the European Coal and Steel Community, European Economic Community and European Atomic Energy Community were not substantively amended[7] from their entry into force in the 1950s until the Single European Act in 1987.

Those three decades were of course periods of exceptional development for the Communities. The innovation and ambition of the founding Treaties were such that there was considerable scope for evolution, and much to implement, debate and resolve, within the original legal framework. Additional challenges and opportunities were presented by the beginning of the process on enlargement starting in the 1970s and the development of supplementary forms of intergovernmental cooperation—notably European Political Cooperation on foreign policy established in 1970 and the Trevi Group of Interior Ministers set up in 1975—outside the original treaty framework.

B. The Single European Act

However, by the 1980s, the pressures for change had grown as reflected in the European Council's Stuttgart Declaration of June 1983.[8] These pressures were driven by a range of factors including the ambition on the part of a number of Member States and those in the EU institutions to take European integration beyond the 1950s' treaty framework into new areas and new methods of cooperation, as well as the concerns, still current some two decades later, to put in place institutional reforms and to ensure that the Communities were able to deal with further enlargement.

---

[5] Merger Treaty (1965) Official Journal 152 of 13 July 1967.

[6] Accession of Denmark, Ireland and the United Kingdom (Adaptation decision 1973) Official Journal L 2 of 1 January 1973; Accession of Greece (1979) Official Journal L 291 of 19 November 1979; Accession of Spain and Portugal (1985) Official Journal L 302 of 15 November 1985.

[7] There were, however, a number of specific or technical amendments and additions: Greenland Treaty (1984) Official Journal L 29 of 1 February 1985; Protocol on the Statute of the European Investment Bank (1975) Official Journal L 91 of 6 April 1978; Treaty amending certain financial provisions (1975) Official Journal L 359 of 31 December 1977; Treaty amending certain budgetary provisions (1970) Official Journal L 2 of 2 January 1971; Merger Treaty (1965) Protocol (No 36) on the privileges and immunities of the European Communities (1965) Official Journal C 321E, 29.12.2006; Protocol on the Netherlands Antilles (1962) Official Journal 150 of 1 October 1964.

[8] Solemn Declaration on European Union, Stuttgart, 19 June 1983, Bulletin of the European Communities, June 1983 6/1983, 24–9.

The Dooge Committee report[9] of March 1985 recommended convening an IGC to agree a new treaty and in the same month the European Council declared its intention to create 'a single large market by 1992'[10] leading to the Cockfield White Paper.[11] The proposed IGC and the White Paper were both endorsed by the European Council in June 1985[12] and the achievement of a single market was a key element in the resulting Single European Act (SEA)[13] which entered into force in July 1987. While significantly extending majority voting, the SEA was otherwise more modest in its scope than many of the proposals which preceded it. But it was the start of an ongoing process of substantive treaty amendment and its approach in amending the existing treaties, strengthening the powers of the European Parliament and setting out new areas of competence was taken up in later treaties.

C. The Maastricht Treaty

Only two years after the SEA's entry into force, two parallel IGCs were convened to discuss Economic and Monetary Union and European Political Union. These picked up on many of the proposals that had been made in the run-up to the SEA—which itself had referred to 'transforming relations' among Member States into a European Union—as well as, in relation to economic and monetary matters, the April 1989 Delors Report.[14] The resulting Treaty on European Union (TEU) or Maastricht Treaty marked the most significant changes to the treaty and institutional framework since the establishment of the European Communities.

Alongside the original three Communities, the TEU created two new areas of cooperation in the areas of Common Foreign and Security Policy (CFSP) and Justice and Home Affairs (JHA) covering criminal and civil justice matters and immigration. These were kept distinct, as separate Titles in the TEU itself, operating on an intergovernmental rather than supranational basis.[15] A new overarching entity, 'the European Union' was established to cover both the existing

---

[9] Report from the ad hoc Committee on Institutional Affairs (Brussels, 29–30 March 1985), Bulletin of the European Communities, March 1985, No 3, 102–10.

[10] European Council Brussels 29 and 30 March 1985, Conclusions of the Presidency, Bulletin of the European Communities 1985, No Supplement 7/85, 15.

[11] Completing the Internal Market, White Paper from the Commission to the European Council (Milan, 28–29 June 1985) COM(85) 310 final, 14 June 1985.

[12] Conclusions of the Milan European Council (28–29 June 1985) Bulletin of the European Communities. June 1985, No 6, 13–16. Denmark, Greece and the UK opposed the convening of an IGC.

[13] Single European Act (1986) Official Journal L 169 of 29 June 1987.

[14] Committee for the Study of Economic and Monetary Union, Report on Economic and Monetary Union in the European Community (12 April 1989).

[15] The 'supranational' or 'Community' method can be characterized as including a preponderance of majority voting and the vesting of significant powers in institutions—the Commission, European Parliament and ECJ—operating independently of the constituent Member States. Intergovernmentalism in this context does not mean traditional government to government diplomacy but rather maintaining governments' control through the Council of Ministers and curtailing many of the elements of the Community method. See P Berman, 'The European Union—Development, Structure and Decision-Making' in I Roberts (ed), *Satow's Diplomatic Methods* (Oxford University Press, 2009) 380.

European Communities and the two new intergovernmental areas.[16] Reforming this 'three pillar structure' which was criticized from the outset for its complexity—it was labelled 'organised schizophrenia'[17] by the then Commission President Jacques Delors—was one of the key issues in the debates leading up to the entry into force of the Lisbon Treaty.

Like the SEA, the TEU expanded the areas of Community competence and the powers of the European Parliament as well as making a series of institutional changes. The most significant additions were the new provisions and institutional arrangements paving the way for Economic and Monetary Union and the introduction of a single currency. However, reflecting the differences between Member States which were to re-emerge in later treaty negotiations, the UK and Denmark secured carve-outs from the EMU provisions and the UK an opt-out from the new social chapter.

The Treaty was signed in February 1992 but, in a foretaste of subsequent events, faced a troubled path to ratification. It was narrowly rejected in a referendum in Denmark, only squeezed through a French referendum in September (the so-called 'petit oui'),[18] faced detailed scrutiny by the German Constitutional Court[19] and was the subject of intense debate in the UK Parliament. The position of Denmark was addressed through the agreement at the Edinburgh European Council in December 1992 of a free-standing Decision, binding in public international law but not amending the EU Treaties themselves, which covered Denmark's position on issues including the single currency, defence implications, JHA and citizenship.[20] The Treaty was approved in a subsequent Danish referendum in May 1993 and entered into force in November 1993.

D. The Amsterdam Treaty

These events did not dampen the appetite for treaty change. The TEU itself provided for yet a further IGC to be held in 1996.[21] This drew on the Westendorp Reflection Group's[22] review of the operation of the TEU and built on the latter's innovations. The resulting Amsterdam Treaty, which entered into force in October

---

[16] 'The Union shall be founded on the European Communities, supplemented by the policies and forms of cooperation established by this Treaty' para 3 Article A, Treaty on European Union.

[17] 'Delors Calls Latest EC Plan Crippling', *International Herald Tribune*, 21 November 1991. Also quoted in D Buchan, *Europe—The Strange Superpower* (Dartmouth, 1993).

[18] 'Un petit "Oui"' *L'Humanité*, 22 September 1992. See also Michael S Lewis-Beck and DS Morey, 'The French "Petit Oui": The Maastricht Treaty and the French Voting Agenda' *Journal of Interdisciplinary History* 38.1 (2007: 65–87).

[19] See *Brunner v European Union Treaty* CMLR [1994] 57.

[20] See Presidency Conclusions of the Edinburgh European Council (11 and 12 December 1992), in Bulletin of the European Communities 12–1992, 12. See also D Howarth, 'The Compromise on Denmark and the Treaty on European Union: A Legal and Political Analysis' (1994) *CMLR* 31: 765–805.

[21] Article N(3).

[22] Report by the Reflection Group: *A Strategy for Europe* (Brussels, 5 December 1995). The text of the report can be found at <http://www.europarl.europa.eu/enlargement/cu/agreements/reflex2_en.htm>.

1999, reinforced the provisions on CFSP, moved civil justice and immigration from the intergovernmental to the Community pillar, and incorporated the Schengen[23] arrangements on the abolition of internal frontier controls into the EU Treaties. It again followed the established pattern of setting out further areas of Community competence, increasing the powers of the European Parliament and extending qualified majority voting. And again, like the TEU, the Amsterdam Treaty provided for a variety of carve-outs for individual Member States.[24]

But the Treaty failed to deliver the institutional reforms which were increasingly regarded as essential to deal with enlargement. Already the EU had grown from 10 States at the time of the SEA to 15 States at the time of the conclusion of the Amsterdam Treaty. With the fall of Communism at the beginning of the decade, an even greater wave of enlargement was anticipated. The need to address the size of the Commission and voting rules in the Council, together with the need for yet a further IGC, were flagged in a Protocol to the Treaty nicknamed the 'Amsterdam leftovers'.[25]

E. The Nice Treaty and Nice Declaration

These leftovers were reheated in the next IGC convened only four months after the entry into force of the Amsterdam Treaty. The resulting negotiations were particularly acrimonious dividing large and small Member States. A deal was finally achieved in the form of the Nice Treaty[26] signed in February 2001. It was the shortest and most modest of the amending treaties to date. It made changes to the Union's institutional arrangements, made further extensions to majority voting and modified the arrangements on enhanced cooperation,[27] but the negotiations left a sense of dissatisfaction and malaise among many of its participants and wider observers. This was reflected in a 'Declaration on the future of the Union' ('the Nice Declaration') adopted by the IGC which called for a 'deeper and wider debate about the future of the European Union'.[28]

---

[23] The Schengen Agreement (1985) and Convention (1990) were originally concluded and developed by some Member States outside the framework of the European Communities and provided for abolition of internal frontier controls.

[24] The UK and Ireland maintained the right to decide whether to opt into civil justice and Schengen measures while Denmark opted out of these altogether and confirmed its non-participation in defence measures.

[25] See the Protocol on the institutions with the prospect of enlargement of the European Union of the Treaty of Amsterdam. See generally D O'Keefe and P Twomey (eds), *Legal Issues of the Amsterdam Treaty* (Hart Publishing, 1999).

[26] Treaty of Nice Official Journal C 80 of 10 March 2001.

[27] Eg, enhanced cooperation now needed the participation of only eight Member States (under Amsterdam closer cooperation required at least a majority) and, in respect of enhanced cooperation under the First Pillar, the national veto held by every Member State was removed. Further, authorization for a non-participating Member State to join an existing enhanced cooperation was to be granted by the Commission (under Amsterdam such decisions were reserved to the Council).

[28] Presidency Conclusions of the Laeken European Council (14 and 15 December 2001): Annex I: Laeken Declaration on the Future of the European Union, in *Bulletin of the European Union* (2001) No 12, 19–23.

This malaise went wider than the acrimony over institutional reform. There was a growing realization that the European Union had grown detached from the citizens that it was intended to serve. Turnout for the European Parliament elections of June 1999 had fallen below 50 per cent;[29] the same low level of support for the European Union was recorded in the Eurobarometer[30] surveys across Member States in 2000 and 2001. The resignation of the Santer Commission in 1999 had done further damage to the Union's reputation. This sense of the EU's unpopularity was reinforced by the rejection of the Nice Treaty itself in a referendum in Ireland in June 2001.[31] The Treaty only entered into force in February 2003 following the adoption of a European Council Declaration at Seville on Ireland's neutrality[32] and a further Irish referendum in October 2002.

An initial period of some 30 years of relative stability had been succeeded by 15 years of increasingly rapid treaty change. Five IGCs and four rounds of substantive treaty amendment had created a complex and opaque treaty framework. Further pressure was added by the German Länder which had threatened to hold up ratification of the Nice Treaty in the Bundesrat insisting on a clearer delimitation of powers in relation to the European Union.[33]

These concerns were picked up in the Nice Declaration[34] which referred to the need to address the democratic legitimacy and transparency of the Union and the delimitation of powers between the EU and Member States, the simplification of the Treaties and the role of national parliaments.

The Declaration also picked up on another parallel development—the Charter of Fundamental Rights[35] which had been 'proclaimed' by the Presidents of the European Parliament, Council and Commission at Nice in December 2000. The Charter had been drawn up on the basis of a European Council Decision the previous year calling for a Charter to make the fundamental rights enshrined in EC law 'more visible to the Union's citizens'.[36] The European Council had entrusted

[29] See <http://www.europarl.europa.eu/parliament/archive/staticDisplay.do?language=EN&id=211>.

[30] Archived Eurobarometer reports can be found at <http://ec.europa.eu/public_opinion/index_en.htm>.

[31] The electorate voted by 53.9% to 46.1% against ratification of the Treaty. See House of Commons Research Paper 01/57 of 21 June 2001, 'The Irish Referendum on the Treaty of Nice'.

[32] See Annex III to the Presidency Conclusions of the Seville European Council of 21 and 22 June 2002. A text of the conclusions is available at <http://www.consilium.europa.eu/ueDocs/cms_Data/docs/pressdata/en/ec/72638.pdf>.

[33] See House of Commons Research Paper 01/49 of 1 May 2001, 'The Treaty of Nice and the Future of Europe Debate'. For a more general discussion, see A Bözel, 'What Can Federalism Teach Us about The European Union? The German Experience' (Royal Institute of International Affairs, 2003).

[34] For the full text of the Declaration on the Future of the Union, see the annexes to the Treaty of Nice, Official Journal C 80 of 10 March 2001. See further B de Witte, 'The Nice Declaration: Time for a Constitutional Treaty of the European Union' *The International Spectator* Vol XXXVI, No 1, January–March 2001.

[35] Official Journal C 364 of 18 December 2000. The full text can also be found at <http://www.europarl.europa.eu/charter/pdf/text_en.pdf>. See also, in general, Lord Goldsmith QC, 'A Charter of Rights. Freedoms and Principles' 38 *CML Rev* 1201–16.

[36] Annex IV to the Conclusions of the Presidency, Cologne European Council, 3–4 June 1999. The full text can be found at <http://www.europarl.europa.eu/summits/kol2_en.htm>.

this task to a novel negotiating process—'a body composed of representatives of the Heads of State and Government and of the President of the Commission as well as of members of the European Parliament and national parliaments'. This Convention, as it was termed, met from December 1999 to October 2000 producing a non-binding text reaffirming the rights, freedoms and principles recognized by the Union. The issue going forward was what status, if any, to give this new document.

This was a significant and wide-ranging agenda. To take it forward the Nice IGC stipulated that the European Council scheduled to take place in Laeken in December would 'agree on a declaration containing appropriate initiatives for the continuation of this agenda' and that yet another IGC would be convened in 2004 'to make the corresponding changes to the Treaties'.

III. The Constitutional Treaty

A. The Laeken Declaration

The Laeken Declaration[37] issued by the Heads of States and Government at the European Council in December 2001 may reasonably be regarded as the launch of the process that led to the conclusion of the Lisbon Treaty. The Declaration was long—some eight pages of densely drafted text—and portentous even by the standard of EU declarations. It announced that:

the Union stands at a crossroads, a defining moment in its existence. The unification of Europe is near. The Union is about to expand to bring in more than ten new Member States, predominantly Central and Eastern European, thereby finally closing one of the darkest chapters in European history: the Second World War and the ensuing artificial division of Europe. At long last, Europe is on its way to becoming one big family, without bloodshed, a real transformation clearly calling for a different approach from fifty years ago, when six countries first took the lead.

The text provided a detailed blueprint for an in-depth review of the structures and operation of the European Union. It identified first the broad challenges, external and internal, facing the Union. Internally, the Declaration referred to the 'democratic challenge facing Europe' and the need to bring the EU's institutions 'closer to its citizens' and to make them 'less unwieldy and rigid and, above all, more efficient and open'. The external challenge was 'Europe's new role in a new globalised world':

Now that the Cold War is over and we are living in a globalised, yet also highly fragmented world, Europe needs to shoulder its responsibilities in the governance of globalisation. The role it has to play is that of a power resolutely doing battle against all violence, all terror and all fanaticism, but which also does not turn a blind eye to the world's heartrending injustices.

---

[37] Presidency Conclusions of the Laeken European Council (14 and 15 December 2001): Annex I: Laeken Declaration on the Future of the European Union, in *Bulletin of the European Union* (2001) No 12, 19–23.

The Declaration followed these broad issues with a range of specific questions on ensuring a better division and definition of competence in the Union including addressing whether the allocation of competence as between the EU and Member States needed to be reorganized; assessing whether the Union's range of legal instruments could be simplified and better defined; increasing the democracy, transparency and efficiency of a much-enlarged Union through institutional reform, improving working methods and increasing the role of national parliaments; and reviewing the complex treaty framework and pillar structure of the Union. The latter point covered the possibility of incorporating the Charter of Fundamental Rights into the Treaties and concluded with the question 'whether this simplification and reorganisation might not lead in the long run to the adoption of a constitutional text in the Union'.

The text of the Declaration had been largely drafted under the auspices of the Belgian Presidency with the assistance of a group of senior politicians from across Europe.[38] But it had its roots firmly in the issues identified in the Nice Declaration and in the range of still unresolved concerns of the past decade, which came starkly to the fore in the post-Nice malaise. The Union had grown big but it had grown flabby. Its treaty and institutional structures were overly complex. It had become remote from its citizens. It needed to get fit for purpose to face the challenges of international security and globalization in the twenty-first century.

The European Council's Declaration concluded by setting out in detail how the problems and questions it raised were to be addressed—by convening a Convention on the Future of Europe drawing together representatives of Heads of States and Government, national parliaments, the European Parliament and the European Commission.[39] The Laeken summit decided that the body would be chaired by the 75-year-old former French President Valéry Giscard d'Estaing with, as Vice Chairmen, two of those involved in drafting the Declaration, former Italian Prime Minister Giuliano Amato and former Belgian Prime Minister, Jean-Luc Dehaene. There would also be a Praesidium to 'lend impetus' to the Convention and to 'provide it with an initial working basis'.

The Convention method had of course already been used the previous year in drawing up the Charter of Fundamental Rights but that had been a smaller body drawing up what was at that time a declaratory, and narrowly focused, text. It had never been used to review the EU Treaties themselves. Support for convening a Convention had grown during 2001 and had been endorsed by Foreign Ministers in October. However, as the Declaration itself acknowledged, the Convention could only 'pave the way' for a further IGC to agree any treaty changes. Under the EU

---

[38] The Group of 'Wise Men' comprising former Belgian Prime Ministers Dahaene of Belgium and Amato of Italy, former Commission President Jacques Delors, former Polish Foreign Minister Gemerek and future UK Foreign Secretary David Miliband.

[39] The Declaration provided that there would be one representative from each government, two from each national parliament, 16 representatives from the European Parliament and two from the Commission. Accession candidate countries could also send representatives from their governments and national parliaments to participate as observers.

Treaties, and as a matter of general treaty law, any amendments to the EU Treaties had to be agreed by the Member States themselves as the Contracting Parties.

B. The Convention on the Future of Europe

The Convention[40] was launched in February 2002. Taking into account alternates and those participating as observers from accession candidate countries and other EU institutions, those taking part in the Convention—the 'conventionnels'—numbered some 220 people. The sheer number and diversity of the participants meant that the roles played by the Chairman, the 13 members of the Praesidium[41] and the Convention Secretary-General[42] were central.

The Convention's work opened with an initial 'listening phase' which lasted until the autumn. The Laeken Declaration had referred to opening a 'Forum' to ensure broad input from civil society. To this end a website was established and special hearings were held in June followed by a 'Youth Convention' the following month. During the same period, the Convention began to get up to speed with its work establishing the first round of the working groups which were to be the main vehicle for the detailed discussion of specific issues.

A total of 11 groups were to be established, each chaired by a member of the Praesidium,[43] and later supplemented by three discussion circles.[44] Most of the topics for the working groups reflected the issues identified by the Laeken Declaration but, perhaps significantly, the core issues of institutional reform, leaving these to be addressed by Giscard d'Estaing. The Chairman and Praesidium, supported by the Secretariat, also prepared the first outline of a proposed new treaty which was presented to the Convention in October.[45]

The structure and nature of the new text was of course a fundamental issue. There was widespread concern to make the EU's treaty framework simpler and more accessible in line with the Convention's objectives. The British Foreign Secretary, Jack Straw, noting the concision of the UN Charter and US

---

[40] For more on the Convention and the origins of the Constitution see Piris, *The Lisbon Treaty: A Legal and Political Analysis* (Cambridge University Press, 2010); G Milton and J Keller-Noellet, *The European Constitution: Its Origins, Negotiations and Meaning* (John Harper Publishing, 2005) and P Norman, *The Accidental Constitution: The Making of Europe's Constitutional Treaty* (2003) Euro-Comment, 2nd rev edn.

[41] Giscard d'Estaing, Amato and Dehaene together with three government representatives from the rotating Presidencies (Alfonso Dastis, Henning Christopherson, Georges Papandreou), two representatives from national parliaments (John Bruton, Gisela Stuart), the European Parliament (Klaus Hänsch and Iñigo Méndez de Vigo y Montojo) and the European Commission (Michel Barnier and Antonio Vitorino) and a representative from the accession candidate States (Alojz Peterle).

[42] Sir John Kerr, later Lord Kerr, former Head of the British Diplomatic Service. At the end of the last session of the Convention, Giscard d'Estaing referred to him as 'one of the most brilliant men I have ever met'; quoted in Peter Norman, above n 40 at 33.

[43] These covered: subsidiarity; the Charter of Fundamental Rights and accession to the ECHR; the EU's legal personality; the role of national parliaments; complementary competences; economic governance; external action; defence; simplification of legislative procedures; freedom, security and justice; and social Europe.

[44] On the Court of Justice, own resources and on budgetary procedures.

[45] <http://register.consilium.europa.eu/pdf/en/02/cv00/cv00369.en02.pdf>.

Constitution, called for a document he could put into his pocket.[46] There were references ensuring that any new text was comprehensible to school children. Various structures were mooted—including bolting a short 'chapeau' text onto the existing EU Treaties—while others worked in parallel on their own texts[47] including the much-discussed 'Penelope' project.[48]

The October outline picked up on the tentative reference 'to a constitutional text' in the Laeken Declaration. It proposed replacing the existing EU Treaties with a single text—a 'Treaty Establishing a Constitution for Europe'—of which the first part would set out the 'Constitutional Structure' including the Union's institutional provisions, the status of the Charter of Fundamental Rights and a new catalogue of the Union's competences.

This provided the vehicle for the next phase of the Convention's work drawing on both the reports of the Working Groups and the first set of draft provisions tabled by the Praesidium in February 2003. This was the busiest period of its work, with hundreds of amendments being proposed and discussed—with particularly intensive debate surrounding Giscard d'Estaing's late tabling of the institutional provisions in April. While Member States' initial engagement and level of representation had varied, as the negotiations intensified so did the level of governments' involvement.

In the closing stages the Legal Services of the Council, Commission and European Parliament were co-opted to help produce the longest section of the draft on Union Policies (largely copied from the existing EU Treaties) and a final text was approved by a significant majority of the Convention members (termed a consensus by the Chairman) in July. It was a weighty document of some 330 pages. Recalling Jack Straw's call for a document that he could put in his pocket, a British diplomat quipped that 'in the Foreign Office we have very large pockets'.[49]

Due in large part to the combined skills of Giscard d'Estaing, Amato, Dehaene and Kerr,[50] the Convention had succeeded in producing from scratch a new, detailed and more or less comprehensive text. This included the proposal that convening a Convention should be the default option for the negotiation of all future treaty amendments—something retained in the Lisbon Treaty.[51] Whether

---

[46] 'A Constitution for Europe' *The Economist*, 11 October 2002.

[47] The texts prepared as contributions to the debate included that produced by a team led by Alan Dashwood of Cambridge University at the request of UK Government officials. See A Dashwood, M Dougan, C Hillion, A Johnston and E Spaventa, 'Draft Constitutional Treaty of the European Union and Related Documents' (2003) 28 *ELRev* 3.

[48] 'Penelope' was a draft Treaty produced by Commission officials at the request of Romano Prodi—named either after the wife of Odysseus who unpicked the cloth on which she was working each evening (akin to the painful process of drafting) or after the daughter of one of those working on the project. Penelope (the text not the daughter) was leaked to the press in December overshadowing the official Commission contribution to the Convention; a copy was also passed by a Commission official to Giscard d'Estaing as he was boarding a train at Gare du Nord in Paris. See Peter Norman, above n 40 at 135–9.

[49] Jack Straw himself referred to the need for a 'poacher's pocket', see *The Economist*, 10 July 2004.

[50] One diplomatic observer referred to the complementary talents of 'Giscard's political and theatrical skills and contact book; Amato's vision; Dahaene's brawn; and Kerr's brain'.

[51] Article 48(4) of the Lisbon Treaty.

the Convention had succeeded in its stated aim of being a transparent, accountable and inclusive forum, or was a more effective negotiating process than a traditional IGC, was more moot.

While all Convention documents were published on its websites, and all its plenary sessions were public, much of its work was done by the Praesidium whose proceedings were confidential. The attempts to reach out to the public were seen by some as artificial, largely focused on those who were already part of the EU culture with the Youth Forum being dismissed as 'Eurocrats in short trousers'.[52] While IGCs were composed of, and required the unanimous agreement of, the actual Contracting Parties—governments democratically accountable through their respective national systems—each with an equal say in the final outcome and each legally responsible for complying with its provisions, the selection and balance of the individual members participating in the Convention could appear arbitrary. One jaded diplomat commented that while the criticism of IGCs was that the public did not know what was going on, in the Convention neither the public nor governments knew what was happening.

The process allowed individuals to advocate personal ideas—such as the distinction between implementing and delegated acts promoted in the Simplification Working Group. This allowed for creativity but by the same token could lead to incorporation of innovations which might not otherwise have been considered necessary. Some commentators also complained that by virtue of its location (in the European Parliament building), working methods and composition, it gave undue weight to the European Parliament, even allowing for its status as the only directly elected EU institution. Certainly MEPs were much better versed in the EU technicalities than their national counterparts and consequently were able to exercise a much greater influence.

While the Secretariat included some able lawyers, there was no legal adviser to the Convention and no professional drafting body—a questionable arrangement for a process preparing a legally binding text, applicable by the ECJ and domestic courts across the European Union, and covering issues of fundamental importance to business and individuals, which were already the subject of 50 years of case law. While the drafting of some substantive provisions could therefore have been better,[53] particular criticism was reserved for the preamble's purple prose topped off by Giscard d'Estaing's personal choice of an introductory quotation from Thucydides.[54]

---

[52] See 'The Convention and Public Opinion: The Fabrication of Interest' in Milton and Keller-Noellet, above n 40 at 42.

[53] See, eg, Article III-365(4) of the Treaty Establishing a Constitution for Europe—on the standing of natural and legal persons to bring proceedings before the Court of Justice of the European Union. That provision is now reproduced, in substance, in Article 263(4) TFEU and is the subject of much commentary and debate. See, eg, K Lenaerts, 'Le traité de Lisbonne et la protection juridictionnelle des particuliers en droit de l'Union' *Cahiers de droit européen*, 2009 No 5–6.

[54] 'Our Constitution . . . is called a democracy because power is in the hands not of a minority but of the greatest number.' This was variously criticized on grounds of mistranslation, Thucydides' own lack of democratic credentials and the inappropriateness of opening a treaty text with a literary quotation.

C. The 2003–04 IGC

The Convention transmitted the draft Constitutional Treaty to the Italian Presidency in July 2003 and the IGC to consider the text started work in October. In order to avoid detailed negotiation on the text, and to limit its work to consideration of the key outstanding institutional issues, the Presidency determined that the IGC would only meet at the level of Heads of State and Government on the basis of work prepared by Foreign Ministers.[55] These meetings addressed some of the most contentious issues which had been left unresolved by the Convention on which opinion between governments was still divided—notably the size of the Commission, future arrangements for majority voting and the Presidency of the Council.[56]

In parallel, there were calls for a group to review the text in detail to ensure that it had the necessary legal rigour.[57] This IGC Working Party of Legal Experts—comprised of representatives of the Member States, Commission and European Parliament—held 23 meetings from October 2003 to April 2004. It was chaired by the Director General of the Council Legal Service, and Legal Adviser to the IGC, Jean-Claude Piris, and the body was colloquially referred to as the Piris Group. Piris played a key behind-the-successive role in successive IGCs—he had been instrumental in devising the Decision on the position of Denmark reached at the Edinburgh Summit[58] and both through his chairmanship of the Legal Experts Groups and his role at European Councils was to be one of the key players in brokering agreement on the Constitutional and Lisbon Treaties.

The Piris Group was the only IGC body meeting on a regular basis and the only one to undertake a line-by-line review of the Convention text. There was a strong presumption in favour of the latter with any changes having to be agreed by consensus. To curb any overeagerness on the part of delegates, the lengthy meetings were held without interpretation (in French) in a cramped and airless room. Despite this, and its strictly technical character, the Piris Group inevitably became a policy negotiation by proxy on sensitive issues. As well as completing a detailed revision of the Convention text, the Group also undertook the first comprehensive review of the numerous Accession Treaty arrangements and Protocols concluded over the previous half-century. But the constraints on the process also imposed limits; thus, for example, the Group was unable to improve the Convention's poor drafting of the new provisions on standing before the ECJ.

Presidency hopes to secure political agreement at the European summit in December foundered on Spanish and Polish concerns about the proposals on

---

[55] There were five meetings of Heads of State and Governments; nine meetings of Foreign Ministers; and two informal meetings at official level.

[56] Other outstanding issues addressed in these negotiations were the provisions on defence, budgetary procedure and the extension of qualified majority voting. On the latter, eg, in the area of criminal justice, the IGC agreed a new 'emergency brake' procedure under which sensitive matters affecting 'fundamental aspects' of a Member State's criminal justice system could be referred to the European Council for decision by consensus.

[57] Termed in the jargon of the IGC, the 'legal verification' of the text.

[58] See p 7 above.

qualified majority voting. These and other points were eventually resolved and a revised treaty text was agreed at the European Council in June 2004 and signed in October.[59]

D. The Treaty Establishing a Constitution for Europe

The text which went forward for ratification by Member States was still largely the product of the Convention. As already proposed in the outline tabled by Giscard d'Estaing two years earlier, it took the form of a single treaty, which abolished the existing EU and EC Treaties, and the existing European Union and European Community, and replaced them with a Constitutional Treaty and a new, single European Union. However, apart from some consequential amendments, the Treaty Establishing the Atomic Energy Community was left outside the new arrangements—reflecting in particular concerns in some Member States about provoking domestic controversy on the issue of atomic energy.

This wholesale replacement of the existing treaties was arguably the most radical innovation.[60] The reference to a 'Constitution', first floated in the Laeken Declaration, was particularly contentious. On one view this was a material change in the nature of the instrument as compared with earlier treaties. It carried associations with national constitutions and this, reinforced by the inclusion of 'symbols of the Union',[61] lent weight to those who (either as critics or supporters) chose to see the Treaty as a step towards statehood. On this view, the new nomenclature might be seized upon in the ECJ and elsewhere, to argue that this was a new kind of instrument instituting a new kind of Union. As the historical evolution of the United States of America had demonstrated such a paradigm shift could not be excluded. In this regard, the inclusion of a new provision explicitly confirming that Member States could leave the Union[62] was a helpful reminder that the Union remained an entity composed of sovereign Member States.

On the other view, the term 'Constitution' was purely descriptive. It reflected the fact that this was, like the treaties it replaced, simply the constituent instrument of the EU just as, for example, the Charter was the constituent instrument of the United Nations. There were solid precedents for using this term to describe the treaties constituting classic intergovernmental organizations—the instruments establishing the International Labour Organization and UNESCO were both called Constitutions.[63] Perhaps because he was speaking in Edinburgh, the British Foreign Secretary Jack Straw, in signalling the UK's acceptance of the term in August 2002, preferred to cite the precedent of golf clubs:

---

[59] Treaty establishing a Constitution for Europe, Official Journal C 310 of 16 December 2004.

[60] From the legal practitioner's perspective it would also have provided a clarity and convenience—for the first time all the primary law including the often obscure accession treaty provisions would have been grouped together in a single text—not found in earlier texts.

[61] Article I-8.

[62] Article I-60.

[63] See the Constitution of the International Labour Organization and the Constitution of the United Nations Educational, Scientific and Cultural Organization.

Golf clubs all across Scotland have constitutions. The point about having a constitution is that it's a clearly understood word describing the basic rules for the operation of an institution, whether it's a golf club, a political party or in this case a European Union.[64]

Another significant aspect of this structural change was the abolition of the pillar structure created by the TEU. There was now a single entity straddling all aspects of the EU's work and while CFSP retained the characteristics of intergovernmental decision-making,[65] the remaining intergovernmental areas of justice and home affairs—cooperation on criminal justice and police matters—were subsumed within in supranational decision-making.

The Constitutional Treaty was divided into four parts. The first part echoed the original desire for a succinct statement of fundamental provisions. It covered issues such as the definition and objectives of the Union, the institutions, membership and citizenship. In particular, it included for the first time a definition and list of the areas of EU competence.[66] Part II incorporated the entire text of the Charter of Fundamental Rights after intensive negotiations to revise parts of the Charter and to prescribe that the Charter was to be interpreted with 'due regard' to the Explanations.[67] Part III, by far the longest part of the Treaty, set out the provisions on the policies and functioning of the Union. These were largely lifted, with the necessary amendments, from the existing treaties and continued to include the detailed provisions on institutional arrangements and procedure which were not included in the first part. The fourth part contained the usual general and final provisions and was followed by 36 Protocols—some new, some consolidating earlier treaty provisions and some restating the Protocols to earlier treaties.

Within these provisions were a range of other innovations reflecting the outcome of the deliberations of the Convention and subsequent IGC including:

- a simplified framework of legal instruments (in which regulations and directives were renamed European laws and framework laws);
- a smaller Commission dispensing with one Commissioner for each Member State;
- a new, permanent President of the European Council;
- a new post of Union Minister for Foreign Affairs straddling both the Commission and Council;

---

[64] Quoted in the *Guardian*, 27 August 2002. The agreement itself also had the form of a classic Treaty concluded, and subject to amendment, by Member States as the Contracting Parties and in the general and final provisions in Part IV referred throughout to 'this Treaty'. Conversely, advocates of the contrary view might have sought to place emphasis on the implied distinction in its title—a Treaty *establishing* a Constitution for Europe. Those seeking to emphasize the Convention's character as a classic Treaty referred to it as the 'Constitutional Treaty'—a term first used in the document tabled by Giscard d'Estaing (see p 15 above), and for convenience used here, but not a term used in the instrument itself.

[65] See n 15 above.

[66] These were largely intended to codify existing categories of competence reflected in earlier Treaties and case law but distinguished for the first time the distinct category of 'supporting, coordinating or complementary action'.

[67] On the Explanations (or 'Commentary') see Goldsmith, above n 35.

- a reinforced role for national Parliaments;
- a new system of 'double majority voting' in the Council;
- new provisions on cooperation in the area of defence;
- the extension of qualified majority voting in some 51 new areas;[68] and
- changes to the nomenclature, jurisdiction and appointments procedure of the ECJ.[69]

In its simplification of the EU's treaty structure and legal instruments, reform of the EU institutions (which made it easier to accommodate future enlargements), definition of EU competences and resolution of the status of the Charter, the Constitutional Treaty had gone a long way to addressing the list of issues in the Laeken Declaration. But perhaps equally significant was what the Treaty did not do. The new areas of EU competence were relatively few compared to earlier EU Treaties and in many cases codified areas where the EU had already acted. Many of the provisions on substantive EU policies were largely untouched and, setting aside the above debates on the significance of a 'Constitution', the new EU retained the characteristics of its predecessors as an organization founded on Member States in which long-standing principles such as free movement remained key. This was not accidental but the product of hard negotiation by those Member States opposed to using the Laeken process to promote an integrationist agenda. In many respects there was arguably just enough to upset both those who had hoped that the Convention would lead to a more supranational, more social European Union and those opposed to any moves in that direction.

E. Non, Nee and the period of reflection

As with other EU Treaties, the Constitutional Treaty provided that it was to be ratified by the Contracting Parties 'in accordance with their respective constitutional requirements'.[70] Such national requirements, and in particular whether a referendum was to be held, varied as between Member States and also as between EU Treaties. Since the ruling of the Irish Supreme Court in *Crotty*[71] in 1987, Ireland had been the most consistent Member State in holding referendums on all the substantive amendments to the EU Treaties.[72] Denmark, which had held referendums on the SEA, TEU and Amsterdam Treaty (but not the Nice Treaty), also confirmed that it would be carrying out a referendum, their Prime Minister

---

[68] See the list in the Commentary on the Treaty Establishing a Constitution for Europe, Command Paper 6459 presented by the Foreign and Commonwealth Secretary, February 2005 at 491. Methods for counting the moves to qualified majority voting, and thus the overall total, varied.

[69] This is only a very selective list. For a comprehensive account of the changes made by the Constitutional Treaty see Piris, above n 40.

[70] Article IV-447, see also Article 48 (as applicable at that time) of the TEU.

[71] *Crotty v An Taoiseach* [1987] IESC 4; [1987] IR 713 (9 April 1987).

[72] This is not an automatic requirement but requires an assessment to be made as to the significance of the changes made.

Anders Fogh Rasmussen stating that 'The EU's constitution is so new and large a document that it would be right to hold a referendum on it.'[73]

Seven other states indicated that they would be holding referendums: France, Luxembourg, the Netherlands, Poland, Portugal, Spain and the UK. But the announcement in May 2004 by UK Prime Minister Tony Blair that he had decided to hold a referendum drew particular attention. While the UK had held a referendum in 1975 on the UK's continuing membership of the European Communities it had never held a referendum on an EU Treaty. Ratification of EU Treaties was a matter for the government once Parliament had enacted the necessary implementing legislation;[74] as with the Maastricht Treaty, the Parliamentary legislative process had therefore been the usual vehicle for scrutiny of EU Treaties. Blair argued that without a referendum it would not be possible to secure parliamentary approval; he also acknowledged that his decision placed great pressure on France, which had previously held a referendum on the Maastricht Treaty, to do the same:

> With deep misgivings, I accepted we had to promise a referendum ... We couldn't get the Constitution through the House of Lords without it, and even the Commons vote would have been in doubt ... Jacques Chirac was ... aggrieved as he felt it presented him with a real problem. In this he was right. If Britain promised a referendum, it put enormous pressure on France to do the same.[75]

The decision of nine Member States to hold referendums on the Constitutional Treaty, including six which had not done so on previous amending EU Treaties, reflected their various views as to the significance of the Constitution. But it was difficult to generalize about their reasons. For some it reflected the assessment that the Constitutional Treaty represented a significant change—by virtue of the character and nature of the instrument itself or the substantive changes that it made. For others, the fact that the entirety of the EU's treaty framework provisions were being ratified, whether new ones or ones simply set out afresh, or indeed just represented a symbolic new departure for the European Union, warranted a referendum.[76]

The first referendum was held in February 2005 in Spain where the Constitutional Treaty was approved by 77 per cent.[77] The Treaty was also approved by 57 per cent in a referendum held in July in Luxembourg. France held its referendum in

---

[73] Quoted in *EU Observer*, 31 May 2003.

[74] Although under the European Parliamentary Elections Act 2002, section 12, the UK Parliament was required to approve the ratification of an EU Treaty which increased the powers of the European Parliament.

[75] Tony Blair, *A Journey* (Hutchinson, 2010) 501. A contemporary British political cartoon showed French President Jacques Chirac being dragged to a guillotine, marked with a 'non', with Tony Blair, in the guise of a French revolutionary crone, looking on in glee.

[76] In his statement to the UK Parliament announcing a referendum, Prime Minister Blair stated that 'The question will be on the treaty, but the implications go far wider—as I believe we all know. It is time to resolve once and for all whether this country, Britain, wants to be at the centre and heart of European decision making or not; time to decide whether our destiny lies as a leading partner and ally of Europe or on its margins.' *Hansard*, 20 April 2004, col 155.

[77] On a turnout of 42%.

May 2005. The rejection of the Constitution by 55 per cent to 45 per cent[78] was a major shock. It was followed by a further rejection of the Treaty three later days in the Dutch referendum by 61 per cent to 39 per cent.[79] Other plans for referendums were shelved or abandoned. The fact that two of the founding Member States had rejected the Constitutional Treaty by significant margins, and with comparatively high turnouts, plunged the European Union into political crisis.

There was inevitably much hand-wringing as to the reasons for the no votes with some eager to blame anything other than the Constitution itself. Surveys in France identified a range of factors of which three appeared to be the most significant: fear that the Treaty would increase unemployment in France; general dissatisfaction with the domestic situation in France; and concerns that the Treaty was too economically liberal and pro-market.[80] The last of these underlined the sometimes mixed, and conflicting, views of the Constitution. While in the UK the Constitution was criticized in some quarters for moving further towards an integrationist, social Europe, for some in France and elsewhere it was criticized as representing a success for proponents of an 'Anglo-Saxon' free market model.[81]

There was also sterile debate as to the legal consequences of the no votes. Dubious reliance was placed on an IGC declaration of ratification.[82] Some sought to argue that there was an obligation on Member States to continue their national ratification procedures. Others argued that the Constitution must now be considered dead. Legally, the Treaty could not enter into force unless and until it had been ratified by all 27 Member States—the issue was whether this was now politically acceptable or feasible.

The French and Dutch referendum results were discussed by Heads of States and Government meeting at the European Council in June. They issued a declaration calling for a 'period of reflection':

...We have noted the outcome of the referendums in France and the Netherlands. We consider that these results do not call into question citizens' attachment to the construction of Europe. Citizens have nevertheless expressed concerns and worries which

---

[78] On a turnout of 69%.

[79] On a turnout of 62%.

[80] TNS-Sofres opinion poll for *Le Monde* and TF1 television quoted in the *Guardian*, 31 May 2005. See also The European Constitution: Post-referendum survey in France, Eurobarometer, The European Commission June 2005 section 2.3. The same three points feature at the top of the list of the reasons for voting no. There were equally a range of reasons underlying the no votes in the Dutch referendum but with concerns about the lack of information and about the loss of national sovereignty appearing to rank as the most significant—see The European Constitution: Post-referendum survey in the Netherlands, Eurobarometer, The European Commission June 2005 section 2.3.

[81] 'Words like "free and fair competition" and "free movement of goods, people and capital" were presented by "no" campaigners of the left as the new gospel of Anglo-Saxon, "ultra-libérale," heartless capitalism, rather than the old religion of the EEC, EC and EU going back to 1957' John Lichfield, the *Guardian*, 30 May 2005. See also Paul Reynolds, 'An Anglo-Saxon Takeover of the EU' BBC News Website, 11 May 2005.

[82] Declaration 30 in the Final Act of the IGC adopting the Constitutional Treaty: 'The Conference notes that if, two years after the signature of the Treaty Establishing a Constitution for Europe, four-fifths of the Member States have ratified it and one or more Member States have encountered difficulties in proceeding with ratification, the matter will be referred to the European Council'.

need to be taken into account. Hence the need for us to reflect together on this situation. This period of reflection will be used to enable a broad debate to take place in each of our countries, involving citizens, civil society, social partners, national parliaments and political parties...[83]

The Heads of State and Government agreed to return to the matter 'in the first part of 2006' to decide how to proceed. As their contribution to the period of reflection, the Commission issued in October 2005 its 'Plan D for Democracy, Dialogue and Debate' which was 'aimed at encouraging wider debate on the future of the EU, between the EU institutions and citizens'.[84]

Other European Union business had of course been continuing throughout the period of the negotiation of the Constitutional Treaty and the subsequent referendums. Most significantly, the largest enlargement in the history of the Union, with the accession of 10 new Member States, had taken place at the beginning of 2004. Some observers indeed argued that the fact this had taken place smoothly and had not impaired the effectiveness of the Union indicated that the Nice Treaty arrangements were sufficient—there was no need for a further treaty. During 2005 and 2006 much of the focus of the EU's work was on other business and in particular the 2007–2013 Financial Perspective.[85]

There had therefore been little progress in deciding the fate of the Constitutional Treaty when Heads of State and Government returned to the issue again at the European Council in June 2006. But even if the enlarged Union was dealing effectively with day-to-day business, the expectations and momentum created by the process leading up to the Constitutional Treaty meant that the sense of crisis created by its rejection was real. The unresolved fate of the Treaty, and of institutional reform, was a continuing distraction from the substantive work of the Union.

The June summit prolonged the period of reflection, calling on the Presidency to present a report to the European Council during the first semester of 2007 containing 'an assessment of the state of discussion with regard to the Constitutional Treaty and explore possible future developments'. The examination of the report would 'serve as a basis for further decisions on how to continue the reform process, it being understood that the necessary steps to that effect will have been taken during the second semester of 2008 at the latest'.[86]

This placed responsibility for taking forward the process onto Germany which would take up the Presidency in the first part of 2007 and onto the shoulders of its Chancellor Angela Merkel.

---

[83] Declaration by the Heads of State or Government of the Member States of the European Union on the Ratification of the Treaty Establishing a Constitution for Europe (European Council, 16 and 17 June 2005) Brussels, 18 June 2005, SN 117/05.

[84] Communication from the Commission to the Council, the European Parliament, the European Economic and Social Committee and the Committee of the Regions—'The Commission's contribution to the period of reflection and beyond: Plan-D for Democracy, Dialogue and Debate' 13 October 2005, COM(2005) 494.

[85] On which leaders had failed to reach agreement at the June 2005 European Council and which was only settled at the end of the following year.

[86] See the Presidency Conclusions of the Brussels European Council, 15–16 June 2006.

IV. The Lisbon Treaty

A. From re-launch to Reform Treaty

One of the initial priorities of the German Presidency was agreement in March of a 'Berlin Declaration' of EU leaders to mark the fiftieth anniversary of the Treaty of Rome.[87] This concluded with the aim of 'placing the European Union on a renewed common basis before the European Parliament elections in 2009'. Differences over the text meant that the Declaration was signed by the Presidents of the Council, Commission and European Parliament, rather than by the Heads of States and Government, but the reference to a 'renewed common basis' was a clear signal of the intention, at least on the part of the Presidency and the EU Institutions, to have a new treaty in place in 2009.

The German Presidency faced wide differences in the positions of Member States. By the time it took office, 18 Member States had ratified the Constitutional Treaty. This included Bulgaria and Romania who had acceded to the European Union on 1 January 2007 and whose Treaty of Accession had provided for alternative arrangements depending on whether or not the Constitution had entered into force by that date.[88] France and the Netherlands had of course rejected the Constitution and the remaining states had formally suspended their ratification procedures.[89]

There were similarly wide differences in the views as to what should be done. Some considered that the whole process of treaty change should simply be abandoned. Some were continuing to press for a continuation of the ratification process. There had been indications that Germany had been considering a new Protocol on social issues[90] to address French concerns, but even if this was feasible, it would not have been sufficient to overcome objections to reviving the Constitution. Others again had suggested 'cherry-picking' the text of the Constitution by taking forward selected provisions on institutional reform or implementing those elements which did not require formal treaty change. Meanwhile, the new French President Nicholas Sarkozy, elected in May 2007, had been calling for a new 'simplified treaty'.[91]

---

[87] This had been called for by the June 2006 European Council which sought a political declaration 'setting out Europe's values and ambitions and confirming their shared commitment to deliver them'. See Presidency Conclusions, ibid.

[88] Official Journal L 157 of 21 June 2005.

[89] Czech Republic, Denmark, Ireland, Poland, Portugal, Sweden and the UK.

[90] See K Barysch, 'The Austrian EU Presidency and the Future of the Constitutional Treaty' Centre for European Policy, January 2006.

[91] 'It is urgent to enable Europe to function efficiently with 27 members. That's the reason I've proposed that we adopt a "simplified treaty" with the aim precisely of remedying the institutional emergency. I spoke of this simplified treaty for the first time over a year ago, in Berlin, then again last September in Brussels... The draft Constitutional Treaty contained a number of measures that everyone, including the "no" camp, recognized would permit the EU to function more efficiently. The "simplified treaty" would reintroduce those measures on which there was a consensus.' Quoted in

The German Presidency undertook extensive bilateral consultations among Member States to ascertain the basis on which they would accept returning to the process of negotiating a new treaty. For a number of Member States this included addressing both concerns about specific issues and the nature and structure of the proposed Treaty itself. For France and the Netherlands, and as reflected in Sarkozy's call for a 'simplified treaty', any new instrument had to be materially different from the Constitution which had already been rejected in their national referendums. For Denmark, a key issue was whether a new treaty would entail the transfer of competences to the European Union and thus require a referendum or the approval of four-fifths of the Folketing. In the UK, the government also made clear its opposition to reviving a constitutional treaty as well as emphasizing four 'red lines' that would need to be met in any new treaty[92]—protection of the UK's existing labour and social legislation; protection of the UK's common law system, and police and judicial processes; maintenance of the UK's independent foreign and defence policy; and protection of the UK's tax and social security system.[93]

Any agreement to re-enter into negotiations on a new treaty would need to be sufficiently precise and comprehensive as to address all these concerns. Another concern was timing. For those within the Presidency and EU institutions, the various institutional issues and decisions on the horizon meant that the ambition of having a new treaty in place by 2009 could only be met if the German Presidency actually re-launched the negotiating process.[94] As well as its bilateral meetings with senior officials ('focal points') from Member States, the Presidency worked closely with the Council Secretariat to examine in detail the possible options for any new instrument.[95] There were, however, only two meetings of the Member States' focal points as a group[96] in May before the German Presidency unveiled its brief report on institutional reform on 14 June.[97] This was discussed three days later at an informal meeting of Foreign Ministers.

The Presidency report was short. Reviewing the results of its consultations with Member States it noted that a number of Member States had 'underlined the

an interview with *Politique Internationale*, Revue no 115, Printemps 2007, reproduced (and translated) at <http://www.ambafrance-uk.org>.

[92] 'The Government's position is that, in view of the results of the French and Dutch referendums, the best way forward now is the traditional approach of an amending treaty rather than the constitutional treaty'. UK Foreign Secretary Margaret Beckett, Parliamentary Written Answer, House of Commons, *Hansard* 14 May 2007, Col 496W.

[93] See 'The Reform Treaty: The British Approach to the European Union Intergovernmental Conference' July 2007, Foreign and Commonwealth Office, Command Paper 7174.

[94] See Piris, above n 40 at 26–9: 'Calculating backwards [from 2009], that meant that the report required from the German Presidency for June 2007 could not be limited to a presentation of different options, or even to a political description of what a possible revision of the treaties should be, but should already present a clear and precise mandate to the IGC'.

[95] Ibid 30–3.

[96] See House of Commons Foreign Affairs Committee, Foreign Policy Aspects of the Lisbon Treaty Third Report of Session 2007–08, 16 January 2008 at 15. There has also been an initial meeting of the focal points in January.

[97] Report from the Presidency to the European Council—Pursuing the Treaty Reform Process. 10659/07, 14 June 2007.

importance of avoiding the impression which might be given by the symbolism and the title "Constitution" that the nature of the Union is undergoing radical change'. It also noted that the concern of others which had ratified the Constitutional Treaty 'to preserve the substance of the innovations agreed upon in the 2004 IGC and to ensure as far as possible the readability and simplicity of the new Treaty'. The report recommended that:

the June European Council agree to the rapid convening of an IGC. It suggests that the European Council give a precise and comprehensive mandate (on structure and content) to the IGC, thus allowing it to finalise its work on a new Treaty before the end of this year. The Presidency proposes a return to the classical method of treaty change. The IGC would therefore be asked to adopt a Reform Treaty amending the existing Treaties rather than repealing them.

The proposal for an immediate IGC based on a detailed mandate reflected the concerns on timing and the need to address, comprehensively and in advance, the issues on the basis of which Member States would agree to come back to the negotiating table.

B. The IGC Mandate

The draft mandate was given to Member States for the first time on 19 June just two days before the start of the European Council. As well as the pressures which this placed on governments in reviewing and analysing the draft, this tight timetable was criticized for impeding effective Parliamentary scrutiny.[98] The subsequent European Council was gruelling even by the standards of EU summits with Heads of State and Government, Foreign Ministers and officials negotiating and drafting around the clock over two and a half days across the whole range of EU treaty issues. Agreement on a mandate for an IGC to negotiate a new 'Reform Treaty' was finally reached in the early hours of the morning of 23 June.

The agreed mandate, annexed to the Presidency Conclusions of the June European Council,[99] was the most detailed ever proposed for an IGC. It set out comprehensively how the proposed treaty was to be structured and even included precise stipulations as to the location and wording of certain provisions. All this ensured that Member States with specific concerns had had these addressed as part of their agreeing to the convening of the IGC and the re-launch of the treaty amendment process.

The mandate stipulated at the outset that the 'constitutional concept...is abandoned'. It went on to provide that a Reform Treaty would be drawn up 'amending the existing Treaties with a view to enhancing the efficiency and democratic legitimacy of the enlarged Union, as well as the coherence of its external action' and that the 'innovations resulting from the 2004 IGC' (that is as set out in

---

[98] See the House of Commons Foreign Affairs Committee Report, above n 96 at 16.
[99] Presidency Conclusions of the Brussels European Council, 21 and 22 June 2007 (11177/1/07 REV 1).

the Constitutional Treaty) would be introduced into the existing treaties, as set out in the mandate, and with a series of modifications 'introduced as a result of the consultations with the Member States over the past six months'. The mandate went on to set out in 24 detailed paragraphs, with lengthy footnotes and supplemented by two substantial annexes, how both the Treaties Establishing the European Union and the European Communities were to be amended.[100]

The overall result was that many of the innovations, and with them much of the drafting, of the Constitutional Treaty were retained. This was particularly the case in relation to the institutional changes including the proposed reduction in the size of the Commission, a new elected President of the European Council, a new external relations post straddling the Commission and Council supported by an external action service, and the introduction of double majority voting in the Council. Also kept were the new provisions on the Union's values and objectives[101] on democratic principles, the new catalogue of competences,[102] the extensions of majority voting and co-decision, the new solidarity clause and new articles on areas of EU competence, the distinction between legislative and non-legislative acts and changes to the budgetary procedure. In particular, as with the Constitutional Treaty, the previously intergovernmental area of criminal justice and police coop-eration was brought within the supranational arrangements.

The original aim of simplifying the Union's architecture was also maintained by abolishing the European Community and extending the scope of the European Union across both Treaties. As a consequence, the Treaty Establishing the Euro-pean Community (TEC) was to be renamed the Treaty on the Functioning of the European Union (TFEU),[103] the Union replaced and succeeded the Community and all references to the 'Community' were replaced by references to the 'Union'. Many saw this as an elegant means of ending the 'organised schizophrenia'[104] created by the Maastricht Treaty—under which they were two legal persons operating in parallel creating particular confusion and inefficiencies in dealings with third countries and organizations—within the existing treaty framework.

---

[100] The approaches taken to the TEU and TEC were prima facie different. In relation to the TEU the mandate provided that 'in the absence of indications to the contrary . . . the text of the existing Treaty remains unchanged'. In relation to the TEC, it was provided that the 'innovations as agreed in the 2004 IGC will be inserted in the Treaty by way of specific modifications'. In other words, the innovations made by the Constitutional Treaty relating to the TEC were to be inserted wholesale, with such changes as set out in the mandate, but in relation to the TEU only those set out in the mandate would be inserted. While this was occasionally relevant to discussions in the IGC Legal Experts Group the practical significance was marginal given on the one hand the detail of the changes set out in relation to the TEU and on the other the number of changes made by the mandate—set out in 24 paragraphs—to the IGC 2004 innovations affecting the TEC.

[101] But with modifications on competition, see below.

[102] But inserted at the front of the TFEU (as the EC Treaty was renamed) rather than the TEU.

[103] When the first document was tabled proposing renaming the EC Treaty, the Treaty on the Function of the Union, some British officials immediately suggested referring to it as TOFU. Unfortunately the abbreviation, while easier to say than the subsequently accepted usage of TFEU, did not survive; no doubt the association with a bland, rubbery and opaque mass was not to everyone's taste.

[104] See section II, C, 'The Maastricht Treaty' above.

The framework was, however, very different from that created by the Constitutional Treaty as the mandate itself emphasized in underlining that the 'constitutional method' had been abandoned. The existing treaties were not themselves abolished and replaced with a new, single text. They remained in place and were to be amended just as they had been amended by the Nice Treaty and earlier agreements. The European Union itself was a continuation of the entity created by the TEU rather than a new entity. As well as dispensing with the term 'Constitution', the provisions on the symbols of the Union (such as the flag and anthem) which had been the focus of some concern under the Constitutional Treaty were also abandoned. Similarly, the term 'Union Minister for Foreign Affairs', which for some had carried associations with statehood, was replaced with the more anodyne 'High Representative of the Union for Foreign Affairs and Security Policy'. The significance one attached to these differences depended to a large extent on the significance that one had previously attached to the new approach, framework and nomenclature introduced by the Constitution.

There were also a number of substantive changes, many of which had been introduced specifically to address concerns raised by individual Member States such as France, the Netherlands, the UK and Denmark. These included expanding and strengthening the provisions relating to the role of national parliaments. The provision on the primacy of EU law included in the Constitutional Treaty was removed and replaced a declaration recalling existing case law. References to the limits on EU competence and the role of Member States, which had already been strengthened in the Constitutional Treaty as compared to earlier treaties, were further reinforced.[105] The planned changes to the nomenclature of EU legal instruments, including substituting 'law' and 'framework law' for regulation and directive, were dropped.[106] A reference to combating climate change was inserted. A new Protocol was agreed on Services of General Economic Interest. Certain new provisions were moved into the Title on Justice and Home Affairs.[107] The introduction of the new rules on double majority voting was delayed until 2014 with a possibility of using the old rules until 2017.

French concerns about the economic liberalism re-emerged in a high-profile spat about the reference to competition. In what was trailed in the media as a last-minute ambush by President Sarkozy, a reference to an internal market 'where competition is free and undistorted' in the new list of Union objectives was removed.[108] There was much debate as to whether this represented anything more than a presentational change to help the French Government respond to domestic concerns. The Treaties contained numerous other references to competition and the

---

[105] This included a new Protocol on shared competence, a Declaration on the delimitation of competences, making clear in the catalogue of competences that Member States again exercise their competence to the extent that the Union had ceased to exercise its competence and making clear the Union exercise of supporting competence was in support of Member States.

[106] Happily removing what would undoubtedly have been the cause of much confusion and complexity for legal practitioners.

[107] With a consequent impact on their applicability to Denmark.

[108] Constitutional Treaty Article I-3.

substantive powers in this area were unchanged. Matters were resolved by the inclusion of a new Protocol[109] making clear that the reference to the internal market in the Union's objectives 'includes a system ensuring that competition is not distorted'. Expert opinion confirmed that the legal position had not changed[110] but the episode was a telling example both of the competing pressures on EU leaders at the summit to address the concerns of their constituents and of how rapid negotiations at the highest level could intrude upon long-established and complex areas of EU law.

A key example of the ways in which the concerns of individual Member States were addressed was provided by the range of changes made in relation to the UK's red lines. By virtue of using a classic amending treaty, the continuing distinct, intergovernmental character of CFSP was underlined by its remaining separate from other EU policies in the TEU. This was further reinforced by a new provision underlining its specific character and institutional arrangements. In addition there were two declarations underlining the continuing responsibility and powers of Member States for foreign policy.[111] In relation to the Charter of Fundamental Rights, a new UK-specific Protocol was agreed guaranteeing, among other points, that the Charter did not extend courts' ability to find that national laws were inconsistent with the rights and principles which it reaffirmed.[112] In relation to Justice and Home Affairs, the UK's (and Ireland's) existing opt-in arrangements were extended to criminal justice and police cooperation—a significant change in view of the latter's transfer to supranational decision-making. Finally,[113] a provision was inserted which explicitly confirmed for the first time that, 'national security remains the sole responsibility of each Member State'[114]—the last point to be negotiated by exhausted EU leaders during the European Council in the early hours of the morning.

C. The 2007 IGC

Unsurprisingly, given its detailed character, the mandate was quickly transformed by the Council Secretariat into a draft treaty text[115] which was transmitted to Member States soon after the opening of the IGC by the Portuguese Presidency in July. As with the Constitutional Treaty, a Group of Legal Experts was formally

---

[109] Protocol No 27 on the Internal Market and Competition.

[110] See R Whish, *Competition Law*, 6th edn (Oxford University Press, 2009).

[111] See also P Berman, 'The Lisbon Treaty: The End of Foreign Office?' Royal Institute of International Affairs, London, January 2010, <http://www.chathamhouse.org.uk>.

[112] On the Protocol, see A Dashwood, 'The Charter of Fundamental Rights and its Protocol. Drawing the Teeth of a Paper Tiger' *Parliamentary Brief* (February 2008) 9–10. During the subsequent IGC, the application of the Protocol was also extended to Poland. In addition, the text of the Charter was removed from the Treaty itself but given the same 'legal value as the Treaties' with the relevant provision in the Treaty (Article 6 TEU) underlining the need to have regard to the Explanations.

[113] The examples here are not of course an exhaustive list of the changes made by the IGC mandate or those made to address UK concerns.

[114] Article 4(2) TEU.

[115] CIG 1/07.

convened under the chairmanship of Jean-Claude Piris comprising representatives of the 27 Member States, the European Parliament and Commission. It was again the only standing group operating during the IGC holding an initial meeting in July and then holding intensive meetings on a regular basis from late August until early October. Operating under similar constraints to the previous Piris Group, it undertook a detailed comparison of the draft Treaty with mandate agreeing some 350 changes including the text of the preamble, the tightening of the drafting of the language on the ECJ's jurisdiction over CFSP and the arrangements for the publication of the text of the Charter and its Explanations.[116]

The Group also negotiated the only substantive issues which had been left open by the mandate—the application of the opt-ins of the United Kingdom, and Ireland, in relation to amendments to justice and home affairs (JHA) measures and to measures building on the Schengen *acquis*. This also extended to cover the jurisdiction of the ECJ in relation to existing intergovernmental JHA measures. The driving factor here was the UK Government's concern to ensure that its opt-in arrangements were watertight and in particular, given the domestic sensitivities relating to the ECJ's jurisdiction over JHA, that it retained the right to decide whether to participate in JHA measures subject to the Court's jurisdiction. This turned into the most protracted and difficult part of the Group's work—and one of the most difficult parts of the entire negotiation of the Lisbon Treaty—taking as much time as had been taken to go through the entirety of the treaty text. Its successful resolution, with agreement on arguably some of the most complex and baroque procedures in the Treaties, paved the way for the publication of a revised draft Treaty on 5 October.[117]

The revised text was discussed at meetings of Foreign Ministers on 15 October and of Heads of State and Government on 18 October. The latter agreed a small number of outstanding issues[118] and confirmed its political agreement of the Treaty which was reissued with amendments on 30 October.[119] Following a review of the different language versions by the lawyer linguists and Member States' representatives in November, the Treaty amending the Treaty on European Union and the Treaty Establishing the European Community, now simply known as the Lisbon Treaty,[120] was formally signed at Lisbon on 13 December 2007.[121]

The publication of the politically agreed text on the eve of Hallowe'en was a gift to political cartoonists. Gothic imagery had already begun to dog the negotiation of the Lisbon Treaty. Accusations that it was simply the disinterred body of the Constitution had already prompted images of the text emerging zombie-like from

---

[116] For a detailed list of the changes agreed by the Legal Group see Piris, above n 40 at 41–3.

[117] CIG 1/1/07 REV 1 and CIG 2/1/07 REV 1.

[118] The composition of the European Parliament, modifications to the Ioannina compromise applicable to majority voting, the number of Advocates General, the role of the European Parliament in relation to the appointment of the High Representative and the spelling of Euro in Cyrillic.

[119] SN 4579/07.

[120] This supplanted the name 'Reform Treaty' used in the IGC mandate.

[121] Published in the Official Journal on 17 December, OJ C 306 1.

the grave. This was now supplemented with cartoons with the caption 'Trick or Treaty?'—a foretaste of the arguments that were to loom in ratification debates as to whether the Treaty was a political sleight of hand in which the rejected Constitutional Treaty had simply been repackaged under a different name.

D. Ratification: from Lisbon to London to Dublin to Karlsruhe to Prague

Of the nine Member States which had called referendums on the Constitutional Treaty, only one Member State, Ireland, determined to hold a referendum on the Lisbon Treaty—just as it had done on all previous amending treaties. In the Netherlands the State Council (Raad van State) had already concluded in September that the new Treaty was 'substantially different' from the Constitution on the basis of which the government concluded that a referendum was not necessary. In France, while it was concluded that the Treaty required a revision to the French Constitution, the government decided that this did not require a referendum and could be done by parliamentary procedure. Denmark followed the same procedure as it had done for the Constitutional Treaty in determining whether a referendum (or approval by four-fifths of the Folketing) was needed—that is, whether it transferred competences to the EU. The new analysis concluded that none of the 11 points on which the Constitutional Treaty were held to transfer power to the EU, and which had informed Denmark's approach to the IGC mandate, subsisted under the Lisbon Treaty.

(i) The UK

The debates over a referendum, and the differences between the Constitutional Treaty and the Lisbon Treaty, were probably most fierce in the UK. The high-profile commitment by Prime Minister Tony Blair to hold a referendum on the Constitutional Treaty,[122] reiterated in political parties' manifestos for the 2005 General Election, focused particular attention on this issue. Both Tony Blair, and his successor Gordon Brown, made clear their view that the Lisbon Treaty did not warrant a referendum. Presenting the agreement on the IGC mandate to Parliament in June 2007, Tony Blair stated:

We have never, on conventional amending treaties, had referendums. We did not on the Single European Act; we did not on Maastricht; we did not on Amsterdam; we did not on Nice. We accepted that the constitutional treaty was in a different bracket precisely because it purported to be a constitution that governed all the various items in Europe. As a result of the changes that we have made, it is impossible to say that.[123]

---

[122] See p 23 above.
[123] *Hansard*, 25 June 2007, col 30.

This was reinforced by the incoming Prime Minister Gordon Brown. Speaking in a BBC interview the same month,[124] he underlined that the UK had achieved its red lines and 'that means that just as in the case of all the other amending treaties, the Nice and Maastricht and so on, that the people would not therefore expect there to be a referendum'.

As with previous EU Treaties, the process of scrutiny and ratification of the Lisbon Treaty was taken forward by way of a Bill amending the European Communities Act.[125] The scrutiny of the Treaty was intense. There were some 25 days of debates in the Commons and Lords on some 515 amendments with 57 divisions, or votes, being held. In addition, Parliamentary Committees issued five separate reports on the Treaty.[126] Given the difficulties in reading and understanding an amending treaty, the UK Government rapidly produced the first consolidated version of the EU Treaties as amended by the Lisbon Treaty[127] as well as a comparative table of the Treaties before and after amendment.[128]

The Bill itself made important and novel concessions to parliamentary control over decision-making on EU matters giving Parliament prior control over the use of certain *passerelles*[129] and introducing for the first time a general requirement for parliamentary approval, by primary legislation, of the ratification of any future changes to the EU Treaties.[130] This provision, nicknamed the, 'thus far and no further clause', was intended to send a clear signal both as to Parliament's reinforced control over future amendments and the government's aversion to further treaty change.[131]

While parliamentary scrutiny of the Treaty covered the entirety of its provisions the most intense arguments, and some of the closest votes, remained focused on the issue of a referendum and the differences between the Constitutional Treaty and

---

[124] Speaking on 24 June 2007 three days before he replaced Tony Blair as Prime Minister.

[125] The European Union (Amendment) Act 2008 (c.7).

[126] House of Commons European Scrutiny Committee: European Union Intergovernmental Conference, Thirty-fifth Report of Session 2006–2007 (HC 1014); House of Lords Constitution Committee 6th Report of Session 2007–2008: European Union (Amendment) Bill and the Lisbon Treaty: Implications for the UK Constitution, Report with Evidence (HL Paper 84); House of Commons Foreign Affairs Committee: Foreign Policy Aspects of the Lisbon Treaty (HC 120-I, 2007–2008); House of Lords European Union Committee 10th Report of Session 2007–08: The Treaty of Lisbon: an impact assessment (HL Papers 62-I and 62-II).

[127] Consolidated Texts of the EU Treaties as Amended by the Lisbon Treaty. Command Paper 7310, January 2008.

[128] A Comparative Table of the Current EC and EU Treaties as Amended by the Treaty of Lisbon. Command Paper 7311, January 2008.

[129] *Passerelles* are provisions which allow less onerous procedural requirements to be followed without the need for formal treaty revision. The *passerelles* agreed under Lisbon are provisions which allow either the European Council or the Council to decide by unanimity to switch a particular legal basis from unanimity to QMV or from a special legislative procedure to the ordinary legislative procedure without having to follow the full ordinary legislative procedure for revising the Treaties.

[130] European Union (Amendment) Act 2008 (c.7), section 5.

[131] 'I can confirm that, not just for this Parliament but also for the next, it is the position of the Government to oppose any further institutional change in the relationship between the EU and its member states. In our view, there is also a growing consensus across Europe that there should be no more institutional change for many years.' UK Prime Minister Gordon Brown, House of Commons, *Hansard*, 22 October 2007, col 22.

the Lisbon Treaty. This was also raised in a high-profile judicial review case brought against the government in the Divisional Court.[132] The Court dismissed the application on a number of grounds[133] but noted that the 'Lisbon Treaty . . . is any view . . . a distinct treaty, agreed more than three years later than the Constitutional Treaty and stemming from a separate mandate and set of intergovernmental negotiations' and noting that 'there are undoubted differences between the treaties'. The Court approached the assessment of the significance of these material differences with a very light touch, noting that it was as a matter of political judgement rather than one for judicial assessment.[134]

This last observation was arguably at the heart of what would remain an irreconcilable dispute. The Court confirmed that the Lisbon Treaty was different from the Constitutional Treaty both in form and substance. But on form, as noted above, whether one regarded the abandoning of the Constitutional approach and nomenclature as important depended on the view one took of their legal and political significance. On substance, the IGC mandate set out a range of changes to the Constitutional Treaty which was added to during the IGC negotiations themselves. In his comparison of the two Treaties, Professor Steve Peers[135] identified 35 substantive differences although the list is arguably somewhat longer.[136] While some of these changes might be of only symbolic significance, others were not. In relation to the UK, it was difficult, for example, to discount the extension of the opt-in to cover criminal justice and police cooperation.[137]

But at the same time, it was equally clear that most of the Lisbon Treaty drew on, and retained, institutional and other innovations introduced by the Constitutional Treaty. In a country such as the UK where there were no set criteria for determining whether to hold a referendum, whether one regarded as more significant the undoubted differences, or the undoubted similarities, between the Constitutional Treaty and the Lisbon Treaty, came down to a matter of political judgement.[138]

---

[132] *R (on the application of Wheeler) v the Office of the Prime Minister and the Secretary of State for Foreign and Commonwealth Affairs* [2008] All ER (D) 333 (Jun).

[133] The Court held that the promise to hold a referendum related to the Constitutional Treaty rather than the Lisbon Treaty (para 26); that even were it taken to refer to a Treaty of equivalent effect there were differences between the two Treaties but as to form (para 32) as on points of substance 'which cannot be dismissed as obviously immaterial' (para 33); that referendum promises could not in any event give rise to enforceable legitimate expectations (para 41); and that given that the applicant's case turned on a failure to introduce a Bill providing for a referendum would involve interference with the proceedings of Parliament (para 51). Given that this was not material to the outcome, the Court's treatment of the selected examples of the substantive differences between the two Treaties was only cursory and fell short of a proper analysis of their effect.

[134] See para 34 of the judgment.

[135] EU Reform Treaty—Analysis of the amended text of the draft Reform Treaty, Professor Steve Peers, 12 October 2007, <http://www.statewatch.org>.

[136] The list of 35 changes omits, eg, the new provision on national security and groups as one change the new Protocols on public services, competition, EU competence and the effect of the EU Charter of Fundamental Rights.

[137] The Divisional Court's treatment of this and the few other differences it examined, while deliberately cautious, fell short of a proper analysis of their effect.

[138] This would be fundamentally changed by the European Union Bill introduced by the Coalition Government in the House of Commons in Autumn 2010 which sets out detailed provisions as to when a referendum would be required to be held on future amendments to the EU Treaties.

Two of the more colourful comments were made by Parliamentarians. Richard Corbett MEP noted that 'just as the Lisbon Treaty is estimated to be 90% the same as the Constitutional Treaty, human beings and mice are 90% the same in terms of their DNA but the difference is pretty important'.[139] On the other side of the argument in the Commons debate on the Treaty a backbencher turned to the back of his Command Paper version of the text and wryly observed that it was printed on paper 'containing 75% recycled content'.[140]

(ii) Germany

The ratification process in Germany was also subject to a court case but one very different from that brought in the UK. As had previously happened with the Maastricht Treaty,[141] the Lisbon Treaty was referred to the German Constitutional Court to determine its compatibility with Germany's Basic Law (*Grundgesetz*). Its judgment of 421 densely drafted paragraphs was delivered on 30 June 2009.[142] The Court held that given the limited democratic accountability at the level of the Union, the EU remaining an association of sovereign national states (*Staatenverbund*) with public authority remaining vested in the peoples of the Union represented through their Member States. It was therefore important to protect democratic accountability and 'constitutional identity' at the state level and the Basic Law placed constraints on the transfer of sovereign powers by organs of the German State to the EU. It was also important for the German Constitutional Court to keep under review whether EU measures remained within the scope of the powers conferred on the Union.[143]

---

[139] Quoted by Stephen Mulvey, 'A Close Look at the Reform Treaty' 3 August 2007, BBC News website.

[140] Mr Ian Davidson (MP for Glasgow, South-West), House of Commons, *Hansard*, 21 January 2008, col 1306. A number of EU leaders also commented on the comparisons between the Constitution Treaty and Lisbon Treaty. German Chancellor Angela Merkel reported to the European Parliament that the agreement on the IGC mandate 'enables us to retain the substance of the Constitutional Treaty' while going further on issues such as climate change, the role of national parliaments and the demarcation of EU competences, Debates, 27 June 2007, <http://www.europarl.europa.eu>. According to the Spanish Prime Minister Jose Zapatero 'a great part of the content of the European Constitution is captured in the new treaties' (quoted in *El Pais*, 23 June 2007) while Irish Taoiseach Bertie Ahern commented that 'they haven't changed the substance—90 per cent of it is still there' (*Irish Independent*, 24 June 2007). For his part, Dutch Prime Minister Jan Peter Balkenende argued that 'the result is really very different to what we had two years ago . . . The outcome fully acknowledges the concerns that the Dutch people expressed through their vote on the referendum', Dutch Government Press Release, 23 June 2007. Valérie Giscard d'Estaing wrote that 'the difference between the original Constitution and the present Lisbon Treaty is one of approach, rather than content' but flagged the importance of the 'concessions made to the British. Having already weakened all attempts at further European integration. Britain has also been allowed to be the odd man out whenever it feels like it' (*The Independent*, 30 October 2007).

[141] The 1994 *Brunner* case, above n 19.

[142] Judgment of 30 June 2009, *Bundesverfassungsgericht*, BvE 2/08, 2 BvE 5/08, 2 BvR 1010/08, 2 BvR 1022/08, 2 BvR 1259/08 and 2 BvR 182/09, available in English at <http://www.bundesverfassungsgericht.de>.

[143] This is necessarily a very telescoped summary of a long and subtle ruling. For a detailed analysis see M Bothe, 'The Judgment of the German Federal Constitutional Court Regarding the Constitutionality of the Lisbon Treaty' *Istituto Affari Internazionali Documenti IAI 0920* and P Kiiver, 'The

The conclusion of the Court was that the Lisbon Treaty itself was compatible with the Basic Law but that the domestic implementing legislation relating to the role of the Bundestag and Bundesrat did not go far enough in ensuring democratic accountability in relation to both possible future transfers of power under the simplified revision procedure,[144] various *passerelles* and Article 352[145] and the application of other provisions under the Treaties. This was addressed by the enactment of a series of domestic legislative measures[146] and Germany ratified the Treaty in September 2009. The German Constitution Court case did more than simply delay German ratification. It underlined the Court's view, reinforced in the Treaty itself, of the centrality of Member States in the EU's legal order. It was a reminder, like earlier rulings on EU matters, of the Court's vigilant approach to the exercise of EU competences and the continuing sensitivities in the relationship between the Court and Union. And it placed potentially significant constraints on the exercise of some of the procedures to be exercised under the Lisbon Treaty.

(iii) Ireland

Just as the UK legislation was completing its passage through the British Parliament in June 2008, there was a significant setback to the ratification process on the other side of the Irish Sea. In a referendum on 12 June, the Irish electorate rejected the Lisbon Treaty by a margin of 53.4 per cent to 46.6 per cent.[147] As with the earlier 'no' votes on the Constitutional Treaty, there was much heated discussion as the reasons for the result. Opinion polls and the Irish Government's own analysis suggested that the reasons were just as diverse as those behind the French result, but prominent among them were the difficulties in understanding the Treaty, the loss of an Irish Commissioner and concerns about the Treaty's impact on Irish neutrality, taxation, ethical issues, workers' rights system and the farming sector.[148] Critics of the Treaty, recalling that this was the only popular vote on the new agreement anywhere in the Union, argued that this should now mark its final demise—the cover of the *Economist* newspaper for that week carried an image of a dead sparrow impaled with an arrow fletched in Irish colours with the headline 'Just Bury It'.

Lisbon Judgment of the German Constitutional Court: A Court-Ordered Strengthening of the National Legislature in the EU' (2010) *European Law Journal*, 16: 578–88.

[144] Article 48(6)(7) TEU providing for certain treaty amendments to be made without recourse to the full treaty revision procedure by way of a new amending Treaty.

[145] Formerly Article 308 TEC allowing for adoption of measures to attain one of the Treaties' objectives where the Treaties have not otherwise provided the necessary powers.

[146] The Integration Responsibility Act, the Act amending the Act on Co-operation between the Government and the Bundestag on EU matters, the Act to Implement Amendments to the Basic Law for the Ratification of the Lisbon Treaty and the Act amending the Act on the Co-operation between the Federal Government and the Länder on EU matters.

[147] With a turnout of 53%.

[148] See House of Commons Research Paper 08/66 of 30 July 2009, 'The Treaty of Lisbon: An Uncertain Future' and the report of the Oireachtas Sub-Commttee: 'Ireland's Future in the European Union: Challenges, Issues and Options' 27 November 2008.

EU leaders had different ideas. The European Council meeting the same month simply noted the outcome of the referendum and agreed 'that more time was needed to analyse the situation' and recorded the Taoiseach Brian Cowen's suggestion to come back to the issue at the October summit.[149] The October meeting only took stock of the Irish Government's analysis of the reasons for the 'no' vote, agreeing to return again to the matter at the December European Council with a view to 'defining the elements of a solution'. But work on this solution intensified in the run-up to the December summit which agreed[150] to address Irish concerns (as set out in a separate statement by the Taoiseach) and in particular to give Ireland 'the necessary legal guarantees' in relation to the Treaty's impact on taxation, Irish neutrality and, as regards justice and home affairs and the legal status of the Charter, on the Irish Constitutional provisions relating to life, education and the family. In addition, in a step back from the institutional reform, it agreed that the European Council would exercise its option under the Lisbon Treaty[151] to keep one Commissioner for each Member State. In exchange, the Irish Government committed itself to seeking ratification by Autumn 2009.

A number of commentators criticized the contrast between this deal, in which the Irish electorate were simply going to be asked to vote again, and the consequences of French and Dutch 'no' votes which had been sufficient to stop the ratification of the Constitutional Treaty.[152] Size it seemed did matter when it came to the impact of national referendums—a perception reinforced by those proponents of the Treaty who argued that the Irish 'no' vote majority of some 25,600 people should not impede a treaty which had already been ratified in most Member States. There were of course precedents for the electorates of Member States being asked to vote again—in the case of Denmark in relation to the Maastricht Treaty and Ireland itself in relation to Nice—and these precedents were very much to the fore in considering the way forward.

The December deal sought to address what were considered to be key concerns behind the Irish 'no' vote. It was followed by intensive discussions in the first part of 2008 to turn its various elements into a package which could be put back to the Irish electorate. There were a number of issues to resolve. Many of the concerns were misconceived—the Lisbon Treaty simply did not have the impact ascribed to it. That might point to a political declaration confirming the (non-)effect of the Treaty similar to that done after the 'no' vote on the Nice Treaty or if something more was required a free-standing Decision of Governments, binding in international law, as was adopted for Denmark in relation to the TEU. The Irish Government was, however, concerned that only a commitment to a new Protocol would be sufficient to satisfy its electorate.[153] That would, however, mean a further

---

[149] Presidency Conclusions, European Council, 19–20 June 2008.
[150] Presidency Conclusions, European Council, 11–12 December 2008.
[151] Article 17(5) TEU.
[152] There were also further ironic references to the apparently supernatural ability of EU Treaties to come back from the dead.
[153] The key concern was that while a Decision might be binding in international law it could not amend, and thus prevail over a clearly contrary provision in the EU Treaties. This should not have been

round of treaty amendment and ratification which others were not prepared to contemplate. In addition, having just completed their own fraught ratification procedures, some Member States were concerned to avoid any impression that Ireland was gaining additional concessions or that their own position on the Treaty was being adversely affected.

The package agreed at the June European Council in 2009 which sought to resolve these points was, on a smaller scale, as carefully balanced and rigorously negotiated as the IGC mandate of two years previously. The Heads of State and Government agreed a legally binding Decision, similar to that agreed for Denmark in 1992, confirming that nothing in the Lisbon Treaty:

- attributing legal status to the Charter of Fundamental Rights or the provisions on justice and home affairs affected the articles in the Irish Constitution on the right to life, education and the family;
- makes any change for any Member State in relation to the EU's competence on tax;
- prejudices the security and defence policy of each Member State, including Ireland's neutrality.[154]

There was in addition a Declaration on Workers' Rights, Social Policy and Other Issues drawing on existing elements in the EU Treaties and EU law.[155] The guarantees were largely crafted in general terms, making clear that they applied to all Member States. The covering European Council[156] conclusions confirmed the retention of one Commissioner for each Member State and also stipulated that 'at the time of the conclusion of the next accession Treaty' the Decision would be enshrined in a Protocol to the EU Treaties. It was equally confirmed that the Protocol would 'clarify but not change either the content or the application of the Treaty of Lisbon'. On this basis, Ireland held a second referendum on the Lisbon Treaty on 2 October resulting in a 'yes' vote of 67 per cent.[157] Ratification by Ireland, and by Poland which had been awaiting the outcome of the Irish vote, followed quickly.

(iv) The Czech Republic

But even this, and the following month's ratification by Poland, was not the end of the story. The Czech Republic still had to ratify. The Lisbon Treaty had been

---

necessary since the need was to confirm, rather than amend, the effect of the Treaties. But the Irish electorate were increasingly alert to the subtle legal distinctions between the various instruments and only a commitment to enshrine the guarantees in the Treaties themselves was held to be sufficient.

[154] This section went into detail to provide reassurance on issues such as the European Defence Agency, a move to a common defence, conscription and the creation of an European army, mutual assistance in the event of an armed attack and military funding underlying the deep concerns about these issues in Ireland.

[155] EU leaders also took note of a unilateral declaration by Ireland on neutrality and defence.

[156] Presidency Conclusions, European Council 18–19 June 2009.

[157] With a turnout of 59%.

referred twice to the Czech Constitutional Court which handed down its second judgment on 3 November, confirming that there was no bar to the ratification. But the Czech President Vaclav Klaus, a long-standing opponent of the Treaty, had continuing (albeit legally unwarranted) concerns about the impact of the Lisbon Treaty and the Charter of Fundamental Rights on the Beneš decrees adopted after the Second World War.[158] This led to yet a further round of negotiation at the October European Council concluding with an agreement on the text of yet a further Protocol, adding the Czech Republic to the UK and Poland Protocol on the Charter of Fundamental Rights, which, like that for Ireland, would be agreed at the time of the next accession Treaty. This final hurdle having been overcome, the Czech Republic deposited its instrument of ratification on Friday, 13[159] November. The Lisbon Treaty entered into force at the beginning of the following month, 1 December 2009, concluding a process which had been launched some nine years earlier by the Nice Declaration.

V. Conclusions

The tortuous history and negotiation of the Lisbon Treaty has had a number of consequences.

Ironically for a process which was meant to increase the transparency and accessibility of the Union's treaty framework, the Lisbon Treaty is arguably as complex as any of the amending treaties which preceded it. Rather than replacing the accretion of treaties, Protocols and other texts with a single, unitary text, the Lisbon Treaty adds yet another layer. There are distinct improvements. The new definition catalogue of competences provides greater clarity on a core aspect of the EU legal order. The subsuming of the EC within the EU ends one of the more criticized aspects of the Maastricht Treaty arrangements, particularly in relation to dealings with third countries and organizations, but does not remove the distinction between supranational and intergovernmental decision-making on external action. Some might also argue that the end of the distinct intergovernmental third pillar for justice and home affairs simplifies the treaty structure, but this has been supplanted by new and highly complex opt-in and transitional arrangements. In addition, the European Atomic Energy Community remains outside the EU framework—a separate body based on a separate treaty.

This complexity is not accidental. It is a product of the difficult compromises and last-minute deals which the conflicting ambitions and successive crises made necessary. The same applies to the plethora of additional Protocols which have been added to the original text—on competition, services of general economic interest, the Charter of Fundamental Rights and competence with yet more Protocols—on Ireland and the position on the Czech Republic—remaining to be added in the

---

[158] See S Peers, 'The Beneš Decrees and the EU Charter of Fundamental Rights' 12 October 2009, Statewatch, <http://www.statewatch.org>.
[159] Yet another gothic touch.

future. Equally the Treaties cannot be properly interpreted and applied without reference to other external texts—not only the usual range of IGC Declarations (to which again must be added the Irish and Czech texts) but also now the Charter of Fundamental Rights and accompanying explanations. To make matters more difficult, the treaty article numbers have all been renumbered for the second time in the EU's history—not out of perversity on the part of the negotiators, but because the bolting together of the various texts, notably in the process of agreeing the IGC mandate and the consequent insertions, deletions and relocation of text meant that the old treaty numbering would have been unworkable.

The process has also left its mark on the drafting of the text. Many of the new institutional provisions remain the product of the Convention. The fact that these were largely crafted by politicians rather than professional diplomats and lawyers means that they have a greater elegance and simplicity but equally much greater scope for ambiguity and interpretation.[160] This has meant that the process of implementation of the Lisbon Treaty has raised its own range of new issues, disputes and negotiations. To take but one example, the provision that the new President of the European Council shall ensure the external representation of the Union 'at his level'[161] leaves open the tricky issue of the division of responsibility with the new High Representative. The temptation and tendency within the Convention to substitute their own language and terminology has meant that there are a range of issues of interpretation and application to address.

Rather than resolving these issues, in the subsequent negotiations there was a reluctance to re-open agreed text save where political concerns made this a priority. Thus as noted above the opaque drafting on standing before the ECJ was never clarified just as there was, save in certain cases, no further elaboration of the institutional provisions. The latter was again not accidental. The determination to secure agreement, and to end the succession of crises which the treaty amendment process had engendered meant that many difficult and important issues—particularly on institutional matters and external relations—have been left to be addressed during the period of implementation. The appointment of the new President of the European Council, Herman Van Rompuy, and the new High Representative, Catherine Ashton, and a special summit in the days leading up to the entry into force of the Lisbon Treaty, was only the start of a process of implementation and negotiation which continues to the present.

The post-Convention negotiations added drafting challenges and innovations of their own. New provisions in areas such as competition, the Charter, the opt-ins in the areas of justice and home affairs, while carefully and rigorously crafted, have often gone to the other extreme from the Convention drafting in their complexity and subtlety. Equally, the domestic ratification process in countries such as Germany and the UK has required additional legislation and safeguards to be introduced at the national level.

---

[160] See Piris, above n 40 at 324.
[161] Article 15(6) TEU.

The drawn-out nature of the negotiations raised yet other issues. In order to avoid the complexities of appointing a new Commission as scheduled in Autumn 2009 under the applicable Nice Treaty arrangements (requiring an immediate reduction in the number of Commissioners) it was necessary to keep the old Commission in office on a caretaker basis. Similarly while the ambition had been to have the Lisbon Treaty in place for the European Parliament elections in 2009, those elections had to take place under the old Nice Treaty arrangements. Member States such as Spain who were to acquire additional MEPs under the Lisbon Treaty, as part of the wider delicate balance of representation across the EU institutions, strongly felt themselves to be disadvantaged. This was addressed by political agreement at the December 2008 European Council, confirmed at the subsequent summit in June 2009, to amend the Treaties to increase temporarily the number of MEPs.[162] Thus, there will need to be yet another Protocol and yet another amendment to the Treaties.

At the political level, while the successive crises would not appear to have done lasting damage to the European Union, the public's confidence in EU decision-making, and in particular the process of treaty amendment, has been shaken. Both among political leaders and public opinion, there is little appetite for further treaty amendment and institutional reform.[163] This has found concrete expression for example in the legislative arrangements in the UK.[164] The opening lines of the Lisbon Treaty referring to *completing* 'the process started by the Treaty of Amsterdam and by the Treaty of Nice' reflect not just the aim to tie up the unresolved issues of institutional reform from these Treaties but also echo the deeper sense of fatigue produced by nine years of negotiation and indeed the ongoing process of treaty reform extending back to the 1980s.

So was it all worth it? From the legal perspective, much remains the same. The fundamental character of the European Union has not changed. The transfers of new competences to the Union are relatively few. The position of Member States, and the delimitation of EU competences, have in many regards been reinforced. The core policies and principles of the Union remain largely the same. On the other hand, there have been significant extensions of qualified majority voting and co-decision. Supranational decision-making has been extended to criminal justice and police matters. There are important new institutional arrangements whose impact, both on internal decision-making and at the international level, remains to

---

[162] See the Presidency Conclusions of the Brussels European Council of 11 and 12 December 2008 (17271/1/08 REV 1) and the Presidency Conclusions of the Brussels European Council of 18 and 19 June 2009 (11225/2/09 REV 2).

[163] A further, limited treaty change under the simplified revision procedure was agreed in principle by Heads of States and Government at the European Council in December 2010 paving the way for the establishment of a European Stability Mechanism for financial crises affecting the Eurozone.

[164] Initially, and more modestly, in the requirements for primary legislation and Parliamentary approval in the European Union (Amendment) Act 2008, ss 5 and 6, but most significantly in the detailed requirements for referendums and primacy legislation proposed in the European Union Bill due to be enacted in 2011.

be determined. As Jean-Claude Piris has observed, 'both teams, the Euro-sceptics and the Euro-enthusiast may claim, to have scored goals with the content of the Lisbon Treaty'.[165] There are elements to reassure and dismay those on all sides of the political debate about the nature and future of the European Union—which is so often what EU decision-making is about.

---

[165] Piris, above n 40 at 46.

2

The Two (or Three) Treaty Solution: The New Treaty Structure of the EU

Marise Cremona

I. Introduction[1]

The Treaty of Lisbon is essentially an amending treaty; it amended the Treaty on European Union and the EC Treaty, renaming the latter the Treaty on the Functioning of the EU (TFEU).[2] These amendments are major ones and include the replacement of the EC by the EU. Nevertheless, we do not see, as the Constitutional Treaty proposed, a complete replacement of the previous treaties with a new legal instrument. Instead, we have the impression of incremental change through amendment, as has happened many times before.[3]

This decision, to act through an amending treaty and to retain the separated treaty structure of the existing constitutional architecture, was obviously predominantly driven by the need to demonstrate first that the Treaty of Lisbon is something different from the Constitutional Treaty (and that the public voice evidenced in the negative referendums on the Constitution had been heard), and second that the new Treaty does not in fact make major constitutional changes to the status quo (and that therefore new referendums did not need to be held). As the IGC Mandate agreed by the European Council in June 2007—which formed the basis for the negotiations of the Treaty of Lisbon—stated, 'The constitutional concept, which consisted in repealing all existing Treaties and replacing them by a single text called "Constitution," is abandoned. . . . The TEU and the Treaty on the Functioning of the Union will not have a constitutional character.'[4] On the other hand, the 'innovations resulting from the 2004 IGC' (and reflected in the

---

[1] Thanks to Bruno de Witte, Paivi Leino-Sandberg, Madalina Moraru and Anna Södersten for helpful conversations; this is not to imply that they share the views expressed in what follows.
[2] In this chapter, the abbreviation 'TEU' refers to the Treaty on European Union in the version in force after 1 December 2009, while 'TFEU' refers to the Treaty on the Functioning of the European Union. The abbreviation 'EC' after a Treaty article refers to a provision of the European Community Treaty in the version in force until 30 November 2009; similarly 'EU' refers to an article of the Treaty on European Union in the version in force until that date.
[3] See B de Witte, 'The Question of the Treaty Architecture: 1957–2007' in A Ott and E Vos (eds), *Fifty Years of European Integration—Foundations and Perspectives* (TMC Asser Press, 2009).
[4] Council doc 11218/07, paras 1 and 3.

Constitutional Treaty) were indeed to be incorporated into the TEU and TFEU.[5] Is the Reform Treaty (as the IGC Mandate called the Treaty of Lisbon) therefore merely about presentation, public relations and a purely cosmetic adjustment, given that the text of the resulting two Treaties is very similar, in essence, to the Constitutional Treaty? What are its implications, as compared on the one hand with the Constitutional Treaty and on the other with the pre-Lisbon state of play?

Prior to the coming into force of the Lisbon Treaty the European Union was essentially based on two treaties[6] and three pillars;[7] the Constitutional Treaty would have simplified matters by replacing these with one treaty and one pillar; following the Treaty of Lisbon we have two treaties and (ostensibly) one pillar: we might call this the 'two treaty solution'. This chapter will first of all examine the two treaty solution as established by the Treaty of Lisbon, and will then focus on the legal relationship between the two Treaties, comparing this structure to the prior relationship between the EU and EC Treaties as well as to the Constitutional Treaty. In a final section we will address the somewhat anomalous and 'forgotten' position of the Euratom Treaty which is actually a third treaty in this two-treaty picture.

My conclusion is that the two treaty solution offered by the Treaty of Lisbon is in fact rather different both from the Constitutional Treaty and—to an even greater extent—from the status quo ante of the pre-Lisbon Treaties. It is more than a purely cosmetic exercise (it does not just disguise the Constitutional Treaty) but at the same time it produces results significantly different from the pre-existing treaty structure. As we shall see, some crucial questions as to the precise relationship between the two Treaties are left unanswered and the Euratom is in a decidedly ambiguous position.

II. The Two Treaty Solution

It might be thought that the division between the two Treaties (TEU and TFEU) is only formal and that the unifying effect of the single Constitutional Treaty has been fully preserved (remembering that even the Constitutional Treaty did not fully dismantle the pillar differentiation). However, the Lisbon Treaty does not merely split the Constitutional Treaty into two. It preserves the basic structure and differentiation between the pre-existing EU and EC Treaties, while making substantial amendments to both. What follows is a very brief summary of the way in which the provisions are distributed between the TEU and the TFEU.

---

[5] Ibid paras 1 and 4.

[6] In fact we had—according to J-C Piris's count—three basic Treaties (EC, TEU and Euratom) with a total of 36 Protocols (of the same legal value as the Treaties to which they are attached), nine amending or supplementary Treaties and six accession Treaties (18 treaties not counting Protocols) all with provisions in force: Jean-Claude Piris, *The Constitution for Europe: A Legal Analysis* (Cambridge University Press, 2006) 57.

[7] Traditionally, the pre-Lisbon EU was regarded as being made up of three pillars: the first encompassing the EC and Euratom (and formerly the Coal and Steel Community); the second being the Common Foreign and Security Policy and the third being Police and Judicial Cooperation in Criminal Matters.

A. The Treaty on European Union

Title I contains the General Provisions, including:

- Creation of the Union, Article 1
- Relations between the TEU and TFEU, Article 1
- Union values, Article 2
- Union objectives, Article 3
- Reserved powers, the equality of the Member States and the loyalty principle, Article 4
- The principles of conferral, subsidiarity and proportionality, Article 5
- Fundamental human rights and accession to the ECHR, Article 6
- Sanction for serious breach of Union values, Article 7
- Relations with neighbours, Article 8

Title II is on democratic principles, including the role of national parliaments, and European Union citizenship (the detailed provisions on citizens' rights are in the TFEU).

Title III provides the institutional framework, but does not include details of decision-making procedures or the jurisdiction of the Court of Justice, which are in the TFEU. It includes among the institutions the European Council and the European Central Bank. It also provides for the office of High Representative for Foreign Affairs and Security Policy.

Title IV is on enhanced cooperation.

Title V contains first, the general provisions on external action and second, the detailed competence-conferring provisions on the Common Foreign and Security Policy (CFSP) and Common Security and Defence Policy (CSDP).

Title VI contains final provisions including:

- Legal personality of the Union, Article 47
- Treaty revision, Article 48
- Membership of the Union, including accession (Article 49) and withdrawal (Article 50)
- Territorial scope, Article 52
- Language versions, Article 55

B. The Treaty on the Functioning of the European Union

Part I contains the common provisions, first giving a description of the TFEU and its relationship to Article 1 TEU.

Title I sets out the categories of Union competence.

Title II contains provisions of general application, including:

- Principles of consistency and conferral

- Horizontal provisions on equality, employment, social protection, discrimination, environment, consumer protection, animal welfare, services of general interest, transparency, data protection

Part II contains specific provisions on nationality-based discrimination and citizenship. Part III is on Union policies and internal action, including:

- Internal market
- Agriculture and fisheries
- Workers, Establishment, Services and Capital
- Area of freedom, security and justice, incorporating amended versions of the former 'third pillar', with chapters on borders, asylum and immigration; judicial cooperation in civil matters; judicial cooperation in criminal matters and police cooperation
- Transport
- Competition, taxation, approximation of laws
- Intellectual property
- Economic and monetary policy
- Employment
- Social policy
- Education and training
- Culture, health, consumer protection, industry, cohesion, research, space, environment, energy, tourism
- Civil protection
- Administrative cooperation

Part IV is on the association of the overseas countries and territories.

Part V is on external action (except CFSP), including trade, development cooperation, economic, financial and technical cooperation, humanitarian assistance, restrictive measures ('sanctions') and procedures for concluding international agreements.

Part VI contains

- the institutional provisions, including those on the jurisdiction of the Court of Justice
- the types of legal act
- decision-making procedures
- procedure for adoption of the budget
- detailed provisions on enhanced cooperation

Part VII contains the final provisions including the flexibility clause (Article 352).

Apart from the two Treaties, the constitutional architecture of the EU includes the 37 Protocols attached to the TEU and TFEU,[8] the Charter of Fundamental Rights,[9]

---

[8] All Protocols are attached to both the TEU and TFEU; some are attached also to the EAEC: on this see below section VII.

[9] By virtue of Article 6(1) TEU the Charter has the same legal value as the Treaties. For the revised Charter as proclaimed on 12 December 2007, see OJ 2007 C 303/1. There is no space in this chapter

and the Treaty establishing the European Atomic Energy Community.[10] The Protocols range in length and substance; some establish a set of detailed rules such as the Statutes of the Court of Justice and European Central Bank, Protocol 7 on the privileges and immunities of the Union, or Protocol 10 on permanent structured cooperation in defence; some set out special rules or derogations for particular Member States; and some are aimed at clarifying particular treaty provisions.

The division and allocation of matters between the two revised Treaties is not as logical as that between Parts I and III of the Constitutional Treaty. Thus, the basic provision on types of competence is in the TFEU (Article 2 TFEU), while the provision on the principles of conferral, subsidiarity and proportionality is in the TEU (Article 5 TEU). The provisions establishing the institutions are in the TEU but those on decision-making, types of legal act and the jurisdiction of the Court are in the TFEU. In fact, neither treaty would be able to stand alone. The TEU would have objectives and institutions but no powers or policies (apart from CFSP). The TFEU would have powers but nothing on the principles governing their exercise, the establishment of the institutions or indeed the creation of the Union.

III. Linking the Two Treaties

The two Treaties provide for a single Union on which competences are conferred (Article 1(1) TEU) and which will 'replace and succeed' the EC (Article 1(3) TEU). Some had already argued in favour of seeing the Union legal order as a single entity.[11] If we regard a legal order as a set of norms all ultimately deriving their authority and legitimacy from the same source, the new interrelationship between the Treaties makes it clear that we are now talking about one single Union legal order, founded on two treaties, not two separate legal orders. Although there are two treaties, they are, as we have seen, incapable of standing alone (this was not true of the former EU and EC Treaties) and together they provide the 'foundation' for the Union. The relationship between the two treaties is established in Article 1 TEU and Article 1 TFEU.

The Union shall be founded on the present Treaty and on the Treaty on the Functioning of the European Union (hereinafter referred to as 'the Treaties'). Those two Treaties shall have the same legal value. The Union shall replace and succeed the European Community.[12]

---

to discuss the relationship between the Charter, the Treaties and general principles of EU law; see further M Dougan, 'The Treaty of Lisbon 2007: Winning Minds, Not Hearts' (2008) 45 *CMLRev* 617, 661–72.

[10] On the EAEC see section VII.

[11] A von Bogdandy, 'The Legal Case for Unity: The European Union as a Single Organization with a Single Legal System' (1999) 36 *CMLRev* 887; C Herrmann, 'Much Ado about Pluto? The Unity of the European Union Legal Order Revisited' in M Cremona and B de Witte (eds), *EU Foreign Relations Law: Constitutional Fundamentals* (Hart Publishing, 2008).

[12] Article 1(3) TEU.

This Treaty and the Treaty on European Union constitute the Treaties on which the Union is founded. These two Treaties, which have the same legal value, shall be referred to as 'the Treaties'.[13]

The two Treaties are of equal value, and EC priority is removed: the reference to the EU Treaty 'supplementing' the EC in the former Article 1(3) EU has disappeared and the Union is now founded on both treaties rather on the 'European Communities,' as previously. The reference to maintaining and building on the Community *acquis* in the former Article 2 EU has also disappeared—in fact all references to the *acquis communautaire* per se have disappeared.[14] If EC priority has disappeared, neither is the TEU with its more general and institutional (not to say constitutional) provisions given a more fundamental status than the TFEU, although we should note that the simplified revision procedure only applies to the TFEU so in some sense the TEU provisions are more entrenched. As Dougan has said, the two Treaties, together with their Protocols, 'should be read as a seamless ensemble of primary law for the Union'.[15]

The merger of the EC into the EU—into a single entity with a single legal personality—is reflected in the treaty structure. The two Treaties are bound more closely together than were the EU and EC Treaties.[16] In a clever piece of drafting, the TEU and TFEU refer to 'the Treaties' not only in Article 1 in each, but throughout. So for example under Article 17(1) TEU, the Commission shall 'ensure the application of the Treaties, and of measures adopted by the institutions pursuant to them'; under Article 19(1) TEU, the Court of Justice 'shall ensure that in the interpretation and application of the Treaties the law is observed'; under Article 18 TFEU, 'Within the scope of application of the Treaties, and without prejudice to any special provisions contained therein, any discrimination on grounds of nationality shall be prohibited.' Under Article 167(4) TFEU, 'The Union shall take cultural aspects into account in its action under other provisions of the Treaties'. Under Article 193 TFEU more stringent protective measures for the protection of the environment adopted by Member States 'must be compatible with the Treaties'. On the other hand, such references to 'the Treaties' are not

---

[13] Article 1(2) TFEU.

[14] It is rather ironic that the term *acquis communautaire* disappears, while other uses of *acquis,* which have developed out of its original use in relation to the Community legal order, remain: see Article 20 (4) TEU which refers to the accession *acquis* in the context of enhanced cooperation, and Article 87(3) TFEU which refers to the Schengen *acquis.*

[15] M Dougan, above n 9 at 624.

[16] Although there were references to the EC Treaty in the EU Treaty, notably in the Common Provisions, there were rather few references to the EU Treaty in the EC Treaty (eg Article 11 EC on closer cooperation referring to Articles 3 and 4 EU; Article 61(a) and (e) EC on the Area of Freedom Security and Justice referring to the third pillar; Article 125 EC on employment referring to the objectives established in Article 2 EU as well as Article 2 EC; Article 268 EC on the budget referring to CFSP administrative expenditure; Article 300 EC referring to procedures for amendment set out in Article 48 EU; Article 301 EC on economic sanctions against third countries; Article 309 EC referring to the procedure established in Article 7 EU). In addition, the procedures for accession and amendment were established by the EU Treaty and applied to the Union as a whole and to all the founding Treaties.

entirely systematic, and tend to replace earlier references to 'this Treaty' in the equivalent provisions in the EC Treaty.

In addition to the use of the term 'the Treaties', the Treaties are linked in other ways. As will have been seen from the above summary of their content, some issues are dealt with by provisions in both treaties with consequent inter-treaty cross-referencing. Thus the principle of enhanced cooperation is established in Article 20 TEU, which refers to the detailed provisions in Articles 326–334 TFEU. The concept of EU citizenship is introduced in Article 9 TEU among the provisions on democratic principles, the detailed provisions being found in Articles 20–24 TFEU. Article 52 TEU provides that the territorial scope of 'the Treaties' is defined in Article 355 TFEU. The citizen's initiative is governed by Articles 11 TEU and 24 TFEU. The provision on the adoption of restrictive measures against third countries (Article 215 TFEU) refers to the prior adoption of a decision under the CFSP chapter of the TEU. One other example might be mentioned here, although the cross-treaty reference is not explicit. Article 8 TEU provides for a 'special relationship' with neighbouring countries, which may involve the conclusion of agreements with those countries containing 'reciprocal rights and obligations' as well as the possibility of joint activities. A number of reasons might be put forward for the placing of this provision right at the start of the TEU, instead of within Part V of the TFEU which deals generally with external relations, including provision for association and cooperation agreements. Its placing here, as well as the references to the 'special relationship' and the establishment of 'an area of prosperity and good neighbourliness' which is 'founded on the values of the Union' not only evoke the policy *acquis* of the European Neighbourhood Policy but suggest that this is about the status of the neighbouring countries vis-à-vis the Union rather than simply an external policy. Be that as it may, it is clear that agreements concluded on the basis of Article 8 TEU may cover all Union competences, including those found in the TFEU, and that the general treaty-making procedures laid down in Article 218 TFEU will apply.[17]

Second, a single set of objectives is applicable to both treaties and all policies. Article 2 TEU establishes the Union's values and Article 3 TEU its overall objectives; the separate objectives, tasks and activities previously set out in Articles 2 EU and 2, 3 and 4 EC have disappeared. A single set of legal acts applies across both treaties and all policy areas (although some acts—legislative acts—are excluded from the CFSP). The consistency provision in the TFEU (Article 7 TFEU) refers to all policies and activities of the Union and to all its objectives (objectives which are defined in the TEU). The only substantive area of activity that is spread between the two Treaties—external action—has a set of 'general principles and objectives'[18] which are explicitly stated to apply both to the CFSP Chapter in the

---

[17] The description of the agreements which may be concluded under Article 8 TEU, in its reference to reciprocal rights and obligations and joint action, resembles closely Article 217 TFEU which provides for the conclusion of association agreements; as the Court of Justice held in case 12/86 *Demirel* [1987] ECR 3719, at para 9, this provision 'empower[s] the Community to guarantee commitments towards non-member countries in all the fields covered by the Treaty'.

[18] Article 21(1) and (2) TEU.

TEU and to Part Five of the TFEU and both of these refer back to these general principles and objectives.[19]

Are there then *any* provisions explicitly specific to one or other Treaty? Such provisions are in fact very limited, both in number and extent. First, the formal provisions on language versions, duration of the Treaties and ratification are separate for each treaty. Article 55 TEU on the authenticity of language versions refers only to 'this Treaty'; however, Article 358 TFEU simply provides that Article 55 TEU shall also apply to the TFEU, thereby making an explicit link. The separate treatment of duration and ratification in Articles 53 and 54 TEU and Articles 356 and 357 TFEU is a technical consequence of having two treaties.

Among the substantive provisions, there are two instances, the first relating to treaty revision, the second to certain treaty-specific competences. Article 48(6) TEU provides that the simplified revision procedure applies only to (parts of) the TFEU, not the TEU. However, the provision itself is contained in the TEU and also specifies the ordinary revision procedure which applies to both treaties. Second, each policy competence is defined within one or other of the Treaties (in most cases the TFEU) and two of the competence categories specified in Article 2 TFEU are expressly linked to one or the other Treaty. Under Article 2(3) TFEU the coordination of the Member States' economic and employment policies is to take place 'within arrangements as determined by' the TFEU itself; this does not imply that the TEU provisions are inapplicable to these policy fields; it appears to be a reference to the specific procedures operating in these two policy sectors and set out in the relevant TFEU provisions (Articles 5(1) and (2), 120–126, and 145–150 TFEU). Then, Article 2(4) TFEU provides that the CFSP competence is to be defined in accordance with the provisions of the TEU; we will consider the position of the CFSP in relation to the overall treaty structure below. In addition, two fields of shared competence make specific reference to the TFEU: the shared competences granted under Article 4(2) TFEU both for social policy and for common safety concerns in public health matters apply to 'the aspects defined in this Treaty'. This, however, seems to be concerned more with the Union/Member State balance of powers in setting limits to the competence granted to the Union than with the relations between the Treaties.

It is clear that the two revised Treaties are intertwined in a way in which the EC and EU Treaties were not; nevertheless they are two separate legal instruments. The question that then arises is what significance, if any, attaches to a provision being placed in one treaty rather than the other? Are the Treaties so connected that a provision's position in one rather than the other is no more (or less) significant than its allocation to a particular Chapter or Title, even in the absence of a specific cross-reference or inclusion of a reference to 'these Treaties'? We can look at this from two perspectives. On the one hand, we can ask to what extent general or horizontal

---

[19] Article 23 TEU; Article 205 TFEU. The provision on relations with neighbouring countries is an anomaly here: it is placed in Article 8 TEU, which falls outside the scope of Article 21(3) requiring respect for these general principles. Still, the wording of Article 21(1) and (2) is sufficiently general to allow for their application to Article 8.

provisions placed in one treaty also apply to the other. On the other hand, we can question the significance of placing the CFSP in the TEU rather than the TFEU. And in what way should our answers to these questions be affected by Article 40 TEU?

IV. Applying Common and General Provisions

As we have seen, the TEU contains a set of 'common provisions', including those on the creation of the EU, provisions on the Union's values and objectives, on the principles of conferral, subsidiarity and proportionality, the principle of sincere cooperation, fundamental human rights and sanctions for serious breaches of the Union's values by a Member State. These provisions are in the TEU but refer to the Union and are clearly intended to be common to the Union as a whole and to govern the TFEU and actions governed by TFEU competences; this is uncontroversial. Thus, for example, if a serious and persistent breach of the Union's values was found under Article 7(2) TEU, the Council may decide under Article 7(3) to 'suspend certain of the rights deriving from the application of the Treaties to the Member State in question', including rights under the TFEU. Similarly, the principles of subsidiarity and proportionality are said in Article 5(1) TEU to apply to the use of the Union's competences and this clearly includes competences conferred by the TFEU (we shall discuss below whether it also includes the CFSP competence conferred by the TEU itself).

The TFEU contains a group of 'provisions having general application' in Title II, namely principles of conferral (again) and consistency (Article 7 TFEU); equality between men and women (Article 8); objectives of high levels of employment, education and public health, and adequate social protection (Article 9); combating discrimination based on sex, racial or ethnic origin, religion or belief, disability, age or sexual orientation (Article 10); environmental protection and sustainable development (Article 11); consumer protection (Article 12); animal welfare (Article 13); services of general economic interest (Article 14); transparency and access to documents (Article 15); data protection (Article 16); and the status of churches and religious organizations (Article 17). Do these have 'general application' across both treaties? Or does their position at the start of the TFEU rather than among the common provisions of the TEU imply that they apply only to the policies contained in the TFEU itself? Or is this positioning simply a reflection of the fact that they represent a gathering together of a number of horizontal provisions formerly found in the EC Treaty? In some cases, indeed, the provisions reflect and expand on values, objectives and principles already found in the TEU (for example, the principles of equality, non-discrimination, social justice, environmental protection and sustainable development) and there is no reason to suppose that they are not intended to apply equally to both treaties. Even where this is not the case, it can surely be argued that provisions of general application should apply across all Union activities and policy sectors, in the absence of an express limitation or derogation. Thus, since Article 13 TFEU links concern for animal welfare to certain specific policies (agriculture, fisheries, transport, internal market, research and techno-logical development and space) it can be argued that there is no *obligation* in respect of other policies, such as external trade. Article 16 TFEU on data protection is subject to a specific provision on data protection in the context of the CFSP (Article 39 TEU); this latter competence is stated to be both 'in accordance with Article 16' and 'in derogation from' paragraph 2 of that provision which contains the decision-making competence. Decisions with respect to establishing data protection rules within the CFSP are thus covered by Article 39 TEU rather than Article 16 TFEU, but the principle of data protection established by Article 16(1) TFEU applies across both treaties and all Union activities.[20]

What then of Article 15 TFEU on transparency and access to documents? To what extent does it encompass action taken under the TEU, and more specifically, action in the framework of the CFSP? Our starting point here must be the fact that we are dealing with one single legal order, albeit containing within it different spheres of activity with different decision-making rules. The Treaty of Lisbon has changed the rule/exception relationship that existed between the EU and EC Treaties: whereas previously, there was no application of EC rules to the EU unless specified,[21] under the Lisbon Treaty the same rules will apply throughout unless a specific exception is made. As we will see in the following section, an exception *is* made in relation to the CFSP, and the question that must be answered is how far that exception extends; would it, for example, cover Article 15 TFEU in the absence of a specific derogation?

V. The Special Nature of the CFSP

The clearest example of the legacy of the EU and EC Treaties is the decision to retain the CFSP provisions in the TEU.[22] This may seem to be anomalous, and in a sense it is, as apart from the Neighbourhood Policy (Article 8 TEU) the CFSP is the only substantive policy competence established by the TEU. However, it is not only an anomalous historical legacy of the pre-existing treaty structure. It emphasizes—and is clearly intended to emphasize—the separation of the CFSP

---

[20] It is notable that whereas Article 16 TFEU refers in general to the right to the protection of personal data, and establishes a competence to legislate 'the processing of personal data by Union institutions, bodies, offices and agencies, and by the Member States when carrying out activities which fall within the scope of Union law', Article 39 TEU only refers to 'the processing of personal data by the Member States when carrying out activities which fall within the scope of [the CFSP]' thereby omitting processing of personal data by the EU institutions when acting within the scope of the CFSP. Since the derogation from Article 16(2) is not qualified this might perhaps be interpreted so as to exclude the latter from the EU's legislative competence; however, this seems both unlikely and contrary to the statement that Article 39 TEU is 'in accordance with' Article 16; according to Piris, the necessary implication is that the acts of the institutions, even within the field of the CFSP, will be covered by Article 16 TFEU and legislation adopted on that legal basis: J-C Piris, *The Lisbon Treaty* (Cambridge University Press, 2010) 265.

[21] Which did not prevent the Court from importing general principles in some cases: see Case C-105/03 *Pupino* [2005] ECR I-5285.

[22] This section will not discuss the impact of the Treaty of Lisbon on the CFSP more generally; for further discussion see chapter 13 below.

competence from other competences, something which was intended in the Constitutional Treaty but which its provisions did not make fully clear. The Constitutional Treaty had placed the CFSP in Part III among the other provisions on the Union's external action. The Lisbon Treaty divides these provisions on external action into three: a set of general provisions, including the EU's objectives, applicable to the whole of external policy (in the TEU); the common foreign, security and defence policy provisions (also in the TEU); and all other aspects of external action, including treaty-making procedures (in the TFEU). Although covered by common principles and objectives, including common strategy formation, the CFSP is thus separated off from other fields of external action.

This separation is not only a matter of placement in the Treaties. The CFSP is treated as a special type of competence in the TFEU (Article 2(4) TFEU), not being listed among the exclusive, shared, supporting, coordinating or supplementary competences but in a separate paragraph. Article 24(1) TEU emphasizes that the CFSP is subject to 'specific rules and procedures', and although exactly what this means is not explained some indications are given. First, the institutional balance in policy-framing, decision-making and implementation is different from other EU policy sectors; there is emphasis on the role of the European Council, the Council and the High Representative as opposed to the Commission and European Parliament.[23] Second, although the Treaty of Lisbon abolished the special types of CFSP instrument introduced by the Treaty of Maastricht (the common position and the joint action), replacing them with 'decisions', these decisions are by default to be adopted unanimously, and—most significantly—legislative acts may not be adopted.[24] Third, the so-called 'flexibility clause', Article 352 TFEU (ex Article 308 EC), may not be used in order to achieve CFSP objectives.[25] Fourth, there is the 'non-affect' clause in Article 40 TEU, which seems designed to separate the CFSP from other policy competences and which will be discussed more fully in the next section. Finally, the jurisdiction of the Court of Justice over 'provisions relating to' the CFSP is strictly limited; the Court may monitor compliance with Article 40 TEU and may also hear cases brought under Article 263 TFEU for

---

[23] The European Council is to establish overall strategy (Articles 22(1) and 26(1) TEU); the Council is to 'frame' the CFSP and take decisions to 'define' and 'implement' it (Article 26(2) TEU); the High Representative is to submit proposals to the Council (Articles 22(2) and 27(1) TEU), ensure the implementation of European Council and Council decisions (Article 27(1) TEU) and (together with the Member States) to put the CFSP into effect (Article 26(3) TEU); the Commission, by contrast, is represented in CFSP policy-making through the High Representative who is a Vice President of the Commission, and it also assists the High Representative through its officials in the External Action Service (Article 27(3) TEU); the European Parliament is to be regularly consulted by the High Representative (Article 26 TEU).

[24] Articles 24(1) and 31(1) TEU; see also Declaration 41. The joint action and common position have been replaced by decisions on operational action (Article 28 TEU) and decisions which 'define the approach of the Union to a particular matter of a geographical or thematic nature' (Article 29 TEU). Decisions are adopted by the European Council or Council; the exclusion of legislative acts excludes the European Parliament from formal participation in decision-making.

[25] Article 352(4) TFEU; see also Declaration 41, which affirms that Article 352 may be used to achieve the Union objectives set out in Article 3(5) TEU 'with respect to external action under Part V of the [TFEU],' in other words non-CFSP external action. It may nevertheless be argued that the breadth of the CFSP competence is such that the flexibility clause is scarcely necessary.

review of the legality of CFSP decisions providing for restrictive measures against natural and legal persons.[26]

The move from one Constitutional Treaty to two treaties, and the corresponding separation of the CFSP and explicit reference to 'specific rules and procedures', underline the distinctive nature of the CFSP. They make it less likely that the Court would seek to minimize the difference, as it might have done in the ambiguous context of the Constitutional Treaty. The special status of the CFSP is not equivalent to a derogation from a fundamental principle, to be interpreted strictly (with the assumption of preference for the Community method).[27] The CFSP is given its own status and space, indicated in particular by Articles 24 and 40 TEU and Article 352(4) TFEU. In some sense the CFSP remains a separate 'pillar' of the EU. However, neither should we exaggerate the separation: the 'specific rules and procedures' do not put into question the single legal order; the chapter on the CFSP is included in the same Title as, and is subject to, the general principles governing the Union's external action; it is part of that external action and part of the same legal system, albeit with a different institutional balance and decision-making procedure; the European Union is a single legal person, a single international actor in both CFSP and non-CFSP fields. Thus, for example, Article 220 TFEU on cooperation with the UN and other international organizations applies to CFSP as well as non-CFSP matters, and under Article 221 TFEU Union delegations will represent the whole of EU policy, including CFSP. Article 222 TFEU, the 'solidarity clause', is a striking example of a provision which brings together both internal and external security, action which may fall within CFSP as well as non-CFSP powers, with an explicit cross reference to Article 31 TEU (CFSP decision-making). Without denying the specificity one may say that there is a presumption that, where no special rule for the CFSP is mentioned, the general rules will apply.

Let us take the example of CFSP decisions. There is nothing to suggest that they are not 'decisions' in the sense of Article 288 TFEU and thus binding legal acts;[28] however, they cannot, according to the 'specific rule' mentioned above, be legislative acts. Therefore they cannot be adopted according to the ordinary legislative procedure,[29] nor may they create delegated powers in the sense of Article 290 TFEU; or confer implementing powers on the Commission under Article 291 TFEU; however, they may provide for implementation by the Council.[30] As non-legislative acts, CFSP decisions are not subject to the procedures established in Protocol 2 on the application of the principles of subsidiarity and proportionality,

---

[26] Article 275 TFEU.

[27] But see D Eisenhut, 'Delimitation of EU-Competences under the First and Second Pillar: A View between *ECOWAS* and the Treaty of Lisbon' (2009) 10 *German Law Journal* 585, 600ff, who argues that the 'primacy of supranational law' should prevail even under the Lisbon regime.

[28] De Witte takes the view that the Treaties are ambiguous here and that the drafters of the Lisbon Treaty probably did not intend the CFSP decision to be the same legal instrument as the Article 288 TFEU decision: B de Witte, 'Legal Instruments and Law-Making in the Lisbon Treaty' in S Griller and J Ziller (eds), *The Lisbon Treaty—EU Constitutionalism without a Constitutional Treaty?* (Springer, 2008) 79, 90.

[29] This is reserved for legislative acts: Article 289 TFEU.

[30] Articles 24(1) and 26(2) TEU.

which apply only to legislative acts. This does not mean, however, that these principles as such are irrelevant to the CFSP: there is no reason, for example, why the principle of proportionality established in Article 5(4) TEU should not be taken into account by the Court of Justice when engaging in judicial review under Article 275(2) TFEU of a CFSP decision imposing restrictive measures. As non-legislative acts, they are not subject to Article 15(2) TFEU which requires the Council to meet in public when considering and voting on a legislative act. However, this does not prevent the application of the right of access to documents relating to CFSP issues under Article 15(3) TFEU, as indeed was the case before the Lisbon Treaty, since Article 255 EC was applicable to the CFSP by virtue of former Article 28(1) EU.[31]

To take a principle of Union law which is not regulated explicitly by the Treaties, what of the direct effect of CFSP decisions? Decisions per se are capable of direct effect under Union law,[32] and without express provision[33] it seems difficult to exclude CFSP decisions as a category from the possibility of direct effect. Whether or not a specific CFSP decision possesses this characteristic will depend on its nature and content and in practice many of them will not entail the granting of individual rights. Others, however, may do so, particularly those imposing restrictive measures which must include 'necessary provisions on legal safeguards',[34] and may be challenged by individuals pursuant to Article 275(2) TFEU. The issue will have to be decided on a case-by-case basis, either by the Court of Justice or, where its jurisdiction is excluded, by a national court.[35]

Since the CFSP is not categorized as either an exclusive, shared, supporting, coordinating or supplementary competence, the Treaties leave undefined the important question of the relationship between Union and Member State powers in this field. By giving the CFSP a separate status, and deliberately not including it among the supporting, coordinating or supplementary competences in Article 6 TFEU, the Treaties make clear that this policy field is not intended merely to complement or support Member States' foreign policies; it is to develop an identity of its own. That said, to what extent do the principles and rules associated with the 'supranational' EC Treaty relating to the principle of sincere cooperation, primacy, or exclusivity in relation to international agreements, now apply to the CFSP? The

---

[31] That is not to say that specific exceptions are not possible. Under Regulation 1049/2001/EC regarding public access to European Parliament, Council and Commission documents, OJ 2001 L 145/43, Article 4(1)(a), access to a document may be refused where its disclosure would undermine the public interest as regards, inter alia, public security, defence and military matters or international relations and there are special procedures for sensitive documents established by Article 9.

[32] Case 9/70 *Grad* [1970] ECR 825, para 5; see also as regards the direct effect of decisions, the Opinion of Advocate General Trstenjak in Case C-80/06 *Carp* [2007] ECR I-4473, para 55 et seq.

[33] cf former EU, Article 34(2)(b).

[34] Article 215(3) TFEU.

[35] This latter possibility, with its opportunity for divergent interpretations at national level, is one major disadvantage of the limits to the Court's jurisdiction over the CFSP. Even if one were to take the view—contrary to that expressed here—that CFSP decisions are by their nature incapable of direct effect as a matter of Union law, national courts might well come to a different conclusion.

principle of sincere cooperation is expressed in Article 4(3) TEU.[36] It refers to 'the Treaties', the Union, and Union objectives in general terms and there is nothing to indicate that it would not apply to all Union policy fields, including the CFSP. There is an additional loyalty clause specific to the CFSP in Article 24(3) TEU, but unlike Article 39 TEU on data protection, there is no indication that this is intended to derogate from Article 4(3). The emphasis in Article 24(3) TEU on the Member States' obligation to support the Union's CFSP and the emphasis elsewhere in the CFSP chapter on the need for the Member States to implement CFSP acts[37] can be seen to counterbalance the fact that the Commission does not have enforcement powers in relation to the CFSP, rather than replacing the general loyalty clause.[38]

The provision on primacy of Union law that was in the Constitutional Treaty has been removed;[39] it reappears as Declaration number 17 which purports to affirm the application of the principle to 'the Treaties' (that is, TEU and TFEU) although the 'well settled case law' to which it refers does not affirm the primacy of EU law but only of EC law. In any event, primacy in the strong sense of the *Simmenthal* case is intended to ensure the application in the national legal order of acts which are directly applicable.[40] Although this may possibly be the case for some CFSP decisions it will certainly not apply to all, and since the Court of Justice has no preliminary ruling jurisdiction over CFSP acts,[41] there will be little opportunity for the Court to declare a CFSP act to have primacy over national law, or (for example) to apply its *Francovich* case law[42] to failures to implement CFSP decisions. As Van Elsuwege points out, to apply a strong doctrine of primacy in

---

[36] Article 4(3) TEU provides: 'Pursuant to the principle of sincere cooperation, the Union and the Member States shall, in full mutual respect, assist each other in carrying out tasks which flow from the Treaties. The Member States shall take any appropriate measure, general or particular, to ensure fulfilment of the obligations arising out of the Treaties or resulting from the acts of the institutions of the Union. The Member States shall facilitate the achievement of the Union's tasks and refrain from any measure which could jeopardise the attainment of the Union's objectives.'

[37] Eg Articles 26(3), 28(2), 29, 32, 42(1) and (3) TEU.

[38] Under Article 24(3) TEU it is for the Council and the High Representative to ensure compliance with the loyalty principle as regards the CFSP; the Court of Justice has no jurisdiction under Article 258 TFEU in respect of provisions relating to the CFSP.

[39] This removal was stipulated by the IGC Mandate agreed by the European Council in June 2007: see above n 4, para 3.

[40] Case 106/77 *Simmenthal* [1978] ECR 629. See further M Cremona, 'The Union's External Action: Constitutional Perspectives' in G Amato, H Bribosia and B de Witte (eds), *Genèse et Destinée de la Constitution Européenne: Commentaire du traité établissant une Constitution pour l'Europe à la lumière des travaux préparatoires et perspectives d'avenir* (Editions Bruylant, 2007) 1173, 1194.

[41] Although the decision of the Court in *Segi* should be borne in mind: C-355/04 P *Segi v Council* [2007] ECR I-01657, paras 52–3, in which the Court held that 'all measures adopted by the Council, whatever their nature or form, which are intended to have legal effects in relation to third parties' must be subject to control by the Court of Justice. CFSP acts affecting individuals are indeed subject to control by the Court via judicial review under Articles 263 and 275(2) TFEU, but the preliminary ruling procedure is part of the 'complete system of legal remedies and procedures' offered to individuals by Union law: Case C-50/00 P *Union de Pequeños Agricultores v Spain (UPA)* [2002] ECR I-6677, para 40.

[42] See Joined Cases C-6/90 and C-9/90 *Francovich & Bonifaci v Italy* [1991] ECR I-5357; Joined Cases C-46/93 and C-48/93 *Brasserie du Pêcheur SA v Germany* and *R v Secretary of State for Transport, ex parte Factortame Ltd* [1996] ECR I-1029.

national legal orders without the possibility of making a preliminary ruling would put the national courts in a potentially precarious position.[43]

It is clear that the CFSP is not an exclusive competence, since these are listed in Article 3(1) TFEU. It also appears not to be a shared competence to which pre-emption applies.[44] However, ambiguity remains: it is not clear from the text whether the provision on exclusive competence to conclude international agreements (Article 3(2) TFEU) applies to the CFSP. On the one hand, as we have already seen, the CFSP appears to be categorized as neither exclusive nor shared competence; on the other hand, this provision is drafted in general terms without reference to specific types of competence and its application to the CFSP is not excluded.[45] Declarations 13 and 14 affirm that the CFSP will not affect the responsibilities of the Member States for the formulation and conduct of their foreign policy, a statement which is designed to reinforce the presumption that pre-emption will not apply to the CFSP as well as to signal that the Union, through the CFSP, is not intended to replace the Member States as international actors.[46]

The CFSP, although enmeshed in the general provisions of the Treaties,[47] thus has a sufficient distinctiveness in terms of the powers of the institutions, the nature of the legal acts adopted and—in particular—the jurisdiction of the Court, to render significant the choice of acting under CFSP or other Union powers, and the position of the CFSP in the TEU, as opposed to the TFEU, is one aspect of this distinction between the alternative bases for action. In making such choices, the institutions will be bound by Article 40 TEU, a provision which appears to be designed to emphasize the separation between the CFSP and other powers.

VI. Separating the Two Treaties? Article 40 TEU

We should make clear at the outset that Article 40 TEU is not concerned directly with the relationship between the Treaties; however, since it deals expressly with the relationship between the CFSP and other EU powers, contained in the TEU and TFEU respectively, it should help us to understand the implications of separating the CFSP from other Union powers by placing it in a different treaty.

---

[43] P Van Elsuwege, 'EU External Action after the Collapse of the Pillar Structure: In Search of a New Balance between Delimitation and Consistency' (2010) 47 *CMLRev* 987, 991.

[44] Article 2(2) TFEU describes shared competence; the CFSP competence is mentioned separately in Article 2(4) TFEU.

[45] In practical terms, the conditions set by Article 3(2) TFEU for exclusive competence are unlikely to apply to the CFSP: legislative acts are not permitted within the CFSP; a CFSP agreement is unlikely to be necessary in order for the Union to exercise an internal competence (the CFSP is entirely external); its conclusion is unlikely to affect 'common rules', as the nature of CFSP instruments, at least thus far, is not to establish common rules.

[46] The formulation of the Member States' foreign policy is of course 'affected' by the CFSP in the sense that they are bound by decisions taken and by the loyalty clauses (Articles 4(3) and 24(3) TEU); presumably what is meant here is that the Member States retain full competence to act, in conformity with these obligations.

[47] See Van Elsuwege, above n 43 at 994–8 for the argument that the CFSP can no longer be regarded as a purely intergovernmental legal system but is evolving into a 'fully integrated part of EU law'.

Its presence and wording reflects well both the change in the relationship between the Treaties as a result of the Treaty of Lisbon and the specificity of the CFSP (its 'special rules and procedures'):

The implementation of the common foreign and security policy shall not affect the application of the procedures and the extent of the powers of the institutions laid down by the Treaties for the exercise of the Union competences referred to in Articles 3 to 6 of the Treaty on the Functioning of the European Union.

Similarly, the implementation of the policies listed in those Articles shall not affect the application of the procedures and the extent of the powers of the institutions laid down by the Treaties for the exercise of the Union competences under this Chapter.[48]

Article 40 differs from its predecessor, Article 47 EU, in a number of ways.[49] First, it deals with a separation not between treaties but between policies and institutional powers. Second, its concern is to maintain the different 'procedures and the extent of the powers of the institutions' in the different policy fields and thus to respect the 'special rules and procedures' for the CFSP. Third, whereas former Article 47 EU referred to the Treaties establishing the European Communities, Article 40 TEU refers only to TFEU competences, and the provision thus no longer covers (or protects) the Euratom Treaty.[50] Fourth, the second paragraph is wholly new and results in a reciprocal protection for the CFSP. This is a logical consequence of the equal value of the two Treaties, asserted in Article 1 of both the TEU and TFEU. It also confirms the conception of the CFSP as a separate policy sphere rather than an exceptional derogation. Thus although the new provision does not weaken the close links between the two Treaties (the distinction it draws being based on policy competences not treaties), it nonetheless serves to emphasize the separation between the TEU-based CFSP and other TFEU-based policies.

The former Article 47 EU helped to keep the EU and EC Treaties separate. Advocate General Mengozzi argued that Article 47 provided a watertight divide between the two, in order to protect the primacy of the Community legal order.[51] The Court of Justice had also emphasized this separation, referring to the Union and Community as 'integrated but separate legal orders',[52] and interpreted its task under Article 47 EU as 'to ensure that acts which, according to the Council, fall within the scope of Title V of the Treaty on European Union [that is, CFSP acts]

---

[48] Article 40 TEU. Articles 3 to 6 TFEU, referred to in para 1, specify the Union's exclusive and shared competences, economic policy coordination and supporting, coordinating or supplementary action—that is, all categories of non-CFSP competence.

[49] Article 47 EU stated more briefly: 'nothing in this Treaty shall affect the Treaties establishing the European Communities or the subsequent Treaties and Acts modifying or supplementing them.'

[50] On the Euratom Treaty, see further below.

[51] 'Article 47 EU aims to keep watertight, so to speak, the primacy of Community action under the EC Treaty over actions undertaken on the basis of Title V and/or Title VI of the EU Treaty, so that if an action *could* be undertaken on the basis of the EC Treaty, it *must* be undertaken by virtue of that Treaty.' Opinion of AG Mengozzi in Case C-91/05 *Commission v Council* (on small arms and light weapons), para 116.

[52] Joined Cases C-402/05 P and C-415/05 P *Yassin Abdullah Kadi and Al Barakaat International Foundation v Council and Commission* [2008] ECR I-06351, para 202, citing the CFI (now the General Court) in case T-315/01 *Kadi* [2005] ECR II-3649, para 120.

and which, by their nature, are capable of having legal effects, do not encroach upon the powers conferred by the EC Treaty on the Community'.[53] Article 47 EU was thus interpreted not simply as a rule which gave priority to the EC Treaty in case of conflict, but as a delimitation or allocation rule designed to ensure that CFSP powers were not used where EC powers could be. Further it was an allocation rule which gave preference to Community powers, so that, according to the Court, in a case where EC and CFSP objectives are equally important, Article 47 did not permit a joint CFSP–EC legal basis and the EC legal base alone must be used.[54]

The new Article 40 TEU, with its reciprocal 'non-affect' clauses, alongside the 'equal value' provisions in both TEU and TFEU, removes the Community priority that was at the heart of Article 47 EU while at the same time emphasizing the separation between CFSP and non-CFSP competence. It may still be read as an allocation provision: with its references to procedures and institutional powers, it looks like a simple reaffirmation of the principle that the appropriate legal base should be chosen for Union acts, in line with the principle of institutional balance, respecting the powers and prerogatives of the institutions and the limits to Union action set out in the Treaty, and not using one legal base to circumvent restrictions laid down in another.[55] But when one comes to ask on what basis a decision might be made in a particular case as between CFSP and other competences—what allocation rule might be applied—it becomes more difficult. The familiar tests of objectives and content[56] are not so helpful. First, as we have seen, we have a single set of objectives for all external action; second, the CFSP is defined to include all of foreign policy (Article 24(1) TEU). In the past, this potential breadth of the CFSP was tempered by two things: first, a specific set of CFSP objectives including such things as international peace and security, and second, Article 47 EU with its Community-priority rule. The first has been subsumed into the Union's general external objectives none of which are expressly linked to the CFSP,[57] and the second has been amended so as to remove the priority accorded to (former) Community competence.

Nevertheless it seems likely that the Court will continue to apply a form of aim and content test based on a pre-Lisbon understanding of the scope of the CFSP. Apart from defence and external aspects of security, the CFSP will presumably include those aspects of foreign policy which are not covered by other express external legal bases such as the common commercial policy and development, or by specific TFEU policy objectives such as environment, migration or energy. However, this distinction between sectoral external relations and so-called 'high'

---

[53] Case C-91/05 *Commission v Council* (SALW/ECOWAS) [2008] ECR I-3651, para 33.

[54] Ibid paras 75–7.

[55] cf Case C-376/98 *Germany v Council & European Parliament* (tobacco advertising) [2000] ECR I-08419, para 79.

[56] Eg Case C-94/03 *Commission v Council* (Rotterdam Convention) [2006] ECR I-1; *Opinion 1/2008*, 30 November 2009.

[57] Article 21(2) TEU; although note that Article 352(4) TFEU assumes that 'objectives pertaining to the common foreign and security policy' can be identified, in prohibiting the use of the flexibility clause for this purpose.

foreign policy is not easy to maintain in practice;[58] it is easy to envisage debate over the respective scope of the CFSP and (for example) Article 212 TFEU as a basis for action aimed at democracy and rule of law promotion, and Article 40 TEU makes it clear that the CFSP has its own sphere of operation and should not be seen merely as a residual competence.[59] This is emphasized by Article 352(4) TFEU which excludes the use of the flexibility clause 'as a basis for attaining objectives pertaining to the common foreign and security policy', referring to the need to 'respect the limits set out in Article 40, second paragraph, of the Treaty on European Union'. This provision is not an attempt to curtail the creeping extension of CFSP powers by forbidding the use of the flexibility clause, since CFSP powers are drawn so widely there could scarcely be any need for Article 352 (although, as Declaration 41 on Article 352 reminds us, there is no power under the CFSP to adopt legislative acts). The reference to the second paragraph of Article 40 makes it clear that it is, rather, intended to 'protect' the CFSP, to prevent the use of Article 352 in a TFEU context so as to circumvent CFSP decision-making prerogatives.

Would the new relationship between the Treaties permit the use of joint CFSP and non-CFSP legal bases? Article 218 TFEU assumes that agreements will be concluded which contain both CFSP and non-CFSP elements, although it only provides explicitly for agreements relating 'exclusively or principally' to the CFSP, which are subject to specific procedural rules. Following previous legal base case law, agreements relating exclusively or principally to a non-CFSP policy would use the relevant non-CFSP legal base. A 'merely incidental' aim or component does not require a separate legal basis.[60] Less easy to predict is whether, where neither policy is predominant nor merely incidental, the Court will take the view that Article 40 TEU precludes, as did its predecessor, the use of joint CFSP and non-CFSP legal bases for an autonomous measure or international agreement—for example, a possible future agreement with a third country on data transfer and retention which may concern data held for the purposes of internal security, criminal investigation and counter-terrorism. Although the revised Treaties remove the priority rule which was the basis for the Court's refusal to accept a joint legal base under the pre-Lisbon regime,[61] it could be argued both that Article 40 reinforces the separation between CFSP and non-CFSP powers, and that the

---

[58] J-V Louis, 'The European Union: From External Relations to Foreign Policy?' EU Diplomacy Papers, 2/2007.

[59] The difficulty of drawing these boundaries is illustrated by case C-130/10 *European Parliament v Council* (currently pending before the Court) in which it is asked to determine the respective scope of financial restrictions adopted for counter-terrorism purposes under Article 75 TFEU and restrictive measures adopted under CFSP powers and Article 215 TFEU: Regulation 1286/2009 was adopted on the basis of Article 215 TFEU; the European Parliament argues that it should have been adopted on the basis of Article 75 TFEU.

[60] Case C-91/05 *Commission v Council* (SALW/ECOWAS) [2008] ECR I-3651, para 73. For a critique of the application of the predominant/incidental purpose analysis where competence boundaries are at issue, see M Cremona, 'Balancing Union and Member State Interests: Opinion 1/2008, Choice of Legal Base and the Common Commercial Policy under the Treaty of Lisbon' (2010) 35 *European Law Rev* 678. Unfortunately, Article 218 TFEU, by using terms such as 'exclusively or principally', invites the Court to maintain this approach.

[61] Case C-91/05 *Commission v Council* (SALW/ECOWAS) [2008] ECR I-3651, paras 75–7.

decision-making procedures are incompatible.[62] In favour of at least the possibility of a joint legal base is the fact that we are no longer dealing with separate legal orders, or legal acts of a wholly different nature, but rather different procedures and institutional roles. And the Court has held that use of the ordinary legislative procedure may be compatible with a provision under which the Council acts as sole legislator,[63] suggesting that it should not be assumed that there is an incompatibility in combining (in the example suggested above) Article 39 TEU and Article 16 TFEU as joint legal bases.[64]

VII. The Ambiguous Position of Euratom

In discussing the post-Lisbon Treaty structure we cannot ignore the position of the European Atomic Energy Community Treaty (EAEC) and in this section we will briefly consider its structural relationship to the Union, without, however, being able here to take a broader perspective on the future of the Euratom within (or without) the Union. Before the Treaty of Lisbon, the Euratom was one of the 'European Communities' which had once included also the European Coal and Steel Community. The former Treaty on European Union stated that the Union was 'founded on the European Communities' (Article 1 EU), the Euratom *acquis* was protected by Article 47 EU alongside the EC *acquis*, and Article 305(2) EC provided that the EC Treaty should not derogate from the EAEC.[65] The position now seems rather different. Most striking, the Union is founded upon the TEU and TFEU (Article 1 TEU); there is no mention of the Euratom or the EAEC either here or elsewhere in the text of either of these founding Treaties, nothing to indicate that the Euratom is part of the Union at all. Indeed, although a Protocol exists on the amendment of the EAEC it is attached to the Treaty of Lisbon and so does not appear among the Protocols attached to the TEU and TFEU in the consolidated versions of the Treaties in the EU's Official Journal.[66] Within the Treaties, all provisions linking the EAEC to the Union and its founding treaties have been placed in the EAEC itself. This has the advantage that changes to the

---

[62] On incompatibility of decision-making procedures, see Case C-300/89 *Commission v Council (Titanium dioxide)* [1991] ECR I-2867, paras 17–21; Case C-94/03 *Commission v Council* [2006] ECR I-1, para 52; Case C-178/03 *Commission v Parliament and Council* [2006] ECR I-107, para 57.

[63] Case C-155/07 *European Parliament v Council* [2008] ECR I-08103, paras 77–9; for a suggestion that the Council's rights of participation are also relevant, see the Opinion of AG Kokott in the same case at para 89.

[64] Clearly this issue needs a more detailed discussion than is possible here; in its legal base case law, eg, the Court has taken the view that different voting rules in the Council may be incompatible (see Case C-155/07 *European Parliament v Council*, above n 63 at para 76). Here the object is only to suggest that the issue is not predetermined. For further discussion reaching a similar conclusion, see Van Elsuwege, above n 43 at 1006–7.

[65] This is not to suggest that the relationship between the EC and EAEC Treaties was entirely clear, even before the Treaty of Lisbon; on this see TF Cusack, 'A Tale of Two Treaties: An Assessment of the Euratom Treaty in Relation to the EC Treaty' (2003) 40 *CMLRev* 117.

[66] At OJ 2010 C 83; the Protocol is at OJ 2007 C 306/199; the amended consolidated EAEC is published at OJ 2010 C 84.

EAEC, and indeed to its relationship to the Union, can be made without the need to amend the TEU and TFEU,[67] but its effect is to render the EAEC almost invisible. Almost, but not completely, since certain of the Protocols to the TEU and TFEU are also annexed to the EAEC,[68] and Protocol 36 on transitional provisions defines 'the Treaties' for the purposes of that Protocol as including the EAEC.

Somewhat paradoxically, given the silence of the TEU and TFEU with respect to the place of the Euratom within the Union, the amendments to the EAEC introduced by Protocol 12 to the Lisbon Treaty in fact tie the EAEC firmly into the Union structures by repealing the existing institutional and decision-making provisions and replacing them with the relevant TEU and TFEU provisions. This is done by a simple reference in Article 106a(1) EAEC to the relevant Articles of the TEU and TFEU. The provisions thus incorporated into the EAEC include the TEU and TFEU provisions on the institutions (excluding the European Central Bank), the Articles on treaty revision (ordinary revision procedure only), accession and withdrawal, the jurisdiction of the Court of Justice, types of legal act and decision-making procedures, including Article 15 TFEU on transparency, and financial and budgetary provisions. On the other hand, the general provisions of the TEU on the Union's values and objectives and on the principles of sincere cooperation, conferred powers, proportionality and subsidiarity are not directly incorporated into the EAEC; nor is Article 6 TEU on fundamental rights. Might these 'common provisions' apply also by inference to the Euratom, on the grounds that they apply generally to the Union in all its activities and that the Euratom is a part of the Union? An indication is given by the somewhat surprising inclusion, among those Articles which *are* directly applicable to the EAEC, of Article 7 TEU, providing for sanctions against a Member State in a serious breach of the Union's values. The inclusion of this provision is presumably intended to ensure that the suspension envisaged by Article 7 in some circumstances of 'certain of the rights deriving from the application of the Treaties' could include rights under the EAEC.[69] But if the sanction extends to suspension of EAEC rights, then consistency requires that at least the values thus protected should also be applicable to the EAEC.

A further indication of the relationship between the TEU, TFEU and the EAEC is given in Article 106a(3) EAEC according to which 'The provisions of the Treaty on European Union and of the Treaty on the Functioning of the European Union shall not derogate from the provisions of this Treaty.' This replaces both Article 305

---

[67] In Declaration 54, attached to the Final Act adopting the Treaty of Lisbon, Germany, Ireland, Hungary, Austria and Sweden note that the core provisions of the EAEC have not been substantially amended since its coming into force and need to be updated; they support the idea of convening an IGC as soon as possible to undertake this reform.

[68] Protocol 1 (on national parliaments); Protocol 3 (on the Statute of the Court of Justice) which also refers to the EAEC in its Article 1; Protocol 6 (on the location of the Union's institutions); Protocol 7 (on privileges and immunities of the EU); and Protocol 36 (on transitional provisions).

[69] Article 106a(2) EAEC provides that references, inter alia, to 'the Treaties' shall be taken as a reference to the EAEC Treaty.

(2) EC and Article 47 EU.[70] Its being placed in the EAEC instead of the EC and EU Treaties emphasizes that the relationship between the EAEC and the Union's two founding Treaties is governed by the EAEC itself. The incorporation of the institutional, lawmaking and budgetary provisions and the non-derogation clause together suggest that the EAEC should be characterized as a special sectoral regime operating within the Union framework.[71] Apart from the fact that these conclusions are drawn by inference rather than made explicit in the Treaties, the oddity persists that the Euratom remains as a separate organization with its own legal personality (Article 184 EAEC) alongside the EU itself, undermining the simplification achieved by the Lisbon Treaty. There is no doubt that these anomalies and the somewhat ambiguous position of the EAEC in relation to the Union's legal regime is the result of uncertainty as to its future, and the legal solutions adopted in structuring the Treaties are designed to make changes to that position relatively easier to implement than if revision to the EU Treaties were required.

VIII. Conclusions

Already, a year after the entry into force of the Lisbon Treaty, we are getting used to working with the new TEU and TFEU. The choice of two treaties as the fundamental structural basis for a single Union system was mandated by history and politics, not by drafters working from a blank sheet of paper, and the drafters of the Lisbon Treaty have done a clever and effective job of 'knitting together' the two Treaties, notwithstanding some seemingly arbitrary choices. Neither treaty will stand alone; they are integrally connected in a way that the former EC and EU Treaties were not. The division of provisions between the two Treaties is influenced by the former treaty structure; it does not reflect a division between institutional and substantive provisions, nor between fundamental principles and detailed implementation (although there are elements of both of these). Most fundamentally, the relationship between the two Treaties is governed by the equal value principle, a fundamental departure from the previous position.

The two Treaties seek to create one Union, with one legal personality and one legal order, but at the same time to differentiate the CFSP from other (external) policy fields. This differentiation is clearer than it was in the Constitutional Treaty, but it is based on differences in procedure and institutional powers, rather than separation between legal orders, as was the case under the pre-Lisbon EC and EU Treaties. It has been argued here that in the absence of express provision the general

[70] Article 305(2) EC has been repealed, and as we have seen, Article 40 TEU makes no mention of the EAEC and indeed is not formulated in terms of treaty relationships.

[71] Care must be taken here; the relationship is perhaps not accurately described in terms of *lex generalis/lex specialis*. As Cusack points out, above n 65 at 127, it may be argued that the EC and EAEC Treaties are (were) equal and autonomous, and this reasoning would equally apply to the EU/EAEC relationship. Comparisons may be drawn with the earlier discussion on the relationship between the CFSP and other non-CFSP policies, although it should be noted that whereas Article 40 TEU is a non-affect clause, Article 106a(3) EAEC is a non-derogation clause.

treaty rules will apply to the CFSP. On the other hand, certain of those express provisions and the nature of the CFSP as a policy field mean that the CFSP will continue to retain distinctive characteristics. In addition, some ambiguities remain, in particular over the basis on which it should be decided whether to use CFSP or other competences to achieve a particular external objective. The relationship between the CFSP and other policy fields is governed by the non-affect clause, which does not prioritize one over the other. Given the single set of objectives for all external action, and the breadth of the potential scope of the CFSP, the classic approach to legal base questions will be difficult to apply, and the differences in institutional balance and choice of instruments may create problems for the practical application of the non-affect clause while maintaining policy coherence. In most cases the choice will be politically uncontroversial, or reached by negotiation. However, in one or two hard cases, the Court will be asked to create a 'choice of legal base' rule, but this time with no treaty-sanctioned priority clause.

Against this picture of consolidation, integration and simplification—at least as regards the treaty structure—the position of the European Atomic Energy Community appears to be anomalous. It is practically invisible if one looks at the TEU and TFEU; it retains its separate identity and sphere of action; however, membership of Euratom is possible only through membership of the Union, and its institutional structures are more closely integrated into the Union framework than before. The precise extent to which it forms part of the Union legal order, subject to the Union's common rules as established in Title I of the TEU, is remarkably ambiguous. The Euratom may well be in a transitional phase; if so, it is fortunate that its relationship with the Union is determined within the EAEC Treaty itself since a further major reform of the Union's treaty structures is unlikely to be attempted in the near future.

3

Lawmaking after Lisbon

Alexander H Türk

The changes brought about by the Lisbon Treaty for lawmaking in the EU reflect the pragmatic approach of the drafters of the Lisbon Treaty to maintain the innovations of the (failed) Constitutional Treaty while avoiding its contentious use of constitutional language. The new hierarchy of norms between legislative and non-legislative acts, an innovation of the Constitutional Treaty, is realized in the Lisbon Treaty with the use of the traditional legal instruments of the Rome Treaties, rather than the allegedly controversial nomenclature of the Constitutional Treaty. The lawmaking design of the Union after Lisbon is therefore characterized by a fusion of traditional elements within the more ambitious constitutional design elaborated in the Constitutional Treaty. This approach, however, raises a number of questions. The shift in the institutional balance in favour of the European Parliament as a result of the new regime brings into sharper relief persistent doubts as to its legitimacy and therefore the legitimacy of the lawmaking process as a whole. In addition, it needs to be questioned whether certain new lawmaking features transplanted from national constitutions, such as the concept of legislation, can justifiably be employed at Union level, and whether others, such as the category of delegated legislation, enhance democratic legitimacy or in fact undermine the traditional forms of European lawmaking. And indeed many of the more unique, but also contentious, lawmaking features of the Union (open method of coordination, involvement of agencies or private parties in Union lawmaking), which have often developed in the shadow of any treaty provisions have been unaffected by the provisions of the Lisbon Treaty, but would perhaps have deserved greater attention.

This chapter will first briefly recall the innovations the Constitutional Treaty offered in response to the reform agenda set out in the Laeken European Council. It will then set out in detail the changes which the Lisbon Treaty has introduced to the Union's lawmaking system. In this respect this chapter will discuss the introduction of the hierarchy of norms with its levels of legislation and subordinate lawmaking. The chapter will then assess which aspects of lawmaking, which developed prior to Lisbon, have been unaffected by the Lisbon Treaty and to what extent a 'constitutional' treatment would have been beneficial.

I. The Road to Lisbon

The lawmaking processes of the European Union after the Nice Treaty had become so complex that a need for reform could hardly be disputed. Lawmaking powers could be found in each of the Union's three pillars providing for different lawmaking procedures with the use of different legal instruments. Consequently, the difficulty arose of deciding under which pillar action could be taken.[1] Even within the EC Treaty more than 20 different lawmaking procedures existed[2] and the proliferation of legal instruments beyond those officially mentioned in Article 249 EC had become a cause for concern.[3] In addition, under the EC Treaty no formal recognition was given to acts adopted on the basis of the EC Treaty and acts which implemented such basic acts at Community level.[4] This could lead to confusion about the hierarchical position of legal acts in EC law.[5] What was more, the legal instruments provided by Article 249 EC resembled more those used in national legal systems as administrative measures and therefore did not adequately convey the nature and quality of at least those European laws which were adopted with the equal participation of the European Parliament.[6] Also, the proliferation of agencies in the European Union had led to a renewed appraisal of the Court's *Meroni* doctrine, which provides that agencies could only adopt executive decisions, and not measures involving political discretion.[7] The request for a greater involvement of agencies in the decision-making process resulted from a strategic retreat of the Commission to focus on its core functions.[8] Finally, the European Community had pursued new forms of governance, which on the one hand sought to involve private parties, such as standardization organizations or social partners, in the Community's lawmaking process and which on the other hand employed the Open Method of Co-ordination where Community competences were weak or non-existent. These attempts to build lawmaking structures without recourse to the 'Community method' did not universally meet with approval.[9]

---

[1] See Case C-176/03 *Commission v Council* [2005] ECR I-7879; Case C-91/05 *Commission v Council* [2008] ECR I-3651 and Case C-440/05 *Commission v Council* [2007] ECR I-9097.

[2] European Convention (The Secretariat), Legislative procedures (including the budgetary procedure): current situation, CONV 216/02 of 24 July 2002, Annex I, available at <http://register.consilium.europa.eu/pdf/en/02/cv00/cv00216.en02.pdf>.

[3] See K Lenaerts and M Desomer, 'Towards a Hierarchy of Legal Acts in the European Union? Simplification of Legal Instruments and Procedures' (2005) 11(6) *ELJ* 744, 746–8.

[4] Under the EC Treaty (EC), Article 202 3rd indent, the Community legislator could delegate powers to the Commission and, exceptionally, the Council for the adoption of implementing acts. The Court of Justice recognized the distinction between basic acts and implementing acts in Case 25/70 *Einfuhrstelle v Köster* [1970] ECR 1161, para 6.

[5] It was only with reference to the legal basis of an act that the hierarchical position of an act as basic act or implementing act could be determined.

[6] See R Schütze, 'Sharpening the Separation of Powers through a Hierarchy of Norms? Reflections on the Draft Constitutional Treaty's Regime for Legislative and Executive Law-making' Working Paper 2005/W-01 (EIPA, Maastricht, 2005) 6.

[7] Cases 9, 10/56 *Meroni v ECSC High Authority* [1957/58] ECR Spec Ed 133.

[8] See European Commission, European Governance: A White Paper, 25.7.2001, COM(2001)428 final.

[9] See C Joerges, 'Integration through De-legalisation' (2008) 33 *ELR* 291.

The European Council's Laeken Declaration of 2001, which set the reform agenda for the upcoming Convention for the Future of Europe, made a number of suggestions to improve the Union's lawmaking processes, which focused on 'simplification of the Union's instruments'[10] and on ways to achieve 'more democracy, transparency and efficiency'.[11] The Convention's Working Group on Simplification understood its mandate in these terms, as it considered simplification not only to mean better comprehension of the Union's lawmaking process, but also to ensure its democratic legitimacy.[12] The Constitutional Treaty reflected the core recommendations of the Working Group on Simplification.[13] It provided for a distinction between legislative acts, delegated acts and implementing acts.[14] The distinction between legislative and non-legislative acts also resulted in a specific nomenclature for each category reserving European laws and European Framework Laws for legislative acts and European Regulations and European Decisions for non-legislative acts. By providing these legal instruments across the previous pillars, the Constitutional Treaty also considerably reduced the number of legal instruments.[15] Moreover, a streamlined co-decision procedure was to become the ordinary legislative procedure[16] thereby extending the participation of the European

---

[10] The Declaration did not merely suggest the need for a better definition and possible reduction of the number of legal instruments; it also raised the question as to whether a distinction between legislative and executive measures should be introduced, as well as asking for a consideration of the use of open coordination and mutual recognition.

[11] The Declaration made the point that democratic legitimacy and transparency of the political institutions could be enhanced through an extension of co-decision and QMV, as well as holding meetings of the Council acting in its legislative capacity in public. A greater role for national parliaments was also presented as a way to provide more democratic legitimacy. Finally, concerns were raised about the efficiency of the decision-making process in an enlarged Union.

[12] See Final Report of Working Group IX on Simplification of 29 November 2002, CONV 424/02. In addition, the Working Group on the 'Role of national parliaments' suggested, not entirely surprisingly, that a greater involvement of national parliaments could also strengthen the democratic legitimacy of the Union. See Final report of Working Group IV on the role of national parliaments of 22 October 2002, CONV 353/02, 2.

[13] The Working Group also suggested that the quality of legislation be improved through greater consultation with interested parties, by having more frequent recourse to self-regulation and co-regulation, by codifying and recasting European law, and by drafting legislation with greater clarity and consistency.

[14] See Constitutional Treaty (CT), Articles I-34 to I-37. Its recommendation to give constitutional status to the open method of coordination was, however, not incorporated into the Constitutional Treaty.

[15] Lenaerts and Desomer, above n 3 at 749. See, however, the ambiguous statement in Article I-33 (2) CT, which requires the legislative authority to refrain from adopting acts other than those provided in the relevant legislative procedure.

[16] See Article I-34(1) CT. This approach suggests that legislative acts were defined on the basis of the procedure in which they were adopted. However, the Constitutional Treaty was not coherent in this approach, as legislative acts could also be adopted in specific cases in accordance with special legislative procedures (see Article I-34(2) CT). More surprising even, certain acts based on the Constitutional Treaty itself could be adopted as non-legislative acts, even though their abstract-general nature would suggest that they be adopted in a legislative procedure (eg Article III-163). See also A Türk, 'The Concept of the "Legislative" Act in the Constitutional Treaty' (2005) *German Law Journal* 1550.

Parliament to the vast majority of acts adopted on the basis of the Treaty. Similarly, on the recommendation of the Working Group, the Council would adopt most acts by qualified majority[17] and would meet in public when exercising its legislative function.[18] On the other hand, the Constitutional Treaty did not follow the recommendation of the Working Group to give constitutional status to the open method of coordination.[19] The silence of the Constitutional Treaty on this issue could be seen as benign neglect of the 'new modes of governance' or a deliberate attempt to reinforce the more traditional modes of lawmaking.

II. The Lisbon Approach: Reform without Constitutional Symbolism

The drafters of the Lisbon Treaty wanted to maintain the changes contained in the Constitutional Treaty without being bound by what they perceived as its controversial constitutional symbolism. This approach is also apparent in the provisions on lawmaking. In its desire to purge any (alleged or real) elements of constitutional character in the Union Treaties, the drafters abandoned the nomenclature for legal instruments introduced by the Constitutional Treaty and maintained the traditional (Community) legal instruments of Regulations, Directives, Decisions as legally binding instruments and Recommendations and Opinions as non-binding legal instruments.[20]

On the other hand, by extending the use of these instruments across all Union activities the Lisbon Treaty removes the specific legal instruments provided in the former third pillar and, to some extent, in the former second pillar[21] and thereby takes up the objective of the Constitutional Treaty to reduce the number of Union instruments.[22] All the same, specific forms of Union legal acts continue to exist under Article 295 TFEU, which explicitly provides for (potentially) binding inter-institutional agreements and under Articles 216 to 219 TFEU on international agreements. The establishment of the Union's budget also constitutes a specific form of act, subject to its own special procedure under Article 314 TFEU. A source of confusion is also introduced by Article 296(3) TFEU, which requires the legislative authority 'to refrain from adopting acts not provided for by the relevant legislative procedure in the area in question' implying that other types of legal instruments can

---

[17] Article I-23(3) CT.

[18] Article I-24(6) CT.

[19] See Final Report of Working Group IX on Simplification of 29 November 2002, CONV 424/02, 7.

[20] See Treaty for the Functioning of the European Union (TFEU), Article 288.

[21] The Treaty on European Union (TEU), Article 24(1)(2), makes it clear that the Union's CFSP 'is subject to specific rules and procedures'. While the Lisbon Treaty removes the old common positions and joint actions, Article 25 TEU contains its special typology of legal instruments.

[22] The new definition of decision in Article 289(4) TFEU allows for its application in CFSP matters, thereby replacing the previous CFSP 'joint actions' and 'common position'. Also, this wider definition will do away with the differentiation between 'normal' and 'atypical' decisions. The latter differentiation had caused confusion in the past because of the differences in the language versions.

be used for acts, which are not adopted in the legislative procedure.[23] It is, however, submitted that flexibility in the choice of legal instruments should only be contemplated for non-legally binding legal instruments.[24]

The Lisbon Treaty also establishes a formal distinction between legislative acts and non-legislative acts in Union law. The realization of a formal hierarchy of norms in Union law, already foreseen in the Constitutional Treaty, requires more reflection, however. It would be questionable to suppose that the idea of a hierarchy of acts was completely absent from European law prior to the entry into force of the Lisbon Treaty. It is worthwhile recalling the Court's ruling in *Köster*,[25] where the Court held that:

[B]oth the legislative scheme of the [EC] Treaty, reflected in particular by the last indent of Article 155 [Article 211 EC], and the consistent practice of the Community institutions establish a distinction, according to the legal concepts recognized in all the Member States between measures directly based on the Treaty itself and derived law intended to ensure their implementation.

The Court's ruling established a hierarchical relationship between the EC Treaty, acts based directly on the EC Treaty (basic acts) and implementing acts.[26] The innovation of the Lisbon Treaty therefore does not consist in inventing a hierarchy of norms in European law, but in the attempt to make it more visible through the formal distinction between legislative and non-legislative acts.

The distinction between legislative and non-legislative acts as part of the hierarchy of norms in Union law is quite obviously based on concepts employed in constitutional states.[27] The reliance on constitutional state models is also apparent in case of delegated acts as non-legislative under Article 290 TFEU, which in its field of application replaces the unique comitology approach with arrangements which are traditionally provided in national constitutional systems to allow the legislator to delegate powers to the executive. It is easy to understand that the Union desires to make the Union's lawmaking process more democratically legitimate, to provide for greater accountability and transparency, but it can be questioned to what extent traditional arrangements enshrined in national constitutions can be justified in the context of Union law.

---

[23] See HCH Hofmann, 'Legislation, Delegation and Implementation under the Treaty of Lisbon: Typology Meets Reality' (2009) 15(4) *ELJ* 482, fn 23 and 491.

[24] See Final Report of Working Group IX on Simplification of 29 November 2002, CONV 424/02, 6–7.

[25] Case 25/70 *Einfuhr- und Vorratsstelle für Getreide und Futtermittel v Köster* [1970] ECR 1161, para 6.

[26] In certain instances Community law even foresaw two levels of implementation (general implementing acts which provided the legal basis for more specific implementing acts), see Case 121/83 *Zuckerfabrik Franken v Hauptzollamt Würzburg* [1984] ECR 2039 and Case C-443/05 P *Common Market Fertilizers v Commission* [2007] ECR I-7209.

[27] See the earlier reference of the Court in *Köster* (above n 4 at para 6), to 'the legal concepts recognized in all the Member States' as an argument in favour of a hierarchy of norms in Community law.

III. Legislation

One of the innovations of the Lisbon Treaty is the formal introduction of a new category of legislative acts. It is worth recalling the rationale given by the Working Group on Simplification for this approach as 'to provide a guarantee that acts with the same legal/political force have the same foundation in terms of democratic legitimacy. The democratic legitimacy of the Union is founded on its states and peoples, and consequently an act of a legislative nature must always come from the bodies which represent those states and peoples, namely the Council and the Parliament.'[28]

This rationale is implicitly based on the assumption that a concept, which constitutes a key characteristic of constitutional states, can also be legitimately employed by the European Union. Such an assumption can be challenged on various grounds. First, the European Union is not a state[29] and the characterization of the Lisbon Treaty as a Constitution in the traditional sense could therefore be seen as questionable.[30] Second, it can be argued that the democratic credentials of the Council and the European Parliament are not sufficient to justify the term 'legislation' for its acts. In particular, the democratic legitimacy of the European Parliament has again been questioned by the German Constitutional Court in its recent Lisbon ruling.[31] Third, the term legislation, if understood as legislation in form rather than legislation in substance, can only be used for those acts, which are adopted in a procedure, in which the directly elected body occupies a central, if not necessarily exclusive, position.[32] These objections will be explored in more detail below.

A. Definition

Article 289(3) TFEU states that '[l]egal acts adopted by legislative procedure shall constitute legislative acts'. This provision seems to indicate that legislative acts are defined by the procedure in which they are adopted. A legislative act can be adopted in accordance with Article 289(1) TFEU in the ordinary legislative procedure, which consists in the joint adoption by the European Parliament and the Council of a regulation, directive and decision on a proposal by the Commission in accordance with Article 294 TFEU, which replicates, with certain modifications, the former

---

[28] See Final Report of Working Group IX on Simplification of 29 November 2002, CONV 424/02, 2.

[29] See W Van Gerven, 'Wanted: More Democratic Legitimacy for the European Union—Some Suppositions, Propositions, Tests and Observations in Light of the Fate of the European Constitution' in J Wouters, L Verhey and P Kiiver (eds), *European Constitutionalism beyond Lisbon* (Intersentia, 2009) 154; A Dyevre, 'The Constitutionalisation of the European Union: Discourse, Present, Future and Facts' (2005) 30 *ELR* 165, 177.

[30] For a more general debate on constitutions and constitutionalism in the European Union, see P Craig, 'Constitutions, Constitutionalism, and the European Union' (2001) 7 *ELJ* 125.

[31] See BVerfG, 2 be 2/08 of 30 June 2009. The judgment is available in English at <http://www.bverfg.de/entscheidungen/es20090630_2bve000208en.html>.

[32] See A Türk, *The Concept of Legislation in European Community Law—A Comparative Perspective*, 1st edn (Kluwer Law International, 2006).

co-decision procedure. However, in accordance with Article 289(2) TFEU legislative acts can also be adopted by way of special legislative procedures in the specific cases provided for by the Treaties. Such legislative procedures allow for the adoption of regulations, directives, or decisions by the European Parliament with the participation of the Council, or by the Council with the participation of the European Parliament.

By defining legislative acts by the procedure in which they are adopted, Article 289(3) TFEU provides therefore for a formal criterion of defining legislative acts, comparable to the approach taken in national constitutional systems, which define legislative acts also by reference to a specific legislative procedure. In contrast to the Constitutional Treaty,[33] the Lisbon Treaty does not limit the adoption of legislative acts to specific legal instruments. Substantive limitations are generally also absent from the definition of legislative acts adopted in national constitutional systems. A substantive limitation on Union legislation is imposed only insofar as legislative acts have to contain the essential elements of an area.[34]

B. Does Union legislation deserve the term 'legislative'?

It might well be the case that the Union after Lisbon does not constitute a state and that the Union Treaties lack the characteristics of a Constitution comparable to that found in nation states. However, it does not follow that the term 'legislation' cannot validly be used in Union law provided it serves a purpose which is functionally equivalent to that employed in states. It has been convincingly argued elsewhere that the European Union has evolved into a constitutional legal order.[35] An autonomous legal order can exist beyond the national state[36] and therefore also within the Union. Also, the objection that the Union lacks a *demos* as basis for an autonomous legal order[37] is based on the questionable assumption that a *demos* can only exist within the confines of a nation state and cannot be based, as in the Union's case, instead on a civic understanding of *demos*.[38] It is therefore equally possible to perceive the constitutional nature of the Union in non-statal terms[39] and to classify it 'among the non-revolutionary, historical types of constitutions'.[40]

---

[33] Article I-33 CT limited the adoption of legislative acts to European Laws and Framework Laws.

[34] Article 290(1)(2) second sentence TFEU.

[35] See Craig, above n 30; A Verhoeven, *The European Union in Search of a Democratic and Constitutional Theory*, 1st edn (Hart Publishing, 2002).

[36] See N McCormick, 'Beyond the Sovereign State' (1993) 56 *MLR* 1; A Verhoeven, *The European Union in Search of a Democratic and Constitutional Theory*, 1st edn (Kluwer Law International, 2002) 296. See also the contributions in C Joerges, I Sand and G Teubner (eds), *Transnational Governance and Constitutionalism*, 1st edn (Hart Publishing, 2004).

[37] See D Grimm, 'Does Europe Need a Constitution?' (1995) 1 *ELJ* 282; PL Lindseth, 'Democratic Legitimacy and the Administrative Character of Supranationalism: The Example of the European Community' (1999) *Columbia LJ* 628; G Majone, 'Delegation of Regulatory Powers in a Mixed Polity' (2002) 8(3) *ELJ* 319.

[38] See JHH Weiler, 'Does Europe Need a Constitution? Demos, Telos and the German Maastricht Decision' (1995) 1 *ELJ* 219, 256; Verhoeven, above n 36 at 160.

[39] McCormick, above n 36 at 2; A Verhoeven, above n 36 at 122.

[40] LFM Besselink, 'The Notion and Nature of the European Constitution after the Lisbon Treaty' in J Wouters, L Verhey and P Kiiver (eds), *European Constitutionalism beyond Lisbon*, 1st edn (Intersentia, 2009) 262.

While the nature of the Union does not a priori exclude the characterization of Union acts as legislation, it could be argued that none of the Union's institutions can be considered as being sufficiently representative in the traditional sense of a national parliament to justify the term legislation for Union acts. This point has again been forcefully made by the German Constitutional Court in its recent Lisbon ruling.[41] The Union is, however, not characterized by the traditional view of national parliaments as representing the nation. Each institution represents a particular interest in the lawmaking process that allows the Union to form a system of functional representation.[42] Despite its distinguishing features, similarities with the national system become apparent when bearing in mind that the legislative process in the nation state also comprises all constitutionally relevant institutions in a deliberative process of lawmaking. Consequently the functional equivalent of legislation at Union level to that of national legislation exists, where the Union institutions participate in the lawmaking process in accordance with the specific function they represent in the Union.[43] Union acts can therefore be considered as legislative where the procedure for the adoption of such acts provides for a sufficient representation of these interests.

There can be little doubt that the ordinary legislative procedure in Article 294 TFEU satisfies these requirements.[44] Acts adopted in this procedure are functionally equivalent to national legislation and are therefore deserving of the term legislation. Doubts arise, however, in respect of acts adopted in a special legislative procedure, which consists of the adoption of acts by the Council either with consultation or consent of the European Parliament or by the European Parliament with the consent of the Council. The majority of cases, in which the special legislative procedure applies, concern the adoption of Council acts after consultation of Parliament.[45] Given the weak input of the European Parliament in this procedure, it is difficult to see on what grounds such a procedure should be regarded as legislative. Moreover, this variant of the special 'legislative' procedure is indistinguishable from procedures which lead to the adoption of non-legislative acts, such as that provided under Article 103(1) TFEU. On the other hand, in those cases, in which the special legislative procedure provides for the adoption of acts by the Council with the consent of Parliament,[46] the European Parliament is given

---

[41] BVerfG, 2 be 2/08 of 30 June 2009. The judgment is available in English at <http://www.bverfg.de/entscheidungen/es20090630_2bve000208en.html>.

[42] See Türk, above n 32 at 217–18.

[43] The Commission represents 'the general interest of the Union' (see Article 17(1) TEU), the interests of the Member States are represented in the Council (see Article 10(2) TEU) and the citizens are represented by the European Parliament (see Article 10(2) TEU). The European Parliament is best placed to protect minority interests and to provide a public forum of communication. Despite efforts to subject Council debates to greater openness (see Article 16(8) TEU), it is still doubtful that the Council can provide such a forum (see ME De Leeuw, 'Openness in the Legislative Process in the European Union' (2007) 32(3) *ELR* 295).

[44] See previously on Article III-396 CT, Türk, above n 16 at 1562–3.

[45] In the following cases the Council acts by unanimity: Articles 21(3); 22(1); 22(2); 64(3); 77(3); 81(3); 87(3); 89; 113; 115; 118(2); 126(14); 127(6); 153(2); 192(2); 194(3); 203; 262; 308(3); 311 (3); 333(2) TFEU. In the following cases the Council acts by QMV: Articles 23; 182(4); 349 TFEU.

[46] In the following cases the Council acts by unanimity: Articles 19(1); 25; 86(1); 223(1) (European Parliament needs majority of its component members); 312(2) (European Parliament

sufficient influence to qualify the procedure as legislative. Similarly, the term legislative is also justified where the special legislative procedure consists in the adoption of an act by the European Parliament with the consent of the Council.[47]

C. Scope of legislative acts

While it contains the definition of legislative acts, Article 289(3) TFEU does not determine when such legislative acts are to be adopted, in other words in which instances the ordinary or special legislative procedure is to be followed. When Article 289(2) TFEU specifies that a special legislative procedure only applies 'in the specific cases provided for by the Treaties', it could be argued that the ordinary legislative procedure applies by default for the adoption of legal acts based on the Treaties. It is, however, clear from the general scheme of the Treaties[48] that the ordinary legislative procedure also only applies where the treaty provision which provides the Union with the competence to act specifically refers to its application.

A survey of the enabling provisions in the Treaties shows that many competences are not exercised in accordance with a legislative procedure, but provide for the adoption of non-legislative acts by the Council,[49] the Commission[50] and the European Central Bank.[51] The reservation in the Union Treaties for the adoption of non-legislative acts therefore creates a considerable gap, in which the legislative procedures do not apply.

While it is not unusual in many constitutional systems for the executive to be granted the power to adopt legal acts based directly on the Constitution, this is usually restricted to acts of an executive nature.[52] On the other hand, it would be inconceivable in national constitutional systems to exclude the adoption of acts of general application which restrict fundamental rights of citizens from the scope of legislative acts. While the exclusion in the Union Treaties of certain lawmaking competences from the adoption in the legislative procedure could be justified on

---

acts with majority of its component members); 352(1) TFEU. In the following cases the Council acts by QMV: Articles 218(6)(a)(v); 311(4) TFEU; Article 2(1) TFEU, Protocol 37.

[47] Articles 223(2) (Council acts by QMV, but in certain cases unanimity is required; also the Opinion of Commission is required); 226 (QMV in Council; also consent of Commission); 228(4) TFEU (QMV in Council; opinion of the Commission is also required).

[48] Article 2(6) TFEU states that 'the scope and arrangements for exercising the Union's competences shall be determined by the provisions of the Treaties relating to each area'. This provision should read together with Article 13(2) TEU, which states that 'each institution shall act within the limits of the powers conferred on it in the Treaties, and in conformity with the procedures, conditions and objectives set out in them'.

[49] Articles 31, 42, 43(3), 66, 70, 78(3), 81(3)(2), 95(3), 98, 103(1), 107(3)(e), 109, 112, 121(4), 122(1) and (2), 125(2), 126(6) and (14), 128(2), 129(4), 138(1), 140(2) and (3), 148(2), 155(2), 188, 213, 218(9), 300(5), 301, 305, 322(2), 329, 346(2) TFEU; Article 64 TFEU, Protocol No 3; Article 41 TFEU, Protocol No 4; Article 6 TFEU, Protocol No 13; Article 5(3) and (4) TFEU, Protocol No 19; Articles 4a(2), (3); 5(2), (3) TFEU, Protocol No 21; Article 10(4) TFEU, Protocol No 36; Article 2 TFEU, Protocol No 37.

[50] See Articles 45(3)(d) and 106(3) TFEU.

[51] See Article 132 TFEU, Article 34 TFEU, Protocol (No 4) on the Statute of the European System of Central Banks and of the European Central Bank.

[52] See Lenaerts and Desomer, above n 3 at 753–4.

grounds of their more administrative nature, other areas seem to have been removed from the ambit of a legislative procedure merely due to their politically sensitive nature. This is, however, difficult to reconcile with the nature of the legislative procedure, which should apply exactly to those legal acts which require a greater degree of democratic legitimacy. Even more confusing is the fact that a large number of these non-legislative acts are adopted in a procedure which is substantially the same as the special legislative procedure which provides for the adoption of Council acts after consultation of the European Parliament.[53] This also demonstrates that legal acts adopted in the consultation variant of the special legislative procedure are in fact regulatory in nature and not legislative.

D. Legal consequences for legal acts characterized as legislative

The importance of the characterization of legal acts as legislative lies in the legal consequences which are attached to such a finding. In the national constitutional systems legislative acts are accorded a privileged position in the national legal order. This privileged position is justified on the ground that the legislative procedure endows such acts with greater democratic legitimacy than other legal acts. It has been shown above that only legal acts adopted in the ordinary legislative procedure and the special legislative procedures requiring the consent of the other branch of the legislative authority can be characterized as legislative in this sense. Where Union law therefore accords legislative acts a privileged position this cannot extend to acts adopted in a special legislative procedure which merely provides for the consultation of the European Parliament.

First, legislative acts stand out in the national legal order due to their specific denomination. In their desire to remove all constitutional trappings from the Lisbon Treaty, the drafters opted, in contrast to the Constitutional Treaty, not to accord Union acts with a special denomination. All the same, even though these acts will be adopted as regulations, directives or decisions, they can still be distinguished from other acts by the adjective legislative being added. It can of course be argued that it is their formal characterization as legislative that reveals the constitutional ambitions of the drafters. Merely not giving them a specific denomination seems in this respect rather pointless.

Second, legislative acts of the Union are granted a limited hierarchical supremacy over other Union acts. The adoption of delegated acts under Article 290 TFEU requires the conferral of such powers in a legislative act. They may not therefore exceed their legislative authorization and be contrary to the provisions of legislative acts. The same is true for implementing acts adopted under Article 291 TFEU, where authorization for their adoption is granted by a legislative act.[54] All the same,

---

[53] See eg Article 103(1) TFEU for the field of competition law, which provides the legal basis for the adoption of non-legislative acts, which, inter alia, shall make provision for fines and periodic penalty payments in case of a violation of Articles 101(1) and 102 TFEU (see Article 103(2)(a) TFEU).
[54] In contrast to delegated acts, Article 291 TFEU does not require a legislative act as the legal basis for an implementing act. This is discussed in greater detail below.

legislative acts only enjoy hierarchical superiority in areas in which they can be validly adopted. It appears that in this respect the legal situation remains the same as before the adoption of the Lisbon Treaty. Moreover, despite a considerable increase in areas where legislative acts are now adopted, the exclusion of the legislative procedure from certain important competence areas creates an issue for the interpretation of Article 52(1) of the Charter, which states that 'any limitation on the exercise of the rights and freedoms recognised by this Charter must be provided for by law'. The link between legislative acts and fundamental rights protection is considered essential in many constitutional systems.[55] It is therefore questionable to allow also non-legislative acts based directly on the Union Treaties to be used as the basis for the limitation of fundamental rights.

Third, most constitutional systems require legislative acts to contain a certain minimum amount of detail to avoid the adoption of essential matters in non-legislative procedures. Even before the adoption of the Lisbon Treaty, the Court had consistently required that 'the basic elements of the matter to be dealt with' have to be contained in the basic act. The Lisbon Treaty enshrines this doctrine now in Article 290(1)(2) TFEU when it states that 'the essential elements of an area shall be reserved for the legislative act and accordingly shall not be the subject of a delegation of power'.[56]

Fourth, the characterization of a legal act as legislative also has legal consequences for certain procedural rights, such as the right to be heard, which does not apply to legislative acts.[57] The rationale for this privilege is that the legislative procedure provides for the functional representation of the relevant interests in the Union and the participation of individuals would upset this institutional balance. This rationale does not apply to non-legislative acts, including those directly adopted on the basis of the Union Treaties, and those legislative acts which are adopted in a special legislative procedure which merely provides for the consultation of the European Parliament.

Fifth, the characterization of legislative acts is also relevant for the application of the principle of subsidiarity. While Article 5(3) TEU refers in general to Union action, the Protocol on Subsidiarity and Proportionality[58] attached to the Lisbon Treaty, in contrast to the Protocol in force before the entry into force of the Lisbon Treaty, only applies to draft legislative acts[59] and also the judicial review clause in Article 8 of the Protocol only concerns legislative acts.[60] Similarly,

---

[55] A Von Bogdandy and J Bast, 'La Loi Européenne: Promise and Pretence' in D Curtin, AE Kellerman, and S Blockmans (eds), *The EU Constitution: The Best Way Forward?*, 1st edn (TMC Asser Press, 2005). See also H Rieckhoff, *Der Vorbehalt des Gesetzes im Europarecht*, 1st edn (Mohr Siebeck, 2007).

[56] Even though Article 291 TFEU does not provide a similar proviso for the conferral of implementing acts, there can be little doubt that this requirement also applies to Union acts conferring implementing powers under the regime of Article 291 TFEU.

[57] See also Article 41(2)(a) of the Charter of Fundamental Rights.

[58] See Protocol (No 2) on the Application of the Principles of Subsidiarity and Proportionality.

[59] See the definition in Article 3 of the Protocol. This is also the case for the right of national parliaments in Article 6 of the Protocol to issue a reasoned opinion as to non-compliance with the subsidiarity principle and the corresponding duty of review by the institutions set out in Article 7(2) and (3) of the Protocol.

[60] Given that Article 5(3)(2) TEU stipulates that the Union's institutions have to apply the principle of subsidiarity 'as laid down in the Protocol', one could even draw the conclusion that the

the Protocol on the Role of National Parliaments applies to draft legislative acts, but not to non-legislative acts based directly on the Union Treaties.[61]

Finally, the characterization of legal acts as legislative is also relevant for judicial review by the Union courts, both in terms of access and substance. Article 263(4) TFEU allows private parties to bring an action against a Union regulatory act which does not entail implementing measures merely on the basis of direct concern, but crucially eliminates the need to show individual concern. It is submitted that this relaxation of the standing requirements does not apply to legislative acts, a challenge of which still requires direct and individual concern.[62] It has been argued elsewhere that the term 'regulatory' should be interpreted as a non-legislative act of general application.[63] It should be noted that also in the legal systems of the Member States direct challenges to legislative acts[64] are the exception and even indirect means of review are not available in all Member States. All the same, the limitation of judicial protection can only be justified in relation to Union legislative acts which are functionally equivalent to national legislation.[65] Acts of general application adopted in the special legislative procedure in which one branch of the legislative authority is merely consulted cannot occupy such a privileged position and should therefore be considered as regulatory acts within the meaning of Article 263(4) TFEU. In substantive terms, the characterization of legal acts as legislative has already led the Union courts to apply a more marginal form of review when considering the compatibility of legislative acts with general principles of Union law.[66] This judicial deference to the Union legislator is justified on the basis of the special procedural characteristics of legislative acts, in particular in cases where the Union legislator has discretion in the political objectives it wants to pursue.

IV. Subordinate Lawmaking

Before the entry into force of the Lisbon Treaty, Article 202, 3rd indent, EC allowed the Community legislator to confer implementing powers on the Commission and, exceptionally, on the Council.[67] The legislative authority could make the exercise of implementing powers by the Commission subject to certain control mechanisms, which consisted in the consultation of committees, comprised of civil

---

principle in Article 5(3) TEU only applies to legislative action of the Union. Clearly, this could not have been the intention of the drafters.

[61] See Protocol (No 1) on the Role of National Parliaments in the European Union.

[62] See, however, S Balthasar 'Locus Standi Rules for Challenges to Regulatory Acts by Private Applicants: The New Article 263(4) TFEU' (2010) 35(4) *ELR* 542.

[63] See A Türk, *Judicial Review in EU Law* (Edward Elgar Publishing, 2009) 168–9. This category also includes non-legislative acts of general application directly based on the Union Treaties.

[64] Legislative acts are here understood as acts adopted in the legislative procedure provided for in the Constitution or by constitutional principles in the Member States.

[65] See Türk, above n 16 at 1569.

[66] See Türk, above n 32 at 232–3.

[67] See HCH Hofmann and A Türk, 'Policy Implementation' in HCH Hofmann and A Türk (eds), *EU Administrative Governance*, 1st edn (Edward Elgar Publishing, 2006).

servants of the Member States. These procedures had to be laid down in advance by a Council decision. The interaction between the Commission and the committees in the adoption of implementing measures has been viewed by the Parliament with great suspicion from the start. It has used the increase in its political, budgetary and legal powers to enhance its position in the comitology process, from which it was initially excluded.[68]

Even though the European Parliament's participation was strengthened in the second comitology decision adopted by the Council in 1999, it was the Constitutional Treaty, which advanced the cause of the European Parliament more dramatically by distinguishing between the categories of delegated legislation, in which the European Parliament was put on an equal footing with the Council, and implementation, in which the traditional comitology process should operate. When the demise of the Constitutional Treaty became apparent, it was difficult to refuse the European Parliament greater control over quasi-legislative acts and an amendment to the 1999 Comitology Decision incorporated the regulatory procedure with scrutiny.[69]

The Lisbon Treaty has left the arrangements of the Constitutional Treaty for the adoption of subordinate laws virtually intact.[70] Article 290 TFEU establishes the category of delegated acts, while Article 291 TFEU provides for the adoption of implementing acts. These provisions represent a political solution to the power struggle over the Commission's subordinate lawmaking powers by putting the European Parliament on an equal footing with Council for the adoption of quasi-legislative acts by the Commission under Article 290 TFEU and by leaving the adoption of implementing acts under Article 291 TFEU subject to the traditional comitology system.[71] However, this dichotomy for the adoption of subordinate rules raises considerable conceptual and legal issues.

A. Delegated acts: Article 290 TFEU

The adoption of delegated acts under Article 290 TFEU can be considered as an intermediate form of lawmaking, lying between the enactment of legislation under Article 289 TFEU and the adoption of implementing acts under Article 291 TFEU.[72] Article 290 TFEU subjects the conferral of quasi-legislative powers to strict conditions, but also provides the legislative authority with extensive powers of control over the exercise of such powers.

---

[68] On the history of comitology, see HCH Hofmann, G Rowe and A Türk, *EU Administrative Law and Policy* (Oxford University Press, forthcoming 2011) ch IX, and the literature referred to therein.

[69] See G Schusterschitz and S Kotz, 'The Comitology Reform of 2006—Increasing the Powers of the European Parliament without Changing the Treaties' (2007) 3 *European Constitutional Law Review* 68; T Christiansen and B Vaccari, 'The Reform of Comitology: Problem Solved or Dispute Postponed?' (2006) *EIPASCOPE* 9.

[70] For a discussion of the arrangements for subordinate rule-making under the Constitutional Treaty, see P Craig, 'The Hierarchy of Norms' in T Tridimas (ed), *EU Law for the Twenty-First Century, Volume I*, 1st edn (Hart Publishing, 2004); Lenaerts and Desomer, above n 3 at 754–6.

[71] See Hofmann, above n 23; Hofmann, Rowe and Türk, above n 68 at chs VIII and XV.

[72] Hofmann, above n 23 at 494–6.

Under Article 290(1) TFEU a legislative act may entrust the Commission with the power to adopt delegated acts of general application.[73] The reference to legislative acts in Article 290(1) TFEU makes it clear that only acts adopted in the ordinary or special legislative procedure can form the basis for the conferral of delegated powers under Article 290 TFEU. This, however, raises the question as to why Article 290 TFEU, with its more extensive rights of control for the European Parliament, should be available for legal acts adopted under a special legislative procedure requiring merely the consultation of Parliament.

Article 290(1) TFEU allows the Commission to be authorized to 'supplement or amend certain non-essential elements of the legislative act'.[74] While the term 'amend' clearly entails the power to insert or delete non-essential elements in the legislative act, it seems more difficult to define the expression 'to supplement'. This interpretative issue is legally important, as it determines the scope of application of Article 290 TFEU vis-à-vis that of Article 291 TFEU, but also politically sensitive as Article 291 TFEU, in contrast to Article 290 TFEU, does not provide the European Parliament with any mechanism of control. It is submitted that the term 'to supplement' should be interpreted as granting the power to adopt legally binding provisions which complement legislative provisions, by their nature often abstract, requiring more detailed specification to become operational.[75] The distinction between the power 'to supplement' under Article 290 TFEU and that 'to implement' under Article 291 TFEU could be based on the Court's distinction between the scope of application for the regulatory procedure on the one hand and the management procedure on the other.[76]

Article 290(1)(2) TFEU requires that the 'objectives, content, scope and duration of the delegation of power shall be explicitly defined in the legislative acts'. Recent case law of the ECJ, at least outside the agricultural area, has already shown a notable trend in imposing more rigorous requirements in respect of the specificity of the authorizing provision adopted under the regime of Article 202, 3rd indent, EC. The legislative branch has without doubt a greater burden to discharge under Article 290 TFEU when specifying the terms of the authorization than has hitherto been the case. The requirements should, however, contribute to making the exercise of delegated powers under Article 290 TFEU more transparent and should also make it easier for the Union courts to determine whether the Commission in

---

[73] Measures of general application are often considered as legislation in substance. On the definition of 'general application', see Türk, above n 32 at 77–185.

[74] This formulation is similar, but not identical to the one used in Article 2(2) of Council Dec 1999/468, as amended, to determine the regulatory procedure with scrutiny.

[75] See eg Article 7 of Directive 2010/40 of the European Parliament and of the Council of 7 July 2010 on the framework for the deployment of Intelligent Transport Systems in the field of road transport and for interfaces with other modes of transport [2010] OJ L207/1; Article 10 of Directive 2010/30 on the indication by labelling and standard product information of the consumption of energy and other resources by energy-related products [2010] OJ L153/1.

[76] Case C-122/04 *Commission v European Parliament and Council* [2006] ECR I-2001, para 44. The Court held that the management procedure applied where the Community legislator 'defined very precisely the principles under which the Commission . . . could approve projects to receive aid', while the regulatory procedure had to be followed, where the Community legislator 'merely created a wide and general framework for the scheme'.

the exercise of such powers has remained within the authorization granted by the legislative branch. All the same, the experience of the German Federal Constitutional Court in interpreting similar requirements of objectives, content and scope in Article 80 of the German Federal Constitution shows that the interpretation of these terms is less than straightforward and raises concerns as to the justiciability of these requirements.[77] Moreover, the limitation of the duration of delegated powers is not unproblematic, as the imposition of sunset clauses in legislation in the field of financial services has shown.[78]

Two specific conditions of delegation can be laid down in a legislative act under Article 290(2) TFEU.[79] First, the European Parliament and the Council as the two parts of the legislative branch can each be allowed to revoke the delegation granted to the Commission.[80] Secondly, the legislative act may provide that 'the delegated act may enter into force only if no objection has been expressed by the European Parliament or the Council within a period set by the legislative act'.[81] Such an objection is, like the act containing a revocation, also a non-legislative act in the form of a decision. Where contained in the legislative act, both conditions could be used in combination.[82]

Article 290 TFEU does not make the exercise of the Commission's power to adopt delegated acts subject to a comitology regime. While the loss of the comitology regime in Article 290 TFEU will be greeted by some with relief, others will perceive this move towards a solution which resembles that adopted in many constitutional states as depriving the European Union of a forum for deliberation[83] and of an effective tool for the adoption of delegated acts by the Commission. The Commission has already indicated in its White Paper on Governance that it would welcome such a step. Moreover, the logic of putting both parts of the legislative authority on an equal footing in respect of the control of the Commission's exercise of its delegated powers would have been seriously undermined if a comitology regime had remained. All the same, some form of comitology, at least in the form of advisory committees, seems necessary. Given the considerable impact that delegated acts would have on the Member States, the Commission might want to

---

[77] See A Türk, 'Delegated Legislation in German Constitutional Law' in M Andenas, and A Türk (eds), *Delegated Legislation and the Role of Committees in the EC* (Kluwer Law International, 2000) 127–81.

[78] It is therefore regrettable that recently adopted Union legislation conferring delegated powers to the Commission quite often contains clauses which limit the duration of such powers. Eg, Article 12 of Directive 2010/40 on the framework for the deployment of Intelligent Transport Systems in the field of road transport and for interfaces with other modes of transport [2010] OJ L207/1, limits the Commission's power to adopt delegated acts to seven years.

[79] There is currently uncertainty as to whether the control mechanisms provided in Article 290(2) TFEU are exhaustive. The English language version suggests that they are not.

[80] See Article 290(2)(a) TFEU.

[81] Article 290(2)(b) TFEU. In contrast to the regulatory procedure with scrutiny under Article 5a of Council Decision 1999/468 laying down the procedures for the exercise of implementing powers conferred on the Commission [1999] OJ L184/23, as amended, the European Parliament's right to object is not limited to specific grounds.

[82] Union legislation frequently uses both control mechanisms; see Directive 2010/40, Articles 13 and 14.

[83] See C Joerges and J Neyer, 'From Intergovernmental Bargaining to Deliberative Political Processes: The Constitutionalisation of Comitology' (1997) 3 *ELJ* 273.

consult the national authorities before exercising its delegated powers,[84] which allows it to make use of the expertise offered by the national authorities as well as to avoid an unforeseen objection to a delegated act. Moreover, the participation of such committees would provide the Council with the necessary information to exercise its power of objection more effectively.

The move away from the traditional comitology regime also brings about a change in the role of the European Parliament in the review of the exercise of delegated powers by the Commission from accountability to control.[85] It can be argued that the increase in direct control by the European Parliament over the Commission's exercise of delegated powers[86] could undermine its efforts of holding the Commission to account (*ex post* control).[87] Moreover, it is submitted that the new control mechanisms for the European Parliament under Article 290 TFEU could lead to a weakening of its overall position in the lawmaking process, as its scarce resources also have to cover a considerably increased legislative load. It is therefore suggested that the European Parliament should focus instead on *ex ante* control by carefully considering the powers of the Commission and then on *ex post* control by holding the Commission to account, but should reserve direct interventions in the process of the adoption of delegated acts to exceptional cases.

B. Implementing acts: Article 291 TFEU

The conferral of powers for the adoption of implementing acts under Article 291 TFEU constitutes the traditional arrangement for delegated lawmaking at Union level.[88] It thereby continues the regime of Article 202, 3rd indent, EC with certain modifications and limitations. First, given the specific provisions in Article 290 TFEU for the conferral of powers to amend or supplement legislative acts, Article 291 TFEU does not apply for the conferral of powers which are within the scope of application of Article 290 TFEU. A second limitation on the scope of application is the condition in Article 291(2) TFEU which allows implementation at Union level only where uniform conditions for such implementation are needed. Article 291(1) TFEU makes it clear that implementation is the task of the Member States.

---

[84] Union legislation delegating powers to the Commission under the regime of Article 290 TFEU emphasizes the need for appropriate consultations by the Commission. See Directive 2010/40, rec 21.

[85] On the difference between these concepts, see M Busuioc, 'Accountability, Control and Independence: The Case of European Agencies' (2009) 15(5) *ELJ* 599.

[86] Before the entry into force of the Lisbon Treaty, the European Parliament could already exercise as co-legislator some *ex ante* control and through the regulatory procedure with scrutiny had also some form of direct control over implementing powers of the Commission. The Lisbon Treaty extends the scope of *ex ante* control considerably by widening the fields in which the European Parliaments acts as co-legislator. Moreover, the power of objection under Article 290 TFEU is no longer linked to legal grounds.

[87] See M Bovens, 'Analysing and Assessing Accountability: A Conceptual Framework' (2007) 13(4) *ELJ* 447; D Curtin, 'Holding (Quasi-) Autonomous EU Administrative Actors to Public Account' (2007) 13(4) *ELJ* 523.

[88] See Hofmann, Rowe and Türk, above n 68 at chs VIII and XV.

In contrast to Article 290 TFEU, the conferral of implementing powers under Article 291 TFEU is not limited to legislative acts, but can be contained in any Union act. This allows a number of different scenarios in which a conferral of implementing acts can be envisaged. Legislative acts can confer implementing powers, with the exception of those which amend or supplement legislative acts, which fall within the scope of Article 290 TFEU. A conferral of implementing powers can also be the subject matter of a non-legislative act based directly on the Treaty.[89] Finally, implementing powers can also be conferred in delegated acts adopted under Article 290 TFEU. Given the comprehensive nature of Article 291 TFEU for the adoption of Union implementing acts, subject of course to the more specific provisions in Article 290 TFEU, it would not seem permissible to pursue the implementation of certain Union acts outside the regime of Article 291 TFEU.[90]

Article 291 TFEU provides for the conferral of implementing powers. It can be expected that the interpretation of the scope of any such power will follow the case law under Article 202, 3rd indent, EC.[91] The Court interpreted the notion of implementation rather generously by including all measures 'however important they may be'[92] of individual and general scope provided that they do not deal with essential elements, which have to be decided in the basic act itself.[93] It is therefore to be expected that Union acts which confer implementing powers have to deal with the essential elements of a matter itself, even though Article 291 TFEU, in contrast to Article 290 TFEU, does not explicitly require this. In its interpretation of Article 202, 3rd indent, EC the Court also had to determine how specific the authorization to adopt implementing acts had to be. While in some cases, which mainly relate to the Common Agricultural Policy (CAP), the Court accepted that 'a provision drafted in general terms provides a sufficient basis for the authority to act',[94] it has taken a more restrictive approach in other cases, in which it demanded that the authorization be 'sufficiently specific' in that it had to 'clearly specify the

---

[89] This again questions the wisdom of classifying legal acts adopted in identical procedures differently. Legal acts which are adopted by the Council in a special legislative procedure, which provides for the consultation of Parliament are subject to the regime of Article 290 TFEU when delegating powers to the Commission to amend or supplement such acts, while non-legislative acts adopted directly on the basis of the Treaty in the same procedure, which delegate the power to the Commission to amend or supplement such acts are subject to the regime of Article 291 TFEU.

[90] Union acts, which provide for the imposition of anti-dumping duties, therefore fall under the regime set out in Article 291 TFEU. See Regulation 182/2011 of the European Parliament and of the Council laying down the rules and general principles concerning mechanisms for control by Member States of the Commission's exercise of implementing powers [2011] OJ L55/13.

[91] See A Türk, 'The Development of Case Law in the Area of Comitology' in T Christiansen and B Vaccari (eds), *21st Century Comitology: The Role of Implementing Committees in the Wider European Union* (EIPA, 2009) 71.

[92] Case 41/69 *Chemiefarma v Commission* [1970] ECR 661, para 65.

[93] See Case 25/70 *Köster* [1970] ECR 1161, para 6; Case C-240/90 *Germany v Commission* [1992] ECR I-5383 para 37; Case C-104/97 P *Atlanta and Others v Council and Commission* [1999] ECR I-6983, paras 70–6; Joined Cases T-64/01 and T-65/01 *Afrikanische Frucht-Compagnie GmbH and Another v Council and Commission* [2004] ECR II-521, paras 119–20; Case C-66/04 *United Kingdom v European Parliament and Council* [2005] ECR I-10553, paras 53–8.

[94] Case C-240/90 *Germany v Commission* [1992] ECR I-5383, para 41.

bounds of the power conferred on the Commission'.[95] The latter approach was prevalent in cases, where 'the Community legislature wishes to delegate its power to amend aspects of the legislative act at issue'.[96] In this case it needed to ensure that 'that power is clearly defined and that the exercise of the power is subject to strict review in the light of objective criteria'.[97] It is submitted that a stricter approach will be taken by the Court in case of conferral of powers to amend non-legislative Union acts which are directly based on the Treaties, whereas a more relaxed approach can be expected in all other cases.

In contrast to Article 290 TFEU, which entrusts the control of delegated acts to the two institutions of the legislative branch, Article 291 TFEU envisages that any control mechanisms are to be in the hands of the Member States, albeit enshrined in a legislative act adopted in the ordinary legislative procedure by Council and Parliament.[98] The reference to the Member States as exercising control over implementing measures ensures the continued relevance of comitology, however, in a modified form as any intervention by the Council and the European Parliament in the implementation process seems excluded. Moreover, the exercise of control mechanisms by the Member States seems to allow giving comitology committees, as forums for representatives of the Member States, a veto in Union lawmaking.[99] This novel approach[100] would recognize the importance that comitology committees play in Union lawmaking and would reinforce the integrated nature of the European administration, but at the same time would also exacerbate the problem of their accountability.

V. Lawmaking in the Shadow of Constitutional Arrangements

For reasons of political expediency, the Lisbon Treaty did not, and arguably could not, go beyond the reforms set out in the Constitutional Treaty. It is therefore not surprising that the Lisbon Treaty does not deal with the less traditional modes of

---

[95] Case 291/86 *Central-Import Münster* [1988] ECR 3679, para 13.
[96] Joined Cases C-154/04 and C-155/04 *Alliance for Natural Health* [2005] ECR I-6451, para 90.
[97] Ibid.
[98] See Regulation 182/2011 of the European Parliament and of the Council laying down the rules and general principles concerning mechanisms for control by Member States of the Commission's exercise of implementing powers [2011] OJ L55/13. The new Comitology regulation contains two procedures, an advisory procedure, in which the relevant committee is merely consulted by the Commission, and an examination procedure, as a result of which the Commission may not adopt implementing measures which are not in accordance with the opinion of the committee or where it fails to obtain a favourable opinion in certain specified cases. A notable innovation in the new Comitology regulation is the appeal committee, to which the Commission can refer those draft acts which it was not allowed to adopt following a negative or no opinion in the comitology committee.
[99] See Article 5(3) and 5(4)(2) of Regulation 182/2011. This veto is, however, subject to a referral to the appeal committee and Article 7 of Regulation 182/2011.
[100] In the *Köster* case, above n 4 at para 9, the Court justified the involvement of committees in the implementation process, by pointing out that they did not have the power to take decisions and thereby would not alter 'the Community structure and the institutional balance'.

EU lawmaking, such as the open method of coordination, regulatory activities of agencies and private parties.

A. Open method of coordination

The areas of most extensive reliance on the open method of coordination (OMC) are also those which form the core of the Europe 2020 Strategy,[101] economic policy and employment.[102] Alongside them, but in a more supplementary role, the OMC has been employed in developing the coordination of policies on social protection, social inclusion, pensions and healthcare.[103] Other policy fields, such as research and education, information society, the environment, immigration, enterprise and youth, are only now emerging as relevant areas in which the OMC may play a role.[104] While differences emerge in its mode of operation of the OMC in different fields, its core features distinguish it from the traditional Community method to the extent that it has been considered as a form of 'new governance'.[105] This account of its character as 'governance' is, however, not undisputed.[106] While the OMC does contain certain new tools and instruments, its institutional structure is not so far removed from some existing administrative structures, such as comitology, agencies or regulatory networks, as has been asserted.[107] The OMC, therefore,

---

[101] See Communication from the Commission, Europe 2020—A strategy for smart, sustainable and inclusive growth, COM(2010) 2020 of 3 March 2010. This new strategy has been endorsed by the European Council, see European Council conclusions, 25 and 26 March 2010, at points 1–10, and 17 June 2010, at points 1–8. The new strategy focuses on three priorities: smart growth (developing an economy based on knowledge and innovation), sustainable growth (promoting a more resource efficient, greener and more competitive economy) and inclusive growth (fostering a high-employment economy delivering social and territorial cohesion). These priorities are to be achieved through five headline targets: 75% of the population aged 20–64 should be employed; 3% of the EU's GDP should be invested in Research and Development; the '20/20/20' climate/energy targets should be met; the school drop-out rate should be brought under 10% and at least 40% of the younger generation should have a university degree; finally, 20 million less people should be at risk of poverty. At the national level, the Member States would translate these objectives into national targets. At the EU level, national efforts would be complemented by seven flagship initiatives of the Commission.

[102] For a typology of areas, see E Szyszczak, 'Experimental Governance: The Open Method of Coordination' (2006) 12 *ELJ* 486, 493–5.

[103] See J Zeitlin, 'The Open Method of Co-ordination and the Governance of the Lisbon Strategy' (2008) *Journal of Common Market Studies* 436, 441–4. All the same, Europe 2020 has reconfirmed the importance of the social dimension of the EU as an integral part of the European 2020 Strategy. One of the three overall priorities is entitled 'inclusive growth', one of the five EU headline targets is expressly devoted to social inclusion, one of the 10 Integrated Guidelines is reserved for social inclusion, and the 'European Platform Against Poverty' is one of seven Commission flagship initiatives.

[104] See Szyszczak, above n 102 at 494.

[105] See G De Búrca, 'The Constitutional Challenge of New Governance in the European Union' (2003) 28 *ELR* 814; S Regent, 'The Open Method of Coordination: A New Supranational Form of Governance?' (2003) 9 *ELR* 190; G De Búrca and J Scott (eds), *Law and New Governance in the EU and the US* (Hart Publishing, 2006); B Kohler-Koch and B Rittberger, 'Review Art: The "Governance Turn" in EU Studies' (2006) 44 *Journal of Common Market Studies* 27.

[106] See C Scott, 'Governing without Law or Governing without Government? New-ish Governance and the Legitimacy of the EU' (2009) 15(2) *ELJ* 160; K Armstrong and C Kilpatrick, 'Law, Governance, or New Governance? The Changing Open Method of Coordination' (2006–2007) 13 *Columbia JEurL* 649.

[107] C Scott, above n 106 at 167–8.

constitutes not so much governing without government, but rather governing without law.[108]

To the extent that this characterization is valid, it raises considerable questions of the legitimacy of the OMC. While it is possible to emphasize the output quality of the OMC as a regulatory mechanism 'in areas where some level of EU regulation is necessary but where it has been difficult to reach consensus on *what* level and *how* this should be achieved',[109] it can also be seen as 'a threat to the rule of law and associated political and legal accountability mechanisms'.[110] It is precisely its informality which causes concerns, as it 'permits its evasion of risks of being tied down and controlled by the regular political process including the constraints of the rule of law'.[111] Similarly, given that democratic legitimacy depends at least in part on the extent to which civil society can be engaged in the process,[112] the dominant position of national and supranational executive bodies in the OMC process raises doubts in this respect.[113] Finally, deliberation and learning,[114] as well as peer pressure, as central components of the OMC, while observable in some cases, seem notably absent where politically sensitive issues arise.[115] Given these doubts about the OMC, it seemed wise not to accord it 'constitutional' status in the Lisbon Treaty.

B. Agencies

Agencies have been entrusted with pursuing different tasks ranging from the provision of information, the provision of services as a basis for the adoption of implementing acts, and even the exercise of specific implementing powers.[116] Agencies undertake these decentralized functions not as autonomous and independent bodies, but rather by providing a unitary administrative framework within which they integrate, usually through committees, a network of national and supranational administrative bodies.[117] All the same, even though some agencies

---

[108] Ibid 163.

[109] Szyszczak, above n 102 at 487.

[110] Scott, above n 106 at 172. See also M Büchs, 'How Legitimate is the Open Method of Co-ordination?' (2008) 46 *Journal of Common Market Studies* 765; V Hatzopoulos, 'Why the Open Method of Coordination is Bad for You: A Letter to the EU' (2007) 13(3) *ELJ* 309; S Borrás and K Jacobsson, 'The Open Method of Co-ordination and New Governance Patterns in the EU' (2004) 11 *Journal of European Public Policy* 185, 199.

[111] C Joerges, 'Integration through De-legalisation' (2008) 33 *ELR* 291, 310.

[112] Scott, above n 106 at 172.

[113] See M Heidenreich and G Bischoff, 'The Open Method of Co-ordination: A Way to the Europeanization of Social and Employment Policies' (2008) 46 *Journal of Common Market Studies* 497, 501–3. See also P Craig, *EU Administrative Law*, 1st edn (Oxford University Press, 2006) 221–4.

[114] Borrás and Jacobsson, above n 110 at 195–7; Heidenreich and Bischoff, above n 113 at 503–4. For a sceptical view on the contribution deliberation can make to accountability, see A Benz, 'Accountable Multilevel Governance by the Open Method of Coordination?' (2007) 13 *ELJ* 505.

[115] See P Craig, above n 113 at 224–8.

[116] Two examples of many: Article 42(5) of the Council Regulation (EC) 207/2009 on the Community trade mark (codified version) [2009] OJ L78/1; Article 62 of the Council Regulation (EC) 2100/94 on Community plant variety rights [1994] OJ L227/1, as amended.

[117] See E Chiti, 'Decentralisation and Integration into the Community Administrations: A New Perspective on European Agencies' (2004) 10 *ELJ* 402.

support the Commission only by collecting information or processing applications, others do make important decisions outside the decision-making process laid down by the Treaties.

The constitutional basis for a delegation of powers to agencies is much more disputed than the rapid increase in these structures would suggest. Articles 290 and 291 TFEU, like Article 202, 3rd indent, EC, cover only the conferral of implementing powers to the Commission or, under Article 291 TFEU, exceptionally, the Council. They do not deal with the delegation of powers to other actors such as agencies. This reinforces the continued validity of the Court's seminal *Meroni*[118] doctrine.[119] Some have argued that a delegation of broader powers to agencies ought not to fall foul of the *Meroni* doctrine, as the Union's institutional balance could be protected 'by a reinforcement or re-balancing of the existing institutions and constitutional guarantees for decision-making'.[120] Others have urged more caution to be shown before the constraints of the *Meroni* doctrine are lessened for the purpose of entrusting to agencies the exercise of discretionary powers, as such a move would weaken the rationales which currently sustain the delegation of powers to agencies.[121] Such a course of action would, therefore, require a careful consideration of the legal and political constraints which would have to be imposed on such agencies.[122] However, not only legal but also political considerations play a role for the more narrowly defined mandate of European agencies.[123] In particular the Commission seems to be anxious not to let the undoubted help that agencies provide in reducing its administrative overload result in a loss of its administrative authority and control.

In reality, some agencies have gained quite considerable influence over the decision-making process, perhaps already stretching the *Meroni* doctrine to its limits. This is not only the case where agencies have been entrusted with the adoption of binding decisions,[124] but also where they play an essential part in the decision-making process. Under Regulation 726/2004[125] the EMEA has been given the task to deliver scientific opinions on applications for the authorization of pharmaceutical products. Even though its opinions are not binding on the

---

[118] *Meroni* case, above n 7.

[119] See Hofmann, above n 23 at 502.

[120] E Vos, 'Reforming the European Commission: What Role to Play for EU Agencies' (2000) 37 *CMLRev* 1113, 1123.

[121] P Craig, above n 113 at 183–5.

[122] Ibid 185–90. See the suggestions in S Griller and A Orator, 'Everything under Control? The "Way Forward" for European Agencies in the Footsteps of the Meroni Doctrine' (2010) *ELR* 3.

[123] R Dehousse, 'Misfits: EU Law and the Transformation of European Governance' in C Joerges and R Dehousse (eds), *Good Governance in Europe's Integrated Market*, 1st edn (Oxford University Press, 2002) 223.

[124] See Council Regulation (EC) 2100/94 on Community plant variety rights [1994] OJ L227/1; Council Regulation (EC) 207/2009 on the Community trade mark (codified version) [2009] OJ L78/1; Regulation (EC) 216/2008 on common rules in the field of civil aviation and establishing a European Aviation Safety Agency [2008] OJ L7911.

[125] Regulation 726/2004 laying down Community procedures for the authorization and supervision of medicinal products for human and veterinary use and establishing a European Medicines Agency [2004] OJ L136/1.

Commission, which takes the final decision in accordance with the applicable comitology procedure, it has been argued that 'the EMEA's opinion appears to condition substantially the discretion of the Commission in taking the final decision',[126] in particular as the Commission 'systematically rubber-stamps EMEA recommendations'.[127] It should be recalled that the ECJ in *Meroni* characterized the conferral of powers there as true delegation precisely because the High Authority, when adopting the final decision, did not call into question the findings of its agencies, although it seemed to have been entitled to do so.[128] The EMEA's scientific opinion is 'likely to include not only purely scientific, but also normative (nationally-flavoured) elements'[129] and therefore seems to trespass on the discretionary territory so firmly protected in *Meroni*. A certain loosening of the *Meroni* constraints can also be detected in the General Court's recent judgment in *Schräder v CPVO*.[130] In light of the importance of agencies in the lawmaking process of the Union, the silence on this issue in the Lisbon Treaty is to be regretted.

C. Rule-making by private actors

Rule-making by private actors has become of increasing relevance in the achievement of Union policies.[131] While the involvement of private parties in EU administrative governance has allowed European legislation to focus on the essential aspects of such policies and to harness the expertise of such bodies and their closer proximity to the relevant policy issues, the retreat of the public authorities in favour of private actors has raised concerns about the legitimacy of private party rule-making. Such disquiet about the delegation of responsibility and power to private parties is most evident in the field of European standardization, where the European Union has entrusted private bodies with the adoption of harmonized European standards. For economic operators, compliance with such standards, although voluntary, confers considerable legal and practical advantages for undertakings engaged in intra-Union trade. By creating incentives for compliance with standards, standardization activity plays an important role in the realization of an internal market for goods.

The debate about the legitimate delegation of responsibilities to private bodies must, however, also take account of the rationales for their involvement. It can also be asked whether the approach to the development of standards on the EU level is in fact fundamentally different from that which applies, and has applied for a considerable period, in many Member States. In the case of standardization on the

---

[126] See E Chiti, 'The Emergence of a Community Administration: The Case of European Agencies' (2000) 37 *CMLRev* 309, 336.

[127] R Dehousse, above n 123 at 223. See also E Vos, above n 120 at 1132.

[128] *Meroni* case, above n 7 at 147–9.

[129] Vos, above n 120 at 1132. See also Chiti, above n 126 at 337.

[130] Case T-187/06 *Schräder v Community Plant Variety Office (CVPO)* [2008] ECR II-3151; upheld on appeal in Case C-38/09 P *Schräder v CVPO* [2009] OJ C82/17.

[131] See Hofmann, Rowe and Türk, above n 68 at chs 9 and 17.

EU level, it was precisely the inability of the legislative branch to deal with the adoption of detailed technical rules that the new regulatory approach was chosen, just as has been the case on the national level. The inclusion of the standardization process in a hierarchy of norms[132] would therefore be ill-advised.[133] Equally, given the procedural and substantive differences between legally binding norms and standards, the finding that the adoption of standards involves political judgements should not lead to the conclusion that the standardization process should be treated in accordance with procedural or substantive principles applicable to Union legislation.[134]

VI. Conclusion

Its desire to avoid the constitutional symbolism of the failed Constitutional Treaty should not disguise the fact that the Lisbon Treaty incorporates in substance quite a number of constitutional features, which can be found in national legal systems. The formal introduction of legislative acts and the new regime of delegated acts demonstrate the willingness of the drafters to pursue a more state-oriented model of lawmaking. This approach is not without problems. On the one hand, the constitutional reform of Union legislation remains incomplete as can be seen from the notion of 'special' legislative acts, which are really regulatory acts in all but name. On the other hand, certain state-oriented aspects of the constitutional reform of the Lisbon Treaty, such as the new category of delegated acts, undermine traditional constitutional features of the Union, such as comitology, which have developed over time providing a crucial link between the Union and its Member States. Moreover, new forms of governance, which accompany the more traditional forms of lawmaking processes in the Union, such as the open method of coordination, the involvement of agencies or the participation of private parties, are treated with benign neglect in the more state-oriented outlook of the new Union.

---

[132] See E Previdi, 'The Organisation of Public and Private Responsibilities in European Risk Regulation: An Institutional Gap between Them?' in C Joerges, K-H Ladeur and E Vos (eds), *Integrating Scientific Expertise into Regulatory Decision-Making: National Traditions and European Innovations* (Nomos, 1997) 241; G Majone, 'The Credibility Crisis of Community Regulation' (2000) 38 *Journal of Common Market Studies* 273, 275.

[133] H Schepel, *The Constitution of Private Governance—Product Standards in the Regulation of Integrating Markets*, 1st edn (Hart Publishing, 2005) 247.

[134] Ibid 257.

4

Does the Lisbon Treaty Provide a Clearer Separation of Competences between EU and Member States?

Lucia Serena Rossi

I. The Absence of a Catalogue of the European Competence in the Founding Treaties and the Role of the ECJ

One of the most significant—and most 'constitutional'—innovations introduced by the Lisbon Treaty is a more detailed and organic discipline of the competences enjoyed by the European Union.[1]

Explicit rules on the delimitation of competences between the EU and the Member States were not included in the founding Treaties, probably because at the beginning of the European integration the principle of conferred power—as a cornerstone of international law—was so obviously implicit in every international convention establishing an international organization that it was not necessary even

---

[1] The legal literature on the subject matter is abundant, see further V Constantinesco, *Compétences et pouvoirs des Communautés européennes* (LGDJ, 1974); K Boskovits, *Le juge communautaire et l'articulation des compétences normatives entre la Communauté européenne et ses États membres* (Bruylant, 1999); V Constantinesco and V Michel, 'Compétences communautaires' in Rép. Droit communautaire, Dalloz, 2002; G De Bùrca and B de Witte, 'The Delimitation of Powers between the EU and its Member States' in A Arnull and D Wincott (eds), *Accountability and Legitimacy in the European Union* (Oxford University Press, 2002) 217; V Michel, *Recherches sur les compétences de la Communauté européenne* (L'Hartmattan, 2003); R Mastroianni, 'Le competenze dell'Unione' in X Il Diritto dell'Unione europea, 2005, 390; A Goucha Soares, 'The Division of Competences in the European Constitution' in 11 *European Public Law*, 2005, 603; U Draetta, 'Le competenze dell'Unione europea nel Trattato di Lisbona' in 47 *Diritto comunitario e degli scambi internazionali*, 2008, 245; T Kostantinides, *Division of Powers in European Union—The Delimitation of Internal Competence between the EU and the Member States* (Kluwer Law International, 2009); K Lenaerts and JA Gutierrez-Fons, 'The Constitutional Allocation of Powers and General Principles of EU Law' in 47 *CMLRev* 2010, 1629; JC Piris, *The Lisbon Treaty, A Legal and Political Analysis* (Cambridge University Press, 2010) 74ff; R Baratta, 'Le competenze interne dell'Unione europea tra evoluzione e principio di reversibilità' in XV Il Diritto dell'Unione europea, 517; P Craig, *Competence and Member State Autonomy: Causality, Consequence and Legitimacy* (electronic copy available at: <http://ssrn.com/abstract= 1474325>); JP Jacqué, 'L'Union, une communauté de valeurs?' 44 *Revue Trimestrielle de Droit Européen* 2008, 1–3;, NA Neuwhal, 'Shared Powers or Combined Incompetence? More on Mixity' in *CMLRev* 1996, 667; and G Tesauro, 'Sovranità degli Stati e integrazione comunitaria' 11 *Il Diritto dell'Unione europea* 2006, 235.

to mention it in the EEC Treaty. According to international law, all the competences belong to the state and no sacrifice of sovereignty can be presumed unless it is expressly established; consequently, an international organization enjoys all and only the competences explicitly mentioned by the founding Treaty. The EEC Treaty affirmed therefore only the principle of mutual respect of the competences among the different European institutions,[2] which related to the exercise of the European competences. However, this principle had some consequences in terms of the general question of National vs Supranational governance, in an inter-institutional balance axed on the so-called 'Community Method'.

The EEC original system of competences—whose structure remained unaltered until the Lisbon Treaty—followed the so-called functionalistic approach. The original Treaty assigned a range of goals to the European Economic Community, which were broadly indicated, and a series of policies as instruments necessary for the pursuit of those goals. Within those policies the EEC Treaty listed the single sectors of competences, not in a general way, but by means of specific legal bases.

The legal basis is the provision of the Treaty indicating the procedure to be followed when the European institutions intend to adopt a piece of legislation in a specific field. The same policy can be subject in its different aspects to different legal bases. The legal basis consists of two elements: the type of majority required in the Council and the involvement of other institutions, namely the European Parliament.

In this way, by establishing the procedure, the treaty provisions also pictured the competence of the Community and of the single institutions. Accordingly, in order to know what competences the Community was given it was necessary to read all of the Treaty.

The main goal of the original Treaty was the Common Market, axed on the four fundamental freedoms, the common commercial policy, the common agricultural policy, free competition and other collateral policies such as transport. The functionalistic approach was also implicit, pertaining to European integration. In fact, the original Article 2 of the EEC Treaty mentioned the promotion of ever closer relations among the Member States.

The system was completed by a general clause of flexibility, allowing the institutions to adopt any measure necessary to achieve, in the functioning of the Common Market, one of the aims of the Community, in cases where the Treaty had not provided for the requisite powers of action (former Article 235 EEC and then Article 308 EC). The practice expanded the application of the flexibility clause, creating new competences such as environment and consumer protection.

The expansion of the European competence over the years has been impressive, with the differentiation and multiplication of specific legal bases. The many revisions of the founding Treaty progressively included new policies and—with the Maastricht Treaty—new pillars. From the original, mainly economic, focus the European competence gradually extended to matters only indirectly related to

---

[2] According to Article 4 of the EEC Treaty, each of the institutions 'shall act within the limits of the powers conferred upon it by this Treaty'.

the market and with significant political implications. In many cases the revisions of the Treaty simply codified what the ECJ case law or the institutional practice had already established. That was the case for environment and consumer protection, codified by the Single European Act, the trans-European networks, introduced by the Treaty of Maastricht, and certain aspects of the Area of Freedom Security and Justice regulated by the Treaty of Amsterdam.[3] Pursuant to the Lisbon Treaty, the European Union may adopt measures in new fields such as space, energy, tourism and a common diplomatic service.

The division of competences between Member States and the European Community (and subsequently the Union) seems therefore to have been gradually shaped not by a predetermined project, but according to specific needs, as Member States become aware of the impotence of their national instruments to cope with increasing complexity and globalization.

As it was pointed out many years ago,[4] the delimitation of competences between the Community and the Member States is by its nature 'mobile'. This is mainly due to the case law of the Court of Justice, which on the one hand endorsed the use of the flexibility clause for expanding the existing competences and, on the other hand, progressively established at the external level (that is, in the international relations of the Community) two principles: parallelism and pre-emption; which not only increased but also made exclusive the Community competence.

Furthermore, the Court enunciated—in the face of the Treaty's silence on the matter—the rules concerning the use of legal basis by the European institutions. Since each legal basis can entail a different involvement of the European Parliament, as well as requiring a different majority within the Council, these cases mainly deal with the conflict of inter-institutional competences. But such conflicts can also be seen as a struggle between the Community/supranational method and the intergovernmental method within the different procedures. The more power is attributed to the non-governmental institutions (European Parliament and Commission) and the less room is left for unanimity, the weaker is the influence of the single Member States.

The relevant case law was elaborated in judgments concerning annulment procedures and regarded both the existence of the European competences and the delimitation of the inter-institutional powers. First, according to the ECJ, the legal basis has to be mentioned by every piece of legislation as a condition of their validity:[5] a simple 'having regard to the Treaty' is not considered a sufficient legal basis.[6] This is important because the legal basis indicates the competence, and not only the procedure. Moreover, the ECJ

---

[3] According to R Schütze, 'Co-operative Federalism Constitutionalised: The Emergence of Complementarity Competences in the EC Legal Order' 31 *ELR* 2006, 167, newly introduced legislative competences mandated the Community legislator to set minimum requirements only on the one hand; but on the other hand, they characterized the function of the legislator as complementing or supplementing national action.

[4] A Tizzano, 'The Powers of the Community' in Commission of the European Communities in A Tizzano (ed), *Thirty years of Community Law* (Office of Official Publications of the EC, 1981).

[5] Case C-440/05 *Commission of the European Communities v Council of the European Union* [2007] ECR I-9097, para 61.

[6] Case 45/86 *Commission of the European Communities v Council of the European Communities* [1978] ECR 1493, para 8.

also noted that the choice of the legal basis could affect the determination of the content of the contested act.[7] Secondly, when the institutions adopt an act Member States tend to prefer the legal basis which allows the Council more freedom with respect to the European Parliament or to rely on more than one legal basis, in order to cumulate the different procedural requirements. The Court affirmed that a double legal basis should be avoided if the measure's centre of gravity mainly relates to one of the relevant matters.[8] A double basis is nevertheless possible if the act concerns two subjects equally: in this case a problem may arise if one of the matters falls in the exclusive competence and the other entails a shared competence, with complications for the control of subsidiarity and—in the case of external relations—of the competence to negotiate.[9] Third, before the entry into force of the Lisbon Treaty several problems of inter-pillar conflicts were raised before the Court, which used Article 47 TEU in order to prioritize the first pillar with respect to the more intergovernmental pillars of CFSP and JHA.[10]

The case law of the Court of Justice has also been the source of the distinction between exclusive and shared competences,[11] which was not defined before the Lisbon Treaty and not mentioned at all in the Treaties before the Maastricht revision.[12]

Even more importantly, the Court affirmed the principle of pre-emption, according to which once—and only to the extent that—the subject is regulated at European level, the states lose their powers. It is interesting to note that the same type of competence (exclusive or shared) can in practice attribute a different power to the European Union, corresponding to the procedures prescribed by the relevant legal basis. In fact, a shared competence subject to unanimity often risks remaining purely potential for the European Union (see for instance the direct tax harmonization).

The principle of pre-emption operates both at intra-EU level and in the external relations of the Union. At the EU level it combines with those of supremacy of the European law on the national legislations and of loyal cooperation: once an act has been adopted by the European institutions, it prevails on the laws of the Member States; the latter must avoid jeopardizing the EU action, for instance by adopting national laws capable of endangering the application of a directive whose term has yet to expire.[13]

---

[7] Ibid para 12.

[8] Case C-178/03 *Commission of the European Communities v European Parliament and Council of the European Union* [2006] ECR I-107, para 42.

[9] See D Verwey, *The European Community, the European Union and the International Law of Treaties* (TMC Asser Press, 2004) 102.

[10] For an overview of the case law and legal literature on the matter, see R van Ooik, 'Cross-Pillar Litigation before the ECJ: Demarcation of Community and Union Competences' in 4 *European Constitutional Law Review* 2008, 399; C Hillion and RA Wessel, 'Competence Distribution in EU External Relations after ECOWAS: Clarification or Continued Fuzziness?' in 46 *CMLRev* 2009, 551; L Paladini, 'I conflitti fra i pilastri dell'Unione europea e le prospettive del Trattato di Lisbona' in 15 *Il Diritto dell'Unione europea* 2010, 87.

[11] Joined Cases 3, 4 and 6–76 *Cornelis Kramer and others* [1976] ECR 1279.

[12] The Maastricht Treaty only indirectly mentioned the exclusive competences with reference to the principle of subsidiarity.

[13] See further, S Weatherill, 'Pre-emption, Harmonisation and Distribution of Competences to Regulate the Internal Market' in C Barnard and J Scott (eds), *The Law of the Single Market: Unpacking the premises* (Hart Publishing, 2002) 41–74. R Schütze, 'Supremacy without Pre-emption? The Very Slowly Emergent Doctrine of Community Pre-emption' in (2006) 43 *CMLRev* 1023.

Before the entry into force of the Lisbon Treaty the Court has constantly expanded the external competence of the European Community[14] also in the field of the external relations, first of all by affirming the principle of parallelism.[15] According to this principle, the internal competence also involves a parallel exclusive external competence of the Community: once an act is adopted at the EU internal level, Member States can no longer negotiate international agreements with third parties which could hinder the effects of EU legislation. The exclusivity of the external competence derives from the pre-emption principle and therefore occurs even when the internal competence is not exclusive.

The Court further extended the field of external exclusive competences in the *Lugano* Opinion,[16] with reference to the potential competence, that is, a shared competence, which has not yet been utilized by the European Community/Union. The Court affirmed that any international negotiation capable of affecting an internal competence that the European institutions have started to exercise—even in very broad terms—must be considered to be of exclusive competence of the Union, thereby preventing the Member States from negotiating in their own name.

Finally, in the recent cases concerning bilateral agreements on foreign investments, the Court, interpreting in a restrictive way the former Article 307 EC (now Article 351 TFEU),[17] further reduced the external competence of the Member

[14] See in general S Amadeo, *Unione europea e treaty-making power* (Giuffrè Editore, 2005); P Koutrakos, *EU International Relations Law* (Hart Publishing, 2006) 77ff; F Casolari, 'La sentenza MOX: la Corte di giustizia delle Comunità europee torna ad occuparsi dei rapporti tra ordinamento comunitario ed ordinamento internazionale' in 12 *Il Diritto dell'Unione europea* 2007, 327; LS Rossi, 'Conclusione di accordi internazionali e coerenza del sistema. L'esclusività della competenza comunitaria' in 90 *Rivista di diritto internazionale* 2007, 1008; M Cremona, 'Defining Competence in EU External Relations: Lessons from the Treaty Reform Process' in A Dashwood and M Maresceau (eds), *Law and Practice of EU External Relations: Salient Features of a Changing Landscape* (Cambridge University Press, 2008) 34.
[15] Case 22/70 *Commission of the European Communities v Council of the European Communities* [1971] ECR 263.
[16] Opinion 1/03 *Competence of the Community to Conclude the New Lugano Convention on Jurisdiction and the Recognition and Enforcement of Judgments in Civil and Commercial Matters* [2006] ECR I-1145. On the approach adopted by the ECJ in this Opinion see N Lavranos, 'Opinion 1/03, Lugano Convention' in 43 *CMLRev* 2006, 1087; E Cannizzaro, 'Le relazioni esterne della Comunità: verso un nuovo paradigma unitario?' in 12 *Il Diritto dell'Unione europea* 2007, 223; LS Rossi, above n 14 at 1012; F Pocar (ed), *The External Competence of the European Union and Private International Law. The EC Court's Opinion on the Lugano Convention. Proceedings of the Round Table Held at Milan University on 16 September 2006* (Cedam, 2007); A Santini, 'The Doctrine of Implied External Powers and Private International Law Concerning Family and Succession Matters' in A Malatesta, F Pocar, and S Bariatti (eds), *The External Dimension of EC Private International Law in Family and Succession Matters* (Cedam, 2008) 31.
[17] For a general survey of the ECJ's case law concerning Article 307 EC, see R Mastroianni, *Diritto internazionale e diritto d'autore* (Giuffrè Editore, 1997) 208ff; R Mastroianni, *Art. 307 TCE* in A Tizzano (ed), *Trattati dell'Unione europea e della Comunità europea* (Giuffrè Editore, 2004) 1372; P Manzini, 'The Priority of Pre-existing Treaties of EC Member States within the Framework of International Law' in 12 *European Journal of International Law* 2001, 781; J Klabbers, *Treaty Conflict and the European Union* (Cambridge University Press, 2009) 115ff. On the BIT's case law, see F Casolari, 'La Corte di giustizia e gli obblighi convenzionali assunti dall'insieme degli Stati membri verso Stati terzi: obblighi comuni o . . . obblighi comunitari?' in 14 *Il Diritto dell'Unione europea* 2009, 267, 308ff; T Eilmansberger, 'Bilateral Investment Treaties and EU Law' in 46 *CMLRev* 2009, 383; N Lavranos, 'Case-note on BITs Judgments' in 103 *American Journal of International Law* 2009, 716; MR Mauro, 'Accordi internazionali sugli investimenti e Unione europea' in 5 *Studi sull'integrazione europea* 2010, 403.

States with regards to bilateral conventions concluded before their accession to the European Union.

The Lisbon Treaty endorses this case law (see below) providing a wide notion of external exclusive competences. Such an extension is connected with the principle of consistency between external and internal action of the EU (Article 21(3) TEU).[18]

II. Fluid Concepts: Values, Aims and Competences

As indicated above, the original Community system of competences was based not on a catalogue but on general objectives and specific legal bases, which regulated both the competence and the procedure.

The Lisbon Treaty establishes a hybrid system of attribution, which is based, on the one hand, on the connection between general aims and specific legal bases—as it was in the pre-Lisbon system—and, on the other hand, on a catalogue. The principles governing the competences of the EU are split by the new Treaty into the TEU and the TFEU. The first Treaty contains the general principles and the latter the list of competences and their definition as well as the single legal basis and the flexibility clause. This is confirmed by Article 1 TFEU, according to which 'this Treaty organizes the functioning of the Union and determines the areas of, delimitation of, and arrangements for exercising its competences'.

As the catalogue is not exhaustive in its main components (the shared competences), the quest for the objectives of the Treaty is still important for exploring the borders of the EU competences. The values and aims of the European Union are wider and more detailed than those mentioned by the previous treaties. The broadening of the European values and aims operated by the Lisbon Treaty could also entail a widening of the cases in which an action of the European Union may be justified and reflects the progressive evolution of the process of integration. Objectives can be seen as potential sources of competence in light of Article 3 § 6 TEU, which makes it clear that 'The Union shall pursue its objectives by appropriate means commensurate with the competences which are conferred upon it in the Treaties'. Moreover, since all objectives need a legal basis in order to become a competence, when no legal basis is connected to any of the EU's aims, it should be possible to make recourse to the flexibility clause, at the conditions set out in Article 352 TFEU. The latter provision allows the Union to take measures necessary to attain one of the objectives set out in the Treaties even in the absence of a legal basis, but only insofar as the relevant action takes place within the framework of the policies defined in the Treaty.[19]

---

[18] On this principle see M Dony and LS Rossi (eds), *Démocratie, cohérence et transparence vers une constitutionnalisation de l'Union européenne* (Editions de l'Université Libre de Bruxelles, 2007).

[19] In this regard it should be noted that although a 'high degree of competitiveness' no longer appears among the list of objectives to be attained (cf Article 2 EC) recourse to the flexibility clause in this domain will still be possible. Indeed, Protocol No 27 on the internal market and competition states that 'considering that the internal market as set out in Article 3 of the Treaty on European Union includes a system ensuring that competition is not distorted . . . the Union shall, if necessary, take

From a theoretical point of view, the difference between values and objectives should be clear: the objectives of the EU may be a ground for competences in connection with a specific legal basis or the flexibility clause while the values of the European Union are intended to orientate the exercise of the competences. In practice, however, there will be some overlapping. The values are introduced by Article 2 TEU: respect for human dignity, freedom, democracy, equality, the rule of law and respect for human rights, including the rights of persons belonging to minorities. But a reference to values is made by Article 3 §1 TEU with regard to the aims of the European Union, according to which one of the aims of the European Union is to promote its own values.[20]

More generally, it is not easy to grasp the difference between the values and objectives of the European Union. Indeed, the latter go far beyond the Area of Freedom, Security and Justice, the internal market and the euro, including 'the sustainable development of Europe based on balanced economic growth and price stability, a highly competitive social market economy, aiming at full employment and social progress, and a high level of protection and improvement of the quality of the environment'.[21] According to the provision noted above, 'the European Union shall promote scientific and technological advance, combat social exclusion and discrimination, and shall promote social justice and protection, equality between women and men, solidarity between generations and protection of the rights of the child. It shall promote economic, social and territorial cohesion, and solidarity among Member States, and shall ensure that Europe's cultural heritage is safeguarded and enhanced.'[22]

The same overlapping of values and objectives can also be found in the provisions on the external action. The Lisbon Treaty indicates a broad list of values for the EU external action, which in part reflect the 'internal' values. In this regard, Article 205 TFEU states that 'The Union's action on the international scene . . . shall be guided by the principles, pursue the objectives and be conducted in accordance with the general provisions laid down in Chapter 1 of Title V of the Treaty on European Union'.

According to Article 3 § 5 TEU, the Union 'shall uphold and promote its values and interests and contribute to the protection of its citizens . . . It shall contribute to peace, security, the sustainable development of the Earth, solidarity and mutual respect among peoples, free and fair trade, eradication of poverty and the protection of human rights, in particular the rights of the child, as well as to the strict observance and the development of international law, including respect for the principles of the United Nations Charter'.

---

action under the provisions of the Treaties, including under Article 352 of the Treaty on the Functioning of the European Union'. This statement is hard to combine with the circumstance that, as will be seen, the 'competition rules necessary for the functioning of the internal market' are exclusive competence of the Union pursuant to Article 3 § 1 b TFEU (see below section V).

[20] According to Article 3 § 1 TEU, 'The Union's aim is to promote peace, its values and the well-being of its peoples.'

[21] Article 3 § 3 TEU.

[22] Ibid.

Similarly, Article 21 TEU blends with no clear delimitation principles (which are values), objectives and specific competences for the external action. According to Article 21 §1 TEU 'The Union's action on the international scene shall be guided by the principles which have inspired its own creation, development and enlargement, and which it seeks to advance in the wider world: democracy, the rule of law, the universality and indivisibility of human rights and fundamental freedoms, respect for human dignity, the principles of equality and solidarity, and respect for the principles of the United Nations Charter and international law.' But the same paragraph also attributes some objectives to the European Union: 'The Union shall seek to develop relations and build partnerships with third countries, and international, regional or global organizations which share the principles referred to in the first subparagraph. It shall promote multilateral solutions to common problems, in particular in the framework of the United Nations.' Specific objectives are also assigned to the Union by the second paragraph of Article 21, in order to define and pursue common policies and actions, and to work towards a high degree of cooperation in all fields of international relations.[23] Article 22 TEU provides the legal basis for adopting the strategic interests and objectives of the Union and the subsequent decision 'in connection with the principles and objectives set out in Article 21'.

The fuzzy borders between values and aims should have a lesser impact on common foreign security and defence policies because the use of the flexibility clause in this field is prevented by Article 352 § 4 TFEU.

The Intergovernmental Conference (IGC) tried to clarify the situation by means of a Declaration number 41 attached to the Lisbon Treaty. According to the Declaration 'the reference in Article 352 §1 of the Treaty on the Functioning of the European Union to objectives of the Union refers to the objectives as set out in Article 3 § 2 and § 3 of the Treaty on European Union and to the objectives of Article 3 § 5 of the said Treaty with respect to external action under Part Five of the Treaty on the Functioning of the European Union. It is therefore excluded that an action based on Article 352 of the Treaty on the Functioning of the European Union would *only* pursue objectives set out in Article 3 § 1 of the Treaty on European Union. In this connection, the

---

[23] 'The Union shall define and pursue common policies and actions, and shall work for a high degree of cooperation in all fields of international relations, in order to: (a) safeguard its values, fundamental interests, security, independence and integrity; (b) consolidate and support democracy, the rule of law, human rights and the principles of international law; (c) preserve peace, prevent conflicts and strengthen international security, in accordance with the purposes and principles of the United Nations Charter, with the principles of the Helsinki Final Act and with the aims of the Charter of Paris, including those relating to external borders; (d) foster the sustainable economic, social and environmental development of developing countries, with the primary aim of eradicating poverty; (e) encourage the integration of all countries into the world economy, including through the progressive abolition of restrictions on international trade; (f) help develop international measures to preserve and improve the quality of the environment and the sustainable management of global natural resources, in order to ensure sustainable development; (g) assist populations, countries and regions confronting natural or man-made disasters; and (h) promote an international system based on stronger multilateral cooperation and good global governance.' The third paragraph of the same Article stipulates that 'the Union shall respect the principles and pursue the objectives set out in paragraphs 1 and 2 in the development and implementation of the different areas of the Union's external action covered by this Title and by Part Five of the Treaty on the Functioning of the European Union, and of the external aspects of its other policies'.

Conference notes that in accordance with Article 31 § 1 of the Treaty on European Union, legislative acts may not be adopted in the area of the Common Foreign and Security Policy'. Therefore, if the exclusion of CFSP is quite clear, the objectives of Article 3 § 1 are not excluded from the scope of Article 352, provided that they are not the sole objective of a proposed EU act.

In conclusion, the vagueness of the delimitation between values and objectives, which can represent grounds for recognizing competences, may turn into a diminution of the role of the principle of conferral, notwithstanding the fact that the latter was the mantra of the Lisbon revision. A more effective barrier to an overflow of competences through the channels of objectives is the restriction of the scope of the flexibility clause (see below).

III. The General Principles on Competences in the Lisbon Treaty: The Obsession with Conferral

An assessment of the general principles affirmed by Article 5 TEU reveals that the Lisbon Treaty intends to submit both the attribution and the exercise of the EU competences to stricter control. This is shown by the attention dedicated to the principles of conferral, subsidiarity and proportionality.

As previously mentioned, the original EEC Treaty only referred to the sharing of competences among institutions,[24] not expressly mentioning the principle of conferral. The latter was introduced many years later, by the Treaty of Maastricht. The Lisbon Treaty makes so many references to this principle that it seems to have become almost an obsession.

The principle is mentioned by Article 3 § 6 TEU, according to which 'the Union shall pursue its objectives by appropriate means commensurate with the competences which are conferred upon it in the Treaties'. It is repeated in Article 4 § 1 TEU ('In accordance with Article 5, competences not conferred upon the Union in the Treaties remain with the Member States') and again in Article 5 TEU, which gives a full definition of the principle (§1 and § 2): 'the limits of Union competences are governed by the principle of conferral. . . . . . Under the principle of conferral, the Union shall act only within the limits of the competences conferred upon it by the Member States in the Treaties to attain the objectives set out therein. Competences not conferred upon the Union in the Treaties remain with the Member States'.

The same principle is recalled by Article 7 TFEU ('the Union shall ensure consistency between its policies and activities, taking all of its objectives into account and in accordance with the principle of conferral of powers').[25] The

---

[24] Today embodied in Articles 13 TEU, 314 TFEU and Declaration number 24.

[25] See also Article 19 TFEU: 'Without prejudice to the other provisions of the Treaties and within the limits of the powers conferred by them upon the Union, the Council, acting unanimously in accordance with a special legislative procedure and after obtaining the consent of the European Parliament, may take appropriate action to combat discrimination based on sex, racial or ethnic origin, religion or belief, disability, age or sexual orientation.'

principle is also echoed in the Charter of Fundamental Rights: Article 51, defining the scope of the latter, affirms that 'this Charter does not establish any new power or task for the Community or the Union, or modify powers and tasks defined by the Treaties'.

The other side of conferral is the repatriation of competences from the EU to the Member States, which makes the conferral reversible. Declaration number 18 concerning the delimitation of competences reiterates the principle of conferral as well as those of subsidiarity and proportionality and—for the first time in the history of the European Union—the concept of repatriation of competences has also been mentioned.

The repatriation of competences can be made at two different levels: by means of the ordinary legislation or through the revision procedure. On one hand, according to the Declaration, the Council may, on the initiative of one or several of its members, request that the Commission submit proposals for repealing a legislative act. On the other hand, the IGC takes note of the Commission's statement that it will devote particular attention to these requests and underlines that the ordinary revision procedure provided for in Article 48(2) to (5) TEU, may be applied in order to amend the founding Treaties, either increasing or reducing the competences conferred on the Union in those Treaties. The last statement is probably superfluous, given that ordinary international law recognizes the right of Contracting Parties to a treaty unanimously to amend it, but it shows the IGC's attitude of suspicion towards the expansion of EU competences.

As specified in Article 48 § 6 TEU, the simplified revision procedure cannot be used to increase the competences conferred on the Union in the Treaties, but nothing is said about using the special revision procedure in order to reduce the EU competences. The above mentioned Declaration could be used for interpreting the Treaty in the sense that the reduction could only be made by means of ordinary legislative procedure.

The 'obsession for conferral'—as well as the focus on reversibility—clearly reveal the distrustful attitude of the Member States towards European competences, but—as previously suggested—this is diluted by the complex interplay of values, objectives and competences. Such distrust was apparent in the negotiation of the Lisbon Treaty, but it is also reflected in the decisions of the Constitutional Courts of the Member States, starting with the *Bunderverfassungsgericht*.[26]

---

[26] See further, Editorial Comments, 'Karlsruhe Has Spoken: "Yes" to the Lisbon Treaty, but...' 46 *CMLRev* 2009, 1023–33; D Symon, 'La Cour de Karlsruhe et le traité de Lisbonne: oui mais...' 19 *Europe* 2009, 1; D Thym, 'In the Name of Sovereign Statehood: A Critical Introduction to the Lisbon Judgment of the German Constitutional Court' 46 *CMLRev* 1795–1822; LS Rossi, 'I principi enunciati della sentenza della corte costituzionale tedesca sul Trattato di Lisbona: un'ipoteca sul futuro dell'integrazione europea?' 92 *Rivista di diritto internazionale* 2009, 993–1019 and E Cannizzaro, 'Continuità, discontinuità e catastrofismo. Sulle reazioni della dottrina al LissabonUrteil' 15 *Il Diritto dell'Unione europea* 2010, 1–18.

IV. Subsidiarity and Proportionality: A Better Control

In contrast with the principle of conferral—which relates to the delimitations of competences among the Member States and the European Union and to the very existence of an European competence—the principles of subsidiarity and proportionality concern the use of the competences. More precisely, they govern the choice of *when* (subsidiarity) and *how* (proportionality) the existing competence can be exploited by the European institutions. Only a brief mention will be made here, as chapter 10 of this book is devoted to those principles.[27]

Subsidiarity should determine the best level of action in areas that do not fall within the EU exclusive competence. After an isolated appearance in the Single European Act (with reference to the environment)[28] those principles entered the Treaty in the Maastricht revision and were dealt with by a specific Protocol attached to the Treaty of Amsterdam. Since its introduction it has always been paraded by the official literature of the European institutions as the cornerstone of the European action.[29] Nevertheless, the observance of the principle is much more formal than substantial. Although a statement on the impact of the proposed measure on the application of the principle usually accompanies all legislative proposals of the Commission, this is often only an exercise of mere rhetoric. In fact, the Commission usually justifies the proposal in terms of scale of action, affirming—with a somewhat tautological reasoning—that an action of the EU is necessary because the proposed measure has cross-border effects and therefore the adoption of national measures could not attain the same result. Of course the real question should be whether and why such a cross-border effect exists, or is at least appropriate.

After the Lisbon revision, Article 5 TEU still remains sufficiently ambiguous to permit such a tautological interpretation of the principle, affirming that 'the Union shall act only if and in so far as the objectives of the proposed action cannot be sufficiently achieved by the Member States, either at central level or at regional and local level, but can rather, by reason of the scale or effects of the proposed action, be better achieved at Union level'. The principle is occasionally reaffirmed by the Treaty with reference to particular cases: Article 113 TFEU, for example, stipulates that provisions for the harmonization of legislation concerning turnover taxes, excise duties and other forms of indirect taxation may be adopted to the extent

---

[27] See A Biondi, 'Les compétences normatives de l'Union' in LS Rossi (ed), *Vers une nouvelle architecture de l'Union européenne* (Bruylant, 2004) 99.

[28] cf Article 130R, no 4 EEC as it became as a result of the Single European Act.

[29] On the division of competences and the principle of subsidiarity, see D Cass, 'The Word That Saves Maastricht: The Principle of Subsidiarity and the Division of Powers within the European Community' 29 *CMLRev* 1992, 1112; H Bribosia, 'Subsidiarité et répartition des compétences entre la Communauté et ses États membres' 5 *Revue du Marché Unique Européen* 1992, 165; NV Barber, 'Subsidiarity in the Draft Constitution' 11 *European Public Law* 2005, 197; V Constantinesco, 'Les compétences et le principe de subsidiarité' 41 *Revue Trimestrielle de Droit Européen* 2005, 305.

that such harmonization is necessary to ensure the establishment and the functioning of the internal market and to avoid distortion of competition.

An important innovation in comparison with the former Article 5 EC is the reference to the regional and local level, which matches the relevance given by Article 4 TEU to local self-government. Nevertheless, it will not be easy for the EU institutions to assess the possible contribution of the diverse levels of local governments within the Member States, since they may be part of very different systems (federal, regional, centralized) and therefore have very different powers.

But the real innovation introduced by the Lisbon Treaty is the new role of the national parliaments laid down in Protocols 1 and 2 concerning the role of national parliaments and the application of the principles of subsidiarity and proportionality.

In fact, the weakest point of the principle of subsidiarity has always been the monitoring of its correct application. The practice before the Treaty of Lisbon showed that no institution of the decisional triangle—despite continuous declarations in support of the principle—has a real interest in strictly controlling the principle's application.

The Commission's main concern is to carry out its proposal and usually it tests the practicability of that through a preliminary negotiation with the national governments, which are sometimes keen to bypass their national parliaments by adopting some legislation at EU level. Moreover the Council is usually interested in the content of the act because when the proposal arrives at the ministerial meetings (or even at the level of Coreper) it has already passed the first steps of negotiation and the question of subsidiarity has been settled, be it explicitly or implicitly. Of course a state which is outvoted in the Council may have an interest in attacking the act before the Court of Justice, invoking the violation of the principle of subsidiarity; but the very few cases before the ECJ to date show how infrequently that event occurs.[30] In general terms, the Court seems to be inspired by a sort of *favor validitatis*, which limits the chances that an act, once adopted, will be annulled.

The European Parliament is also usually more interested in the substance of the act than in subsidiarity. Furthermore, to raise the question of subsidiarity means that the European Parliament has to deny its competence in favour of the national parliaments.

In the case of violation of the principle of subsidiarity it is each national parliament which is dispossessed of its prerogatives. For this reason, conferring an

---

[30] Although the principle of subsidiarity has regularly been invoked before the ECJ, the Court has yet to annul an act for breaching the principle: Case C-84/94 *United Kingdom of Great Britain and Northern Ireland v Council of the European Union* [1996] I-5755; Case C-233/94 *Federal Republic of Germany v European Parliament and Council of the European Union* [1997] ECR I-2405; Case C-377/98 *Netherlands v European Parliament and Council* [2001] ECR I-7079; Case C-491/01 *The Queen v Secretary of State for Health, ex parte British American Tobacco (Investments) Ltd and Imperial Tobacco Ltd* [2002] I-11453; Joined Cases C-154/04 and C-155/04 *The Queen, on the application of Alliance for Natural Health and Nutri-Link Ltd v Secretary of State for Health (C-154/04)* and *The Queen, on the application of National Association of Health Stores and Health Food Manufacturers Ltd v Secretary of State for Health and National Assembly for Wales (C-155/04)* [2005] ECR I-6451; Judgment of 8 June 2010, Case 58/08 *The Queen, on the application of Vodafone Ltd and Others v Secretary of State for Business, Enterprise and Regulatory Reform*, nyr.

ex ante control on the matter of subsidiarity to the national parliaments may represent the correct solution to the problem of making subsidiarity an effective—and not a merely abstract—instrument.[31] Although the procedures provided for by the two Protocols have probably been designed in order not to allow too strict and punctual a review, the control on subsidiarity has now been conferred on the sole subjects—the national parliaments—which have the real interest in using it. Although the control established by the Lisbon Treaty (which has been strengthened in comparison with that provided for by the Constitutional Treaty) has more political than legal force it is unlikely that it will be ignored by the European institutions.[32]

Still, the judicial position of national—and regional—parliaments remains weak as far as the *ex post* control is concerned. If they want to bring a claim to the Court of Justice they have either to go through their national governments or to play the 'uncomfortable' role of non-privileged applicants, charged with the (impossible) burden of proving that the act concerns them directly and individually. Such a judicial review will therefore be strongly influenced by the internal dynamics (between Parliament and government); the German Constitutional Court has paved the way for a strict parliamentary control, but in other states such as Italy, it seems unlikely that the National Assembly will challenge what the government approves within the Council. Such dynamics—as well as the control on subsidiarity—will also involve the regional assemblies, which will have to settle the matter with their national government.

Similar reasoning can be made with regard to the principle of proportionality, which relates to the choice of the instruments used by the European institutions for implementing their action[33] and applies to all EU competences. More precisely than the pre-Lisbon rules, Article 5 TEU specifies that 'the content and form' of Union action shall not exceed what is necessary to achieve the objectives of the Treaties. The reference to the content may influence the choice of the type of harmonization (minimal as opposed to total), while the mention of the form of the EU action may suggest the adoption of directives instead of regulations. The borders between a test of proportionality and a control on the content of the EU proposal can sometimes be very thin. As the Protocols do not extend to proportionality the same procedures of the control on subsidiarity, the national parliaments will be able to influence the European institutions in the decision-making process only through their influence on national governments.

The application of the two Protocols noted above is one of the most challenging issues of the Lisbon Treaty. Will the national Assemblies be capable of really influencing EU decision-making? Will they establish an effective inter-parliamentary

---

[31] See also JV Louis, 'National Parliaments and the Principle of Subsidiarity—Legal Options and Practical Limits' 4 *European Constitutional Law Review* 2008, 429.

[32] M Dougan, 'The Treaty of Lisbon 2007: Winning Minds, Not Hearts' 45 *CMLRev* 2008, 617, 641 and 658.

[33] See G De Búrca, 'The Principle of Proportionality and its Application in EC Law' 13 *Yearbook of European Law* 1993, 105; E Ellis (ed), *The Principle of Proportionality in the Laws of Europe* (Oxford University Press, 1999).

communication (more effective than the existing, and irrelevant, COSAC) or will they go through the European Parliament? The latter's offer to help the national parliaments to connect may go some way to alleviating its concern of being bypassed by national parliaments. An alliance between the European Parliament and national parliaments against the Council and the national governments could develop in the near future.

Be that as it may, the Lisbon Treaty will force national parliaments to pay greater attention to the EU lawmaking process, increasing the democratic control on the exercise of the European competences.[34]

V. The 'Catalogue' of Competences

The idea of a catalogue of competences was expressed many times by advocates of legal certainty. However, it was fiercely opposed by the supporters of the creative role of the Court of Justice in the European integration process, claiming that a written catalogue would 'freeze' such a role.

In Declaration number 23 on the future of the Union (26 February 2001) attached to the Treaty of Nice, the IGC raised the question of 'how to establish and monitor a more precise delimitation of powers between the European Union and the Member States, reflecting the principle of subsidiarity'.

The Lisbon Treaty, following the path mapped out by the Treaty establishing a Constitution for Europe, introduces for the first time a description of the EU competence into the Treaty. This description is enshrined in Title I of the Treaty on the Functioning of the European Union. Article 2 TFEU describes three kinds of competence: exclusive, shared and supporting actions. According to Article 2 § 6 TFEU the scope of and arrangements for exercising the Union's competences shall be determined by the provisions of the Treaties relating to each area.

The catalogue partly takes inspiration from the case law of the ECJ, and partly innovates, introducing new elements.

Exclusive competence is defined as an area in which only the Union may adopt legally binding acts, while Member States can only legislate if such a power is delegated to them by the EU or to implement Union acts. The fields of exclusive competences are strictly enumerated by Article 3 TFEU: three of them (custom union, common commercial policy and conservation of marine biological resources under the common fisheries policy) had already been defined as exclusive by the ECJ.

With reference to the common commercial policy, Article 207 § 6 TFEU establishes some limits, specifying that the exercise of that competence shall not affect the delimitation of competences between the Union and the Member States, and shall not lead to harmonization of legislative or regulatory provisions of the Member States insofar as the Treaties exclude such harmonization.

---

[34] Although, as noted, the application of the principle of proportionality is not specifically addressed in the specific Protocol on subsidiarity and proportionality and escapes the reach of the national parliaments' *ex ante* control over EU acts.

The exclusive character of the monetary policy for the Member States of the eurozone is easy to understand. Quite surprisingly, Article 3 TFEU qualifies as exclusive also the competence of 'establishing the competition rules necessary for the functioning of the internal market'. Such a qualification—that is at least less general with respect to the Giscard Draft of the Constitutional Treaty, which foresaw that all the internal market would fall within the exclusive competence of the European Union—found no support in the previous case law of the Court of Justice.[35]

Although the qualification of such a competence as exclusive is clear by now, one may wonder at the rationale for considering as exclusive the rules on competition, deemed necessary for the functioning of the internal market. Perhaps the negotiators of the Lisbon Treaty had in mind state aids when they drafted Article 3 TFEU: only the rules on state aids could be reasonably taken away from the Member States' competences, but the same could not be said about the discipline of cartels and abuse of a dominant position. Furthermore, Protocol number 27 is quite contradictory in affirming that 'considering that the internal market as set out in Article 3 of the Treaty on European Union includes a system ensuring that competition is not distorted, . . . to this end, the Union shall, if necessary, take action under the provisions of the Treaties, including under Article 352 of the Treaty on the Functioning of the European Union'. An exclusive competence should not need authorization to use the flexibility clause.

Acknowledging the *Lugano Opinion* of the Court of Justice,[36] Article 3 TFEU adopts a very broad notion of exclusive external competence: 'the Union shall also have exclusive competence for the conclusion of an international agreement when its conclusion is provided for in a legislative act of the Union or is necessary to enable the Union to exercise its internal competence, or in so far as its conclusion may affect common rules or alter their scope'.[37]

It is therefore interesting to remark that notwithstanding (or perhaps thanks to) the 'conferral obsession' the same Lisbon Treaty widens the sphere of the EU exclusive competences.

In the field of shared competences both the European Union and the Member States can adopt legally binding acts, but the EU action, once taken, has a pre-emptive effect on the competence of the Member States: as specified by Article

---

[35] After the entry into force of the Lisbon Treaty the ECJ has acknowledged that Regulation 1/2003 and the principles it establishes form part of the 'competition rules necessary for the functioning of the internal market' (Case C-550/07, *Akzo Nobel Chemicals* [2010] nyr, para 45).

[36] Opinion 1/03, above n 16.

[37] It should also be remembered that Declaration No 36 annexed to the Final Act of the IGC which adopted the Treaty of Lisbon confirms that Member States may negotiate and conclude agreements with third countries or international organizations in the areas covered by Chapters 3, 4 and 5 of Title V of Part Three of the Treaty (ie the area of freedom, security and justice) insofar as such agreements comply with the Union law. According to G Gaja and A Adinolfi, *Introduzione al diritto dell'Unione europea* (Editori Laterza, 2010), 220–1, such a Declaration contests the EU external exclusive competence in the field of jurisdiction, recognition and enforcement of judgments in civil and commercial matters, as affirmed in the Lugano Opinion.

2 § 2 TFEU, 'States shall exercise their competence to the extent that the Union has not exercised its competence'.

Pre-emption is strictly connected with the primacy of EU law, on the one hand, and the principle of sincere cooperation, on the other: once the EU act has been adopted, it prevails on the national legislations and Member States are bound to respect and implement it. However, the preclusive effect of pre-emption does not transform the exclusive competence. In fact the occupation is not necessarily irreversible: the same Article stipulates that the Member States shall again exercise their competence to the extent that the Union has decided to cease exercising its competence. Moreover, as has been noted above, Declaration number 18 expressly refers to abrogation of EU legislation at the request of the Member States.

Most of the EU competences are shared with Member States: this is a residual category, embracing all the competences not referred to by Article 3 (exclusive) or Article 6 (supporting actions) of the same Treaty. The list provided for by Article 4, § 2 TFEU is merely illustrative, indicating only the 'principal' areas: internal market; social policy, for the aspects defined in the TFEU; economic, social and territorial cohesion; agriculture and fisheries, excluding the conservation of marine biological resources (which is exclusive); environment; consumer protection; transport; trans-European networks; energy; area of freedom, security and justice; common safety concerns in public health matters, for the aspects defined in the TFEU. This list includes the cornerstones of the European Union (internal market; agriculture; Area of Freedom, Security and Justice) as well as new competences like energy.

The third category of competence provided for by the Lisbon Treaty concerns actions carried out by the Union in order to support, coordinate or supplement the actions of the Member States.

The fields of the supporting, coordinating or supplementing actions are defined by Article 6 TFEU: protection and improvement of human health; industry; culture; tourism; education, vocational training, youth and sport; civil protection; administrative cooperation. Apart from civil protection and tourism, these fields of competence are not new but, since their introduction by the Single European Act, they have always been defined by the related legal basis not as full competences but only matters in which the Community Action could complete that of the Member States.[38] It is a merit of the Lisbon Treaty to have codified this category which stands in between shared competences and competences totally

---

[38] In the context of the Lisbon strategy, areas such as employment, education and vocational training have been addressed through the open method of coordination (OMC), which involves the adoption of soft law measures which are binding on the Member States in varying degrees, but that never take the form of regulations, directives or decisions. On the OMC mechanism, see S Smisman, 'Reflexive Law in Support of Directly Representative Polyarchy: Reflective-Deliberative Polyarchy as Normative Frame of the OMC' in O De Schutter and S Deaking (eds), *Social Rights and Market Forces: Is the Open Method of Coordination of Employment and Social Policies the Future of Social Europe?* (Bruylant, 2005); DM Tubek and LG Trubek, 'Hard and Soft Law in the Construction of Social Europe: The Role of the Open Method of Coordination' 3 *European Law Journal* 2005, 343 and B Lange and N Alexiadou, 'How to Govern for Solidarity? An Introduction to Policy Learning in the Context of Open Methods of Coordinating Learning Policies in the European Union' in M Ross and Y Borgmann-Prebil (eds), *Promoting Solidarity in the European Union* (Oxford University Press, 2010) 235.

reserved to Member States, even if in the case of new competences (that is, civil protection and tourism) such a codification may lead to a limitation of the EU intervention.[39]

Similar to the shared competences, such actions are submitted to the respect of the principles of subsidiarity and proportionality. But unlike shared competences this kind of competence presents two limits. First, they have no pre-emption effect, the states remaining free, notwithstanding the EU action, to adopt national measures in the same field. Nevertheless, the action of Member States does not seem to be totally free, as it has to respect general principles of EU law such as, for instance, non-discrimination on grounds of nationality, as well as the duty of sincere cooperation. Secondly, the action of the EU cannot lead to harmonization of Member States' laws or regulations (Article 2 § 5 TFEU).

In addition to the three categories mentioned above, the Lisbon Treaty cites other special competences, whose character is less easy to define. It should be recalled that all the competences not expressly defined otherwise have to be considered as shared. Whether or not such policies are to be considered as areas of shared competences may have significant implications such as pre-emption and harmonization.

Article 2 § 3 TFEU stipulates that Member States shall coordinate their economic and employment policies within arrangements, which the Union shall have competence to provide. Since it is clear that they are competences of the Member States and that the Union is only competent to provide a coordination it seems difficult to consider them as shared, notwithstanding the fact that they are not mentioned among the coordination actions. The situation is even more complicated because economic policy is strictly related to the monetary policy, which is for the eurozone an exclusive competence of the EU. That provision has to be read in connection with Article 5 TFEU. According to the latter, 'the Member States shall coordinate their economic policies within the Union. To this end, the Council shall adopt measures, in particular broad guidelines for these policies. Specific provisions shall apply to those Member States whose currency is the euro. The Union shall take measures to ensure coordination of the employment policies of the Member States, in particular by defining guidelines for these policies. The Union may take initiatives to ensure coordination of Member States' social policies'. Such competences are typically submitted to the open coordination method with no harmonization option. This is confirmed by Articles 149 and 153 TFEU, which expressly exclude harmonization in certain economic and social fields.

A special competence is also defined by Article 2 § 4 TFEU, which stipulates that the Union 'shall have competence, in accordance with the provisions of the Treaty on European Union, to define and implement a common foreign and security policy, including the progressive framing of a common defence policy'. If the text allows one to consider CFSP as a shared competence, the position of the defence policy is less clear. Even if it is only a competence *in fieri*, that is, potential, it should

---

[39] M Gestri and F Casolari, 'Il turismo nel Trattato di Lisbona: un personaggio non più in cerca di autore' in *Rivista italiana di diritto del turismo*, forthcoming.

nevertheless be considered as shared; moreover, in this field it is provided that the European Defence Agency will promote harmonization of operational needs and adoption of effective, compatible procurement methods.[40]

Similar problems arise from Article 4 § 3 TFEU, devoted to the shared competences, according to which 'in the areas of research, technological development and space, the Union shall have competence to carry out activities, in particular to define and implement programmes; however, the exercise of that competence shall not result in Member States being prevented from exercising theirs'. This is a special shared competence with no pre-emption effect, but unlike in support actions, harmonization could be possible.

The same could be said with reference to Article 4 § 4, according to which 'in the areas of development cooperation and humanitarian aid, the Union shall have competence to carry out activities and conduct a common policy; however, the exercise of that competence shall not result in Member States being prevented from exercising theirs'.

Apart from the cases mentioned above it must be recalled that the Lisbon Treaty expressly excludes harmonization in certain fields of shared competences, such as the implementation of the principle of non-discrimination (Article 19 TFEU), integration of third-country nationals (Article 79 TFEU) and crime prevention (Article 84 TFEU).

In conclusion, the delimitation among the different kinds of competences made by the Lisbon Treaty is not so clear-cut, especially with reference to the shared competences, representing the largest category. Not only is there a grey area of special cases surrounding them, but the relevant degree of pre-emption may determine to what extent a field of shared competence remains open to the action of the Member States.

In fact the Treaty could provide a real catalogue of competences, explaining who—the Union or the Member States—has the competence in a given period. As the latter keep their power to legislate until the European institutions cover the field with EU legislation, only the actual exercise of a shared competence can decide the exact extension in any moment of the respective powers of the Union and Member States. In any given moment of the process of European integration, the real catalogue is represented by the *acquis*. For this reason writing an a priori catalogue of the EU competences can only be a theoretical exercise, confined to the potential competences and not embracing the actual exercise of the latter.

As the borders between the potential and the exercised EU competences continuously change as a result of the effect of pre-emption and primacy, the competences left to the Member States change almost on a daily basis.

Therefore, the 'catalogue' provided for by the Lisbon Treaty is very general; nevertheless it is useful for clarifying that in certain fields, pre-emption is not allowed, and consequently Member States will be able to legislate regardless of whether an EU act has already been adopted.

---

[40] See for instance Article 45(1)(b) TEU.

VI. The Declining Role of the Flexibility
Clause(s) after the Lisbon Treaty

The original system of the Community competences, based on objectives and legal bases, was completed by the flexibility clause (originally Article 235 EEC, then Article 308 TCE), an instrument for filling the gaps that in practice proved to be almost a simplified revision mechanism.[41] In fact such a procedure prevented a new competence being submitted to a revision of the Treaty, even if the required unanimity made it impossible to bypass the will of any of the Member States.

For its part, the Court of Justice interpreted the condition of the 'necessity for the functioning of the Common Market' extremely broadly, thereby allowing an expansion of the existing competences.[42] The revisions of the Treaty (Single European Act, Maastricht, Amsterdam, Nice) then accepted such expansions, by creating corresponding legal bases.

After the entry into force of the Single European Act, however, the Council started to use Article 235 EEC also in fields subject to the new cooperation procedure, jointly with other legal bases such as the general basis for harmonization in the Internal Market (Article 110 A EEC). The addition of the two different procedures (unanimity and consultation of the European Parliament plus qualified majority and cooperation) created a procedure in which unanimity combined with cooperation: this had the result politically of making the opinion of the European Parliament useless (as the cooperation procedure imposed unanimity for the acts not accepted by the Parliament). For that reason, after the Single European Act the litigation about legal bases grew impressively, propelled by the Commission which supported the position of the European Parliament, still lacking at the time an active *locus standi* before the Court of Justice.[43]

The attitude of the Court regarding the use of the flexibility clause then became more restrictive. The ECJ established that the provision on implied powers is merely residual, and therefore the institutions can only use it when no other legal basis covers the subject; but in any case a double basis cannot hinder the prerogatives of a European institution. As new competences were introduced along with several revisions of the founding Treaties, there was progressively less room for Article 235 EEC.

The text concerning the use of the flexibility clause remained unchanged until the Lisbon Treaty, which introduces some innovation, at the same time broadening the field of application of the clause, but also limiting its possible use.

---

[41] For a general survey see R Schütze, 'Organized Change towards an "Ever Closer Union": Article 308 EC and the Limits to the Community's Legislative Competence' 22 *Yearbook of European Law* 2003, 79.

[42] LS Rossi, *Il buon funzionamento del Mercato Comune* (Giuffrè Editore, 1990).

[43] The competence of the Parliament was recognized only with the ECJ judgment in Case C-70/88 *Parliament v Council* [1990] ECR I-2041, then partially included in the Treaty (with Maastricht) and fully granted (by the Nice Treaty).

The scope of the new clause (Article 352 TFEU)[44] is extended to 'the policies defined in the Treaties', including the freedom, security and justice area, but not to the CFSP (Article 352(4)).[45] Moreover, any acts adopted on the ground of the flexibility clause shall respect the limits set out in Article 40 § 2 TEU, that is, it cannot trespass the borders of the CFSP. On the other hand, as the Lisbon Treaty introduces new policies which are expressly regulated such as energy and space cooperation, the institutions are prevented from using the clause in those areas.

The Lisbon Treaty surrounds the flexibility clause with a set of limits. A special legislative procedure is provided for, according to which the Council must decide unanimously with the consent (under the Nice Treaty a simple opinion was required) of the European Parliament. Moreover, the new Treaty requires the Commission to draw national parliaments' attention to proposals based on the flexibility clause. Such a provision, in line with the general control of subsidiarity and proportionality, fills a gap left by the previous treaties: as the use of the flexibility clause entails an expansion of the EU competences without a revision of the Treaty, the national parliaments would be deprived of the power to ratify, and consequently, to reject it.

A further limit regards the impossibility of using the flexibility clause in order to harmonize the Member States' laws or regulations when the Treaties exclude harmonization (described in the previous section). Moreover, by virtue of Article 353 TFEU the simplified revision procedure cannot apply to the revision of the flexibility clause.

In Declaration number 42 on Article 352 TFEU, the IGC underlines that 'in accordance with the settled case law of the Court of Justice of the European Union, Article 352 of the Treaty on the Functioning of the European Union, being an integral part of an institutional system based on the principle of conferred powers, cannot serve as a basis for widening the scope of Union powers beyond the general framework created by the provisions of the Treaties as a whole and, in particular, by those that define the tasks and the activities of the Union. In any event, this Article cannot be used as a basis for the adoption of provisions whose effect would, in substance, be to amend the Treaties without following the procedure which they provide for that purpose'.

Article 352 is not the only flexibility clause provided for by the TFEU. Special flexibility clauses are incorporated in Articles 21 and 77 TFEU. The first affirms that if action by the Union should prove necessary to attain the objective of free movement of citizens and the Treaties have not provided the necessary powers, the European Parliament and the Council, acting in accordance with the ordinary legislative procedure, may adopt provisions with a view to facilitating the exercise of the related rights. For the same purposes and if the Treaties have not provided the

---

[44] See D Chalmers, G Davies and G Monti, *European Union Law*, 2nd edn (Cambridge University Press, 2010) 214. For a recent judicial application of Article 352 TFEU see Joined Cases C-402/05 P and C-415/05 P *Yassin Abdullah Kadi and Al Barakaat International Foundation v Council of the European Union and Commission of the European Communities* [2008] ECR I-6351, para 224ff.
[45] See also Declaration number 41, noted above.

necessary powers, the Council, acting in accordance with a special legislative procedure (unanimity in Council and consultation with the European Parliament), may adopt measures concerning social security or social protection.

With regard to the policies on border checks, asylum and immigration, Article 77 TFEU stipulates that, if action by the Union should prove necessary to facilitate the exercise of the right of free movement of citizens, and if the Treaties have not provided the necessary powers, the Council, acting in accordance with a special legislative procedure (unanimity with consultation of European Parliament), may adopt provisions concerning passports, identity cards, residence permits or any other such document. This provision shall not affect the competence of the Member States concerning the geographical demarcation of their borders, in accordance with international law.

Such special flexibility clauses, both connected to the free movement of EU citizens, expand those formerly provided for by Article 18 EC Treaty, which were—on the other hand—subject to the co-decision procedure.

A restrictive approach towards the use of the flexibility clause has recently been expressed in the European Council of 16–17 December 2010, where preference was given to the simplified revision procedure with respect to the procedure envisaged by Article 352 TFEU (or an extensive interpretation of Article 122 TFEU) in order to adopt a new stability mechanism. On the other hand, following the Lisbon judgment of the national constitutional court, the German government must be preliminarily authorized by the national parliament with a constitutional law before voting in the Council the adoption of an EU act based on the flexibility clause procedure. For the German government, this procedure is even less attractive than the parliamentary ratification of the EU Treaty required by (ordinary or special) revision procedures, where the government negotiates and then the German Parliament ratifies. As Article 352 TFEU requires unanimity in the Council, the German *Lissabon Urteil* casts a long shadow on the future of the flexibility clause.

VII. Concluding Remarks: A New Philosophy

The Lisbon Treaty entails a systematic reflection on the competences of the European Union, which has a constitutional value (and in fact this is one of the few 'Constitutional' parts that have been resumed from the Constitutional Treaty). An overall assessment of the new Treaty shows that the philosophy underlying the original EU system has been modified.

The new Treaty gives the European Union some new fields of competence, and it widens the exclusive ones (especially in the EU external relations). But, on the other hand, the system becomes much more rigid. The clear will of the Member States (but many of the new rules originate in the Constitutional Treaty as approved by the Giscard Convention) has been to rein in the powers of the EU institutions, regarding them with a certain amount of suspicion.

The principle of conferral has been obsessively stressed, becoming the mantra of the new philosophy. Repatriation of powers has been foreseen. A more effective and more democratic control will be applied to the exercise of the European competences. A sort of catalogue has been written into the Treaty. Recourse to the flexibility clause has been limited. Therefore, in contrast with the past, the EU competences will no longer be able to 'spontaneously' emerge from practice, that is, outside the boundaries of the Treaty, and without democratic control.

The fear of a continuous and uncontrolled expansion of the EU competences is not new (the principles of subsidiarity and proportionality were introduced with the aim of limiting the exercise of European powers) and has recently been expressed by the German Constitutional Court (surprisingly with reference to the first Treaty seriously regulating the European competences). As a flexible system of competences has so far been one of the reasons of the evolution of the European legal order towards a more supranational structure, one may wonder whether a more rigid system may have consequences for the future of European integration.

On the one side, it is clear that the EU legislative institutions will be submitted to stricter control when they adopt a new act; as for the European Court of Justice, its creative function will be somewhat limited by a clearer demarcation of powers between the EU and the Member States. But this does not seem to interrupt the legislative capacity of the European Union, nor to paralyse the interpretative function of the Court of Justice. In particular, the concept of pre-emption can still leave a large margin of interpretation and evolution both in the shared and in the external competences.

A flexible and fuzzy system of competences was suited to the original European system, based on functionalism. But the child has grown up. The European Union does not only have economic goals, as the bulk of the current European competences has grown impressively and the EU legal order progressively resembles a federal state. Clearer and stricter rules on the conferral and exercise of competences are part of a process of democratization and constitutionalization of the European Union. For these reasons they should be welcomed not only by those who fear, but also by everyone who welcomes, a future European Federation.

5

Treaty Revision Procedures after Lisbon

Bruno De Witte

I. Introduction

The Lisbon Treaty is the latest link in the long chain of revisions of the found-ing Treaties of the European Union. It did not seek to break that chain and the Lisbon Treaty was carefully presented by its authors—the Member States of the Union—as 'just' an amendment of the *existing* treaties, which was accomplished according to the *existing* rules of change which have remained basically the same ever since the 1950s. The Lisbon Treaty is thus firmly situated within the European treaty revision tradition, as described in section II of this chapter. Yet, this last revision process took much longer than any of the previous ones, and much longer than originally expected. Between 2002 and 2009, there were many unexpected political events and also a number of legal innovations and inventions that were grafted on the traditional treaty revision mechanism; section III of this chapter briefly discusses the specific legal features of the latest revision round. The Lisbon Treaty also alters the 'rules of change' for the future. This 'revision of the revision' denotes the will of the governments to differentiate the rules on treaty amendment so as to make them more flexible in some circumstances. The new Article 48 TEU does not remotely look like the old Article 48 TEU; its text is much longer and it introduces some entirely new modes of amending the Treaties (see the analysis in section IV). And yet, one may doubt whether the new revision rules have adequately equipped the European Union of 27 states for facing future pressures for change. Despite the 'treaty fatigue' that accompanied the entry into force of the Treaty of Lisbon, further amendments of the founding Treaties will unavoidably be needed. Indeed, the first post-Lisbon revision of the Treaties was undertaken only six months after the Lisbon Treaty's entry into force. The new treaty revision regime may still be too rigid and restrictive to allow for the timely adaptation of primary EU law to new external challenges and new political priorities.

II. The Treaty Revision Tradition (1951–2009)

The main instrument of constitutional change in the European Union, throughout the six decades since the creation of the Coal and Steel Community in 1951, was the conclusion of a revision treaty, that is, an international agreement between the member states of the European Communities, and later the European Union, making amendments to the 'founding treaties'. This was also true for the latest reform round which was not only the most protracted of all, but also particularly ambitious, since it involved—at least in its first phase, until the late spring of 2005—a self-conscious attempt at creating a formal Constitution for Europe. Despite that ambitious object-ive, there was never any doubt about the fact that an international treaty would, once again, be used as the legal instrument to attain it. Indeed, although the aim of the authors of the Constitution was to *repeal* (and replace) the existing treaties,[1] the adoption of the Constitution was seen by all the leading actors—and without much controversy—as involving, formally speaking, a *revision* of the current treaties in accordance with the procedure of Article 48 TEU, rather than the creation of a wholly new legal edifice. The Constitutional Treaty's Article IV-447 confirmed that the Treaty had to be 'ratified by the High Contracting Parties in accordance with their respective constitutional requirements' before it could enter into force, which corres-ponded to the requirement in the last sentence of Article 48 TEU. In fact, this Article IV-447 used the coded language typical of the law of international treaties ('ratify', 'enter into force', 'High Contracting Parties') and was perhaps the clearest formal confirmation that the Constitutional Treaty was indeed, in the view of its drafters, a genuine international treaty. The very same language is, of course, repeated in Article 6 of the Lisbon Treaty, which is that treaty's entry-into-force clause.

From the perspective of public international law, all the major revision treaties of the last 25 years, from the Single European Act to the Lisbon Treaty, were amendments of multilateral treaties, the legal regime of which is set out in Articles 39 to 41 of the Vienna Convention on the Law of Treaties. Article 39 contains the very simple default rule that a treaty may be amended by an agreement between all the parties, and that the normal rules on the conclusion of treaties apply to this amending agreement. This default rule may be set aside by the parties when concluding the original (to-be-amended) treaty. The international law regime of treaty amendment is, thus, one of utmost flexibility: the Contracting Parties are free to arrange for the later amendment of their treaty in the way they wish.[2] Indeed, a large and increasing number of multilateral treaties contain such a special amend-ment procedure, which is generally aimed at facilitating adaptation to changing circumstances, often by allowing for the amendment of a treaty without the agreement of all the parties. Article 48 TEU—the amendment clause applying to the latest EU revision round[3]—was an example of a specific amendment clause

---

[1] See Article IV-437 of the Treaty establishing a Constitution for Europe.

[2] See A Aust, *Modern Treaty Law and Practice* (Cambridge University Press, 2000) 214: 'It is wrong to think that the Vienna Convention is a rigid structure which places obstacles in the way of treaty modification: rather, it allows states to include in treaties such amendment provisions as they wish.'

[3] I refer here to Article 48 TEU as it stood prior to the entry into force of the Lisbon Treaty. The new revision clause, as amended by the Lisbon Treaty and as applicable to future revisions, is also numbered Article 48 TEU. The fact that the number remained the same is entirely coincidental because almost all other provisions of the EU Treaty were renumbered as of 1 December 2009. On the new version of Article 48, see further in this chapter.

that, contrary to most others, did *not* provide more flexibility than the default rule of Article 39 Vienna Convention. It required the agreement of *all* the parties (in this case, the Member States of the EU) for the valid adoption of an amendment and, in addition, it required a degree of involvement of the EU institutions in the preparation of the revision, and the subsequent ratification by each state according to its own constitutional requirements.

European Union treaty revisions are thus firmly embedded within the legal regime of the international law of treaties. This has a number of practical legal consequences. *First*, with respect to the drafting, conclusion and entry into force of the revision treaties, the specific rules of Article 48 can be supplemented, where needed, by the general rules of international treaty law. For example, the device of putting certain matters in a separate Protocol rather than in the main text of the treaty, and above all the careful distinction between binding Protocols and non-binding Declarations, which played a very important role in the latest intergovernmental conference (IGC),[4] rely on an implicit understanding of the meaning of those terms which is rooted in the international law of treaties. Secondly, with respect to the judicial control of treaty revisions, the European Court of Justice has confirmed several times that they were not acts of an EU institution and that the Court therefore had *no* authority to review them,[5] nor indeed the treaties of accession to the EU.[6] Thirdly, with respect to their application and enforcement in the national legal orders of the Member States, the international legal nature of treaty revisions means that in many Member States—and contrary to the orthodox understanding of the Court of Justice's primacy doctrine—EU law is applied on the basis of general constitutional doctrines about the domestic effect of international treaties.

Admittedly, the legal dynamics of European integration has not resulted exclusively from those repeated treaty revisions. Particularly during the period preceding the Single European Act, but also later on, we have seen other mechanisms of informal constitutional change at work in the European Community and the European Union, namely the creative interpretation of existing treaty rules by the European Court of Justice, the use of inter-institutional agreements and practice to flesh out the institutional provisions of the treaties and to prepare for the next formal revision,[7] and, most clearly, the generous use made by the Council of the 'gap-filling clause' of Article 235 EEC Treaty (later renumbered as Article 308 TEC and now, since the Treaty of Lisbon, as Article 352 TFEU). However, despite the important role played by these alternative instruments, formal treaty revisions have been, by far, the most important instrument of constitutional change.

Treaty revision was a success story during what could retrospectively be called its golden age, from 1985 to 1999, when amendments were successfully made and

---

[4] The Treaty of Lisbon has 13 Protocols and 65 Declarations, some of which clearly served to defuse last-minute tensions during the negotiations. See 'Editorial Comments: Protocology' (2009) *CMLRev* 1785.

[5] Case C-235/94 P *Olivier Roujansky v Council* [1995] ECR I-7, para 11.

[6] Case C-313/89 *Commission v Spain* [1991] ECR I-5231, para 9.

[7] See, eg, D Kietz and A Maurer, 'The European Parliament in Treaty Reform: Predefining IGCs through Interinstitutional Agreements' (2007) *European Law Journal* 20.

implemented in accordance with the traditional method of intergovernmental conferences followed by national ratifications. However, this method was increasingly criticized for putting an undue constraint on the adaptation of the European Union to changing needs and also for excluding citizens and public opinion from the process of institutional change. Misgivings arose, in particular, after the difficult ratification process of the Maastricht Treaty, with a failed first referendum in Denmark and an almost failed referendum in France. They became more widespread after the Treaty of Amsterdam, and came to be shared by most of the governments themselves after the disappointing functioning and results of the IGC leading to the Treaty of Nice, in 2000.

One type of criticism related to the continued adherence to traditional diplomatic forms of treaty negotiation 'behind closed doors' which increasingly appeared ill-suited to the crucial questions of democracy and governance that are invariably dealt with on the occasion of treaty revision. It took the dreadful European Council meeting of Nice, in December 2000, to convince the political leaders of the Member States that their traditional mode of negotiation was no longer suited to the complexity and constitutional importance of the matter at issue.

A second type of criticism related to the particularly rigid nature of the specific revision procedure adopted for the EU Treaties. The practice of multilateral international organizations shows that their founding charters can usually be changed without the need for a unanimous agreement of all the members (and, indeed, without national referendums).[8] Various kinds of special majorities allow for amendments of the treaties establishing the United Nations Organization, the International Labour Organization, the World Health Organization, the World Trade Organization and the Council of Europe, to name but a few. The European Union is thus exceptional among international organizations with a large membership in requiring the unanimous consent of all the Member States for changes in the founding instrument. The unanimity requirement for revision of the European Treaties was originally not much of a problem, when there were only six members. In a Union with 27 Member States, however, the unanimity rule for treaty amendment has become a major obstacle to change. It involves the risk that the dynamics of integration be halted, or made subject to blackmail, by a single Member State. The governments favouring the status quo are, in fact, put in an advantageous position compared to those favouring changes in the European Union's constitutional framework: a new rule, considered by a large majority of the states to be an improvement, can be blocked by one recalcitrant state.

Of course, it is precisely the vital impact that European treaty changes have on the Member States which explains the heavy insistence by the governments of those states on maintaining an individual veto right. The fact remains, though, that this rigidity makes treaty revisions very difficult tasks. It explains why European treaty amendments, despite their formal success, were never entirely satisfactory and were always accompanied by 'leftovers' (that is, questions on which the negotiators could

---

[8] See an overview in CF Amerasinghe, *Principles of the Institutional Law of International Organizations*, 2nd edn (Cambridge University Press, 2005) 447–63.

not agree and that were postponed until the next revision round), and increasingly also by opt-outs and special regimes for Member States which had difficulties with one or other element of the package.

III. The Specific Features of the 2002–2009 Treaty Revision Round

The latest revision round, although formally subject to the 'rules of change' laid down in Article 48 TEU, which remained exactly the same as the ones that had structured the earlier treaty revisions, was nevertheless quite distinctive in institutional terms. During the 'golden age' of treaty revision, stretching from 1985 to 1999, the amendment process had displayed a number of political routines and institutional practices that were repeated from one intergovernmental conference to the next.[9] The latest revision round departed from some of those established features. Its main innovation was the crucial role played in the amendment process by a new body, the Convention (subsection (a) below), but the subsequent stages of the process, namely the two intergovernmental conferences and the two national ratification processes, also displayed some unusual legal and institutional features (subsection (b) below).

A. A new actor: The Convention (2002–2003)

The most spectacular innovation occurred when the European Council, in its Laeken Declaration of December 2001, decided to call a Convention, to be composed of a variety of mainly non-governmental actors, in order to prepare the formal treaty revision negotiations among the governments.

For many years, European federalists had rejected the IGC regime as utterly unsuitable for the task of drawing up a coherent constitutional future for Europe. The radical alternative to the IGC which they proposed was the 'Philadelphian' model of a constitutional convention that would proclaim the 'United States of Europe', bypassing the obstruction of the national governments. This model was at the heart of Altiero Spinelli's European federalism,[10] although the 'Draft Treaty on European Union' which he promoted, was adopted in 1984 by the European

---

[9] For an account of the institutional practices of treaty amendment in that period, see B De Witte, 'The Closest Thing to a Constitutional Conversation in Europe: The Semi-Permanent Treaty Revision Process' in P Beaumont, C Lyons and N Walker (eds), *Convergence and Divergence in European Public Law* (Hart Publishing, 2002) 39. For political science perspectives, comparing the institutional dynamics of the various IGCs, see BPG Smith, *Constitution Building in the European Union—The Process of Treaty Reforms* (Kluwer Law International, 2002); D Beach and C Mazzucelli (eds), *Leadership in the Big Bangs of European Integration* (Palgrave Macmillan, 2007); and G Mateo González, *Hacia una Constitución Europea: Las Conferencias Intergubernamentales en la EU* (Tirant Lo Blanch, 2008). For a specific study of the amendment process leading to the Treaty of Nice, see F Laursen (ed), *The Treaty of Nice: Actor Preferences, Bargaining and Institutional Choice* (Brill, 2006). For an interesting insider's account of the mechanisms and dynamics of the Amsterdam IGC, see B McDonagh, *Original Sin in a Brave New World* (Institute of European Affairs, 1998).

[10] See the contributions to A Glencross and AH Trechsel (eds), *EU Federalism and Constitutionalism: The Legacy of Altiero Spinelli* (Lexington Books, 2010).

Parliament, rather than by a self-standing convention. In 1990, the European Parliament adopted, along the same lines, a resolution on the constitutional basis of the European Union.[11] This was a fully elaborated text with a constitutional character which, however, was presented by the European Parliament as merely the 'basis' of the definitive draft Constitution which it was prepared to adopt after the Member States would have acknowledged its right to do so (see point 2 of the resolution). The states never did, of course. On the contrary, they formally started, only a few days after the adoption of the Parliament's resolution, an IGC conducted along traditional lines which was successfully concluded, one year later, at Maastricht. Since then, the idea of a European constitutional convention as an *alternative* mechanism to the IGC had turned, again, into a utopian scheme which was occasionally proposed by academics of the federalist persuasion, but was no longer officially promoted by any European or national institution.

Surprisingly though, the European Council itself decided, at its meeting of Cologne in 1999, to put into operation an embryonic constitutional assembly by creating a quadripartite *body*, composed of representatives of the European Parliament, of national parliaments, of the Commission and of the Member State governments, for drafting a Charter of Fundamental Rights for the European Union. This body soon decided to call itself a 'Convention'. Although it did not actually claim for itself the power to *adopt* the Charter (that was left to the political institutions of the EU[12] after the green light had been given by the European Council), the Convention acquired a high degree of institutional legitimacy, which made it virtually impossible for the Member State governments to reject or even modify its proposals when they examined them at the Biarritz European Council of October 2000.

The inclusive composition of that Convention, and the relatively open and deliberative method of work adopted for drafting the Charter,[13] became particularly attractive when contrasted with the bitter bickering that occurred, some months later, at the IGC summit in Nice.[14] In the text of the Declaration on the Future of the European Union, which was appended to the Nice Treaty, the governments admitted that there was a need for a 'deeper and wider' reform debate than the one the IGC had been conducting. For this purpose, the governments agreed that the next intergovernmental conference, scheduled for 2004, would have to be preceded by an open debate involving a large number of political institutions and wider groups in society. No direct reference was made, at this stage, to the 'Convention method' (as it came to be called), but the Belgian Presidency managed in the second

---

[11] OJ 1991, C 19/65.

[12] Charter of Fundamental Rights of the European Union—Solemn Proclamation by the European Parliament, the Council and the Commission, OJ 2000, C 364/1.

[13] See G De Búrca, 'The Drafting of the EU Charter of Fundamental Rights' (2001) *European Law Review* 126, and F Delouche-Gaudez, 'La convention pour l'élaboration de la Charte des droits fondamentaux: Une méthode "constituante"' in R Dehousse (ed), *Une constitution pour l'Europe?* (Presses de Sciences Po, 2002) 177.

[14] See the summary press report, 'Nice Shambles Boosts Support for Convention' *European Voice* 14–20 December 2000, 1.

half of 2001 to obtain the consent of all the Member State governments on the creation of a new Convention,[15] whose composition was to be similar to the Convention that drafted the Charter of Rights, but whose task would prove to be incomparably more ambitious and demanding.

The decision taken in December 2001 by the Laeken European Council to establish a Convention on the Future of the Union was a bold experiment which profoundly affected the European Union's treaty amendment regime, even though it only complemented the procedure foreseen in Article 48 TEU without formally modifying it. The Convention mechanism sought to address the lack of democratic representation in treaty reform by the massive involvement of members of the European Parliament and of the national parliaments of the Member States. For the European Parliament, this was a major boost of its capacity to influence institutional reform, allowing it to cease to be a critic from the sidelines in order to become a major actor in its own right.[16] The involvement of the members of national parliaments allowed for a meaningful input of those national parliaments prior to the final agreement on the revised text (thus avoiding the fait accompli situation of earlier treaty revisions) and the revision treaty could be expected, logically, to meet with greater goodwill among the national parliaments when they would be called to approve it afterwards.

The Convention mechanism effectively allowed breakthroughs on certain taboo issues that had proved intractable for previous IGCs, such as the granting of a legal personality to the European Union, and the merger of the Community and the Union. Tenacious veto positions held by individual governments on such questions became untenable now that rational arguments had to be offered (and could not be found) to convince the Convention assembly. Whether the Convention was truly more representative, and more deliberative, than an IGC is quite another matter. Some studies of the Convention's operation point to the leading role played by the Convention's Praesidium and its secretariat, and the relatively minor role played by the delegates of national parliaments and of civil society.[17] The work of the

---

[15] See, on the negotiations preceding the Laeken Declaration, P Magnette, 'La constitutionnalisation des traités européens—Forces et limites de la méthode conventionnelle' in O De Schutter and P Nihoul (eds), *Une Constitution pour l'Europe. Réflexions sur les transformations du droit de l'Union européenne* (Larcier, 2004) 23, 34–7.

[16] See O Costa, 'La Convention dans la stratégie constituante du Parlement européen: aboutissement ou recul?' in O Beaud et al (eds), *L'Europe en voie de Constitution. Pour un bilan critique des travaux de la Convention* (Bruylant, 2004) 201.

[17] For some interesting accounts of the way the Convention operated, see P Norman, *The Accidental Constitution—The Story of the European Convention* (Eurocomment, 2003); A Lamassoure, *Histoire secrète de la Convention européenne* (Éditions Albin Michel, 2004); J Pollak and P Slominski, 'The Representative Quality of EU Treaty Reform: A Comparison between the IGC and the Convention' (2004) *European Integration* 201; J Ziller, *La nuova costituzione europea*, 2nd edn (Il Mulino, 2004) chapter III; C Closa, 'The Convention Method and the Transformation of EU Constitutional Politics' in EO Eriksen, JF Fossum and A Menendez (eds), *Developing a European Constitution* (Routledge Studies on Democratizing Europe, 2004) 183; P Magnette and K Nicolaidis, 'The European Convention: Bargaining in the Shadow of Rhetoric' (2004) *West European Politics* 381; S Puntscher-Riekmann and W Wessels (eds), *The Making of a European Constitution—Dynamics and Limits of the Convention Experience* (VS Verlag für Sozialwissenschaften, 2006); F Deloche-Gaudez, 'La Convention européenne sur l'avenir de l'Europe: Ruptures et continuités' in G Amato, H Bribosia and

Convention was much more accessible than that of a typical IGC, but the effort to involve the broader public through the creation of a Forum and through meetings with selected interest groups was largely unsuccessful.[18] There was no structured presence of non-governmental organizations in the Convention working groups, unlike what happens, occasionally, in multilateral treaty negotiations. The reform debate was, on the whole, unable to bridge the distance between the European Union and the general public. Moreover, the rapid rhythm of the Convention's drafting, particularly in its later stages, did not leave time for a considered debate of the main options at the level of each country separately. On some questions, mainly those relating directly to the composition and role of the EU institutions, intergovernmental negotiations took place in the shadow of the Convention, and pre-empted its choices. All in all, the Convention proved to be an ambiguous organ which, as Carlos Closa put it, combined features of an institutional arena for experts, an embedded diplomatic conference and a constitutional assembly.[19]

In contrast with the original scenario delineated in the Laeken Declaration according to which the Convention would present the intergovernmental conference with recommendations or policy options, the Convention very soon decided to elaborate and adopt a complete draft Treaty establishing a Constitution of Europe, which the IGC could have approved as a complete package, and without making any changes, if it had wished to do so. This shift in the nature of the Convention's output took place with the tacit acceptance of the Member State governments' representatives in the Convention and was not challenged either by the ensuing IGC. Although that IGC did look carefully at the Convention's Draft, and made some changes to it, the Convention's work nevertheless formed the basis for the governmental negotiations and its fundamental elements were not called into question by the IGC.

B. The two intergovernmental conferences and the two national ratification processes (2003–2009)

Although many of the reforms presented in the Convention's draft Treaty eventually found their way into the Lisbon Treaty, it took a very long time for this to happen. The Convention was immediately followed, in the summer of 2003, by an intergovernmental conference similar to the previous ones, with the usual mix of transparency as far as access to official documents is concerned, and opaqueness as to the actual content of the negotiations. In terms of its internal organization, this IGC operated differently from the earlier ones in that its meetings were mainly held at the political level of the foreign affairs ministers, and the heads of government

---

B De Witte (eds), *Genesis and Destiny of the European Constitution* (Bruylant, 2007) 47; and contributions by several authors in *European Law Journal* 2005, issue no 4. For a very critical view: H Rasmussen, 'The Convention Method' (2005) *European Constitutional Law Review* 141.

[18] See MF Labouz,'La société civile européenne dans le cadre de la Convention' in C Philip et P Soldatos (dir.), *La Convention sur l'avenir de l'Europe* (Bruylant, 2004) 209.

[19] C Closa, above n 17 at 195 (and his elaboration of each of the three elements at 195–204).

meeting in the European Council.[20] The lower, operational, level of the so-called preparatory group, which played a central role in previous IGCs, was omitted this time, although there were still many informal meetings between civil servants to prepare the ministerial meetings, and between legal experts to 'improve' the draft adopted by the Convention.[21]

Despite this effort at speeding up the IGC by limiting the occasions for 'technical' debates, it eventually took more time than expected, and two subsequent European Council meetings respectively under Italian and Irish Presidency, to reach final agreement on the Treaty establishing a Constitution for Europe. The national ratification processes that started in late 2004 were marked by some important constitutional court judgments (in Spain and France) and, above all, by a sudden profusion of national referendums to precede or follow parliamentary approval. After the two negative referendums in France and the Netherlands, the ratification processes were stopped in the remaining countries, and the Constitutional Treaty was left in a legal limbo for ever after: it was not formally repealed, but no further steps were taken to make it enter into force.

Instead, a second intergovernmental conference was eventually called, in June 2007, to revise the Treaties as they stood. This IGC was, this time, not preceded by a Convention. In formal terms, it took the EC and EU Treaties, as last amended at Nice, as its starting point, although in practice the defunct Constitutional Treaty was used as the matrix from which the new 'Reform Treaty' (as it tended to be called for a while) was sculpted. This second intergovernmental conference was very different from any of those that had preceded it in the history of European integration. Its most striking feature was the fact that the European Council meeting of June 2007 that formally launched the IGC did not limit itself (as on earlier occasions) to set out a broad and vague mandate for the negotiators, but contained a detailed collection of texts which had already been negotiated *before* the formal start of the IGC, namely by means of very secretive bilateral meetings between the German Presidency and its governmental counterparts during the Spring of 2007.[22] Also, unlike what had happened in the 2003–04 IGC and indeed in the earlier Amsterdam and Nice IGCs, the positions of the various governments were not made public in the form of IGC memoranda. The actual intergovernmental conference, which took place between June and October 2007, operated mainly as a technical drafting body, although a few substantive issues which had not

---

[20] This modification was deliberately introduced by the Italian Presidency that conducted the first phase of the IGC, in an effort to limit the agenda of the IGC to 'essential' political matters. See R Cangelosi, 'Le conferenze intergovernative e il ruolo dell'Italia: dall'Atto Unico alla conclusione della CIG del 2003' in LS Rossi (ed), *Il progetto di Trattato-Costituzione. Verso una nuova architettura dell'Unione europea* (Springer, 2004) 9, 42 ff. For a short survey of the operation of the 2003–04 IGC, see J-C Piris, *The Lisbon Treaty—A Legal and Political Analysis* (Cambridge University Press, 2010) 17–19.

[21] See J Ziller, above n 17 at 140–2.

[22] The text of the IGC mandate is annexed to the Conclusions of the Presidency after the European Council of 19–20 June 2007. For a glimpse of the preparatory diplomatic phase during the first half of 2007, see J-C Piris, above n 20 at 29–33, and A Maurer, *Le sauvetage du traité constitutionnel: retour sur un dossier prioritaire de la présidence allemande'* Note du Cerfa no 46, September 2007 (<http://www.ifri.org>).

been resolved by the time of the European Council of June had still to be resolved.[23] The end result of those secretive diplomatic efforts, the Lisbon Treaty as signed in December 2007, constituted a curious mix of many provisions that had been broadly and publicly debated in the Convention and the first IGC, and a smaller number of provisions that were new and had not been the object of any public deliberation. The secrecy was, to a large extent, functional to the objective, shared by all the governments, to make the Lisbon Treaty *seem* very different in nature from the Constitutional Treaty so as to facilitate the national ratification processes by obviating the need for referendums. That strategy worked well, except in the one country, Ireland, in which the holding of a referendum remained unavoidable for internal constitutional reasons.

The entry into force of the Lisbon Treaty was facilitated by a last-minute ingenious use of the resources offered by international law. When faced with the first negative referendum in Ireland on the Lisbon Treaty, the Member State governments sought a solution which would allow the Irish government to call a second referendum without amending the Lisbon Treaty which had been duly signed by all states, and in the meantime ratified by many of them. The solution was found in an elaborate 'Package for Ireland' approved at the European Council meeting of June 2009. A central element of that package was constituted by the 'Decision of the Heads of State or Government of the 27 Member States of the EU, Meeting within the European Council, on the Concerns of the Irish People on the Treaty of Lisbon.'[24] So, the members of the European Council—with the exception of the President of the Commission—decided to switch hats during their meeting and, instead of acting as members of the European Council, acted as representatives of their governments in order to 'agree'[25] on this 'decision'. Their intention was to produce a text which (1) would be binding, and not a mere political declaration, (2) would not modify the Lisbon Treaty but give a solemn interpretation of some of its provisions in the sense proposed by Ireland; and (3) would not require ratification by any of the national parliaments but would operate immediately. Those three goals were reached through a legal sleight of hand, and the authors of the document carefully avoided specifying its legal nature. Arguably, the 'Decision on Ireland' can best be qualified as an international treaty in simplified form or 'executive agreement';[26] it was precisely the fact that the Decision did not purport to modify the Lisbon Treaty that explains why it could be adopted as an executive agreement, without requiring parliamentary ratification. This legal construction was clearly inspired by the precedent of the Decision on Denmark, which had also been adopted by the Heads of State or Government in the margin of a European Council meeting (in December 1992) in order to help

---

[23] See J-C Piris, above n 20 at 40–6, for a discussion of the mode of operation of that 'second' IGC and of the subject matter that was still on the negotiation table.

[24] The text of the Decision can be found in Annex 1 of the Presidency Conclusions of the European Council meeting of 18/19 June 2009.

[25] The words 'have agreed' figure in the last sentence of the preamble of the Decision.

[26] As is well known, treaties between states do not need to be called either 'treaty' or 'convention' or 'agreement'. The terminology is indifferent: what counts is the expression of the intention to be bound.

Denmark mend its temporary inability to ratify the Maastricht Treaty after a failed referendum.[27]

This additional recourse to international law at a crucial moment of the treaty revision process should not hide the fact that the Lisbon Treaty also affected the central role of public international law in matters of EU Treaty revision in an unexpected way. Indeed, the Lisbon Treaty attributes the 'same legal value as the Treaties'[28] to a document which is not a treaty, namely the EU Charter of Fundamental Rights and Freedoms. The Charter was adopted in 2000 (and re-adopted in slightly modified form in 2007) by the presidents of the three main political institutions of the EU and can therefore not be qualified as an international treaty. For the first time in the history of the EC and EU, written primary law now comprises an element which does not have the nature of an international treaty—although the way in which this happened was legally impeccable, since the Charter was given its primary law status by means of a treaty, namely the provision of the Lisbon Treaty inserting the new text of Article 6 into the TEU.

IV. The Reform of the Revision Rules by the Lisbon Treaty

After the brief discussion of how the treaty revision regime evolved through the turbulent institutional practice of the past decade, we will now examine how that revision regime has been formally modified by the Lisbon Treaty and how, therefore, it will apply to the future treaty amendments that will, inevitably, be proposed. Despite the institutional reform fatigue among the Member State governments, the text of the current TEU and TFEU is not, and cannot possibly be, a definitive document carved in stone for generations to come. Those treaties will have to evolve and the question arises whether and how the new treaty revision rules will allow them to evolve. After considering the way in which reform of treaty revision became part of the overall constitutional reform debate in the past decade, we will examine, in turn, the various alternative modes of treaty revision that will apply in the future: the ordinary revision procedure, the two simplified revision procedures, and finally the indirect revision procedures linked to the accession or withdrawal of states.

A. The debates on the reform of treaty revision (1999–2009)

The Group of Wise Men chaired by the former Belgian Prime Minister Dehaene, who were called by the Commission, in 1999, to shed their light on the upcoming

---

[27] For the argument that the Decision on Denmark was also an international treaty in simplified form, see B De Witte, 'The Process of Ratification and the Crisis Options: A Legal Perspective' in D Curtin, AE Kellermann and S Blockmans (eds), *The EU Constitution—The Best Way Forward?* (TMC Asser Press, 2005) 21, 32; and D Curtin and R van Ooik, 'Denmark and the Edinburgh Summit: Maastricht without Tears' in D O'Keeffe and P Twomey (eds), *Legal Issues of the Maastricht Treaty* (Wiley Chancery Law, 1994) 341, 353–8.

[28] Article 6(1) TEU.

post-Amsterdam IGC, suggested splitting up the European Treaties into a 'funda-mental' and a 'less fundamental' part, and possibly to combine this distinction with a differentiation in the treaty *amendment procedure*: the fundamental provisions would continue to be revised according to the cumbersome procedure of Article 48 EU Treaty, whereas the more technical provisions would then be amendable according to a more flexible and less time-consuming procedure.[29] This potential differentiation in amendment rules was probably the prime political motive for the Commission's keen interest in this idea of splitting up the Treaties.[30] On a request of the Commission, the Robert Schuman Centre of the European University Institute then submitted two separate, though related, reports during the year 2000: one on reorganization of the Treaties, and one on the reform of the treaty amendment procedures. The latter report, which proposed rather radical changes in treaty revision,[31] added that a reform of the rules of changes could be connected to a reorganization of the Treaties, but not necessarily so. In fact, though, the idea of a reorganization of the Treaties, which soon attracted much political support, con-veys almost naturally the thought of a hierarchy of norms within primary EU law. This seemed to be the approach adopted, for instance, in the Franco-German Declaration of Nantes of November 2001 in which the two governments declared that they agreed on the idea of '*une division des traités en une partie constitutionnelle et une partie infra-constitutionnelle plus facile à faire évoluer*'. One month later, this issue was officially put on the EU's reform agenda in the form of some of the many questions contained in the Laeken Declaration, namely whether the existing Treaties should be merged, whether this merged document should then be split into a basic treaty and a rest treaty, and whether there should be a 'distinction between the amendment and ratification procedures for the basic treaty and for the other treaty provisions'.

Despite this initial interest in experimenting with the EU's 'rules of change', the question of the reform of treaty revision did not figure prominently in the work of the Convention on the Future of Europe. The subject was not entrusted to any of the working groups of the Convention, and the Convention's Praesidium waited until a very late stage before making concrete proposals. The first textual proposal, submitted by the Praesidium on 2 April 2003, was very conservative, and basically repeated the existing treaty amendment procedure of Article 48 TEU. Members of

---

[29] Von Weizsäcker, Dehaene and Simon, *The Institutional Implications of Enlargement* (18 October 1999) 12–13 (<http://europa.eu.int/igc2000/repoct99_en.pdf>).

[30] In its immediate reaction to the report of the Wise Men, the Commission stated that a reorganization of the Treaties would, in its view, have two advantages: greater clarity about the essential elements of the EU system, and greater flexibility for the non-fundamental provisions. However, it dwelled particularly on the latter advantage (*Adapting the institutions to make a success of enlargement*, Commission contribution to the preparations for the Intergovernmental Conference on institutional issues, 10 November 1999, IP/99/826, at 8).

[31] In particular, the report proposed to replace the consensus rule by some kind of super-qualified majority decision rule for amending the Treaties, combined with the possibility for reluctant Member States to opt out from the non-institutional amendments (EUI, Robert Schuman Centre, *Reforming the Treaties' Amendment Procedures. Second Report on Reorganization of the European Union Treaties* (July 2000) (available at <http://europa.eu.int/comm/archives/igc2000/offdoc/discussiondocs>).

the Convention made many proposals to change that first text. In a first stage, they put successful pressure on the Praesidium to include the Convention method as a normal feature of future treaty revisions, preceding the formal IGC;[32] in a second stage, they tried to convince the Praesidium of the need to introduce more flexible procedures for altering specific parts of the Constitutional Treaty, either by eliminating the requirement of formal national ratifications or by eliminating the requirement of the unanimous agreement of all Member States. Those efforts were much less successful, as they had to compete with other pressing concerns during the hectic final weeks of the Convention, so that the final draft Treaty adopted by the Convention was quite modest on the matter of simplified revisions. Paradoxically, the representatives of the governments, during the IGC that followed the Convention, were more innovative than the Convention and developed two fully-fledged simplified revision procedures that were eventually placed, together with the ordinary procedure proposed by the Convention, in the Articles IV-443 to IV-445 of the Treaty establishing a Constitution for Europe.[33]

Nothing much was changed to this text after 2004. On the question of revision procedures, the Lisbon Treaty repeats almost word-for-word the provisions contained in the Constitutional Treaty (although they were of course put in a different place, back to their familiar location in Article 48 TEU rather than in the final Part IV of the Constitutional Treaty). The question of future treaty amendment was simply not a subject that captured the attention of the governments when they sought to distinguish the Lisbon Treaty from its immediate predecessor.

B. The ordinary revision procedure(s)

Paragraphs 2 to 5 of Article 48 TEU, as amended by the Lisbon Treaty, are entitled 'Ordinary revision procedure'. The word 'ordinary' indicates that the procedure described there is applicable to any amendment of the Treaties and their Protocols, unless the amendment comes within the scope of one of the simplified revision procedures described in paragraphs 6 and 7 or provided for in specific articles of the Treaties. The ordinary procedure also applies, arguably, to amendments of the EU Charter of Rights. The Charter itself does not have a revision clause, but has actually been revised already, when the same organs that adopted the original Charter in Nice in December 2000 (namely the presidents of the Commission, of the Council and of the European Parliament) adopted a slightly amended version in Strasbourg on 12 December 2007, in conjunction with the signature of the Treaty of Lisbon. However, the status of the Charter as primary EU law results

---

[32] This change was incorporated in the Praesidium's second draft text which it submitted at the end of May 2003, CONV 728/03 of 26 May 2003.

[33] For a more detailed analysis of the evolution of the treaty revision clauses during the operation of the Convention and the (first) IGC, see H Klinger, *Der Konvent—Ein neues Institut des europäischen Verfassungsrechts* (Verlag C.H. Beck, 2007) 225–37; D Triantafyllou, 'Les procédures d'adoption et de révision du Traité constitutionnel' in G Amato, H Bribosia and B De Witte (eds), *Genèse et destinée de la Constitution européenne—Genesis and Destiny of the European Constitution* (Bruylant, 2007) 223, 234–42.

from the reference in Article 6(1) TEU which grants 'the same legal value as the Treaties' to the Charter 'as adapted at Strasbourg, on 12 December 2007'. Because of the latter words, Article 6 TEU would have to be amended, according to the ordinary revision procedure, in order to give primary law status to any future version of the Charter.

The ordinary revision procedure confirms two essential features of the previously existing treaty revision rules contained in ex-Article 48 EU Treaty, namely the requirement of a common accord to be reached between all 27 governments at an intergovernmental conference, followed by the ratification of that agreement by all 27 states separately, in accordance with their own constitutional rules and requirements.

Among the changes brought by the Lisbon Treaty, the first to be noted relates to the initiation of treaty revisions, since the European Parliament is now formally entitled to take an initiative for treaty reform alongside the single Member States and the Commission. The actual decision to launch a treaty revision procedure is firmly kept in the hands of the European Council, acting, as is specified in the text of Article 48, by a simple majority of its members.

The most significant change, compared to the previous text of Article 48, is the formal integration of the Convention method as a normal feature for future revisions. Those future Conventions shall be 'composed of representatives of the national Parliaments, of the Heads of State or Government of the Member States, of the European Parliament and of the Commission, that is, the same components as the 2002/3 Convention, though the numbers for each group are not specified'.[34] It is clearly confirmed that the Convention will not affect the formal power of treaty negotiation and conclusion that will be entrusted, as before, to an intergovernmental conference. The Convention's role is modestly defined as that of adopting 'by consensus a recommendation to a conference of representatives of the governments of the Member States'. However, the Convention's role had been described in equally modest terms by the Laeken Declaration of 2001, and this did not prevent the 2002–03 Convention from adopting a complete draft text of the treaty rather than a mere 'recommendation'. The new Article 48 thus creates a new ad hoc organ of the European Union, the Convention, to be convened for a single purpose, namely the revision of the Constitution. A degree of direct parliamentary involvement in treaty reforms is thereby entrenched for the future.

However, it will be possible for the European Council to propose that revisions should be decided directly by an IGC without a prior Convention, if the nature of the revision does not justify the setting-up of a cumbersome Convention. The European Council can decide such a change of track towards the 'old' (pre-Lisbon) Article 48 procedure by a simple majority but subject to the consent of the European Parliament, which seems an effective means of ensuring that the European Council will not abuse this possibility of acting without a Convention. The very first treaty revision after the entry into force of the Treaty of Lisbon made use of this 'abbreviated ordinary procedure': a Protocol was adopted and signed by

---

[34] It is also not specified *who* will decide on those numbers. Presumably, this will be decided by the European Council, the institution that will launch future revision procedures.

the Member States allowing for 18 extra members of the European Parliament to be elected or appointed, in addition to those who were elected in June 2009 according to the Nice Treaty rules on the composition of the Parliament.[35] As the Lisbon Treaty had not yet entered into force in June 2009, the new rules on the composition which it contains could not yet be applied, and the Protocol was meant to remedy that problem. This treaty amendment now needs to be ratified by all 27 Member States, which will require some time, although the initiators of the amendment hope that it will enter into force well before the next European elections!

So, both in its normal mode and in its simpler Convention-less mode, the ordinary revision procedure continues to require 27 separate national ratification acts even for treaty amendments which all the governments find uncontroversial. As a feeble response to the difficulties caused by this post-signature stage which is governed by national constitutional law,[36] a new paragraph 5 was inserted into Article 48 which is applicable to both modes of the ordinary procedure and provides that '(i)f, two years after the signature of a treaty amending the Treaties, four fifths of the Member States have ratified it and one or more Member States have encountered difficulties in proceeding with ratification, the matter shall be referred to the European Council'. This enigmatic sentence, which already appeared in the Convention's draft Constitutional Treaty, does not indicate what the European Council will be able to do in such future situations of ratification crisis. It certainly does not allow the European Council to set aside the requirement of ratification by all states, but it encourages it to invent creative solutions such as those which it experimented in December 1992 (when dealing with the case of Denmark and the Maastricht Treaty), in June 2002 (when dealing with the case of Ireland and the Nice Treaty) and in June 2009 (when dealing with the case of Ireland and the Lisbon Treaty). On those earlier occasions, the European Council intervened, in fact, when one single state 'encountered difficulties' to ratify, rather than waiting for four-fifths of the other countries to have ratified. Thus, the new paragraph 5 is both unnecessary (it instructs the European Council to do something which it has been doing repeatedly in the past without specific authorization) and impractical (by its reference to the four-fifths of States). Still, it is a modest reminder of the misgivings that at least some governments had about the collective decision to preserve the requirement of national ratifications by all states for future treaty revisions.

---

[35] Protocol amending the Protocol on Transitional Provisions annexed to the Treaty on European Union, to the Treaty on the Functioning of the European Union and to the Treaty establishing the European Atomic Energy Community, signed on 23 June 2010, OJ 2010, C 263/1. The mini-IGC that adopted this amendment was convened by a European Council decision of 17 June 2010 (OJ 2010, L 160/5) which refers, in its recital 4, to the European Parliament's consent on the choice of not convening a Convention.

[36] On the legal and political issues raised by the post-signature phase of EU treaty revisions, see B De Witte, *The National Constitutional Dimension of Treaty Revision—Evolution and Recent Debates*, Second Walter van Gerven Lecture (2004). For a collection of case studies about the national (non-) ratifications of the Constitutional Treaty, see A Albi and J Ziller (eds), *The European Constitution and National Constitutions: Ratification and beyond* (Kluwer Law International, 2007).

The rigidity caused by this second, national, phase of treaty revision is precisely what the Lisbon Treaty sought to address by including, in Article 48 TEU, two simplified revision procedures, which are both characterized by the absence of formal ratifications (at least, on first view!). We will now turn to examine the characteristics of those new procedures, and their fields of application.

C. The simplified revision procedures

In addition to the ordinary-procedure-without-Convention, mentioned above, Article 48 TEU now also provides for structural alternatives to the mainstream revision procedure. Those alternatives are listed and described in paragraphs 6 and 7 of Article 48 TEU under the heading 'simplified revision procedures', which—as will be argued—is perhaps a deceptively optimistic way of presenting them.

One must remember, at the outset, that simpler ways to amend particular bits of primary EU law have existed before. For example, the Statute of the Court of Justice, which was annexed to the EC Treaty in the form of a Protocol (and therefore with full treaty status) could be amended, already long before Lisbon, by means of a unanimous Council decision[37]—with the exception of the most sensitive part, Title I of the Statute, which could only be modified through the ordinary revision procedure of Article 48 TEU. Such mini-revision clauses continue to exist under the Treaty of Lisbon. In the case of the Statute of the Court of Justice, Article 281 TFEU now states that amendments will be decided (again, with the exception of some parts of the Statute) by means of the co-decision procedure. This creates a unique situation in which the European Parliament will become the co-author of treaty amendments.

The novelty brought by the Lisbon Treaty is that we now have two standard simplified procedures, applicable to a wider range of cases, and whose legal regime is now incorporated within Article 48 TEU, rather than being mentioned in the particular corner of the Treaty to which a simplified mechanism applies. Of those two procedures, only the one described in paragraph 7 introduces a genuine measure of flexibility in treaty amendment. It is commonly called the *passerelle* (which can be translated as 'footbridge' or, perhaps more appropriately, as 'gateway') because it allows the EU institutions to shift from one decision-making system to another within a given policy area. In all the areas and cases where the Treaties continue to provide that the Council must act by unanimity, a European Council decision (itself taken by unanimity and with the consent of the European Parliament) will be enough to remove the unanimity lock in a particular case or area, and allow the Council to act henceforth by qualified majority. Similarly, the European Council will be able to introduce the 'ordinary legislative procedure' (that is: co-decision) in all the areas and cases in which the Treaties still provide for a different (normally, more intergovernmental) procedure. In other words, a further deepening of integration by making EU decision-making less intergovernmental

---

[37] See, eg, the Council Decision of 20 December 2007 amending the Protocol on the Statute of the Court of Justice, OJ 2008, L 24.

will, to some extent, be possible without the need for setting up an IGC and, above all, without the need for constitutional ratification of these changes by all the Member States separately. The scope of application of this simplified procedure is limited by Article 353 TFEU (to which, confusingly, Article 48 fails to cross-refer): decisions about the EU's own resources and about its multi-annual financial framework, decisions based on the 'flexibility' clause of Article 352 TFEU (ex Article 308 TEC) and sanctions against states violating fundamental rights or the EU's other fundamental values, cannot be made subject to the co-decision procedure and/or qualified majority voting by means of the *passerelle*. In addition, one must note the existence, scattered throughout the Treaties, of the so-called *passerelles spéciales* which apply to specific policy areas instead of the general clause of Article 48(7).[38] When all is said and done, the scope of application of the general *passerelle* is actually quite limited.

Moreover, each national parliament will be able to stop any such simplified amendment based on Article 48(7) by expressing its opposition within a six-month period following the European Council decision (that decision will, obviously, not enter into force during this period). The two-phased approach to treaty revision is thus not entirely abandoned.[39] The difference with the ordinary revision mechanism is that national parliaments, instead of being required to give their positive approval to proposed amendments, will have the option of expressing their disagreement by vetoing a proposed amendment. It is not clear from the text whether, in countries with bicameral parliaments, each of the two chambers will possess this veto power. The original version of this mechanism, as submitted by the Italian Presidency during the 2003 IGC, provided that a revision decision could be stopped if 'X' national parliaments expressed their opposition, whereby 'X' stood for an unspecified number higher than one. However, the single parliament veto appeared in the 'post-Naples' IGC document of 5 December 2003 and remained there until the end of the negotiations.[40] It was put there on the insistence, above all, of the British government. Despite the preservation of a single-parliament veto power, this reform is significant because it puts the responsibility for formally approving an amendment on the shoulders of the Member State representatives in the European Council (and the members of the European Parliament)—not unlike what happens in some federal states, where the approval of constitutional

---

[38] Those treaty provisions are, again, not cross-referred to by Article 48. See Article 81(3) TFEU (measures concerning family law), Article 153(2) (certain fields of employment and social security law), Article 192(2) TFEU (certain environmental policy matters), Article 312(2) TFEU (multi-annual financial framework). The broadest of the *passerelles spéciales* is included in Article 31(3) TEU and refers to the whole common foreign and security policy. In addition to that, the text of the Treaties contains a number of 'evolution clauses' which allow for the scope of EU competence in a given field to be extended by means of unanimous Council or European Council decisions (see, eg, Article 86(4) on the powers of the European Public Prosecutor). For a table listing both the evolution clauses and the special *passerelles* see J-C Piris, above n 20 at appendix 3, 361–4.

[39] The national parliaments do not possess a similar veto power under the *passerelles spéciales* mentioned in the previous footnote (except for the one about family law), so that those *passerelles* will actually be easier to use.

[40] See D Triantafyllou, above n 33 at 240, fn 58.

reforms is given by the 'territorial chamber' in which the Member State interests are represented rather than by the Member States' parliaments or populations directly. The Treaties will, in this case, no longer be amended by another international agreement but by a unilateral decision of an organ of the European Union. This phenomenon, which is quite common in the law of international organizations, had remained exceptional in the EU legal order thus far.

The other simplified revision procedure introduced by the Treaty of Lisbon, which is laid down in Article 48, paragraph 6, has a broader scope. It is going to apply to amendments of 'Part Three of the Treaty on the Functioning of the European Union relating to the internal policies and action of the Union', all together some 171 treaty articles—subject to one major exception: if the proposed amendment of an internal policy provision leads to an increase in the European Union's competences, then the ordinary revision procedure will have to be used instead. So, for example, if the Member States wanted to modify the current Article 153(5) TFEU, and remove the sentence which currently excludes the use of the EU's social policy competences with regard to the right of association and the right to strike, they could not do so according to the simplified procedure, because that amendment would involve an expansion of EU competences. But if, to take another example, the Member States decided to abolish or amend the misleading Article 45(4) TFEU which still states—as in 1957—that the free movement of workers does not apply to employment in the public service, this could hardly be considered as an indirect increase in the EU's competences, given that this derogation clause has long been emptied of most of its content by the case law of the Court of Justice, so that here the simplified revision procedure could be used. The scope of this simplified procedure, unlike the one in paragraph 7, seems thus rather fuzzy and will give rise to controversies. One could consider the Court of Justice to be the appropriate organ to decide such 'borderline' cases relating to the use of one or other amendment procedure, as part of its normal role of interpreting the Treaties, but there is in fact no special head of jurisdiction that would allow the Court to be consulted on such questions. The only way in which the Court could possibly be involved in disputes about the scope of Article 48(6) is through an *ex post* annulment of the European Council decision for violation of the conditions set in Article 48(6).[41]

Upon a closer examination of the procedure prescribed by paragraph 6, it soon appears that this is not really a simplified procedure at all. As in the paragraph 7 procedure, discussed above, there will be no need for a Convention or an IGC; the amendment will rather be 'adopted' directly by the European Council acting by unanimity of its members. But—and here is the crucial difference with paragraph 7—that decision will be subject to 'approval' by each Member State under its own constitutional requirements. One may expect these constitutional requirements to

---

[41] One may note, in this respect, that the Lisbon Treaty has now specified, in Article 263 TFEU (the successor of Article 230 EC) that actions for annulment can also be brought against decisions of the European Council 'intended to produce legal effects vis-à-vis third parties'. Would a treaty amendment be considered as a decision producing such effects?

involve, in most if not all Member States, a consultation of the national parliament and probably also a positive vote of approval by the parliament. If one also considers the fact that adopting a unanimous European Council decision is not necessarily a simpler feat than reaching an agreement at an IGC (the actors being essentially the same . . .),[42] one may well wonder whether the paragraph 6 procedure is really any simpler than the ordinary revision procedure without a Convention. Moreover, unlike the latter, it does not require the consent of the European Parliament, thus making it also a distinctly undemocratic revision procedure.

D. Revision through accession or withdrawal

For many years now, amendments of the Treaties also result from the *accession* of new Member States. Accession is now, like before the Treaty of Lisbon, dealt with in Article 49 TEU, although the text of that article, in its post-Lisbon version, does not entirely correspond to the pre-Lisbon version. Article 49 mentions that accession treaties can imply 'adjustments to the Treaties' (meaning the TEU and the TFEU). What was primarily meant when those words were first included is that accession treaties would be able to make changes to the Treaty rules that are closely connected to the individual states: rules dealing with the composition of the institutions, with languages, with the territorial scope of application of the Treaties, etc. But the term 'adjustments' can also be given a broader meaning so as to encompass changes to other provisions of primary law, that are not intrinsically related to the enlargement but are politically convenient. The Treaty of Athens concluded with the 10 new Member States contains some examples of this, and many observers have speculated about the possibility of 'smuggling in' treaty amendments on the occasion of the accession of the next Member State, which will probably be Croatia. The European Council itself has endorsed this wider reading of the term 'adjustments' by agreeing that the Decision on Ireland, adopted in June 2009 (on which, see above), would be elevated to the status of Treaty Protocol on the occasion of the first accession of a new Member State;[43] clearly, addressing the particular concerns of Ireland is an 'adjustment' that is not specifically required by the need of accommodating Croatia into the EU institutional framework.

The Lisbon Treaty explicitly allows, for the first time, the *withdrawal* of a Member State from the EU. Article 50 TEU, which sets out the procedure to be followed, provides for an agreement between the Union and the withdrawing state setting out the practical arrangements for this withdrawal. Since this agreement will be concluded by the Union and not (also) by all its Member States, it will be incapable of modifying the treaty provisions that refer, directly or indirectly, to the withdrawing state (for example; the rules on the Treaties' scope of application or on

---

[42] The fact that an IGC can act as rapidly as the European Council if there are no serious divergences between the EU countries is illustrated by the first post-Lisbon Treaty amendment, mentioned above, which took only six days between the convening of the IGC and the signature of the amendment.

[43] See European Council meeting of 18–19 June 2009, Conclusions of the Presidency, para 5 (iv).

the Treaty languages). So, unlike the accession procedure, the withdrawal procedure will not function as an additional treaty revision procedure. The remaining Member States will, after withdrawal, need to organize an IGC in accordance with the ordinary revision procedure in order to clear the Treaty text from its direct and indirect references to the defaulting country.

The withdrawal clause is, however, relevant for the question of treaty revision in an entirely different way. It could happen, in the future, that country X, being the only one that fails to ratify a revision treaty, declares its wish to leave the European Union, thereby allowing the other states to go ahead with the revision. This rosy scenario does not seem very plausible, though. Why would a country decide to renounce the benefits of EU membership only because it does not agree with proposed changes to the rules of primary EU law? There is, however, a more devious way in which withdrawal and revision could become linked. Faced with the inability of one or more states to either sign or ratify a revision treaty, the remaining states could decide to collectively withdraw from the European Union and reconfigure a new organization, a 'European Union *plus*'. This would leave the original rump-EU unable to function in the absence of most of its Member States. The withdrawing states could seek to justify their action on the basis mentioned in Article 62 of the Vienna Convention, namely that a 'fundamental change of circumstances' makes it impossible for them to continue as parties of the original Treaties. More particularly, they would have to argue that the original objectives of the European Treaties can no longer be achieved under the existing Treaties. This would pre-suppose that the proposed revisions are of a very radical nature—otherwise, it is difficult to make the argument of the fundamental change of circumstances. More generally, this scenario would seem legally very dubious in that it would allow, in an indirect but effective way, to achieve the objective of excluding recalcitrant states, something which the Treaties do not currently contemplate or allow.

V. Conclusion: The Past and Future of Treaty Revision

The existing rules of treaty revision have been modified by the Lisbon Treaty in a number of ways, but the essence remains untouched: as before, all changes will have to be approved by all the Member States' governments and submitted to some kind of approval (whether a formal authorization to ratify or not) by the national parliaments of each country separately. Given the turbulent history of the most recent treaty revision operation, how likely is it that meaningful amendments of the Treaties will still be possible in the future?

The continuing rigidity of EU primary law is particularly problematic in view of its sheer volume. Not only is the text of the instruments of primary law (essentially, now, the TEU and the TFEU) very long and sometimes extremely detailed,[44] but

---

[44] The TEU has 55 Articles, and the TFEU has 358 Articles. Furthermore, the Lisbon Treaty has 13 Protocols (with treaty status), which were added to the Protocols made on earlier treaty reform occasions, most of which were not repealed by the Lisbon Treaty. Then there is the separate Euratom

the Court of Justice has added to this a large amount of court-made constitutional law through the dynamic interpretation of written norms and through the creation of new, unwritten norms of primary law (that is, the general principles of Union law). The various treaty reforms that have happened in the course of the last 20 years have mainly *added* new constitutional rules, but almost never have the Member States agreed to 'de-constitutionalize' particular norms, so as to put back into the democratic arena matters which had previously been entrenched in the founding Treaties. Thus, there has been a constant trend to increase the volume of constitutional law, accompanied by an increasing difficulty to modify those very constitutional rules.

The drafters of the European Constitution assumed optimistically that the rigid revision formula, which they preserved, would not stop the Constitution from evolving in the future. That optimism seems misplaced in view of the difficulties faced by the Constitutional Treaty itself, and in view of the complicated horse-trading which led to its salvation by means of the Lisbon Treaty. Sooner or later, the Member States of the European Union will need to confront the 'taboo' of the unanimity requirement for any kind of treaty amendment. They should consider replacing the consensus rule by some kind of super-qualified majority rule for amending the Treaties, or at least certain parts of the Treaties. In this hypothesis, the assent of the European Parliament would be required, as an alternative democratic input to compensate for the fact that single national parliaments will lose their veto power. Of course, there is no realistic prospect that the Member State governments will agree, in the next few years, to such a symbolically important change. And yet, this is vital for the future of the European integration process. There are so many detailed rules in the founding Treaties which will need to be adapted to changing needs. If the Member States want to continue to reap the benefits of the European integration process, they must allow the EU treaty framework to be adaptable to changing circumstances and priorities, even at the cost of occasionally being confronted with amendments that they do not like. Otherwise, EU constitutional law, rather than protecting the values of the European states and promoting their cooperation, will become an intolerable burden that inhibits the course of European integration. There is, in other words, a need to continue to reflect on finding a new balance between rigidity and flexibility in the European Union's rules of change.[45]

Treaty, and the Charter of Rights (which, as argued above, has the status of primary law and is subject to the ordinary treaty amendment procedure). When counting the number of articles (and, indeed, the number of words) one would find that the primary law of the European Union is more voluminous than any of the national constitutions of European countries.

[45] See also the reflections on this point by R Dehousse, 'Au-delà du Plan B: comment réformer les clauses de révision des traités?' in G Amato, H Bribosia and B De Witte (dir.), *Genèse et destinée de la Constitution européenne* (Bruylant, 2007) 939, by H Bribosia, *Réviser les traités européens : plaidoyer en faveur de la suppression du veto* Notre Europe Policy Paper no 37 (2007) and by J Baquero Cruz, 'Alternativas a las condiciones de revisión y entrada en vigor—Cambiar las reglas del cambio: una cuestión urgente para la Unión Europea' in I Méndez de Vigo (dir.), *Qué fue de la Constitución Europea? El tratado de Lisboa: un camino hacia el futuro* (Planeta, 2007) 293.

6

'Don't Mention Divorce at the Wedding, Darling!': EU Accession and Withdrawal after Lisbon

Allan F Tatham

I. Introduction

Accession to and withdrawal from the European Union cannot be regarded simply as the obverse and reverse of the same coin. On the one hand, the conditions and processes for accession are long established, based on a combination of Treaty Articles, European Council conclusions and practice.[1] On the other hand, withdrawal from the Union is an innovation of the Lisbon Treaty,[2] neither tried nor tested. This analysis will consider briefly the historical context of each process before continuing to look at the relevant Articles of the Treaty on European Union,[3] including their own criteria and procedures, as well as a providing a short commentary on them.

II. Enlargement

A. Historical context

From their very inception, the European Treaties[4] proclaimed the endeavour of integration as 'an ever closer union of the peoples of Europe', by implication

---

[1] AF Tatham, *Enlargement of the European Union* (Kluwer Law International, 2009) chapters 8 and 9, 193–237 and 239–69, respectively.

[2] Treaty of Lisbon amending the Treaty on European Union and the Treaty establishing the European Community, signed at Lisbon, 13 December 2007: [2007] OJ C306/1.

[3] Consolidated version of the Treaty on European Union: [2010] OJ C83/13.

[4] Treaty establishing the European Coal and Steel Community ('ECSC'), signed on 18 April 1951, entered into force on 24 July 1952: 261 UNTS 141, No 3729. Treaty establishing the European Economic Community ('EEC') and Treaty establishing the European Atomic Energy Community ('EAEC'): both signed on 25 March 1957 and both entered into force on 1 January 1958: 294 UNTS 3, No 4300 and 294 UNTS 259, No 4301, respectively.

enjoining states to participate in this process. The issue of enlargement itself[5] has been present on the European integration agenda almost since the establishment of the Communities in the 1950s.[6]

The three founding Treaties[7] each provided[8] that any European state might apply to become a member of the Community, addressing its application to the Council which, after obtaining the Commission's opinion, would act by means of a unanimous vote. The conditions of admission and the adjustments to the Treaties (required by reason of accession) were to be the subject of an agreement between the Member States and the applicant state. Such agreement had to be submitted to all the contracting states for ratification in accordance with their respective constitutional rules.

These provisions remained largely unaltered before the Lisbon Treaty entered into force. One technical innovation, achieved through the 1992 Maastricht Treaty,[9] was the replacement of the three different accession clauses with one single clause.[10] In addition, two textual alterations can be indicated: the first being the need for obtaining the consent (then referred to as the 'assent') of the European Parliament for any accession, as introduced by the Single European Act;[11] and, secondly, the reference to the then Treaty on European Union, Article 6(1),[12] introduced by the 1997 Amsterdam Treaty,[13] which paragraph stated: 'The Union is founded on the principles of liberty, democracy, respect for human rights and fundamental freedoms, and the rule of law, principles which are common to the Member States.' The presence of this paragraph required the respect of these

---

[5] A wealth of detailed analysis has already been provided on the legal aspects of enlargement: M Maresceau (ed), *Enlarging the European Union* (Longman, 1997); G Avery and F Cameron, *The Enlargement of the European Union* (Sheffield Academic Press, 1998); A Ott and K Inglis (eds), *Handbook on European Enlargement: A Commentary on the Enlargement Process* (TMC Asser Press, 2002); M Cremona (ed), *The Enlargement of the European Union* (Oxford University Press, 2003); C Hillion (ed), *EU Enlargement: A Legal Approach* (Hart Publishing, 2004); and S Blockmans and S Prechal (eds), *Reconciling the Deepening and Widening of the European Union* (TMC Asser Press, 2007).

[6] In fact, the first approach to the Communities was made by Israel in October 1958, followed by Greece (June 1959) and Turkey (August 1959): D Urwin, *The Community of Europe: A History of European Integration since 1945*, 2nd edn (Longman, 1995) 116.

[7] The relevant provisions were Article 98 ECSC, Article 237 EEC and Article 205 EAEC.

[8] Article 98 ECSC was slightly different to the other two: 'Any European State may request to accede to the present Treaty. It shall address its request to the Council, which shall act by unanimous vote after having obtained the opinion of the High Authority. Also by a unanimous vote, the Council shall fix the terms of accession. It shall become effective on the day the instrument of accession is received by the government acting as depository of the Treaty.'

[9] Treaty on European Union: [1992] OJ C191/01.

[10] Through the Maastricht Treaty, the then Article O TEU (now Article 49 TEU) replaced the respective provisions of the three founding treaties (Article 98 ECSC, Article 237 EEC and Article 205 EAEC) thereby permitting a putative Member State to accede simultaneously to all the Treaties on which the EU was then based: K Laenerts and P van Nuffel (R Bray (ed)), *Constitutional Law of the European Union* (Sweet & Maxwell, 1999) para 6-006, 274.

[11] Single European Act: [1987] OJ L169/1.

[12] According to the Lisbon Treaty numbering, Article 6(1) TEU is now Article 2 TEU, as amended.

[13] Treaty of Amsterdam amending the Treaty on European Union, the Treaties establishing the European Communities and related acts: [1997] OJ C340/1.

principles by states as one of the conditions not only of membership but also of an application for membership.[14]

The 2004 Treaty establishing a Constitution for Europe[15] continued the method of evolutionary development and most of the changes it made[16] were retained in the Lisbon Treaty.[17]

B. Lisbon Treaty: Article 49 TEU

Building upon previous Articles and practice, the amendments under the 2007 Lisbon Treaty have led to several changes to the accession clause, Article 49 TEU, that now provides:

Any European State which respects the values referred to in Article 2 and is committed to promoting them may apply to become a member of the Union. The European Parliament and national Parliaments shall be notified of this application. The applicant State shall address its application to the Council, which shall act unanimously after consulting the Commission and after receiving the consent of the European Parliament, which shall act by a majority of its component members. The conditions of eligibility agreed upon by the European Council shall be taken into account.

The conditions of admission and the adjustments to the Treaties on which the Union is founded, which such admission entails, shall be the subject of an agreement between the Member States and the applicant state. This agreement shall be submitted for ratification by all the contracting states in accordance with their respective constitutional requirements.

The 2007 Lisbon Treaty has occasioned various textual alterations to Article 49(1) TEU and linked provisions: the list of values (formerly called 'principles') has been extended, due to the changes in Article 2 TEU,[18] to include human dignity and equality; putative Member States must not only respect these values but also commit themselves to promoting them; and, further, the new list in Article 2 TEU is followed by the statement that '[t]hese values are common to the Member States in a society of pluralism, tolerance, justice, solidarity and non-discrimination'.

In addition, any application for membership must be notified to the European and national parliaments, thereby emphasizing their increased visibility in the accession process; the consent of the European Parliament is now by a majority

---

[14] Avery and Cameron, above n 5 at 23.

[15] Treaty establishing a Constitution for Europe: [2004] OJ C310/1.

[16] As laid down in Article I-58 CT.

[17] However, the first sentence of Article I-58 CT was not kept; it read: 'The Union shall be open to all European States which respect the values referred to in Article I-2.' This 'openness' clause which focuses on the EU's common values might be seen as no more than confirmation of previous practice. After all, the Union has not so far failed to admit any state with which it has entered into enlargement negotiations and has thus always remained 'open' to new Member States as part of its vocation.

[18] Article 2 TEU now provides: 'The Union is founded on the values of respect for human dignity, freedom, democracy, equality, the rule of law and respect for human rights, including the rights of persons belonging to minorities. These values are common to the Member States in a society in which pluralism, non-discrimination, tolerance, justice, solidarity and equality between women and men prevail.'

rather than the previous absolute majority of MEPs; and, lastly, the European Council's own eligibility conditions are to be observed. Article 49(2) TEU remains unaltered by the Lisbon Treaty.

III. Criteria for Membership

Article 49 TEU remains an imperfect guide to enlargement[19] and forms merely the departure point for the principles which have been developed through practical experience and inserted into the enlargement process framework.[20] The criteria, which states must satisfy before acceding to the Union,[21] have evolved and expanded since the first membership applications.[22]

A. Copenhagen criteria

Apart from the geographical criterion that the applicant must be a European state and the list of values of the Union in Article 2 TEU (incorporated by express reference into Article 49 TEU),[23] various European Councils have added further political, economic, legal, administrative and institutional conditions. The Lisbon Treaty changes have now included the requirement to take into account the conditions of eligibility defined by the European Council, which change was not expressly foreseen in the 2004 Constitutional Treaty. These enlargement criteria, themselves based on previous developments,[24] were set out by the European Council at Copenhagen in June 1993[25] with respect to the eventual accession of the Central and Eastern European countries (CEECs).[26] These 'Copenhagen criteria', to which the Madrid European Council of December 1995[27] added a fifth, are: (i) that the candidate country has achieved stability of institutions guaranteeing democracy, the rule of law, human rights and respect for and protection of minorities; (ii) the existence of a functioning market economy; (iii) the capacity

---

[19] Avery and Cameron, above n 5 at 23.

[20] D Booss and J Forman, 'Enlargement: Legal and Procedural aspects' (1995) 32 *CML Rev* 95, 100.

[21] KE Smith, 'The Evolution and Application of EU Membership Conditionality' in M Cremona (ed), *The Enlargement of the European Union* (Oxford University Press, 2003) chapter 5, 105, 109–21.

[22] C Preston, 'Obstacles to EU Enlargement: The Classical Community Method and the Prospects for a Wider Europe' (1995) 33 *Journal of Common Market Studies* 451; Booss and Forman, above n 20 at 100–4.

[23] Tatham, above n 1 at chapter 8, 193, 202–18 and 232–6.

[24] European Council, 'Declaration on democracy', Copenhagen, 7–8 April 1978: EC Bull 3-1978, 6; and European Commission, 'Europe and the Challenge of Enlargement': EC Bull, Supplement 3-1992, point 7.

[25] Presidency Conclusions, European Council, Copenhagen, 21–22 June 1993: EC Bull 6-1993, point I.13. See, eg, Tatham, above n 1 at chapter 8, 193, 206–32; and M Maresceau and E Montaguti, 'The Relations between the European Union and Central and Eastern Europe: A Legal Appraisal' (1995) 32 *CML Rev* 1327, 1332–3.

[26] K Inglis, 'EU Enlargement—Membership Conditions Applied to Future and Potential Member States' in K Inglis and A Ott (eds), *The Constitution for Europe and an Enlarging Union: Unity in Diversity?* (Europa Law Publishing, 2005) chapter 10, 225–56.

[27] Presidency Conclusions, European Council, Madrid, 15–16 December 1995, Part A, III.A, para 6.

to cope with the competitive pressure and market forces within the Union; (iv) the ability to take on the obligations of membership, including adherence to the aims of political, economic and monetary union; and (v) the administrative and judicial capacity guaranteeing the effective implementation of the *acquis*, the entire corpus of European law and legal practice.[28] The 1994 Essen European Council further required that associated countries had to cooperate at the intra-regional level among themselves as well as have good relations with their neighbours.[29]

While the above criteria referred to the candidate countries, the Union's own capacity to absorb new members,[30] while maintaining the momentum of European integration, was also considered in the general interest of both the Union and the candidate countries: this criterion will be further considered later.

B. Conditionality

A new principle of enlargement, conditionality, also emerged in relation to the CEECs. At the 1997 Luxembourg European Council,[31] it was agreed that even though negotiations could be opened with those candidate countries that satisfied the political criteria, conclusion of such negotiations would be conditional on their fulfilment of the economic criteria and satisfactory adoption of the *acquis*. The Accession Partnerships[32]—requested by the European Council, drafted by the Commission and enacted by the Council—went a step further and conditioned reception of Union pre-accession aid to the fulfilment of the criteria. Thus the principle of conditionality involves continuous Union scrutiny (particularly by the Commission)[33] in all spheres of the candidate country's preparations for membership.

Following the first CEEC accessions in 2004, the Commission developed a new strategy for enlargement policy[34] based on consolidation of existing commitments, better communication to citizens to improve the legitimacy of the process, and application of fair and rigorous conditionality to the candidate countries so that they would be ready to fulfil their obligations as Member States and implement Union policies. Such conditionality implied that the Union could both demand

---

[28] Tatham, above n 1 at chapter 12, 327, 327–53.

[29] Presidency Conclusions, European Council, Essen, 9–10 December 1994: EU Bull 12-1994, point I.54. The need for 'good neighbourly relations' would thus avoid importing into the EU any conflicts or instability connected with the accession of new Member States and is intertwined with the need for minority rights protection in the Copenhagen criteria. The criterion was partly derived from the EU preference to negotiate with groups of states already enjoying close relationships with each other: Preston, above n 22 at 455–6.

[30] Tatham, above n 1 at chapter 8, 193, 230–1.

[31] Presidency Conclusions, European Council, Luxembourg, 12–13 December 1997.

[32] Tatham, above n 1 at chapter 10, 271, 288–91. For the Western Balkan States, these instruments are called the European Partnerships: Tatham, ibid chapter 11, 307, 324–5.

[33] The Commission provides annual reports on the progress made by candidate countries in their preparations for accession which requirement was introduced vis-à-vis the CEECs: Presidency Conclusions, European Council, Luxembourg, 12–13 December 1997, para 29. See generally Tatham, above n 1 at chapter 9, 239, 247–8.

[34] European Commission, Communication 'Enlargement Strategy Paper': COM(2005) 561. For the latest see European Commission, Communication 'Enlargement Strategy and Main Challenges 2009–2010': COM(2009) 533 final.

fulfilment of the accession criteria (duly rewarding candidates making progress) as well as suspend the accession negotiations at any stage where such criteria were not met.[35] This has indeed happened both in relation to Croatia[36] and Turkey, with the latter's negotiations still suspended at this time.[37]

IV. Procedure for Membership

The wording of Article 49 EU maintains the traditional outline mechanism for accession thereby permitting further elements to be included, as necessary.[38] For example, after the candidate country has lodged its application but before negotiations are opened, the Commission delivers a prior opinion containing an initial analysis of the political, economic, legal and administrative implications of the accession, together with identification of themes that will have to be negotiated.[39] Without being bound by this opinion,[40] the Council issues a summary assessment of the possibilities for accession and decides whether or not negotiations should be opened. A further opinion is provided once the negotiations are completed which, together with the consent of the European Parliament, allows the Council to decide unanimously whether to conclude the accession process with the necessary treaty.

The procedure for conducting negotiations is contained in a Council Decision[41] while the Member States, meeting in the Council, actually conduct them with the candidate country in the form of an Intergovernmental Conference (IGC). The

---

[35] Negotiating Framework for Turkey, 3 October 2005, Luxembourg: <http://www.jeanmonnet-program.org/papers/01/01380.rtf>. Visited 8 August 2010. Para 5 states: 'In the case of a serious and persistent breach in a candidate state of the principles of liberty, democracy, respect for human rights and fundamental freedoms, and the rule of law on which the Union is founded, the Commission will, on its own initiative or on the request of one third of the Member States, recommend the suspension of negotiations and propose the conditions for eventual resumption.' Although equally applicable to Croatia and other future candidates from the Western Balkans, this conditionality was a direct warning to Turkey: C Hillion, 'Negotiating Turkey's Membership to the European Union: Can the Member States Do as They Please?' (2007) 3 *Eur Constitutional L Rev* 269, 270.

[36] Continuing disputes over border demarcations with Slovenia, particularly the maritime boundary between the two nations and Slovenia's access to the Adriatic Sea, prompted Slovenia to block accession talks in December 2008. After the two states had reached an agreement in November 2009, which the Slovene population supported in a referendum on 6 June 2010, the negotiations were revived.

[37] The Commission recommended the suspension of negotiations: European Commission, Communication, 'Accession Negotiations with Turkey': COM(2006) 773; EU Bull 11-2006, point 1.25.22. The Council approved it: General Affairs and External Relations Council, Conclusions on enlargement: EU Bull 12-2006, point 1.25.1. This approval was endorsed by the European Council: Presidency Conclusions, European Council, Brussels, 14–15 December 2006, para 10.

[38] This has been the approach used since the first enlargement in 1973: see J-P Puissochet, *The Enlargement of the European Communities* (AW Sijthoff, 1975).

[39] In order to reinforce conditionality, the European Council at Luxembourg 1997 required the Commission to update its opinions every year until the CEECs' accessions. These annual updates to the opinions were originally termed Regular Reports but developed in time into Progress Reports.

[40] The Council did not follow the Commission's Opinion in respect of Greece: European Commission, *Opinion on Greek application for membership*: EC Bull, Supplement 2-1976, 7. Council rejection of Opinion and decision to open negotiations: EC Bull 1-1976, points 1101–11, 6–9.

[41] Avery and Cameron, above, n 5 at 28.

Commission also participates in the process: first, it is charged with undertaking a formal process of examination of the *acquis*, known as 'screening',[42] in order to assess the state of preparation of the candidate for opening negotiations in specific areas and to obtain initial indications of issues most likely to arise in the negotiations; and secondly in the negotiations it proposes the common positions to be taken by the Council which unanimously adopts them. Although the Member States or other Union institutions are not bound to act in this way, they usually agree with the Commission thereby rendering it the most powerful player in the whole process. The Commission also drafts the Accession or European Partnerships that are issued by the Council.

V. Commentary

The Lisbon Treaty amendments to Article 49 TEU concerning the modalities of accession evince incremental change of the mildest nature. Most of the 'customary' elements of enlargement[43] continue to remain excluded and thus underline the Union's continuing reluctance to codify (in treaty form) such elements. That treaty framework is a strength, allowing customary enlargement practice to be nurtured and to thrive within its interstices, thereby maintaining a necessary flexibility in respect of each enlargement round without having the process 'set in stone'. In this way, the Union institutions can respond more quickly to developments on the ground and not feel hemmed in by treaty provisions that require unanimity among Member States to change.

For example, in respect of future enlargements and as a way of assuaging various Member States' concerns regarding the opening of negotiations with Croatia and Turkey (and foreseeing further problems with FYROM and other Western Balkan States in the future),[44] the European Council agreed in 2004[45] on a revised framework for every future round of negotiations. According to the new formulation, a negotiating framework is to be created 'according to own merits and specific situations and characteristics of each candidate State'. From one perspective, this is clearly a reassertion of the EU's previous practice in relation to candidate countries but which became rather lost in the negotiating processes to the CEEC 'big bang' enlargement. From another perspective, it could be seen to represent the EU's abandonment of its classical model of negotiating in groups of countries. This would underline a wariness on the part of the Union and its Member States vis-à-vis the remaining (potential) candidates—particularly (though not exclusively) in such matters as human and minority rights protection, fighting corruption, judicial

---

[42] Tatham, above n 1 at chapter 9, 239, 254–7.

[43] D Kochenov, 'EU Enlargement Law: History and Recent Developments: Treaty—Custom Concubinage?' (2005) 9 European Integration online Papers, no 6, 20: <http://www.eiop.or.at/eiop/texte/2005-006a.htm>. Visited 12 June 2010.

[44] S Blockmans, 'Consolidating the Enlargement Agenda for South Eastern Europe' in Blockmans and Prechal, above n 5 at chapter 4, 59, 82.

[45] Presidency Conclusions, European Council, Brussels, 16–17 December 2004, para 23.

independence and judicial and public administration reform—and the need to ensure a greater level of delivery on these issues before their being considered fit for membership.

As if to underline this necessity of differentiation, the 2010 Negotiating Framework for Iceland,[46] already a member of the EEA and linked to the EU through various other legal agreements (for example, participation in the Schengen area, like Norway), has a markedly different content compared to that of Turkey.[47]

A. Values

Concerning actual changes in content, the addition of human dignity and equality to Article 2 TEU, and the need for prospective Member States to promote such values (together with freedom, democracy, the rule of law and respect for human rights, including minority rights) may result in significant impacts on the progress towards accession of the (potential) candidate countries. It represents, nevertheless, a clear indication to such countries as well as to Member States, of those EU values to which all Members must not only aspire but also actively practise. Allied to these values is the subsequent phrase in Article 2 TEU, 'These values are common to the Member States in a society in which pluralism, non-discrimination, tolerance, justice, solidarity and equality between women and men prevail.'

The expression of both the values and social concepts through the accession clause, by reference to Article 2 TEU, clearly affect the future dynamics of enlargement, and the evaluation of their fulfilment or otherwise still leaves in the hands of the Union and ultimately the Member States, the power of final arbiter of membership. As veto players in the accession procedure, both Union and Member States have to strike a balance between common core criteria that all candidate countries must satisfy, together with distinct criteria that are peculiar to one candidate country:[48] failure to do so could open the Union to charges from the candidates of discrimination and unequal treatment between them.

B. Parliamentary participation

Also of possible significance to (potential) candidate countries is the clear indication that the European as well as national parliaments are expressly included in the accession process from the very beginning. In the context of recent and general trends, the role of the European Parliament in the Union decision-making process has been increased while the information provided to and interaction with national

---

[46] Negotiating Framework for Iceland, July 2010, Brussels: <http://ec.europa.eu/enlargement/pdf/iceland/st1222810_en.pdf>. Visited 8 August 2010.

[47] Negotiating Framework for Turkey, above n 35.

[48] Eg, in its 2005 Negotiating Framework for Turkey, above n 35 at paras 4 and 6, in addition to contributing to a favourable climate for a comprehensive settlement on the Cyprus question and normalization of bilateral relations, the Union enjoined Turkey to implement provisions relating to freedom of expression, freedom of religion, women's rights, ILO standards including trade union rights and minority rights.

parliaments—as a way to reduce the Union's democratic deficit—have improved.[49] The indication would appear to be that the parliamentary dimension of enlargement needed to be enhanced, by explicitly including Member State parliaments.

On the one hand, this new wording could broaden the domestic debate on the enlargement process and so bring decision-making closer to the citizens thereby contributing to their understanding of the process, as previously advocated by the Commission in its 2005 Communication, as well as to increase the legitimacy of enlargement.[50] On the other hand, however, the Union might be able to pass the responsibility for refusal of entry to a candidate country onto the shoulders of a national representative assembly which—for whatever reason—had voted against that candidate's membership: keeping the unanimity requirement for enlargement in Article 49(2) EU serves to reinforce the likelihood of this happening in an EU of 27 or more Member States. This confirms the existence of a number of veto players at the European and national levels. As a consequence, not only might the European Parliament veto the accession of an applicant, but the Member States each possess a double veto option: first in the context of the Council vote; and second in the need for national ratification.

Two further points should be raised: one concerns the conditions of admission and the adjustments to the Treaties on which the Union is founded; the other concerns ratification by all Contracting Parties in accordance with their respective constitutional requirements.

C. Adjustments to the Treaties

Turning to the first point, the adjustments contained in the accession treaty cover adaptations to EU secondary legislation,[51] transition periods and temporary derogations, safeguard clauses, postponement clauses[52] and institutional changes.[53] Since EU law, in principle, applies completely from the date of accession,[54] any transition periods for adopting outstanding *acquis* must be fixed and limited, and

---

[49] Consolidated versions of the Treaty on European Union and the Treaty on the Functioning of the European Union, Protocol No 1 on the Role of National Parliaments in the European Union: [2010] OJ C83/201.

[50] S Piedrafita, 'The Treaty of Lisbon: New Signals for Future Enlargements?' 2008/1 EIPASCOPE 33, 36: <http://www.eipa.eu>. Visited 14 June 2010.

[51] Joined Cases 31–5/86 *LAISA v Council* [1988] ECR 2285, paras 9–12. Such agreements, while allowing for the necessary adjustments to the European treaties, may not amount to a disguised fundamental amendment of such treaties for which another provision—Article 48 TEU—is to be used. Article 48 TEU, like Article 49 TEU, has a mandatory character: Case 43/75 *Defrenne v SABENA* [1976] ECR 480, para 58.

[52] Postponing accession was provided for in relation to Bulgaria and Romania for up to one year if there were a serious risk that either state was 'manifestly unprepared to meet the requirements of membership by the date of accession' in a number of important areas. It will be interesting to note whether or not the Union will be tempted to increase that period of postponement in relation to future accession countries: Article 39 of the Act concerning the conditions of accession of the Republic of Bulgaria and Romania and the adjustments to the treaties on which the European Union is founded: [2005] OJ L157/203.

[53] Institutional changes will be discussed more fully in relation to integration capacity.

[54] Case 258/81 *Metallurgiki Halyps A.E. v Commission* [1982] ECR 4261, para 8.

any derogations from applying it have to be partial and restricted in order not to impede the evolution of the Union. Yet the 2005 Negotiating Framework on Turkey states:[55] 'Long transitional periods, derogations, specific arrangements or permanent safeguard measures . . . may be considered.' The implication seems to be that the Union expects that Turkey's integration into the Union will be a long and exceptional process, probably taking more time than any previous enlargement.

Safeguard clauses come into play after accession and can be requested by any Member State for its protection from the Commission which issues the measures in an emergency procedure. From the first enlargements, such measures have been available for several years after accession in respect of protecting a particular economic sector or particular area against serious deterioration.[56] The 2003 and 2005 accession treaties[57] extended these measures against new Member States' failures to meet their commitments in the Internal Market and the Area of Freedom, Justice and Security (formerly Justice and Home Affairs). In a new and important development, the 2005 Negotiating Framework for Turkey mentions *permanent* safeguard clauses in such fields as free movement of persons, structural policies and agriculture.[58] This has the effect of allowing the Union or any Member State, whenever it feels justified after Turkish accession, for example, to suspend permanently the right of Turkish nationals to move freely within the EU. In so limiting their right to move, such nationals would be discriminated against on the grounds of their nationality, thereby infringing a basic value enshrined in the Treaties since the very inception of the integration process in the 1950s. By allowing the Union and its Member States legally to flout their own common European values would be an affront to the state concerned and difficult to justify legally.[59]

D. Member States' constitutional requirements

Domestic constitutional arrangements of the parties to the accession treaty may include the need to put such membership to a national referendum, in particular for the acceding country. This has been followed, to some extent, in most accession rounds as a means to gain popular legitimacy for accession[60] although such referendums do not always prove to be harbingers for eventual membership:

---

[55] Negotiating Framework for Turkey, above n 35 at para 12.

[56] Eg, Article 37 of the Act concerning the conditions of accession of the Czech Republic, the Republic of Estonia, the Republic of Cyprus, the Republic of Latvia, the Republic of Lithuania, the Republic of Hungary, the Republic of Malta, the Republic of Poland, the Republic of Slovenia and the Slovak Republic and the adjustments to the Treaties on which the European Union is founded: [2003] OJ L236/33; and Article 36 of the Act of Accession 2005 (Romania and Bulgaria) (above n 52).

[57] Articles 38 and 39 of the Act of Accession 2003 (CEECs, Cyprus and Malta) (ibid); and Articles 37 and 38 of the Act of Accession 2005, above n 52.

[58] 2005 Negotiating Framework for Turkey, above n 35 at para 12.

[59] U Becker, 'EU-Enlargements and Limits to Amendments of the E.C. Treaty', Jean Monnet Working Paper 15/01: <http://www.jeanmonnetprogram.org/papers/01/01380.rtf>. Visited 10 July 2010; and Hillion, above n 35 at 272–82.

[60] Tatham, above n 1 at chapter 9, 240, 267–8.

for example, domestic referendums, post signature of the accession treaty, resulted in Norway's rejection of membership twice (1972 and 1994).[61]

More intriguing is the option, only exercised once so far, for a current EU Member State to hold a referendum on the accession of another. This was the case in 1972 when France used a referendum to approve primarily British (as well as Irish and Danish) accession with, domestic political concerns being in fact of paramount concern—for the then French President, Georges Pompidou, it was a way of dealing with political opposition.[62] In a more recent example, in 2005, France amended its Constitution[63] to require a referendum to be held on any post-2007 accessions, a provision clearly aimed at preventing eventual Turkish accession, unpopular in France. Although subsequently amended,[64] it does bear eloquent witness to the severe reservations in some Member States to a possible Turkish accession. There is no EU rule prohibiting a Member State from holding a national referendum to approve membership of the Union by another country. Use of this by some states could effectively derail a state's accession even after the relevant agreement is signed.

Beyond the changes in its wording, the actual operation of Article 49 TEU in the future will have impacts—both direct and indirect—on candidate countries and the EU alike: direct in the sense that the evolution of the concept of 'European' and common values are intimately and inextricably linked; and indirect in the sense that the criterion on integration capacity on the part of the Union will likely play a greater role in the decisions surrounding enlargement.

E. European identity and common values

The interconnection between the notion of 'European' and Union values is linked to the long-established and inclusive concept of 'European identity' dating from 1973:[65]

The Nine wish to ensure that the cherished values of their legal, political and moral order are respected, and to preserve the rich variety of their national cultures. Sharing as they do the same attitudes to life, based on a determination to build a society which measures up to the needs of the individual, that are determined to defend the principles of representative democracy, of the rule of law, of social justice—which is the ultimate goal of economic

---

[61] M Sæter, 'Norway and the European Union. Domestic Debate Versus External Reality' in L Miles (ed), *The European Union and the Nordic Countries* (Routledge, 1996) chapter 9, 133, 141–5.

[62] Tatham, above n 1 at chapter 9, 240, 267.

[63] Constitutional Act No 2005-204, s 2 introduced into the 1958 Constitution, Article 88-5 that stated: 'Any government bill authorizing the ratification of a Treaty pertaining to the accession of a State to the European Union and to the European Communities shall be submitted to referendum by the President of the Republic.'

[64] Article 88-5 is not applicable to accessions that result from an Intergovernmental Conference whose meeting was decided by the European Council before 1 July 2004 by virtue of s 47 of the Constitutional Act 2008-724 of 23 July 2008.

[65] Heads of State or Government Summit Conference, Copenhagen, 14–15 December 1973, Annex II, 'Declaration on Europe's Identity': EEC Bull 12-1973, 118.

progress—and of respect for human rights. All these are fundamental elements of the European identity.

It was also observed[66] that the originality and dynamism of European identity was derived, inter alia, from the diversity of cultures within the framework of a common European civilization, the attachment to common values and principles, the increasing convergence of attitudes to life and the awareness of having specific interests in common.

This construction of a united Europe has remained open to other European nations who share the same ideals and objectives, and accordingly[67] the term 'European' combines geographical, historical and cultural elements and its essence is regarded differently by each succeeding generation.[68]

As European identity is rooted in common values,[69] the constitutionalization[70] of those values in the body of the TEU is a significant development. The criteria for accession have been extended by the statement which follows the list of values in Article 2 TEU, the implication being that any state wishing to join the Union must also be 'a society of pluralism, tolerance, justice, solidarity and non-discrimination'. Consequently, these values and societal principles are intrinsically linked to European identity in the early twenty-first century.

Interestingly, in view of future enlargements, the clear absence of religion or belief as a common value in Article 2 TEU may be regarded as indicative of a Union wishing to stay open to the evolution of a European identity that could integrate states and societies where Islam forms the belief of the majority or large numbers of their citizens.[71] However, the values in Article 2 TEU derive their origins from a combination of culture, religion and humanism. The Preamble to the TEU (as modified by the Lisbon Treaty) provides: 'Drawing inspiration from the cultural, religious and humanist inheritance of Europe, from which have developed the universal values of the inviolable and inalienable rights of the human person, freedom, democracy, equality and the rule of law.' This is said[72] to represent a consensus between the Member States that the constitutional values of the Union

---

[66] Ibid.

[67] European Commission, 'Europe and the Challenge of Enlargement': EC Bull, Supplement 3-1992, point 7.

[68] Laenerts and van Nuffel, above n 10 at para 6-007, 274.

[69] Presidency Conclusions, Tampere European Council, 15–16 October 1999, 'Towards a Union of Freedom, Security and Justice: Tampere Milestones', para 1: 'from its very beginning European integration has been firmly rooted in a shared commitment to freedom based on human rights, democratic institutions and the rule of law. These common values have proved necessary for securing peace and developing prosperity in the European Union. They will also serve as a cornerstone for the enlarging Union.'

[70] N Walker, 'Constitutionalising Enlargement, Enlarging Constitutionalism' (2003) 9 *Eur LJ* 365; and C Hillion, 'The Copenhagen Criteria and Their Progeny' in Hillion, above n 5 at chapter 1, 1, 10–16.

[71] However, if 'Europe' is defined in cultural terms, it has been queried whether religion might still be considered as covered by this cultural reference, especially in modern European society: E de Souza, 'Enlargement of the EU', Bruges Political Research Papers, No 4/2007, European Political and Administrative Studies, College of Europe, Bruges (2007), 10, 18.

[72] R McCrea, 'Religion as a Basis of Law in the Public Order of the European Union' (2009) 16 *Columbia J Eur Law* 81, 85.

derive from a balance or mix of (largely Christian) religious,[73] humanist and cultural influences: such values reflect the 'value pluralism'[74] at the foundations of the Union, according to which conflicts between differing rights or approaches are regarded as normatively acceptable, their resolution being made by means of a balancing between the conflicting elements as opposed to giving priority to one over the other in some sort of hierarchy. Indeed, it is argued[75] that forms of religion which are unable to accept certain European cultural norms or to accommodate the humanist and secular elements of European culture—which require significant limitations of the influence of religion over law and politics—will find it difficult to cope with the European way or ways of life. The Union has already indicated, within the context of enlargement, that failure to maintain limits on religious influence over law and politics is incompatible with EU membership, for example, Romania was required to repeal its laws criminalizing homosexual behaviour.[76]

F. The EU's integration capacity

The Union's capacity to integrate new Member States also looms large over any enlargement, entailing reform of the functioning and decision-making processes of the EU institutions. In all these reforms, Turkey remains the elephant in the enlargement room, not for cultural, religious or political reasons but rather from demographic and socio-economic ones.

The onus is on the EU to achieve the necessary technical adaptations to take account of the new Members. These adaptations, to be found in the Treaties and EU secondary legislation, include the size and composition of the central EU institutions as well as other institutions and organs based in Brussels and throughout the EU; the weighting of votes in the Council; the addition of new official languages; and the extension of the territory of the Union.

Underlining the express issue linkage between institutional innovation and enlargement in an ever larger EU, the June 2006 European Council[77] asked the Commission to report to it on the Union's capacity to integrate new Members. In reply, the Commission[78] noted that the Union's capacity in this respect was

---

[73] The importance of the Christian churches to the integration project may be seen in Article 17 TFEU: '(1) The Union respects and does not prejudice the status under national law of churches and religious associations or communities in the Member States. (2) The Union equally respects the status under national law of philosophical and non-confessional organisations. (3) Recognising their identity and their specific contribution, the Union shall maintain an open, transparent and regular dialogue with these churches and organisations.'

[74] J Bengoetxea, N MacCormick and L Morial Soriano, 'Integration and Integrity in the Legal Reasoning of the European Court of Justice' in G de Búrca and JHH Weiler (eds), *The European Court of Justice* (Oxford University Press, 2001) 43, 64.

[75] McCrea, above n 72 at 89 and 119.

[76] R McCrea, 'Restrictions on Religion in a Liberal Democratic Polity: Christianity, Islam and the Partial Secularity of the European Union' (2008) 27 *Ybk Eur L* 195.

[77] Presidency Conclusions, European Council, Brussels, 15–16 June 2006, para 53.

[78] European Commission, Communication, 'Enlargement Strategy and Main Challenges 2006–2007, Including annexed special report on the EU's capacity to integrate new members': COM(2006) 649 final.

determined by two factors:[79] (a) maintenance of the momentum to reinforce and deepen European integration by ensuring the EU's capacity to function; and (b) assurance that candidate countries were ready to take on the obligations of membership when they joined by fulfilling the rigorous conditions set. It then stated:[80] 'The capacity of the Union to maintain the momentum of European integration as it enlarges has three main components: institutions, common policies, and budget. The Union needs to ensure that its institutions continue to act effectively, that its policies meet their goals, and that its budget is commensurate with its objectives and with its financial resources.' Of importance in regard to budgetary issues is the fact that the Negotiating Framework for Turkey[81] takes an important step forward by specifying the content of the integration capacity condition, namely, that Turkey cannot accede before the Member States have decided on the EU budget for the period from 2014.

The EU's capacity to integrate new Member States is thus coming to play an increasingly greater role in accession conditionality and remains a condition over which candidate or accession countries can exercise no direct influence. Understandably, in the present economic climate, budgetary matters have assumed a much greater importance and, for example, the problems of funding of regional and common agricultural policies, in an ever larger Union, are particularly stark.

However, it is the link between population and institutional participation, based on the principle of digressive proportionality,[82] that appears as Banquo's ghost at the EU feast. Even the modification of the digressive proportionality principle fails to take properly into account the possibility of fluctuating populations: predicted demographics for Europe show most countries will experience a contraction in population during the next 20–50 years while Turkey's will continue to flourish.[83] The impact of these changes could have important consequences. In relation to the European Parliament, for example, and despite the new 751-MEP limit in the Lisbon Treaty, the proportionate allocation of seats will remain unstable in the coming years with small countries particularly fearful of losing comparative representation. In fact, with a projected membership to include the Western Balkan States, the remaining EFTA countries and Turkey, the EU could in time have a population of over 585 million: on present figures, a ceiling of 751 MEPs would still result in an approximate average of one MEP representing approximately 779,000 people.[84] Based on that, Turkey would become the largest nation in the EU, even surpassing Germany.[85]

[79]   Ibid 15.

[80]   Ibid 20.

[81]   The 2005 Negotiating Framework for Turkey, above n 35 at para 13.

[82]   In the absence of an actual 'mathematical formula,' the EEC and subsequently the EU used the principle of digressive proportionality, according to which so many seats in the European Parliament are awarded between Member States on the basis of population bands.

[83]   S Kurpas et al (eds), 'The Treaty of Lisbon: Implementing the Institutional Innovations', CEPS Special Report, Joint Study CEPS, EGMONT and EPC, Brussels, November 2007, 65: <http://aei. pitt.edu/11751/>. Visited 21 July 2010.

[84]   A little better than the former limit of 700 MEPs which would have resulted in one MEP on average per 835,714 inhabitants.

[85]   European Commission, 'Opinion on Turkey's Request for Accession to the Community' 20 December 1989: SEC(89) 2290 final/2, paras 5–6.

VI. Withdrawal

A. Historical context

Until the advent of the 2004 Constitutional Treaty, neither the original founding Treaties nor the succeeding treaties contained a provision allowing Member States to withdraw or secede—either in a negotiated or a unilateral manner[86]—from the Union.[87]

In fact, it was arguable whether or not such an inherent right existed under the European treaties in the absence of an express provision. Without entering into detailed discussion on the point, prior arguments had essentially centred on the characteristics that protagonists considered inured to the then Community legal order:[88] on the one hand, if Community law were qualified as part of public international law, then writers tended to derive a right of withdrawal from the principles expressed in the Vienna Convention on the Law of Treaties 1969[89] or under customary international law; while, on the other hand, authors determining the Community as an autonomous legal order[90] or attributing to the Community some state-like character tended to regard withdrawal as barred[91] or, at the most, its exercise was highly circumscribed and rarely to be undertaken.

Despite these fundamental divergences, the common view before the Lisbon Treaty came into force was that the Community/Union Treaties 'concluded for an unlimited period'[92] did not allow a unilateral or free right to withdraw.

---

[86] On the subject of seceding from international organizations, see the older monographs: N Singh, *Termination of Membership of International Organizations* (Steven & Sons, 1958); N Feinberg, 'Unilateral Withdrawal from an International Organization' (1963) 39 *British Ybk Intl L* 189; and M Akehurst, 'Withdrawal from International Organisations' (1979) 32 *CLP* 143.

[87] See generally, P Soldatos, 'Durée et Dénonciation des Traités de Rome' (1969) 47 *Revue de droit international des sciences diplomatiques et politiques* 257; PD Dagtoglou, 'How Indissoluble is the Community?' in PD Dagtoglou (ed), *Basic Problems of the European Community* (Basil Blackwell, 1975) 258; C-D Ehlermann, 'Mitgliedschaft in der Europäischen Gemeinschaft. Rechtsprobleme der Erweiterung, der Mitgliedschaft und der Verkleinerung' (1984) 19 *Europarecht* 113; F Götting, *Die Beendigung der Mitgliedschaft der Europäischen Union* (Nomos Verlag, 2000); and A Waltemathe, *Austritt aus der EU—sind die Mitgliedstaaten noch souverän?* (Lang, 2000).

[88] Dagtoglou, ibid 261–9; JA Hill, 'The European Economic Community: The Right of Member State Withdrawal' (1982) 12 *Georgia J Intl & Comparative L* 335, 337–41 and 344–55; JHH Weiler, 'Alternatives to Withdrawal from an International Organization: The Case of the European Economic Community' (1985) 20 *Israel LR* 282, 282–8; and T Bruha and C Nowak, 'Recht auf Austritt aus der Europäischen Union? Anmerkungen zu Artikel I-59 des Entwurfs eines Vertrages über eine Verfassung für Europa' (2004) 42 *Archiv des Völkerrechts* 1, 1–6.

[89] Vienna Convention on the Law of Treaties (Vienna, 23 May 1969: 1155 UNTS 331).

[90] Case 6/64 *Costa v ENEL* [1964] ECR 585, 593.

[91] In *Costa*, ibid 590, the ECJ stated: 'The transfer by the States from their domestic legal system to the Community legal system of the rights and obligations arising under the Treaty carries with it a *permanent limitation of their sovereign rights, against which a subsequent unilateral act incompatible with the concept of the Community* cannot prevail.' (Emphasis added.) Since a Member State seeking to secede from the Community would have undertaken actions incompatible with Community law and since that law was superior to national law, the latter was overturned: secession was therefore, legally speaking, impossible.

[92] Except the 1951 ECSC Treaty the lifespan of which was limited under Article 97 to 50 years. It entered into force on 24 July 1952 and consequently came to an end on 23 July 2002.

Nevertheless there was strong evidence to suggest the existence of an inherent right of withdrawal, but rather one conducted in a negotiated manner.[93]

Thus, no Member State protested against the United Kingdom's right to withdraw,[94] when the Labour government was elected in 1974 with a manifesto pledge to hold a referendum on the issue. Although the issue of withdrawal was never put to the test as a large majority voted in June 1975 in favour of staying in the EEC,[95] it was assumed on all sides that Britain could have left if she had so wished.[96] Since their foundation, only two entities have actually left the Communities, Algeria and Greenland.

B. Algeria

The issue of Algeria occurred very early in the life of the Communities, at a time when it was still an integral part of France,[97] comprising (on the eve of independence in 1962) 15 *départements*[98] and which had elected their own representatives to the French National Assembly since 1870.[99] As with the overseas *départements* of France at that time,[100] Algeria did not fall within the list of overseas countries and territories (OCTs)[101] associated with the EEC under Articles 131–136 EEC. Rather it was included in the EEC[102] but only governed by the provisions of the 1957 Treaty to the

---

[93] S Berglund, 'Prison or Voluntary Cooperation? The Possibility of Withdrawal from the European Union' (2006) 29 *Scandinavian Political Studies* 147, 150.

[94] K Widdows, 'The Unilateral Denunciation of Treaties Containing no Denunciation Clause' (1983) 53 *British Ybk Intl L* 83, 102.

[95] Tatham, above n 1 at chapter 2, 7, 23–5; and REM Irving, 'The United Kingdom Referendum, June 1975' (1976) 1 *ELR* 3, 3.

[96] TC Hartley, 'International Law and the Law of the European Union: A Reassessment' (2001) 72 *British Ybk Intl L* 1, 22.

[97] France had incorporated Algeria in 1848.

[98] French administration for northern Algeria was separated from that in the south: France had made northern Algeria an integral part of France in 1848 and by 1959 this area was made up of 13 *départements*. The four territories of Southern Algeria (also known as Sahara) had been annexed in 1902. The 1947 Algerian Statute (20 septembre 1947), altered their status and they were divided into *départements* and in 1957 were further reorganized into two *départements*. The two Saharan *départements* were reattached to Algeria by Décret 62-535 (Journal Officiel de la République Française, 3 mai 1962, 4483) and responsibility was transferred from the French government minister in charge of the Sahara to his colleague the Minister responsible for Algerian affairs. Algeria, at the time of independence, thus covered 15 *départements*.

[99] However, out of a population of nearly 11 million in 1962, only about one and a half million were French citizens with the right to vote (making up about 15% of the total population). Most of the some 6.5 million people of voting age in Algeria were not French citizens and therefore not entitled to vote for National Assembly elections.

[100] The others being: Martinique and Guadeloupe in the West Indies, French Guiana in South America, and Réunion in the Indian Ocean.

[101] The OCTs (listed in Annex IV to the 1957 EEC Treaty) were non-European countries and territories which had special relations with Belgium, France, Italy and the Netherlands (generally colonial possessions). They were to be associated with the EEC, the purpose of such association being the promotion of the economic and social development of the OCTs and the establishment of close economic relations between them and the EEC as a whole (Article 131 EEC).

[102] P Lampué, 'L'application des traités dans les territoires et départements d'outre-mer' (1960) *Annuaire français de droit international* 907, 915. On the case law and statutory rules on the application of international treaties in Algeria while part of France, see Lampué, ibid 918–19 and 922–3.

extent listed under Article 227(2) EEC[103] as might be extended by unanimous vote in the Council of Ministers on a proposal from the Commission.[104]

Independence from France on 1 July 1962 and thus secession from the EEC was ultimately concluded through bilateral negotiations (between France and Algerian groups opposed to French rule), culminating in the Evian accords[105] and confirmed through separate popular referendums in metropolitan France and Algeria.[106] The withdrawal of Algeria did not result in any revision of France's level of participation in Community institutions: in particular, the number of French representatives in the European Parliamentary Assembly was not reduced,[107] thus maintaining parity in its number of members (36) with the other large Member States of that time, West Germany and Italy.

Of particular interest, however, was that post independence the relevant provisions of the EEC Treaty[108] continued to apply. In fact, the Algerian president Ben Bella sent a letter (dated 24 December 1962) to the President of the EEC Council of Ministers, in which he requested the provisional maintenance of the relevant Articles of the EEC Treaty, pending future definition of EEC–Algeria relations.[109] By implication, then, from July to December 1962, the EEC Treaty had continued to apply to independent Algeria without any official overtures either from that state or the Community. The receipt of the letter was acknowledged by the Council on 24 January 1963, setting out the EEC's interest in the problem and its intention to study it.[110] The European Commission also answered positively, assuring the Community's respect for former responsibilities, especially in financial matters.[111]

---

[103] These were: the free movement of goods; agriculture, with the exception of Article 40(4) EEC; the liberalization of services; the competition rules; the safeguard measures provided for in Articles 108, 109 and 226 EEC; and the institutions.

[104] This was done with regard to the competition rules on cartels and dumping issues by the Commission and the Council as well as the rules on free movement of capital, Articles 67–73 and 106 EEC. See Council Decision (EEC) on the application to Algeria and to the French overseas departments of the provisions of the Treaty concerning capital movements: [1959–1962] OJ Spec Ed 48.

[105] Journal Officiel de la République Française, 20 mars 1962, 3019. These accords had three objectives: providing for a ceasefire between the French and the Algerian forces; the independence of Algeria; and cooperation between France and Algeria after independence. Relations between the EEC and Algeria were not directly raised in these negotiations neither were they mentioned in the accords themselves.

[106] M Flory, 'La fin de la souveraineté française en Algérie' (1962) *Annuaire français de droit international* 905, 915–19. See also the Declaration of President Charles de Gaulle recognizing Algerian independence: Journal Officiel de la République Française, 4 juillet 1962, 6483.

[107] This was probably due to the French constitutional rule according to which deputies of the National Assembly have a nationwide mandate. This was provided for in the first French Constitution (3 September 1791): 'Representatives appointed in the departments shall not be representatives of a specific department but of the Nation as a whole, and cannot be given a specific mandate.' It is now contained in the 1958 Constitution of the Fifth Republic, Articles 24 and 25, and it is rather the Senate, indirectly elected, which ensures representation of the territorial communities of the Republic.

[108] As set out in Article 227(2) EEC and including by reference Council Decision (EEC) on the application to Algeria and to the French overseas departments of the provisions of the Treaty concerning capital movements: [1959–1962] OJ Spec Ed 48.

[109] P Tavernier, 'Aspects juridiques des relations économiques entre la C.E.E. et l'Algérie' (1972) 8 *Revue trimestrielle de droit européen* 1, 9–10.

[110] Bulletin de la CEE, 1963/3, 35; and Conseils des Ministres, '7e aperçu des activités des Conseils' (1963) 90.

[111] Commission européenne, '6e rapport sur l'activité de la Commission' 228.

Before the EEC and Algeria eventually concluded their first comprehensive bilateral agreement in 1976,[112] it was a moot point as to whether Article 227(2) EEC continued as the legal basis for relations between them[113] or that that provision was progressively emptied of its contents in the years after independence due to new rules introduced by Algeria, the EEC or its Member States, particularly regarding the customs union and agri-products.[114] From the Algerian example, it might be possible to conclude that neither side wished to see a sudden and complete rupture between them and they thus allowed an indeterminate legal situation to continue due to important political and economic considerations, especially in relation to France.

C. Greenland

The situation in respect of Greenland was ultimately a more complex process than that of Algeria. The island had been a colony until 1953 and had then been incorporated into the Kingdom of Denmark and directly ruled from Copenhagen. In the 1972 Danish referendum for EEC membership, the overwhelming majority of the electorate in Greenland had voted against[115] and this contributed to the pressure for the eventual creation of home rule, with a Greenlandic parliament and government.[116] Denmark reserved one of its seats in the European Parliament for a Greenlandic MEP and, in the Council of Ministers, it became the practice that observers from Greenland would accompany the Danish member where the Council decided on issues concerning Greenland.[117]

After home rule was eventually introduced in 1979,[118] the new Greenlandic government called for a referendum on membership of the Communities which, in 1982, produced a small majority in favour of withdrawal.[119] The Danish government, which still represented Greenland in matters of external policy, had announced prior to the vote that it would respect the result of the referendum. It thus acted upon the request of the Greenlandic government and requested the

---

[112] The Co-operation Agreement between the EEC and Algeria and the Interim Agreement on the advance implementation of certain provisions of the Cooperation Agreement were signed on 26 April 1976: [1976] OJ L141/2.

[113] A Mameri, 'L'adhésion de l'Algérie à la C.E.E.' (1968) *Revue algérienne des sciences juridiques, économiques et politiques* 429–35; and Tavernier, above n 109 at 22–9.

[114] L Ananiades, *L'association aux Communautés européennes* (LGDJ, 1967) 99–100; M Flory, 'La succession d'Etats en Afrique du Nord' (1966) *Annuaire de l'Afrique du Nord* 21, 21–2; Tavernier, above n 109 at 6–21.

[115] According to the figures, about 70% of voters in Greenland opposed EEC accession, while 63.5% of voters in the whole of the Kingdom of Denmark were in favour: F Harhoff, 'Greenland's Withdrawal from the European Communities' (1983) 20 *CML Rev* 13, 17; and HR Krämer, 'Greenland's European Community (EC)-Referendum, Background and Consequences' (1982) 25 *German Ybk Intl L* 273, 273.

[116] R Friel, 'Providing a Constitutional Framework for Withdrawal from the EU: Article 59 of the Draft European Constitution' (2004) 53 *ICLQ* 407, 409; and Krämer, ibid 278.

[117] Harhoff, above n 115 at 19–20; and Krämer, above n 115 at 275–6.

[118] I Foighel, 'Home Rule in Greenland: A Framework for Local Autonomy' (1980) 17 *CML Rev* 91.

[119] The figures were 52% in favour of withdrawal and 46.1% against: Harhoff, above n 115 at 13; and Krämer, above n 115 at 273.

Council[120] to amend the Treaties in order to allow for the withdrawal of Greenland and its transfer to the status of OCT. The Council asked the Commission and the European Parliament for their opinions on the Danish government's request.[121] In spring 1983 both institutions responded favourably: the Commission delivered its opinion[122] in which it recommended that Greenland be offered OCT status together with specific additional arrangements; the European Parliament endorsed the Commission's position.[123] Little legal debate arose in respect of Greenland's withdrawal, although a minority of MEPs objected to the Communities' easy acquiescence to such withdrawal.[124] The Council then requested the Commission to provide detailed practical proposals in relation to Greenlandic fishery issues, which were duly presented.[125]

Thereafter, in late 1983, the Danish government entered into negotiations on behalf of the island with the other Member States to decide expediently on Greenland's withdrawal from the EEC and its transformation into an OCT:[126] agreement was reached in early 1984.[127] This resulted in the necessary consequent amendments to the Treaties[128] (passed on the basis of then Article 236 EEC[129] according to which the unanimous consent of the Member States could alter or amend the existing Treaties) which took effect—after the last Member State ratification—with the withdrawal of Greenland on 1 February 1985.

Greenland's withdrawal contained a number of unique features[130] including the fact that: (a) it is an overseas, non-European territory, disconnected from Europe on the basis of factors, inter alia, geographical, cultural, social, climatic, ethnic and economic;[131] (b) it is a former colony linked to a Member State and any attempt to prevent its withdrawal would have smacked of colonialism; and (c) it did not represent a secession of a Member State but rather the redefinition of the Kingdom of Denmark through internal home rule: thus Denmark continued its membership of the Communities and, due to Greenland's small population of about 50,000 inhabitants at that time,[132] there was no impact from this population loss, for example, on the number of Danish MEPs or on Denmark's qualified-majority voting strength in the Council of Ministers.

---

[120] EC Bull, Supplement 1/83, 6.
[121] On the basis of Articles 96 ECSC, 236 EEC and 204 EAEC.
[122] COM(83) 66 final.
[123] The report of the Legal Affairs Committee of the European Parliament, EP Doc. 1-264/83, together with a motion for a resolution and an explanatory statement endorsing the Commission's proposal of February 1983, was tabled on 29 April 1983.
[124] EP Doc. 1-264/83, 17.
[125] COM(83) 593 final. Additional proposals were submitted in early February 1984.
[126] F Weiss, 'Greenland's Withdrawal from the European Communities' (1985) 10 *ELR* 173.
[127] [1984] OJ C73/3.
[128] Treaty amending, with regard to Greenland, the Treaties establishing the European Communities ('Greenland Treaty'): [1985] OJ L29/1.
[129] See also Articles 96 ECSC and 204 EAEC.
[130] Harhoff, above n 115 at 21–2 and 31–2; Friel, above n 116 at 411; and Weiss, above n 126 at 185.
[131] For a more detailed analysis of these issues see Harhoff, above n 115 at 21–7; and Krämer, above n 115 at 276–81.
[132] Krämer, above n 115 at 275.

Set against these singular features, there are a number of points which allowed some lessons to be drawn for future withdrawals from the Union:[133] (a) Denmark did not attempt a unilateral withdrawal for Greenland but rather a negotiated one with its fellow Member States: in making this concession, it avoided or significantly reduced the risk that other Member States might have rejected the application; (b) the Council, before exercising its powers to amend the Treaties, sought the opinion of the Commission and Parliament; (c) the process was agreed to unanimously by the Member States which greatly facilitated the expedited and non-contentious withdrawal of Greenland; (d) Denmark retained its general role during the negotiations with the other Member States in the Council of Ministers, albeit reflecting the limited nature of Greenland's withdrawal as opposed to any possible full Member State secession; and (e) the acceptance of the Greenland Treaty by the Member States was predicated on the introduction of arrangements which permitted the maintenance of close and lasting links between the Community and Greenland[134] so that withdrawal appears to infer automatically the need to forge the basis of a new relationship.[135] Such issues had, in varying degrees, an impact on subsequent Treaty developments.

D. Introduction of the concept of withdrawal into the Union

The possibility of providing an express treaty basis for withdrawal from the Union was initially broached by the 2002–2003 Convention on the Future of Europe.[136] Yet despite the importance of such provision, there was a paucity of submissions made to the Convention on the issue: namely, those of Dashwood;[137] Lamassoure;[138] and Badinter.[139] Nevertheless, those submissions generally reflected the three potential models for withdrawal mechanisms:[140] (a) state primacy, where a Member State has an absolute, immediate and unilateral right to withdraw from a federation. This was essentially advocated by Dashwood and meant that the Member State had an unconditional right which did not require permission from EU institutions; (b) federal primacy, where a Member State is absolutely prohibited from withdrawing. Lamassoure did discuss the fact that in a federal[141] restructuring

---

[133] Friel, above n 116 at 410–11.

[134] Greenland Treaty, above n 128, Preamble, Recital 2.

[135] Friel, above n 116 at 410.

[136] See <http://european-convention.eu.int/>. Visited 15 May 2010. Friel, above n 116 at 423–4; and M Jovanović, *Constitutionalizing Secession in Federalized States: A Procedural Approach* (Eleven International Publishing, 2007) 161.

[137] Submission of Peter Hain, UK Minister for Europe, of draft Treaty on Union by Prof Alan Dashwood, Conv 345/1/02 REV 1: <http://register.consilium.europa.eu/pdf/en/02/cv00/cv00345-re01.en02.pdf>. Visited 14 June 2010.

[138] Contribution from Alain Lamassoure, Conv 235/02: <http://register.consilium.europa.eu/pdf/en/02/cv00/cv00235.en02.pdf>. Visited 14 June 2010.

[139] Contribution from Robert Badinter, Conv 317/02: <http://register.consilium.europa.eu/pdf/en/02/cv00/cv00317.en02.pdf>. Visited 14 June 2010.

[140] Friel, above n 116 at 422–3; Jovanović, above n 136 at 162–3.

[141] Lamassoure, above n 138 at 8. The federal model was rejected as being unlikely to be sufficiently acceptable to the people of Europe: basically while people in Europe are supportive of the component parts of the Union, they may resist a model which would present these parts as a whole.

of the EU, the rule should be 'once a member, always a member' but regarded this and the confederal[142] model as extremes. He therefore proposed a community option allowing withdrawal but 'subject to strict and deterrent conditions'; and (c) federal control, where a Member State retains its sovereign right to withdraw, subject to negotiations with and the approval of the remaining states in the federation, thereby emphasizing the process as a mutually negotiated activity. Badinter's proposal, given in a more detailed manner, firmly followed this option and was closer to what was actually drafted for Article I-60 of the 2004 Constitutional Treaty. Although it never entered into force, its contents were later reproduced in the Lisbon Treaty with only minor technical changes.[143]

VII. Lisbon Treaty: Article 50

The Lisbon Treaty consequently introduced the legal possibility of withdrawal from the Union for the first time, thereby[144] underlining the recognition of the Member States as 'Masters of the Treaty'[145] and their continuing sovereignty in this respect. A Member State is now able, according to Article 50 TEU, to 'decide to withdraw from the European Union in accordance with its own constitutional arrangements'. The Article, as discussed in point 4 below, also outlines the procedure for withdrawal.

VIII. Criteria for Withdrawal

No criteria for withdrawal are set out in Article 50 TEU unlike some of the accession criteria set out in Article 49 TEU. Perhaps the best clue is found in the phrase that a Member State might withdraw from the Union, 'according to its own constitutional arrangements'. While this means different procedures for each state, the fact that the state is withdrawing from the Union implies that it is still bound by

---

[142] Lamassoure, above n 138 at 6. The confederal model was rejected as being unworkable in an enlarging EU, as it would tend to exacerbate present difficulties, eg deepening the democratic deficit, reducing accountability, and heightening conflict between states and the Union.

[143] See generally, Friel, above n 116 at 424–7; Bruha and Nowak, above n 88 at 14–24; and J Herbst, 'Observations on the Right to Withdraw from the European Union: Who are the "Masters of the Treaty"?' (2005) 6 *German LJ* 1755.

[144] According to, eg the Spanish Constitutional Tribunal in its ruling on the 2004 Constitutional Treaty, 13 December 2004, DTC 6603-2004: [2005] 1 *CMLR* 981; the German Federal Constitutional Court in the *Lisbon Treaty* judgment, 30 June 2009: [2010] 2 *CMLR* 712; and the Hungarian Constitutional Court, 14 July 2010, *Dec 143/2010 (VII.14) AB*.

[145] The German Court had previously ruled that the Member States remained the 'Masters of the Treaty' in its 1993 judgment on the constitutionality of the German ratification of the 1992 Maastricht Treaty: *Brunner*, 12 October 1993: [1994] 1 *CMLR* 57. For the seminal discussion of this point, see U Everling, 'Sind die Mitgliedstaaten der Europäische Gemeinschaft noch Herren der Verträge? Zum Verhältnis von Europäischem Gemeinschaftsrecht und Völkerrecht' in R Bernhardt et al (eds), *Recht zwischen Umbruch und Bewahrung: Festschrift für Hermann Mosler* (Springer Verlag, 1993) 173.

Union values in the manner of its withdrawal. In particular, it could be argued that the values of democracy, the rule of law, freedom, solidarity and equality—Articles 2 and 49 TEU—are equally applicable to withdrawal.[146] In this sense, the withdrawal, although occurring in a Member State, impacts on all of them so that compliance with such value criteria would be the optimal means of departure from the Union: moreover, since a negotiated withdrawal from the Union has always been a possibility, this clause merely confirms that fact.

Compliance with such values would probably entail the seceding state to gain the support of its population directly through a popular referendum, before commencing the Union side of the withdrawal procedure.[147] It may be contended that a 'Union-conform' way would be to proceed by sufficient domestic consensus between government, parliament and electorate before negotiating with the Union to ensure a continuing relationship, post withdrawal. In such circumstances, 'sufficient' would probably need more than a mere simple majority of votes since some level of weighted or qualified majority vote would render the outcome of the vote more legitimate and binding, and therefore less open to any subsequent challenge.[148]

Nevertheless, a referendum is not always considered necessary in this respect and a parliamentary vote on the issue might suffice, especially where the government is elected on a promise of withdrawal and secures a sufficient majority to so act. This was, in fact, the position of the British Labour Party which promised, in 1981, that if it were elected to power then Britain would withdraw from the EEC without even holding a national referendum.[149]

The possible alternative, a unilateral withdrawal, would encounter problems and run counter to Union values. While theoretically possible for a state to use its own constitutional processes to denounce a treaty (and a matter confirmed by Article 4(2) TEU on the respect for national identity),[150] notify the Council and then sit on its haunches waiting for two years to elapse for the withdrawal to become final without negotiating an agreement, its impact would be wholly negative and would almost certainly sour relations between the withdrawing state and the Union.[151]

---

[146] But cf arguments against this proposition: Herbst, above n 143 at 1756.

[147] Jovanović, above n 136 at 165–95.

[148] In respect of referendums, Norman has advocated a qualified majority (W Norman, 'The Ethics of Secession as the Regulation of Secessionist Politics' in M Moore (ed), *National Self-determination and Secession* (Oxford University Press, 1998) 34, 53) while Weinstock advocated a supermajority (D Weinstock, 'Constitutionalizing the Right to Secede' (2001) 9 *Journal of Political Philosophy* 182, 197). Jovanović, above n 136 at 193–4, notes the different majorities required in different secession referendums under various domestic constitutions.

[149] 'European Community: We'll Love You and Leave You', *The Economist*, 25 July 1981, 53.

[150] Eg, in the United Kingdom, the British government would merely need a simple majority in both Houses of Parliament to repeal the European Communities Act 1972: AF Tatham, 'The Sovereignty of Parliament after Factortame' (1993) 28 *Europarecht* 188.

[151] Herbst argues that this two-year period is so short that the exit clause seems to posit a unilateral right of withdrawal: Herbst, above n 143 at 1757–8.

IX. Procedure for Withdrawal

Article 50 TEU provides that a Member State opting to withdraw from the Union must notify the European Council of its intention to do so. The European Council is to set out the guidelines according to which the Union will negotiate and conclude a withdrawal agreement with that Member State, taking account of the framework for the future relationship between the Union and the state. This agreement would be negotiated in accordance with Article 218(3) TFEU[152] with the Commission submitting recommendations to the Council and the latter adopting a decision to open negotiations. The agreement would be concluded by the Council acting by a qualified majority, after having obtained the consent of the European Parliament. The Treaties would cease to apply to the withdrawing state either from the date of entry into force of the withdrawal agreement or, failing that, two years after the notification of its intention to withdraw. Exceptionally, the European Council—in agreement with the Member State concerned—can unanimously decide to extend this period. Finally, the member of the European Council or of the Council representing the withdrawing Member State may not participate in the discussions of those institutions or in decisions concerning it.

Where a former, withdrawn state asks to rejoin the Union, its request would have to follow the same accession procedure under Article 49 TEU as applies to any new candidate country.

In the absence of a detailed procedure and taking Greenland's withdrawal as a partial precedent, the Council could (reflecting the practice too of Article 49 TEU on enlargement) request Opinions of the Commission and the European Parliament before proceeding to commence the withdrawal process at Union level. The Council would therefore garner the views (and possible support) of the main Union institutions before starting negotiations. In addition, the Council could ask for proposals from the Commission which could utilize current models on which to base its advice. Such pre-existing models, as discussed in the Commentary below, could easily be employed to prevent a complete rupture in relations between the Union and the withdrawing state.

X. Commentary

The introduction of Article 50 TEU now at least renders the Union institutionally prepared to face the prospective trauma were a Member State to seek to withdraw, without imperilling the continuation of further integration among the

---

[152] Consolidated version of the Treaty on the Functioning of the European Union: [2010] OJ C83/47. Article 218(3) TFEU provides: 'The Commission, or the High Representative of the Union for Foreign Affairs and Security Policy where the agreement envisaged relates exclusively or principally to the common foreign and security policy, shall submit recommendations to the Council, which shall adopt a decision authorising the opening of negotiations and, depending on the subject of the agreement envisaged, nominating the Union negotiator or the head of the Union's negotiating team.'

remaining Member States.[153] Nevertheless, this withdrawal clause presents numerous difficulties.

A. Threat of withdrawal as a bargaining chip

From a general point of view,[154] the threat to withdraw under Article 50 TEU would be plausible at any time which would allow the exit of the Member State from the Union to be a relevant factor or bargaining chip in every important decision, thereby encouraging strategic behaviour.[155]

Thus where factors—for example, social, cultural, political, economic—modify the relation of costs and benefits of Union membership[156] and reduce the value of such membership, the option of withdrawal becomes relevant.[157] The heterogeneity of the Union of 27 Members which, after Lisbon, bases its decision-making processes generally on qualified majorities[158] in the Council, greatly increases the likelihood of a Member State being outvoted (and so losing benefits) threatening withdrawal. Such a threat would act as a means of receiving compensatory payments from the Union[159] to sugar the pill of swallowing an initially disadvantageous development as a necessary part of the integration process.

Withdrawal must therefore be seen as a potent weapon, if a state were outvoted in Council on a particularly sensitive national issue and were unable or unwilling to fulfil its legal duties under Article 4(3) TEU of sincere cooperation with other Member States and of Union loyalty. In the hands of a large Member State, it is a trump card: where a vital national interest is at stake, to threaten withdrawal to gain more concessions from other states clearly[160] evokes memories of de Gaulle's 'empty chair' policy of the 1960s which paralysed the operation of the Council of Ministers.[161] Yet, while the clause strengthens the hand of a large

---

[153] J-V Louis, 'Monetary Policy and Central Banking in the Constitution' in ECB, *Legal Aspects of the European System of Central Banks: Liber Amicorum Paolo Zamboni Garavelli* (European Central Bank, 2005) 27, 29.

[154] C Sunstein, 'Constitutionalism and Secession' (1991) 58 *U Chicago LR* 633, 647.

[155] The Article could thus be prone to abuse: J Zeh, 'Recht auf Austritt' (2004) 2 *Zeitschrift für Europarechtliche Studien* 173, 204–5.

[156] S Lechner and R Ohr, 'The Right of Withdrawal in the Treaty of Lisbon: A Game Theoretic Reflection on Different Decision Processes in the EU,' CEGE Discussion Papers, No 77, October 2008, Center for European, Governance and Economic Development research, Georg-August-Universität, Göttingen (2008), 4: <http://www.uni-goettingen.de/de/60920.html>. Visited 21 June 2010.

[157] Ibid 7.

[158] Qualified majority voting, when introduced, was regarded as the exception rather than the rule. With the Lisbon Treaty amendments, qualified majority voting in the Council has become the norm: Article 16(3) TEU. From 1 November 2014, the formula for determining a qualified majority will change to one based on the 'double majority' principle, ie, a system based upon (i) number of Member States; and (ii) population: Article 16(4) TEU. See J Fairhurst, *Law of the European Union*, 8th edn (Pearson Education, 2010) 129–32.

[159] Lechner and Ohr, above n 156 at 7–8.

[160] J Klabbers and P Leino, 'Death by Constitution? The Draft Treaty Establishing a Constitution for Europe' (2003) 4 *German LJ* 1293, 1299; and Lechner and Ohr, above n 156 at 8.

[161] The withdrawal clause thus appears to countenance the resurrection of the spectre of the 1966 Luxembourg Accords: see J Lambert, 'The Constitutional Crisis 1965–66' (1966) 5 *Journal of Common Market Studies* 140; NP Ludlow, *The European Community in the Crises of the 1960s: De Gaulle*

Member State, it weakens that of a small and most medium-sized states; their vulnerability would be exacerbated if they walked away from the EU card table, thereby leaving them politically and economically broke.[162]

B. Unilateral withdrawal possible

The withdrawal clause, while clearly advocating a negotiated secession as the optimum solution, nevertheless presents the departing Member State with a unilateral right to do so.[163] This conclusion is based[164] on three particular points: (a) the wording of Article 50 TEU, highlighting the fact that a withdrawal takes place in accordance with a Member State's own constitutional arrangements; (b) the seceding state is under no treaty obligation to conclude an agreement with the rest of the Union and can thus merely sit out two years before its withdrawal decision becomes final; and (c) the right to withdraw is not preconditioned on a change to EU constitutional law that a Member State cannot accept, that is, the right is unrestricted.[165]

C. The EU's disintegration capacity

As already considered with respect to enlargement and the Union's capacity to integrate new Member States, on withdrawal the Union would need to examine its capacity to cope with secession of a state or states. Even the voluntary withdrawal of certain states could substantially weaken the Union, jeopardizing its survival: for example, in respect of the EMU, French or German withdrawal would place a considerable and unbearable strain on the stability of the common currency;[166] or a British withdrawal would seriously undermine deepening cooperation in security or foreign policy matters. However, the withdrawal of a small or medium-sized state would have relatively less impact on the Union as a whole.

The secession agreement would need to address the profound impact withdrawal would have on, inter alia, institutional changes in Union and budgetary matters; as well as the nature of the continuing relationship with the Union.

Challenges the Community (Routledge, 2006); and L van Middelar, 'Spanning the River: The Constitutional Crisis of 1965–1966 as the Genesis of Europe's Political Order' (2008) 4 *Eur Constitutional LR* 98.

[162] Moreover, in another twist of the bargaining process, the seceding state—in the absence of express wording to the contrary in Article 50 TEU—is not prohibited from unilaterally rescinding its notice of withdrawal any time before the two-year period has elapsed.

[163] Herbst, above n 143 at 1756; R Smits, 'The European Constitution and EMU: An Appraisal' (2005) 42 *CML Rev* 425, 464–5; and Zeh, above n 155 at 201.

[164] P Athanassiou, 'Withdrawal and Expulsion from the EU and EMU: Some Reflections', Legal Working Paper Series, No. 10, December 2009 (Frankfurt am Main: European Central Bank, 2009), 24: <http://www.ecb.europa.eu>. Visited 10 July 2010.

[165] Smits, above n 163 at 464.

[166] J Emmanouilidis, 'Withdrawal or Creation of a New Union—A Way out of the EU's Constitutional Dilemma?' *Spotlight Europe* 2007/02, June 2007, Bertelsmann Stiftung, Gütersloh/ Center for Applied Policy Research, Munich (2007), 3.

D. Impact on EU institutions and budget

Turning to institutional matters, these in part reflect the issues addressed as a result of enlargement with withdrawal having the reverse impact on the operation of the Union institutions. There are also issues peculiar to withdrawal: with the exception of the withdrawal itself, the seceding state's representative in the Council would seem to be able to continue to participate fully in its discussions and decision-making. Moreover, there is no express prohibition on the seceding state's MEPs from deliberating and voting for the European Parliament's consent to the withdrawal agreement. Similarly, no mention is made of what would happen to seceding Member State nationals employed by the Union institutions,[167] neither is there any indication as to how the seceding state's judges in the European courts would continue with their work, especially in respect of new cases arising between notification and the effective date of withdrawal.[168] On budgetary matters, for example, it is a moot point as to whether or not the withdrawing Member State would be obliged to pay its outstanding contributions to the Union[169] or even reimburse monies to the Union.

E. Continuity of relations

As for continuing bilateral relations, this would depend on the attitude of the seceding Member State and the reasons for its departure. Consequently, it might be offered the possibility of joining the EEA[170] or establishing bilateral relations along the lines that Switzerland[171] or Turkey[172] enjoy. Nevertheless, the premise of all these agreements is to deepen integration with the EU and in particular its internal market, to varying, progressive degrees. Thus the agreements remain models but it is questionable whether or not they would be effective in respect of a state going in the opposite direction, by seceding from the Union. If withdrawal were to last longer than two years, the Council could extend the period; alternatively, as with Algeria, the provisions of the European Treaties (probably beyond budgetary and institutional matters) could be temporarily kept in force in the withdrawing state by mutual agreement.

---

[167] Herbst, above n 143 at 1757.
[168] Friel, above n 116 at 426.
[169] Herbst, above n 143 at 1757.
[170] On the EEA Agreement generally, see S Norberg et al (eds), *The European Economic Area. EEA Law: A Commentary on the EEA Agreement* (Fritzes, 1993). For more on the institutional framework, its operation and the need to ensure homogeneity between the EU and EEA–EFTA legal orders: A Łazowski 'EEA Countries (Iceland, Liechtenstein and Norway)' in S Blockmans and A Łazowski (eds), *The European Union and Its Neighbours* (TMC Asser Press, 2006) chapter 4, 95, 108–37.
[171] See generally S Breitenmoser, 'Sectoral Agreements between the EC and Switzerland: Contents and Context' (2003) 40 *CML Rev* 1137; and R Schwok and N Levrat, 'Switzerland's Relations with the EU after the Adoption of the Seven Bilateral Agreements' (2001) 6 *Eur Foreign Affairs Rev* 335.
[172] Tatham, above n 1 at chapter 6, 118, 142–53.

XI. Conclusions

It may be considered somewhat otiose to observe that Articles 49 and 50 TEU are at least similar in the fact that they provide only a general outline as to how and on what basis states may accede to or secede from the Union: for Article 49 TEU, decades of experience have given flesh to the bare bones of the treaty provision while future practice and interpretation will again substantially contribute to the evolving conditionality and procedural requirements; for Article 50 TEU, a rather bare skeleton exists and while academic discourse attempts to add substance to the body,[173] it would probably take the actual use or threat to use the provision which would stimulate the EU institutions to outline their understanding of its operation through the means it has already employed under Article 49 TEU, for instance, with European Council Conclusions.

Although the Member States and the main EU political institutions are involved expressly in both Articles, they nevertheless secure slightly different roles. For example, enlargement requires an agreement with every Member State while withdrawal is negotiated only with the Council.

Putting a withdrawal clause into the TEU might allay the worries of some Member States that view its presence at least as a safeguard to any future situation, where they might feel locked into an unstoppable process through which national sovereignty continues to bleed to the Union. The possibility of staunching this flow, even if never used, might have a more psychological impact on domestic political discourse on the Union.

Lastly, the use of both procedures might actually occur where a current Member State loses one of its component parts through secession:[174] this would be an Algerian or Greenlandic scenario with the current state retaining its membership (with adjustments, for example, in the number of its MEPs, its budgetary contributions and receipts, etc) but with the prospect of that seceded part applying subsequently to join the Union as a state in its own right. Alternatively, a Member State might disintegrate into its component parts—a possible 'Czechoslovak Velvet Divorce'[175] scenario where two or more new states would wish to accede in the place of one previous state.[176] Again, institutional arrangements would need to take into account the relative weighting between the former component parts of the erstwhile state, and their respective budgetary and financial contributions and receipts would need recalibration. In both cases, the Union would be able to 'contain' the changes within the institutional and financial limits previously imposed on the pre-truncated Member State.

---

[173] Friel, above n 116 at 427 in reference to the similarly worded Article 59 CT.

[174] On this point in respect of Scotland and the dangers inherent in such a move, see M Happold, 'Independence: In or out of Europe? An Independent Scotland and the European Union' (2000) 49 *ICLQ* 15, 33–4.

[175] See generally E Stein, *Czecho/Slovakia: Ethnic Conflict, Constitutional Fissure, Negotiated Breakup* (University of Michigan Press, 1997).

[176] The main contender for this option, at this time, is Belgium and its splitting into separate entities for the Flemish and Walloon communities (which neglects what would happen in such a scenario to the German community in Eupen-Malmedy, with its own self-government and equality with the other two communities recognized under the Belgian constitution since 1993).

7

The Charter of Fundamental Rights

David Anderson and Cian C Murphy[1]

I. Introduction

Ten years after its 'solemn proclamation' by the EU institutions, the EU Charter of Fundamental Rights has been given legal force by the Treaty of Lisbon and thus is incorporated into European constitutional law. This chapter traces the Charter's development from a proposal to make rights more visible to its current status as a legally binding catalogue of civil, political, social and economic rights. It surveys the rights protected by the Charter, their sources and the horizontal provisions governing their scope and application, both generally and in the Member States that have sought to limit their effect. The rapidly growing case law of the European Courts on the Charter, both in Luxembourg and in Strasbourg, is analysed with a view to assessing the Charter's likely future impact in litigation. The Charter to a large extent codifies rights already acknowledged by the European Court of Justice and draws strength from that very fact. Nonetheless, the act and manner of codification is likely to give fresh impetus to human rights litigation, not only against the EU institutions but against the Member States and will even, through the Council of Europe, influence the wider Europe outside the EU.

II. Origins and Evolution of the Charter

The genesis of the Charter lies in the decision of the European Court of Justice, in *Opinion 2/94*,[2] that the EC Treaty as it then stood did not grant competence to the European Community to accede to the European Convention on Human Rights (ECHR). Following the Opinion, the Member State governments might have amended the Treaties to provide a legal basis for accession to the Convention. This would, however, have required unanimity that did not exist. In place of accession, the German Presidency of the EU proposed a Charter of Fundamental Rights for the Union. The Presidency Conclusions of the Cologne European Council on 4 June 1999 proclaimed that:

---

[1] The authors wish to thank Tanya Aplin, Stephen Coutts, Tom Hickman an Miguel Poiares Maduro for comments on an earlier draft.

[2] *Opinion 2/94 on Accession by the Community to the EHCR* [1996] ECR I-1759.

Protection of fundamental rights is a founding principle of the Union and an indispensable prerequisite for her legitimacy... There appears to be a need, at the present stage of the Union's development, to establish a Charter of fundamental rights in order to make their overriding importance and relevance more visible to the Union's citizens.[3]

The initial motivations for the Charter were mixed. Some alluded to the Charter as the creation of 'grand new designs for their own sake', commenting that there were many other measures that would have been more useful in improving the quality of human rights protection within the Union and in its policies towards the outside world.[4] It may well be, indeed, that enthusiasm for the Charter derived in some quarters from factors barely connected with the wish to improve human rights protection: in particular, the federalizing desire to create a constitution for the Union more closely resembling that of a state, or thoughts of replacing or rendering redundant the Council of Europe as the ultimate protector of human rights standards within the Union and its Member States.[5] Others saw little merit in the Charter for any reason, as may perhaps be inferred from the UK government's consistently expressed view that the Charter 'should take the form of a political statement, rather than a legal text to be incorporated into the Treaties'.[6]

It would be wrong, however, to diminish the significance of the achievement. Strong protection of individual rights, whatever its political or constitutional motivations, serves both as a compass for the formulation of policy and a necessary judicial safeguard for the individual against the growing legislative and administrative power of the Union. As UK experience with the Human Rights Act 1998 has demonstrated, such protection can be strengthened by the enactment of legislation which 'brings rights home' by giving them explicit effect in a familiar legal order.[7] There was always a chance that the greater visibility envisaged in the Cologne Presidency Conclusions would translate, eventually, into a stronger legislative and judicial focus on fundamental rights protection in the EU legal order. Eleven years later this process is under way.

After the Cologne Presidency Conclusions, the European Council set up a 'body' to draft the proposed Charter. Once the body was assembled, it adopted the rather grand title of 'Convention'. However, opinions differed on the purpose and value of the Charter even within the Praesidium that constituted the Convention's leadership. Whereas the Member States tended towards a declaratory text that

---

[3] Cologne European Council, 'Presidency Conclusions' 3 and 4 June 1999.

[4] Philip Alston and JHH Weiler, 'An "Ever Closer Union" in Need of a Human Rights Policy: The European Union and Human Rights' in P Alson (ed), *The EU and Human Rights* (Oxford University Press, 1999) chapter 1, 66.

[5] For a contemporaneous analysis of the tensions between the EU and Council of Europe, as reflected eg in the case of *Matthews v UK* [1999] 28 EHRR 361, see D Anderson, 'Shifting the Grundnorm and Other Tales' in D O'Keeffe (ed), *Judicial Review in European Union Law, liber amicorum in honour of Lord Slynn of Hadley* (Kluwer, 2000) chapter 22, 349–60.

[6] Answer to written question of Mr Mitchell MP, Hansard HC Deb 30 November 1999, vol 340, c81W.

[7] Secretary of State for the Home Department, *Rights Brought Home: The Human Rights Bill* Cm 3782 24 October 1997.

would, at most, be politically binding, the European Commission and European Parliament intended to draft a more significant document.[8] The speeches of the President of the Convention, Roman Herzog, and the two Vice Presidents, Mendez de Vigo (European Parliament) and António Vitorino (European Commission) at the outset of the process demonstrate this internal division. The Convention's Secretariat, principally consisting of civil servants from the European Council, acted as a 'restraining influence'.[9]

The outcome was in the nature of a compromise. The Charter was not incorporated into the Treaties, via the Treaty of Nice. Rather, it was 'solemnly proclaimed' by the European Parliament, Council of Ministers and European Commission (but not the Member States) at Nice on 7 December 2000.[10] It is indicative of the Charter's early status that it was included in the 'C' series of the Official Journal, rather than the 'L' series that is reserved for law.[11] Nonetheless, the proclamation was not the 'formal funeral' for the Charter that some thought it might be.[12] Although it lacked for the time being the binding force of law, the Convention members had decided to proceed on the basis that the Charter should be drafted 'as if' it might become legally binding.[13] Its 54 Articles—which are for the most part replicated in the Charter as finally adopted in 2007—were thus drafted with an eye to the possibility of judicial enforcement.[14]

After the proclamation, attention turned to the European judiciary to ascertain what effect the Charter might have in European litigation. In this regard, Advocates General and the Court of First Instance (since renamed the General Court) led the way, before the Court of Justice first mentioned it in a 2006 judgment concerning a challenge by the European Parliament to the Family Reunification Directive.[15] However, these cases suggested that the courts of the Union were reluctant to accord full legal force to the Charter in the absence of clear guidance from the political institutions. It remained for the Member State governments to determine its fate.

---

[8] G De Búrca, 'The Drafting of the European Union Charter of Fundamental Rights' (2001) *ELRev* 126, 134.

[9] Ibid.

[10] In reality the declaration lacked solemnity: 'the Charter was signed in five minutes, in the presence of the Heads of State and Governments, and neither Mrs Fontaine [European Parliament President] nor Mr Prodi [European Commission President] were allowed time to deliver the speeches they had prepared for the occasion'. 'Editorial Comments: The EU Charter of Fundamental Rights Still under Discussion' (2001) 38 *CMLRev* 1, 1.

[11] P Eeckhout, 'The EU Charter of Fundamental Rights and the Federal Question' (2002) 39 *CMLRev* 945, 946.

[12] AJ Menéndez, 'Chartering Europe: Legal Status and Policy Implications of the Charter of Fundamental Rights of the European Union' (2000) 40(3) *JCMS* 471, 472.

[13] CHARTE 4105/00.

[14] OJ 2000, C364/1 of 18 December 2000.

[15] Case C-540/03 *European Parliament v Council* [2006] ECR I-5769, para 38. See below text at n 90 for discussion.

At the time of the 2004 Intergovernmental Conference (IGC) the Charter became part of a larger debate on rationalizing EU constitutional law.[16] Thus, the Laeken Declaration instructed a Convention on the Future of Europe to consider, among other matters, 'whether the Charter of Fundamental Rights should be included in the basic treaty'.[17] The task of considering this and other questions in the Declaration was given to a 'Convention' that emulated the body which had drafted the Charter itself.[18] The Convention's Working Group II was assigned the task of considering how the Charter might be incorporated and the implications of such incorporation. The question as to whether the Charter should be incorporated was strictly reserved to the Convention's Plenary.[19] Despite this reservation, the Working Group's final report called for consideration of incorporation 'in a form which would make the Charter legally binding and give it constitutional status'.[20] The Constitutional Treaty, as agreed by the Convention and the later IGC, contained the full Charter as Part II of a three-part text.[21]

The means of this incorporation came under criticism. Sir Francis Jacobs described the Constitutional Treaty as 'wholly unwieldy, a colossus'. Furthermore, he noted that 'the Charter as it emerges in Part II of the Constitutional Treaty is unsatisfactory' and 'is likely to disappoint expectations: to deliver less than it promises'.[22] Some of these criticisms relate to the substance of the Charter and not the manner of incorporation into the Treaty. However, the form of incorporation—an approach that included not just the substantive provisions but also the lengthy preamble—was hardly an example of good draftsmanship.

The rejection of the Constitutional Treaty by the French and Dutch voters ended hopes of ratifying the Constitutional Treaty and with it this form of incorporation. When the Member State governments assembled once more to consider a new treaty, the grander ambitions of the Constitutional Treaty were abandoned. As part of the reconfiguration of the Treaty, it was decided to remove the Charter from the text of the Treaty and instead to insert a cross reference to the Charter in Article 6 of the revised EU Treaty. The intention to

---

[16] Four unresolved matters remained left over from the Nice IGC: the status of the Charter, the role of national parliaments in EU affairs, the division of competences and treaty simplification. See G De Búrca and JB Aschenbrenner, 'European Constitutionalism and the Charter' in S Peers and A Ward (eds), *The European Union Charter of Fundamental Rights* (Hart Publishing, 2004).

[17] European Council, 'Laeken Declaration on the Future of the European Union' Annex I to 'Presidency Conclusions' 14 and 15 December 2001.

[18] For a discussion of the use of the Convention to draft human rights policy see A Williams, 'EU Human Rights Policy and the Convention on the Future of Europe: A Failure of Design' (2003) *ELRev* 794.

[19] The terms of reference for the Working Group were contained in a Memorandum from the Secretariat of the Convention to its Members. See document CONV 72/02, Brussels 31 May 2002.

[20] The draft final report is Working Group II Working Document 25, Brussels 14 October 2002. Members' comments on the draft may be found in Working Group II Working Document 26-REV 1, Brussels 18 October 2002. The final report presented to the Plenary is CONV 354/02, Brussels 22 October 2002.

[21] The horizontal provisions of the Charter were amended prior to inclusion in the Constitutional Treaty. These amendments and their significance are considered in section IV below.

[22] FG Jacobs, *The Sovereignty of Law: The European Way. The Hamlyn Lectures 2006* (Cambridge University Press, 2007) 150–1.

make this amendment was set out in the Presidency Conclusions of June 2007. The fact that the Charter was no longer to be included in the Treaty was only mentioned in a footnote.[23] On 12 December 2007 the (slightly amended) Charter was solemnly proclaimed once more and signed by the Presidents of the European Parliament, the Council and the European Commission. The next day the Treaty of Lisbon was signed by representatives of the Member State governments in the Portuguese capital.

After Lisbon, the Charter—paradoxically, in view of the emphasis of the Cologne Presidency Conclusions on making rights 'more visible to the Union's citizens'—is not contained in the body of the EU Treaty or even in its protocols. Its absence, though perhaps thought important from a political point of view, is without legal significance: Article 6(1) TEU declares that the Charter 'shall have the same legal value as the Treaties'. The attribution of legal force to the Charter remained a highly sensitive matter for two Member States. As a result, a Protocol was added to the Treaty on the application of the Charter to the UK and Poland.[24] Ratification by the final Member State—the Czech Republic—also required a political commitment to include a Protocol on the Charter's application to the Czech Republic in a future treaty.[25] The significance of the Protocol is returned to below. Since its adaptation in 2007, the Charter has not been further amended (despite a brief flirtation with the idea of rendering it in poetic form).[26] Any amendment would presumably also require amendment to Article 6(1) TEU, which refers to the Charter 'as adapted at Strasbourg, on 12 December 2007', if it were to have legal effect via the Treaties.

III. The Protection of Rights by the EU Charter

Despite the desire to make rights more accessible to European citizens, the Charter is not a simple text to read or understand. Here we address the rights and their sources, the difficult distinction between rights, freedom and principles and the relationship with the ECHR.

A. The rights protected and their sources

Articles 1–50 of the EU Charter contain what are referred to in the title of the Charter as 'fundamental rights' and in the last paragraph of its preamble as 'rights, freedoms and principles'—echoing Article 6(1) TEU. The rights are organized in

---

[23] European Council, 'Presidency Conclusions', 21 and 22 June 2007.

[24] Protocol on the Application of the Charter of Fundamental Rights of the European Union to Poland and to the UK.

[25] 'EU Grants Czech Republic Lisbon Treaty Concession' *The Guardian* 30 October 2009.

[26] The EU Fundamental Rights Agency issued in 2010 a tender for poets to rewrite the instrument as an epic poem to raise awareness of its content for European citizens. The project was eventually abandoned following a public outburst by Commissioner Viviane Reding who claimed that 'the language of the Charter is already clear and direct' *EU Observer* 29 April 2010.

six Titles—I: Dignity; II: Freedoms; III: Equality; IV: Solidarity; V: Citizens'
Rights; and VI: Justice. Though that scheme is generally coherent, the names of
the Titles are not an infallible guide to their contents: for example, a majority of the
Articles in V: Citizens' Rights have at least some application to those who are not
citizens of the Union.[27] Title VII, 'General provisions governing the interpretation
and application of the Charter', contains the horizontal provisions, in accordance with
which the rights, freedoms and principles in the Charter must be interpreted.[28]

The sources of the provisions in Titles I–VI are set out in the 'explanations', an
updated version of those prepared under the authority of the Praesidium of the
Convention.[29] The sources most frequently cited in the explanations are the
ECHR,[30] the EC and EU Treaties,[31] the European Social Charter[32] and the Community Charter on the Fundamental Social Rights of Workers.[33] Other international
treaty sources range from the Geneva Convention relating to the status of refugees to
the New York Convention on the Rights of the Child.[34] Judgments of the Court of
Justice are a principal source, for example, of the freedom to conduct a business and
the right to good administration.[35] The constitutional traditions of Member States are
referred to a number of times, usually as a subsidiary source.

It is difficult to point to any right for which there is no template in international
or European Treaties, or the case law of the Court of Justice:[36] but the catalogue of
fundamental rights contained in the Charter is by any standards extensive. To the
extent that the Charter applies to acts of the Member States, it will have the effect of
introducing some principles that have not been acknowledged as fundamental
rights in national law. Where the UK is concerned, that is most obviously the
case in relation to the social and economic rights in Title IV. Even within the
category of orthodox civil liberties, however, new ground is broken by the rule on
the retroactivity of a more lenient penal law,[37] which has not hitherto formed part
of English criminal law or of the ECHR case law.[38]

---

[27] The right to good administration applies to 'every person' (Article 41). The rights regarding
access to documents, the European ombudsman and petitioning the European Parliament apply to
citizens of the Union and to natural and legal persons residing or having their registered office in a
Member State (Articles 42–44). Freedom of movement and residence may be granted to nationals of
third countries legally resident in a Member State (Article 45).

[28] Article 6(1) TEU, third indent.

[29] OJ 2007 C 303/17. The explanations do not have the status of law but are referred to in Article 6
(1) TEU, third indent, and in Article 52(7) of the Charter itself as a source to which 'due regard'
should be paid by Union and national courts in interpreting the Charter.

[30] 19 Articles, including most of the provisions of Titles II and VI.

[31] All the Title V rights, among others.

[32] 13 Articles, including all but the last two Articles of Title IV.

[33] An additional source of some Title III and many Title IV provisions.

[34] Articles 18 and 24 respectively.

[35] Articles 16 and 41 respectively.

[36] Perhaps the closest to a 'new' right is Article 13 ('Freedom of the arts and sciences'), which
provides that 'The arts and scientific research shall be free of constraint' and that 'Academic freedom
shall be respected'. The Explanations note that this right is deduced primarily from the right to
freedom of thought and expression: whether it is so limited in practice remains to be seen.

[37] Article 49(1).

[38] CC Murphy 'The Principle of Legality in Criminal Law under the European Convention of
Human Rights' (2010) *European Human Rights Law Review* 192.

B. Rights, freedoms and principles

Its use in the title of the EU Charter suggests that the phrase 'fundamental rights' is intended as a catch-all term, encompassing not only the classic universal guarantees of freedom from interference by the state but also the right to participation in certain aspects of political, social and economic life and certain rights restricted only to citizens of the Union. The same is true of the German legal term *Grundrechte*, which appears to have been the origin of the term 'fundamental rights' in the case law of the Court of Justice,[39] and which applies to the range of rights and freedoms that are guaranteed by the Basic Law of the Federal Republic.

The words 'right' and 'freedom' are distinguished in the preamble and in a number of Article titles: see for example Articles 2, 3, 6, 9 and 14, which are said to be rights, and Articles 10–13, 15 and 16 which are said in their titles to be freedoms. No consistent or legally relevant distinction is, however, drawn in the Charter between the concepts of right and freedom. Thus, what are described as the 'rights' to liberty and security, private and family life, education, property and asylum are all present in Title II: Freedoms, and the conflation of the two concepts is exemplified by Article 11 which, like its counterparts in the Universal Declaration of Human Rights and the ECHR, protects 'the right to freedom of expression'.[40]

Of greater potential significance is the distinction between rights/freedoms on the one hand, and 'principles' on the other, a distinction which is made in the Preamble, echoed in Article 51(1) 'respect the rights, observe the principles' and given more precise legal effect by Article 52. Article 52(5) provides that the provisions of the Charter which contain principles 'may be implemented' by Union institutions and Member States, and that 'they shall be judicially cognisable only in the interpretation of such acts and in the ruling on their legality'. No such restriction is placed on the 'rights and freedoms' or 'rights' referred to elsewhere in Article 52.

The distinction is evidently intended to be a significant one, given that principles do not give rise to direct claims for positive action by the Union's institutions or Member States.[41] However, it depends upon the existence of a dividing line between provisions of the Charter that contain 'rights' and those that contain 'principles': and the Charter was not drafted with such a distinction in mind.

---

[39] The phrase is not taken from the ECHR, whose full title is the European Convention for the Protection of Human Rights and Fundamental Freedoms. The first cases in which the Court of Justice referred to 'fundamental human rights' and 'fundamental rights' as an integral part of the general principles of Community law were cases in which reliance had been placed on principles derived from the German Basic Law: Case 29/69 *Stauder v City of Ulm* [1969] ECR 419, para 7; Case 11/70 *Internationale Handelsgesellschaft* [1970] ECR 1125, para 4.

[40] Article 19 Universal Declaration of Human Rights, Article 10 ECHR.

[41] As stated in the explanations with regard to Article 52 by reference, inter alia, to existing case law on the precautionary principle. If taken literally, however, the curious result will ensue that the mis-implementation of a principle could be condemned as invalid, whereas in the event that a 'principle' is not implemented, that principle would apparently not be allowable even as an aid to the interpretation of related provisions of law.

Principles which appear unenforceable in the absence of implementing measures (for example the Article 27 principle that workers must be guaranteed information 'under the conditions provided for by Union law and national laws and practices', and the Article 30 provision for protection in the event of unjustified dismissal) are expressly described in their titles or their texts as rights. Conversely, the only provision referring to 'principles' in its title is Article 49: 'Principles of legality and proportionality of criminal offences and penalties'. Yet that Article confers rights that the Court of Justice has long felt able to apply without the need for implementing legislation.[42]

The explanations shed limited light on the problem when they cite Articles 25, 26 and 37 (concerning, respectively, the rights of the elderly, the integration of persons with disabilities and environmental protection) as examples of principles, and Articles 23, 33 and 34 as provisions containing 'both elements of a right and of a principle'.[43] Only one of those six examples (Article 34) includes the phrase 'in accordance with the rules laid down by Union law and national laws and practices', which might have been thought to be a good indicator of a 'principle' requiring implementation;[44] and that is an Article which, despite being qualified in all respects by that phrase, is said in the explanations to include elements of a right. In the absence of precise guidance, the distinction between rights and principles, though important, seems set to remain obscure and unpredictable.

C. The relationship with the ECHR

Some ECHR rights are simply copied into the Charter. For example, the Article 3 prohibition on torture and inhuman or degrading treatment or punishment is replicated in Article 4 of the Charter. Others are updated in minor respects: 'correspondence' in Article 8 ECHR is replaced by 'communications' in Article 7 of the Charter; while others are reformulated more significantly. An example of the latter tendency is Article 8(1) ECHR, which is broken into its component parts, as they have been elaborated by the Strasbourg case law, and spread over Article 3 (integrity of the person), Article 7 (respect for private and family life) and Article 8 (protection of personal data).

Painstaking attempts, watched with close attention from Strasbourg, have been made to ensure that the Charter is interpreted consistently with the ECHR.[45] The central mechanism is Article 52(3), which provides that insofar as the Charter

---

[42] Case C-63/83 *R v Kent Kirk* [1984] ECR 2689, para 22. See also Article 23, which describes the judicially enforceable right to equality between women and men as 'the principle of equality'.

[43] It is not plain whether these hybrid Articles contain separate rights and principles or whether the concepts of rights and principles are blended in a single provision.

[44] In the light particularly of Article 1(2) of the UK–Poland Protocol, discussed at section IV, B below, which states 'for the avoidance of doubt' that nothing in Title IV creates justiciable rights applicable to Poland or the UK except insofar as they have provided for such rights in their national law. It should be noted, however, that not all the Title IV rights are qualified in that way: see Articles 29 (access to placement services); 31 (working conditions); 32 (child employment); and 33(2) (maternity protection).

[45] References to the Charter in the case law of the European Court of Human Rights are considered in section V,B below.

contains rights which correspond to rights guaranteed by the ECHR, the meaning and scope of Charter rights shall be the same as those laid down by the ECHR. That statement is, however, qualified by the next sentence, which provides that Article 52(3) 'shall not prevent Union law providing more extensive protection'. This suggests that the ECHR is intended to function as a floor but not necessarily as a ceiling.[46]

There are obvious examples of Charter provisions which do provide more extensive protection than the ECHR. Thus, Article 21 of the Charter on non-discrimination goes further than Article 14 ECHR as the former is applicable even outside the scope of the other protected rights.[47] The right to a fair hearing under Article 47 of the Charter is not limited, as is Article 6(1) ECHR, to disputes relating to civil rights and obligations. Even where Charter and ECHR provisions are identical in scope, Article 52(3) may be assumed, consistently with the Strasbourg case law on the duties of contracting states, to permit a more generous interpretation of the Charter right.[48]

Under the Convention scheme, the permitted grounds for interference with qualified rights such as Articles 8–11 ECHR are specified individually in the second paragraph of those Articles. The Charter takes the alternative approach of a general clause: Article 52(1) allows proportionate limitations to be made, if they are provided for by law, are necessary and genuinely meet objectives of general interest recognized by the Union or the need to protect the rights and freedoms of others. Any impression that no limits are placed on the permitted grounds for derogation is, however, illusory, because the effect of Article 52(3) is to prohibit derogations on grounds other than those sanctioned in the ECHR. The attractive simplicity of the single derogation clause is thus also illusory. The Charter is not a self-contained document: a copy of the ECHR needs to be at hand for the purpose of assessing the scope of the power to derogate from the rights that it guarantees.

D. An exhaustive catalogue of rights?

While the Charter's catalogue of rights is extensive, it would be surprising if the Court of Justice were to treat it as exhaustive. By its amendments and additions to the ECHR, the Charter itself acknowledges that the formulation of fundamental rights is a dynamic process. Furthermore, Article 6(1) TEU, which recognizes the Charter and accords it the same legal value as the Treaties, is followed by Article 6 (3) which provides that fundamental rights as guaranteed by the ECHR and as they result from the constitutional traditions common to the Member States shall constitute general principles of the Union's law. The freedom of the Court of

---

[46] Article 53 of the Charter, with its reference to the ECHR and Member States' constitutions, also evidences this point.

[47] It also goes further than the 12th Protocol to the ECHR by expressly including genetic features, disability, age and sexual orientation as grounds on which discrimination shall be prohibited.

[48] Save possibly in those relatively uncommon cases where two rights are in opposition to one another, with the result that a generous interpretation of one implies a narrow interpretation of the other.

Justice to identify and develop fundamental rights not contained in the Charter appears thereby to be expressly preserved.

Difficult questions may arise as to whether such judicially developed fundamental rights are subject to the same or analogous restrictions, as regards their application, as the rights contained in the Charter. Those seeking to restrict the application of the Charter (or restrict the development of fundamental rights more generally) will no doubt argue that the scope to rely on fundamental rights, similar to those in the Charter, is limited by the doctrine of *lex specialis*, and that even where such reliance is permitted, the limitations on the enforceability of the Charter rights should apply by analogy. The Precise scope of the Charter in relation to Member States has not yet been resolved—as has been pointed out by more than one Advocate General—since its coming into force with the Lisbon Treaty.[49]

IV. Application of the Charter Rights

The scope of application of the Charter is indicated by the first of its 'horizontal' provisions, Article 51, and by a number of Protocols, notably the UK–Poland Protocol, to the Treaty of Lisbon. These are considered in turn, followed by comments on the UK–Ireland Protocol on the area of freedom, security and justice and some recent UK case law on the application of the Charter rights.

A. Article 51 of the Charter

Article 51(1), as stated in the explanations, establishes that the Charter applies primarily to the institutions, bodies, offices and agencies of the Union, in compliance with the principle of subsidiarity. The institutions are defined in Article 13(1) TEU, and 'bodies, offices and agencies' is a comprehensive formulation, from which no authority set up by the Treaties or by secondary legislation is likely to be excluded.[50]

More problematic is the interpretation of Article 51 as it applies to the Member States. By its terms, the Charter applies 'only when they are implementing Union law'.[51] On the face of it, this is a narrow formulation, reflecting those cases in which fundamental rights have been held to apply to Member States when giving effect in national law to the requirements of EU rules.[52] However, other cases—also referred to in the explanations—stand for the significantly broader proposition that funda-

---

[49] Case C-108/10 Ivana Scattolon Opinion of Bot AG of 5 April 2011, paras 116–12 and Joined Cases C-83/09 and C-1/10 Magatte Gueye and Valentin Sanchez Salmeron Opinion of Kokott AG of 12 May 2011, para 77.
[50] cf the use of the same formulation in Articles 15 and 16 TFEU.
[51] For a discussion of the drafting of this clause, see P Eeckhout, 'The EU Charter of Fundamental Rights and the Federal Question' (2002) 39 *CMLRev* 945, at 954.
[52] Case 5/88 *Wachauf* [1989] ECR 2609, para 19; Case C-292/97 *Karlsson* [2000] ECR I-2737, para 37. These cases (each of which is cited in the explanations) concern national implementation of Community milk quota rules.

mental rights may be invoked in relation to measures that *come within the scope* of Union law—a formulation which includes measures taken by Member States with a view not to implementing but to *derogating from* Union rules.[53]

Whatever the literal words of Article 51, it seems inconceivable that the Court would retreat from the position established in relation to the general principle of fundamental rights and interpret the Charter as applicable to Member States only when giving effect to Union law. The High Court in England has indeed already ruled that a Member State, in exercising a power of derogation, is acting within the material scope of Union law for the purposes of the applicability of the Charter.[54] Yet once it is accepted that the Charter can apply also to national measures derogating from Union law, its application becomes potentially extremely broad. The remarkable range of national activity falling within the scope of the 'four freedoms'—particularly the free movement of goods and the freedom to provide services—is evident from cases such as *Carpenter*,[55] *Karner*[56] and *Derwin*.[57] When the deportation of a third country national has to comply with fundamental rights because of its incidental effect on occasional cross-frontier service provision by the deportee's husband (*Carpenter*), and when an apparently domestic concern such as the banning of fox hunting in England has (at least arguably) to be reviewed for compliance with general principles of EU law because of its possible impact on the import of hunting horses from Ireland, and the desire of Belgians to visit England to hunt (*Derwin*), it will be apparent that the scope of EU law, and thus the applicability of the Charter to national measures, may, with a little lawyerly or judicial imagination, be rendered very broad indeed. Early indications are that the Court may indeed be encouraged to take a broad view of the applicability of the Charter to actions of the Member States.[58]

Article 51(2), building on Article 6(1), second indent, and the reference in Article 51(1) to 'the limits of the powers of the Union as conferred on it in the Treaties', confirms that the Charter does not in itself serve as a distinct legal basis for competences and tasks not otherwise provided for. This point is reaffirmed by Declaration number 1 attached to the Lisbon Treaty.[59] Similarly, by Article 52(2), rights recognized by the Charter for which provision is made in the Treaties shall be exercised under the conditions and within the limits defined by the Treaties. This seems clear and uncontentious. The likely influence of the Charter will not be as a distinct legal basis for legislation, or as a means of bypassing the legal bases set out in the Treaties, but as an aid to the interpretation of the Treaties and measures adopted under them, and as a benchmark against which the validity of such measures—as well as of national measures falling within the scope of Union law—may be judged.

---

[53] Case C-260/89 *ERT* [1991] ECR I-2925, para 43.

[54] *R (Zagorski) v Secretary of State for Business, Innovation & Skills* [2010] EWHC 3110 (Admin), paras 66–71: see further below under section IV, D.

[55] Case C-60/00 *Carpenter* [2002] ECR I-6279.

[56] Case C-71/02 *Karner* [2004] ECR I-3025.

[57] *R (Derwin and others) v Attorney General* [2007] QB 305 (Court of Appeal), [2008] 1 AC 719 (House of Lords).

[58] Case C-34/09 *Zambrano*, Opinion of Sharpston AG of 30 September 2010, paras 156–77. See below text at n 100.

[59] 'Declaration Concerning the Charter of Fundamental Rights of the European Union' OJ C 306/ 249 17.12.2009.

B. The UK–Poland Protocol

Speaking in October 2001, the then UK Minister for Europe, Keith Vaz, claimed 'This is not a litigator's Charter. Nobody can sue on it. Nobody will be able to litigate on it'. Vaz proceeded to suggest that the Charter would be about as persuasive an authority as the *Beano* or *The Sun*.[60] To similar effect, the Prime Minister himself claimed that it was 'absolutely clear that the Charter of Fundamental Rights is not going to be justiciable in British courts or alter British law'.[61] While Messrs Blair and Vaz appear to have been proven wrong, discord between the legal status of the Charter and political acceptance of that status remains.

Having succeeded in limiting the Charter's effect when it was first agreed in 2000, the proposed incorporation of the Charter by the Lisbon Treaty led to renewed calls in the UK for an opt-out. The principal aim of the UK Protocol was to limit the impact of the economic and social rights in the Charter in the UK's legal systems. During the drafting of the Charter, it was the UK that argued for such rights to be limited by reference to 'national laws and practices'.[62] This limitation is cited in relation to workers' rights and collective bargaining,[63] social security,[64] health care[65] and access to services of general economic interest.[66] Article 52(6) adds that full account shall be taken of national laws and practices as specified in the Charter. In addition to these provisions, the UK insisted upon a Protocol to the Lisbon Treaty, which subsequently attracted the support of Poland. The Czech Republic, which already has a Declaration to the Lisbon Treaty addressing the Charter, extracted an agreement to take the benefit of the UK–Poland Protocol when the Member States next enter into a treaty.[67]

A threshold question in relation to the Protocol is whether it provides a limited opt-out from the Charter in favour of specific Member States (Poland, the UK and in due course the Czech Republic), or whether it simply clarifies the uniform effect of the Charter across all Member States. The text of the Protocol is not wholly clear on the point. In favour of the former proposition is the fact that Poland and the UK are singled out in the title of the Protocol, in its preamble and in each of its Articles. Furthermore, the 11th recital—which 'reaffirms' that the Protocol is without prejudice to the application of the Charter 'to other Member States'—might be

---

[60] *The Times* 14 October 2000.

[61] 'EU Leaders Agree on Reform Treaty' *BBC News* 23 June 2007.

[62] Lord Goldsmith noted of this reference to 'national laws and practices' that it 'was a reference that was (rightly) reported at the time, extremely important to the UK and for which we had to fight very hard'. Lord Goldsmith QC, 'A Charter of Rights, Freedoms and Principles' (2001) 38 *CMLRev* 1201 at 1213.

[63] Articles 27, 28, 30.

[64] Article 34.

[65] Article 35.

[66] Article 36.

[67] The Czech Declaration does little more than reiterate statements from the Charter itself, the explanations and Article 6 TEU regarding the scope and impact of the Charter. 'Declaration by the Czech Republic on the Charter of Fundamental Rights of the European Union' OJ C 306/267 17.12.2009.

taken to imply a differential application to Poland and the UK. In favour of the latter proposition, however, is the 8th recital, which notes the wish of Poland and the UK 'to clarify certain aspects of the application of the Charter' (without geographical limitation). It thus provides a possible explanation of why those states are singled out: as states which requested a clarification (which, once obtained, is of general scope) rather than states in which the Charter is to have some lesser degree of application. In addition, Article 1(2) of the Protocol uses the words 'for avoidance of doubt', as if confirming in relation to two Member States a proposition that can be derived generally from the Charter.

The UK government is certain to argue that the Protocol is an aid to understanding (and limiting) the applicability of the Charter. It appears to have decided, however, that such arguments are likely to be more productive before the Court of Justice if they are coupled with an acceptance that the application of the Charter is uniform, rather than contending for special treatment for the two named Member States. Thus, Lord Goldsmith, UK Attorney General when the Charter was first negotiated, has stated:

It will be clear the UK Protocol does not in any way constitute an 'opt out' in the sense of trying to disapply certain rights to UK citizens. That would be neither necessary nor desirable given that the UK fully accepts the rights reaffirmed in the Charter.

To similar effect, Daniel Denman, who was involved in negotiating the Protocol on behalf of the UK, has written (albeit in a personal capacity):

Although the Protocol is in terms that are specific to the United Kingdom and Poland, it does no more than set out some of the implications of the way in which EU law gives effect to the Charter. So every proposition in the Charter, although it only refers to the United Kingdom and Poland, is equally true for every other Member State.[68]

The European Union Committee of the House of Lords, echoing evidence it had received from the then Lord Chancellor, Jack Straw, concluded in similar vein:

The Protocol should not lead to a different application of the Charter in the United Kingdom and Poland when compared with the rest of the Member States.[69]

It appears unlikely, even if the UK government were to argue for it, that the Court of Justice would interpret the Protocol as providing for differential application of the Charter as between different Member States.

Turning to the operative provisions, Article 1(1) of the Protocol notes that the Charter does not:

extend the ability of the Court of Justice of the European Union, or any court or tribunal . . . of the United Kingdom, to find that the laws, regulations or administrative provisions,

---

[68] D Denman, 'The Charter of Fundamental Rights' (2010) 4 *EHRLR* 349–59, 355.
[69] 'The Treaty of Lisbon: An Impact Assessment', 10th Report of Session 2007–2008, HL Paper 62–1, 5.42, 5.96 and 5.103(d). The members of the Committee (whose conclusions, however, carry no judicial weight) included Lord Mance, then a Law Lord and now a member of the Supreme Court.

practices or action of... the United Kingdom are inconsistent with the fundamental rights, freedoms and principles that it reaffirms.

The key term here is 'extend'. Article 1(1) makes it clear that the Charter cannot of itself afford a *new* competence to the courts of Poland, the UK or the Union. However, it does not limit their *existing* competences. Since national and EU courts have long possessed the competence to measure national law within the scope of EU law against the yardstick of EU fundamental rights, freedoms and principles, and since those rights freedoms and principles are said only to be *re-affirmed* by the Charter, it will no doubt be argued—with some force—that the Article 1(1) prohibition on the extension of powers has little if any practical effect. As Lord Goldsmith expressed the point:

As the Charter reflects only existing rights, the underlying rights will continue to have effect in the UK, as in all Member States, as they always have done.[70]

He went on to suggest that were the courts to 'seek to conjure new or extended rights out of the Charter, then the UK's Protocol would indeed have teeth'. This may be correct. However, it is not easy to see how Article 1(1) of the Protocol could prevent the Court of Justice from identifying 'new or extended rights' as aspects of the general principles of law whose continuance is assured by Article 6(3) of the TEU. That is an ability that the Court of Justice has always possessed, and that the Charter cannot therefore be accused of extending.

   The solidarity rights in Title IV receive special treatment in Article 1(2) of the Protocol, which declares 'in particular and for the avoidance of doubt' that nothing in Title IV creates justiciable rights applicable to Poland or the UK except insofar as is provided for in their national laws.[71] The phrase 'for the avoidance of doubt' appears to suggest that no special rule is intended to apply to the UK and Poland. It may therefore be that Article 1(2) of the Protocol is admitted as an aid to the interpretation of Article 52, which governs the scope of the Charter rights and principles in all cases. The authority accorded to 'principles' in Article 52(5) appears similar to the authority accorded to solidarity provisions in Article 1(2) of the Protocol: in each case, they are to be judicially cognizable (or to create justiciable rights) only when implemented by national legislation.[72]

---

[70] The Rt Hon Lord Goldsmith QC, 'The Charter of Fundamental Rights: Speech to BIICL' 15 January 2008.
   [71] 'Solidarity rights' are actually far less controversial in Poland than they are in the UK, as may be seen from Declaration 62 to the Lisbon Treaty, which pays tribute to the struggle for solidarity rights in that Member State and declares that Poland 'fully respects social and labour rights, as established by European Union law': 'Declaration by the Republic of Poland Concerning the Protocol on the Application of the Charter of Fundamental Rights of the European Union in Relation to Poland and the United Kingdom', OJ C 306/249, 17.12.2009. Declaration 61 would suggest that the concerns which impelled the then Polish Government to associate itself with the Protocol had more to do with 'public morality, family law, as well as the protection of human dignity and respect for human physical and moral integrity': Declaration by the Republic of Poland on the Charter of Fundamental Rights of the European Union', OJ C 306/270, 17.12.2009.
   [72] It seems difficult, however, to argue, consistently with the explanations, that the 'principles' referred to in Article 52(5) are coterminous with the Title IV provisions referred to in Article 1(2) of

Six of the solidarity provisions already contain a reference to 'national laws and practices'[73] and so it is unlikely that Article 1(2) of the Protocol offers any further limitation on them. However, a further six solidarity provisions do not contain this reference: right of access to placement services, fair and just working conditions, prohibition of child labour and protection of young people at work, family and professional life, environmental protection and consumer protection.[74] Several of these Articles are not formulated as rights as such but rather as broad statements of social principle. For example, Article 33(1) declares that the family 'shall enjoy legal, economic and social protection'. Article 37 calls for a 'high level of environmental protection' while Article 29 requires Union policies to 'ensure a high level of consumer protection'. Article 1(2) of the Protocol appears to confirm that none of these provisions can be justiciable in the UK or in Poland (or, it would seem, in any other Member State) unless it is so provided in their national law. In relation to those Articles, therefore, the Protocol may prove to be of real legal significance—if, that is, the same conclusion cannot be reached by the limitation on the justiciability of 'principles' accorded by Article 52(5) of the Charter.

Article 2 of the Protocol provides that where a provision of the Charter refers to national laws and practices, it shall only apply to Poland and the UK to the extent that the rights or principles that it contains are recognized in the law or practices of those states. This appears not to be a further limitation, but rather a clarification of what should already be obvious from the references to national law and practice in the Charter: that those provisions operate as limits on the operation of the relevant Charter principles.[75]

C. The UK–Ireland Protocol

The UK–Ireland Protocol on the area of freedom, security and justice may also impact on the application of the Charter in the UK.[76] That Protocol exempts the UK and Ireland from measures adopted under Title V of Part Three of the Treaty on the Functioning of the European Union. Thus, the UK participates in the area of freedom, security and justice on a measure-by-measure basis considering each legislative proposal on its merits. A question which is likely to arise is whether or not the Charter and jurisprudence based on the Charter applies in the UK where that

the Protocol. As discussed in section III, B above, the examples of 'principles' given in the explanations are inconsistent with the suggestion that 'principles' are limited to Title IV, or indeed with the suggestion that they are restricted to provisions which are expressly stated to take effect only under the conditions provided for by national laws and practices.

[73] Articles 27, 28, 30, 34 (all three parts), 35 and 36.

[74] Articles 29, 31, 32, 33, 37 and 38 respectively.

[75] A point reinforced by Article 52(6) of the Charter. For a well-known application of this principle in the context of Article 28 of the Charter (right to collective bargaining and action), see Case C-438/05 *International Transport Workers' Federation* (*Viking*) [2007] ECR I-10779, para 44. For a discussion see C Barnard, 'The "Opt-Out" for the UK and Poland from the Charter of Fundamental Rights: Triumph of Rhetoric over Reality?' Conference Paper 11–12 April 2010 at 12–15.

[76] Protocol on the Position of the United Kingdom and Ireland in Respect of the Area of Freedom, Security and Justice.

Member State has not opted in to a measure. A literal application of the Article 51 test on 'implementing Union law' suggests that the UK should not be bound by the Charter in such instances. However, if the Charter applies more broadly within the 'scope' of EU law, the answer is less clear. It seems at least possible that UK justice and home affairs legislation might be considered to remain within the scope of EU law, even in circumstances where the UK had not opted-in to a Union measure. The Member State would be derogating from the harmonized rules by not opting-in, but would still be acting within the scope of EU law when it adopted national legislation in this sphere.[77] The applicability of the Charter under these circumstances will need to be tested before the courts. It may be difficult to conceive of an appropriate test case as the advantages to an applicant of invoking the Charter over the ECHR in cases of domestic criminal justice may be minimal due to the equivalent protection given to the relevant rights. However, the existing case law suggests that it would be foolish to bet against some such litigation arising in the coming years.

D. UK case law on the Charter

The status of the Protocol arose soon after the coming into force of the Lisbon Treaty in a case variously known as *S, NS* and *Saeedi*.[78] The claimant asylum-seeker sought unsuccessfully to rely on the Charter to contest the decision of the UK government to return him under the Dublin Regulation to Greece, where he said his Charter rights would not be respected—a claim supported by the United Nations High Commissioner for Refugees. Cranston J noted without comment the conclusions of the European Union Committee to the effect that the UK and Poland were not put in a special position by reason of the Charter,[79] before concluding that:

Given the Polish and United Kingdom Protocol, the Charter cannot be directly relied on as against the United Kingdom although it is an indirect influence as an aid to interpretation.[80]

In the ensuing appeal, the Secretary of State conceded the applicability of the Charter to the appellant's case but continued to dispute the scope of protection provided. The Court of Appeal referred the matter to the Court of Justice for consideration of, among other questions, the scope and applicability of Articles 1, 4, 18, 19(2) and 47 of the Charter.[81] The final question referred is whether the

---

[77] Compare the rejection by the English High Court, in a somewhat different context, of the argument 'that in the present case the Defendant has decided not to legislate and that it is difficult to see how a Member State, in deciding not to legislate, can be described as "implementing EU law" even if, had it done so, it would have been acting under a power of derogation conferred by the EU Regulation': *R (Zagorski) v Secretary of State for Business, Innovation & Skills* [2010] EWHC 3110 (Admin), paras 69–70. See further below under section IV, D.

[78] *R (S) v Secretary of State for the Home Department* [2010] EWHC 705 Admin; *R (NS) v Secretary of State for the Home Department* [2010] EWCA Civ. 990.

[79] [2010] EWHC 705 Admin, para 58.

[80] Ibid para 155.

[81] The case has been registered as C-411/10 *NS v Secretary of State for the Home Department* OJ C 274/21, 9.10.2010.

answer to the preceding questions are 'qualified in any respect' by the Protocol. As such, the Court of Justice is being invited to offer a definitive opinion on the status of the Protocol in EU law. The Opinion of Advocate General Trstenjak has come to a similar conclusion noting that the question could be 'easily answered'.[82] At the time of writing it remains to be seen whether the Court follows the Advocate General's lead. Whatever the outcome of *Saeedi*, claimants in the UK seem certain to argue for an extensive application of the Charter in order to take advantage of rights or remedies that are not available to them under the Human Rights Act. Since the majority of Charter rights are not derived from the ECHR, and since a breach of EU law (unlike a breach of a Convention right under the Human Rights Act) carries with it the possibility of disapplying even primary legislation, there are strong incentives for developing such arguments.

An imaginative attempt to apply the Charter, on the basis of its allegedly broader scope *ratione personae* than the ECHR, has already been made in the case of *R (Zagorski) v Secretary of State for Business, Innovation & Skills*.[83] The claimant, a death row prisoner in Tennessee, sought to rely upon the Charter in order to require the UK government to prevent the export of a drug used in lethal injections. The Human Rights Act was of no use because Article 1 ECHR requires rights and freedoms to be secured only to those within the jurisdiction of contracting states.[84] The applicant argued, however, that the Charter contained no equivalent jurisdictional limitation. Rejecting that argument, Lloyd Jones J held that an equivalent limitation on the personal application of the Charter was afforded by the stipulation in Article 52(3) that the 'scope' of Charter rights was to be the same as that of the equivalent ECHR rights. Were it to be otherwise, 'the Charter would confer such rights on anyone, anywhere in the world, regardless of whether they have any connection with the EU'.[85] Lloyd Jones J also commented on the UK–Poland Protocol, noting that Article 1(1) could be read as precluding the claim under the Charter. However, he declined to rule on this ground because of the reference pending before the Court of Justice in *Saeedi*. The *Zagorski* judgment evidences both the potential for imaginative litigation based on the Charter and the need for courts to read the various human rights instruments in tandem with each other.

Other national courts have of course also made use of the Charter. A reference to the Court of Justice from a Belgian court asks if Article 35 of the Charter, which provides for 'a high level of human rights protection' precludes Belgium from permitting the manufacture, importation, promotion and sale of smoking tobacco.[86] In Germany, the Higher Regional Court in Stuttgart has used the Charter to read a proportionality requirement into national legislation on the European Arrest Warrant.[87] There is likely to be a steady stream of traffic from national courts to

---

[82] Case C-411/10 *N.S.v Secretary of State for the Home Department* Opinion of Trstenjak AG, para 167.
[83] *R (Zagorski) v Secretary of State for Business, Innovation & Skills* [2010] EWHC 3110 (Admin).
[84] Ibid paras 53–9.
[85] Ibid paras 72–4.
[86] Case C-267/10 *André Rossius v État belge* OJ C 221/22, 14.8.2010.
[87] *General Public Prosecution Services v C* 1 Ausl. (24) 1246/2010 (OLG (Stuttgart)). See J Vogel and JR Spencer, 'Case Comment: Proportionality and the European Arrest Warrant' (2010) *Criminal Law Review* 474 for a translation and brief comment on the judgment.

both Luxembourg and Strasbourg as the limits of Charter protection are tested in the coming years.

V. Use of the Charter before the European Courts

Although only legally binding since the coming into force of the Lisbon Treaty, the Charter has been invoked by both the EU Courts and the European Court of Human Rights since soon after its proclamation. It has become a strong persuasive and eventually binding source of rights before the EU Courts and provided the impetus for review of leading case law in Strasbourg.

A. The Charter before EU Courts

Given the failure of the Convention which drafted it to agree the appropriate role for the Charter in the EU legal order, the task of articulating that role naturally fell to the Courts. Advocates General were the first to invoke the Charter, followed by the Court of First Instance and the Court of Justice. The first, incidental reference to the Charter came from Advocate General Alber in an Opinion concerning the Italian postal service.[88] The first citation by the Court of First Instance merely involved the citation with approval of the rights to sound administration and to an effective remedy.[89] Thus, the Charter was used simply to confirm rights already existing in the EU legal order. Early references to the Charter therefore suggest that the Courts were no clearer on its appropriate use than were the political institutions.

The first reliance on the Charter by the Court of Justice was prompted by its citation in the preamble to the Family Reunification Directive.[90] The Parliament challenged the validity of the Directive, citing a breach of the rights of children as protected by Article 24 of the Charter (among other sources). The Council disputed the use of the Charter, claiming it did not constitute a source of Community law. The Court favoured the Parliament's argument. The Court used the text of the preamble to the Directive and the preamble to the Charter itself to effectively hoist the Council on its own petard. It noted that the Directive claimed to be in compliance with the Charter and that the Charter itself merely affirmed rights already existing in EU law.[91] Although the Parliament was unsuccessful in the claim on its merits, the case clearly established the Charter as a useful benchmark in EU law. It also evidenced the link between legitimacy and potency: the desire to legitimate the Directive by citing the Charter in the preamble rendered the Charter a benchmark against which the substantive law could be reviewed.

---

[88] Case C-340/99 *TNT Traco* [2001] ECR I-4112. A detailed account of early opinions is not offered here. See P Eeckhout, 'The EU Charter of Fundamental Rights and the Federal Question' (2002) 39 *CMLRev* 945, at 948–50.
[89] Case T-54/99 *max.mobil v Commission* [2002] ECR II-313.
[90] Case C-540/03 *Parliament v Council* [2006] ECR I-5769.
[91] Ibid para 38.

The Charter was used in a more systematic fashion by Advocate General Maduro in a case concerning legal privilege and anti-money-laundering legislation.[92] The Advocate General noted that the Charter, then not legally binding, could have a 'dual function'. First, it might give rise to a presumption of the existence of a right, which would need to be confirmed by reference to accepted authorities (for example, the ECHR). Second, where a right does exist in the legal order, the Charter is useful 'for determining the content, scope and meaning' of the right in question. Where a right exists and is interfered with, the Advocate General suggested that the Court should have recourse to Article 52(1) of the Charter to determine the lawfulness of that interference. Such use of the Charter amounts to the strongest possible form of persuasive authority as the only requirement for further authority is to confirm the presumption raised by the Charter which subsequently is used to determine the nature of the right.

Given the reliance on the Charter in the pre-Lisbon years, it was already a familiar part of the legal landscape even before it was given binding force by the Treaty. However, according it 'the same legal value as the Treaties' can only increase its prominence. In the first year of the post-Lisbon settlement, the Charter was cited on 24 occasions by Advocates General, twice by the General Court and in 30 judgments of the Court of Justice.[93] Two recent cases evidence the potential for the Charter to have a broader constitutional impact: *Kücükdeveci* and *Ruiz Zambrano*. The former case concerned a claim of age discrimination based on a German employment law that did not take periods of work served prior to the employee's 25th birthday into account when calculating the notice period prior to dismissal. The German law was incompatible with the requirements of Directive 78/2000, the transposition period for which had passed prior to the applicant's dismissal. However, as the respondent was a private party, the general prohibition on horizontal direct effect would ordinarily have hindered Ms Kücükdeveci's case. Nonetheless, the Court of Justice held that the principle of non-discrimination on grounds of age was a general principle of EU law which was given 'specific expression' in the Directive.[94] The Court also made reference to Article 21(1) of the Charter which declares that '[a]ny discrimination based on ... age ... shall be prohibited'.[95] As a result the Court held that:

It follows that it is the general principle of European Union law prohibiting all discrimination on grounds of age, as given expression in Directive 2000/78, which must be the basis of the examination of whether European Union law precludes national legislation such as that at issue in the main proceedings.[96]

The Court proceeded to examine the matter at hand and concluded that the principle, as given expression by the Directive, precluded the German national

---

[92] C-305/05 *Ordre des barreaux francophones et germanophone* [2007] ECR I-5305.
[93] Data based on a search of the Eur-lex database on 26 November 2010.
[94] Case C-555/07 *Kücükdeveci v Swedex GmbH & Co* Judgment of the Court of Justice (Grand Chamber) of 19 January 2010, para 21.
[95] Ibid para 22.
[96] Ibid para 27.

legislation. The case appears to further erode the prohibition on the horizontal direct effect of directives.[97] To the existing list of exceptions to this prohibition it is necessary to add the proviso that unimplemented directives may have horizontal effect where they constitute the expression of a general principle of EU law. The Court of Justice's decision does not set out criteria to explain which principles may be relied upon in this way and which may not. The reference to 'general principles' may hearken to more fundamental values than simply the rights, freedom and principles contained in the Charter.[98] Nonetheless, in both *Viking* and *Kücükdeveci* the Charter was held to be evidence of the existence of a general principle.[99] Thus, *Kücükdeveci* underlines the potential significance of the Charter as a tool of EU law. If Charter rights are considered either to be, or to evidence the existence of, 'general principles' then where a directive gives effect to such a right it may be held to have horizontal effect prior to the directive being transposed. As a result, while the Charter cannot extend the Union's competences it may be used to facilitate the swifter implementation of EU law in national legal orders. This is most likely to be the case when the directive in question is one which intends to give further effect to fundamental rights protection.

The Opinion of Advocate General Sharpston in *Ruiz Zambrano* offers the potential for the Charter to have an even greater impact.[100] The latter part of the Opinion addressed the need to determine with certainty what 'the scope of Union law' means when fundamental rights are at issue. While the solution was not required for the case before her, she proposed a new formula for the determination of this question. The Advocate General argued that the scope should depend, for the purpose of the applicability of the Charter to the acts of the Member States, on the existence of a material EU competence, even if that competence had not yet been exercised.[101] Four reasons were offered for this new formula: first, it avoids the need to create 'fictitious' links with EU law; second, it keeps EU fundamental rights protection within the boundaries of EU competences; third, it would encourage Member States to adopt minimum rules on protection in key areas—for example, immigration and criminal law; and fourth, it would be consistent with a coherent idea of European citizenship.[102] On the latter point Advocate General Sharpston finds common cause with Advocate General Maduro, who argued in *Centro Europa 7* that an EU citizen was entitled to travel to another Member State saying 'civis europeus sum' and be treated 'in accordance with a common code of fundamental values'.[103] However, if Advocate General Sharpston's solution were adopted, it appears that the , Charter would be applicable in a case such as *Carpenter*[104], even if the

---

[97] As most readers will know, there were previously three ways in which that prohibition was eroded: (1) by the Court of Justice's broad conception of the 'state'; (2) by the requirement that national law be interpreted in a manner that conforms with unimplemented directives; and (3) by requiring national law to be set aside if it has not met with procedural or technical requirements laid down in a directive. See S Prechal, *Directives in EC Law* 2nd edn (Oxford University Press, 2006) 255–60.

[98] For a wider discussion see A Wiesbrock 'Case Note' (2010) 11(5) *German Law Journal* 539.

[99] *Viking*, above n 75 at para 43.

[100] C-34/09 *Gerardo Ruiz Zambrano v Office national de l'emploi* Opinion Sharpston AG of 30 September 2010.

[101] Ibid para 163.

[102] Ibid paras 165–70.

[103] C-380-05 *Centro Europa 7 Srl* [2008] ECR I-349.

[104] Case C-60/00 *Carpenter v Secretary of State for the Home Department* [2002] ECR I-6279.

applicant's husband had never exercised a free movement right. The federalizing effect of such a choice was clear to the Advocate General, who noted that such a change 'requires both an evolution in the case-law *and* an unequivocal political statement from the constituent powers of the EU (its Member States), pointing at a new role for fundamental rights in the EU'.[105] Such an evolution would be a long and uncertain process but the recent case law suggests that if it does occur the Charter is likely to play a role. The ECJ did not address the Advocate General's proposition in its judgment in *Ruiz Zambrano*. However, the Court did hold that Member States were precluded from taking action that would deprive a Member State national of 'genuine enjoyment of the substance of the rights attaching to the status of European Union citizen—even if that national had never travelled to another Member State.[106] Taken together, *Kücükdeveci* and *Ruiz Zambrano* suggest there may be scope for a renewed legal integration in the EU, with the Court of Justice as the driver and fundamental rights as the engine.

B. The Charter and the European Court of Human Rights

A less widely anticipated development than the use of the Charter by the Union courts is the role that it has begun to play in the jurisprudence of the European Court of Human Rights. The first reference to the Charter came in 2001 when Judge Costa's separate opinion in *Hatton & Others v UK* referred to Article 37 of the Charter as an example of the growing recognition of the importance of environmental rights.[107] In 2002 it was regarded as a persuasive authority in a joint partly dissenting opinion of Judge Sir Nicholas Bratza and Judges Fuhrmann and Tulkens.[108] Later that year the Grand Chamber confirmed the Charter's status as an authority when it was considered in both *Goodwin* and *I*.[109] Subsequently, the Court has accepted what might be described as the orthodox view regarding the Charter and its significance in the EU legal order. In *Bosphorus*, the Strasbourg Court declared that:

Although not fully binding, the provisions of the Charter of Fundamental Rights of the European Union were substantially inspired by those of the Convention, and the Charter recognises the Convention as establishing the minimum human rights standards.[110]

The Court observed that the Constitutional Treaty would have made the Charter 'primary law' for the EU. In 2007 the Grand Chamber held that the explanations attached to the Charter 'do not have equal authority as the Charter' but that they are a 'valuable tool of interpretation'.[111] Most recently, in *Neulinger and Shuruk*, it observed that the Charter 'became legally binding with the entry into

---

[105] Ibid para 173.
[106] Case C-34/09 *Gerardo Ruiz Zambrano v Office National de L'emploi* Judgment of the Court of 8 March 2011.
[107] *Hatton & Others v United Kingdom* [2002] 34 EHRR 1.
[108] *Fretté v France* [2002] 38 EHRR 438.
[109] *Christine Goodwin v UK* [2002] 35 EHRR 18; *I v UK*.
[110] *Bosphorus v Ireland* [2006] 42 EHRR 1, para 159.
[111] *Eskelinen & Others v Finland* [2007] 45 EHRR 43, para 30.

force of the Lisbon Treaty'.[112] Thus, the Strasbourg judiciary have kept a watchful eye on the Charter's evolving legal status and have used it where appropriate.

The use of the Charter as a persuasive authority is demonstrated by decisions in a number of cases relating to transsexual and same-sex marriage. In *Goodwin*, the European Court departed from its earlier jurisprudence on the rights of transsexuals following gender reassignment surgery.[113] The Court found that the failure to allow a transsexual to change the sex recorded on their birth certificate was a violation of Article 8 ECHR. In relation to Article 12 ECHR (right to marry), the Court noted that, unlike the Convention article, the language of Article 9 of the Charter omitted, 'no doubt deliberately' the phrase 'man and woman'. It concluded that these words could no longer be interpreted in a strictly biological sense and that the applicant's status as a transsexual should not be a barrier to her exercising her right to marry. As such, it found a violation of Article 12 ECHR. The case of *I v UK*, decided on the same day, also followed this logic.[114] While it appears from the text of the judgment that the impetus for the re-evaluation of the Court's case law was the evolving social and political recognition of the rights of transsexuals across Europe,[115] its invocation as evidence of the new international consensus demonstrates the Charter's status as a persuasive authority in Strasbourg.

The limits of that persuasiveness have recently been tested in *Schalk and Kopf*. The 2010 case concerned a challenge to Austria's failure to permit same-sex marriages. The Court held that, in a historical context, it was clear that the right to marry was understood as being exercised by a man and woman.[116] Furthermore, it held that there is no 'European consensus' on same-sex marriage.[117] It distinguished the situation of couples seeking same-sex marriage to that of a couple wherein one party is a post-operative transsexual. Turning to the Charter, the Court acknowledged that Article 9, which did not contain a 'man and women' clause, was now legally binding in the EU. However, it noted that the explanations of the Article made reference to national law and observed that 'marriage has deep-rooted social and cultural connotations which may differ largely from one society to another'.[118] Thus, while it found that the Article 12 ECHR right cannot be limited to opposite-sex couples, states were not yet under an obligation to permit same-sex marriage. In a concurring opinion, Judge Malinverni (joined by Judge Kovler) strongly denied the applicability of Article 9 to the interpretation of the Convention on this point. While *Schalk and Kopf* may simply be an idiosyncratic example of reliance on the Charter it may also be evidence of some trends in the case law. First, the Court has used the Charter not just to revise, but effectively to reverse its previous case law. Second, the Court's actions in doing so have not always attracted unanimous support.

---

[112] *Neulinger and Shuruk v Switzerland* Judgment of the Grand Chamber 6 July 2010, para 55.
[113] *Christine Goodwin v UK* [2002] 35 EHRR 18.
[114] *I v UK* [2003] 36 EHRR 53.
[115] See A Mowbray, 'An Examination of the European Court of Human Rights' Approach to Overruling its Previous Case Law' (2009) *Human Rights Law Review* 179, 194.
[116] *Schalk and Kopf v Austria* Judgment of the Court (First Section) 24 June 2010, para 55.
[117] Ibid para 58.
[118] Ibid para 62.

One of the most dramatic reverses in ECtHR jurisprudence in recent years, *Scoppola (No 2)* involved the reinterpretation of Article 7 ECHR as a result of the Charter.[119] In direct contradiction of its earlier case law, the European Court held that the *nullum crimen* principle in the Convention must now include the retrospective application of a more lenient penalty. The Court's judgment made reference to a number of international instruments which contained the *lex metior* rule including the American Convention on Human Rights, the Rome Statute on the International Criminal Court and the case law of the International Criminal Tribunal for the former Yugoslavia. The Court also made reference to Article 49 of the Charter and the ECJ decision in *Berlusconi and Others*, which found the principle to be part of the common constitutional traditions of the Member States.[120] It therefore held that a consensus had emerged in Europe that the *lex metior* rule was part of European human rights law and as a result found a violation of Article 7 ECHR.[121]

In response to the majority's decision in *Scoppola*, a dissenting opinion criticized the Court's reversal of its earlier case law.[122] The dissent noted that the *X v Germany* precedent had been followed 'relatively recently' in decisions concerning Bulgaria and the UK.[123] While the dissent acknowledged that the Convention was a living instrument, it argued that 'no judicial interpretation, however creative, can be entirely free of constraints'. It concluded that the majority opinion had 're-written' Article 7 ECHR 'to accord with what they consider it ought to have been'. This, the dissent concluded, 'oversteps the limits'. This dissent, which is written with strong references to both textual and teleological approaches to judicial interpretation, reflects an uneasiness on the part of certain members of the judiciary when it comes to significantly revising rights. Although the Charter was not explicitly mentioned in the opinion, the disquiet expressed might cast doubt over the willingness of all of the judiciary to use the Charter as a vehicle for the evolution of rights.

The Charter has been explicitly discussed in various other concurring and dissenting opinions. In *Martinie v France* three judges issued a separate concurring opinion which suggested that certain aspects of the right to a fair trial should be 'fundamentally reviewed' in light of Article 47 of the Charter.[124] In *VO v France* Judge Ress dissented from the majority decision not to find a violation of Article 2 ECHR, noting that he considered that 'Article 2 applies to human beings even before they are born'.[125] The judge claimed that this interpretation was 'consistent' with the Charter's approach. The Charter itself does not pronounce on whether there are rights for the unborn, an

---

[119] *Scoppola v Italy (No 2)* Judgment of the Court (Grand Chamber) 17 September 2009.

[120] Joined Cases C-387/02, C-391/02 and C-403/02 *Silvio Berlusconi and others* [2005] ECR I-03565; *Scoppola v Italy (No 2)* Judgment of the Court (Grand Chamber) 17 September 2009, para 105.

[121] *Scoppola v Italy (No 2)* Judgment of the Court (Grand Chamber) 17 September 2009, para 106.

[122] Partly Dissenting Opinion of Judge Nicolaou, Joined by Judges Bratza, Lorenzen, Jociené, Villiger and Sajó.

[123] *X v Germany* [1984] 7 EHRR 152; *Zaprianov v Bulgaria* Admissibility Decision of the Court (First Section) of 6 March 2003; *Le Petit v UK* Judgment of the Court (Fourth Section) of 15 June 2004.

[124] *Martinie v France* [2006] 42 EHRR 15.

[125] *VO v France* [2005] 40 EHRR 259.

issue so far avoided in EU law.[126] It may be that the judge was referring to Article 1 of the Charter which declares human dignity to be inviolable. The existing case law of the European Court of Human Rights on Article 3 ECHR and its prohibition on inhuman and degrading treatment suggests that Article 1 of the Charter might offer fertile ground for judicial interpretation in future.

The Charter occupies a peculiar position for the Strasbourg Court. It is, as the Court has noted, legally binding for 27 of its Members, at least within the scope of EU law. On the other hand, looked at more formally, the Charter can be described as effectively part of an international agreement (the Lisbon Treaty) to which barely half of the Council of Europe members are party. Viewed in this light, it may be overzealous to use the Charter to revolutionize rights protection across all Council of Europe states. However, the case law of the Strasbourg Court to date does suggest a willingness to review the level of protection in light of the Charter. This willingness to revise Convention protection must be considered alongside Article 52 of the Charter which provides for at least equivalent protection of Convention rights under the Charter system. If the Strasbourg Court uses the Charter to revise the Convention, and the Convention interpretation in turn influences the Charter, the result may be ongoing improvement in the level of protection. The relationship between the two courts is referred to in Declaration 2 to the Lisbon Treaty which 'notes the existence of a regular dialogue between the Court of Justice of the European Union and the European Court of Human Rights; such dialogue could be reinforced when the Union accedes to that Convention'.[127] Therefore, those interested in fundamental rights in Europe will need to keep an eye on Strasbourg as well as on Luxembourg to assess the Charter's significance.

VI. Conclusion

By affording the Charter the same legal value as the Treaties, the Member States and institutions—for their various motives—have finally articulated a detailed bill of rights for the EU. That in itself is gratifying for those who saw the Charter as a vehicle for improving the constitutional and political legitimacy of the Union. Together with the creation of the Fundamental Rights Agency, it has also provided a focus for a system of EU human rights protection that will be less reliant than previously on the Council of Europe and that is already beginning to influence the Strasbourg system.[128] It could be argued that nothing much has changed on the judicial plane. The horizontal provisions, supplemented by the UK–Poland Protocol, impose tight prohibitions on the use of the Charter as a legal basis, or as a vehicle for extending the powers of the

---

[126] Case C-159/90 *SPUC v Grogan* [1991] ECR I-4685.

[127] 'Declaration on Article 6(2) of the Treaty on European Union' OJ C 306/249, 17.12.2009.

[128] Though suggestions of an incipient disconnection—or takeover—must be balanced by the Strasbourg-friendly Article 52(3) of the Charter and Article 6(3) TEU, and, more fundamentally, by the requirement that the Union accede to the ECHR, whose significance and implementation is discussed elsewhere in this volume.

Union. While the Charter will be used as a basis for interpreting (and, where appropriate, striking down) both EU measures and national measures falling within the scope of EU law, the general principle of fundamental rights—expressly preserved in the post-Lisbon regime—has long been available for this purpose.

It may well be, however, that the act of codification proves more significant than these dry facts suggest. The Charter may never achieve in Europe the level of popular awareness enjoyed by the Bill of Rights in the United States. But the domestication in a single place of so comprehensive a range of rights will prompt European lawyers, judges and students to read them, to become familiar with them and to apply them. Reduced to written form and given the authority of the Treaties, they have the potential to be developed more consistently and more coherently than is possible when rights have to be identified and applied by judges on a case-by-case basis. One must hope, also, that it will improve the quality of policy-making and legislation within the Union—for while that topic lies outside the scope of this chapter, it is a mistake to judge the efficacy of any human rights instrument by reference only to those matters which come to court.[129]

The subjection of Union and national rules to such a powerful and open-textured instrument does require enormous faith to be placed in the Court of Justice, its ultimate arbiter. Arguments over fundamental rights go, after all, to the heart of what different Member States hold dear, whether it is a particular social model, or economic model, or concept of personal morality. Sensitivity will be required to resolve the inevitable battles about such legal issues as the location and significance of the distinction between rights and principles, the applicability of the Charter outside the territory of the Union, the nature of the link with Union law that is required to trigger Charter protection and the degree to which it applies (if at all) 'horizontally' as against non-public bodies.

The best argument for the Charter is the simplest, and one which should appeal to Europhile and Europhobe alike: the need for robust and accessible judicial protection for individuals against the ever-increasing powers of the Union and of the Member States when acting within the scope of Union law. It is thus a particularly appropriate companion to perhaps the most important of all the Lisbon Treaty developments: the merging of the pillars and the extension of judicial control over such areas as asylum, immigration, national security and criminal justice. Advocate General Sharpston has suggested that in 'the long run, only seamless protection of fundamental rights under EU law . . . matches the concept of EU citizenship'.[130] The reference to the 'long run' was well judged, because as she pointed out, the achievement of that aim will require action by political, as well as legal, institutions. In the meantime, however, the Charter is likely to be invoked in a substantial number of cases. If they are decided wisely, it has the potential to be an effective vehicle for the advancement of civil liberties, fairness and democratic values in the Union.

---

[129] In this respect the scrutiny by the European Commission since 13 March 2001 of all legislative proposals for compliance with the Charter is to be welcomed. See SEC(2001) 380/3, COM(2005) 172 final.

[130] C-34/09 *Gerardo Ruiz Zambrano v Office national de l'emploi* Opinion of Sharpston AG, 30 September 2010, para 170.

8

Accession to the ECHR

Giorgio Gaja

I. Introduction

Under international law the European Convention for the Protection of Human Rights and Fundamental Freedoms (ECHR) is not yet binding for the EU. The EU is not a party to the ECHR. Unlike what possibly occurred with GATT '47, the fact that all the EU Member States are parties to the ECHR does not imply that the EU is also bound in relation to the powers that Member States transferred to the EU. Thus, as was stated in *Matthews v United Kingdom* by the European Court of Human Rights (European Court), 'acts of the EC as such cannot be challenged before the Court because the EC is not a Contracting Party'.[1] Applications to the European Court made against the EC were held by the European Court to be inadmissible *ratione personae*.[2] The same Court maintained in *Bosphorus v Ireland* that, even when an act of the EC appeared to be the origin of an infringement of the ECHR because a Member State was required to implement it, only the Member State could be held responsible.[3] It is clear that accession of the EU to the ECHR is the condition for the ECHR to become legally binding for the EU under international law and for the EU to be held responsible for the infringement of an obligation under the ECHR.

The question whether the EC and later the EU should accede to the ECHR was the object of a lengthy debate among the Member States. One major legal obstacle was represented by the need to amend the Treaties before accession could take place. This was expressed by the European Court of Justice (ECJ) in Opinion 2/94: 'Such modification of the system for the protection of human rights in the Community, with equally fundamental institutional implications for the Community and for the Member States, would be of constitutional significance and would therefore be such as to go beyond the scope of Article 235 [of the EC Treaty]. It

---

[1] ECHR Reports 1999-I 251, 265 (para 32).
[2] This had been expressly stated by the European Commission of Human Rights already in *Confédération Française Démocratique du Travail v the European Communities*, alternatively their Member States (a) jointly and (b) severally Application 8030/77 (1978) 13 DR 231 (para 3).
[3] ECHR Reports 2005-VI 107, 152 (para 137).

could be brought about only by way of Treaty amendment.'[4] After Opinion 2/94, occasions to amend the Treaties in order to make accession possible came with the intergovernmental conferences (IGCs) which led to the Treaties of Amsterdam and Nice but were not seized. The failed Treaty establishing a Constitution for Europe had attempted to provide the necessary legal basis by stating that the EU 'shall seek accession' to the ECHR. The Treaty of Lisbon went one step further. Article 6(2) TEU now reads: 'The Union shall accede to the European Convention for the Protection of Human Rights and Fundamental Freedoms. Such accession shall not affect the Union's competences as defined in the Treaties.' This text does not only provide the legal basis for accession. It makes accession mandatory, although it is clear that accession does not depend only on the will of the EU. Twenty states that are not members of the EU are parties to the ECHR and their consent is also required for accession to take place. Anyway, Protocol No 8 to the Treaties makes it clear that an agreement on accession would have to be concluded and that it should address some complicated questions.

A basic willingness on the part of all the states parties to the ECHR to accept accession of the EU was expressed by an amendment to Article 59 of the ECHR. According to the original text of this Article, only members of the Council of Europe, and thus states, could become parties to the ECHR. A new paragraph providing that 'the European Union may accede to the Convention' was introduced by Protocol No 14 to the ECHR, which entered into force on 1 June 2010. While Protocol No 14 does not specify whether further modifications to the ECHR will be required, the explanatory report to this Protocol says that they 'will be necessary in order to make such accession possible from a legal and technical point of view'[5] and referred to 'a report identifying those issues' that had been adopted in 2002 by the Steering Committee for Human Rights (CDDH).[6]

A new instrument could have provided both for the possibility of the EU becoming a party to the ECHR and for all the other amendments. The provision in Protocol No 14 was thus not strictly necessary. However, acceptance of the amendment to Article 59 of the ECHR by all the states party to the ECHR showed that none of these states had a fundamental objection to accession. This opens the way to meaningful negotiations.

II. The Agreement on Accession

The report adopted by the CDDH discussed the question whether the amendments to the ECHR that accession of the EU will require should be adopted in a protocol to the ECHR or in an agreement on accession.[7] The difference between

---

[4] Opinion 2/94 [1996] ECR I-1759, 1789 (paras 34–5).
[5] 'Explanatory Report' to Protocol No 14, para 101.
[6] 'Study of Technical and Legal Issues of a Possible EC/EU Accession to the European Convention of Human Rights', Doc. DG-(2002)006 of 28 June 2002.
[7] Ibid paras 1–20.

the two options is that a protocol would be concluded only by the states party to the ECHR and would have to be accompanied by accession by the EU as a separate act, while an agreement on accession would be concluded by the EU with all the states party to the ECHR. The EU would take part in the negotiations concerning the amendments whichever option was taken and the final result would in practice be the same.

The explanatory report to Protocol No 14 to the ECHR noted that 'it was considered advisable not to refer to a possible accession treaty in the current protocol so as to keep all options open for the future'.[8] However, the fact of providing in a protocol the possibility for the EU to accede no doubt facilitates the option of concluding an agreement on accession. With regard to the ECHR, standard practice is to include all amendments in protocols, but this could be done in a later protocol consolidating the text.

Protocol No 8 to the Treaties and Article 218(6) and (8) TFEU refer to an 'agreement' on accession. While this wording clearly points to an agreement on accession as the preferred option, it cannot be taken as an absolute requirement from the point of view of EU law. Should the text be in substance negotiated by the EU, there would be indeed little difference between the conclusion of an agreement and the adoption of a protocol to the ECHR. The requirements concerning the agreement on accession could easily be transposed to the acceptance by the EU of the ECHR as amended by the protocol.

The negotiations currently conducted by a working group of the CDDH with the European Commission clearly pursue the aim of adopting an accession agreement. At the time of writing, the text under negotiations is defined as 'Draft Revised Accession Agreement' (Doc. CDDH-UE(2011)10, Appendix III). It will be referred to in the following paragraphs as 'Draft Agreement'.

Protocol No 8 to the Treaties sets out a number of conditions for the agreement on accession to be concluded. The actual inclusion in the agreement of provisions in line with Protocol No 8 will depend on the outcome of the forthcoming negotiations. However, only an agreement on accession that is compatible with what is required by Protocol No 8 could be regarded as lawful under EU law.

The procedural requirements set forth in Article 218 TFEU for the conclusion of the agreement on accession are rather cumbersome. This may seem at odds with the obligation for the EU to accede to the ECHR which is stated in Article 6(2) TEU.[9] One may wonder why, instead of facilitating the conclusion of an agreement on accession, the TFEU requires the Council to obtain the consent of the European Parliament (Article 218(6)(a)(ii)) and then take a unanimous deliberation (Article 218(8)); moreover, 'the decision concluding this agreement shall enter into force after it has been approved by the Member States in accordance with their respective constitutional requirements' (Article 218(8) TFEU). The combination and overall

---

[8] 'Explanatory Report' to Protocol No 14, para 101.
[9] A Gianelli, 'L'adesione dell'Unione europea alla CEDU secondo il Trattato di Lisbona' (2009) *Il Diritto dell'Unione Europea* 678, 696–7.

weight of these requirements finds no parallel with regard to any other agreement to be concluded by the EU.

The requirement that Member States approve the agreement does not make much sense, because it adds little to the need for the same states to ratify the agreement or a protocol in their capacity as parties to the ECHR. The other procedural requirements may be explained by the importance of the actual content of the agreement, which will touch on some politically sensitive issues, some of them listed in Protocol No 8 to the Treaties.

There are signs that several EU institutions intend to influence the outcome of the forthcoming negotiations. While stressing that 'technical impediments should not be allowed to delay the process', the European Parliament requested in a resolution adopted on 19 May 2010 to 'be consulted and involved throughout the negotiation process'.[10] Not surprisingly, the Court of Justice also shows a keen interest and may eventually play a decisive role, since one of the Member States will probably request an opinion of the Court under Article 218(11) TFEU on whether the accession agreement is compatible with the Treaties.

III. The Scope of Rights and Obligations Arising for the EU

Article 6(2) TEU states that accession to the ECHR 'shall not affect the Union's competences as defined in the Treaties'. This is reiterated in the first sentence of Article 2 of Protocol No 8 to the Treaties, according to which the agreement relating to the accession of the EU 'shall ensure that accession of the Union shall not affect the competences of the Union or the powers of its institutions'. Although a neutral term such as 'affect' is used here, the main concern is obviously that the competences of the EU should not be extended as a consequence of accession. This is expressly stated in Article 6(1) TEU with regard to the Charter of Fundamental Rights. Although the wording is different, the concern underlying the two paragraphs of Article 6 TEU seems identical.

It has often been observed that various rights that are conferred by the ECHR and the related protocols have little to do with the activities of the EU. This remark has lost some weight with the progressive expansion of competences of the EU. However, one could still consider that certain human rights are unlikely to be associated with the EU: for instance, rights concerning the fairness of a criminal trial or the right not to be tortured. However, while the EU has not been given the function of promoting these rights, there are acts of EU institutions, concerning for example extradition or expulsion, which should prevent the risk that these rights be infringed, as they would be if a person were extradited or expelled towards a state where torture is likely to be inflicted on him or her. Moreover, when regulating the movement of goods, the EU may contribute to prevent torture by prohibiting

---

[10] Resolution of 19 May 2010 on the institutional aspects of the accession of the European Union to the European Convention for the Protection of Human Rights and Fundamental Freedoms, para 35.

transfer of instruments that may be used for torturing, as was done in Regulation 1236/2005/EC.[11] This points to the conclusion that it would be hard to make a distinction between human rights that are relevant only for a state and those that are relevant also for the EU. All human rights seem to be, at least potentially, relevant for the EU.

The definition of competences of the EU is important insofar as the ECHR sets out a positive obligation. There is nothing in the ECHR which implies that on accession the EU should take on competences that it does not already have. International organizations have a limited capacity, which one cannot reasonably expect to see expanded when they accede to a human rights treaty. It would not be strictly necessary to state in the agreement on accession that the obligations that the EU will acquire under the ECHR do not go further than the actual competences of the EU. However, given the requirement set out in both Article 6(2) TEU and Article 2 of Protocol No 8 to the Treaties, the agreement on accession will no doubt contain a clause specifying that competences of the EU are only those defined in the Treaties and that they are not extended by accession. Article 1(2)(c) of the Draft Agreement runs as follows:

Accession to the Convention and the Protocols thereto shall impose on the European Union obligations with regard only to acts, measures or omissions of its institutions, bodies, offices or agencies, or of persons acting on their behalf. Nothing in the Convention or the Protocols thereto shall require the European Union to perform an act or adopt a measure for which it has no competence.

If the agreement also intended to prevent the EU from implementing positive obligations in the field of concurrent competences that the EU has not yet exercised, certain restrictions concerning the scope of obligations arising from accession for the EU would have to be stated accordingly.

Restrictions of EU rights under the Convention do not necessarily have to correspond to those that relate to the obligations of the EU in view of its limited competences. The EU could promote the protection of all human rights in its external relations in accordance with Article 21(2) TEU, even if it does not have the competence to promote some of those rights internally. However, it is likely that the restrictions that will be defined in the agreement on accession with regard to EU obligations under the ECHR will have an impact on the rights that will be conferred on the EU under the same Convention. Non-member states will probably insist on reciprocity. Thus, it is likely that restrictions due to the limited competences of the EU will similarly affect rights and obligations of the EU under the Convention.

With the proviso that competences of the EU as defined in the Treaties will not be affected, Article 6(2) TEU requires the EU to accede to the ECHR. Thus, the agreement on accession should contain in principle an acceptance of all the

---

[11] Council Regulation (EC) 1236/05 concerning trade in certain goods which could be used for capital punishment, torture or other cruel, inhuman or degrading treatment or punishment [2005] OJ L 200/1.

obligations under the ECHR. The TEU provision does not mention any of the Protocols to the ECHR which protect additional rights: Protocols Nos 1, 4, 6, 7, 12 and 13.

Article 2 of Protocol No 8 to the Treaties contains a reference to the Protocols but only in order to state that the agreement on accession 'shall ensure that nothing therein affects the situation of Member States in relation to the European Convention, in particular in relation to the Protocols thereto, measures taken by Member States derogating from the European Convention in accordance with Article 15 thereof and reservations to the European Convention made by Member States in accordance with Article 57 thereof'. One can leave aside the question of the legal position of Member States under the ECHR. Whether they have ratified a Protocol or not, or made a reservation or declaration at the time of ratification of the Convention or a Protocol, there seems to be no reason why accession by a different subject of international law, like the EU, should affect the status of any Member State under the Convention or its Protocols.

The fact that Article 59 of the ECHR, as amended by Protocol No 14, only mentions accession to the 'Convention' and does not specifically refer to the additional Protocols is not significant, because it certainly does not exclude the EU from becoming a party also to any of the Protocols. The only issue is whether the EU is in fact going to accept any of the additional Protocols. This depends on a political choice. Moreover, it is not something that needs to be settled once and for all when the agreement on accession is concluded. However, one could expect this agreement to provide for the acceptance of Protocols Nos 1 and 6, which have already been ratified by all the EU Member States, and envisage that further protocols may be accepted by the EU in the future. According to Article 1(1) of the Draft Agreement, the European Union 'hereby accedes to the Convention and to Protocols Nos. 1 and 6 of the Convention', while Article 59(2) of the Convention will be amended by Article 1(2) of the same Draft Agreement so that it would read: 'The European Union may accede to this Convention and the Protocols thereto'.

The explanations of the Charter of Fundamental Rights refer to Protocols Nos 1 and 4 and also mention, with regard to Article 50 of the Charter, one provision in Protocol No 7. While the European Parliament recommended accession to be extended to 'all the protocols concerning rights corresponding to the Charter of Fundamental Rights',[12] Protocols Nos 4 and 7 also protect rights to which no reference was made in the explanations to the Charter and which certain states would be reluctant to see recognized in the agreement on accession.

The question remains whether all the procedural requirements that are set forth in Article 218 TFEU for the agreement on accession would apply also to the acceptance of a Protocol to the ECHR by the EU should this occur at a later stage. The answer should be in the negative, in view of the fact that the acceptance of an additional Protocol would not imply any modification of the agreement on accession, but only

---

[12] Above n 10 at para 4.

an extension of its scope. A unanimous decision of the Council after obtaining the consent of the European Parliament should be regarded as sufficient.

Various provisions in the ECHR and the related Protocols contain references to states as the respective Parties. For instance, the second sentence of Article 11(2) ECHR, concerning freedom of assembly and association, reads as follows: 'This article shall not prevent the imposition of lawful restrictions on the exercise of these rights by members of the armed forces, of the police or of the administration of the State'. There is no reason why the same restrictions should not be invoked also by the EU. The agreement on accession could make a long list of all the provisions in which the term 'State' should be replaced by 'Party', in order to include also the EU. A simpler solution would be to provide a general clause stating that all the references to states contained in the ECHR and the additional Protocols will be understood as applying also to the EU. This would not rule out the possibility of envisaging some exceptions to the general solution of placing the EU at the same level as any state party to the ECHR. The amendments to Article 59(2)(d) and (e) of the Convention which are set forth in Article 1(2) of the Draft Agreement follow this approach.

IV. Participation of the EU in the Control Bodies

Article 1(a) of Protocol No 8 to the Treaties requires the agreement on accession to make 'the specific arrangements for the Union's possible participation in the control bodies of the European Convention'.

As far as the European Court of Human Rights is concerned, a judge should be appointed in respect of the EU, since Article 20 ECHR says that 'the Court shall consist of a number of judges equal to that of the High Contracting Parties'. There does not seem to be any reason for ruling out the possibility that one of the judges be appointed in respect of the EU and entitled to sit as 'ex officio member' in a Chamber or the Grand Chamber according to Article 27(2) ECHR when the EU is the Party concerned. While there could be other judges in the Court who are familiar with EU law, it would be difficult to ensure that they are always present in a Chamber when the EU is a respondent, since they have been elected in respect of another Party and may be otherwise engaged.

The appointment of a judge for the EU should follow the general procedure under Article 22 ECHR. Accordingly, the judge would be 'elected by the Parliamentary Assembly with respect to each High Contracting Party by a majority of votes cast from a list of three candidates nominated by the High Contracting Party'. A recent press release of a Council meeting mentions the issue of the 'representation of the EU in the Council of Europe bodies . . . such as Parliamentary Assembly for what concerns appointment of Judges to the European Court of Human Rights'.[13] The European Parliament in its resolution mentioned above requested to be

---

[13] 2998th Council Meeting, Justice and Home Affairs, Brussels, 25 and 26 February 2010, Press release 6855/1/10 Rev. 1.

involved 'in drawing up the list of candidates' and invoked 'the right of the European Parliament to appoint/send a certain number of representatives to the Parliamentary Assembly of the Council of Europe when the latter elects judges to the European Court of Human Rights'.[14] Article 7 of the Draft Agreement provides for a delegation of the European Parliament to 'be entitled to participate, with the right to vote, in the sittings of the Parliamentary Assembly of the Council of Europe whenever the Assembly exercises its functions related to the election of judges in accordance with Article 22 of the Convention'. One may wonder whether this is really necessary, in view of the fact that there are deputies from the 27 Member States in the Assembly and that they constitute the majority.

Participation of the EU in the Committee of Ministers has to reckon with the fact that this is one of the main organs of the Council of Europe. Including a full member appointed by the EU in the Committee would involve an amendment to the Statute of the Council of Europe.[15] An amendment would not be required if the EU was only entitled to appoint an observer with the right to take part in the discussions without a vote. The EU observer could be present at all the meetings in which the Committee exercises its supervisory functions under Article 46 of the Convention and not only when the EU is the Party concerned. The absence of a right to vote would be relatively unimportant, since the Committee decides with the majority of two-thirds of the representatives of states entitled to sit on the Committee, presently 32 out of 47 representatives. Again, the large number of representatives of Member States would seem to make the attribution of a right to vote to the EU representative unnecessary. However, Article 8(1) of the Draft Agreement allows the European Union to participate 'with a right to vote' in the decisions of the Committee of Ministers 'under Article 26, paragraph 2, Article 39, paragraph 4, Article 46, paragraphs 2 to 5 or Article 47 of the Convention'. This list includes the exercise by the Committee of Ministers of its powers to supervise the execution of all judgments rendered by the European Court of Human Rights.

V. The Extent of Supervision of EU Conduct

Accession of the EU to the ECHR implies that the EU will be submitted to the judicial control of the European Court of Human Rights with regard to any application that may be brought against the EU by a state party to the ECHR or by an individual concerning the infringement of an obligation under the ECHR. This is clearly recognized by Article 1(b) of Protocol No 8 to the Treaties, which requires the agreement on accession to provide for 'the mechanisms necessary to

---

[14] Above n 10 at para 7.
[15] An amendment to the statute would not be necessary because an amendment to the ECHR would operate as *lex specialis* according to G Ress, 'The Legal Relationship between the European Court of Human Rights and the Court of Justice of the European Communities According to the European Convention on Human Rights' in H-J Blanke and S Mangiameli (eds), *Governing Europe under a Constitution: The Hard Road from the European Treaties to a European Constitutional Treaty* (Springer, 2005) 279, 291–2.

ensure that proceedings by non-Member States and individual applications are correctly addressed to Member States and/or the Union as appropriate'.

An exemption of the EU from the supervision of the European Court of Human Rights, that the agreement on accession may conceivably contain, would make accession to the Convention practically meaningless. The idea that an equivalent protection of human rights within the EU would justify a presumption of compliance with obligations under the ECHR was expressed by the European Court in *Bosphorus v Ireland* with regard to an application made against a Member State that had implemented its obligations under an EC regulation. The Court then found that:

State action taken in compliance with said legal obligations is justified as long as the relevant organisation is considered to protect fundamental rights, as regards both the substantive guarantees offered and the mechanisms controlling their observation, in a manner which can be considered at least equivalent to that for which the Convention provides ... If such equivalent protection is considered to be provided by the organisation, the presumption will be that a State has not departed from the requirements of the Convention when it does no more than implement legal obligations flowing from membership of the organisation. However, any such presumption can be rebutted if, in the circumstances of a particular case, it is considered that the protection of Convention rights was manifestly deficient.[16]

The European Court fully endorsed this approach in several further decisions, including one concerning the compliance with obligations under Article 6 ECHR in relation to preliminary proceedings before the ECJ, in the case *Kokkelvisserij v The Netherlands*.[17]

While a restriction of supervision by the European Court of Human Rights may find some justification when the conduct leading to an alleged infringement of the ECHR is that of a state and not that of the organization which is at the origin of the breach, any presumption of equivalent protection seems to be out of place when the application directly concerns the conduct of the respondent Party. It would be hard to justify the presumption of equivalent protection with regard to the EU as a respondent thus determining an exemption from supervision, while the same presumption would not apply to a state which may in fact offer a more complete system of protection of human rights.

Under Article 33 ECHR, any Party to the Convention 'may refer to the Court any alleged breach of the provisions of the Convention and the Protocols thereto by another High Contracting Party'. By declaring that nothing in the agreement on accession 'shall affect Article 344 TFEU', Article 3 of Protocol No 8 to the Treaties intends to prevent the possibility of a Member State addressing an application to the European Court of Human Rights against another Member State when the dispute concerns the 'interpretation or application of any Treaties'. According to Article 344 TFEU, 'Member States undertake not to submit a dispute concerning the interpretation or application of the Treaties to any method of settlement other

---

[16] ECHR Reports 2005-VI 107, 158 (paras 155–6).
[17] ECHR Reports 2009-I . . . (para 3).

than those provided therein'. This is intended to cover also disputes concerning EU secondary legislation, as the ECJ stated in the *MOX* case with regard to the corresponding provision in the EC Treaty.[18] Disputes between Member States relating to EU law should not be brought to an international court or tribunal other than the ECJ. Thus, according to Article 344 TFEU a Member State is prevented from seizing the European Court of Human Rights if the alleged infringement of the ECHR by another Member State has occurred when applying EU law.

The same rationale applies to disputes concerning an infringement of the ECHR that a Member State would bring against the EU, since the interpretation or application of EU law would necessarily be involved. These disputes are not expressly covered by Article 344 TFEU nor are those that the EU could bring to an international court or tribunal against a Member State. However, to the extent that an application of the EU against a Member State also concerns the interpretation or application of EU law, it would come under the same principle.

The obligations that Member States and the EU have under EU law with regard to disputes would not as such require to be restated in the agreement on accession. The need to consider the obligations that are stated in Article 344 TFEU in the agreement on accession arises from the presence in the ECHR of a provision (Article 55) which sets out for the parties to the ECHR an obligation not to 'avail themselves of treaties, conventions or declarations in force between them for the purpose of submitting, by way of petition, a dispute arising out of the interpretation or application of this Convention to a means of settlement other than those provided for in this Convention'. Article 55 ECHR thus intends to assert the 'monopoly of the Convention institutions for deciding disputes arising out of the interpretation or application of the Convention'.[19] Thus, when a dispute between Member States of the EU relates to the interpretation or application of both the ECHR and EU law, these Member States would be placed under conflicting obligations. The agreement on accession provides an opportunity for preventing a possible conflict. Article 3 of Protocol No 8 would require the competence of the ECJ to prevail. This is reflected in Article 6(2) of the Draft Agreement, according to which 'Article 55 of the Convention shall not be understood as preventing the operation of Article 344 of the Treaty on the Functioning of the European Union'. The same solution should also cover the disputes between the EU and Member States to which reference has been made above.

VI. The Respective Roles of the EU and its Member States as Respondents

It may happen that an application is directed to the European Court of Human Rights against a party which is not responsible for the alleged infringement of the

---

[18] Case C-459/03 *Commission v Ireland* [2006] ECR I-4635, 4713–14 (paras 150–2).
[19] *Cyprus v Turkey* Application 25781/94 (1996) 86-A DR 104, 138.

ECHR. This would normally lead to a decision of inadmissibility *ratione personae*. In the relations between the EU and Member States the identification of the responsible entity may be controversial, especially when the Member State implements an EU act. Should there be discretion in the implementation, there should be little hesitation in attributing the act to the Member State, as the European Court of Human Rights held with regard to legislation implementing an EC directive in *Cantoni v France*.[20] In *Bosphorus v Ireland* the same Court considered the seizure of an aircraft in the implementation of an EC regulation, which gave no discretion to the Member State concerned. The Court concluded that this type of act also had to be attributed to the Member State because it 'fell within the "jurisdiction" of the Irish State, with the consequence that [the] complaint [was] compatible *ratione loci, personae et materiae* with the provisions of the Convention'.[21] This approach is consistent with Article 4(1) of the draft of the International Law Commission on the responsibility of states for internationally wrongful acts. According to this text, '[t]he conduct of any State organ shall be considered an act of that State under international law, whether the organ exercises legislative, executive, judicial or any other functions, whatever position it holds in the organization of the State, and whatever its character as an organ of the central Government or of a territorial unit of the State'.[22] The fact that a state organ acts on the basis of an obligation under international law or under EU law does not affect the attribution of that act to the state.

The agreement on accession could include a special rule on attribution, to the effect that the conduct of a state would be attributed to a Member State when it exercises its discretion and to the EU when the state implements a binding act of the Union to the extent that the act does not leave discretion.[23] This solution would imply that only the entity which is at the origin of the alleged infringement of an obligation under the ECHR would be held responsible and could defend the measure concerned. Moreover, that same entity would be in a position of remedying the breach if one was ascertained by the European Court of Human Rights. Should the responsible entity be the EU, the Member State would be exonerated even when the relevant conduct had been taken by one of its organs. It is true that Article 2, second sentence, of Protocol No 8 to the Treaties requires the agreement on accession to 'ensure that nothing therein affects the situation of Member States in relation to the European Convention'. However, this is to be understood as intending to protect Member States from receiving additional burdens, not as preventing Member States from being relieved from their responsibility in relation to acts that they have taken in compliance with an EU act.

---

[20] ECHR Reports 1996-V 1614.
[21] ECHR Reports 2005-VI 107, 152 (para 137).
[22] *Yearbook of the International Law Commission 2001*, Vol II, Part Two, 40.
[23] The possible existence of a special rule concerning attribution in the relations between the EU and Member States was envisaged in the 'Report of the International Law Commission, Sixty-first session (4 May–5 June and 6 July–7 August 2009)', General Assembly, Official Records, Sixty-fourth session, Supplement No 10 (A/64/10) 173–5.

When the alleged infringement of the ECHR is caused by a state act implementing EU law, it may sometimes be difficult to identify whether the act in question comes within the state's discretionary power and therefore only the state may be held responsible for it or whether the responsibility lies, in full or in part, with the EU. Article 1(b) of Protocol No 8 to the Treaties sets out that the agreement on accession should include 'the mechanisms necessary to ensure that proceedings by non-member states and individual applications are correctly addressed to the Member States and/or the Union as appropriate'. This may appear to be concerned with the need for applicants to avoid the risk of the European Court of Human Rights finding their application inadmissible *ratione personae*. However, the main underlying concern seems rather that the EU be a party to proceedings which involve the interpretation and application of EU law.

Although in principle an applicant should be free to choose whether to direct its application against the one or the other party to the ECHR, the agreement on accession could provide that the EU be notified by the Registry of any application that concerns the interpretation or application of EU law and that the EU be given the option to be added as co-respondent. This solution would ensure that the EU would be in a position of defending the compatibility with the ECHR of any provision of EU law that was invoked in an application. It would then be open to the Court to decide whether any infringement was to be attributed to the EU or to the Member State concerned.

The need to add a co-respondent in proceedings before the European Court of Human Rights may also exist in the reverse case, when an application is addressed against the EU but considers also the conduct of one or more Member States. Although in this case the role of the EU for the interpretation and application of EU law would already be safeguarded, it may be appropriate to notify the state concerned and give it an opportunity to defend the national measure at stake. This option could be left to the judicial discretion of the European Court.

The Draft Agreement does not provide for the attribution to the European Union of the conduct of state organs implementing acts of EU institutions. Article 4(1) only envisages the addition of the European Union as a co-respondent in a new paragraph to be added to Article 36 of the ECHR. This paragraph would read as follows:

The European Union or a Member State of the European Union may become a co-respondent to proceedings by decision of the Court in the circumstances set out in the Agreement on the Accession of the European Union to the European Convention for the Protection of Human Rights and Fundamental Freedoms. A co-respondent is a party to the case. The admissibility of an application shall be assessed without regard to the participation of a co-respondent in the proceedings.

This paragraph also covers the possibility for a Member State to request the European Court of Human Rights to be added as co-respondent when an application is directed against the European Union. According to the Draft Agreement this possibility is, however, limited to the case when the alleged violation 'calls into question the compatibility with the Convention rights at issue of a provision of the

Treaty on European Union, the Treaty on the Functioning of the European Union or any other provision having the same legal value pursuant to those instruments' (Article 4(3)).

The more frequent case will be that of an application which is directed against one or more Member States and concerns the implementation of an act of an EU institution. The European Union may then 'become a co-respondent to the proceedings in respect of an alleged violation notified by the Court if it appears that such allegation calls into question the compatibility with the Convention rights at issue of a provision of European Union law' (Article 4(2)).

Should the Court add the European Union as a co-respondent and later decide in favour of the applicant, in the opinion of the 'Draft revised explanatory report' of the working group which elaborated the Draft Agreement the co-respondent would then be held responsible 'only for the legal basis' of the act or omission (Doc. CDDH/UE(2011)11, paragraph 43). However, the finding of the Court concerning the co-respondent may then range, according to the circumstances, from the exclusion of any responsibility to the full responsibility for the breach.

VII. Ensuring the Correct Interpretation of EU Law

An application directed against one or more of the Member States, as with regard to any other party to the ECHR, would have to comply with the requirement that 'all domestic remedies have been exhausted' according to Article 35(1) ECHR. In the case of the EU, remedies include, apart from those set out in the Treaties, the remedies that are provided by Member States when they may lead to challenging the validity of acts of EU institutions through a preliminary reference to the ECJ. However, according to the case law of the European Court of Human Rights, although the infringement of a right that the ECHR guarantees is required to have been alleged in substance, the ECHR need not be specifically invoked by the applicant when resorting to domestic remedies.[24] Moreover, since a reference to the ECJ entirely depends on the decision of a national court and not on a request by the party to judicial proceedings, the fact that the applicant did not submit such a request cannot be considered as a failure in exhausting local remedies. If the agreement on accession introduced the requirement for the applicant to have made a specific request to the national court for a preliminary reference, this would unduly raise the bar of admissibility of applications directed against the EU.

The current system of judicial remedies concerning acts of EU institutions cannot ensure that the interpretation of an act or its validity will always have been examined by the Court of Justice before they are considered by the European Court of Human Rights. The reason may be that the national court may have omitted to make a preliminary reference or else that the validity of the act cannot be

---

[24] *Guzzardi v Italy*, Series A No 39, 23 (para 72). The Court then found that local remedies had been exhausted by the applicant since he had 'derived from the Italian legislation pleas equivalent, in the Court's view, to an allegation of a breach of the right guaranteed by article 5 of the Convention'.

challenged under the Treaties, as for instance in matters of foreign and security policy when the exceptions outlined in Article 24(1) TEU and Article 275 TFEU do not apply. This situation may increase the risk that the European Court of Human Rights will not appraise a provision of EU law in the same way as this would be done by the ECJ. It has to be noted that a parallel risk exists with regard to all the other parties to the ECHR and may lead to a judgment that finds a violation of the ECHR on the basis of an interpretation of a law of a particular state that would not have been shared by the highest court in the same state.

Article 1 of Protocol No 8 to the Treaties sets out that the agreement on accession 'shall make provision for preserving the specific characteristic of the Union and Union law'. Declaration Number 2 adopted by the Lisbon Conference also stresses that the specificities of EU law should be kept. The reference in the same declaration to a dialogue between the ECJ and the European Court of Human Rights points to the need that the latter Court takes the jurisprudence of the ECJ into account when addressing questions of EU law. Pressure from the ECJ is directed at enhancing its role as the ultimate interpreter of EU law. In a press release the Council significantly described as an objective of the forthcoming negotiations 'the preservation of the monopoly of the Court of Justice of the EU in the interpretation of EU law'.[25] The word 'monopoly' is clearly an exaggeration, which shows the determination to give the ECJ an additional role.

Current proposals concern the establishment of a mechanism that is designed to allow the ECJ to express its views on an issue concerning the interpretation or application of EU law which is pending before the European Court of Human Rights, when the ECJ has not been previously given this opportunity. According to Article 4(6) of the Draft Agreement:

In proceedings to which the European Union is co-respondent, if the Court of Justice of the European Union has not yet assessed the compatibility with the Convention rights at issue of the provision of European Law as under paragraph 2, then sufficient time shall be afforded for the Court of Justice of the European Union to make such an assessment and subsequently for the parties to make observations. The European Union shall ensure that such assessment is made quickly so that the proceedings before the European Court of Human Rights are not unduly delayed.

This provision would imply the suspension of proceedings before the European Court of Human Rights, while the ECJ is seized either by a direct referral from the European Court or by a request from the EU Commission.

The mechanism is designed to remedy a situation that may be regarded as inconsistent with Article 13 of the ECHR, which requires all the parties to provide effective remedies for the protection of the rights that the ECHR confers.[26] It also serves the purpose of allowing the ECJ to give to the provisions of EU law an interpretation that may be regarded as consistent with the ECHR.

---

[25] Above n 13.

[26] Cf FG Jacobs in his contribution printed in Parliamentary Assembly, 'The accession of the European Union/European Community to the European Convention on Human Rights' (Doc. 11533) 18.

This procedure would place the EU in a privileged position in relation to the other parties to the ECHR, since issues concerning their laws are routinely examined by the European Court of Human Rights without making any reference to the national courts even if the latter have not yet examined those issues. This privilege would be significant even if the European Court of Human Rights was not formally bound by the interpretation given by the ECJ.

The introduction of the procedure thus envisaged in the Draft Agreement would require an amendment to the TFEU. The possible outcome of this procedure has not yet been defined. It would be reasonable to empower the ECJ to set aside the provision of EU law in question, to the extent that the ECJ finds it incompatible with the ECHR rights at issue.

VIII. Effects of Accession to the ECHR on the Status of the Convention under EU Law

The status of the ECHR under EU law before accession is not entirely clear. Article 6(3) TEU refers to fundamental rights as guaranteed by the ECHR and the constitutional traditions common to the Member States as 'general principles' of EU law. This points to a binding standard within EU law. Part of this standard is represented by the ECHR and arguably by those additional Protocols which have been ratified by all the Member States.[27] Even if the reference to 'general principles' may indicate a standard which is lower than that directly established by Treaty provisions, the fact that the need to respect the ECHR is set out in a provision of the TEU suggests a status which is equivalent to that of other provisions in the Treaties.

Accession to the ECHR will not modify this situation. Article 6(3) TEU will continue to apply. Although the ECHR will become an EU agreement and, on that basis, would acquire a status which is lower than that of Treaty provisions, the status of the ECHR within EU law is enhanced by the fact that Article 6(2) TEU makes accession mandatory. Certainly, a systematic interpretation of the Treaties may lead, within EU law, to certain restrictions of the effects of some provisions of the ECHR. On the other hand, the European Court of Human Rights could find that the EU infringed the ECHR even when this was due to the Treaties: for instance, because they do not generally allow remedies for breaches of human rights in matters of foreign and security policy. However, this would not make the ECHR prevail over provisions in the Treaties from the perspective of EU law. Under that scenario, compliance with the ECHR as hypothetically resulting from a judgment of the European Court of Human Rights would require the Treaties to be amended according to Article 48 TEU.

---

[27] My views on these questions were developed in 'The Protection of Human Rights under the Maastricht Treaty' in D Curtin and T Heukels (eds), *Institutional Dynamics of European Integration. Essays in Honour of Henry G. Schermers* (Martinus Nijhoff, 1994) 549.

PART II

INSTITUTIONAL FRAMEWORK

9

The Lisbon Treaty and the Court of Justice

Francis G Jacobs

The changes in the judicial system of the European Union introduced by the Lisbon Treaty are the most far-reaching in the Union's history. They are for the most part welcome as reinforcing the role of the Courts in upholding the rule of law in the EU. But they pose great challenges to the Courts.

The following sections discuss the principal changes affecting the judicial system.

I. Changes in the Institutional Provisions

The most straightforward changes affecting the judicial system are those set out in the institutional provisions of the Treaty on the Functioning of the European Union (TFEU). The provisions governing the Courts are to be found in Part Six, Title I, Section 5 of the Treaty, headed 'The Court of Justice' (Articles 251–281).

A. Nomenclature

The term 'The Court of Justice' itself now requires some explanation. In the revised nomenclature introduced by the Lisbon Treaty, the Court of First Instance is re-named the General Court (in French it is re-named simply 'le Tribunal'); and the judicial panels are re-named specialized courts, of which there is currently one, the European Union Civil Service Tribunal. The Court of Justice retains, as the Court itself preferred, its long-established title.

The new terminology is appropriate; the title 'Court of First Instance', in particular, never seemed right, and is certainly no longer appropriate since that court has become, for some classes of case, the principal court, and for certain cases, a court of appeal. The term 'specialized court' is preferable to 'judicial panel', and recognizes that there can no longer be any constitutional objection to the creation of new courts under the Treaty. But the term 'Court of Justice' is now used also as a collective term for the Union courts: Article 19(1) of the Treaty on European Union, as amended by the Lisbon Treaty, provides somewhat confusingly: 'The Court of Justice shall include the Court of Justice, the General Court and specialised courts.' In the remainder of this chapter, the term 'Court of Justice' is used to mean the Court of Justice in the narrower and original sense.

B. Jurisdiction generally

As regards the jurisdiction of the Courts, some of the changes seem of rather limited scope, but collectively they are liable to change the character of the judicial system and perhaps to reflect the changing character of the European Union itself.

In formal terms, there are changes in each of the three main types of cases before the Court: enforcement action by the Commission against Member States; judicial review of Union measures; and references for preliminary rulings. They may be considered briefly in turn.

(i) Enforcement actions by the Commission

The Lisbon Treaty simplifies the procedure for imposition by the Court of pecuniary sanctions on Member States where they fail to comply with an earlier judgment of the Court following infringement proceedings brought by the Commission. The Commission can then bring further proceedings proposing the imposition of a financial penalty. Previously, in such 'follow-on' proceedings, the Commission had to issue a reasoned opinion specifying the points on which the Member State had not complied with the judgment, and had to specify time limits within which the Member State had to take the requisite measures. Now the Commission can take a 'follow-on' case to the Court without the need for those prior steps; the only requirement is that the Commission first gives the Member State the opportunity to submit its observations.

A further significant change simplifies the procedure in cases where the action brought by the Commission against a Member State targets the Member State's failure to notify measures transposing a directive. Here the Commission need not, under the amended provisions, bring a second action before the Court in order to propose a penalty to be imposed by the Court: instead, the Commission may specify in its initial application the penalty which it considers appropriate.

(ii) Judicial review of Union measures

Under Article 263 of the TFEU, which corresponds to the former Article 230 EC, review by the Courts extends to the following categories of measures:

- Legislative acts;
- Acts of the Council, of the Commission and of the European Central Bank, other than recommendations and opinions;
- Acts of the European Parliament and of the European Council intended to produce legal effects vis-à-vis third parties;
- Acts of bodies, offices or agencies of the Union intended to produce legal effects vis-à-vis third parties.

The expression 'legislative acts' is new in this context but is defined by Article 289(3) as legal acts adopted by legislative procedure. It appears from Article 289(1) and (2) that those legislative acts are regulations, directives and decisions in the adoption of which the Council and the Parliament take part, so that the head 'legislative acts' covers much the same territory as the corresponding provisions of the previous Treaty—regulations, directives and decisions.

Under the previous Treaty, the Courts had jurisdiction over acts of the European Parliament, the Council, the Commission and the European Central Bank. Review now extends also, however, on the one hand to acts of the *European Council*, and on the other hand to acts of *bodies, offices or agencies* of the Union.

While challenges to the *European Council* might be expected to be relatively rare, it is symbolically significant that jurisdiction now extends for the first time to the supreme political authority of the Union, which under Article 15(2) of the TEU now comprises the Heads of State or Government of the Member States together with its President and the President of the Commission. Although the European Council has broad political powers and does not exercise legislative functions, it does have powers to take a remarkably wide range of decisions having legal effect, ranging from the determination of the existence of a serious and persistent breach of the Union's values by a Member State to the decision following an 'emergency brake' on the adoption of a CFSP decision.[1]

The extension of judicial protection to measures taken by *bodies, offices and agencies* of the Union follows on the protection provided under the Charter of Fundamental Rights. The Charter recognizes that fundamental rights may require protection from all sources of Union action. Accordingly, it is provided by Article 51 that, 'The provisions of this Charter are addressed to the institutions, bodies, offices and agencies of the Union'. (The expression 'bodies, offices and agencies', broadly denoting all authorities of the Union other than the Institutions, is now regularly used: see for example Articles 15 and 16 of the TFEU.)

Equally, it seems right that judicial protection should extend beyond fundamental rights to all forms of illegality, and that any Union measure intended to produce legal effects vis-à-vis third parties should be open to challenge, regardless of its source. Potentially this could result in a substantial increase in the case-load of the Courts.

It is a striking fact that under the Lisbon Treaty judicial review is made available against all authorities of the Union—although not in all circumstances—from the highest to the lowest. This can be seen as a reaffirmation of one important aspect of the rule of law, well expressed by Dr Thomas Fuller in 1733, 'Be you never so high, the Law is above you'.[2]

That deals with the question *against* whom, or against what entities, judicial review actions can be brought. Then there is the question *by* whom they can be brought.

---

[1] For a list of articles in the TEU and the TFEU which enable the European Council to take decisions having legal effects, see Jean-Claude Piris, *The Lisbon Treaty: A Legal and Political Analysis* (Cambridge University Press, 2010) Appendix 6.

[2] Fuller, *Gnomologia: Adagies and Proverbs* (1733), sentence no 943: see Tom Bingham, *The Rule of Law* (Allen Lane, 2010) Chapter 1, fn 8.

Standing before the Court

First, as before, actions may be brought by a Member State, the European Parliament, the Council or the Commission without the need to establish a legal interest in taking proceedings (Article 263, second paragraph of the TFEU). These are sometimes referred to as 'privileged applicants'.

Second, action may also be brought, but only for the purpose of protecting their prerogatives, by others: by the Court of Auditors, by the European Central Bank and now, under the Lisbon Treaty, by the Committee of the Regions (Article 263, third paragraph of the TFEU).

Third, there is a significant development for actions by individuals and corporate bodies ('any natural or legal person'). Previously under Article 230 of the EC Treaty, unless the measure was addressed to him, such an applicant had to satisfy requirements both of 'direct concern' and of 'individual concern'—the latter requirement being strictly interpreted. The scope for protection of individuals and companies against *regulatory* acts is increased under the Lisbon Treaty which maintains the requirements of direct and individual concern in general but for regulatory acts removes the condition that the act should be of *individual* concern to the applicant. That condition has often made it difficult or impossible for individuals and companies to take cases to the Court. In the case of regulatory acts Article 263, fourth paragraph of the TFEU, maintains the requirement, more appropriate and generally easier to satisfy, that the act is of *direct* concern to the applicant. The article also requires that the act does not entail implementing measures. (In that event, however, those implementing measures would themselves be likely to be open to challenge.)

The widening of access to the Court for challenges to regulatory acts, removing the requirement of individual concern, follows sustained criticism of the Court's case law on the limited standing for individuals. In the *UPA* case,[3] the Court of Justice declined to change its stance, but the issue became live in the debates under the constitutional convention on the Constitutional Treaty. Although the Court, when maintaining its position in *UPA*, suggested in its judgment that any change in the law was a matter of treaty amendment, it nevertheless conveyed to the Convention its view that no treaty amendment was needed.

The saga is perhaps unique in the history of the European Community, in that the Court's view was overridden. Previously, treaty amendments concerning the Court's jurisdiction had frequently endorsed and in effect ratified changes which prefigured in the Court's own case law; this was the case, for example, with actions brought against the European Parliament and with actions brought by the European Parliament; in both cases, the Treaty did not confer jurisdiction on the Court; in both situations, the Court nevertheless asserted jurisdiction, and in both, the Court's solution was subsequently introduced into the Treaty. In such cases, the Court had taken an expansive view of its jurisdiction, arguably justified by concern for the rule of law.

---

[3] Case C-50/00 P *Unión de Pequeños Agricultores v Council* [2002] ECR I-6677.

It is remarkable also that the treaty amendment in issue here, on standing for individuals, goes once again in the direction of extending the Courts' jurisdiction. However, the extent of the new jurisdiction is uncertain. The scope of the term 'regulatory acts' is not clear; the term is used nowhere else in the Treaty, and, in contrast to the term 'legislative acts', it is not defined. The reluctance of the authors of the Treaty to define its terms is well known. English law sometimes seems to go to the opposite extreme. The term 'regulatory act' would be likely to be defined if it appeared in an English legislative text.

Tom Bingham in his book *The Rule of Law*[4] gives a good example of the propensity of English law to insist on definition: the example is not 'regulatory act' but 'regulation'. The Banking Act 1979 Appeals Procedure (England and Wales) Regulations 1979 provide that, 'Any reference in these regulations to a regulation is a reference to a regulation contained in these regulations.'

While the term 'regulatory act' is not defined with similar precision or indeed at all, it does seem clear, however, that the term should be given a broad scope, since what is in issue here is no less than the right of access to a court, a right generally recognized today as fundamental. The importance of the right was recognized in the powerful judgment of the European Court of Human Rights in the *Golder* case[5] in 1975, in which it held that Article 6(1) of the Convention must be understood as guaranteeing the right of access to a court although such a right was not explicitly formulated in that provision; that right is quite simply central to the rule of law.[6] Indeed, the right is recognized by the Court of Justice, for example, and in different forms, in such leading cases as *Johnston*[7] and *Kadi*.[8]

Guidance on the meaning of the term 'regulatory act' might be sought in the preparatory work on the Treaty, but such guidance is less appropriate to a constitutional text and can often be misleading, and the Court has in general rightly preferred to interpret the Treaty provisions in the light of their object and purpose. That would plainly necessitate a broad interpretation.

In any event, since the Treaty appears to classify acts other than individual measures as legislative or regulatory, the appropriate meaning of 'regulatory act' might seem to be any act which is not a 'legislative' act. That indeed would reflect the legal situation in several Member States, where legislative acts cannot be challenged before the courts directly at the suit of individuals, but secondary measures—delegated legislation and the like—can be so challenged. The position is different, broadly speaking, only in those Member States having a constitutional court (or occasionally the Member State's Supreme Court rather than a specialized constitutional court) of a kind which does have jurisdiction to review even primary legislation at the suit of an individual; not all constitutional courts, however, have such jurisdiction.

---

[4] Tom Bingham, above n 2 at 7.
[5] *Golder v United Kingdom*, Series A, No 18, Judgment of 21 February 1975.
[6] Judgment of 21 February 1975, Series A, No 18.
[7] Case 222/84 [1986] ECR 1651.
[8] Case C-402/05 *P Kadi v Council and Commission* [2008] ECR I-6351.

It is clear from the scale of criticism of the past case law that this reform will be widely welcomed, at any rate if it is given an appropriately broad application.

(iii) References for preliminary rulings

In line with the changes made for direct actions challenging Union measures, the jurisdiction to rule on the validity and interpretation of acts of the institutions (and of the European Central Bank) is extended by Article 267 of the TFEU (formerly 177, then 234) to cover acts of bodies, offices and agencies of the Union. Since the Court's jurisdiction includes rulings on validity as well as interpretation of the acts in question, the legality of all Union measures adopted under the Treaties can be challenged indirectly by this route, although only where the national court decides to make such a reference.

Article 267 also includes a new paragraph affecting, for the first time, the procedure before the Court of Justice on a reference: it provides that where, in the case pending before the national court, a person is in custody, the Court of Justice shall act with the minimum of delay.

II. The Jurisdiction of the Court of Justice in Relation to Freedom, Security and Justice

The main changes here follow from the abolition of the 'three-pillar' system introduced by the Maastricht Treaty. Under that system, the jurisdiction of the ECJ remained largely unchanged under the first pillar—the so-called Community pillar. But under the Maastricht Treaty the new second and third pillars were closer in some respects to the traditional intergovernmental method, and the role of the Community institutions—Parliament, Commission, Court of Justice—was more limited. Indeed, the jurisdiction of the Court of Justice was excluded, with narrow exceptions, under the then second pillar (Common Foreign and Security Policy) and was considerably limited under the then third pillar (Justice and Home Affairs).

The position became more complex under the Amsterdam Treaty. Some matters were transferred from the third pillar to the first (Community) pillar. But they were made subject to variable systems of jurisdiction. Indeed for the first time the jurisdiction of the Court depended in some instances on 'opt-ins' by Member States.

Meanwhile the remainder of the third pillar continued under the Amsterdam Treaty, but under the new title 'Provisions on police and judicial cooperation in criminal matters'.

The resulting patchwork system was widely regarded as opaque, incoherent and generally unsatisfactory.

The Lisbon Treaty is a great improvement in this regard. It does away with the much-criticized three-pillar structure, and makes major changes in relation to Justice and Home Affairs—now under the title *Area of Freedom, Security and Justice*; and this leads to substantial extensions in the jurisdiction of the Court.

Subject to certain transitional provisions,[9] the Treaty extends the normal system of jurisdiction to the area of freedom, security and justice, which is fully integrated into the TFEU. It includes ensuring the absence of internal border controls—although, regrettably, not for all Member States, among those which have excluded themselves being the United Kingdom.

The Title 'Area of Freedom, Security and Justice' now comprises the following subjects:

- Policies on border checks, asylum and immigration;
- Judicial cooperation in civil matters;
- Judicial cooperation in criminal matters;
- Police cooperation.

There may well be a substantial body of legislation in these areas. The ambitious 'Stockholm Programme' of the Swedish Presidency in the second half of 2009 seeks to define the framework for EU police and customs cooperation, rescue services, criminal and civil law cooperation, asylum, migration and visa policy for the period 2010–14. The programme touches on many sensitive areas of policy and has proved highly controversial. It is very clear that the Court of Justice will have to tread a careful path in what may prove to be a metaphorical minefield.

There is one express limitation on the Court's jurisdiction, but that limitation is itself of rather limited scope. The Court does not have jurisdiction, in the areas of judicial cooperation in criminal matters and police cooperation, to review 'the validity or proportionality of operations carried out by the police or other law-enforcement services of a Member State or the exercise of the responsibilities incumbent upon Member States with regard to the maintenance of law and order and the safeguarding of internal security': see Article 276 of the TFEU.

There are also regrettably complex transitional provisions in relation to police cooperation and judicial cooperation in criminal matters.[10]

Thus the Treaty for the most part extends the jurisdiction of the Court in its entirety to the Area of Freedom, Security and Justice. In contrast, the Treaty still broadly excludes the jurisdiction of the Court over the Common Foreign and Security Policy.

III. The Jurisdiction of the Court of Justice over the Common Foreign and Security Policy

The Treaty, with very limited exceptions, excludes the jurisdiction of the Court over the Common Foreign and Security Policy (CFSP).

---

[9] Under the transitional provisions, the more limited jurisdiction of the Court over measures adopted before the entry into force of the Lisbon Treaty under the former third pillar (Title VI of the former TEU) continues to apply for five years after its entry into force.

[10] See Article 10 of Protocol no 36.

The exceptions are specified in Article 275 of the TFEU. Under that Article there are in this area just two aspects within the jurisdiction of the Court.

First, the Article preserves the principle, developed by the Court's case law, that the Court is responsible for ensuring that the implementation of the CFSP does not affect the competences of the Union under what were previously 'first-pillar' provisions. This maintains the idea that CFSP acts must not encroach upon the powers conferred on the Community by the EC Treaty, which now appears as a reference to the principle in Article 40 of the TEU that the implementation of the CFSP should not affect the exercise of the Union's competences. The Court now has explicit jurisdiction to rule on that issue.

Second, the Court has a role in protecting individual rights in the implementation of the CFSP, a role increasingly recognized by the case law and by the Treaties. There have recently been several cases before the General Court and the Court of Justice where, for example, coercive measures against persons alleged to belong to terrorist organizations have been challenged, and one of the key issues has been the availability of judicial remedies. The rule of law requires that even terrorists—or those alleged to be terrorists—are entitled to a degree of judicial protection. The Treaty recognizes this. Where the measures taken by the Council under the CFSP adversely affect individuals or corporations—as the Treaty (Article 275) puts it, 'decisions providing for restrictive measures against natural or legal persons', which are now the subject of a special Title, consisting of a single article, Article 215—the Court (here, in the first place, the General Court) has jurisdiction to review the legality of those decisions.

Again the Treaty appears to recognize the need for upholding, in these specific sectors, the rule of law and the protection of fundamental rights.

IV. Fundamental Rights and the Court of Justice

The Treaty makes two major changes of a more general character on fundamental rights. It requires the Union to accede to the European Convention on Human Rights. And it gives legal force to the European Union's Charter of Fundamental Rights: the Charter now has 'the same legal value as the Treaties' (Article 6(1) of the TEU). These developments are considered elsewhere in this book; here they are examined for their impact on the Court of Justice.

A. Accession to the European Convention on Human Rights

Article 6(2) of the Treaty on European Union, as amended by the Lisbon Treaty, imposes an obligation on the European Union to accede to the European Convention on Human Rights (ECHR). That obligation raises many questions, but should be considered here mainly in terms of its likely impact on the position of the Court of Justice.

As is well known, initially the Court of Justice refused to accept challenges to EC measures on grounds of fundamental rights, apparently fearing the impact on the primacy of EC law. Gradually, and perhaps partly in response to the concerns expressed by national constitutional courts, it shifted to a diametrically opposite position. Ultimately, the Court even seemed excessively concerned, sometimes bringing in human rights principles when they appeared superfluous. In that change of heart, the Court increasingly relied on the ECHR, and its jurisprudential formulation ('The Union shall respect fundamental rights, as guaranteed by the [ECHR] and as they result from the constitutional traditions common to the Member States, as general principles of Community law') was taken over in the Maastricht and Amsterdam Treaties.

In any event, the Court of Justice succeeded in developing its case law to take full account of the Convention; moreover it cited regularly, in recent years, the case law of the Strasbourg Court—an exception to its usual practice of not citing external case law of any kind—and regularly deferred to Strasbourg. The two Courts regularly met, and relations between them were excellent. The position was in practice as if the EU were already subject to the Convention. Acknowledging the respect for human rights in the recent case law of the ECJ, the Strasbourg Court in the *Bosphorus* judgment in 2005[11] decided that it would not review the decision by the ECJ of a human rights issue: the Strasbourg Court accepted that in such circumstances there was a presumption (albeit rebuttable) that the EU provided protection of human rights equivalent to that provided by the Convention.

It might indeed have been thought that the situation as it stood was eminently satisfactory, and that there was no need for EU accession to the Convention—a course which would probably create at least as many problems as it solved. However, it appeared that the die was cast. On the political level, it was urged that accession was needed to comply with the EU's human rights agenda, or even for symbolic reasons. Members of both Courts expressed support for accession.

There seems no doubt that accession will change the relationship between the two Courts. Accession must be based on equal treatment: the EU will be in the same position as the 47 States Parties to the Convention.[12] There will therefore be no place for the *Bosphorus* presumption—unless, as seems improbable, the European Court of Human Rights were to extend some form of the presumption to all the States Parties. To extend the presumption might have the effect that, at least in certain areas, where a state provided effective judicial protection of human rights, there would be a rebuttable presumption that decisions by the national authorities respected human rights and provided equivalent protection to the Convention, and that there was therefore at first sight no need for the Strasbourg Court to review the contested decision. The idea seems far-fetched; but it, or some variant of it, surely deserves further study. Some middle way needs to be found between the routine application of such a presumption by the Strasbourg Court and the present situation in which that Court is called upon to review tens of thousands of applications each year, is itself unable to decide cases within a reasonable time,

---

[11] *Bosphorus v Ireland* ECHR [2005] No 45036/98.
[12] It is not clear that there is in fact complete equality: it is sometimes suggested that Russia has obtained certain forms of favourable treatment.

and is unable to devote the necessary resources to the examination of the truly important cases.

As regards the European Union, while accession to the ECHR does not seem one of the more pressing concerns, it should not be thought that there are no benefits to be gained from EU accession. There may be scope for genuine improvements in the protection of human rights within the EU, which might be facilitated by EU accession to the ECHR. Three examples may be mentioned by way of illustration.

First, there are areas where the ECJ plainly does not have jurisdiction. A clear example is the *Matthews* case.[13] The applicant, being resident in Gibraltar, had no right to vote in elections to the European Parliament. That was a consequence of the Act on direct elections to the Parliament, an Act in effect equivalent in status to the Treaties and thus one whose validity could not be challenged before the ECJ.

Despite the extensions to the jurisdiction of the ECJ introduced by the Lisbon Treaty, there are still gaps, as indicated above: for example, in relation to the CFSP, where the Courts are still almost wholly excluded.

Second, there are areas where the ECJ does potentially have jurisdiction, but has failed to exercise it. The clearest example here restricts the standing of individuals to challenge EU measures. The test, as we have seen, has been amended by the Lisbon Treaty, but much will depend on how the new test is interpreted. If it remains too restrictive, it will certainly be scrutinized by the Strasbourg Court, which has already been alerted to the difficulty and which, as we have seen above, attaches high importance to the right of access to a court.

Third, there are serious issues arising in particular from the enforcement by the European Commission of the competition rules. Concern has been expressed by many commentators about the functions and powers of the Commission, which appears to combine the roles of investigating, prosecuting, finding and punishing infringements of the competition rules. Does that situation meet the requirements of Article 6(1) of the ECHR (and Article 47 of the Charter)? In particular, if, by virtue of the huge fines now imposed by the Commission, the proceedings are tantamount to criminal in their nature, are they accompanied by the necessary procedural guarantees? And in the absence of such guarantees, is the level of judicial review, either by the General Court or by the Court of Justice, sufficient to satisfy the need for full judicial scrutiny? I express no concluded view on these issues, but it is clearly questionable whether the EU Courts have adequately addressed concerns of this kind, which may be particularly serious because of their systemic character. It seems that accession to the Convention may lead the Courts to do so, or may lead the Strasbourg Court to react.

In some of the above areas, therefore, accession by the EU to the ECHR could prove of real value for the more effective protection of fundamental rights.

---

[13] *Matthews v United Kingdom* ECHR [1999] No 24833/94.

B. The Charter of Fundamental Rights

Article 6(1) of the Treaty on European Union, as amended by the Lisbon Treaty, provides, as already mentioned, that the Charter of Fundamental Rights 'shall have the same legal value as the Treaties'.

The Charter was drawn up following a German initiative during its Presidency in the first half of 1999. The Charter was solemnly proclaimed by the European Parliament, the Council and the Commission at Nice on 7 December 2000. However, it was not incorporated into the Treaties and was not given legally binding force until the Lisbon Treaty.

There are still today some reservations about the Charter. At the time when the Charter was conceived it may have seemed a good idea that the European Union should have its own Charter of Rights, suited to its own competences, and expressing its own values. But the Charter as it emerged from a lengthy gestation process seems unsatisfactory in several respects. Some of the unsatisfactory features are intrinsic, others external.

To mention briefly some of the main points:[14]

1. Certain provisions of the Charter are intended to do no more than reproduce the rights set out in the European Convention on Human Rights: but they express them in a different form and in a different language, which seems a recipe for confusion.

2. The Charter may also generate confusion in that it includes both judicially enforceable rights, like the Convention rights, and other rights, social or economic, which can today very well be recognized as fundamental rights but which, at least in some respects, are not obviously justiciable.

3. As is expressly required in Article 6(1) of the Treaty, rights apparently proclaimed without qualification in the Charter have to be understood in the light of 'explanations'—the qualifications added during the negotiations—which may significantly reduce or alter their scope, and may make their interpretation more complex.

4. Contrary to first impressions, the Charter is not an all-purpose human rights instrument for the European Union. It is addressed only to the EU institutions, and to the Member States only when they are implementing EU law. This limit is likely to cause much confusion; and indeed the intended borderline between the case where a Member State is exercising its own competence and the case where it is implementing EU law is not always easy to draw.

The Charter seems likely also to engender confusion with the European Convention on Human Rights, which is binding on the 47 Member States of the Council of Europe. The Charter moreover risks dividing Europe, with the 27 EU Member States subject to the Charter as well as the Convention, the other 20 to the Convention alone.

---

[14] See the author's Hamlyn lectures, *The Sovereignty of Law: The European Way* (Cambridge University Press, 2007) 151.

And the question must be asked: was it necessary for the EU Member States to be subject, within three uncoordinated legal systems, to three different Bills of Rights—their own constitutional Bill of Rights, the European Convention and the Charter?

It might well be thought that the European Convention on Human Rights should continue to be seen as the principal human rights standard for the EU. It carries with it a largely well-judged body of case law developed by an experienced and specialized court. It provides a common standard across Europe, reflecting, and perhaps helping to develop, shared values, while exceptionally making provision, where appropriate, for local differentiation. To avoid fragmentation in human rights standards in Europe, it will surely be desirable to continue to regard the Convention as the primary instrument. The Convention has acquired a special value as a pan-European system. Moreover the role of the EU in relation to the Convention is crucial: it must act so as to strengthen rather than weaken that system.

But the Charter is there and cannot be ignored. It can certainly play an important role in relation to the rights not contained in the Convention, notably the fundamental social and economic rights. Even if these rights cannot always be seen as self-standing and judicially enforceable rights, they may still serve as standards which can be invoked when interpreting EU legislation in those fields.

The Charter, to the extent that it now provides effective protection of a wide range of fundamental rights, could also serve a further valuable function. The Charter has been introduced, or even imposed, on the ground that, in some quarters, the view prevailed that the protection of fundamental rights in the European Union's judicial system was inadequate because there was no EU 'catalogue' of fundamental rights. The introduction of such a catalogue should be seen as meeting those concerns, so that there are no longer grounds for national courts to arrogate to themselves the task of reviewing compliance by the European Union with fundamental rights in any area where the Court of Justice has jurisdiction.

V. Appointments to the Courts

A. Judges and Advocates General

The link between judges and Member States is more clearly brought out by the Lisbon Treaty. There has been a gradual evolution on that link in successive treaties. In the original Community of six Member States, there were seven judges. There was no requirement in the Treaty as to the nationality of the judges, or even any requirement that they should be nationals of a Member State. The invariable practice, however, was that there should be a judge from each Member State. In the early years, when there was a smaller number of Member States, an additional judge was appointed if that was necessary to ensure that there should be an uneven number of judges. The Statute of the Court provides that an uneven number of judges must sit in each case.

The Nice Treaty expressly linked the number of judges with the number of Member States, providing that the Court should consist of one judge per Member State (Article 221 EC as amended by the Nice Treaty). The number of judges accordingly rose from 15 to 25 with the 2004 enlargement of the European Union, and from 25 to 27 with the 2007 enlargement.

Under the Lisbon Treaty the Court consists of 'one judge from each Member State' (Article 19(2) of the TEU). The General Court 'shall include at least one judge per Member State'.

In the original Community there were two Advocates General; the number has progressively increased, and is currently eight (the proportion of Advocates General to judges is now almost exactly the same as in the original Community). However, it has been the practice that there should always be an Advocate General from each of the largest Member States (currently France, Germany, Italy, Spain and the United Kingdom), and that they alone can be reappointed; the Advocates General, like the judges, have a six-year term which according to the Treaty is renewable. However, the Advocates General from the other (currently 22) Member States serve one term only, and there is a system of rotation among those states.

The Treaty provides, as before, that, if the Court of Justice so requests, the Council, acting unanimously, may increase the number of Advocates General (Article 252 of the TFEU). A declaration annexed to the TFEU adds, however, that, if the Court so requests, three additional Advocates General may be appointed.

As Jean-Claude Piris records, at the end of the Lisbon IGC Poland succeeded in obtaining a declaration that, if three additional Advocates General are appointed, 'Poland will . . . have a permanent Advocate General'.[15] Mr Piris adds, 'The Court of Justice might not be very keen on such an increase in the number of advocates general. In any case, it is up to it to request the increase.'[16] To date, it has not done so.

One issue raised by the Lisbon Treaty is whether, given the substantial increase in the Court's jurisdiction, the existing number of judges and Advocates General will be sufficient. But it is likely to be politically difficult—and may be undesirable—to increase their number.

B. Appointment of members of the Court

Another important issue affecting the Court, when the Constitutional Treaty was being drawn up and in anticipation of the 2004 enlargement of the Union, was the procedure for appointment of members of the Court. Some of the then members of the Court had drawn attention to that issue and had informally expressed their views.[17] That approach apparently encouraged the United Kingdom to raise the issue in the negotiations on the Constitutional Treaty.

---

[15] Declaration no 38.
[16] Piris, above n 1 at 233.
[17] With a view to focusing attention on the issue, a high-level conference on the subject of appointments to the European Courts was arranged in Brussels by the *Institut d'études européenes* under the direction of Professor Jean-Victor Louis.

The raising of the issue in no way implies dissatisfaction with the *outcomes* of the existing procedures in general; rather, it reflects concern about the principles which should govern judicial appointments, both to ensure that members have the appropriate qualities and to guarantee judicial independence. Before the Lisbon Treaty, the Treaties simply provided that appointments of judges and Advocates General were to be made by common accord of the governments of the Member States. In practice, the Member States apparently endorsed with little scrutiny each other's nominations. It should be mentioned that some Member States (including the United Kingdom, the Netherlands and Slovenia) had introduced rather more transparent internal procedures for selecting candidates, but the practice of appointment by common accord at EU level had remained unchanged.

The Lisbon Treaty (Article 255 TFEU), following the Constitutional Treaty, makes a radical change in the appointment procedure. It provides for the establishment of a panel to assess candidates for the Court of Justice and for the General Court and to give an opinion on their suitability to perform the duties of Judge and Advocate General. The panel comprises seven persons; they are chosen from among former members of the Court of Justice and the General Court, members of national supreme courts and 'lawyers of recognised competence', one of whom is proposed by the European Parliament.

It is of interest that the first decisions appointing members under the new procedure refer to the positive opinion of the panel. It should indeed be possible to assume that, if an opinion were not positive, the candidate would not be appointed, and that the Member State would be required to nominate a new candidate. And indeed at the time of writing (October 2010) it appears that on two very recent occasions a candidate proposed for the General Court has not been given a positive opinion and that in both cases the Member State concerned has proposed a new candidate.

The establishment of the Civil Service Tribunal in 2005 provided a good precedent: a committee of seven, including several former members of the ECJ and the CFI, was set up, and there was a public call for applications for membership of the Tribunal. The Committee produced, from the 243 applications received, a list of the best qualified, taking account of the need for a balanced composition on a broad geographical basis and with respect to the national legal systems represented. The selection made by the Committee was rapidly approved by the Council.

C. Reappointment of existing members

In principle half the members of the Court of Justice come up for reappointment every three years. 'Every three years there shall be a partial replacement of the Judges and Advocates General' (Article 253, second paragraph of the TFEU). But, despite the term 'replacement' the Treaty adds that, 'Retiring Judges and Advocates General may be reappointed' (fourth paragraph). The position is similar for the General Court.

Several difficulties arise from the need for renewal after the relatively short six-year term. First, there is a difficulty of principle: not every Member State has recognized what might seem, in the interest of judicial independence, an unwritten constitutional principle: the principle that existing members should automatically be reappointed in the absence of valid reasons relating to those members themselves. Indeed, far from accepting such a principle, one Member State has tended to regard appointment of a judge for a single term as the norm, and has regularly failed to reappoint the judge. Incidentally, the effect of that policy is to weaken the influence of the judge from such a Member State compared with others having greater experience at the Court.

But there is also the risk that a failure to reappoint an existing member, apparently well qualified to be reappointed, might cast doubt on the independence of members of the Court. That has probably not been an issue in practice; but the principle of judicial independence (applying of course to both judges and Advocates General) is of such fundamental importance that any appearance or risk of a threat should be avoided as far as possible. It is therefore desirable that the new procedures introduced by the Lisbon Treaty will address non-renewal as well as initial appointment of judges and Advocates General.

VI. Conclusions

The changes in the judicial system introduced by the Lisbon Treaty are broadly to be welcomed as strengthening the rule of law in the European Union. Taken in a different sequence from that followed above, the following general comments may be made by way of conclusion.

The new provisions on appointment of members of the Courts may improve the quality of members and the quality of the appointment procedure, and also serve to improve respect for judicial independence.

Accession of the European Union to the ECHR, while not one of the more pressing concerns, may bring benefits which cannot be gauged in advance. There may be scope for genuine improvements in the protection of human rights within the EU, which might be facilitated by EU accession to the ECHR.

The introduction of the Charter of Fundamental Rights poses numerous problems, especially in relation to the ECHR. There are compelling reasons, where the Charter and the ECHR overlap, for continuing to give priority to the ECHR. On other rights, the Charter could provide a useful set of standards.

The legal status given to the Charter should also be seen as meeting concerns about the protection of fundamental rights in the EU, so that there are no longer grounds for national courts to arrogate to themselves the task of reviewing compliance by the European Union with fundamental rights in any area where the Court of Justice has jurisdiction. In such cases a strong presumption of equivalence should apply.

The various extensions of the jurisdiction of the Courts under the Lisbon Treaty are to be welcomed in a Union based on the rule of law. They are remarkably systematic, filling in many of the lacunae in the Union's provisions governing judicial review. The credit for this must go to the proposed Constitutional Treaty, where the new provisions were first formulated and which led, through its novel procedure, to a more systematic and coherent approach than might have been possible under the traditional method of treaty change by intergovernmental conference. But credit is also due to the Member States, which unanimously agreed the new provisions, some of which, as we have seen, will once more tighten procedures against the Member States themselves.

The new provisions represent, taken in their entirety, a major advance for the European Union. But it cannot be denied that they also present challenges of a novel kind for the Courts; and they may even require, sooner rather than later, some re-shaping of the Union's judicial system. That, however, is an issue for another day.

10

Subsidiarity in the Courtroom

Andrea Biondi

I. Introduction

There are several areas of EU law that are best avoided, as entering into them can prove dangerous. One of these areas is the application of the principle of subsidiarity; one of the most debated, analysed, criticized, despised and, in very few cases, loved concepts of EU law.[1] It is thus difficult to add anything new to the very sophisticated and wide literature on the subject, and furthermore, it is practically unavoidable to become embroiled in too many subtexts and variations. However, a collection of essays on post-EU treaty ratification would not be complete without a chapter on subsidiarity. At least some precautionary measures need to be adopted and the scope of the discussion must be delimited. The approach of this contribution is therefore rather partial and by no means 'new': the judicial applicability of the subsidiarity principle. It is argued that it might be high time for judges to be more involved. Since its introduction in the Treaty of Maastricht, the principle of subsidiarity has played a positive role as a 'remainder' of the peculiarity of the EU governance model whereby competences are not attributed exclusively to a single Central Sovereign but they can variably be allocated to different and most appropriate regulatory levels. However, apart from a sort of conscious awareness about the presence of such a principle, a *'state of mind'*,[2] its practical application has been, at best, minimal. Certainly we did not see any 'judicial' application. Generally, the reluctance of the European Court of Justice could be justified in terms of separation of powers as the Court was cautious in substituting its own judgment for that of the institutions, in assessing a choice which was ultimately perceived as political. This

---

[1] See inter alia DJ Edwards, 'Fearing Federalism's Failure: Subsidiarity in the European Union' 44 *Am J Comp L* (1996) 537; G De Búrca, 'Reappraising Subsidiarity's Significance after Amsterdam' Jean Monnet Paper at <http://www.jeanmonnetprogram.org/papers/99/990701.html> and 'The Principle of Subsidiarity and the Court of Justice as an Institutional Actor' (1998) *Journal of Common Market Studies* 217–35; N McCormick, 'Problems of Democracy and Subsidiarity' (2000) *EPL* 531–42; A Estella, *The EU Principle of Subsidiarity and its Critique* (Oxford University Press, 2002); R Schütze, *From Dual to Cooperative Federalism. The Changing Structure of European Law* (Oxford University Press, 2009).

[2] Commission Report to the European Council on the Adaptation of Community Legislation to the Subsidiarity Principle, COM(93) 545.

chapter argues that, instead, it is time for the Court to take subsidiarity seriously as judicial application is the only way of making this doctrine a true operational principle of governance in the EU and confer on it the constitutional importance it deserves. A more pronounced role is also required by the changes introduced by the Treaty of Lisbon and in particular by the new Protocol (No 2) on the Application of the Principles of Subsidiarity and Proportionality, which confers on Member States, at the request of the national parliaments, the right to bring proceedings on the ground of a possible infringement of the principle of subsidiarity.[3] It might be simply that to 'trust the Court' is just a solution because of the lack of any better alternatives, but as history of EU integration teaches, sometimes judicial adjudication—even if a bit clumsy—serves the purpose of awakening certain sleepy treaty provisions. So, time for a trip to Luxembourg.

II. Subsidiarity So Far

In an ideal world, subsidiarity can function 'upwards' at the international level, or 'downwards' to the nation state, or to regional and local level. In its 'purest' form subsidiarity should make internationalization and regionalization co-existing and not mutually exclusive; a constitutional settlement that operates with the full acknowledgement of the simultaneous necessity of national and supranational regulation and on the need for a fair balancing of conflicting interests, with a call for all the different political actors to be fully involved. Indeed, there exist 'two aspects to the subsidiarity principle: decentralization, but also a corollary function of integration, where effectiveness demands that a problem be solved in a common framework'.[4] In the real world, however, rules are needed and despite the slippery contours of this multiform and multifaceted principle, it would be wrong to claim that we need to start from scratch.

Since its introduction in the Treaty of Maastricht it has been gradually accepted that subsidiarity can operate mainly, if not exclusively, as a '*process*': its application would be satisfied insofar as the procedural requirements for deciding what is the best and most appropriate level of competence allocation is complied with. The principle of subsidiarity is encapsulated in Article 5(3) TEU, which states that in areas which do not fall within its exclusive competence, the Union is to act only if and insofar as the objectives of the proposed action cannot be sufficiently achieved by the Member States, either at central level or at regional and local level, but can rather, by reason of the scale or effects of the proposed action, be better achieved at Union level. Therefore, the Union needed, in accordance with the principle of

---

[3] On the role of national parliaments see chapter 12 in this collection: R Corbett, 'The Evolving Roles of the European Parliament and of National Parliaments'.

[4] See the Commission Report to the European Council on the Adaptation of Community Legislation to the Subsidiarity Principle, COM(93) 545, which suggests that, 'far from having the effect of freezing Community action, the dynamic of the subsidiarity principle should make it possible to expand it if required, or limit or even abandon it when action at community level is no longer warranted'.

subsidiarity, to execute only tasks that the Member States could not perform effectively by themselves. Thus, Article 5 TEU already contains some procedural steps that need to be undertaken: subsidiarity applies to areas of shared competences (another dangerous area of EU law to be avoided!); the need to act together (scale and externalities); verification of Member States' capacity; and finally conferral to the Union. Protocol 30 on the Application of the Principles of Subsidiarity and Proportionality added to the Treaties by the Treaty of Amsterdam tried to further 'proceduralize' the application of the subsidiarity principle by placing the burden on EU institutions, mainly the European Commission, to comply with a series of necessary steps: (i) whether a certain measure has a cross-border dimension that cannot be satisfactorily regulated by Member States; (ii) actions by Member States alone or lack of Community action would conflict with the requirements of the Treaty or would otherwise significantly damage Member States' interests; (iii) action at Community level would produce clear benefits by reason of its scale or effects compared with action at the level of the Member States. It should also be restated that the principle of subsidiarity is directed to the EU political institutions and does not apply to the Court's interpretation of the scope of EU powers under the Treaty.

For many, all of these rules do not amount to much. Certainly, the role played by subsidiarity can be described at best as 'regulatory'. In all the years since its introduction, there has been a concerted and growing effort especially by the European Commission to identify such a concept as a tool for better lawmaking, indeed, better regulation. All of the Commission annual reports on the application of subsidiarity and proportionality stress the 'better lawmaking' value. The Commission sees its role discharged if the following three steps are taken: a preliminary analysis in roadmaps which are published for major initiatives when the Commission legislative programme is agreed; these roadmaps provide a preliminary description of a planned Commission initiative and aim to allow all interested actors to be informed in a timely manner. Secondly, a fuller analysis of subsidiarity as part of the impact assessment process, taking into account views expressed during stakeholder consultations and finally, a justification in terms of subsidiarity and proportionality in the explanatory memorandum and recitals of each legal proposal is required.[5] In short, and decontaminated from a 'euro-Brussels speak', we are talking about a regulatory tool. Increasing legislative quality is of course a laudable aim and sectorial studies reveal some interesting results on what kind of impact subsidiarity had on the lawmaking powers of EU institutions.[6] In the same vein, there have been various attempts to apply an economic approach to subsidiarity that tends to equate this principle with efficiency. As has been often argued, the test should essentially

---

[5] Report from the Commission on subsidiarity and proportionality (17th report on better lawmaking covering the year 2009)/com/2010/0547 final/.

[6] R Wesseling, 'Subsidiarity in Community Antitrust Law: Setting the Right Agenda' 22 *Eur L Rev* 35 (1997); M Dawson, 'EU Law "Transformed"? Evaluating Accountability and Subsidiarity in the "Streamlined" OMC for Social Inclusion and Social Protection' European integration online papers (eiop); M Doherty, 'Judicial Review in the European Community: The Environment, Subsidiarity and the Question of Intensity' 22 *Liverp L R* (2000) 101.

be a functional one, leading to the proper allocation of efficiency of public economic functions to the relevant level of governments. Thus, Article 5 TEU criteria can be 'measured' in terms of economies of scale and cross-border externalities, the need to 'act in common' and the 'better achieved' requirements can thus be objectively verified.[7] An economic approach has its merits but, perhaps it also has the paradoxical effect of making subsidiarity slightly rigid and somehow too predictable, depriving it at the same time of any constitutional significance. Thus an extra dimension needs to be added, and whether one likes it or not, adjudication provides one accordingly. Still, we are often reminded that subsidiarity is not exactly a 'legal' principle but to use a now famous quote:

[I]n divided-power systems, the most effective defences against centralising pressures are to be found in the political process rather than the judiciary. If this is true for federal systems, should it not be so a fortiori for the Community system, where Member States enjoy more powers? Defining at what level a task is better accomplished is primarily a political problem: it should be therefore left to the political process.[8]

Thus, if it is a political principle it is not justiciable and the courts should not be involved.

III. The European Court of Justice and Subsidiarity

The recognition that subsidiarity 'is first and foremost a political principle'[9] should lead to the conclusion that justiciability is excluded. Yet this is not correct. The Court of Justice has confirmed in the relentless series of cases that have come before it, that the principle is in fact justiciable. Thus, for instance, it quickly confirmed, moving away from a previous contrary Advocate General's Opinion,[10] that there had to be a role for subsidiarity in the area of the internal market and that the Court would scrutinize its use in this field.[11] Further, the EU courts have often referred to

---

[7] T Padoa Schioppa, 'Economic Federalism and the European Union' in K Knop (ed), *Rethinking Federalism: Citizens, Markets and Governments in a Changing World* (University of British Columbia Press, 154). See also the various contributions in *Forum: Subsidiarity in the European Union* (Intereconomics, September/October 2006).

[8] R Dehousse, 'Does Subsidiarity Really Matter?' EUI, EUI Working Papers no 92/93 (1992). See also AG Toth, 'Is Subsidiarity Justiciable?' (1994) 19 *ELR* 268.

[9] Commission Report to the European Council on the Adaptation of Community Legislation to the Subsidiarity Principle, COM(93) 545.

[10] See the Opinion of Advocate General Fennelly in Case C-376/98 *Germany v Parliament and Council* [2000] ECR I-8419, para. 142, where it was argued that 'the exercise of Community competence under Articles 57(2) and 100A of the Treaty is exclusive in character and that the principle of subsidiarity is not applicable. There can be no test of "comparative efficiency" between potential Member State and Community action'.

[11] See the Court's judgment in Case C-491/01 *British American Tobacco and Imperial Tobacco* [2002] ECR I-11453, para 179, where it held that 'the principle of subsidiarity applies where the Community legislature makes use of Article 95 EC (now Article 114 TFEI), inasmuch as that provision does not give it exclusive competence to regulate economic activity on the internal market, but only a certain competence for the purpose of improving the conditions for its establishment and functioning'.

this principle as an interpretative aid or a supporting argument in the judicial *ratio decidendi*[12] so no question about justiciability, however, the Court's application of the concept and the level of review it has exercised have been of a minimalist nature. The Court has readily accepted in a number of cases raising subsidiarity pleas, that where the Community institutions have power to act, it is inevitably the Community institutions that are best placed to exercise that power. In the *BAT* judgment, the Court adopted a circular agreement—first it stated that as the objective of the directive in question on the manufacture, presentation and sale of tobacco products, was to eliminate the barriers raised by the differences between the Member States' laws,

[S]uch an objective cannot be sufficiently achieved by the Member States individually and calls for action at Community level, as demonstrated by the multifarious development of national laws in this case. It follows that, in the case of the Directive, the objective of the proposed action could be better achieved at Community level.[13]

This perfunctory scrutiny and the deployment of reasoning confounding the existence and exercise of conferred powers, arguably deprive judicial inspection of the use of subsidiarity of all meaningful purpose. Furthermore, the Court has in the past demanded little proof that the concept of subsidiarity had even been considered by the relevant institutions. In the *Biotechnological Inventions* case, the Court, in an infamous passage dealing with subsidiarity, suggested that compliance with the principle was 'necessarily implicit' in the preamble to the relevant Directive, which stated that, in the absence of action at Community level, the development of the laws and practices of the different Member States impeded the proper functioning of the internal market.[14] Alarmingly, the Court was able to conclude, rejecting the subsidiarity plea in the *Biotechnological Inventions* case, that the Directive stated 'sufficient reasons on that point'.[15] More recent cases portray a similar hesitance on the part of the Court to interfere with the margin of discretion of the legislative institutions by engaging in a rigorous scrutiny of the deployment of subsidiarity.

Thus, in Case C-518/07 *Commission v Germany*,[16] the Court found that a directive on data processing fell within the scope of what is now Article 114 TFEU. Germany tried, in vain, to invoke the principle of subsidiarity, alongside the principle of proportionality, to protect its long-established supervisory national arrangements on the protection of data, thus disputing the need to make any alterations in order to comply with its transposition obligations under the relevant European legislative measure. The Court's brief conclusion on the subsidiarity plea does not appear to contain any indication of a new and developing approach to

---

[12] See T Tridimas, *The General Principles of EU law* (Oxford University Press, 2006) 184. He refers for instance to Case C-114/01 *Avesta Polarit Chrome* [2003] ECR I-8725 and Case C-103/01 *Commission v Germany* [2003] ECR I-5369.

[13] Case C-491/01 *Ex parte British American Tobacco* [2002] ECR I-11453, paras 180–3; Case C-84/94 *UK v Council (Working Time)* [1996] ECR I-5755, paras 46–7; Case T-326/07 *Cheminova v Commission* [2009] ECR II-02685, paras 251–61.

[14] Case C-377/98 *Netherlands v European Parliament and Council* [2001] ECR I-7079, para 33.

[15] Ibid.

[16] Case C-518/07 *Commission v Germany* (Judgment of 9 March 2010) [2010] ECR I-1885.

subsidiarity monitoring: the judgment is in fact exemplary of the ephemeral treatment of the concept to date. In the specific circumstances of the case, the Court may have been particularly reluctant to unravel an already adopted legislative measure in the context of proceedings brought for failure of one of the Member States to fulfil its obligations. At the same time, however, the Court's recent judgment in the *Vodafone* case[17] similarly displayed little evidence of a new era in subsidiarity monitoring. The case involved a challenge to the Roaming Regulation,[18] which established Community-wide maximum prices in respect of roaming on public mobile phone networks across the Member States. The question arose as to whether the measure could be found to be invalid on the basis that subsidiarity had been infringed through the imposition of a price ceiling in respect of retail roaming charges. In the Opinion[19] of Advocate General Maduro, the decision to regulate maximum retail prices for roaming services at Community rather than national level required specific justification.[20] He also urged the Court to take a stance on a possible breach of the subsidiarity principle. He argued that neither the objective pursued by a Community measure, nor the intent of the legislator, can be considered decisive when determining compliance with the subsidiarity principle.[21] Instead, subsidiarity monitoring must entail a scrutiny of the possible problems or costs involved in leaving the matter to be addressed by the Member States. The Advocate General concluded that the Community legislator had, in fact, been in a better position than the national legislator to regulate the retail rates of roaming prices, the 'decisive' argument stemming from 'the cross-border nature of the economic activity to be regulated'.[22] In reaching this conclusion, the Advocate General emphasized the duty of the Court with respect to subsidiarity monitoring, highlighting the difference between the Court substituting its judgment for that of the Community legislator and simply compelling it instead to take subsidiarity seriously.[23] Despite

---

[17] Case C-58/08 *Vodafone Ltd, Telefónica O2 Europe plc, T-Mobile International AG, Orange Personal Communications Services Ltd v Secretary of State for Business, Enterprise and Regulatory Reform* (Judgment of 8 June 2010) [2010] ECR I nyr.

[18] Regulation (EC) No 717/2007 of the European Parliament and of the Council of 27 June 2007 on roaming on public mobile telephone networks within the Community and amending Directive 2002/21/EC (OJ 2007 L 171, 32).

[19] Opinion of AG Maduro in Case C-58/08 *Vodafone Ltd, Telefónica O2 Europe plc, T-Mobile International AG, Orange Personal Communications Services Ltd v Secretary of State for Business, Enterprise and Regulatory Reform* (Opinion of 1 October 2009) [2010] ECR I nyr.

[20] Ibid para 28.

[21] Ibid fn 19, para 30. In the view of the Advocate General, '[F]irst, the judgment to be made under the principle of subsidiarity is not about the objective pursued but whether the pursuit of that objective requires Community action. Certain Community objectives (which in themselves justify the existence of a Community competence) may be better pursued by the Member States (with the consequence that the exercise of that competence is not justified). Second, the intent of the Community legislator is not sufficient to demonstrate compliance with the principle of subsidiarity. The latter requires that there be a reasonable justification for the proposition that there is a need for Community action. This must be supported by more than simply highlighting the possible benefits accruing from Community action.'

[22] Ibid. In the view of the Advocate General, it was reasonable for the Community legislator to conclude that national regulatory authorities would not have attached the same 'degree of priority' to the Community rights protected under the challenged regulation, while the Community had a 'special interest' in protecting the particular economic activity in question (see para 34).

[23] Ibid.

the clear invitation of its Advocate General, and despite referring for the first time to the Amsterdam Protocol, the CJEU reiterated its low-profile approach and concluded that the Community legislature, by introducing a common approach, implicitly satisfies the principle of subsidiarity. However, in my view at least, the Court made an attempt to engage in some discussion by pointing out that it would be absurd—because of the interdependence of retail and wholesale charges for roaming services, to leave the fixing of wholesale prices to Member States' action.

[A]ny measure seeking to reduce retail charges alone without affecting the level of costs for the wholesale supply of Community-wide roaming services would have been liable to disrupt the smooth functioning of the Community-wide roaming market. For that reason, the Community legislature decided that any action would require a joint approach at the level of both wholesale charges and retail charges, in order to contribute to the smooth functioning of the internal market in those services.[24]

Although there might be some positives to be taken from the *Vodafone* judgment, it cannot be argued that the position of the Court has substantially changed, despite several calls for increased judicial involvement. The Advocate General in the *Vodafone* judgment has not in fact been alone in advocating a more rigorous judicial scrutiny of compliance with the subsidiarity principle. Thus, for instance, the European Union Committee of the House of Lords, in anticipation of the Constitutional Treaty, embarked on an evaluation of subsidiarity monitoring and concluded its enquiry expressing the hope that the Court would take 'a more critical approach to subsidiarity, particularly in ensuring that the justification for action at Union level is adequate'.[25] A similar concern was expressed early on by Advocate General Léger,[26] who considered how useful it could be, for the purpose of ensuring a proper application of the principle of subsidiarity, for the obligation to state reasons in the Treaty 'to be enforced with particular rigor whenever the Community legislature takes action to lay down new rules'.[27] In the view of the Advocate General, given the role played by subsidiarity in allocating powers between the Member States and the Community, it did not appear excessive to expect the Community institutions 'systematically to state reasons for their decisions'.[28] Rather, it was mandatory for the Community measures to 'indicate, either implicitly or explicitly, but in any event clearly' the relevant authority basis, 'even if only to state, where this is the case, that the principle of subsidiarity does not come

---

[24] Ibid fn 19, para 77. Although as it was observed by AG Maduro, 'Once maximum wholesale rates are fixed and once the requirement for a finding of SMP before regulatory intervention could take place was removed, the Community could have empowered national regulators to set maximum retail prices for roaming services if they felt that the retail rates charged by providers in their State were excessive', at para 28.

[25] House of Lords EU Committee, 'Strengthening national parliamentary scrutiny of the EU—the Constitution's subsidiarity early warning mechanism' Report with Evidence, 14th Report of Session 2004–05, at <http://www.publications.parliament.uk/pa/ld200405/ldselect/ldeucom/101/10102.htm>.

[26] Opinion of AG Léger in C-233/94 *Germany v Parliament and Council (Deposit guarantee directive)* [1997] ECR I-2405.

[27] Ibid para 87.

[28] Ibid fn 26, para 89.

into play'.[29] Nonetheless, the Court has so far been reluctant to enforce convincingly even this procedural aspect of subsidiarity and, in the specific case at hand, the Court appears to have adopted reasoning diametrically opposed to that of the Advocate General.[30]

The reasons for such a 'minimal' approach are potentially numerous. Apart from trite worries of political interference, perhaps a thorough judicial scrutiny of the use of subsidiarity might appear counterintuitive insofar as it requires the Court to question acts already adopted and probe into the *acquis communautaire*. It is interesting to note that, in an early resolution, the European Parliament expressed concern that subsidiarity might be used as a pretext to call into question all that had been achieved at the Union level, stressing that the application of subsidiarity should not under any circumstances result in a weakening of EU law.[31] It is perhaps this underlying bipolar ethos of the principle of subsidiarity, commanding, on the one hand, the preservation of national autonomy, and, on the other, a centralizing premise based on arguments of comparative efficiency, that has made the Court reluctant to interfere with the political bargains struck by the legislative institutions. Or, perhaps, as it has been summarized with an excellent title, subsidiarity is just the wrong idea, in the wrong place, at the wrong time.[32]

IV. Lisbon, Subsidiarity and the Court

There is, however, always room for improvement and the potential for change. Among the many protocols annexed to the Treaty of Lisbon, one of the most significant is certainly Protocol (No 2) on the Application of the Principles of Subsidiarity and Proportionality. The most significant changes relate of course to the enhanced role of national parliaments in monitoring compliance with the principle of subsidiarity both by redefining the Commission's obligations and through the establishment of a formal scrutiny procedure (yellow card

---

[29] Ibid fn 26, para 90.

[30] The Court in C-233/94 *Germany v Parliament and Council (Deposit guarantee directive)* [1997] ECR I-2405, para 28 held that, 'on any view, the Parliament and the Council did explain why they considered that their action was in conformity with the principle of subsidiarity and, accordingly, that they complied with the obligation to give reasons as required under Article 190 of the Treaty. An express reference to that principle cannot be required'.

[31] European Parliament Resolution on the Commission reports to the European Council—on the application of the subsidiarity principle in 1994 (COM(94) 0533 - C4-0215/95) entitled 'Better Law-making' on the application of the subsidiarity and proportionality principles, on simplification and on consolidation—1995 (CSE(95) 0580 - C4-0561/95) entitled 'Better Law-making 1996' on the application of the subsidiarity and proportionality principles, on simplification and on consolidation (CSE(96) 0007 - C4-0015/97) on the application of the subsidiarity and proportionality principles (interim report) (CSE(96) 0002 - C4-0355/96) [C (1997) 167, 34]. The European Parliament in the resolution noted with concern the lack of progress made during 1994–96 in essential areas of the internal market, condemning the way the use of subsidiarity had influenced this state of affairs, and called on the Commission to demonstrate that the principle of subsidiarity had not been applied to the detriment of the *acquis communautaire*.

[32] G Davies, 'Subsidiarity: The Wrong Idea, in the Wrong Place, at the Wrong Time' (2006) 43 *CMLRev* 63.

procedure).[33] The Protocol also contains further attempts to subject the principle of subsidiarity to some stricter rules. For instance, it is provided in Article 5 that the 'reasons for concluding that a Union objective can be better achieved at Union level shall be substantiated by qualitative or, wherever possible, quantitative indicators'. Further, all proposals have to take into account their financial implications and in the case of directives, of their implications for the rules to be put in place by Member States including, where necessary, the regional legislation. The Commission has also promised to review its control mechanisms and present its findings in its next report on subsidiarity.[34] Of particular relevance in the context of our discussion is, however, Article 8 of the Protocol which introduces a new form of action for a breach of subsidiarity. Article 8 provides that:

The Court of Justice of the European Union shall have jurisdiction in actions on grounds of infringement of the principle of Subsidiarity by a legislative act, brought in accordance with the rules laid down in Article 263 of the Treaty on the Functioning of the European Union by Member States, or notified by them in accordance with their legal order on behalf of their national Parliament or a chamber thereof. In accordance with the rules laid down in the said Article, the Committee of the Regions may also bring such actions against legislative acts for the adoption of which the Treaty on the Functioning of the European Union provides that it be consulted.

Procedurally speaking, this new form of action does not change much as the ordinary action for judicial review under Article 263 TFEU will be used. More radical options such as conferring directly on national parliaments' locus standi before the Court have been discarded. So it will be for the governments to act should the national parliament so request. Still, the Protocol formulation seems to actually require Member States to make such an action available to their parliaments.[35] A new element is also that the Committee of the Regions (CoR) acquires standing to bring Article 263 proceedings, albeit only in regard to those acts on which it was consulted.[36]

The Protocol certainly reaffirms the political dimension of the subsidiarity principle as it does purposefully devolve to political institutions, national

---

[33] See R Corbett, above n 3.

[34] Report from the Commission on Subsidiarity and Proportionality (*17th report on Better Law-making covering the year 2009*) COM(2010) 547.

[35] The procedural arrangements are of course at the discretion of each Member State but they can be introduced via ordinary instruments and do not need constitutional amendments. See Presidium Notes CONV 724/1/03 REV 1, 144.

[36] It should be added that the Protocol also requires that the Commission should consult widely and where appropriate, take into account the regional and local dimension of the action envisaged (Article 2). Any draft legislative act should contain a detailed statement making it possible to appraise compliance with the principles of subsidiarity and proportionality. The statement should contain some assessment of the proposal's financial impact and, in the case of a directive, of its implications for the rules to be put in place by Member States, including, where necessary, the regional legislation. The reasons for concluding that a Union objective can be better achieved at Union level shall be substantiated by qualitative and, wherever possible, quantitative indicators. Draft legislative acts shall take account of the need for any burden, whether financial or administrative, falling upon the Union, national governments, regional or local authorities, economic operators and citizens, to be minimized and commensurate with the objective to be achieved (Article 5).

parliaments, the task of subsidiarity monitoring. However, its Article 8 specifically compels the CJEU to take sides on the application of subsidiarity. What should be expected then? First of all, legal challenges will surely be brought. The Committee of the Regions, strengthened by its extended role as a consultative body, has already signalled its intention of making use of Article 8.[37] According to the CoR former president,

[W]e see this new right to challenge EU laws in court more as a deterrent than an actual threat. We are convinced that this new possibility will deepen our relations with other EU institutions and national parliaments. We will exercise this right with caution, but with great conviction in cases where we feel it is necessary to defend the subsidiarity principle in EU lawmaking.[38]

As for national parliaments, they are equally active. The UK Parliament has already[39] made use of the Lisbon procedure[40] by objecting, on the basis that it contravenes the principle of subsidiarity, to the proposed Directive[41] relating to the admission of third-country nationals as seasonal workers. The objection of the House of Lords essentially suggests that action at the EU level is not necessary in an area, like immigration, which does not fall within the exclusive competence of the European Union, and where the needs of Member States differ, for example, as regards the numbers of workers needed, the times at which and for which they are needed, and the work for which they are needed. The Swedish Parliament has 'sanctioned' instead the proposal for amendments to the current EU regulations on deposit guarantee schemes. It objected, in particular, to the introduction of an obligation of a credit mechanism between national schemes, as a last resort for managing temporary financial needs.[42]

V. Judicial Review of Subsidiarity—Misconceptions, Procedure and Substance

If it is to be taken for granted that sooner or later litigation will be brought, the questions to be addressed are therefore: can we expect a new and developing case

---

[37] The Lisbon Treaty enables the CoR to be consulted by the European Parliament, not just by the Commission and the Council. The areas for which the CoR has the right to be consulted by the three institutions have also been extended and new areas such as energy and climate change are included.

[38] <http://www.euractiv.com/regional./regions-hope-wield-new-powers-lisbon-treaty>.

[39] HL Paper 35, 2010–11, 13 October 2010 at <http://www.publications.parliament.uk/pa/ld201011/ldselect/ldeucom/35/35.pdf>.

[40] Article 6 of the Protocol (No 2) on the Application of the Principles of Subsidiarity and Proportionality.

[41] Commission proposal for a Directive of the European Parliament and of the Council on the conditions of entry and residence of third-country nationals for the purposes of seasonal employment (COM(2010) 379; Council doc 12208/10). The proposal establishes a fast-track procedure for the admission of third-country seasonal workers and provides for the facilitation of the re-entry of a seasonal worker in a subsequent season.

[42] Statement by the Committee on Finance 2009/10: FiU42 Subsidiarity check of a proposal for a Directive on deposit guarantees schemes.

law on subsidiarity monitoring? Is the Court equipped for this new task? What kind of justiciability test would need to be employed? In short, is it a good or bad idea to have the Court involved?

First, the Protocol in interlocking the Court within a very (perhaps too) detailed procedural grid has the effect of getting rid of a common misconception. There is a certain tendency in identifying subsidiarity with the idea that European integration should be able to incorporate and respect constitutional diversities and the allocation of competence in different national systems. Thus the Protocol on subsidiarity is often mentioned in the same breath as the new Article 4 of the Lisbon Treaty which clearly acknowledges that Member States are legally able to organize their constitutional structure as they wish and that the Union shall respect these differences. It is sometimes suggested therefore, that subsidiarity could become a tool that should be used by the Court in accepting these constitutional divergences. The traditional case law of the Court is in fact very rigid in establishing that any internal constitutional differences need to be overlooked in the interest of the uniform application of EU law. Time and time again the Court has reaffirmed that, 'a Member State cannot plead provisions, practices or situations prevailing in its domestic legal order, including those resulting from the constitutional organisation of that State, to justify the failure to observe obligations arising under Community law'.[43] Such a monolithic approach has in my view already been altered in the recent case law of the Court and we might not need to look to subsidiarity for support. Even in core areas such as state aid and the internal market there are clear signs. As far as state aid is concerned, the Court has now explicitly recognized the relevance of internal federal arrangements for the application of EU law. In cases dealing with differential tax rates adopted by a region or other infra-state bodies the Court found that a measure did not constitute aid if three conditions are satisfied: (i) the measure must be adopted by a regional or local authority constitutionally separate from the central government (institutional autonomy); (ii) it must be adopted without the central government being able to directly intervene in the determination of its content (procedural autonomy); and (iii) the financial consequences of the measure must not be offset by other regions or by the central government (economic autonomy).[44] The second example comes from those cases where the Court is required to balance the need to guarantee free trade with the preservation of certain national public aims. Traditionally, the 'negative integration' provisions of the Treaty that require Member States to remove any obstacles on free movement have been applied by the Court to any kind of national regulatory measures and any possible justifications put forward by Member States were subject to intense scrutiny. In several recent high-profile cases the Court seems instead to have embraced a sort of 'margin of appreciation' assessment, whereby the

---

[43] Case C-212/06 *Government of the French Community and Walloon Government* [2008] ECR I-1683, para 58, with further references.
[44] Case C-88/03 *Portugal v Commission* [2006] ECR I-7115; Case T-211/04 *Gibraltar v Commission* [2008] ECR II-3745; and Joined Cases C-428/06 to C-434/06 *UGT–Rioja and Others* [2008] ECR I-6747.

intensity of scrutiny diminishes in consideration of the interests of the Member State in question. The *Omega* judgment is a good example. It concerned a German law banning certain games (a 'laserdrome') involving players shooting at each other. The Court considered German law to have violated the right to provide an economic service in other Member States but justified such a provision on the grounds that the game in question was an affront to human dignity—a clear acknowledgement of the importance of human dignity rights enshrined in the German Constitution.[45] These examples raise the problem of national constitutions being used to avoid the application of EU law or possibly endangering the uniform application of EU law; they are nonetheless 'signs' of a more mature and multilevel constitutionalism.[46]

At the same time, other problems are raised—for instance, on the vagaries of the application of the principle of proportionality sometimes indicated as the 'easy one' to apply in contrast to that of subsidiarity. The Protocol with its emphasis on the role of national parliaments (and their governments) instead puts the Court in a rather advantageous position as it focuses its jurisdiction with a 'file of the case' compiled only after a lengthy 'discovery' between national parliaments and the Commission: legislative proposal plus objections by national parliaments plus reply from the Commission. The Lisbon Treaty thus by providing an enhanced role for national parliaments, allowing them to express their views on whether draft legislative proposals, can facilitate a more penetrating judicial review. The assessment of the national parliaments may be in fact of value to the Court in its inspection of subsidiarity insofar as it will provide a potential counterpoint to the arguments presented by the legislative measure itself and the Community institutions promoting it. Still, it is clear that we need at least to formulate some ideas on what criteria the Court could employ in deciding on whether the principle of subsidiarity has been complied with or not. It would therefore be the duty of the Court to require EU institutions to demonstrate a need 'to act in common', or if you prefer an economic take—to make sure that the EU institution subjects any measure to a verification of the existence of either economies of scale or cross-border externalities. As for the actual test and intensity of scrutiny that the CJEU should apply once the case is brought, commentators tend to distinguish between substantive and procedural review, usually emphasizing the latter as the only possible and feasible way forward.[47] In reality, as in any form of judicial review, procedure is always substantial and it all depends on the intensity of scrutiny. Thus if we accept for the sake of argument that the 'file of the case' will be based on competing reconstruction but masterful analysis on behalf of the Commission and the national parliaments on the comparative efficiency of a certain proposal, the Court will be confronted with not such an unusual situation as it will be for the

---

[45] Case C-36/02 *Omega* [2004] ECR I-9609, see also Joined Cases C-338/04 and C-359-360/04 *Placanica* [2007] ECR I-1891; and Case C-137/09 *Josemans* [2010] ECR I-nyr.
[46] See Davies, above n 32.
[47] See the discussion in B Flynn, The Legal Enforceability of Reformed Subsidiarity, IEAP, WP, 2005/W/07 and I Cooper, 'The Watchdogs of Subsidiarity: National Parliaments and the Logic of Arguing in the EU' (JCMS 920006) 281.

Court to conduct a full review as to whether the Commission and national parliaments applied the relevant rules of law properly. The Court obviously cannot take the place of the Commission or national parliaments on issues where both must carry out complex economic and ecological assessments in this context. However, it would be up to the Court to verify, 'that the measure in question is not vitiated by a manifest error or a misuse of powers, that the competent authority did not clearly exceed the bounds of its discretion and that the procedural guarantees, which are of particularly fundamental importance in this context, have been fully observed.'[48] This is the standard formulation used by Community courts in reviewing Commission decisions; a standard that can be used with vigour and intensity. In the *Tetra Laval* case the Court famously held that:

Whilst the Court recognises that the Commission has a margin of discretion with regard to economic matters that does not mean that the Community Courts must refrain from reviewing the Commission's interpretation of information of an economic nature. Not only must the Community Courts, inter alia, establish whether the evidence relied on is factually accurate, reliable and consistent but also whether that evidence contains all the information which must be taken into account in order to assess a complex situation and whether it is capable of substantiating the conclusions drawn from it.[49]

Therefore, without asking a judge to substitute their views for that of a legislator, it is not impossible for courts to assess whether qualitative and, wherever possible, quantitative indicators that the Protocol on subsidiarity requires to be taken into account have been reliable and well funded. The national parliament–Commission–CJEU subsidiarity review as incarnated by the Protocol procedure also has the advantage of intervening *ex ante* before the actual adoption. As observed by Hoffman and Türk, albeit in a much more general context, this model of judicial review not only has the advantage of measures being reviewed in close temporary proximity to their adoption but also that in a procedure that is after all determined by EU law in which the national authorities participate, 'those national authorities operate under the rules and principles of Community law and fall within the scope of Community law',[50] making judicial review less complicated. It is perhaps interesting to refer to a judgment that is seldom mentioned in the list of 'subsidiarity' cases. In the *Polish and Estonians NAPs* case[51] the CFI (now General Court) made a very rare reference to the principle of subsidiarity. The case concerned Directive 2003/87/EC

---

[48] Case T-13/99 *Pfizer Animal Health v Council* [2002] ECR II-3305, paras 166 and 171; Case T-70/99 *Alpharma v Council* [2002] ECR II-3495, paras 177 and 182; and Case T-392/02 *Solvay Pharmaceuticals v Council* [2003] ECR II-4555, paras 126 and 188.

[49] Case C-12/03 P *Commission v Tetra Laval* [2005] ECR I-987, para 39; see also Case C-413/06 P *Bertelsmann and Sony Corporation of America v Impala* [2008] ECR I-4951; and Case C-525/04 *Spain v Lenzing* [2007] ECR I-9947, para 57; and Case C-290/07 P *Commission v Scott* [2010] ECR I-0000. See in general A Fritzsche, 'Discretion, Scope of Judicial Review and Institutional Balance in European Law' *CMLR* (2010) vol 47, fn 2, 361.

[50] H Hofmann and A Türk, 'Legal challenges in EU Administrative Law by the Move to an Integrated Administration' in H Hofmann and A Türk (eds), *Legal challenges in EU Administrative Law* (Edward Elgar, 2009) 355, 374.

[51] Cases T-183/07 and T-263/07 *Poland v Commission* [2009] ECR II-3395, under appeal C-504/09P.

aimed at reductions of greenhouse gas emissions.[52] The Directive establishes a scheme for emission allowance trading within the EU and provides that each Member State develops a national allocation plan (NAP) stating the total quantity of allowances that it intends to allocate for that period and how it proposes to allocate them. In the case of incompatibility with the criteria listed in the Directive, the Commission may reject all or part of the NAP. In the judgment, the General Court annulled in their entirety the Commission's decisions rejecting the Estonian and Polish national allocation plans. On the substance the Court held that the Commission substantially failed to provide any adequate data and that the Commission rejected the NAPs on the basis of reasoning which was merely based on, 'the evocation of doubts as to the reliability of the data used by Estonia and Poland'. For what is relevant in the context of our discussion, the General Court after reminding itself of the need to apply a subsidiarity analysis, held that the case of environmental protection is clearly an area of shared competence where it would be for the EU institutions to prove to what extent the powers of the Member State and, therefore, its freedom of action, are limited by EU law and in this case the relevant Directive.

To go back to our Protocol-based judicial review action, as has been noted by Wyatt, there might be two likely scenarios: in the first, in the absence of a yellow card the case would be arguably prima facie unfounded (and it is unlikely it would be brought anyway). In the second, when national parliaments have actually raised a yellow card and the Commission has maintained its draft it would be likely that the Courts would put the burden of proof onto the Commission to prove that the national parliament has made a manifest error, however, still within the relevant EU benchmark.[53]

VI. Conclusions

As has been seen, the Court has in the past exercised a minimalist review of the subsidiarity principle. The confounding of the existence and exercise of Community powers has meant that there has generally been little possibility to examine the substantive grounds of challenge raised in subsidiarity pleas. Even more alarmingly, judgments such as the *Biotechnological Inventions* case suggest that even the procedural checks on the deployment of subsidiarity have been of a modest nature. Admittedly, insofar as subsidiarity review requires the Court to probe into an already adopted legislative measure, which the Court may have even concluded that the institutions were competent to enact, it entails an unenviable task for the

---

[52] Directive 2003/87/EC of the European Parliament and of the Council of 13 October 2003 establishing a scheme for greenhouse gas emission allowance trading within the Community and amending Council Directive 96/61/EC (OJ 2003 L 275, 32), as amended by European Parliament and Council Directive 2004/101/EC of 27 October 2004 (OJ 2004 L 338, 18).
[53] D Wyatt, 'Could a "Yellow Card" for National Parliaments Strengthen Judicial as well as Political Policing of Subsidiarity?' in *Croatian Yearbook of European Law & Policy,* University of Zagreb, Vol 2 (2006) 1.

judiciary. The phrasing of the act and the reasons stated for the act's adoption will not usually offer much indication that subsidiarity may have been infringed. Yet, if subsidiarity is to be taken seriously, the Court must engage in both a rigorous procedural and substantive review of the consideration attributed to subsidiarity as a legal principle. In accordance with Protocol (No 2) on the Application of the Principles of Subsidiarity and Proportionality, the Court should ensure that the reasons for concluding that a Union objective can be better achieved at Union level are substantiated by qualitative or, wherever possible, quantitative indicators. As seen above, this exercise does not entail the Court substituting its judgment for that of the Community legislator, but rather compelling it instead to take subsidiarity seriously. The underlying bipolar ethos of the principle of subsidiarity, mandating, on the one hand, the preservation of regional autonomy, and, on the other, a centralizing premise based on arguments of comparative efficiency, means that the Court will continue to have an arduous task. Nevertheless, it is a task that, especially in the light of the Lisbon reforms and the concomitant possibility for the Court to look for guidance in reasoned opinions produced by national parliaments, the Court should be well equipped to carry out. A rigorous scrutiny of the deployment of subsidiarity will ensure that the Court is diligently fulfilling its judicial review responsibilities and 'developing a culture of subsidiarity could make a decisive contribution to strengthening public confidence in European cooperation'.[54] As has been argued in the immediate aftermath of the insertion of the principle of subsidiarity in the Treaty of Maastricht, the Court has already shown its abilities of skilful navigation in applying equally vague concepts such as proportionality.[55] Likewise, regardless of whether one agrees or not with the stance taken by the Court, the debate on the principle of conferral contained in Article 5(1) TFEU has acquired at least as much concrete dimension following the tobacco litigation and its ensuing case law.

In conclusion, although the majority of commentators see the involvement of the Court of Justice in monitoring subsidiarity not as a positive development as it drags the supreme judicial body into the political arena, it could be argued that the Court is in fact the more appropriate forum. It is a body independent from all other institutions and has been operating virtually as a supreme court for the EU now for more than 50 years. Thus, although it might be a difficult task, the Treaty of Lisbon provides an opportunity for the Court to rise to the challenge, or, to borrow the words of Advocate General Maduro in supporting a more active role for the Court, 'we are not requiring the Court to substitute its judgment for that of the Community legislator but simply to take Subsidiarity seriously'. This in turn might have the effect of making subsidiarity a true operational principle of governance in the EU.[56]

---

[54] Opinion of the Committee of the Regions on Guidelines for the Application and Monitoring of the Subsidiarity and Proportionality Principles (2006/C 115/08), para 1.4.

[55] J Steiner, 'Subsidiarity under the Maastricht Treaty' in D O'Keeffe and P Towney (eds), *Legal Issues of the Maastricht Treaty* (Wiley, 1994) 49, 62.

[56] Case C-376/98 *Germany v European Parliament and Council* [2000] ECR I-8419; Cases C-434/02 & C-210/03 *Arnold Andre* and *Swedish Match* [2004] ECR I-11825 [2004] ECR I-11893; and Case C-380/03 *Germany v European Parliament* [2006] ECR I-11573.

11

The European Union after the Lisbon Treaty: An Elusive 'Institutional Balance'?

Thomas Christiansen

I. The Notion of Institutional Balance

Until the Lisbon Treaty, the institutional architecture of the European Union had seen relatively few major reforms since the formation of the Communities in the 1950s. The 1965 Merger Treaty had indeed united previously separate institutions that had been working in parallel, the transformation of the parliamentary assembly into a directly elected legislature at the end of the 1970s and the creation of the European Council as a regular meeting of Heads of State and Government all changed the shape of the original blueprint. However, the basic pattern of an institutional triangle of Parliament, Council and Commission tasked with legislative decision-making, watched over by a European Court of Justice, had been preserved over the decades. Much of the recent reforms contained in successive treaty revisions changed the relations between these three institutions, with the progressive extension of co-decision between European Parliament and Council in the legislative procedure being the most important aspect in this regard.

Institutional balance, in a basic understanding of the term, is about the absence of any single institution among these three having fundamentally more weight and influence in the politics of the Union than the other two. In the past, a degree of balance has been achieved due to three cross-cutting 'cleavages' that in turn separate and unite the institutions vis-à-vis one another:[1]

- first, Parliament and Council work together as the two chambers of the EU's legislature, whereas the Commission acts as the Union's sole executive;

---

[1] Obviously the use of 'cleavages' here is not in line with the understanding of societal cleavages as developed by Lijphart and others (see A Lijphart, 'Consociational Democracy' *World Politics* 21, no 2 (December 1969)) but is used here in a wider sense of institutional divisions reflecting opposing logics underlying the European integration project.

- second, Commission and Council (Secretariat) both follow a bureaucratic logic, being populated mainly by administrative officials, whereas the European Parliament is the sole parliamentary body in the EU's institutional architecture; and

- third, the European Parliament and the Commission as supranational institutions both represent the common European interest, whereas the Council as an intergovernmental institution stands for the collective interests of the Member States.

It is arguably this last dimension about the supranational/intergovernmental divide in the Union that is most often implied when questions about institutional balance are raised.[2] And it is in this respect that there has been most debate recently, given that the European Parliament has seen its powers significantly increased through the Lisbon Treaty, while at the same time many observers have raised the spectre of rising intergovernmentalism as a result of the Lisbon Treaty changes.[3]

This chapter will analyse the impact of the Lisbon Treaty in terms of these inter-institutional relations and discuss the degree to which there has been a change, if not a threat, to the institutional balance in the European Union. The main conclusion, as we will seek to show, is not that the institutional balance has been dramatically upset by the changes arising from Lisbon, but that the very notion of an institutional triangle—be it in balance or not—is increasingly difficult to maintain in the post-Lisbon Union. The chapter starts out with an overview of the main institutional reforms contained in the new Treaty, before discussing the driving forces that led to these changes. The subsequent section then looks in some detail at the new inter-institutional relations that arise from these arrangements in operation. It does so by distinguishing developments in four different domains of institutional interaction, namely strategic leadership, external relations, coordination of macro-economic policy, and administrative governance. Within each of these domains, there is now a more complex web of relations, given the arrival of new actors on the scene, and the resultant picture is a much more complicated geometry than the comparatively simple institutional triangle described above.

II. The Lisbon Treaty: Key Institutional Reforms

The institutional structure of the European Union has been significantly reformed with the coming into force of the Lisbon Treaty. The main reforms involve the creation of a semi-permanent President of the European Council,[4] the establishment

---

[2] See eg S Crossick, *Community Method vs Intergovernmentalism* (posted on blogactiv.eu on 23 September 2010) <http://crossick.blogactiv.eu/2010/09/23/community-method-vs-intergovernmentalism/>(accessed on 5 April 2011).

[3] U Puetter, 'Consolidating Europe's New Intergovernmentalism—European Council and Council Leadership in Economic Governance and CFSP under the Lisbon Treaty' paper presented at the UACES conference 'The Lisbon Treaty Evaluated', London (January 2011).

[4] S Kurpas et al (eds), 'The Treaty of Lisbon: Implementing the Institutional Innovations' (EPC, Egmont, CEPS) 48–59.

of a European External Action Service, a new role of the High Representative as Vice President of the European Commission and chair of the Foreign Affairs Council of the EU—a new configuration of the Council of the European Union that is formally separate from the General Affairs Council. Furthermore, the powers of the European Parliament have been extended, with important new policy areas—agriculture, trade, justice and home affairs—now falling under the co-decision procedure.[5] The European Parliament also acquired the power to approve international agreements of the Union and to elect the President of the European Commission, leading to the further politicization of EU decision-making. The size of the European Commission, in terms of the number of Commissioners, was also supposed to be the subject of reform, with a reduction in this number to two-thirds of the number of Member States from 2014 onwards,[6] but this reform has been abandoned in negotiations seeking to secure a positive outcome in the second Irish referendum on the Lisbon Treaty.[7] Instead, it has been decided to maintain the link between Commissioners and Member States, giving in particular smaller Member States a continued opportunity to influence the decision-shaping process in the EU. Further important innovations coming with the Lisbon Treaty include the European Citizens Initiative, the new powers for national parliaments[8], and the elevated status of advisory bodies such as the Economic and Social Committee and the Committee of the Regions.

The two key changes in terms of institutional balance within the Union are the establishment of the posts of European Council President and High Representative for Foreign Policy. In order to evaluate the impact of these changes, it is important to look in some detail at the tasks and responsibilities of these posts. According to the Treaty,[9] the new President of the European Council:

- will convene the European Council meetings (four per year; when the situation requires, the President will convene a special meeting of the European Council);

- ensures the preparation and continuity of the work of the European Council in cooperation with the President of the Commission, and on the basis of the work of the General Affairs Council;

- endeavours to facilitate cohesion and consensus within the European Council;

- presents a report to the European Parliament after each of the meetings of the European Council;

- ensures the external representation of the Union on issues concerning its common foreign and security policy, without prejudice to the powers of the

---

[5] Ibid 5–21.
[6] Treaty on European Union, Article 17(5) Official Journal of the European Union, Consolidated Version of the Treaty on European Union, Brussels (2008).
[7] Presidency of the Council of the European Union, 'Presidency Conclusions of the Brussels European Council 11–12 December 2008' (13 February 2009), Article 2.
[8] See the discussion in Chapter 12 of this book.
[9] Treaty on European Union, Article 15(6) Official Journal of the European Union, Consolidated Version of the Treaty on European Union, Brussels (2008).

High Representative for Foreign Affairs (HR)/ Vice President of the European Commission (VP);

- will be assisted by the General Secretariat of the Council and have his private office.

The High Representative for Foreign Affairs and Vice President of the European Commission, does not have to worry about a potential lack of workload. If anything the 'double-' or indeed 'triple-hatting' of that post has been leading to concerns about overload. According to the formal provisions,[10] the High Representative:

- shall conduct the Union's CFSP (and CSDP) and shall contribute by proposals to the development of that policy, which she shall carry out as mandated by the Council;
- shall preside over the Foreign Affairs Council;
- shall represent the Union for matters relating to the CFSP. She shall conduct political dialogue with third parties on the Union's behalf and shall express the Union's position in international organizations and at international conferences;
- shall be assisted by a European External Action Service (EEAS);
- shall ensure coordination of the civilian and military aspects of conflict management;
- shall ensure the consistency of the Union's external action;
- shall be one of the Vice Presidents of the Commission and shall be responsible within the Commission for responsibilities incumbent on it in external relations and for coordinating other aspects of the Union's external action;
- is bound by Commission procedures for Commission-related responsibilities.

Overall, the Lisbon Treaty introduces many of the provisions of the Constitutional Treaty (which failed in the ratification stage), which in turn means that a lot of these reforms codify existing practices and/or carry forward the underlying trend of greater institutionalization of the European Union, often based on case law from the European Court of Justice.[11] It constitutes the culmination of a long period of almost constant treaty reform that began with the negotiation of the Single European Act in 1985, but also brings that phase of European integration to a close: even if the Lisbon Treaty does not turn out to be the 'constitutional settlement' for the coming 50 years that some had expected it

---

[10] Treaty on European Union, Article 18 Official Journal of the European Union, Consolidated Version of the Treaty on European Union, Brussels (2008).

[11] For a more detailed debate concerning the continuous nature of EU treaty reform, see eg B de Witte, 'The Closest Thing to a Constitutional Conversation in Europe: The Semi-Permanent Treaty Revision Process' in P Beaumont, C Lyons, and N Walker (eds), *Convergence and Divergence in European Public Law* (Hart Publishing, 2002) 137–60; or T Christiansen and C Reh, *Constitutionalizing the European Union* (Palgrave Macmillan, 2009).

to be,[12] it appears unlikely that a major reform involving formal treaty change will be politically possible in the coming years.

At the same time, the coming into force of the Lisbon Treaty itself required a process of implementing new provisions—a process that has lasted for several years. It is only in the course of this implementation process that crucial details, and in some cases the very meaning of the new provisions, will become clear. The Treaty contains not only several transition periods but also many 'incomplete contracts' which need to be resolved as new institutional and procedural provisions are operationalized.[13] Cases in point include the detailed arrangements for the EEAS and the framework for delegated acts and implementing measures (comitology), both of which were for a long period the subject of some controversy among the institutions.[14] The Lisbon Treaty's long gestation period as well as its lengthy and unpredictable implementation process demonstrate the extent to which treaty change is a continuous process—a process which will in the future also be carried forward by the use of *passerelle* clauses, ECJ jurisprudence and further institutional changes being adopted outside the formal treaty framework. The recent agreements among the Member States and the EU institutions in order to address the debt crises of several Eurozone countries—as discussed below—is a timely illustration of this pattern.

III. The Driving Forces behind Institutional Reform

Before discussing the effects of these reforms on the question of institutional balance in the European Union, it is useful to establish the driving forces behind these changes. Much of the impetus behind the reform of both the Lisbon Treaty and the Nice Treaty had been the 'Eastern enlargement' of the Union.[15] The prospect, and the eventual accession, of 12 new Member States was expected to

---

[12] A Moravcsik, 'The European Constitutional Settlement' *World Economy* 31, no 1 (January 2008) 158–83. See also *European Voice*, 'Dehaene challenges Giscard on 50-year Treaty Claim' (Brussels   03.07.2003),   <http://www.europeanvoice.com/article/imported/dehaene-challenges-giscard-on-50-year-treaty-claim/47876.aspx> (accessed on 5 April 2011).

[13] See H Kassim and A Menon, 'The Principal-agent Approach and the Study of the European Union: Promise Unfulfilled?' *Journal of European Public Policy* 10, no 1 (March 2003) 121–39 for a discussion of the incomplete contracts concept in the context of European integration.

[14] For a discussion of the challenges of implementing the new provisions in the EEAS, see inter alia J Bátora, 'A Democratically Accountable European External Action Service: Three Scenarios' *European Integration Online Papers* 14 (2010) 1–20. And Wessels, Wolfgang, and Franziska Bopp, 'The Institutional Architecture of CFSP after the Lisbon Treaty—Constitutional Breakthrough or Challenges ahead?' *Challenge Liberty and Security Research Report No.10*, 2008. For a discussion of the issues surrounding the reform of comitology, see T Christiansen, 'Administrative Fusion in the European Union: Reviewing a Decade of Comitology Reform' in U Diedrichs, A Faber, F Tekin, and G Umbach (eds), *Europe Reloaded: Differentiation or Fusion?* (NOMOS Verlag, 2009).

[15] For a discussion of the link between enlargement and institutional reform, see inter alia T Christiansen and C Reh, above n 10; B Steunenberg, 'Enlargement and Institutional Reform in the European Union: Separate or Connected Issues?' *Constitutional Political Economy* 12, no 4 (2001) 351–70; N Walker, 'Constitutionalising Enlargement, Enlarging Constitutionalism' *European Law Journal* 9, 365–85, July 2003.

overburden the EU's decision-making system and endanger the efficiency and effectiveness of the Union to address the challenges it faces.

This concern about the anticipated negative effects of enlargement had three separate dimensions: first, the simple 'numbers game' of a rise from 15 to 27 (or more) implies that decisions taken under unchanged procedural rules would be harder to arrive at as more potential 'veto players' enter the fray. Second, the fact that most of the new Member States can be considered as small or medium-sized countries has been a concern to those (mainly from the larger Member States) worried about the future imbalance between smaller and larger Member States (something that has particular resonance with respect to the composition of a European Commission in which all Commissioners are equal); and, third, there was concern for the leadership in a Union in which individual countries would only hold the Presidency every 13 years or more, meaning that the 'Presidency experience' would be unique and within Member States—old or new—there would be very little, if any, institutional memory on how to handle the diverse and complex tasks that come with running the Council. This would in turn have negative repercussions for policy-continuity in the EU as business would be constantly handed over from one to another, new and inexperienced, Presidency.

There were other driving forces behind the treaty reform process of the past decade—such as the long-standing search for coherence in EU foreign policy in the face of changing global politics[16] and the desire by Europe's political class to address long-standing concerns about the Union's perceived 'democratic deficit'[17]—but enlargement was clearly the main one. It is against that background that it is appropriate to evaluate the changes arising from the Lisbon Treaty in terms of whether and how they addressed the above concerns.

The picture is somewhat skewed, however, by the fact that the treaty reform, which was meant to prepare the EU *before* the arrival of the accession of the new Member States, in the end occurred some five years after the main wave of Eastern enlargement. This meant that the reforms came late and addressed a 'problem' that had largely failed to appear—the above concerns which had been widespread ahead of enlargement did *not* lead to any slowdown or standstill of the EU's decision-making system. The main EU institutions did work well after 2004, and in fact in some respects performed better—more efficiently—than prior to enlargement. This is true both with respect to their internal functioning as well as their interaction in the legislative process or in the area of centralized policy-implementation (comitology).[18]

---

[16] See S Nuttal, 'Coherence and Consistency' in C Hill and M Smith (eds), *International Relations and the European Union* (Oxford University Press, 2005) 91–112, for a discussion of this issue.

[17] For key contributions to the debate about the absence or presence of a 'democratic deficit' in the European Union, see A Moravcsik, 'Reassessing Legitimacy in the European Union' *Journal of Common Market Studies* (November 2002) 40, no 4 603–24; G Majone, 'The Common Sense of European Integration' no 5 (August 2006) *Journal of European Public Policy* 13, 607–26; and A Foellesdal and S Hix, 'Why There is a Democratic Deficit in the EU: A Response to Majone and Moravcsik' *Journal of Common Market Studies* 44, no 3 (September 2006) 533–62.

[18] See the contributions to E Best, T Christiansen, and P Settembri (eds), *The Institutions of the Enlarged European Union* (Edward Elgar, 2008) for an analysis of the impact of Eastern enlargement on the individual institutions and decision-making processes in the EU.

The one area where there have indeed been difficulties has been treaty reform, that is, decision-making *about* the operation of institutions and procedures for legislative decision-making. Here it has taken the Union almost 10 years from the agreement on the Nice Treaty to the coming into force of the Lisbon Treaty, and the arrival of the new Member States in 2004–07 played a role in the problems the EU had to find agreement on fundamental changes to its institutional arrangements. The key issue here has been the balance—or rather the lack of it, as some observers might see it—between large and small- or medium-sized Member States. It was, and is, this (im)balance after accession that is seen to have repercussions with regard to a number of institutional questions:

- First, as discussed above, the number of members of the European Commission, where every Member State has one Commissioner and decisions are taken by simple majority;

- second, decision-making in the Council, where there has been a move away from qualified majority voting with weighted votes to a new system of double-majority voting (majority of Member States and majority of population);

- third, decision-making inside the European Parliament, where the total number of MEPs has been fixed at 750 + 1 and the distribution of seats across Member States has been revised in order to make it more proportional; and

- finally, as already discussed, the arrangements for the Presidency, where the larger number of smaller (and new = less experienced) Member States holding the Presidency has been counter-balanced by the appointment of the semi-permanent President of the European Council and the new role of the High Representative for Foreign Policy who will also chair the Foreign Affairs Council.

Addressing these (as well as many other) issues occupied EU decision-makers for the past decade, and while the reform debates on these questions where *triggered* by Eastern enlargement, the fault-lines and disagreements often divided the Union in different ways: small states across the Union sought to maintain, if not to strengthen the communitarian character of the EU, something that implied a support for a European Commission that was seen, by many, as having been weakened by a more intergovernmental trend in the Union, and that would lose out even further by the appointment of new centre of leadership in the Council and the European Council.[19] It was in response to this rearguard action among the smaller Member States in defence of the European Commission that the High Representative was also appointed as Vice President of the Commission, thus acting as a 'bridge' between the institutions of Council and Commission in the area of external relations in which either has competences.

---

[19] The divisions among smaller and larger Member States in the European Convention preparing the Constitutional Treaty is discussed in B Crum, 'Politics and Power in the European Convention' *Politics* 24, no 1 (February 2004) 1–11; and P Norman, *The Accidental Constitution* (EuroComment, 2005).

Also with respect to the issue of Council voting, the new Member States as such had not been the ones making agreements difficult, but rather an alliance between Poland and Spain that sought to defend the Nice Treaty voting system, and who were ultimately placated with a delayed introduction of the new double-majority from November 2014.[20] And when it came to the delays in the ratification of treaty reforms, it was chiefly in the old Member States that difficulties were encountered: Ireland initially rejecting the Nice Treaty in a popular referendum, followed by France and the Netherlands rejecting the Constitutional Treaty, and then again Ireland rejecting the Lisbon Treaty in the first referendum in 2008.[21] Indeed, two new Member States—Poland and the Czech Republic—also turned out to be 'awkward partners' during the treaty change ratification process when the Presidents of both countries threatened to veto the Lisbon Treaty that had otherwise been approved by all Member States.

In conclusion, treaty reform was seen to be required because of the large number and the particular nature of new Member States, and this had been the main driving force over almost 15 years of continuous reform debate. Ironically, the arrival of the new Member States did *not* cause significant problems for the everyday functioning of the European Union, but made it more difficult to achieve these elusive reforms.

IV. From Triangle to . . . ?: The New Complexity of Inter-institutional Relations in the EU

At the outset, the Union's institutional architecture was outlined in terms of a fairly simple and enduring triangle of Commission, Parliament and Council. The previous sections have shown the extent to which this traditional image has changed through the addition of new institutions and actors. In particular, the Council has become a more complex set of institutions due to the elevation of the European Council into an institution in its own right, the creation of an elected President of the European Council, the greater independence of the High Representative who, while acting as Commission Vice President, is also chairing the Foreign Affairs Council, and the formation of the EEAS as a hybrid organization of Commission, Council Secretariat and national diplomatic services.[22] The arrival of the European Council President and the transformation of the role of the High Representative in turn have a major impact on the rotating Presidency—an

---

[20] See *European Voice*, 'Growing Tensions as Leaders Prepare for Treaty Showdown' (11.10.2007).

[21] See T Christiansen, 'The EU Reform Process: From the 'European Constitution' to the Lisbon Treaty' in M Carbone (ed), *National Politics and European Integration: From the Constitution to the Lisbon Treaty* (Edward Elgar, 2010) for an overview of the negotiation and ratification process.

[22] See S Duke, 'Providing for European-Level Diplomacy after Lisbon: The Case of the European External Action Service' *The Hague Journal of Diplomacy* 4, no 2 (September 2009) 211–33, for a discussion of the wider issues involved in setting up the EEAS.

institution that nevertheless remains important in the context of the Union's legislative work.[23]

Looking at this changing landscape, one can still regard the European Council and the Council as the exponents of the intergovernmental dimension (even though the relationship between these two is now more fraught with difficulty and the European Council President as a permanent feature complicates this picture) while the European Commission and Parliament remain as the institutionalization of supranationalism in the Union. The main difficulty is with the hybrid nature of both the High Representative and the EEAS which she directs: both are to a large extent operating within the ambit of the European Commission (and could therefore be seen as supranational actors) but many observers also consider the High Representative and the EEAS as manifestations of an increasing 'intergovernmentalization' of the Union.[24] This is not the place to make such judgements, which in any case depend on the way in which these new actors *act* rather than on the formal stipulations on the basis of which they were set up. What needs to be recognized, however, is that the High Representative and the EEAS *are* new actors which can be expected to perturb previous institutional arrangements.

As a consequence, the traditional institutional triangle as outlined at the beginning of this chapter has been overlaid with a wider set of relationships involving these new actors. The following bilateral relations are the main elements of this new complexity:

- European Parliament – Commission
- European Council President – Commission President
- Commission – High Representative
- High Representative – European Council President
- European Council President – rotating Presidency

The following section will briefly discuss the key issues arising with respect to each of these relations.

A. European Parliament and European Commission

The two institutions have formalized their relations through a framework agreement (FA), laying down some of the key principles in their interaction.[25] The new FA

---

[23] For a discussion of the impact of the Lisbon changes on the rotating Presidency see B Crum, 'Accountability and Personalisation of the European Council Presidency' *Journal of European Integration* (2009) 685–701 and S Kurpas et al (eds), 'The Treaty of Lisbon: Implementing the Institutional Innovations' (EPC, Egmont, CEPS, 2007) 39–56; D Allerkamp, 'The Presidency Effect after the Lisbon Treaty: The Consequences of the Demotion of the Rotating Council Presidency' UACES Conference Paper, London (2011).

[24] The contribution by J Howarth and A-M le Gloannex in G Avery and A-M Le Gloannec (eds), *EU Foreign Service: How to Build a More Effective Common Policy* (Europe In The World Working Paper No 28) Brussels: EPC, 2007, 28–34, discusses the different logics at work in the formation of the EEAS.

[25] European Parliament and European Commission, 'Framework Agreement on relations between the European Parliament and the European Commission' *Official Journal of the European Union* Brussels, 20 November 2010, 47–62; see J Stacey, 'The European Commission and Informal Politics

has been seen as far-reaching in accommodating demands from the European Parliament in terms of access to documents and participation in Commission expert groups, and the Council formally protested that some of these provisions went beyond the permissible limits of the Treaty. However, this is far from a strong alliance between two supranational institutions, as there are also many divisive issues. This concerns both specific dossiers—the new rules for delegated and implementing acts is one case in point—as well as wider issues of strategy, where the European Parliament is often dissatisfied with the Commission's lack of leadership. However, these are not necessarily new developments, and even though the new powers of the European Parliament will have an impact not only on the European Commission, but also on the Council (which has already threatened legal action),[26] on the whole this relationship is arguably least changed of all those being analysed here.

B. The Presidents of the European Council and of the European Commission

This, on the other hand, is an entirely new leadership, confronting the Commission and its President with a range of challenges. In terms of projecting leadership both internally, towards the European public, and externally, towards third countries, the spotlight now falls on Herman Van Rompuy, when previously it was shared between Jose Manuel Barroso and the rotating President of the (European) Council. Moreover, going beyond the public perception of 'who is in charge of the Union', the arrival of the European Council President on the scene has also impacted on the power of initiative of the Commission. The 'monopoly of legislative initiative', historically regarded as one of the key planks of Commission power (and thus as an essential element of the 'community method') is increasingly compromised by a European Council which is now meeting more frequently, which is better organized and which is developing a tendency to set a more detailed agenda for the Union—an agenda that in turn limits the Commission's power to launch its own initiatives.

C. The European Commission and the High Representative/European External Action Service

Both the HR and the EEAS were created as a sort of bridge between Commission and Council, with the execution of external relations not falling clearly into the

---

in the European Union' in T Christiansen and C Neuhold (eds), *International Handbook on Informal Governance* (Edward Elgar, 2012) for a discussion on the implications for the European Commission.

[26] In a formal statement, the Council complained that the FA was 'modifying the institutional balance as set out in the Treaty' and threatened 'to submit to the Court of Justice any act or action of the European Parliament or of the Commission performed in application of the provisions of the Framework Agreement that would have an effect contrary to the interests of the Council and the prerogatives conferred upon it by the Treaties'. See Council of the European Union, 'Framework Agreement on Relations between the European Parliament and the Commission', *Official Journal of the European Union*, Brussels, 23 October 2011, 1.

ambit of one or the other institution. In practice, however, Catherine Ashton is not primarily perceived as a member of the Commission, despite her appointment as Commission Vice President, but rather as an agent of the Member States. The Commission, in turn, has reacted defensively with regard to the setting-up of the EEAS, with the move of DG RELEX and DG DEV seen as a loss, and with reservations about cooperation in areas such as operational financial instruments. Most importantly, the Commission decided early in the process that the key departments for external economic relations, DG TRADE and EuropeAid, would not be part of the new service, but would remain within the Commission. Because of this, the perennial search for coherence and consistency in EU external relations will continue to face institutional boundaries dividing responsibilities for 'political' and 'economic' external relations.

D. The European Council President and the High Representative

These two newly established positions both carry huge weight in terms of the external representation of the Union—the European Council President at the level of Heads of Government and State, and the High Representative at the level of foreign ministers. This arrangement requires close cooperation, replacing to a large degree the role previously played by the Prime Minister and Foreign Minister of the Member State holding the rotating Presidency. The shared responsibility for foreign representation is complicated by the fact that the High Representative is, as discussed above, 'triple-hatted' and potentially overburdened, whereas the European Council President has comparatively limited duties in preparing and chairing four to six European Council meetings annually, and will therefore have sufficient time to devote to foreign policy. The significance of this relationship is amplified by the fact that foreign ministers are not participating in the meetings of the European Council any more; making the High Representative—who is participating in the European Council—the conduit between the Foreign Relations Council and the European Council.

E. The European Council President and the rotating Presidency

As mentioned above, the new roles of European Council President and High Representative replaced important functions previously held by the rotating Presidency. This concerns not only external relations but also the symbolic link between the most senior political offices in the Member State and the leadership of the EU, and carries with it the potential for rivalry between the respective Prime Ministers and the European Council President. In addition, the previous decision to hold all European Council meetings in Brussels, rather than in the Member States, also limits the opportunities for the rotating Presidency to demonstrate leadership in the EU, and the difficulties that occurred during the Spanish Presidency in 2010 provided an illustration of the kind of problems that might arise because of this. It needs to be remembered, however, that the rotating Presidency remains crucial for the management of Council business in all other areas, and in particular for the legislative work of the Union. The outcome might be a kind of 'division of labour', with the European Council President concentrating on the 'high politics' issues whereas the rotating Presidency takes care of routine business and as such is focused on 'low politics'.[27]

V. Inter-institutional Relations in Practice

Having reviewed the changes to the key institutional relations resulting from the Lisbon Treaty, we can now look at the new dynamics in EU policy-making in certain key areas. In the subsequent sections we will briefly look at developments in four areas of activity in the EU after the Lisbon Treaty: strategic leadership; macro-economic coordination; external relations; and administrative governance.

A. Foreign policy

External relations is one of the key areas in which the institutional changes of the Lisbon Treaty were meant to improve the long-standing quest for greater coherence. However, in the implementation phase the evidence has rather pointed towards greater friction among the various actors. With regard to the setting up of the EEAS, there had been criticism by both the European Parliament and some Member States about the appointment of individual officials, while at the same time observers identified greater influence by the larger Member States than of the Commission in the new organization. These are indications of a possibly latent struggle for influence over external relations between the Commission, European Parliament and Member States while the EEAS is searching for its own institutional identity.

While there has been much criticism of the limited profile the EEAS has developed in the first years of its life, the absence of open conflict indicates the rather minimalist interpretation of the role by Catherine Ashton, somewhat in contrast to the way in which Javier Solana executed his role as HR previously. As a result, concerns have been voiced by those who are more communitarian-minded that a 'slow start' to the office might mean that its powers may be curtailed in the long run. Certainly, much of the early analysis has pointed to the way in which the larger Member States have appointed low-profile politicians to these two offices, and at the same time ensuring that their nationals hold key positions in the 'second tier' as secretary-generals in the Council Secretariat and the EEAS.

The question is what implications these developments might have for the rotating Presidency of the Council. Formally speaking, the main changes here are that, in terms of management of the Council business, the Presidency will cease to represent the EU at the highest level and that it will cease to chair the Foreign Affairs Council as well as the majority of the CFSP working groups. At the

---

[27] See the discussion in D Allerkamp, 'The Presidency Effect after the Lisbon Treaty: The Consequences of the Demotion of the Rotating Council Presidency' UACES Conference Paper, London (2011).

same time, the Presidency will remain the liaison (for the Council) with other institutions in terms of programming, priorities, execution and reporting (except concerning European Council meetings) and will prepare the 18-month working programme, within the Trio format (that is, in cooperation with the High Representative for her fields and in close cooperation with the President of the European Council and the Commission in other policy areas).

In analysing the impact on the rotating Presidency, it needs to be remembered that it has always had (at least) two dimensions: on the one hand, the symbolic, political functions of representation at the highest level, and, on the other hand, the very important but often invisible work of preparing and chairing the large number of Council working groups, of managing the legislative activity and maintaining the momentum in the search for solutions in the intergovernmental bargaining process of EU decision-making. The Lisbon Treaty reforms have had the paradoxical effect that in terms of external representation, the function of Prime Ministers and Foreign Ministers has now been eclipsed by the European Council President and the High Representative, whereas in terms of the Presidency's administrative workload the demands on national administrations remains largely unchanged. In effect, the rotating Presidency is now a 'Presidency minus foreign policy'.

A further observation needs to be made about the future of the EU's delegations—quasi-embassies in third countries—which until Lisbon had been part of the European Commission. With the creation of the EEAS these have become part of that service, under the political control of the High Representative. This implied wider changes, in particular the appointment of Council Secretariat officials and seconded national diplomats to positions in the delegations. The immediate result has been a game of moving chairs as key ambassadorial appointments have been made, and these new arrangements will require time to settle in. But in the medium to long term one can expect the delegations to grow in size and political weight, and to eventually take on a larger diplomatic role alongside the embassies of the Member States. One initial dynamic has already been the fact that with the end of the rotating Presidency, that Member State's embassy does not take a leading coordination function in third countries any more.

Finally, it cannot be ignored that the European Parliament is becoming more of an actor in EU external relations in the post-Lisbon era. The main driver behind this development is the European Parliament's acquisition of assent powers over international agreements of the Union—new muscles which the Parliament immediately flexed when it blocked the SWIFT agreement the Commission had negotiated with the United States. The vote caused much upheaval and led not only to great pressure exerted on MEPs from the Commission and the Member States, but also sustained lobbying from senior officials in the US administration (including phone calls from Secretary of State Clinton to European Parliament President Buzek). The European Parliament's initial veto over the agreement indicated that it is a real force to reckon with in the foreign relations of the Union, at least insofar as they require formal agreements. The European Parliament also sought to influence decisions about the structure of the EEAS, even though here it has only indirect powers over the budgetary decisions of the service.[28]

B. Macro-economic coordination

The ratification and implementation of the Lisbon Treaty was to a significant degree overshadowed by the global financial and economic crisis. The global crisis had great repercussions in Europe, but affected some Member States more than others. Crucially, it hit a European Union in which there was a long-standing divide between Eurozone members and non-members. And while certain non-Member States were hit hard by the crisis—Latvia was one country in point—there was a wider impact on the Eurozone as it became clear that individual Eurozone members were facing defaults on their sovereign debt. There is no space here to chart in detail the impact of, and the response to, the resulting 'Euro-crisis', but a brief look at the way in which the EU managed this crisis also reveals something about the emerging institutional balance after the Lisbon Treaty.

In order to assess this institutional dimension to the EU's crisis-management, one needs to go back to the prior arrangements for macro-economic coordination which had *not* been changed by the new Treaty.[29] The status quo ante was the original Maastricht Treaty arrangement under which decision-making for monetary policy-making had been centralized with the creation of the European Central Bank, whereas fiscal decisions and macro-economic decision-making remained in the hands of the Member States and were merely coordinated at the European level. While the Growth and Stability Pact, adopted after the Maastricht Treaty, laid down certain 'stability criteria' that Member States are expected to observe in the management of their public finances, there had been a long-lasting inter-institutional tension about the enforcement of these criteria. This also included a court case between the European Commission and the Council about the degree to which these criteria are binding and whether the sanctions must be imposed on Member States not complying. It was an argument carried by the Council when the ECJ ruled that it was ultimately down to the Member States to decide whether or not to impose sanctions in cases of non-compliance.

Against this background, the financial crisis, leading to a massive increase in public spending in the context of bail-outs for commercial banks and stimulus packages to support economic recovery, caused further strains in the management of the Eurozone. While most Member States ended up violating the stability criteria in the turmoil of this crisis, for some the new pressures aggravated pre-existing problems to

---

[28] See European Parliament, 'SWIFT: European Parliament Votes Down Agreement with the US' (<http://www.europarl.europa.eu/sides/getDoc.do?language=en&type=IM-PRESS&reference=20100209IPR68674>, accessed on 5 April 2011). See also *European Voice*, 'A Year of Living Dangerously' (25 November 2010) for a wider discussion of how this and other actions by the European Parliament have affected the institutional balance in the EU.

[29] See U Puetter, 'Europe's Deliberative Intergovernmentalism—the Role of the Council and European Council in EU Economic Governance' *Journal of European Public Policy* no 18, March (2011) 1–30, for a discussion of the wider institutional implications of the economic crisis management.

such an extent that the budgetary situation became unsustainable. Under attack by speculative financial markets, a number of Eurozone members faced massive increases in the interest rates at which they could borrow from international financial markets and ultimately were in danger of default on the public debts. Given the impact that these developments had on the single currency, this led to requests for assistance from the remaining EU members.

The search for a permanent resolution is ongoing, but the short-term solution arrived at in 2010 was the creation of a European stability mechanism which would provide sizeable loans to Greece, Ireland and other Eurozone members potentially effected at interest rates below market rates—a solution that had to be found outside the treaty structure because the EU budget cannot be used to provide loans to Member States. Due to the intergovernmental nature of decision-making arrangements in this field, and given the political significance and controversy surrounding the decisions that were being taken, the European Council became the forum in which the search for solutions was being conducted. This in turn elevated Herman Van Rompuy to the status of crisis-manager, but it also led to a close cooperation between him and Commission President Barroso, given that it is in the European Commission where expertise on economic and financial matters reside at the level of the Union. At the same time, it also brought the distinction between Council and Eurogroup to the fore, with much of the crisis management prepared—pre-cooked—in the Eurogroup, presided over by Luxembourg's Prime Minister Juncker, before then being formally adopted by the European Council.

It is too early to say what the institutional repercussions of these ongoing developments have been, but one may hazard a guess that the greater institutional-ization of the European Council and the appointment of a permanent President has aided the crisis management. Clearly, the rotating Presidency, held frequently by non-Eurozone members, is in principle less well able to provide sustained leader-ship in such a crisis, and even less so at the level of Heads of State and Government. In this context, the Euro-crisis and the European Council President constituted a 'good match', because it also provided an opportunity for Herman Van Rompuy to demonstrate both the relevance and the permanence of his post, and in the process expanded its role. The meaning of potentially limited tasks such as the preparation of European Council meetings developed into permanent political activity in the search for both short-term and long-term solutions to the crisis. The situation also brought about a new *esprit* of partnership between the Commission and European Council, in particular as proposed institutional mechanisms such as the 'European semester'—the early monitoring of fiscal plans in Eurozone Member States—will require greater cooperation between the two institutions in the future.

C. Strategic leadership

When discussing the question of leadership in the post-Lisbon EU, it should be remembered that in addition to the multiplication of (European) Council Presidents there are even more Presidents in the EU system. The European Parliament President, for example, has become more powerful, not directly as a result of the Lisbon Treaty, but as a consequence of the way in which the European Parliament has extracted concessions from the European Commission in the course of its appointment. The new Framework Agreement, adopted in conjunction with the approval of the new Commission in early 2010, contains several provisions that provide the European Parliament with greater leverage vis-à-vis the Commission, including, for example, the participation of the European Parliament President in selected meetings of the College of Commissioners. More importantly, the roles of the elected Chair of the Eurogroup and the President of the European Central Bank need to be mentioned. As the EU crisis management during the spring of 2010 in response to the Greek debt crisis and the agreement on protective measures to stabilize the Euro exchange rate demonstrated, these actors are also extremely important in the leadership of the EU and in the search for a coherent representation of the European interest.

In the light of these observations, judgements about the future evolution of political leadership in the European Union are difficult. Providing leadership and direction for the EU seems not, at least, to have become any simpler. Given the new posts and appointments, a lot will depend on the personal chemistry between the individual politicians involved. In the past, it had been noted that the good working relations between Javier Solana and Chris Patten had been crucial for the effectiveness of the original High Representative appointment after the job was created by the Amsterdam Treaty. At this stage, Herman Van Rompuy and Catherine Ashton seem to be working well together, but given the way in which each of their positions has encroached on the previous responsibilities of national Prime Ministers and foreign ministers, respectively, there is a greater need for good cooperation not only at the European level, but also between EU and national politicians.

With respect to leadership in the internal policies of the Union, the key relationship involves the EC President and the Commission President. One early indication in this respect is that some sort of division of labour might develop which involves Herman Van Rompuy being occupied with facilitating and indeed managing bargaining among Heads of State and Government while the Commission and its President are dominant when it comes to the legislative agenda of the Union. If managed well, this might be a mutually beneficial arrangement, and one that is furthered by the communitarian reflexes of Herman Van Rompuy and the intergovernmental sensitivities of Barroso—a pattern that has so far helped to avoid the potentially conflictual dynamics of their offices.

Finally, we will need to see what impact the Lisbon changes will have on the national Presidency. As mentioned earlier, there is a chance that the symbolic representation of a Member State's leadership of the EU that was hitherto encapsulated by holding the Presidency will be lost given that neither Prime Ministers nor foreign ministers will lose much of the limelight that the EU used to award them in the past. At the same time, Member States will continue to have to carry much of the administrative burden of managing the EU's legislative business during their Presidency. The result may be perceived as a no-win situation for individual states, benefiting ultimately only the 'Big Three' of Germany, France and Britain that are able, unlike the other Member States, to shape policies informally outside the formal institutional structure.

Experience so far suggests that Herman Van Rompuy, the first holder of this position, has assumed an influential position behind the scenes in searching for compromise and brokering agreements (for example, in the context of searching for a solution to the Greek debt crisis), even though initial confrontations with the Spanish Presidency (for example about the EU–US summit meeting) have high-lighted the potential for rivalry between the President of the European Council and rotating Presidency. An important part of the explanation is the style of Herman Van Rompuy—his apparent skill in searching for compromise and persuasion behind the scenes suggests that he is able to avoid conflict, but also that he might be able to achieve, over the course of his term, a subtle expansion of the influence of the role of European Council President. The close cooperation between Herman Van Rompuy and the Belgian Presidency in the second half of 2010 assisted a maximalist definition of the role of the European Council President.[30] At the same time, the development of the President's private office, including plans for a separate building in Brussels, raises questions about the relationship with the Council and the Council Secretariat—in the long run the 'Office of the President' may develop into an institution in its own right.

Also, in terms of the elusive search for simplification, the new arrangements are, if anything, a step backwards, as from now on new centres of power and authority have to coordinate with one another, not only horizontally across President of the European Council, HR/VP, Presidency and Commission President, but also vertically as it has become clear that in the chain of decision-making in certain areas a dossier can change hands from the representative of the High Representative (chairing a Council working group) to the representative of the Presidency (chairing COREPER) back to the High Representative (chairing the Foreign Affairs Council)—a process that will add new challenges to an already complex decision-making system.

The limited experience of EU politics since the coming into force of the Lisbon Treaty therefore demonstrates that the question of leadership has not become any easier under the new regime. It is, as yet, an unfinished story but it is already clear that there are huge demands placed on the system, and on the individual actors, in terms of coordination and cooperation. In good time, the need for constant compromise across institutional boundaries in the achievement of common and coherent policies might lead to an effective decision-making complex in Brussels, but in the current phase of transition there is also much uncertainty and friction in the search for the right balance between communitarian and intergovernmental solutions to European problems.

D. Administrative dimension

Beyond the personal and the political level, these developments also have an administrative dimension in which the new arrangements have thrown up a large

---

[30] See S van Hecke and P Bursens, 'The EU, Belgium and the 2010 Presidency: Back to Basics' *EURACTIV* (<http://www.euractiv.com/en/future-eu/eu-belgium-and-2010-presidency-back-basics-analysis-500710> accessed on 5 April 2011).

number of new questions. Chief among these are the way in which the EEAS will work, and how it will impact on the internal functioning of both the European Commission and the Council Secretariat. Looking first at the Commission, one has to note that there will in the future be a greater institutional division between the former DG RELEX (which has become part of the EEAS) and the other DGs and agencies of the Commission dealing with related issues (enlargement, trade, development, humanitarian aid). This means that while at the *political* level the double-hatting of the High Representative has brought the Council and Commission closer together, at the *administrative* level the establishment of the EEAS will create new divisions. Overall, the hoped-for increase in coherence in EU external relations arising from the Lisbon Treaty will continue to be a challenge.

With respect to the impact on the Council Secretariat, a similar process of moving foreign and security issues out of the existing administration and into the new EEAS will cause a new split, but in this case it is perhaps quite welcome. The Council Secretariat had only quite recently acquired the executive functions in foreign and military matters, and this development has actually been at odds with the traditional focus of the Council secretarial on legislative and institutional questions.[31] With the diplomatic and military elements leaving the Council Secretariat in the direction of the EEAS, it will be able to re-focus on its traditional role of supporting the Presidency in the legislative process.

What remains unclear at this point is whether the European Council President's administrative support will be part of the Council Secretariat, or whether yet another secretariat will populate the institutional landscape in Brussels.[32] The indications are that the European Council President, with a separate staff and building, will in time come to be considered as a distinct institution, outside the traditional Council structure (though probably sharing logistical, translation and other support services). This growth of new 'institutions' such as the EEAS and the European Council President emphasizes that the institutional architecture in Brussels is more and more moving beyond the traditional understanding based on a supranational/intergovernmental divide.

VI. Conclusions

In many ways, the implementation of the new Lisbon Treaty provisions demonstrates that the new arrangements are still in the process of evolving and that there

---

[31] For a discussion of the internal tensions within the Council Secretariat over the past decade, see T Christiansen and S Vanhoonacker, 'At a Critical Juncture? Change and Continuity in the Institutional Development of the Council Secretariat' *West European Politics* 31, no 4 (July 2008) 751–70. For a more long-term history of the evolution of the Council Secretariat, see M Mangenot, 'The Invention and Transformation of a Governmental Body: The Council Secretariat' in J Rowell and M Mangenot (eds), *A Political Sociology of the European Union* (Manchester University Press, 2010).

[32] See M Mangenot, 'Le Secrétariat général du Conseil au service du Conseil européen' paper presented at the conference, 'The Commanding Heights of the European Union: The European Council: Institution, Actors, Resources' Brussels, 10–11 March 2011.

remains much uncertainty over their ultimate impact. With regards to foreign affairs, where the Lisbon Treaty was meant to deliver a step-change in terms of improved coherence and effectiveness, the EEAS may—after a long period of gestation—ultimately become a successful tool in projecting European interests and values abroad. However, in the eyes of many observers, the road towards operational capability has been long and fraught with difficulties, and the execution of EU foreign policy remains distinctly modest. European responses to international crises—the 2010 earthquake in Haiti, the 2011 nuclear disaster in Fukushima and the 2011 Libya conflict—all demonstrated the continuing differences among the Member States rather than the unity of the EU. These deep-seated divisions within the Union will not vanish even in the face of an ultimately more effective institutional arrangement. Instead of looking forward to the development of a genuinely *common* European foreign policy, it might be more meaningful to expect at the European level the development of (more long-term) analytical and policy-planning capacities that go beyond what is available in the Member States.

So far, the implementation of the institutional provisions of the Lisbon Treaty has proven to be more complex and time-consuming than expected, especially in the light of the long gestation period of the new Treaty. In the first year after the coming into force of the Treaty, the focus has been more on personalities than on institutional features. While the assessment of individual performance might appear straightforward, the search for a new post-Lisbon institutional balance is proving rather elusive. The traditional 'triangle' between Parliament, Council and Commission has given way to more complex and still somewhat fluid institutional arrangements whose impact also differs across different domains.

With regard to one key cleavage mentioned at the outset—the opposition of supranational and intergovernmental forces at the heart of the Union—the balance sheet is difficult to determine: on the one hand, the European Parliament appears in the eyes of most observers as the clear 'winner', having gained greater powers in legislation and in foreign affairs. On the other hand, the Commission is generally perceived to have 'lost' some of its key responsibilities in the management of external relations, with the 'loss' of DG Relex and the delegations. More generally, the decline of the 'Community Method' has to some extent continued, as an increasing number of key areas—economic policy, foreign policy, competitiveness—are governed through non-binding coordination mechanisms, rather than legislation.

What makes the assessment of where we stand with regard to the long-standing and inherent supranational-intergovernmental tensions within the Union more difficult is above all the growing institutionalization of intergovernmental processes, something which can also be seen as the increasing 'communitarization' of institutions and policies such as the European Council, the CFSP and macro-economic coordination. This means that the traditional balance between the Commission and the Parliament on one side, and the Council and the rotating Presidency on the other side, has been replaced by a more complex arrangement with a heightened demand for negotiation and coordination across various institutional boundaries. In this new landscape, the European Council President and the High Representative are not only individual personalities representing the collective interests of the Member States, but also come with emerging institutions that are going to develop their own identity within the political, social and organizational networks of Brussels.

The result of this greater number of players, and of the growing complexity that comes with that, is an evolving institutional landscape in which the search for institutional balance is becoming increasingly elusive. Ironically perhaps for a treaty that was meant to increase the Union's ability to project a more coherent and effective foreign policy, the immediate effect of the Lisbon changes has been a more inward-looking Europe trying to come to terms with the self-imposed challenges arising from its own institutional innovations.

12

The Evolving Roles of the European Parliament and of National Parliaments

Richard Corbett

As in other matters, the Lisbon Treaty can, in terms of the parliamentary dimension, best be seen as an evolution rather than a revolution. It is the latest of a series of steps that have taken place over the last two decades with successive revisions of the treaties and of the institutional structure—through the 1986 Single European Act, the 1992 Maastricht Treaty, the 1997 Amsterdam Treaty, the 2001 Nice Treaty and now the Lisbon Treaty. Lisbon has not made any radical change to the field of competence of the European Union, but it *has* taken further a process of change in the way in which its competences are exercised. One of the main aims of the Treaty was to enhance the democratic accountability of the European Union and in this respect the increased powers of the European Parliament and the greater potential role of national parliaments are significant. Indeed, they are highlighted in a new section, right at the start of the Treaty, entitled 'Provisions on Democratic Principles', containing Articles 9 to 12.

I. The European Parliament

The strengthening of the EU's democratic credentials by strengthening the directly elected Parliament is a striking feature of the successive treaty changes. All of the treaties mentioned above (and, preceding them, the 1970 and 1975 Budget Treaties too) have increased at least some aspect of the European Parliament's powers.

A. Legislative powers

In terms of legislative powers, the European Parliament had, essentially, just a consultative role right the way up to the Treaty of Maastricht, which introduced a co-decision procedure for just a handful of Treaty articles and, at the time, in a more Council-friendly procedure than now. The procedure was changed to Parliament's advantage with the Treaty of Amsterdam, and its scope was also enhanced. Its scope was then enhanced further with the Treaty of Nice and now again with the Treaty of Lisbon, which made it the Ordinary Legislative Procedure. We now have parliamentary power over almost all areas of EU legislation, where it jointly decides legislation with the Council in what amounts to a bicameral legislature at European level.

How does this work? The bottom line is simple: only if Parliament and Council agree on a text in identical terms can it be passed into law. The detail is more complex: there are up to three readings in each institution, allowing them to consider the Commission's proposal and each other's amendments.

If, after two readings each, there are still outstanding differences, the proposal is referred to a conciliation committee,[1] which has six weeks to negotiate a compromise. If agreement is reached within the committee, both Parliament and Council must approve the outcome in a third reading within six weeks, failing which, the proposal falls. If conciliation fails to produce an agreement, the proposal equally falls. The six-week time limits may, by agreement, be extended to eight weeks. At all stages in procedure, there are informal contacts between the institutions, not least through what has become known as the 'trilogue',[2] to explore and negotiate compromises.[3]

What this system is intended to ensure, is that there is a double check before any European legislation can be adopted. Proposals for legislation must prove acceptable to the representatives of the national governments in the Council (and, indeed, a large majority of them, as a qualified majority in the Council requires a high threshold of support), and also acceptable to the representatives directly elected by citizens. The primary focus of the members of one of the institutions is to examine matters from the perspective of the national interest, as seen by the government of the day. The other institution is organized not in national delegations but in political groups, examining proposals primarily from an ideological or political perspective. We shall examine this further below.

B. International agreements

The step-by-step evolution of Parliament's powers is also clear, if we look at its power to approve (or not) international agreements entered into by the European Union. Parliament was first given such powers with the Single Act, but only for Association Agreements and Accession Treaties. With the successive changes to the European Treaties, that has now been expanded step by step and now virtually any international agreement entered into by the European Union of any significance

---

[1] Composed of all the members of the Council or their representatives and an equal number of MEPs, with the assistance of the Commission.

[2] Composed of the relevant Commissioner, the President in Office of the Council and a small delegation from the Parliament usually including the relevant rapporteur and committee chair.

[3] If one looks still more closely, there are further levels of detail that govern the co-decision procedure. In particular, the Treaty provides that, at second reading, if the Commission does not accept an amendment, then the Council can only adopt it by unanimity. This power is tempered, however, by the fact that this does not apply at the conciliation stage where Parliament and Council can agree over the heads of the Commission, and anyway the Commission has an interest in garnering support of a qualified majority for its proposal, and this indeed entails accepting amendments, sometimes reluctantly.

requires the approval of the European Parliament. This was spectacularly illustrated by Parliament's rejection on 11 February 2010 of the SWIFT agreement with the USA on the transfer of banking data.

Because Parliament's approval will ultimately be required for international agreements, it is now in a strong position to insist politically that its views be taken into account during the definition of the negotiating mandate by the Council and during negotiations themselves. The Treaty now provides[4] for the Parliament to be 'immediately and fully informed at all steps of the procedure' of negotiating with international agreements.

The day-to-day conduct of the EU's external relations will now come under the European External Action Service (EEAS), headed by the Vice President of the Commission/High Representative of the Union for Foreign Affairs and Security Policy (a post sometimes described as the 'EU Foreign Minister', a title it was actually formally given under the abandoned Constitutional Treaty). As Vice President of the Commission, the incumbent is accountable to Parliament, must attend a public hearing prior to Parliament's approval of the Commission, and is subject to all the parliamentary rights of questioning and scrutiny (and the ultimate sanction of dismissal of the college) as is the case for every other Commissioner.

C. Commission's appointment and accountability to the European Parliament

We can also see this step-by-step change in terms of the Commission's appointment and accountability to the European Parliament. Under the original treaties, the Commission was simply appointed by national governments, for a four-year term of office. Step by step, with Maastricht, with Amsterdam, and with Lisbon, that has changed. Since Maastricht, we have a Commission appointed for a five-year term of office coinciding with that of the European Parliament. Also with Maastricht, Parliament gained the right to confirm the appointment of the Commission in a vote of confidence (and it insisted on public hearings with each Commissioner prior to its vote). It was also initially given (by Maastricht) the right to be consulted on the choice of President of the Commission, then (by Amsterdam) to confirm the choice of President and now (with Lisbon) the terminology in the Treaty is that Parliament 'elects' the President of the Commission. The procedure requires the European Council to propose (since Nice by qualified majority voting (QMV)) to Parliament a candidate 'taking into account the elections to the European Parliament and after having held the appropriate consultations'.[5] If the candidate does not secure the necessary majority, the European Council must propose a new candidate under the same procedure.

Thus, the European Council must nominate a candidate capable of attaining a majority in Parliament—indeed, an absolute majority of members of the house. This potentially makes the nomination similar to that of a Head of State choosing a

---

[4] Article 218(10) TFEU.   [5] Article 17(6) TEU.

candidate Prime Minister who is capable of enjoying a parliar
may well lead to European political parties nominating the
mission President ahead of the European election campai

Once appointed, the President now, also through succ.
the right to jointly agree with national governments on the cana..
portfolios, reshuffle portfolios midterm and even, should that be neces..
a member of the Commission.

Parliament retains, unchanged by Lisbon, the power to dismiss the Commission. This power, which Parliament enjoyed from the beginning, seemed rather theoretical until early 1999 when it was illustrated in a spectacular way with the dramatic resignation of the Santer Commission when it became clear that there was the necessary majority in Parliament for a vote of no-confidence. In combination with the treaty changes mentioned above, it justifies the statement, added to the Treaties by Lisbon, that 'The Commission, as a body, shall be responsible to the European Parliament'.[6]

Besides involvement in the election of the Commission, Parliament elects the European Ombudsman and is consulted (also with public hearings) on the choice of the President and members of the Board of the European Central Bank and of the Court of Auditors. It has also claimed the right (and successfully exercised it) to invite individuals appointed as heads of European Agencies or as EU ambassadors to third countries to appear for hearings before the relevant parliamentary committee. The consequences of Parliament being strongly dissatisfied with such an appointment have not yet been tested.

D. Rights of scrutiny over delegated legislation

Another way in which Parliament's powers have evolved concerns its rights of scrutiny over delegated legislation. All legislatures have a system of delegating detailed implementing measures to the executive. At EU level too, the Council and Parliament can confer such powers on the Commission. However, the EU system has been a matter of considerable complexity and controversy.

This is because the Council established, in the 1960s and '70s when it was sole legislator, a system whereby the Commission must act in conjunction with committees of national civil servants who often had the power to block the Commission decision and refer the matter to the Council.

The sheer number of such committees gave rise to the term 'comitology'. Only such a committee, and not Parliament, had a right to examine and refer back a proposed implementing measure, and a blocked decision was referred back to Council alone with no parliamentary involvement.

Over the years, Parliament fought a long battle to reform the system and achieved, through inter-institutional agreements and changes to the framework adopted by Council, a degree of success: in 1988, the 'Plumb–Delors' agreement

---

[6] Article 17(8) TEU.

.ween Parliament and the Commission obliged the latter to send Parliament
·roposals transmitted to comitology committees; in 1994, a *Modus Vivendi* agreed
by all three institutions laid down that the Commission would be obliged to 'take
account to the greatest extent possible' of the views of Parliament; in 1999, a new
comitology system was adopted by Council, which, inter alia, provided for Parliament to receive all agendas, minutes, the composition of committees, and all draft
measures tabled, and for it to be able to object if a proposed measure exceeded the
scope of powers delegated, in which case the measure had to be re-examined; in
2002, the Commission acknowledged that, for financial services legislation, Parliament could formally comment on the substance and not just on the scope of
delegated measures and that it could incorporate a 'sunset clause' in the legislation,
such that the delegation of implementing powers ceases after four years, unless
renewed; in 2006, after intense negotiations between the institutions, Parliament
finally obtained, under a new 'regulatory procedure with scrutiny' (RPS), a right to
block individual implementing measures that have a general scope and can be
described as 'quasi-legislative' in nature, but not administrative or purely executive
decisions.

Lisbon entrenches and slightly modifies the results of this step-by-step evolution.
It provides[7] for two categories of Commission implementing decisions. Under the
first, called 'delegated acts', both Parliament (by a majority of its Members) and
Council (by a qualified majority) can reserve the right to object to any proposed
measure, thereby blocking it. Furthermore, the legislation can provide for either
institution to revoke the delegation of powers to the Commission at any time. This
will broadly apply to the field that previously fell under the RPS procedure. Under
the second category, 'implementing acts', Lisbon provided simply for legislation, to
be approved under co-decision, to lay down in advance the mechanisms for control.
After intense negotiations between Parliament and Council, it was agreed in
December 2010 to keep a modified version of the old 'comitology' system, but
with entrenched rights for informing Parliament and the public, including a public
register of information on committee proceedings containing, inter alia, a list of
committees and their composition, their agendas, the drafts transmitted to them,
the summary records of their proceedings and the results of any votes. Parliament is
given the possibility (as is the Council) to indicate to the Commission that it
considers that a draft implementing measure exceeds the implementing measures
provided for in the basic act. In such cases the Commission is to review the draft
measure, and must inform the co-legislators as to whether it intends to maintain,
amend or withdraw the draft implementing act.

The distinction between the two new categories of delegated and implementing
act is by no means obvious and will remain controversial, not least because the
choice of act in individual cases has very different implications for Parliament's
powers. It is now given a powerful role as regards delegated acts, but much less so as
regards implementing acts. Parliament will thus be confronted by hard choices as to

---

[7] Articles 290 and 291 TFEU.

what to delegate, and what not, which act should apply, and how much importance it should attach to these points in its legislative negotiations with the Council and Commission. It is likely to try to get as many measures as it can classed as delegated acts and not as implementing acts.

E. General scrutiny

As regards more general scrutiny, Parliament has a number of ways and means of exercising supervision over the Commission (and to a degree over other institutions). This is done, most routinely, through its right to question (through written questions or oral questions at question time), to examine and debate statements or reports and to hear and cross-examine Commissioners, Ministers and civil servants and the Governor of the Central Bank in its committees. The new full-time President of the European Council is required by the Lisbon Treaty[8] to report to Parliament after each of its meetings. He has supplemented this with a variety of other regular contacts with Parliament, including a meeting with leaders of its political groups immediately after each European Council meeting.

It is also Parliament which examines the accounts and votes (or not) 'discharge' to the other institutions (and to its own authorities) on the execution of the budget. This is a power which derives from the 1975 Budget Treaty and is not fundamentally changed by Lisbon. The consequence of Parliament failing to grant discharge to the Commission are not spelt out in the Treaty, but many consider that it is tantamount to a vote of censure on the Commission. Indeed, controversy surrounding the discharge led within months to the resignation of the Santer Commission in 1999.

Parliament also has the right to take the other institutions to the Court. Initially, the Treaty allowed it to do so only in a highly restricted number of circumstances. This has also been enhanced, step by step, with the Nice Treaty representing a particular improvement in Parliament's role, allowing it to turn to the Court to defend its interest against the other institutions or to ensure correct application of treaties by the other institutions, not least the Council. This power has been of significant importance in defending Parliament's rights. At the same time, its own actions are subject to judicial review by the Court.

F. Budget

When it comes to the budget, the Lisbon Treaty also provides for a sort of co-decision procedure whereby both institutions must agree on every item in the whole budget. Prior to that, as a result of the 1970 and 1975 Budget Treaties, each institution had the final say over different categories of expenditure, provided they remained within jointly agreed ceilings. This gave rise to frequent arguments about whether expenditure was categorized as 'obligatory' (over which the Council had the final say, notably agriculture) or 'non-obligatory' (over which Parliament had

---

[8] Article 15(6) TEU.

the final say, notably the structural funds, research and the environment). In this field, Lisbon is the first treaty modification for over 30 years. The new procedure features a mammoth negotiation between Parliament and Council on the whole budget, with trade-offs, and the danger of brinkmanship. Indeed its first use, in Autumn 2010, saw the failure of the conciliation committee to agree, with the Commission being obliged to submit a new draft budget and the resumption of negotiations, this time successfully.

Formally,[9] the Commission must submit a draft budget for the following year by 1 September and the Council must adopt a position on it by 1 October. If Parliament accepts the Council's position (or takes no decision within 42 days) the budget is approved as such. If Parliament adopts amendments, and the Council does not accept them within 10 days, the matter is referred to the conciliation committee[10] which has 21 days to reach agreement on a 'joint text'. If it fails to do so, the procedure must start again with a new Commission proposal. If it does agree, both Parliament and the Council must approve the joint text within 14 days (though in the event of one institution not taking a position, it is deemed to have acquiesced with the position of the other). Only if Parliament explicitly rejects the text does it automatically fall and the whole procedure must start again with a new Commission proposal. If the Council rejects the joint text, while Parliament approves it, then the procedure continues with Parliament able, within 14 days, to amend the joint text by re-adopting its initial amendments by a majority of its members comprising a three-fifths majority of votes cast. This latter possibility is, however, extremely unlikely, as it assumes that a qualified majority of Council members would agree the text in the conciliation committee and subsequently reject it in the Council meeting itself. In practice, it is the negotiations on a joint text, and the final vote in Parliament to approve or reject the outcome, which will count.

G. Constitutional development

Last, but not least, the European Parliament was given by Lisbon a formal role in terms of the constitutional development of the European Union. Lisbon recognizes formally, for the first time, that the European Parliament has the right to propose a revision to the Treaties[11] be it under the ordinary revision procedure or a simplified procedure. The ordinary procedure for treaty revision will include, unless the European Parliament agrees otherwise, a Convention composed of MEPs and members of national parliaments as well as representatives of the Commission and national governments, to prepare (and hopefully reach consensus on) the treaty changes prior to an intergovernmental conference (IGC) and national ratifications.

Simplified revision procedures can be used to modify Part III of the Treaty (internal policies), provided that there is no increase in the EU's field of competence. It obviates the need for an IGC or Convention, simply requiring a unanimous European Council

---

[9] Article 314 TFEU.
[10] Composed of each member of the Council or their representative and an equal number of MEPs.
[11] Article 48 TEU.

decision after consulting the European Parliament, followed by national ratification. Another simplified procedure, transferring a matter subject to a special legislative procedure to the ordinary legislative procedure (co-decision), or authorizing the Council to act by a qualified majority instead of unanimity, can be decided by the European Council, acting unanimously with the consent of the European Parliament, which must be given by a majority of its component members.[12] The use of the so-called 'flexibility clause'[13] also requires the consent of the European Parliament, as does any agreement setting out the arrangement for the withdrawal of a Member State from the Union. As we saw above, Parliament's consent is already required for accession of a new Member State to the Union.

* * *

The European Union is unique among international structures in having an elected parliament among its institutions. The reasons for this are twofold: some saw the creation of a directly elected parliament as a means towards a more 'federal' system whereby the Union institutions would derive their legitimacy directly from citizens instead of via national governments, while others simply saw the need to compensate for the loss of national level parliamentary power, inherent in pooling competences at European level, by a common European level parliamentary scrutiny complementing, rather than replacing, joint governmental decision-taking.

The organization of the Parliament along political lines, rather than national lines, does not mean that the national allegiances disappear entirely—any more than political considerations disappear in the Council of Ministers. Nonetheless, it is clear that the political cleavages are the key ones in the Parliament whose political Groups have become more cohesive over time. While not having as strict a 'whipping' system as parties in national parliaments, the positions taken by the Groups—and the negotiations between them—are what counts in determining the parliamentary majorities. This, after all, reflects the nature of the choices in the issues at stake. When dealing with legislation, typical policy choices are, for example, about whether you want higher environmental standards, but at greater cost, or not? Higher standards of consumer protection or leave it to competition? More protective employment legislation or leave it to the market? On these subjects, there will be different views within each Member State, irrespective of the position taken by their Ministers in the Council. These views are represented in Parliament, which contains members from opposition parties as well as governing parties in every Member State. There is a higher degree of pluralism in Parliament than in the Council.

There are over 150 national parties that coalesce into seven Groups, most of which correspond to political families with which citizens in most member states are familiar, such as Liberals, Socialists, Christian Democrats or Greens. Some smaller groups are more ad hoc, but are still formed on the basis of political affinity. Most groups are the parliamentary arm of a European political party: a federation of corresponding national parties that not only possess a group in the European Parliament but often organize caucus meetings of their Ministers prior to Council or European Council meetings.

---

[12] Article 48(7) TEU.   [13] Article 352 TFEU.

To some, the Parliament, as the only directly elected EU institution, is the voice of the citizen in European decision-taking. To others, it is just an expensive talking shop. Compared to national parliaments, it lacks the right (which most of them have in theory, though many do not exercise it much in practice) to initiate legislation (as the first draft of legislation must emanate from the Commission) and its budgetary powers concern only expenditure, not the sources of revenue. On the other hand, it exercises its significant legislative powers in a forceful way (most national parliaments rarely amend or reject government proposals), and it makes astute use of its powers of appointment and scrutiny of the executive. Because it is not controlled by the executive or any 'governing majority', it can use its independence to considerable effect.

Yet it is dogged by image problems. It is obliged by the Member States to divide its activities between Brussels (three weeks out four) and Strasbourg (for four days a month). Its systems for assisting Members with their costs, although reformed in 2009, continue to be criticized. The multiplicity of languages means that its debates lack the cut and thrust found in some national parliaments. The bulk of its work is done in committee, far from the limelight. The growth of its powers is only recent, and it is still perceived as being toothless, although this perception is slowly changing. There is no highly visible direct link between the outcome of the parliamentary elections and the composition of the executive, which is what voters are used to at national level in European countries. The turnout in European elections is lower than in national elections in the Member States, though about the same level as US Congressional elections.

Under the Lisbon Treaty, its size is capped at 751 members with a minimum of six and a maximum of 96 seats per Member State according to their size, distributed according to the principle of 'degressive proportionality'. However, as the last European elections took place before the entry into force of the Lisbon Treaty, 736 MEPs were elected in 2009, ranging from five for Malta to 99 for Germany. A minor treaty change will add the extra MEPs midterm, while allowing Germany to keep its extra three until the 2014 elections. Any seats for a newly acceding country will be additional to the 751 until the following elections allow an overall adjustment.

II. National Parliaments

The role of national parliaments in European Union affairs is also one that has evolved over the years, with the Lisbon Treaty codifying this evolution and making some further adjustments.

Until 1979, the European Parliament was itself composed of members of national parliaments, designated by them. This link was broken once the European Parliament became a directly elected body, within which the number of members with a 'dual mandate' rapidly diminished (from some 20 per cent in 1979 to just over 6 per cent by 1999) and indeed was eventually made illegal as of 2004.

Most national parliaments continued to monitor European affairs, and in particular to scrutinize the actions of their own governments, but in various ways and to varying degrees. However, they all had a responsible parliamentary committee, and the latter collectively, and with the European Parliament, established a Conference of European Affairs Committees in 1989 (known by its French abbreviation, COSAC), on a proposal of Laurent Fabius, who was at that time both President of the French National Assembly and a Member of the European Parliament's committee on Constitutional Affairs. COSAC has met biannually since then, hosted by the parliament of the country holding the Council presidency, and with the European Parliament providing interpreters and expertise. It has been a forum to exchange best practice, and has also enabled those MPs most closely involved in European affairs in each national parliament to get to know each other. Through the Amsterdam Treaty, COSAC was given the right to submit 'contributions' to the EU institutions. It has established a small secretariat on the premises of the European Parliament in Brussels, as have no fewer than 26 national parliaments.

The Treaties originally recognized a role of national parliaments only obliquely, in those cases where EU decisions required approval by Member States 'in accordance with their respective constitutional requirements', which in most Member States normally meant parliamentary approval. These decisions included the accession of new Member States, treaty changes and decisions on the budgetary 'own resources' of the European Union.

A declaration annexed to the Maastricht Treaty encouraged a greater involvement of national parliaments through the exchange of information and meetings between them and the European Parliament, and through national governments ensuring that they 'receive Commission proposals for legislation in good time for information and possible examination'. The Amsterdam and Nice Treaties included protocols on the role of national parliaments, providing for a six-week period for national parliaments to examine proposals before Council deliberated on them, though initially Amsterdam restricted this to the field of Justice and Home Affairs.

The Lisbon Treaty, reflecting the fact that much of its substance was drawn from the abandoned Constitutional Treaty, which was prepared by a Convention that included representatives of national parliaments, strengthens the role of national parliaments in a number of ways.

In the section on democratic principles on which the Union is based, Article 12 TEU highlights the role of national parliaments, listing a number of ways in which they 'contribute actively to the good functioning of the Union': by being informed of proposals and policies (which enables them to control their government's European activities better), by taking part in Conventions preparing future changes to the Treaty, by cooperating with each other and with the European Parliament, by taking part in treaty revision procedures, and through a new innovation giving then a particular role in the application of the principle of subsidiarity.

This latter point is spelt out in a special Protocol[14] appended to the Treaty, which contains an innovative procedure allowing national parliaments to send, within eight weeks of receiving a legislative proposal, a reasoned opinion to the EU

---

[14] Protocol No 2 on the Application of the Principles of Subsidiarity and Proportionality.

institutions stating why they consider that the draft legislative act does not comply with the principle of subsidiarity.

If one third of the total number of votes allocated to national parliaments (two votes each for unicameral parliaments, one vote per chamber for bicameral parliaments) consider that the principle has been violated, then the draft must be reviewed. (This is colloquially known as the 'Yellow card procedure'.) If such reasoned opinions reflect more than half of the votes attributed to national parliaments, and if it is in the context of the ordinary legislative procedure, and if the Commission maintains its proposal, then a special vote must take place in the Council and in the European Parliament, each of which can kill off the procedure there and then (by a simple majority in the European Parliament or by a majority of 55 per cent of the members of the Council). (This is known as the 'Orange card procedure'.)

The yellow card and orange card procedures have attracted much comment. It is unlikely that they will be frequently used, if at all. The Finnish Parliament, which has had a mechanism for subsidiarity control since Finland joined the European Union, has never found a Commission proposal to be in breach of the principle. The first year of the operation of the system, with national parliaments perhaps being keen to try it out, saw no proposal being objected to by more than small handfuls of chambers, and usually not more than one. Nonetheless, the procedures do constitute an important and visible safeguard to fall back on, if need be, to prevent over-centralization of powers.

The procedures are, however, likely to contribute to another development. Their existence, combined with the new provisions on forwarding documents directly to national parliaments, and the whole debate that has surrounded national parliaments as a consequence, is likely to mean that a greater number of parliaments will in future pay close attention to the shaping of European policy in their country, and on the substance, rather than just on subsidiarity. More may avail themselves of the opportunity of holding prior meetings with their Minister before he or she attends a Council meeting, as is already standard practice in the Nordic countries. They will certainly have better opportunities to scrutinize documents at earlier stages in EU procedures. There will also be a greater flow of information back and forth, both among national parliaments and between them and the European institutions.

The Treaty now states explicitly that Commission consultation documents, the annual legislative programme, as well as 'any other instrument of legislative planning or policy', will now be forwarded directly to the national parliaments by the Commission and that Council agendas and minutes of deliberative meetings are to be forwarded directly as well, and the annual report of the European Court of Auditors.[15] Moreover, the period within which no agreement may be reached on a draft legislative act, in order to allow time for national parliamentary scrutiny, is extended from six to eight weeks.

---

[15] These requirements are laid down in Protocol No 1 on the Role of National Parliaments.

Indeed, the Commission already anticipated this treaty change through the so-called Barroso initiative in 2006, and regularly receives in return submissions from national parliaments (some 200 per year). Immediately following the entry into force of the Treaty, Barroso wrote in December 2009 to the Presidents (Speakers) of the EU's 40 upper and lower national parliamentary chambers on ways in which the Commission intended to improve the flow of information. This included sending all draft legislative acts and consultation documents electronically at the same time as they are sent to the European Parliament and/or the Council; sending at the end of each week a reminder list of documents that have been sent so that, in the case of non-receipt of a document by a national parliament having an impact on the deadline mentioned under the yellow card and orange card procedures, the deadline (for that Parliament) can be adjusted accordingly; undertaking not to consider the month of August for the purpose of calculating deadlines and inviting national parliaments to distinguish in their opinions as far as possible between subsidiarity aspects (if any) and comments on the substance of a proposal.

The national parliaments are given a special role in the field of freedom, security and justice.[16] Arrangements for involving national parliaments both in the political monitoring of 'Eurojust'[17] and in the political evaluation of 'Europol'[18] are to be laid down in regulations to be adopted by co-decision between the European Parliament and the Council.

National parliaments are also brought into the process of future treaty change. They are given the right to be involved in any major treaty reform through the Convention method used for the draft Constitution, whereby any intergovernmental conference to revise the Treaty must be preceded by a Convention composed of members of the national parliaments, of the European Parliament, of the Commission and of a representative of each government.[19] Of course they retain the right to ratify such treaty changes (except where national procedures provide otherwise, for example, a referendum), as they also do for any revision of policies in Part 3 of the TFEU Treaty under the simplified revision procedure (with no Convention or IGC). They are also given the right to block changes of procedure where the European Council can decide to allow the Council to act by a qualified majority instead of unanimity, or to change from a special legislative procedure (mere consultation of the European Parliament) to the ordinary legislative procedure (co-decision), even if only a single national parliament makes known its opposition within six months of the date of being notified of any such initiative.[20] The same applies to Council decisions to move a measure on aspects of family law with cross-border applications to the ordinary legislative procedure (QMV and co-decision).[21]

---

[16] Article 12(c) TEU and Article 70 TFEU.
[17] Article 12(c) TEU and Article 85 TFEU.
[18] Article 12(c) TEU and Article 88 TFEU.
[19] Article 48(3) TEU.
[20] Article 48(7) TEU as well as Article 6 of Protocol No 1 on the Role of National Parliaments in the European Union.
[21] Article 81(3) TFEU.

Finally, national parliaments are given the right to go to the European Court of Justice on grounds of infringement of subsidiarity.[22]

The Lisbon Treaty provisions affecting national parliaments are thus quite numerous, but have clear limitations. Their direct scope is relatively limited, especially when compared to the new powers given to the European Parliament. There are also wider structural and institutional constraints. National parliaments have little time to devote to the nitty-gritty detail of many EU issues. Moreover, many of them have only small staffs, whether devoted to substantive issues in the committees or to practical logistical matters, such as capacity for translation of their opinions into other languages. Above all (and unlike the European Parliament), most national parliaments in Europe are in a classic government/opposition structure where governing majorities mean that there is, in practice, often little or no scope to amend government texts or reverse their policies. And also unlike the European Parliament, which is working full time on EU matters, national parliaments have less time, expertise and staff resources to devote to EU matters. Their procedures, practices and timetables all diverge.

Moreover, the successive stages of EU lawmaking can sometimes make it difficult for national parliaments to follow what is going on, and thus to have any kind of impact on the process. This is arguably reinforced by the greater emphasis in recent years on first reading deals in co-decision, which involve early negotiations between Council and Parliament that national parliaments find difficult to follow. Indeed some national parliaments have already expressed their concerns on this issue.

Yet, the Lisbon Treaty provides a clear incentive for further inter-parliamentary cooperation. The idea of an Inter-parliamentary Agreement (similar to Inter-institutional Agreements between the European Parliament, Council and Commission) is implicit in Article 9 of Protocol 1 on the Role of National Parliaments.

The instruments of European Parliament–national parliament cooperation are thus likely to be further developed. Existing mechanisms, such as the 'IPEX' system for exchanging EU information electronically between parliaments, the Conference of Speakers, and COSAC can all be used, as can networks of officials. National parliament officials in Brussels now meet with all their counterparts most Monday mornings to share information not just on subsidiarity matters but on wider concerns. They also help to draw up lists of EU proposals which are of common interest to parliaments, or which are already being actively examined by one or more parliaments. Joint meetings of equivalent parliamentary committees (Joint Parliamentary Committees) and joint meetings on specific general topics (Joint Parliamentary Meetings) are likely to be more frequent. The possibility of a 'second COSAC', devoted to defence issues, has even been suggested. More national parliaments will make use of opportunities to meet with MEPs from their country or even give them a formal role in their work, though that particular aspect is likely to be more developed within party political structures.

---

[22] Article 8 of Protocol No 2 on the Application of the Principles of Subsidiarity and Proportionality.

III. Final Remarks

Although the Lisbon Treaty has taken further the step-by-step evolution of parliamentary power in the context of the European Union, and has done so both by strengthening the powers of the European Parliament and by reinforcing the role of national parliaments, the debate on the 'democratic legitimacy' of the Union is set to continue.

First, of course, the strengthening of parliamentary powers is just one of the means sought to strengthen its legitimacy. Others include the adoption of the Charter of Rights, the obligation imposed on the Council to meet in public when deliberating on and adopting legislation,[23] the strengthening of the Committee of Regions, the requirement for dialogue with civil society[24] and the 'citizens' initiative'.[25] Most of these have yet to be tested in practice.

Second, discussion will continue on the best way of electing the European Parliament. Some have suggested that a proportion of its members be elected on trans-national lists in a single Europe-wide constituency (as a means of enhancing the European aspect of election campaigns), but this would require a unanimously agreed treaty revision. More likely is an evolution, not needing any treaty revision, whereby European political parties put forward their candidates for President of the European Commission before the European elections, thereby making this choice a feature of the election campaign.

The European institutions will always suffer from the handicap of being more distant from citizens than are national or local institutions. That is a good reason not to act at European level unless there is a clear advantage in doing so. But to the extent that European-level action *is* deemed necessary, it is important that it be done in the most transparent, democratic and accountable way possible. The strengthening of parliamentary powers in the context of the European Union must be seen in that context.

---

[23] Article 16(8) TEU.
[24] Article 11(1), (2) and (3) TEU.
[25] Article 11(4) TEU.

PART III
EXTERNAL RELATIONS

13

The EU's Common Foreign and Security Policy after Lisbon: From Pillar Talk to Constitutionalism

Piet Eeckhout

I. Introduction

The Treaty of Lisbon is generally described as doing away with the three-pillar structure of the European Union. We are advised no longer to engage in so-called 'pillar talk', as there is now a unified EU legal system.[1] There is no better indication of this unification than the single legal personality which has been created for the whole of the EU construct (Article 47 TEU). And it would certainly be great to be able to remove the pillars from our collective attempts at imaging and imagining the EU: a temple with only three, unequal pillars constituted a rather inelegant picture. However, notwithstanding the attempt to unify the EU's legal and institutional system, the Treaty of Lisbon certainly did not remove all differences between the Common Foreign and Security Policy (CFSP) and the EU's other policies. The provisions on the CFSP continue to be located in the TEU, in contrast with those on other policies. Decision-making is intergovernmental: the European Council and the Council call the shots, they decide unanimously, and the Commission, the Parliament, and the Court of Justice have but a limited role to play. No legislation can be made under the CFSP heading. The instruments used are different from standard EU legal acts. The CFSP competences are undefined, in the sense of being neither exclusive nor shared.

There is much that can and needs to be said about the EU's evolving attempt, *post* Lisbon, to set up a genuine foreign policy, and this contribution is of limited scope.[2] It focuses on some of the essential changes to the system which the Lisbon Treaty introduced. As will be seen, pillar talk cannot as yet be avoided. There is an incontrovertible need to delimit the CFSP from other EU policies, because the

[1] M Dougan, 'The Treaty of Lisbon 2007: Winning Minds, not Hearts' (2008) 45 *CMLRev* 624.
[2] See further J-C Piris, *The Lisbon Treaty—A Legal and Political Analysis* (Cambridge University Press, 2010) chapter VII; P Craig, *The Lisbon Treaty—Law, Politics, and Treaty Reform* (Oxford University Press, 2010) chapter 10; P Eeckhout, *EU External Relations Law*, 2nd edn (Oxford University Press, 2011) chapters 5 and 11.

decision-making mechanisms are very different. However, there is also a need to move beyond pillar talk, and to analyse the CFSP from the perspective of constitutionalism. Is it really proper for the CFSP to be intergovernmental, which means that it is dominated by executives? Are there adequate checks and balances? Again, this contribution does not aim to provide a definitive analysis. More modestly, it seeks to draw attention to at least some of the constitutional defects. It focuses on three areas of Lisbon innovation: the scope and nature of the CFSP competences (including their delimitation from other competences); the legal acts employed to conduct the CFSP; and the institutional innovations, in particular the office of the High Representative and the European External Action Service.

II. Scope and Nature of the Competences to Conduct a Common Foreign and Security Policy

The TEU and TFEU, as amended by the Treaty of Lisbon, are extremely short as regards the scope and nature of the EU's competence to conduct a CFSP. The scope of the EU's competence in CFSP matters is not particularly well defined. Article 24(1) TEU provides:

The Union's competence in matters of common foreign and security policy shall cover all areas of foreign policy and all questions relating to the Union's security, including the progressive framing of a common defence policy that might lead to a common defence.

As can be seen, there are two elements to this definition. On the one hand, the CFSP covers all areas of foreign policy; on the other, it extends to all questions relating to the EU's security. The former element is not further defined in the TFEU. The latter, by contrast, forms the object of an entire section, with the heading 'Provisions on the Common Security and Defence Policy' (hereafter, CSDP). According to Article 42(1) TEU, the CSDP shall provide the EU with an operational capacity drawing on civilian and military assets, which may be used on missions outside the EU for peace-keeping, conflict prevention and strengthening international security in accordance with the principles of the UN Charter. This is elaborated upon in Article 43(1) TEU, which provides that the tasks referred to in Article 42(1):

[s]hall include joint disarmament operations, humanitarian and rescue tasks, military advice and assistance tasks, conflict prevention and peace-keeping tasks, tasks of combat forces in crisis management, including peace-making and post-conflict stabilization. All these tasks may contribute to the fight against terrorism, including by supporting third countries in combating terrorism in their territories.

Article 42(2) TEU further provides that the CSDP shall include the progressive framing of a common EU defence policy, which will lead to a common defence, when the European Council, acting unanimously, so decides.[3]

---

[3] On the CSDP, see Piris, above n 2 at 265–79.

There is thus an enormous contrast between the relatively precise and detailed description of the scope and content of the security and defence element of the CFSP, and the totally undefined foreign policy element. The pre-Lisbon version of the TEU was different in this respect, in the sense that it set out a specific set of CFSP objectives,[4] which could be called in aid of determining the scope of 'all areas of foreign policy'. The Treaty of Lisbon has replaced these specific CFSP objectives with a set of overall objectives for EU external action. Article 21(2) TFEU provides:

The Union shall define and pursue common policies and actions, and shall work for a high degree of cooperation in all fields of international relations, in order to:

(a) safeguard its values, fundamental interests, security, independence and integrity;
(b) consolidate and support democracy, the rule of law, human rights and the principles of international law;
(c) preserve peace, prevent conflicts and strengthen international security, in accordance with the purposes and principles of the United Nations Charter, with the principles of the Helsinki Final Act and with the aims of the Charter of Paris, including those relating to external borders;
(d) foster the sustainable economic, social and environmental development of developing countries, with the primary aim of eradicating poverty;
(e) encourage the integration of all countries into the world economy, including through the progressive abolition of restrictions on international trade;
(f) help develop international measures to preserve and improve the quality of the environment and the sustainable management of global natural resources, in order to ensure sustainable development;
(g) assist populations, countries and regions confronting natural or man-made disasters; and
(h) promote an international system based on stronger multilateral cooperation and good global governance.

In the literature it is often indicated that this means that the scope of the CFSP can no longer be determined by reference to the objectives pursued.[5] Such statements

---

[4] See old Art 11(1) TEU:

The Union shall define and implement a common foreign and security policy covering all areas of foreign and security policy, the objectives of which shall be:

— to safeguard the common values, fundamental interests, independence and integrity of the Union in conformity with the principles of the United Nations Charter;

— to strengthen the security of the Union in all ways;

— to preserve peace and strengthen international security, in accordance with the principles of the United Nations Charter, as well as the principles of the Helsinki Final Act and the objectives of the Paris Charter, including those on external borders;

— to promote international co-operation;

— to develop and consolidate democracy and the rule of law, and respect for human rights and fundamental freedoms.

[5] C Herrmann, 'Much Ado about Pluto? The "Unity of the Legal Order of the European Union" Revisited' in M Cremona and B De Witte (eds), *EU Foreign Relations Law—Constitutional Fundamentals* (Hart Publishing, 2008) 47.

need to be qualified, however. Objectives (d) to (g) clearly refer to non-CFSP areas of external action, that is, development cooperation, trade, environmental protection and humanitarian aid. Objective (c), on the other hand, concerning the preservation of peace, the prevention of conflicts, and the strengthening of international security, is clearly at the heart of the CFSP. Objectives (a), (b) and (h), lastly, are more of a cross-sectoral nature.

Those are the objectives and subject matter of the CFSP. The legal nature of the EU's competences to conduct the CFSP are as ill-defined as their scope.

Article 2(4) TFEU simply provides that the Union shall have competence, in accordance with the provisions of the TEU, to define and implement a common foreign and security policy, including the progressive framing of a defence policy. The nature of that competence is not clarified, in contrast with the preceding paragraphs of Article 2, which define exclusive and shared competences. It has always been clear of course that the CFSP is not an exclusive competence, but the concept of shared or concurrent competence has been employed to characterize it.[6] The Lisbon Treaty drafters nevertheless chose not to define the CFSP competence as shared with the Member States. One reason for this may be that shared competences are described as having a pre-emptive effect. Article 2(2) TFEU provides, inter alia, that, in areas of shared competence, the Member States shall exercise their competence to the extent that the Union has not exercised its competence. The same provision also defines such competence as authorizing both the EU and the Member States to legislate and adopt legally binding acts. Article 24(1) TEU, however, excludes the adoption of legislative acts within the scope of the CFSP. In that sense, too, the CFSP is not a shared competence. It is not an area of general lawmaking, or normative action, where EU acts have a pre-emptive effect on national competence.

III. Delimitation of TEU and TFEU
External Competences

The above discussion shows that the scope and nature of the EU's powers under the CFSP do not lend themselves to a strict legal analysis, because of the open texture of the Treaty provisions and the lack of authoritative interpretation through case law. However, when it comes to the interaction between the CFSP and the EU's other external policies and powers one can hardly be satisfied with some general reflections. It matters a lot whether a decision is taken under the TEU or the TFEU: decision-making procedures are different, parliamentary and judicial scrutiny is different, and so are the legal effects of the decisions.

---

[6] Eg R Gosalbo Bono, 'Some Reflections on the CFSP Legal Order' (2006) 43 *CML Rev* 364.

The paradox of the relationship between the CFSP and other EU external action—indeed, one could say the original sin of overall EU external action—is that the CFSP *supplements* the TFEU with a less integrated policy,[7] and yet is intended to cover *all areas* of foreign and security policy. But commercial policy, development cooperation policy, etc are of course also forms of foreign policy. As Koskenniemi points out, everyone agrees that it is difficult to separate foreign policy from other aspects of policy and that the most credible conception of security is the comprehensive one.[8] This original sin of EU external action produces many effects. Within the supranational context of other EU policies it creates concerns about contamination by the CFSP. Those concerns have an obvious institutional dimension: as the Council is the central CFSP institution, with only limited roles for the Commission and the Parliament, the latter institutions do not like to see certain types of decisions effectively transferred to the CFSP.[9] Moreover, there has been concern that CFSP decisions, taken unanimously under intergovernmental procedures, could contain instructions for the other EU policies, and could be seen as hierarchically superior.[10] Those concerns were present at the inception of the pillar structure. Accordingly, the pre-Lisbon TEU contained a number of provisions which were aimed at avoiding undue interference with (then) EC policies. Article 2 TEU provided that one of the Union's objectives was 'to maintain in full the acquis communautaire and build on it with a view to considering to what extent the policies and forms of co-operation introduced by this Treaty may need to be revised with the aim of ensuring the effectiveness of the mechanisms and the institutions of the Community'. It thus appeared to foreshadow a gradual integration of the pillars. The central provision on the matter was (old) Article 47 TEU:

Subject to the provisions amending the Treaty establishing the European Economic Community with a view to establishing the European Community...and to these final provisions, nothing in this Treaty shall affect the Treaties establishing the European Communities or the subsequent Treaties and Acts modifying or supplementing them.

This provision was clearly intended to protect the *acquis communautaire*, and to prevent intergovernmental contamination of supranational decision-making. To vary the pillar image, Article 47 TEU aimed to compartmentalize the Community, on the one hand, and the CFSP (as well as Police and Judicial Co-operation in Criminal Matters), on the other.

---

[7] Although it must be noted that the Treaty of Lisbon has deleted the notion, in (old) Article 1 TEU, of the CFSP supplementing other policies.

[8] M Koskenniemi, 'International Law Aspects of the Common Foreign and Security Policy' in M Koskenniemi (ed), *International Law Aspects of the European Union* (Kluwer Law International, 1998) 36.

[9] See eg Commission, *Report on the Operation of the Treaty on European Union* (EC Commission, May 1995) as reported by G Edwards, 'Common Foreign and Security Policy' (1994) 14 *YEL* 545.

[10] CWA Timmermans, 'The Uneasy Relationship between the Communities and the Second Union Pillar: Back to the "Plan Fouchet"?' (1996/1) *LIEI* 61.

A. The *Small Arms and Light Weapons* judgment

In the light of the concerns over the relationship between the pillars, it comes as no surprise that the Court was asked to decide when measures adopted under the (then) second and third pillars 'affected', in the words of Article 47, the EC Treaty.[11] After a series of judgments which concerned the first and the third pillar,[12] the Court was asked to rule in a case involving the delimitation of CFSP and EC competences. *Small Arms and Light Weapons* (hereafter, *SALW*) concerned a Council decision implementing a joint action with a view to an EU contribution to ECOWAS in the framework of that organization's Moratorium on Small Arms and Light Weapons.[13] The Commission claimed that the joint action, and the decision implementing it, fell within the shared competences on which Community development policy was based, and that such shared competences were just as much protected by (old) Article 47 TEU as the areas of exclusive competence.

Although (old) Article 47 TEU has been substantially amended by the Treaty of Lisbon, the judgment continues to be important for delimiting CFSP competences from those in other areas of external action. A complete analysis of the judgment cannot be presented here.[14] The focus is on the basic principles underpinning the Court's approach to the issues.

Analysing the issues, the Court considered it necessary to determine whether the provisions of the contested decision affected competences enjoyed by the Community under the EC Treaty, on the ground that those provisions could have been adopted on the basis of that Treaty. (Old) Article 47 TEU aimed to maintain and build on the *acquis communautaire*. A measure having legal effects adopted under (old) Title V of the TEU affected the provisions of the EC Treaty within the meaning of (old) Article 47 TEU whenever it could have been adopted on the basis of the EC Treaty, it being unnecessary to examine whether the measure prevented or limited the exercise by the Community of its competences. If it was established that the provisions of a measure adopted under the TEU, on account of both their aim and their content, had as their main purpose the implementation of a policy conferred by the EC Treaty on the Community, and if they could properly have been adopted on the basis of the EC Treaty, the Court had to find that those

---

[11] See also A Dashwood, 'Article 47 TEU and the Relationship between First and Second Pillar Competences' in A Dashwood and M Maresceau (eds), *Law and Practice of EU External Relations* (Cambridge University Press, 2008) 70; D Curtin, *Executive Power of the European Union—Law, Practices, and the Living Constitution* (Oxford University Press, 2009) 179–94.

[12] Case C-170/96 *Commission v Council (Airport Transit Visas)* [1998] ECR I-2763; Case C-176/03 *Commission v Council (Environmental Penalties)* [2005] ECR I-7879; and Case C-440/05 *Commission v Council (Shipsource Pollution)* [2007] ECR I-9097.

[13] Case C-91/05 *Commission v Council (SALW)* [2008] ECR I–3651. The decision is published in [2004] OJ L359/65. ECOWAS stands for Economic Community of West African States.

[14] For comment see also B Van Vooren, 'EU–EC External Competences after the Small Arms Judgment' (2009) 14 *EFAR* 7 and 'The Small Arms Judgment in an Age of Constitutional Turmoil' (2009) 14 *EFAR* 231; A Dashwood, 'The Law and Practice of CFSP Joint Actions' in M Cremona and B De Witte, above n 5 at 65–77; G De Baere, *Constitutional Principles of EU External Relations* (Oxford University Press, 2008) 283–94; C Hillion and R Wessel, 'Competence Distribution in EU External Relations after *Ecowas*: Clarification or Continued Fuzziness?' (2009) 46 *CML Rev* 551.

provisions infringed (old) Article 47 TEU. It was not relevant whether in an area such as development cooperation—which did not fall within the exclusive competence of the Community and in which, therefore, the Member States were not precluded from exercising, individually or collectively, their competences—such a measure could have been adopted by the Member States in the exercise of their competences. Moreover, the question of whether the provisions of such a measure fell within the competence of the Community related to the attribution and, thus, the very existence of that competence, and not its exclusive or shared nature. It was therefore necessary to determine whether the contested decision infringed (old) Article 47 TEU inasmuch as it could have been adopted on the basis of the provisions of the EC Treaty.[15]

The Court then recalled that the objectives of EC development cooperation policy were broad, and established, on the basis of a number of documents from the EU institutions, that certain measures aiming to prevent fragility in developing countries, including those adopted in order to combat the proliferation of small arms and light weapons, could contribute to the elimination or reduction of obstacles to the economic and social development of those countries. Nevertheless, a concrete measure aiming to combat such proliferation could be adopted by the Community under its development cooperation policy only if that measure, by virtue of its aims and its content, fell within the scope of the competences conferred upon the Community. That was not the case if such a measure, even if it contributed to the economic and social development of the developing country, had as its main purpose the implementation of the CFSP. The Court then referred to the principles emanating from its case law on the delimitation of legal bases in the EC Treaty. If examination of a measure revealed that it pursued a twofold aim or that it had a twofold component, and if one of those was identifiable as the main one, whereas the other was merely incidental, the measure had to be based on a single legal basis, namely that required by the main aim or component. It followed that measures combating the proliferation of small arms and light weapons did not fall within the competences of the Community in the field of development cooperation if, on account of their main aim or component, they were part of the pursuit of the CFSP. With regard to a measure which simultaneously pursued a number of objectives or which had several components, without one being incidental to the other, the Court had held that such a measure had to be founded, exceptionally, on the various corresponding legal bases. However, and this was a crucial finding by the Court, under (old) Article 47 TEU, such a solution was impossible with regard to the delimitation of EU and EC competences. Since (old) Article 47 precluded the Union from adopting, on the basis of the EU Treaty, a measure which could properly be adopted on the basis of the EC Treaty, the Union could not have recourse to a legal basis falling within the CFSP in order to adopt provisions which also fell within a competence conferred by the EC Treaty on the Community.[16]

---

[15] *SALW*, above n 13 at paras 58–63 of the judgment.
[16] Ibid paras 64–77.

The Court then carried out an extensive analysis of the aims and content of the contested decision. It concluded that the contested decision contained two components, neither of which could be considered to be incidental to the other, one falling within Community development cooperation policy and the other within the CFSP. This meant that (old) Article 47 TEU had been infringed and that the decision had to be annulled.[17]

The *SALW* judgment established three important principles. First, (old) Article 47 TEU protected all EC competences, be they exclusive or shared. If, having regard to the aim and content of an act, it could have been adopted under the EC Treaty, it was impossible to adopt it under the TEU. Whether or not the Member States were capable of adopting the act, individually or collectively, because it came only within the shared competences of the EC, was irrelevant. This meant that the Member States could not act collectively under the CFSP in cases where they were entitled to act collectively, outside the EU framework. The CFSP could thus cover all areas of foreign and security policy, but where the EC Treaty conferred upon the Community competences for a specific form of foreign policy, such as commercial policy and development cooperation, those competences took precedence. They were, one could say, *lex specialis*. However, as *lex specialis* they were not to be interpreted narrowly, but rather on their own terms, in no way confined by the TEU provisions on the CFSP.

Secondly, the only qualification to this first principle was that, as in other areas of external action, the delimitation of the respective competences had to be done focusing on the main purpose or component of the measure in issue. This meant that the EU could adopt CFSP measures with an incidental effect on trade, development cooperation, or other EC matters. It also meant that there could be cases, like *SALW*, where there were two purposes or components, neither of which was incidental to the other.

In the latter cases, the third principle came into play: in contrast with other external competences, the Court as a matter of principle excluded recourse to a dual legal basis in such cases. (Old) Article 47 TEU simply precluded such a dual legal basis. The Court did not further elaborate on the reasons for this finding. Advocate General Mengozzi drew attention in a footnote to the incompatibility of the decision-making processes under, respectively, the TEU and the EC Treaty.[18] Clearly, this rejection of a dual legal basis may make it more difficult to pursue a coherent EU external policy, since it precludes the use of all-encompassing legal instruments, having both foreign policy and other EU policy dimensions.

B. Article 40 TEU

It remains to be seen whether, after the entry into force of the Treaty of Lisbon, those principles continue to be valid. The legal relationship between the CFSP and

---

[17] Ibid paras 108–10.   [18] Ibid Opinion AG Mengozzi, fn 76.

other forms of EU external action is substantially modified by the Treaty of Lisbon. Article 40 TEU, which replaces (old) Article 47 TEU, provides:

The implementation of the common foreign and security policy shall not affect the application of the procedures and the extent of the powers of the institutions laid down by the Treaties for the exercise of the Union competences referred to in Articles 3 to 6 of the Treaty on the Functioning of the European Union.

Similarly, the implementation of the policies listed in those Articles shall not affect the application of the procedures and the extent of the powers of the institutions laid down by the Treaties for the exercise of the Union competences under this Chapter.

As can be seen, this provision not only protects EU competences under the TFEU (former EC competences), but also works the other way round, to protect CFSP competences. It therefore appears to introduce a more balanced approach to questions of delimitation. Furthermore, the new provision does not generally preclude that one Treaty affects the other, but refers, more specifically, to the application of the procedures and the extent of the powers of the institutions laid down by the Treaties for the exercise of the various EU competences.

The amendment of this provision is not the only significant modification. The current Treaties no longer contain provisions such as (old) Articles 1 to 3 TEU. (Old) Article 1 provided that the Union was founded on the Communities, *supplemented* by the policies and forms of cooperation (that is, CFSP and Police and Judicial Cooperation in Criminal Matters (PJCCM)) established by the TEU. (Old) Article 2 TEU provided that one of the objectives of the EU was to maintain in full the *acquis communautaire*. (Old) Article 3 referred to the EU's single institutional framework which had to respect and build upon the *acquis communautaire*.

Also relevant, no doubt, are the attempts to create a more integrated legal framework for external action. The CFSP is no longer characterized by a set of objectives of its own, as referred to above; instead, Articles 3(5) and 21 TEU list and describe the EU's objectives for its external action as a whole. There is also an attempt to institutionalize this integrated framework by creating the double-hatted position of the High Representative, served by the European External Action Service.

Against that revised Treaty background, what is one to make of the new Article 40 TEU? Which of the principles established by the Court in *SALW*, if any, continue to be valid?

It is clear that on the basis of Article 40 the Court can in future be asked to review, not just whether a CFSP act ought to have been adopted under other EU competences, provided for by the TFEU, but also whether an act adopted under the TFEU is in reality a CFSP act. That in itself does not, however, mean the withdrawal of the principle that a CFSP act which could have been adopted, in the light of its aim and content, under the (current) TFEU, violates (current) Article 40 TEU; that is, the first principle emanating from *SALW*. If anything, (current) Article 40 TEU is more specific in that respect. The implementation of the CFSP may not affect the TFEU procedures and the powers of the institutions under the TFEU for the exercise of TFEU competences. The facts of *SALW* clearly come within those terms: as the contested decision also had an aim and component of development cooperation, for that purpose the relevant procedures under (current) Articles 208 to 211 TFEU should have been employed, involving all three EU political institutions, the Commission, the Parliament and the Council, under the ordinary legislative procedure. It is difficult to see any basis for a more restrictive reading of (current) Article 40 TEU.

It is true of course that the new provision also protects the CFSP. On a first reading that may lead one to think that the CFSP is no longer purely supplementary, and that, as was mentioned, some kind of more 'balanced' approach is required for the delimitation of competences; an approach requiring, in some cases, that TFEU competences give way to the CFSP. There are, however, two difficulties with such an argument.

First, the scope of the CFSP continues to be as ill-defined as before. Indeed, some commentators point out that the absence of specific CFSP objectives in the TEU make it even more difficult to define that scope.[19] That is probably exaggerated, as it is clear that the CFSP continues to be focused on questions of peace and international security. Nevertheless, those aims are very broad—does not development aid or free trade also contribute to peace and international security? And so is the reference in Article 24(1) TEU to 'all areas of foreign policy'—which again could easily be seen to encompass development cooperation and trade. Yet it is clear that one of the purposes of (new) Article 40 TEU is to safeguard the EU's competences in those specific matters, and the applicable decision-making procedures and involvement of the various institutions. The better view is that the relationship between the CFSP and other competences is in the nature of *lex generalis* and *lex specialis*.[20] That means that an analysis of whether (current) Article 40 TEU is violated, because a CFSP act affects TFEU procedures and competences, will need to be conducted along the lines of *SALW*.

Secondly, the Court's approach in *SALW* effectively introduced a balanced delimitation, by applying the test of the main purpose or component. It so happened that in the case at hand the Court found two indissociably linked purposes and components, but the Court also expressly recognized that a CFSP act could, in principle, incidentally affect non-CFSP matters such as development cooperation.[21] Of course, that also means that a non-CFSP act, adopted under the TFEU, may incidentally affect the CFSP. It is not clear what methodology to applying (current) Article 40 TEU would constitute a more balanced approach.

In *SALW* the Court focused nearly exclusively on the aims of the contested decision, as its content—financial support and technical cooperation—could equally come within the scope of the CFSP as within that of development cooperation. There is of course an element of subjectivity, so to speak, in determining the aims of a measure. The institutions adopting the measure will often have considerable discretion in determining and expressing those aims. It is clear that the Court

---

[19] Herrmann, above n 5.
[20] See also M Cremona, 'Defining Competence in EU External Relations: Lessons from the Treaty Reform Process' in A Dashwood and M Maresceau, above n 11 at 46.
[21] *SALW*, above n 13 at paras 73–4.

in *SALW* sought to reduce the scope for such discretion by analysing a whole series of political documents and statements, to support the conclusion that the decision had both development and CFSP aims. That approach carries the risk that, in practice, it will often have to be concluded that a measure has more than one aim, in particular, after the entry into force of the Treaty of Lisbon. Since there is now a unified set of objectives for EU external action, the institutions will often, in their policy-making, refer to several objectives. Indeed, they are required to do so (see, for example, Article 205 TFEU). Such multiplicity of objectives will not make the task of delimiting the CFSP and other external competences any easier. Moreover, the objectives of the CFSP are so broadly defined—'preserve peace, prevent conflicts and strengthen international security' (Article 21(2)(c) TEU)—that many acts can be seen to pursue them.

A final question concerning Article 40 TEU is whether a dual legal basis continues to be excluded, and whether therefore the third principle emanating from *SALW* remains in place. Can acts with a dual purpose or component, one within the scope of the CFSP, the other within that of a TFEU competence, ever be adopted on a dual legal basis? At least for one type of act, namely, international agreements concluded by the EU, the provisions of the TFEU suggest that this is conceivable.[22] Article 218 TFEU contains procedural provisions on the conclusion of agreements, which apply to both CFSP agreements and to other agreements. Under Article 218(3), it is respectively the Commission or the High Representative which makes recommendations to the Council for the opening of negotiations; the High Representative has this power 'where the agreement envisaged relates exclusively or principally to the common foreign and security policy'. Furthermore, Article 218(6) TFEU sets out the procedure for concluding the agreement, and provides for the involvement of the European Parliament 'except where agreements relate exclusively to the common foreign and security policy'. Those provisions strongly suggest that an agreement may contain provisions coming within the scope of the CFSP as well as other provisions. Indeed, it would be rather nonsensical if, notwithstanding all the attempts to create a unified legal framework for EU external action, the EU would not be capable of concluding an agreement with a third country which contains elements of foreign policy as well as other forms of cooperation, or provisions on trade, or the environment, etc. If, nonetheless, the Court were to decide that Article 40 TEU does not permit a dual legal basis for the conclusion of an agreement, at least the agreement itself should continue to be unified, and the institutions could simply conclude it by way of two decisions, one concerning the CFSP elements, and the other for the remaining provisions.

However, also for autonomous EU acts, a case can be made for allowing a dual legal basis, in the TEU and the TFEU, where an act has a twofold purpose or component. Unfortunately, the Court did not, in *SALW*, clarify why a dual legal basis is excluded, other than by referring to (old) Article 47 TEU. As was men-

---

[22] See also RA Wessel, 'Cross-Pillar Mixity: Combining Competences in the Conclusion of EU International Agreements' in C Hillion and P Koutrakos (eds), *Mixed Agreements Revisited—The EU and its Member States in the World* (Hart Publishing, 2010) 30.

tioned, Advocate General Mengozzi was more specific, and considered that the respective CFSP and EC procedures were incompatible. There is indeed long-standing case law of the Court of Justice on when different procedures for decision-making can and cannot be combined, and on when an act can or cannot be adopted on a dual legal basis in the light of these differences. In the 1991 *Titanium Dioxide* case the Court had established that it was not possible to combine the so-called cooperation procedure (the predecessor to the current ordinary legislative procedure, but not yet involving full co-decision by the Parliament) with a procedure requiring unanimity in the Council, because that would divest the cooperation procedure (involving a qualified majority in the Council) of its substance.[23] However, more recent case law has become substantially more liberal in this respect. In *International Fund for Ireland* the Court considered that (old) Articles 159 and 308 EC should have formed the legal basis of the act in issue, notwithstanding the fact that the former article provided for the co-decision procedure and the latter for unanimity.[24] Similarly, in *Kadi and Al Barakaat* the Court accepted the combined application of (old) Articles 60, 301 and 308 EC, notwithstanding the fact that the first two articles provided for decision-making by qualified majority, without involving the Parliament, whereas Article 308 EC provided for unanimity and consultation of the Parliament.[25] In the light of this more liberal case law, the question can at least be raised of whether there are genuinely huge obstacles to an act being based on, say, both the CFSP provisions in the TEU, and Article 209 TFEU on development cooperation, which provides for the ordinary legislative procedure. As in *International Fund for Ireland*, that procedure would simply need to be combined with unanimity in the Council.

If, however, a dual legal basis continues to be excluded, how should the institutions proceed in the case of an act with a dual purpose or component (like the decision in *SALW*)? Which procedure ought to be followed? It must be emphasized that the Court did not state in *SALW* that the EC procedure was to be preferred. It simply annulled the CFSP act, without indicating how the institutions should have proceeded. Now that Article 40 TEU also protects the CFSP method of decision-making, it is difficult to contend that the TFEU procedures should take precedence over those of the CFSP. The only solution appears to be for the act to be split in two: one with a main or predominant CFSP purpose or component; the other with a main or predominant TFEU purpose of component. How that should work in the case of an act with a single content and a dual purpose, such as the financial support and technical cooperation of the *SALW* decision, remains a mystery.

It may finally be noted that specific cross-pillar issues arise in the area of sanctions, or what the Treaties now call 'restrictive measures' (Article 215 TFEU).

---

[23] Case C-300/89 *Commission v Council (Titanium Dioxide)* [1991] ECR I-2867, para 18.
[24] Case C-166/07 *European Parliament v Council (International Fund for Ireland)* [2009] ECR I-7135, para 69.
[25] Joined Cases C-402/05 P and C-415/05 P *Kadi and Al Barakaat v Council and Commission* [2008] ECR I-6351, paras 235–6. For further analysis of the issue of dual legal basis, see RH Lauwaars and RH van Ooik, 'De problematiek van de dubbele rechtsgrondslagen in het Europese recht' (2010) 58 *SEW* 293–305.

IV. Acts of the CFSP

Article 25 TEU provides that the EU shall conduct the CFSP by:

(a) defining the general guidelines,
(b) adopting decisions defining:

  (i)   actions to be undertaken by the Union;
  (ii) positions to be taken by the Union;
  (iii) arrangements for the implementation of the decisions referred to in points (i) and (ii); and by

(c) strengthening systematic co-operation between Member States in the conduct of policy.

It may be useful to indicate how these provisions on the EU's CFSP instruments have evolved through the various treaty amendments. The original version of the TEU did not contain the above enumeration as such. It spoke of systematic cooperation between the Member States and of the gradual implementation of joint actions in areas where the Member States had important interests in common (Article J.1(3)). Member States were to inform and consult one another, and the Council could define common positions to which national policies had to conform. Member States were also to coordinate their action in international organizations and at international conferences (Article J.2). The Treaty provided for a procedure for the adoption of joint actions, but did not define the concept itself (Article J.3).

The Treaty of Amsterdam attempted to create more precision through an enumeration, in (then) Article 12 TEU, which included principles and guidelines; common strategies; joint actions; common positions; and systematic cooperation between Member States. It also offered some type of definition of joint actions (old Article 14(1) TEU) and of common positions (old Article 15 TEU). It introduced common strategies, decided by the European Council, and 'to be implemented by the Union in areas where the Member States have important interests in common' (old Article 13(2) TEU).

The Treaty of Lisbon again modified the list of available instruments. Instead of having to use the peculiar concepts of 'joint actions' and 'common positions' the Council now simply adopts 'decisions'. It is to be noted that the legal concept of an EU 'decision' is modified by Article 288 TFEU: former Article 249 EC implied that decisions were by definition addressed to particular persons,[26] whereas Article 288 TFEU no longer requires a particular connection between a decision and an addressee, but also allows decisions of a general nature.[27] The use of decisions for the conduct of the CFSP also needs to be assessed in the light of the exclusion of legislative acts in the context of the CFSP.

---

[26] 'A decision shall be binding in its entirety upon those to whom it is addressed.'
[27] 'A decision shall be binding in its entirety. A decision which specifies those to whom it is addressed shall be binding only on them.'

The replacement of joint actions and common positions with decisions does not mean that the distinction between actions and positions is abandoned. As set out above, Article 25 TEU speaks of decisions defining either actions to be undertaken or positions to be taken by the Union. That distinction is elaborated upon in Articles 28 and 29 TEU. The former provision addresses 'operational action', the latter concerns 'decisions which shall define the approach of the Union to a particular matter of a geographical or thematic nature'. As the CFSP decisions need to identify the TEU provisions on which they are based, the distinction between joint actions and common positions to some extent survives.

However, the post-Lisbon TEU removes 'common strategies' as a specific CFSP instrument. The ostensible purpose of common strategies was to create a general policy framework, in certain broader areas, leading to more coherent and unified CFSP actions. That idea is taken one step further by the current TEU, in the sense that, what are now called 'decisions of the European Council on the strategic interests and objectives of the Union' cover both the CFSP and other areas of EU external action. Article 22 TEU, which follows the TEU provision setting out the EU's overall objectives as regards external action, contains the relevant provisions.

Articles 22(1) and 26(1) TEU define the role of the European Council in the conduct of the CFSP. Article 22(1) provides that: 'On the basis of the principles and objectives set out in Article 21, the European Council shall identify the strategic interests and objectives of the Union.' It further provides that the relevant decisions:

[s]hall relate to the common foreign and security policy and to other areas of the external action of the Union. Such decisions may concern the relations of the Union with a specific country or region or may be thematic in approach. They shall define their duration, and the means to be made available by the Union and the Member States.

Article 26(1) TEU further provides that the European Council shall identify the Union's strategic interests, and determine the objectives of and define the general guidelines for the CFSP.

As was mentioned, the ostensible purpose of decisions on strategic interests and objectives (former common strategies) is to create a general policy framework, in certain broader areas, leading to more coherent and unified CFSP actions. Indeed, the extension of this instrument to other areas of EU external action follows that same logic. The European Council is clearly an important actor in CFSP matters, and in EU external action generally. Nearly every European Council meeting devotes considerable time to international affairs and external relations, and the Presidency Conclusions invariably contain policy statements and guidelines for further EU action.

There is, however, also a significant institutional and decision-making dimension to decisions on strategic interests and objectives. Pursuant to Article 31(2) TEU the Council acts by qualified majority 'when adopting a decision defining a Union action or position on the basis of such a European Council decision, by way of derogation from the standard unanimity requirement. Throughout the inception and life of the CFSP there has been intense debate about the voting rules in the Council. Unanimity is regarded as safeguarding national sovereignty, whereas qualified majority is advanced as indispensable for effective decision-making. This debate took place at Amsterdam and in the Convention on the Future of Europe. Decisions on strategic interests and objectives are thus also akin to a form of ceasefire in the constitutional politics of the EU as regards voting rules in CFSP matters.[28]

The broad, inclusive nature of decisions on strategic interests and objectives raises questions concerning their relationship with TFEU policies. As with decisions on actions and positions, the Treaty does not clarify whether the EU institutions are bound by them when acting within the framework of the TFEU. Again this is left to the consistency requirement for which the Council, the Commission and the High Representative are responsible.

V. The Exclusion of Legislative Acts

It is useful, at this point of the analysis, to examine the express exclusion of legislative acts in the context of the CFSP. Remarkably, the TEU twice contains exactly the same phrase, 'The adoption of legislative acts shall be excluded', in Articles 24(1) and 31(1). What is the scope and effect of this exclusion?

The reference to 'legislative acts' finds its origins in the ill-fated Constitution for Europe, which would have introduced a general distinction between legislative and non-legislative acts.[29] Under its provisions, European decisions were labelled as non-legislative acts. The legislative acts encompassed European laws, and such an act was defined as a legislative act of general application, binding in its entirety and directly applicable in all Member States; and European framework laws, which were described as a legislative act binding, as to the result to be achieved, upon each Member State to which it was addressed, but leaving to the national authorities the choice of form and methods. The Constitution for Europe did not in terms exclude the adoption of legislative acts in the framework of the CFSP, but as it only allowed the adoption of CFSP decisions (as does the current TEU), it was obvious that legislative acts were excluded.

The current versions of the TEU and the TFEU are not of course identical to the Constitution for Europe. The Treaty of Lisbon largely abandoned the concepts of legislative and non-legislative acts, keeping the existing instruments of regulations, directives, decisions, recommendations and opinions (Article 288 TFEU). However, it kept the denomination of ordinary and special 'legislative' procedures for the adoption of EU legal acts (Article 289(1) and (2) TFEU). All of those

---

[28] S Peers, 'Common Foreign and Security Policy' (1997) 17 *YEL* 546 suggests that this was the real purpose of introducing common strategies; A Dashwood, 'External Relations Provisions of the Amsterdam Treaty' in D O'Keeffe and P Twomey (eds), *Legal Issues of the Maastricht Treaty* (Chancery Law, 1994) 212 speaks of the primary purpose.

[29] See Articles I-33–I-35.

procedures involve at least the Parliament and the Council. Moreover, the TFEU specifies that 'Legal acts adopted by legislative procedure shall constitute legislative acts' (Article 289(3) TFEU).

The exclusion of legislative acts for the conduct of the CFSP could simply be understood, in accordance with the above TFEU provisions, as confirming that the ordinary or special legislative procedures do not apply to CFSP decision-making. However, such a straightforward reading is difficult to justify in the light of the principle of effective treaty interpretation. Indeed, it is most clear from the TEU provisions on CFSP decision-making that CFSP decisions are not adopted in accordance with either the ordinary or a special legislative procedure, as the Parliament is not involved. There was therefore no need to confirm, twice, that legislative acts are excluded: the provisions on decision-making already implied such an exclusion.

A purely formal reading of the exclusion of legislative acts is thus unpersuasive. There are, moreover, strong arguments in support of a more substantive reading;[30] a reading which excludes general normative action in the framework of the CFSP.

The first argument is based on the democratic principles underpinning the EU, as now set out in Articles 9 to 12 TEU. Article 10, in particular, describes how the functioning of the Union shall be founded on representative democracy. It points out that citizens are directly represented at Union level in the European Parliament, and that Member States are represented in the European Council and the Council by their (heads of) governments, themselves democratically accountable to either their national parliaments or their citizens. Article 10(3) confirms that every citizen shall have the right to participate in the democratic life of the Union and that decisions—a concept clearly used in a generic sense—shall be taken as openly and as closely as possible to the citizen.

As the European Parliament has no direct say in CFSP matters, the CFSP decisions benefit from only one type of representative democracy: through Member State representation in the European Council and the Council. It could well be argued that this explains the exclusion of legislative acts, understood as general normative action. The latter clearly affects European citizens directly, and should therefore only result from decision-making involving the Parliament, which directly represents those citizens. Regulations and directives adopted under the TFEU involve such general normative action, even if directives are not directly applicable and require national implementation: they are nevertheless binding as to the results, which more often than not encompass creating rights and obligations for EU citizens. CFSP decisions should not involve that kind of normative action. Such an understanding of representative democracy justifies a reading of the exclusion of legislative acts for the conduct of the CFSP which precludes general normative action, in particular action which purports to create rights and obligations.

---

[30] cf A Türk, *The Concept of Legislation in European Community Law—A Comparative Perspective* (Kluwer Law International, 2006) 77–185; K Lenaerts and M Desomer, 'Simplification of the Union's Instruments' in B de Witte (ed), *Ten Reflections on the Constitutional Treaty for Europe* (RSCAS, 2003) 110–11.

A second argument in support of such a reading is derived from the principle that the Union is founded on the rule of law (Article 2 TEU).[31] In the conception of the Court of Justice, that principle implies that all acts of the institutions are subject to review as regards their conformity with the basic constitutional charter, the (then) EC Treaty.[32] Clearly, the exclusion of the Court's jurisdiction over CFSP decisions (see Article 275 TFEU) constitutes a breach in this foundational principle. However, it is a breach which is more tolerable if general normative action is excluded in the context of the CFSP.

There are signs that the Court itself may share such a conception. In *Segi* it was confronted with a challenge, by way of an action in damages, against a common position listing Segi, a Basque group, as a terrorist organization. The common position was based on the pre-Lisbon TEU provisions concerning both the second and the third pillars. Segi's listing was in fact characterized as a third pillar act. The case had first been brought to the (then) Court of First Instance (CFI), which had established that the then TEU did not provide for an action in damages against the institutions, and therefore dismissed the application. On appeal, the Court of Justice could only confirm that finding. However, as to whether this finding was in conformity with the right to effective judicial protection, the Court made the following analysis. The background to this analysis is that, at the time, the Court had some jurisdiction for third pillar measures: it could hear actions for annulment brought against framework decisions and decisions, and references from national courts on the interpretation and validity of framework decisions and decisions, but it could not hear such actions or references as regards common positions.

The Court first admitted that the system of remedies as regards the third pillar was less extensive than that under the (then) EC Treaty. Nevertheless, the appellants could not validly argue that they were deprived of all judicial protection. As was clear from (then) Article 6 TEU, the Union was founded on the principle of the rule of law and it respected fundamental rights as general principles of Community law. It followed, according to the Court, that the institutions were subject to review of the conformity of their acts with the Treaties and the general principles of law, just like the Member States when they implemented the law of the Union. Here it was to be noted that (then) Article 34 TEU provided that the Council could adopt acts varying in nature and scope. Under Article 34(2)(a) TEU the Council could 'adopt common positions defining the approach of the Union to a particular matter'. A common position required the compliance of the Member States by virtue of the principle of the duty to cooperate in good faith, which meant in particular that Member States were to take all appropriate measures, whether general or particular, to ensure fulfilment of their obligations under EU law. However, the Court also stated that a common position was not of itself supposed

---

[31] cf Gosalbo Bono, above n 6 at 347, where he states that the principle of the rule of law is applicable to the CFSP.

[32] Case 294/83 *Les Verts v European Parliament* [1986] ECR 1339, para 23, as confirmed in Joined Cases C-402/05 P and C-415/05 P *Kadi and Al Barakaat v Council and Commission* [2008] ECR I-6351, para 281.

to produce legal effects in relation to third parties. That was why, in the system established by the then TEU, only framework decisions and decisions could be the subject of an action for annulment before the Court of Justice. The Court's jurisdiction, as defined by Article 35(1) TEU, to give preliminary rulings also did not extend to common positions but was limited to rulings on the validity and interpretation of framework decisions and decisions, on the interpretation of conventions established under Title VI and on the validity and interpretation of the measures implementing them.

The Court then continued as follows. Article 35(1) TEU, in that it did not enable national courts to refer a question to the Court for a preliminary ruling on a common position but only a question concerning the acts listed in that provision, treated as acts capable of being the subject of such a reference for a preliminary ruling all measures adopted by the Council and intended to produce legal effects in relation to third parties. Given that the procedure enabling the Court to give preliminary rulings was designed to guarantee observance of the law in the interpretation and application of the Treaty, it would run counter to that objective to interpret Article 35(1) TEU narrowly. The right to make a reference to the Court of Justice for a preliminary ruling therefore had to exist in respect of all measures adopted by the Council, whatever their nature or form, which were intended to have legal effects in relation to third parties. As a result, it had to be possible to make subject to review by the Court a common position which, because of its content, had a scope going beyond that assigned by the TEU to that kind of act. Therefore, a national court hearing a dispute which indirectly raised the issue of the validity or interpretation of a common position adopted on the basis of Article 34 TEU, and which had serious doubts whether that common position was really intended to produce legal effects in relation to third parties, would be able, subject to the conditions fixed by Article 35 TEU, to ask the Court to give a preliminary ruling. It would then fall to the Court to find, where appropriate, that the common position was intended to produce legal effects in relation to third parties, to accord to it its true classification, and to give a preliminary ruling.[33]

The Court thus displayed a willingness to review the use of common positions under the then third pillar, and considered that such common positions were precluded from producing legal effects in relation to third parties. That was the justification, and indeed the condition, for its exclusion of jurisdiction to be justified.

Those considerations can easily be transposed to current CFSP decisions. The only justification, and indeed a condition, for the exclusion of the Court's jurisdiction is that CFSP decisions cannot produce legal effects in relation to third parties. The amended TEU and TFEU recognize this, because the Court does have jurisdiction, pursuant to Article 275 TFEU, to review 'the legality of decisions providing for restrictive measures against natural or legal persons adopted by the Council on the basis of Chapter 2 of Title V of the Treaty on European Union' (the

---

[33] Case C-355/04 P *Segi v Council* [2007] ECR I-1657, paras 50–4.

CFSP chapter). This exception confirms the principle that, in a Union governed by the rule of law, all acts of the institutions producing legal effects in relation to third parties must be reviewable. It does not, on the other hand, imply that general normative action is permitted under the CFSP. Article 275 TFEU talks about restrictive measures against natural or legal persons, and clearly recognizes that such decisions are adopted in the context of the CFSP. However, such restrictive measures do not of necessity involve general normative action. They may be in the nature of administrative decisions concerning individual cases.

General normative acts can therefore only be adopted under the TFEU, where the Court has full jurisdiction. The exclusion of legislative acts for the conduct of the CFSP, thus understood, is the counterpart of the exclusion of the Court's jurisdiction. It should furthermore be noted that, pursuant to current Article 40 TEU, it would be open to the Court to advance such an understanding of the nature and indeed the limitations of CFSP acts, and to police it. Article 40 clarifies that the CFSP shall not affect the procedures and the extent of the powers of the institutions for the exercise of Union competences under the TFEU. Clearly, if the Treaties are to be read as precluding CFSP decisions from producing legal effects in relation to third parties by way of general normative action, such acts being reserved to decision-making under the TFEU, then this concerns the procedures and the powers of the institutions for the exercise of Union competences under the TFEU.

The conclusion at this point, on the basis of the EU's democratic principles and of the principle of the rule of law, is that the exclusion of legislative acts for the conduct of the CFSP is to be understood as an exclusion of general normative action producing legal effects in relation to third parties. If that conclusion is correct, two further questions arise. First, what is the scope of this limitation; what kind of acts does it preclude? Secondly, does the current CFSP practice conform to the limitation?

As regards the first question, clearly, a CFSP decision cannot contain general provisions producing legal effects in relation to third parties which are directly applicable in the Member States. In other words, they cannot have an effect equal to that of general regulations adopted under the TFEU. This appears to imply that CFSP decisions cannot have direct effect, and that the principle of the primacy of EU law does not extend to them, at least not in the meaning normally attributed to those concepts in EU law. Indeed, direct effect means that, of its own force, a provision of EU law has effect in national law. The principle of primacy means that such a provision prevails over any inconsistent national law. Unavoidably, a general act which has such effects, in and on national law, will produce legal effects in relation to third parties. It is therefore arguable that the exclusion of legislative acts for the conduct of the CFSP implies that CFSP acts do not have direct effect and do not prevail over national law.

That may not be the end of the matter, however. CFSP decisions do not in terms purport to have direct effect or to prevail over inconsistent national law. They do not define their legal effects. The TEU itself only clarifies that the Member States are under an obligation to comply. It is the Member States which are bound by the

CFSP decisions (also pursuant to the duty of sincere cooperation in Article 4(3) TEU—see further the Court's statements on the binding nature of third pillar common positions in *Segi*, as set out above). Is that sufficient for the purpose of the exclusion of legislative acts? Since CFSP decisions do not of themselves have any effect in and on national law, are they, by definition, not legislative acts? It is submitted that that would be an approach which is too formal. The analogy with directives comes to mind. Directives are not directly applicable in the laws of the Member States, but need to be transposed. Nevertheless, most directives clearly have a strong legislative scope. They purport to produce legal effects for third parties, subject to their transposition into national law, which in any event, as a matter of law, is a foregone conclusion: Member States need to achieve the directive's result and are under an obligation to transpose. CFSP decisions, even if equally binding, are not permitted to have legislative scope. They cannot, to use a non-hypothetical example, provide that Member States need to ensure that acts of terrorism shall be established as serious criminal offences.[34] The exclusion of legislative acts must extend to the normative content of the decisions in issue. An analysis of that content cannot be avoided on the mere basis that a CFSP decision is only binding on the Member States and is not as such directly applicable.

Does the CFSP practice conform to those limitations?[35] It is not clear that it does. In particular, the practice as regards restrictive measures stands out as a cause for concern. Decisions on restrictive measures (formerly common positions) contain detailed and extensive provisions which, in substance, have a normative content.[36]

The best example is the latest decision concerning Iran.[37] That decision involves restrictions on imports and exports; on technical assistance; on investment; on financial services; on the transfer of funds; on the entry into and transit through the Member States of listed persons; and on the freezing of funds. It is true that such decisions are usually implemented, at least in part, by means of regulations adopted under Article 215 TFEU. That, however, does not mean that the CFSP decisions have no legislative scope, or that such scope is justified. Not all aspects of the relevant CFSP decisions acquire a TFEU counterpart: restrictions on the sale and export of arms, and on the entry and transit of persons, are never incorporated in the Article 215 regulations (or their Articles 301 and 60 EC predecessors). Moreover, even if one were to accept that the principle of the exclusion of legislative acts is somehow remedied by also taking action under the TFEU, the CFSP decisions ought not to be as detailed as they usually are, for then the TFEU regulations constitute a mere transposition of what is effectively CFSP legislative action.

---

[34] Common Position 2001/930 on combating terrorism [2001] OJ L344/90.
[35] Dashwood, above n 11 at 54 and 64, notes that certain pre-Lisbon joint actions had legislative purposes 'presumably as the least inappropriate instrument available'.
[36] cf Gosalbo Bono, above n 6 at 364.
[37] Council Decision concerning restrictive measures against Iran and repealing Common Position 2007/140 [2010] OJ L195/39.

VI. The Office of the High Representative for Foreign Affairs and Security Policy

The Treaty of Lisbon has introduced the office of the High Representative of the Union for Foreign Affairs and Security Policy, a major institutional innovation in the sphere of external action.[38] It has its origin in the Constitution for Europe, and the original name of EU Minister for Foreign Affairs indicates the ambition of the Treaty drafters. It is clear from the work of the Convention on the Future of Europe that this so-called double-hatted office was introduced mainly to ensure coherence and efficiency between the various institutions and actors.[39] Indeed, because of the constitutional and institutional gap between the CFSP and other areas of EU external action, the EU had developed parallel administrations, in the Council and the Commission, dealing with external policies. As is clear from the above analysis, the Treaty of Lisbon in no sense removes the special character of the CFSP and its awkward relationship with other EU external policies. Instead, it attempts to create an institutional bridge, through the office of the High Representative and indeed the creation of the EEAS. It remains to be seen whether that institutional bridge will be effective in reducing inter-institutional tension and conflict, or whether the creation of a new office and a new institution, the EEAS, will increase the scope for in-fighting.

The new office of the High Representative has its own pedigree. For some time already, there had been a growing desire to put a face to the CFSP through the appointment of a distinguished politician responsible for moving the CFSP forward and for representing the EU in CFSP matters. The Treaty of Amsterdam thus created the position of the High Representative for the CFSP, occupied by Mr Solana, who was at the same time Secretary-General of the Council. The creation of that position was already an important development.[40] Whereas the (old) TEU described his or her role as that of assisting the rotating Presidency of the Council, the practice in the context of implementing joint actions went further. They did not, as a rule, provide for an important role for the Presidency, but instead conferred powers on the High Representative and on the EU's Political and Security Committee (PSC). In the EU's military operations, the role of the PSC was preponderant. In other matters there was a more important role for the High Representative.

---

[38] See also Piris, above n 2 at 243–9; J Wouters, D Coppens and B De Meester, 'The European Union's External Relations after the Lisbon Treaty' in S Griller and J Ziller (eds), *The Lisbon Treaty— EU Constitutionalism without a Constitutional Treaty?* (Springer-Verlag, 2008) 150–6; C Kaddous, 'Role and Position of the High Representative of the Union for Foreign Affairs and Security Policy under the Lisbon Treaty' in ibid 206; Curtin, above n 11 at 100–3.

[39] European Convention, Final Report of Working Group VII on External Action, CONV 459/ 02, at 4–5.

[40] E Decaux, 'Le processus de décision de la PESC: vers une politique étrangère européenne?' in E Cannizzaro (ed), *The European Union as an Actor in International Relations* (Kluwer, 2002) 20.

The new office of the High Representative builds on that practice. However, the powers of the High Representative are much more extensive than those of her pre-Lisbon predecessor. An analysis of the provisions of the TEU referring to the High Representative show that there are, broadly speaking, five types of powers (understood in a broad sense as encompassing responsibilities and duties).

The first is a power to make proposals. Article 18(2) TEU, which speaks about the office in general terms, provides that the High Representative shall contribute, by her proposals, to the development of the CFSP. Further provisions refer to more specific rights of proposal. Article 22(2) TEU, concerning European Council decisions on the Union's strategic interests and objectives, provides that the High Representative and the Commission may submit joint proposals. Article 27(1) instructs the High Representative to contribute, through her proposals, towards the preparation of the CFSP. Along the same lines, Article 30(1) provides that the High Representative may refer any question relating to the CFSP to the Council. More specific rights of proposal concern the appointment of a special representative with a mandate in relation to particular policy issues (Article 33 TEU), and the setting up of a start-up fund for the urgent financing of CFSP initiatives (Article 43(3) TEU).

The second power is that of chairing the Foreign Affairs Council (Article 27(1)). Part of that power is the right to convene extraordinary Council meetings, in an emergency (Article 30(2)). There is no further indication of the role of the chair, but it is clear in any event that it is an important one, if only because the chair sets the agenda.

The third power is one of implementation and supervision. Article 18(2) TEU already indicates that the High Representative 'shall conduct the Union's [CFSP]'. Article 24(1) similarly provides that the CFSP 'shall be put into effect' by the High Representative (and by the Member States), a phrase which is repeated in Article 26 (3) TEU. Similarly, Article 27(1) provides that the High Representative shall ensure the implementation of the decisions adopted by the European Council and the Council.

A further indication of what implementation of the CFSP involves is given by Article 24 TEU. That provision determines that the CFSP must be conducted within the framework of the (general) principles and objectives of external action, and that the policy must be based on the development of mutual political solidarity among Member States, the identification of questions of general interest, and the achievement of an ever-increasing degree of convergence (Article 24(2)). The Member States must support the Union's policy actively and unreservedly in a spirit of loyalty and mutual solidarity and must comply with Union action; they must also work together to enhance and develop their mutual political solidarity and refrain from any action contrary to the Union's interests or likely to impair its effectiveness as a cohesive force in international relations (Article 24(3)). The provision ends by stating that the Council and the High Representative 'shall ensure compliance with these principles' (also Article 24(3); see also Article 26(3) TEU).

There is therefore also a supervisory and enforcement role for the High Representative, to some degree similar to the role which the Commission has, in other areas of EU policy, 'to ensure the application of the Treaties' (Article 17(1) TEU).

However, in contrast with the Commission, the High Representative has no legal means to ensure Member State compliance with the CFSP, such as the opportunity to bring an action before the Court of Justice. It remains to be seen whether the limited political instruments in the hands of the High Representative will be sufficient for this purpose.

The High Representative further supervises the special representatives which may be appointed (Article 33 TEU). In the context of the CSDP tasks referred to in Article 43(1) TEU (joint disarmament operations, humanitarian and rescue tasks, military advice and assistance tasks, etc) the High Representative shall ensure coordination of the civilian and military aspects of such tasks.

Lastly, under the heading of implementation and supervision one may also refer to the High Representative's duty regularly to consult the European Parliament on the main aspects and the basic choices of the CFSP and to inform it.

A fourth power—or duty in fact—concerns the 'Holy Grail' of ensuring consistency in the EU's external action. Article 18(4) indicates that the fact that the High Representative is also one of the Commission's Vice Presidents, responsible for Commission responsibilities in external relations, is aimed at ensuring such consistency. Article 21(3) TEU again emphasizes the need for consistency between the different areas of external action and between these and other EU policies, and instructs the Council and the Commission, assisted by the High Representative, to ensure that consistency and to cooperate to that effect.

A fifth power concerns the external representation of the EU as regards the CFSP, and coordination of external action by the Member States. Article 27(2) provides that the High Representative shall represent the Union for CFSP matters, and that she shall conduct political dialogue with third parties on the Union's behalf and shall express the Union's position in international organizations and at international conferences. Furthermore, Article 34(1) instructs the High Representative to organize the coordination of Member States' action in international organizations and at international conferences. Article 34(3) envisages that the High Representative will be invited to present the Union's position before the UN Security Council, when that position concerns a subject which is on the Security Council's agenda.

As can be seen, this is a tremendous range of powers and responsibilities. There can be serious doubts as to whether one person could ever accomplish all of those tasks. The High Representative is of course assisted, in particular by the EEAS. Delegation of some of the High Representative's functions will no doubt take place. Nevertheless, the combination of participation in the Commission's work, the chairing of the Foreign Affairs Council, and the external representation of the EU would seem to be a very tall order indeed.

VII. The European External Action Service

Article 27(3) TEU provides that the High Representative shall be assisted by a European External Action Service, which shall work in cooperation with the diplomatic services of the Member States and comprise officials from relevant departments of the General Secretariat of the Council, and of the Commission, as well as staff seconded from national diplomatic services of the Member States.[41] The Article further provides that the organization and functioning of the EEAS shall be established by a decision of the Council, acting on a proposal of the High Representative after consulting the European Parliament and after obtaining the consent of the Commission. As with the office of the High Representative, the idea is clearly to bridge the gap between the Commission and Council departments responsible for external action. However, the inclusion of diplomatic staff from the Member States also shows that this new EU diplomatic service is intended to build on and work in close cooperation with national administrations.

The EEAS was set up in July 2010 by Council decision,[42] after an intense negotiation between the various institutions. It is beyond the scope of this overview to provide a full analysis of its genesis. It will no doubt take some time to see what the effects of the creation of this EU 'Foreign Office', 'State Department', or 'Ministry for Foreign Affairs' will be on EU external action and what kind of role it may come to play.

The EEAS is set up as 'a functionally autonomous body of the European Union, separate from the General Secretariat of the Council and from the Commission with the legal capacity necessary to perform its tasks and attain its objectives' (Article 1(2) of the decision). It is placed under the authority of the High Representative (Article 1(3)) and is made up of a central administration and of the Union delegations to third countries and to international organizations (Article 1(4)). The inclusion of Union delegations is not as such provided for in the Treaties: Article 221 TFEU simply provides that Union delegations in third countries and at international organizations shall represent the Union, and that they shall be placed under the authority of the High Representative. However, it clearly makes institutional sense to integrate the Union delegations with the Brussels 'Foreign Office'.

As regards staff, the EEAS comprises officials and other servants of the EU, including personnel from the diplomatic services of the Member States appointed as temporary agents (Article 6(2)). As regards the Council, the departments and staff transferred are those covering the CFSP and the CSDP. As regards the Commission, the transfer includes nearly the entire Directorate-General (DG) for External Relations and parts of the DG for Development. This reflects to some extent the Commission portfolio of the current High Representative, which is limited to external relations. The Commission continues to have its own DGs for Development; Enlargement; Humanitarian Aid and Civil Protection; and Trade.

---

[41] See also Wouters, Coppens and De Meester, above n 38 at 156–60; S Vanhoonacker and N Reslow, 'The European External Action Service: Living Forwards by Understanding Backwards' (2010) 15 *European Foreign Affairs Review* 1.

[42] Council Decision 2010/427 Establishing the Organization and Functioning of the European External Action Service [2010] OJ L201/30.

The task of the EEAS is, first of all, to support the High Representative (a) in fulfilling her CFSP and CSDP mandate; (b) in her capacity as President of the Foreign Affairs Council; and (c) in her capacity as Vice President within the Commission (Article 2(1) of the EEAS decision). However, the EEAS shall also assist the President of the European Council, the President of the European Commission, and the Commission in the exercise of their respective functions in the area of external relations (Article 2(2)). When fulfilling those tasks, the EEAS must also cooperate with a range of institutions and actors. It must support, and work in cooperation with, the diplomatic services of the Member States, as well as the General Secretariat of the Council and the services of the Commission, in order to ensure consistency between the different areas of the Union's external action and between those areas and its policies (Article 3(1)). The EEAS and the Commission services must consult each other on all matters relating to EU external action, except on matters covered by the CSDP. The EEAS must also extend appropriate support and cooperation to the other institutions and bodies of the Union, in particular to the European Parliament (Article 3(4)). The preamble to the EEAS decision emphasizes that the Parliament will fully play its role in the external action of the Union, including its functions of political control as provided for in Article 14(1) TEU, as well as in legislative and budgetary matters.

The EEAS decision also contains specific provisions on EU delegations. Such delegations shall comprise EEAS staff and, where appropriate for the implementation of the Union budget (which is a Commission responsibility) and Union policies other than those under the remit of the EEAS, Commission staff (Article 5(2)). The delegations therefore serve both the EEAS and the High Representative, on the one hand, and the Commission, on the other. This is exemplified by the provision which enables not only the High Representative and the EEAS to give instructions to heads of delegations, but also the Commission, 'in areas where the Commission exercises the powers conferred upon it by the Treaties' (Article 5(3)). Moreover, the Union delegations 'shall have the capacity to respond to the needs of other institutions of the Union, in particular the European Parliament, in their contacts with the international organizations or third countries to which the delegations are accredited'.

VIII. Conclusions

The sphere of action of the CFSP is defined in the broadest terms, as encompassing all areas of foreign and security policy. Whereas before Lisbon the CFSP was governed by its own set of objectives, that is no longer the case, and this has made the task of defining the scope of this policy even more difficult than before. A lot of different activities are undertaken within the framework of this policy, but increasingly, it appears that its specificity is concentrated in security and defence matters, where the TEU clarifies the kind of activities which the EU is destined to undertake. Another important strand of the CFSP is the policy on sanctions ('restrictive measures').

If the CFSP were to exist in isolation, its broad definition, indeed its lack of real definition, would not necessarily raise many issues. However, the CFSP is constitutionally juxtaposed to other EU external policies, by virtue of Article 40 TEU. The Court polices the boundaries between the CFSP and competences and policies under the TFEU. Its judgment in *SALW* continues to be relevant, even if Article 40 TEU looks both ways, in contrast to (old) Article 47 TEU. Thus, the CFSP may not trespass on TFEU external action territory. As the latter continues to expand, the CFSP may indeed shrink to security and defence policy. Its vocation to cover all areas of foreign and security policy is thus much qualified: there should be a footnote to Article 24(1) TEU stating that this provision applies only insofar as there is no other EU external competence.

The way in which the Court policed the borders between the EC Treaty and the TEU also confirmed that there is a unified concept of EU law, and the Treaty of Lisbon has sealed that development. The TEU and the TFEU are organically linked, and competences therefore have to be allocated. A development cooperation measure, for example, cannot be taken under the CFSP. The institutional provisions of the Lisbon Treaty wholly confirm this unified concept, by creating the position of the High Representative and the EEAS. It is to be hoped that this will lead to the better coordination and greater effectiveness of external policies. There will, however, still be scope for institutional turf battles. The High Representative may unify the external action administration, but decision-making procedures remain different (for example, unanimity in CFSP matters) as does the role of the various institutions.

The analysis of the instruments of the CFSP shows that this policy continues to be in a somewhat precarious state, from a legal and institutional perspective. The various legal instruments are ill-defined and the practice does not bring much clarity. The precise legal effects are uncertain, be it in relation to the Member States, to the EU institutions, or to individuals. The institutional lacuna of lack of Court jurisdiction has prevented authoritative clarification.

However, it is at the level of parliamentary involvement and judicial scrutiny that much remains to be done. The Court of Justice does not have general jurisdiction in CFSP matters,[43] and the European Parliament is merely consulted as regards CFSP decision-making. Here, unfortunately, the Treaty of Lisbon made only limited progress. The current state of affairs, it is submitted, is unacceptable in a polity governed by the rule of law. CFSP policies show signs of significant expansion, in particular in their natural terrain of security and defence policies. There is now a string of decisions on actions involving military operations. All these policies are excessively dominated by the executive. The focus of debate should not continue to be the well-worn battle between supranationalism and intergovernmentalism, but should turn to issues of accountability. The latter is clearly no luxury in times when the EU is involved in military operations and the war against terrorism. The exclusion of legislative acts, introduced by the Lisbon

---

[43] See chapter 9 by Francis Jacobs for an analysis of the limitations to the Court's jurisdiction in CFSP matters.

amendments, is to be taken seriously as meaning that the CFSP cannot be used for the purpose of general normative action. In the area of restrictive measures (sanctions), in particular, it is questionable whether the institutions comply with that instruction. Overall, the CFSP should be further scrutinized from a perspective of constitutionalism.

14

The Reform of the Common Commercial Policy

Markus Krajewski

I. Introduction

The Treaty of Lisbon introduced a number of significant institutional and substantial changes in the law governing the external relations of the European Union.[1] Many of these were already foreseen in the Treaty establishing a Constitution for Europe.[2] In particular, the Lisbon Treaty preserved the provisions of the Constitution Treaty regarding the common commercial policy, which is why the respective analyses of these provisions remain by and large valid.[3]

The Lisbon Treaty's changes of the law of the common commercial policy deserve special attention for at least two reasons: first, external trade policy is still the most important field of EU external relations in practical terms.[4] The EU is one of the key players of the multilateral trading system and increasingly pursues bilateral and regional trade agreements with strategic partners throughout the world.[5] Second, the debates about the scope, nature and instruments of the common commercial policy as well as the changes introduced through the treaty reforms of Amsterdam and Nice suggest that this policy field is characterized by a set of fundamental constitutional disputes.[6] They concern the distribution of competences between the

---

[1] For a general overview see J Wouters, D Coppens and B De Meester, 'External Relations after the Lisbon Treaty' in S Griller and J Ziller (eds), *The Lisbon Treaty—EU Constitutionalism without a Constitutional Treaty?* (Springer, 2008) 143–203.

[2] On these changes see M Cremona, 'The Draft Constitution: External Relations and External Action' (2003) *CMLRev* 40, 1347–66.

[3] R Leal-Arcas, 'The EU Constitutional Treaty and International Trade' in F Laursen (ed), *The Rise and Fall of the EU's Constitutional Treaty* (Brill/Nijhoff, 2008), 25; C Tietje, 'Die Außenwirtschaftsverfassung der EU nach dem Vertrag von Lissabon' in C Tietje and G Kraft (eds), *Beiträge zum Transnationalen Wirtschaftsrecht*, Vol 83 (2009) 9.

[4] A Dimopoulos, 'The Effects of the Lisbon Treaty on the Principles and Objectives of the Common Commercial Policy' (2010) *EFARev* 15, 153.

[5] M Bungenberg, 'Going Global? The EU Common Commercial Policy after Lisbon' (2010) *European Yearbook of International Economic Law* 1, 123, 126. See also European Commission, *Global Europe—Competing in the World, A Contribution to the EU's Growth and Jobs Strategy* (2006).

[6] See the ECJ's leading cases on the matter: Opinion 1/75 *Local Costs* [1975] ECR 1355; Opinion 1/78 *Natural Rubber Agreement* [1979] ECR 2125; Opinion 1/94 *WTO* [1994] ECR I-5267. The

Union and its Member States, the powers and functions of the EU's institutions and the values and policy goals underlying the formation of the common commercial policy.[7] The present contribution will therefore analyse the changes of external trade policy focusing on principles and objectives, competences and institutions. It begins by situating the common commercial policy in the framework of the Treaties and then moves to a discussion of the substantive and procedural reforms of the common commercial policy introduced by the Treaty of Lisbon.

II. Location and Context of the EU's External Trade Law

The provisions on the common commercial policy in the Treaty on the Functioning of the European Union (TFEU) can be found in Articles 206 and 207 TFEU which amend and modify former Articles 131(1) and 133 of the Treaty Establishing the European Community (TEC). Article 131(2) TEC, which contained a reference to the favourable effect of the abolition of customs duties between Member States on the competitive strength of undertakings, has been abolished because the provision had no specific legal meaning and was redundant. Furthermore, the Lisbon Treaty eliminated the former Article 132 TEC on the harmonization of state aid for exports to third countries, because this provision was never used.[8] It should be noted that export aids are in any event a subject matter covered by the scope of Article 133 TEC (now Article 207 TFEU).[9] Finally, Article 134 TEC on requisite measures in case of trade diversion or economic difficulties due to the execution of the common commercial policy was also not included in the reformed provisions on trade policy, because it was deemed incompatible with the internal market and has not been applied since 1993.[10]

Articles 206 and 207 TFEU form Title II of Part V of the Treaty on the Functioning of the European Union, which is entitled 'External Action by the Union'. Unlike the Constitutional Treaty which also included the provisions on the common foreign and security policy (CFSP) in this part of the Treaty,[11] the

---

literature on this subject is abundant, see eg S Meunier and K Nicolaïdis, 'Who Speaks for Europe? The Delegation of Trade Authority in the EU' (1999) *JCMS* 37, 477–501; M Cremona, 'EC External Commercial Policy after Amsterdam: Authority and Interpretation within Interconnected Legal Orders' in JHH Weiler (ed), *The EU, the WTO, and the NAFTA: Towards a Common Law of International Trade?* (Oxford University Press, 2000) 5–34; HG Krenzler and C Pitschas, 'Progress or Stagnation?: The Common Commercial Policy after Nice' (2001) *EFARev* 6, 291–313; C Herrmann, 'Common Commercial Policy after Nice: Sisyphus Would Have Done a Better Job' (2002) 39 *CMLRev* 7–29 and P Koutrakos, '"I Need to Hear You Say It": Revisiting the Scope of the Common Commercial Policy' (2003) *YEL* 22, 409–33.

[7] M Krajewski, 'External Trade Law and the Constitution Treaty: Towards a Federal and More Democratic Common Commercial Policy?' (2005) *CMLRev* 42, 91, 92–3.

[8] European Convention, Draft Articles on external action in the Constitution (April 2003 Draft of the Constitution), 23 April 2003, CONV 685/03, 55.

[9] Opinion 1/75, *Local Costs* [1975] ECR 1355, 1362.

[10] April 2003 Draft of the Constitution, above n 8 at 55.

[11] On the common framework of the EU's external actions in the Constitution Treaty see Cremona, above n 2 at 1352–3.

Lisbon Treaty kept the CFSP in the Treaty on European Union (TEU).[12] The separation of the CFSP from the other external policies resembles the former pillar structure of the European Union which included the CFSP in the second pillar while the common commercial policy—as the 'façade' of the common market[13]—constituted an element of the first pillar, the European Community. Furthermore, both the Constitution and the Lisbon Treaty maintain institutional and legal differences between the CFSP and the traditional external policies of the European Community.

Unlike the CFSP the other external policies, such as development cooperation (Articles 208–211 TFEU), economic, financial and technical cooperation (Articles 212–213 TFEU), humanitarian aid (Article 214 TFEU) and restrictive measures (Article 215 TFEU) are included in the TFEU's Part V. Part V also contains a general provision (Article 205 TFEU) which stipulates that the EU's external policies shall be guided by the principles and objectives laid down in the general provisions on the Union's external action in the Treaty on European Union. Furthermore, the rules applying to the conclusion of international agreements (Articles 216–219 TFEU) and the relations with third countries and international organizations (Articles 220 and 221 TFEU) as well as the solidarity clause (Article 222 TFEU) are also included in Part V of the TFEU. All provisions of this part of the TFEU constitute the context of the common commercial policy.

III. Principles and Objectives

The common commercial policy is subject to two layers of principles and objectives: Article 206 TFEU, which is based on former Article 131(1) TEC contains the specific trade policy objectives and can be considered the inner layer of objectives. The general objectives and principles of Union's external policy as laid down in Article 21 TEU also apply to the common commercial policy by reference of Article 205 TFEU. They form an outer layer of principles and objectives for the common commercial policy. There is, however, no hierarchy between the two layers and all objectives are of equal relevance for the common commercial policy.

A. Specific policy objective: gradual trade liberalization

The specific policy objectives of the common commercial policy according to Article 206 TFEU continue to be the harmonious development of world trade, the progressive abolition of restrictions on international trade and lowering of customs and other barriers. In addition, Article 206 TFEU introduces the abolition of restrictions on foreign direct investment as a further objective which was not part of Article 131(1) TEC. This reflects the extension of the scope of the common commercial policy to foreign direct investment according to Article 207(1) TFEU.[14]

---

[12] Articles 23–41 TEU.
[13] P Eeckhout, *The European Internal Market and International Trade* (Clarendon Press, 1994) 344.
[14] See below IV.B.iv.

The objectives of Article 206 TFEU refer to trade liberalization, but they do not indicate a free trade policy. Instead, the wording indicates that the process of trade liberalization shall be a gradual one.[15] In this respect, the objectives of Article 206 TFEU resemble the objectives of the world trading system.[16]

The Treaty of Lisbon did not change the contents of the specific policy objectives of the common commercial policy much (with the exception of the inclusion of investment liberalization), but it modified their addressees and legal nature. While the TEC referred to the Member States as actors, Article 206 TFEU uses the Union as grammatical subject and underlines the predominant role of the Union as an actor in external trade policy. More importantly, Article 206 TFEU turns the gradual trade liberalization into a binding objective.[17] Article 131(1) TEC only contained an aspiration ('Member States aim to contribute to'). Contrary to this, Article 207(1) TFEU uses the word 'shall', which denotes an obligatory character of the liberalization objective.

The binding nature of this trade policy objective introduced through the Lisbon Treaty has been interpreted as a prohibition of the removal of liberalization commitments such as tariff concessions or market access commitments in services because such a 'step back' would contradict the objective of gradual trade liberalization.[18] This reading of Article 206 TFEU seems too strict. It overlooks that the Union is only obliged to *contribute* to trade liberalization, but not to pursue it under any circumstances. Furthermore, Article 206 TFEU states the objectives of the external trade policy, but not its means. The removal of tariff concessions or of services market access commitments is a particular trade policy instrument, which may also contribute to the gradual liberalization of trade in the long run. For example, the modification and partial removal of GATS concessions of the EU as a result of the Union's enlargement in 2004[19] lead to the harmonization of services concessions within the EU and contributed to an overall lowering of trade restrictions as stipulated in Article V:4 GATS. Whether or not a tariff or market access commitment can be withdrawn or modified is not a question to be answered on the basis of Article 206 TFEU, but by the respective rules of the World Trade Organization (WTO) in particular Article XXVIII GATT and Article XXI GATS. In any case, all trade measures, be they liberalizing or not, must be scrutinized on the basis of the general external policy objectives and principles.

---

[15] Dimopoulos, above n 4 at 155–7.

[16] See the preambles of the Marrakesh Agreement Establishing the World Trade Organization and of the General Agreement on Tariffs and Trade 1947 ('substantial reduction of tariffs and other barriers to trade and to the elimination of discriminatory treatment in international commerce').

[17] Dimopoulos, above n 4 at 160.

[18] Ibid 161.

[19] See Council for Trade in Services, Communication from the European Communities and its Member States, Certification, Draft Consolidated GATS Schedule, 9 October 2006, S/C/W/273. On the distribution of competences to implement these modifications see ECJ, Opinion 1/08 *Modification of GATS Schedules* [2009] ECR I-11129.

B. General external policy objectives and principles

The Treaty of Lisbon significantly increased the objectives and principles of the common commercial policy by submitting it to the general external policy objectives and principles. Article 205 TFEU stipulates that all external policies 'shall be guided by the principles, pursue the objectives and be conducted in accordance with the general provisions laid down in Chapter 1 of Title V of the Treaty on European Union'. In addition, Article 207(1) TFEU states specifically that the common commercial policy shall be conducted 'in the context of the principles and objectives of the Union's external actions'.[20] While the wording of Article 207(1) TFEU only requires the pursuit of the common commercial policy in the context of the general principles and objectives, Article 205 TFEU clarifies the obligatory nature[21] of the framework established by the general objectives and principles: the common commercial policy has to be conducted in accordance with those objectives and principles.

These principles and objectives can be found in Article 21 TEU. They include, 'democracy, the rule of law, the universality and indivisibility of human rights and fundamental freedoms, respect for human dignity, equality and solidarity, and respect for the United Nations Charter and international law'. Furthermore, according to Article 21(2) TEU the Union shall define and pursue common policies, inter alia, in order to:

foster the sustainable economic, social and environmental development of developing countries, with the primary aim of eradicating poverty, encourage the integration of all countries into the world economy, including through the progressive abolition of restrictions on international trade and help develop international measures to preserve and improve the quality of the environment and the sustainable management of global natural resources, in order to ensure sustainable development.

These goals reflect and reinforce the general objectives of the Union's relations with the 'wider world' according to Article 3(5) TEU.[22]

It should be noted that both Articles 3(5) and 21 TEU contain references to classical trade policy objectives: Article 3(5) TFEU refers to 'free and fair' trade and Article 21 TFEU calls for an encouragement of the integration of all countries into the world economy which shall be achieved, inter alia, 'through the progressive abolition of restrictions on international trade'. It is therefore clear that the general obligations and principles of the external policy do not abandon or supersede

---

[20] Cremona, above n 2 at 1363 also highlights the significance of this addition to the provisions on the common commercial policy.

[21] Dimopoulos, above n 4 at 165 ('mandatory nature').

[22] This provision states, 'In its relations with the wider world, the Union shall uphold and promote its values and interests and contribute to the protection of its citizens. It shall contribute to peace, security, the sustainable development of the Earth, solidarity and mutual respect among peoples, free and fair trade, eradication of poverty and the protection of human rights, in particular the rights of the child, as well as to the strict observance and the development of international law, including respect for the principles of the United Nations Charter.'

gradual trade liberalization as an objective. However, it is equally clear that the common commercial policy should not only aim at gradual liberalization of trade, but also non-economic policy objectives, such as human rights, equality and solidarity, sustainable development and the preservation and improvement of the quality of the environment.[23] Articles 205 and 207(1) TFEU explicitly require the common commercial policy to contribute to these objectives rather than simply to focus on the reduction of barriers to trade. By placing the common commercial policy into the larger framework of such policy goals, the Lisbon Treaty deviates substantially from previous reforms of trade policy through the Amsterdam and Nice Treaties.[24]

Submitting the common commercial policy to the general external policy objectives and principles may have practical implications: As the pursuance of the goals mentioned in Article 21 TEU through the common commercial policy is a binding obligation, the Union's organs will have to consider them in the formulation and implementation of the EU's external trade policy. Consequently, the Council and Commission need to explain and justify a particular trade policy measure with reference to the objectives and goals mentioned in Article 21 TEU. This could be supported by the requirement of environmental, social and development impact assessments of all trade agreements and unilateral measures. It could also be argued that trade relationships with countries which openly reject the principles mentioned in paragraph 1 of Article 21 TEU (democracy, the rule of law, the universality and indivisibility of human rights and fundamental freedoms, principles of the United Nations Charter and international law) would require specific justifications and an explanation why these relations would not further harm the pursuance of those principles on a global level.

Binding the common commercial policy to the general goals and objectives of the Union's external policies has been criticized in the literature because it would lead to a 'politicisation' of trade policy.[25] These fears are unfounded and based on a misconception of trade policy. Trade liberalization has never been an end on its own. Neither the European Treaties nor the treaties of the multilateral trading system indicate such an understanding of trade liberalization. Already the GATT 1947 stipulated that trade liberalization should contribute to such goals as raising standards of living and ensuring full employment. The WTO agreement preamble broadened these objectives to include sustainable development, protecting and preserving the environment and the concerns of developing countries. Furthermore, trade policy measures have been used and continue to be used to support political developments, both positive and negative. In this respect, trade policy has always been political. The novelty of the Treaty of Lisbon is that it recognizes that trade policy may pursue non-economic objectives and that it stipulates which non-economic objectives the EU should pursue through its trade policy. This also indicates which objectives may not guide trade policy. For example, using trade sanctions as a reaction to the election of a particular

---

[23] Dimopoulos, above n 4 at 169.
[24] Ibid 162.
[25] Bungenberg, above n 5 at 128.

government could not be justified on the basis of the Treaty of Lisbon, because it would contradict the democratic principles mentioned in Article 21(1) TEU as long as the election was free and fair.

This raises the question how potential conflicts between trade liberalization and the other objectives mentioned in Article 21 TEU could be addressed. At the outset, it should be remembered that all objectives are of equal value and should therefore be pursued on a mutually reinforcing basis. In fact, Article 21 TEU seems to be based on the assumption that there is only little potential for conflict between those objectives in the first place. The goals of Article 21 TEU are also sufficiently general to suggest a wide scope of political discretion for the institutions of the EU to assess whether there is (a potential) conflict between those objectives and how to avoid it. If the political organs of the Union deem trade liberalization as a valuable instrument to foster human rights, the Treaties would not seem to hinder such an approach. However, in the case of an unavoidable conflict the different objectives would have to be balanced based on the principle of proportionality. For example, if the liberalization of basic public services would clearly lead to unacceptable social exclusion from the supply of these services in a particular country, the protection of the right to water and health may trump the objectives of trade liberalization. If such a clear causal relationship could be shown it would be the task of the European Court of Justice to assess whether a particular trade policy violates the principles of Article 21 TEU.

IV. Competences

The nature and scope of the Community's (now Union's) competence with regard to the common commercial policy has been a 'constitutional construction site' of growing complexity since the early days of the European Economic Community.[26] The Treaty of Lisbon clarifies some of the pertinent and disputed issues, but also raises new questions.

A. Exclusive nature

Article 3(1)(e) TFEU explicitly holds that the Union shall have exclusive competence in the area of the common commercial policy. This codifies the ECJ's case law[27] which has consistently held that the Member States do not have the power to enter into international agreements or legislate on matters of the common commercial policy.[28] According to Article 2(1) TFEU, exclusive competence means that only the

---

[26] P Eeckhout, *External Relations of the European Union—Legal and Constitutional Foundations* (Oxford University Press, 2004) chapter 2.

[27] F van den Berghe, 'The EC's Common Commercial Policy Revisited: What Does Lisbon Add?' (2009) *Global Trade and Customs Journal* 4, 275, 279; D Leczykiewicz, 'Common Commercial Policy: The Expanding Competence of the European Union in the Area of International Trade' (2005) *German Law Journal* 6, 1673, 1674.

[28] Opinion 1/75 *Local Costs* [1975] ECR 1355, 1363–4.

Union may legislate and adopt legally binding acts. Member States can only do so if they have been empowered by the Union or when they implement Union Acts. According to Article 3(2) TFEU the exclusive competence also includes the conclusion of an international agreement 'when its conclusion is provided for in a legislative act of the Union or is necessary to enable the Union to exercise its internal competence, or insofar as its conclusion may affect common rules or alter their scope'. Similarly, Article 216(1) TFEU holds that the Union may conclude international agreements 'where the conclusion of an agreement is necessary in order to achieve, within the framework of the Union's policies, one of the objectives referred to in the Treaties, or is provided for in a legally binding Union act or is likely to affect common rules or alter their scope'. Both provisions are based on the ECJ's doctrine on implied external powers.[29] According to this doctrine, the Union not only enjoys external powers if and insofar as the Treaties explicitly confer such powers, but also implicit powers, which follow from internal competences.[30] The three alternatives of Articles 3 (2) and 216(1) TFEU are based on different aspects of the implied powers doctrine.[31] The first alternative, that is the conclusion of an agreement which is provided for in a legislative Act of the Union, seems to be taken from Opinion 1/94,[32] the second alternative, that is the conclusion is necessary to enable the Union to exercise its internal competence, can be traced to Opinion 1/76[33] and the third alternative, that is the conclusion of an agreement may affect common rules or alter their scope, is taken from the *AETR* judgment.[34]

B. Scope

The first sentence of Article 207(1) TFEU holds that the scope of the common commercial policy includes trade agreements relating to trade in goods and services and the commercial aspects of intellectual property as well as foreign direct investment.

(i) Policy instruments

The common commercial policy traditionally comprises an autonomous and an international policy dimension. The former employs internal EU legislation regulating trade while the latter covers the negotiation and conclusion of international agreements. Article 207 TFEU clarifies that the Union's exclusive competence in the field of the common commercial policy according to the Lisbon Treaty would

---

[29] J-M Grave, 'The Impact of the Lisbon Treaty on Customs Matters: A Legal Analysis' (2010) *Global Trade and Customs Journal* 5, 95, 98. See also M Cremona, *A Constitutional Basis for Effective External Action? An Assessment of the Provisions on EU External Action in the Constitutional Treaty* EUI Working Papers LAW No 2006/30, 9.

[30] For a comprehensive overview see Eeckhout, above n 26 at chapter 3.

[31] Wouters, Coppens and De Meester, above n 1 at 174–80.

[32] Opinion 1/94, WTO [1994] ECR I-5416, para 94.

[33] Opinion 1/76 *Laying-up Fund for Inland Waterway Vessels* [1977] ECR 741, 756, para 5.

[34] Case 22/70 *Commission/Council (AETR)* [1971] ECR 263, 275, para 22.

include the negotiation and conclusion of agreements (external competence) as well as the implementation of these agreements (internal competence). Article 207(3) TFEU mentions the negotiation and conclusion of international agreements and Article 207(2) TFEU refers to the implementation of the common commercial policy. This not only covers measures of the autonomous trade policy, but also the implementation of trade agreements.

(ii) Trade in services

The scope of the common commercial policy concerning trade in services has been subject to a 15-year-long 'saga' of treaty changes and disputes between the Member States and the EU's institutions.[35] The controversy was finally resolved by the Lisbon Treaty.

According to Article 207 TFEU the common commercial policy covers all aspects of trade in services. The Union is therefore exclusively competent to agree and implement trade agreements with provisions on services. The Lisbon Treaty abandons the 'shared competence' concerning agreements relating to trade in cultural and audiovisual services, educational services, and social and human health services which was contained in Article 133(6) subparagraph 2 TEC.[36] The only remains of this sectoral carve-out is the third subparagraph of Article 207(4) TFEU, which requires unanimity in the Council for the conclusion of trade agreements concerning these services in particular circumstances.[37] This increase in the Union's competence of the common commercial policy strengthens the negotiating power of the Commission in international trade negotiations. However, it should be noted that the sectoral carve-out of Article 133(6) subparagraph 2 TEC concerned a set of politically and socially sensitive services, including services of general interest. The abolishment of the shared competence in this area substantially limits the Member States' influence on trade policy affecting these services and may have significant implications for Member States' policies in these areas.[38] It also affects the democratic legitimacy of the common commercial policy, because national parliaments are no longer responsible for the ratification of trade agreements which would (also) cover these services.

(iii) Commercial aspects of intellectual property

The scope of the common commercial policy concerning intellectual property rights remains restricted to the 'commercial aspects' of these rights. Article 207

---

[35] M Krajewski, 'Of Modes and Sectors—External Relations, Internal Debates and the Special Case of (Trade in) Services' in M Cremona (ed), *New Developments in EU External Relations Law* (Oxford University Press, 2008) 172, 188–95.

[36] Opinion 1/08 *Modification of GATS Schedules* [2009] ECR I-0000, para 125 et seq.

[37] See below V, A.

[38] On these implications see M Krajewski, 'Protecting a Shared Value of the Union in a Globalized World: Services of General Economic Interest and External Trade' in J W van de Gronden (ed), *The EU and WTO Law on Services* (Kluwer Law International, 2008) 173, 206–13.

TFEU keeps the term 'commercial aspects of intellectual property', which has no direct equivalent in international trade law: the relevant WTO's agreement refers to trade-related aspects of these rights.[39] While there is a general agreement that the linguistic difference between commercial aspects and trade-related aspects is not of great significance and that the term commercial aspects of intellectual property rights refers to the WTO's TRIPS agreement, the nature of this reference has been disputed. Some commentators have argued that the reference is a dynamic one which would also include changes in the TRIPS agreement.[40] Others have held that the reference is static, linking the common commercial policy to the TRIPS at the time of its conclusion while any changes would require the exercise of a special competence in Article 133(7) TEC.[41] According to this provision, the Council was empowered to extend the application of the common commercial policy to international agreements on intellectual property insofar as they were not covered by the common commercial policy yet. The Lisbon Treaty abandoned this possibility. This has two implications: first, the Council can no longer enlarge the scope of the common commercial policy to non-commercial aspects of intellectual property. Second, if one assumes that the reference to commercial aspects of intellectual property is a static one, the abolishment of Article 133(7) TEC would deprive the Union of the possibility to negotiate and conclude changes in the TRIPS agreement. This would lead to a reduction of the scope of the common commercial policy which was not intended by the drafters of Lisbon (and Constitution) Treaty.[42] It is therefore more appropriate to assume that Article 207 TFEU contains a dynamic reference to the TRIPS agreement. In conclusion, the Treaty of Lisbon extends the exclusive competence of the European Union to all three 'pillars' of the WTO (trade in goods, trade in services and trade-related aspects of intellectual property rights).[43]

(iv) Foreign direct investment

While the increase and clarification of the scope of the common commercial policy regarding trade issues has not been subject to much political or academic controversy, the extension of the common commercial policy to foreign direct investment attracted considerable scholarly interest[44] and has already triggered legislative and

---

[39] M Cremona, 'A Policy of Bits and Pieces—The Common Commercial Policy after Nice' (2001) *Cambridge Yearbook of European Legal Studies* 4, 61, 71.

[40] Krenzler and Pitschas, above n 6 at 302.

[41] Cremona, above n 39 at 72; Herrmann, above n 6 at 18–19.

[42] Krajewski, above n 7 at 111.

[43] Eeckhout, above n 26 at 55; Leal-Arcas, above n 3 at 29; Bungenberg, above n 5 at 132.

[44] A Dimopoulos, 'Regulation of Foreign Investment in EU External Relations Law', PhD dissertation, European University Institute, 2010; C Herrmann, 'Die Zukunft der mitgliedstaatlichen Investitionspolitik nach dem Vertrag von Lissabon' (2010) *Europäische Zeitschrift für Wirtschaftsrecht*, 207–12; T Eilmansberger, 'Bilateral Investment Treaties and EU Law' (2009) *CMLRev* 46, 383–429; J Ceyssens, 'Towards a Common Foreign Investment Policy?—Foreign Investment in the European Constitution' (2005) *Legal Issues of Economic Integration* 32, 259–91; J Karl, 'The Competence for Foreign Direct Investment—New Powers for the EU' (2004) *Journal of World Investment and Trade* 5, 413–48. See also the contribution by Federico Ortino and Piet Eeckhout, chapter 15 of this volume.

policy proposals from the Commission.[45] Foreign direct investment usually refers to long-term investment in a foreign country and can be distinguished from short-term portfolio investment.[46] Portfolio investments are therefore not covered by Article 207 TFEU.[47] It has been argued that the Union would have an implied external competence relating to portfolio investments based on the provisions of the free movement of capital (Articles 63–66 TFEU).[48] This argument ignores the express intention of the drafters of the Lisbon Treaty to limit the EU's competence to foreign direct investment. Furthermore, the argument cannot explain why the inclusion of foreign direct investment in Article 207 TFEU was necessary in the first place, because an implied external competence based on the free movement of capital would also cover foreign direct investment.

As a consequence of the limitation of the Union's competence to foreign direct investment, agreements covering foreign direct investment and portfolio invest-ment like most investment protection treaties do not fall within the exclusive external competence of the Union.[49] This leads to a split of the competence to negotiate and conclude investment agreements. The Union is exclusively compe-tent concerning those aspects of the agreement which relate to foreign direct investment, the Member States remain competent concerning portfolio invest-ments. The practical consequence is that all investment agreements which cover both aspects of investment need to be concluded as mixed agreements.[50]

Another even more controversial issue concerns the substantive scope of the competence regarding foreign direct investment.[51] At the outset it should be under-lined that the wording of Article 207 TFEU does not refer to investment protection and therefore leaves the question about the contents of the Union's competence regarding foreign direct investment open. The majority view in the literature holds that Article 207 TFEU covers not only issues of investment liberalization but also of investment protection. Some authors argue that this coverage should extend to all typical forms of investment protection including measures regarding expropriation.[52] This is also the view of the European Commission.[53] Others want to restrict the Union's investment competence to so-called performance standards, that is, non-discrimination, fair and equitable treatment and full protection and security,[54]

---

[45] European Commission, 'Towards a Comprehensive European Investment Policy' 7 July 2010, COM(2010) 343 final; Proposal for a Regulation Establishing Transitional Arrangements for Bilateral Investment Treaties between EU Member States and Third Countries, 7 July 2010, COM(2010) 344 final.

[46] OECD, 'International Investment Law: Understanding Concepts and Tracking Innovations' (2008) 47; European Commission, 'Towards a Comprehensive Investment Policy' above n 45 at 3.

[47] Ceyssens, above n 44 at 275.

[48] European Commission, 'Towards a Comprehensive Investment Policy', above n 45 at 8.

[49] EC Schlemmer, 'Investment, Investor, Nationality, and Shareholders' in P Muchlinski, F Ortino and C Schreuer (eds), *The Oxford Handbook on International Investment* (Oxford University Press, 2009) 49, 55–8.

[50] Bungenberg, above n 5 at 135; Tietje, above n 3 at 16.

[51] On this debate see also Wouters, Coppens and De Meester, above n 1 at 171–3.

[52] Bungenberg, above n 5 at 144; Herrmann, above n 44 at 211.

[53] European Commission, 'Towards a Comprehensive Investment Policy', above n 45 at 5.

[54] On these standards see also R Dolzer and C Schreuer, *Principles of International Investment Law* (Oxford University Press, 2008) 119–94.

because the principle of neutrality vis-à-vis the Member States' systems of property ownership (Article 345 TFEU, ex Article 295 TEC) excludes an EU competence regarding expropriation.[55] Both views lead to the consequence that the Member States would lose the exclusive competence to negotiate, conclude and implement investment protection agreements and that the Union would acquire the competence to negotiate new and re-negotiate old investment protection agreements. This would revolutionize the investment protection policy in Europe: until now, EU bilateral agreements did not contain provisions on investment protection. Bilateral investment protection treaties remained within the competence of the Member States. Some Member States, such as Germany and the UK, are currently parties to more than 100 bilateral treaties with different countries.[56] The Member States would lose the competence to determine the scope, contents and partners of these agreements if the common commercial policy is understood to include investment protection.

It is submitted that the extension of the common commercial policy to foreign direct investment could and should be read more narrowly only referring to those aspects of foreign direct investment which concern investment liberalization and those which have a close link to trade.[57] This reading of Article 207 TFEU is supported by context, object and purpose of the provision and by its negotiating history. According to Article 206 TFEU the Union aims to contribute to 'the progressive abolition of *restrictions* on international trade and on foreign direct investment' (emphasis added). The abolition of restrictions on foreign direct investment refers to so-called pre-establishment restrictions on market access, but not to post-establishment standards of investment protection.[58] While it is true that the absence of international standards of investment protection may deter foreign investors, the notion of 'restrictions' relates to restrictive measures and not to an investment-unfriendly environment.[59]

It should also be noted that the term 'foreign direct investment' is not a term of international investment protection law. It is typically not used in bilateral investment treaties. If the drafters of the Lisbon Treaty wanted to confer the competence to conclude typical investment protection agreements to the Union why did they use the limited concept of foreign direct investment which would not give the Union the competence to conclude a single bilateral investment treaty on its own?

The negotiating history of the inclusion of foreign direct investment in the common commercial policy also supports a more narrow reading. As the inclusion was already part of the Draft Constitution Treaty adopted by the European Convention in 2003, the Convention deliberations are a point of reference. During the early phase of the Convention's work, the Working Group on External Action

---

[55] Tietje, above n 3 at 14. On this argument see also Dimopoulos, above n 44 at 127 et seq.

[56] Dimopoulos, above n 44 at 371.

[57] A similar view is proposed by Ceyssens, above n 44 at 279–81, who wants to exclude expropriation and standards of protection on the basis of the limitation of competences now laid down in Article 207(6) TFEU, but maintains that the scope of the common commercial policy is not limited to market access issues, ibid 286. On Article 207(6), see below section C.

[58] Krajewski, above n 7 at 114; Leczykiewicz, above n 27 at 1678.

[59] This is argued by Ceyssens, above n 44 at 177 and Herrmann, above n 44 at 206–7.

did not discuss an extension of the common commercial policy to investment at all and made no proposal in this regard. When the Convention Praesidium proposed the extension of the common commercial policy to foreign investment it argued that this was necessary because 'financial flows supplement trade in goods and represent a significant share of commercial exchanges'.[60] This indicates the assumption of a close link between investment and trade, but made no reference to investment protection. It is therefore not clear whether the Praesidium wanted to include investment protection in the first place or intended a more narrow scope of the notion of investment. The proposal was not discussed in detail. However, some Convention Members rejected it and called for the deletion of foreign direct investment mostly without any differentiated reasoning.[61] The only exception was the representative of the British government and then Minister for Europe Peter Hain, who suggested that the reference to foreign direct investment should be explicitly limited to investment negotiations in the WTO. He explained this with the perceived intention of the Commission to negotiate a multilateral investment agreement in the WTO. In addition, he clearly indicated that the reference to foreign direct investment would not 'remove Member State competence to conduct bilateral investment activity'.[62] There are no other documented references to investment protection or bilateral investment treaties in the Convention deliberations.

Had the Convention intended to include investment protection treaties in the common commercial policy, these issues would have been debated in the Convention. It is hardly imaginable that representatives from 15 Member States governments and parliaments would have abandoned the legal basis for hundreds of Member States' international agreements without discussion.[63]

It should also be remembered that the deliberations of the Convention took place at the same time as the EC and its Member States were engaged in the debates and discussions about investment policies in the WTO.[64] This also supports the view that the proponents of the inclusion of foreign direct investment in the common commercial policy were predominantly concerned with the EC's negotiating mandate in the WTO and were not necessarily thinking about bilateral investment treaties concluded by the EU.

C. Limitations of the exercise of competences

Article 207(6) TFEU contains a limitation of the exercise of the competences of the common commercial policy according to which the exercise of these competences 'shall not affect the delimitation of competences between the Union and the

---

[60] Draft Articles on external action (April Draft), above n 8 at 43.
[61] See the compilation of suggestions at the Convention's website, <http://european-convention.eu.int/Docs/Treaty/pdf/866/global866.pdf> (accessed 20 August 2010).
[62] Proposal by Mr Hain contained in the compilation of amendments, above n 61.
[63] Similar doubts are expressed by Cremona, above n 29 at 31.
[64] HG Krenzler and C Pitschas, 'Die Gemeinsame Handelspolitik nach dem Entwurf des Europäischen Verfassungsvertrags—Ein Schritt in die richtige Richtung' (2005) *Recht der Internationalen Wirtschaft* 51, 801, 805.

Member States, and shall not lead to harmonisation of legislative or regulatory provisions of the Member States in so far as the Treaties exclude such harmonisation'. Article 207(6) TFEU contains two elements which are closely connected: the first part of the provision stating that the delimitation of competences between the Union and the Member States shall not be affected by the exercise of the competences in the field of the common commercial policy reiterates the general principle of limited and specific conferral of competences (Articles 4(1) and 5(1) and (2) TEU). In the context of external policies this excludes a so-called 'inverse AETR effect' by which an implicit internal competence could be derived from an explicit external competence.[65] The second element of Article 207(6) TFEU holds that the exercise of the trade competence may not lead to harmonization where the Treaty expressly prohibits this. This applies in particular to those areas in which the Union is only competent for 'supporting, coordinating and complementary action', such as education and health (Article 6(a) TFEU). As the Lisbon Treaty conferred the Union with the exclusive competence to conclude trade agreements covering services, the Union may conclude agreements covering education and health as well. However, the Union may not implement such an agreement if these agreements would require harmonization measures, because the Union lacks the competence to harmonize in these areas. Consequently, the Union's external competence ('treaty-making') may extend beyond the scope of its internal competence ('treaty-implementing').

Such an incongruence between internal and external competences would not be a deviation from the *AETR* doctrine and its codification in Article 3(2) TFEU because this doctrine only provides for parallel competences if an internal competence exists. It does not affect the possibility that an external competence can exist without a parallel internal competence. In fact, the ECJ mentioned the possibility of an incongruence between external and internal competences in Opinion 1/75 ('Local costs') when it held that it was without prejudice to the treaty-making powers of the EC if the implementation of the agreement were to be the responsibility of the Member States.[66]

An incongruence of external and internal competences is not uncommon in federal systems. Often the federation has an all-inclusive competence to conclude international agreements, but cannot implement them as long as the relevant legislative power rests with the states.[67] As a consequence, the federation has to consult the states before it concludes an agreement which requires implementation by them. A similar requirement of the Union to consult the Member States before the conclusion of an agreement which requires implementation by the Member States could be based on the principle of sincere cooperation between Union and Member States which is expressively laid down in Article 4(3) TEU.[68] This

---

[65] Wouters, Coppens and De Meester, above n 1 at 174; Cremona, above n 29 at 32.
[66] *Local Costs* [1975] ECR 1355, above n 9 at 1364.
[67] See Krajewski, above n 7 at 117–18.
[68] On the principle of cooperation concerning international agreements see also ECJ, Opinion 2/00 [2001] ECR I-9756, para 8 with further references to the case law.

particular consequence of Article 207(6) TFEU can be seen as a step towards further 'federalization' of the Union's external relations. Instead of only 'centralizing' additional external powers at the Union level, the Lisbon Treaty requires policy coordination and cooperation at different government levels. Such policy coordination and cooperation is a typical element of federal systems in which the central level is competent to act externally, but does not have the internal competence to legislate in all matters and therefore depends on the sub-central units of the system (provinces, cantons, *Länder*, etc) to implement international agreements.

V. Institutions

The central reforms of the common commercial policy regarding institutional matters concern the decision-making in the Council (qualified majority voting/unanimity) and the role and powers of the European Parliament. The Lisbon Treaty introduced smaller amendments regarding the former and major changes regarding the latter.

A. Decision-making in the Council

Article 207(4) TFEU holds that the Council should decide by qualified majority voting regarding the negotiation and conclusion of international agreements. This rule already existed before the Lisbon Treaty. Subparagraphs 2 and 3 of Article 207 (4) TFEU contain exceptions from this principle.

Article 207(4) subparagraph 2 TFEU requires unanimity for the negotiation and conclusion of agreements regarding trade in services, commercial aspects of intellectual property and foreign direct investment 'where such agreements include provisions for which unanimity is required for the adoption of internal rules'. This provision applies the principle of parallelism to the decision-making in the Council: the negotiation and conclusion of international agreements shall be governed by the same majority requirements as internal legislation with the same content. This reflects the sensitivity of services and foreign direct investment for national regulatory autonomy and shows that the Member States were reluctant to lose the control over international agreements in this field. However, unanimity in the Council with regard to services and investment agreements is only required if respective internal legislation also needs to be adopted by a unanimous Council. If the Council can adopt legislation by qualified majority, it can also conclude international agreements in the same way.

Subparagraph 3 of Article 207(4) TFEU requires unanimity in the Council for the conclusion of agreements in the field of trade in cultural and audiovisual services, where these risk prejudicing the Union's cultural and linguistic diversity and in the field of trade in social, education and health services, where these risk seriously disturbing the national organization of such services and prejudicing the responsibility of Member States to deliver them. This provision raises a number of questions. At the outset it should be noted that it only covers the conclusion of agreements, and not the negotiation, which distinguishes it from subparagraphs 1 and 2. Hence, the negotiating process will not be influenced by the unanimity rule of subparagraph 3. Another aspect of the scope of subparagraph 3 concerns its sectoral coverage, which could be determined on the basis of the standard classification of services (CPC) used by the WTO.[69]

The interpretation of the term 'cultural and linguistic diversity', which is new in the context of the common commercial policy, poses a greater challenge. The term used to exist only in Article 149(1) TEC. The Lisbon Treaty also uses it in Article 3 (3) TEU which states that the Union 'shall respect its rich cultural and linguistic diversity, and shall ensure that Europe's cultural heritage is safeguarded and enhanced.' However, the term is not defined. Apart from the ambiguity of this term, the operation of Article 207(4) subparagraph 3(a) TFEU also requires an assessment of the risk posed by a trade agreement to the Union's linguistic and cultural diversity. Assessing such a risk raises difficult legal and factual questions.[70] It is not clear how this risk assessment could be implemented in practice.

Subparagraph 3(a), unlike 3(b) does not aim to protect a particular value of the Union, but the organizational and institutional necessities for the provision of services in the three sectors at the national level. It therefore seeks to protect the national autonomy in this context. The provision can therefore be seen as the last pocket of resistance of the Member States against the complete incorporation of services into the common commercial policy.

Both subparagraphs 3(a) and 3(b) require an assessment of the risk posed by an international agreement to the organizational context of the provision of a service. The exception from qualified majority voting in subparagraphs 3(a) and (b) requires a Member State calling for a unanimous vote to specifically invoke one of these subparagraphs and explain why and how the agreement concerned would pose a risk to the Union's cultural and linguistic diversity or to the provision of health, social and education services. If the other Council members do not share this view and the decision is taken by qualified majority voting, only a judgment by the ECJ would provide ultimate clarity.[71]

Arguably, these interpretative uncertainties could render subparagraph 3 non-operational. As a consequence the Council could either decide to conclude all agreements involving audiovisual, cultural, health and education services by unanimous vote in order to avoid risking a violation of the voting requirements or

---

[69] WTO, Services Sectoral Classification List, 10 July 1991, MTN.GNS/W/120, reproduced as part of the Guidelines for the Scheduling of Specific Commitments under the GATS of 23 March 2001, WTO-Document S/L/92. Audiovisual services include motion picture and videotape production and distribution services and television and radio production and transmission services. Cultural services include a variety of services broadly associated with literature, art, music and history, such as museums, archives and theatre services. Education services include primary, secondary, higher and adult education. Health services include hospital services, and possibly also medical services of doctors, nurses, midwives and physiotherapists, which are actually considered professional services. Social services are not further specified in the WTO classification, but could include social work, care and community services.

[70] Leal-Arcas, above n 3 at 31–2; Krenzler and Pitschas, above n 64 at 808.

[71] Krenzler and Pitschas, above n 64 at 808.

Member States could refrain from invoking subparagraph 3 in the first place. The actual practice will most likely depend more on the political context of the issues concerned and less on legal niceties.

In any event, a trade agreement which includes issues requiring unanimity and issues requiring only a qualified majority will be concluded in its entirety by unanimous vote in the Council according to the 'Pastis' principle.[72] This could in particular be the case for agreements concluding future rounds of multilateral trade negotiations, which typically include a large variety of subjects.

B. Role and function of the European Parliament

The Lisbon Treaty significantly enhanced the role and the function of the European Parliament in the field of the common commercial policy. One commentator even argued that the increased importance of the parliament is the most important change of the common commercial policy.[73] The role of the Parliament has been modified regarding the negotiations, conclusion and implementation of international trade agreements and regarding autonomous trade policy measures.

Article 207(2) TFEU clearly stipulates the European Parliament's function as a co-legislator with regard to the implementation of agreements and the adoption of internal autonomous trade policy measures.[74] The provision refers to the ordinary legislative procedure (Article 294 TFEU) which is the former co-decision making procedure (Article 251 TEC) in all but name. Consequently, the European Parliament has the right to make amendments and also has a final veto power with regard to internal measures.

The European Parliament also gained a special right to be informed with regards to negotiations of international agreements. According to Article 207(3) subparagraph 2 TFEU the Commission shall inform the special committee of the Council (the former 'Committee 133', now the Trade Policy Committee) and the European Parliament on the progress of such negotiations. Even though the Commission already informed the Parliament on trade issues prior to the entry into force of the Lisbon Treaty on the basis of an inter-institutional agreement, the additional reference to the Parliament in Article 207(3) TFEU enhances the role of the Parliament because it is legally binding[75] and because it requires the Commission to inform the European Parliament in the same way as the Council's Trade Policy Committee on trade negotiations. Given the fact that the Commission consults with this committee on a weekly basis, the inclusion of the Parliament in Article

---

[72] P Lamy, 'The Convention and Trade Policy: Concrete Steps to Enhance the EU's International Profile' 5 February 2002, available at <http://europa.eu.int/comm/commissioners/lamy/speeches_articles/spla146_en.htm> (accessed 20 July 2004): '. . . under the Pastis principle, a little drop of unanimity can taint the entire glass of QMV [qualified majority voting] water'. See also Leal-Arcas, above n 3 at 30.

[73] S Woolcock, 'The Potential Impact of the Lisbon Treaty on European Union External Trade Policy' *SIEPS European Policy Analysis* 8–2008, 1.

[74] Cremona, above n 29 at 31.

[75] Woolcock, above n 73 at 5.

207(3) TFEU goes beyond the current practice and sends a clear signal to the other EU organs, in particular the European Commission, that the European Parliament is supposed to play an active role in external trade policy.

Regarding the conclusion of trade agreements, Article 207(3) TFEU refers to the general rules on the conclusion of international agreements in Article 218 TFEU.[76] This provision contains two means of parliamentary participation concerning the conclusion of international agreements. In general, the European Parliament needs to be consulted before the Council concludes an agreement (Article 218(6) subparagraph 2(b) TFEU). The only exception to this rule concerns agreements relating exclusively to the common foreign and security policy. However, no exception exists for trade agreements. This distinguishes the TFEU from the TEC, which excluded trade agreements from parliamentary consultation.

The Treaty of Lisbon requires parliamentary consent in five specific categories of cases according to Article 218(6) subparagraph 2(a) TFEU. Among others, parliamentary consent is necessary for 'agreements covering fields to which either the ordinary legislative procedure applies, or the special legislative procedure where consent by the Parliament is required'. Hence, whenever an international agreement covers an area, to which the ordinary legislative procedure applies, its conclusion requires the consent of the European Parliament. As mentioned, Article 207(2) TFEU requires the establishment of the framework for implementing the common commercial policy in accordance with the ordinary legislative procedure. The European Parliament is hence not only a co-legislator for the implementation of international agreements, but also needs to give its consent to the conclusion of the agreement.

It is therefore safe to assume that the European Parliament's consent is required for the conclusion of all international agreements which need to be implemented in accordance with the provision of Article 207(2) TFEU.[77] However, this does not answer the question whether the Parliament's consent is required for agreements which do not need to be implemented because they do not contain any requirements which need to be transformed into domestic law. For example, changes in the WTO's Dispute Settlement Understanding (DSU) would not need to be implemented domestically because the DSU is only applicable at the international level. It could therefore be argued that Article 207(2) TFEU does not apply to changes of the provisions of the DSU. As a consequence, parliamentary consent for the conclusion of an international agreement changing provisions of the DSU would not be necessary. Therefore, if such an agreement would be concluded independently of the results of the other current WTO negotiations, it is possible that the European Parliament's consent would not be necessary. However, since Article 218 TFEU would abandon the exception for trade agreements from the general consultation requirement, the European Parliament would need to be consulted.

---

[76] On this see Wouters, Coppens and De Meester, above n 1 at 181 et seq.
[77] Grave, above n 29 at 108; Wouters, Coppens and De Meester, above n 1 at 185; Cremona, above n 29 at 15.

The new requirement of parliamentary consent to the conclusion of international agreements is an improvement from the perspective of democratic legitimacy and ought to be welcomed. The limitation of this right to agreements which need implementation in internal law is disappointing, but may not be too significant in practice. In any case, the requirement of parliamentary consent will strengthen the European Parliament's influence in the negotiation process of international agreements, which is arguably just as important as the right to accept or reject an agreement.

When assessing the overall level of democratic legitimacy of external trade policy according to the Lisbon Treaty, it must be remembered that all areas of trade policy fall into the exclusive competence of the Union. Hence, Member States' parliaments are no longer required to ratify trade agreements.[78] This in turn reduces their influence on those agreements and the level of legitimacy they confer upon the common commercial policy. In particular because of the reduced influence of national parliaments on the common commercial policy, the Lisbon Treaty does not substantially decrease the deficit of democratic legitimacy of this policy area even if the increased role of the European Parliament would fill the gap in parliamentary scrutiny due to the exclusion of the Member States' parliaments.[79]

VI. Conclusion

The Lisbon Treaty changed the constitutional law of the common commercial policy in a number of important aspects. Overall, it can be concluded that these changes make the Union's external trade policy more federal, but not necessarily more democratic. The Union gained a comprehensive external competence which covers all fields of the current multilateral trading system. The extent of the Union's competences regarding foreign investment remains disputed: against an apparent academic and political consensus that the Union is competent to conclude investment protection agreements, this chapter claimed that contextual, teleological and historic arguments support a more narrow view.

It has also been shown that Article 207 TFEU does not provide the Union with full internal competence to adopt legislation to implement respective agreements. Hence, the Union needs to coordinate with the Member States before such an agreement can be concluded. This is a situation which can be found in many federal systems and is therefore neither unusual nor impractical. The coordination between Union and Member States is facilitated by the fact that a number of issues still require unanimity in the Council. Many of those issues which require unanimity in the Council for the conclusion of an international agreement are also the issues for which the Union does not have internal competence. Therefore, the voting rules require coordination and a common accord of the Member States in matters where the internal competence of the Union is limited.

---

[78] Wouters, Coppens and De Meester, above n 1 at 186.
[79] See also Woolcock, above n 73 at 5, who points out that the parliamentary scrutiny of the Member States' parliaments has not been very effective in practice.

The necessity to implement an international agreement of the Union will nevertheless put political pressure on the Member States to adopt the relevant legislation. The formal competence of the Member States to implement an international agreement may in fact not leave the Member States a large margin of discretion.

The Lisbon Treaty increased the rights of the European Parliament regarding the conclusion of trade agreements. However, this improvement is partly outweighed by the fact that the national parliaments lost the right to ratify trade agreements which minimized their influence on external trade policy. The Lisbon Treaty therefore repaired some democratic defects of the previous constitutional law of the common commercial policy, but also introduced new problems.

15

Towards an EU Policy on Foreign Direct Investment

Federico Ortino and Piet Eeckhout

I. Introduction

From the entry into force of the Treaty of Lisbon, the common commercial policy extends to 'foreign direct investment' (Article 207(1) TFEU), and aims at the progressive abolition of restrictions on such investment (Article 206 TFEU). In the light of the exclusive nature of the EU's commercial policy competence (Article 3 (1) TFEU), this constitutes one of the most important expansions of the EU's competences in the whole of the Lisbon Treaty. Foreign direct investment is the object of the rapidly growing field of international investment law, an important branch of international economic law. The Member States have in the past been the main European actors in this field, with only limited EU involvement. They are parties to a dense network of bilateral investment treaties (BITs). The complete transfer of competences to the EU—complete in the sense that the EU's competences are exclusive, not shared—will therefore entail a massive shift in policy.

The origins of this new provision lie, as is the case for most of the Lisbon Treaty, in the ill-fated Constitution for Europe. The proceedings of the Convention which drafted the Constitution do not shed much light on the purpose or scope of the new powers.[1] It is clear though, that for quite some time, the EU has attempted to include investment-related issues in its external economic policies. The original plans for the Uruguay Round had a strong focus on investment, but the Round only produced the Agreement on Trade-Related Investment Measures

---

[1] See generally J Ceyssens, 'Towards a Common Foreign Investment Policy? Foreign Investment in the European Constitution' (2005) 32 *LIEI* 259; A Radu, 'Foreign Investors in the EU—Which "Best Treatment"? Interactions between Bilateral Investment Treaties and EU Law' (2008) 14 *ELJ* 237; L Mola, 'Which Role for the EU in the Development of International Investment Law?' Society of International Law Working Paper No 26/08; T Eilmansberger, 'Bilateral Investment Treaties and EU Law' (2009) 46 *CML Rev* 383; M Bungenberg, 'Going Global? The EU Common Commercial Policy after Lisbon' in C Hermann and JP Terhechte (eds), 1 *European Yearbook of International Economic Law* (2010) 135–51; F Benyon, *Direct Investment, National Champions and EU Treaty Freedoms* (Hart Publishing, 2010) chapter 10.

(TRIMs) as a specific investment instrument. The EU was then involved in the (also ill-fated) negotiations on a Multilateral Agreement on Investment. Bilateral agreements concluded by the EU often include provisions on establishment or investment.[2]

As a matter of fact, the common commercial policy has included some investment matters for a number of years now—since the Treaty of Nice expanded it to trade in services. GATS mode 3 involves the supply of services through commercial presence (Article 1(2)(c)), which means any type of business or professional establishment (Article XXVIII(d)). GATS includes commitments as regards both market access and national treatment for mode 3, so effectively covers certain forms of investment in the services sector. Where a WTO member enters into full commitments under mode 3, it is required to provide access to its market to foreign services companies and to ensure non-discrimination (national treatment) of such companies (Articles XVI and XVII GATS). This extension to what is effectively investment flows from the broad conception of international trade in services. As services are intangible, the goal of trade liberalization of necessity requires a focus, not just on the products themselves, but also on the persons or companies supplying them. To some extent, this justifies the distinction between investment issues in the services sector—included in GATS and in the common commercial policy, and those in the goods sector—limited to TRIMs. However, as globalization progresses, trade and investment matters are increasingly entwined, and newer forms of protectionism are often investment-related.[3] In that sense, the inclusion of foreign direct investment in the common commercial policy makes a lot of sense. From an international perspective, on the other hand, trade and investment have also to some extent developed as parallel universes. There is no broad-based multilateral agreement on investment. Instead, states increasingly conclude and apply BITs, which typically include many forms of investment and of investment protection, and provide for investor-state arbitration, which stands in stark contrast with inter-state trade dispute settlement. The Commission reports that EU Member States have concluded close to 1,200 BITs with non-member countries.[4] It is thus clear that a common policy on investment cannot be produced overnight, and that a lot of work and time will be required to transform Member State policies into an EU policy. It is also clear that the question of the scope of the EU's new powers is vital.

This contribution focuses on two main issues: the scope of the EU's new competence regarding foreign investment (section I) and some of the challenges facing the EU in shaping a common investment policy (section II).

---

[2] Ceyssens, ibid 265–8.

[3] cf P Eeckhout, 'The Scales of Trade—Reflections on the Growth and Functions of the WTO Adjudicative Branch' (2010) 13 *JIEL* 4.

[4] Communication from the Commission, *Towards a Comprehensive European International Investment Policy*, COM(2010) 343 final, at 4.

II. The Scope of the New Competence

This section first examines the notion of foreign direct investment, as referred to in the TFEU. It starts by defining the types of foreign investment which come within the new commercial policy competence of the EU. It finds that portfolio investment is not included, and investigates whether other EU competences enable the EU to extend its new policies to such investment. The analysis then turns to the forms of investment protection which are standard in BITs, to see whether the new competence enables the EU to provide for all those forms of protection. Finally, it considers the fate of the existing BITs between Member States and third countries.

A. The notion of 'foreign direct investment'

Articles 206 and 207 TFEU speak of 'foreign direct investment'. The term 'foreign' no doubt refers to investments from the EU into third countries, and to investments by third-country nationals or companies in the EU. This conforms to the logic of the common commercial policy, which regulates both imports and exports. The term 'direct investment', on the other hand, is not a new concept in EU law. Article 64 TFEU, part of the chapter on capital and payments, employs it. As is well known, the Treaty provides in Article 63 for the free movement of capital and payments between Member States, and between Member States and third countries. This is without prejudice, however, to existing restrictions 'in respect of the movement of capital to or from third countries involving direct investment—including in real estate' (Article 64(1) TFEU). The EU legislator can also adopt measures on capital movement involving direct investment (Article 64(2) TFEU). The Court of Justice has interpreted the concept of direct investment to mean 'investments of any kind undertaken by natural or legal persons and which serve to establish or maintain lasting and direct links between the persons providing the capital and the undertakings to which that capital is made available in order to carry out an economic activity'.[5] That definition is based on an older capital movement directive,[6] which in turn corresponds to widely accepted definitions of the International Monetary Fund (IMF) and the Organization for Economic Co-operation and Development (OECD).[7] The Court distinguishes between direct investment and portfolio investment: the former includes 'investments in the form of participation in an undertaking through the holding of shares which confers the possibility of effectively participating in its management and control', whereas the latter involves 'investments in the form of the acquisition of shares on the capital market solely with the intention of making a financial

---

[5] See eg Case C-446/04 *Test Claimants in the FII Group Litigation* [2006] ECR I-11753, para 181.
[6] Directive 88/361/EEC for the implementation of Article 67 of the Treaty [1988] OJ L178/5.
[7] See further Commission Communication, above n 4 at fn 4, and Ceyssens, above n 1 at 274.

investment without any intention to influence the management and control of the undertaking'.[8]

The distinction is clearly transposable to the notion of foreign direct investment in Article 207(1) TFEU. It is important for the purpose of determining to what extent the new commercial policy competence covers forms of investment protected under standard BITs. The latter, indeed, often extend to portfolio investment in the sense of short-term financial participation in undertakings, as well as the mere enjoyment of movable and immovable property; intellectual property rights; and monetary claims under contracts.[9] In its Communication on investment policy the Commission also distinguishes between direct investment and portfolio investment.[10] Therefore, without it being necessary at this stage to offer a complete definition of the notion of foreign direct investment, it is clear that it does not encompass all forms of investment which are covered by standard BITs concluded by Member States. Thus, for these BITs to be fully substituted by EU investment agreements, there needs to be a further legal basis in the Treaties. Furthermore, for the EU to be able to make legal claims to a position as the sole actor, its competences need to be exclusive, not shared with the Member States. In case of shared competences, the Member States are likely to insist that so-called mixed agreements be concluded, involving joint participation by the EU and its Member States.[11]

The following section will explore to what extent the TFEU provisions on movement of capital provide further treaty-making powers, which may complement Article 207.

B. Free movement of capital and implied powers

In its Communication on a European international investment policy, the Commission claims that the treaty provisions on capital and payments complement the EU's exclusive competence under the common commercial policy, and provide for an implied exclusive competence. The Commission's reasoning is as follows.[12] It points out that the articulation of investment policy should be consistent with the TFEU chapter on capital and payments, which provides that, in principle, all restrictions on payments and capital movements, including those involving direct as well as portfolio investments, both between Member States and between Member States and third countries, are prohibited. The Commission recognizes that that chapter does not expressly provide for the possibility to conclude inter-

---

[8] See lastly Case C-171/08 *Commission v Portugal*, judgment of 8 July 2010, para 49, with further references.

[9] Commission Communication, above n 4 at 3. See also Ceyssens, above n 1 at 274–5; Eilmansberger, above n 1 at 394; Bungenberg, above n 1 at 147; J-C Piris, *The Lisbon Treaty—A Legal and Political Analysis* (Cambridge University Press, 2010) 282.

[10] Commission Communication, above n 4 at 3.

[11] On mixed agreements see C Hillion and P Koutrakos, *Mixed Agreements Revisited* (Hart Publishing, 2010).

[12] Commission Communication, above n 4 at 8.

national agreements on investment, including portfolio investment. However, with reference to Article 3(2) TFEU, the Commission claims that, to the extent that international agreements on investment affect the scope of the common rules set by the chapter on capital and payments, the exclusive EU competence to conclude agreements in this area would be implied.[13] If the Commission's analysis were correct, one would have to conclude that substantially all forms of investment covered by BITs are now within the EU's exclusive competence.

There are, however, serious doubts whether the Commission's reasoning conforms to the law of EU external competence. Assuming that Article 3(2) TFEU merely codifies the principles governing exclusive implied powers,[14] the starting point of our analysis must be to identify the substantive competences for which the TFEU provides in the area of capital movement. Indeed, the Court invariably takes great care to define the EU's substantive competences in implied powers cases.[15] It is only once those competences are defined, that the further question whether they are exclusive can be answered.

Article 63 TFEU establishes the rule of free capital movement, also between Member States and third countries. A number of further provisions determine the scope for EU legislation, or other measures, in this area. First, Article 64(2) TFEU confers on the EU competence to adopt measures, in accordance with the ordinary legislative procedure, 'on the movement of capital to or from third countries involving direct investment—including investment in real estate—establishment, the provision of financial services or the admission of securities to capital markets'.

---

[13] Article 3(2) TFEU provides: 'The Union shall also have exclusive competence for the conclusion of an international agreement when its conclusion is provided for in a legislative act of the Union or is necessary to enable the Union to exercise its internal competence, or insofar as its conclusion may affect common rules or alter their scope.'

[14] For further literature see I Macleod, ID Hendry and S Hyett, *The External Relations of the European Communities* (Oxford University Press, 1996) 47–55; C Kaddous, *Le droit des relations extérieures dans la jurisprudence de la Cour de justice des Communautés européennes* (Helbing & Lichtenhahn, 1998) 240–55; A Dashwood and J Helikoski, 'The Classic Authorities Revisited' in A Dashwood and C Hillion (eds), *The General Law of EC External Relations* (Sweet & Maxwell, 2000) 3–19; D O'Keeffe, 'Exclusive, Concurrent and Shared Competence' in ibid 179–99; J-V Louis, 'La compétence de la CE de conclure des accords internationaux' in J-V Louis and M Dony (eds), *Commentaire J Megret—Relations extérieures* (Etudes européennes, 2005) 59–71; P Koutrakos, *EU International Relations Law* (Hart Publishing, 2006) chapter 3; R Holdgaard, *External Relations Law of the European Community—Legal Reasoning and Legal Discourses* (Wolters Kluwer, 2008) chapter 4 and 97–119; G De Baere, *Constitutional Principles of EU External Relations* (Oxford University Press, 2008) 16–29 and 43–58; P Mengozzi, 'The EC External Competences: From the *ERTA* Case to the Opinion in the Lugano Convention' in M Poiares Maduro and L Azoulai, *The Past and Future of EU Law—The Classics of EU Law Revisited on the 50th Anniversary of the Rome Treaty* (Hart Publishing, 2010) 213; P Eeckhout, 'Bold Constitutionalism and beyond' in ibid 218; C Hillion, '*ERTA*, *ECHR* and *Open Skies*: Laying the Grounds of the EU System of External Relations' in ibid 224; R Post, 'Constructing the European Policy: *ERTA* and the *Open Skies* Judgments' in ibid 234; R Schütze, *From Dual to Cooperative Federalism—The Changing Structure of European Law* (Oxford University Press, 2009) chapter 6; P Eeckhout, *EU External Relations Law*, 2nd edn (Oxford University Press, 2011) chapter 3.

[15] See eg Case 22/70 *Commission v Council* [1971] ECR 263 (*AETR*); *Opinion 1/76 re Inland Waterways* [1977] ECR 741; *Opinion 2/91 re ILO Convention No 170* [1993] ECR I-1061; *Opinion 1/94 re WTO Agreement* [1994] ECR I-5267; Case C-467/98 *Commission v Denmark* [2002] ECR I-9519 (*Open Skies*); and *Opinion 1/03 re Lugano Convention* [2006] ECR I-1145.

Although the reference to the ordinary legislative procedure suggests that this provision aims at the adoption of internal EU legislation, the law on implied powers has clarified that such a competence may be used for the conclusion of an international agreement. However, it is clear that the scope of the competence conferred by Article 64(2) does not extend to all portfolio investments. Direct investment is the opposite of portfolio investment. Measures concerning the provision of financial services or the admission of securities to capital markets may affect portfolio investment, but clearly do not cover all aspects of such investment.

Second, Article 66 TFEU enables the Council to take safeguard measures, where, in exceptional circumstances, movements of capital to or from third countries cause, or threaten to cause, serious difficulties for the operation of economic or monetary union. Such safeguard measures, if ever adopted, would of course extend to portfolio investment. But again this does not constitute a general competence to regulate portfolio investments from third countries in the Member States. It does not, for example, confer competence to guarantee 'national treatment' or 'fair and equitable treatment' as regards portfolio investments.

Third, the same reasoning can be applied to the EU's competences under Articles 75 and 215 TFEU. Article 75 permits the adoption of regulations, aimed at preventing and combating terrorism, which define a framework for administrative measures with regard to capital movements and payments, such as the freezing of funds, financial assets or economic gains belonging to, or owned or held by, natural or legal persons, groups or non-state entities. Article 215 TFEU enables the Council to adopt restrictive measures involving 'the reduction, in part or completely, of economic and financial relations with one or more third countries'. Again these measures may affect portfolio investments, but do not confer general competence to regulate such investments.

It is therefore difficult to see on what basis the EU could claim a general competence to conclude international agreements on the protection of foreign portfolio investment. It is even more difficult to establish a basis for exclusive competence. Article 4(2)(a) provides for shared competence in internal market matters. This is confirmed by Article 65(1) TFEU, which recognizes that the Member States may still adopt certain measures restricting capital movements, for example 'measures which are justified on grounds of public policy or public security'.

Of course, such shared competence does not exclude the operation of the *AETR* principle, according to which there is exclusive competence to the extent that internal legislation may be affected, or its scope altered.[16] However, as Advocate General Maduro noted in two cases involving investment treaties, the EU has so far not made use of the competences under Article 64(2) or 66 TFEU. In other words, there is as yet no internal legislation which may be affected or whose scope may be altered by an investment agreement covering portfolio investment. Nor could it be

---

[16] *AETR*, ibid.

argued that the *Opinion 1/76* type exclusive implied powers extend to portfolio investment.[17] The Court has indeed stated the principle that there may be excusive implied powers, even in the absence of any internal acts being affected, where the conclusion of an international agreement is necessary to enable the EU to exercise its internal competences. But it has accepted such exclusive competence only in *Opinion 1/76* itself. To paraphrase what the Court stated in the *Open Skies* cases:[18] there is as regards portfolio investment no internal competence which could be effectively exercised only at the same time as the external competence, the conclusion of the international agreement thus being necessary in order to attain objectives of the Treaty that could not be attained by establishing autonomous rules.

The Commission appears to consider that, purely on the basis that the Treaty provides for free movement of capital and payments between Member States and third countries, exclusive EU competence to conclude agreements covering the making and protection of portfolio investments is implied. That is, with respect, a reasoning which is too broad-brush. It fails to distinguish the scope of one of the fundamental freedoms from the question of (external) competence. In fact, it is not clear on what Treaty basis the EU has shared competence to regulate all aspects of portfolio investment between the Member States and third countries, let alone exclusive competence.

C. What type of measures come under the new competences?

A further question is what type of measures affecting foreign direct investment come within the new competences. There is no need to produce a complete typology or definition of such measures. Standard BITs contain a number of basic norms, and the EU's policy will no doubt build on those BITs and also attempt to make use of those norms.[19] They include: most-favoured-nation and national treatment; fair and equitable treatment; full security and protection; and protection from unlawful expropriation.[20] In the literature, including in this volume,[21] it has been argued that a distinction needs to be made between investment liberalization (market access), covered by the new competence, and the standards of protection listed above, which all concern the post-investment phase, and are said not to be included. That argument is not convincing. It is clear that, in the context of making investment decisions, economic actors are not only concerned about access to the relevant market, but are equally interested in legal stability post-investment. Moreover, GATS mode 3, which is within the scope of Article 207 TFEU, already extends to post-investment protection: commitments are made for both market access and national treatment. The EU clearly could not

---

[17] *Opinion 1/76*, above n 15.
[18] *Commission v Denmark (Open Skies)*, above n 15 at paras 59–63.
[19] Commission Communication, above n 4 at 5.
[20] Ibid 8. cf Andrew Newcombe and Lluis Paradell, *Law and Practice of Investment Treaties: Standards of Treatment* (Wolters Kluwer, 2009) and Peter Muchlinski, Federico Ortino and Christoph Schreuer (eds), *The Oxford Handbook of International Investment Law* (Oxford University Press, 2008).
[21] See chapter 14 by M Krajewski.

pursue a meaningful and effective policy on foreign direct investment if it were not able to negotiate on standards of post-investment protection.[22] In this respect, it makes little sense to distinguish between the various norms referred to above. Insofar as the relevant investments are covered by the notion of 'foreign direct investment', there is little justification for limiting EU competence to providing for, for example, national treatment, and not fair and equitable treatment, or full security and protection. The international practice, which is a relevant factor for determining the scope of the common commercial policy,[23] supports such a broad approach.

However, there is one possible limitation which is worth exploring a little further. Standard BITs often offer protection from expropriation, and it has been contended that the effect of Article 345 TFEU is to exclude EU competence to conclude investment agreements offering such protection. Article 345 provides that the Treaties shall in no way prejudice the rules in Member States governing the system of property ownership. On its face this may seem a strict prohibition, but the Court of Justice has rarely if ever accepted arguments based on this provision, although such arguments are frequently put forward. In *Ospelt*, for example, a case concerning free movement of capital and Austrian legislation on a prior authorization procedure for the acquisition of agricultural and forestry plots, the Court recalled that the systems of ownership remained subject to the fundamental rules of Community law, including those of non-discrimination, freedom of establishment and free movement of capital.[24] It is true that that principle is not as such applicable to the issue before us, which is one of EU competence, and not of compatibility of Member State legislation with the EU's basic freedoms. However, also where the EU's legislative activity is involved, the Court has not been willing to construe Article 345 as a strict limitation. *Spain v Council* concerned a challenge to a regulation concerning the creation of a supplementary protection certificate for medicinal products (effectively providing for the extension of patent protection for pharmaceutical products to take account of time lost for the purpose of obtaining an authorization to put the products on the market).[25] Spain argued that the Community had no power to regulate substantive patent law, and could harmonize only those aspects relating to the exercise of industrial property rights which were capable of having an effect upon the achievement of the general objectives laid down in the Treaty. Such action could not take the form of a new industrial property right. The Court replied that (current) Article 345 TFEU did not reserve a power to regulate substantive patent law to the national legislature, to the exclusion of any Community action in the matter.[26] The analysis of Advocate General Jacobs

---

[22] Ceyssens, above n 1 at 277; Eilmansberger, above n 1 at 395.

[23] *Opinion 1/75 re Understanding on a Local Cost Standard* [1975] ECR 1362-3.

[24] Case C-452/01 *Ospelt v Schlössle Weissenberg Familienstiftung* [2003] ECR I-9743, para 24, with reference to Case 182/83 *Fearon* [1984] ECR 3677, para 7 and Case C-302/97 *Konle* [1999] ECR I-3099, para 38.

[25] Regulation 1768/92 Concerning the Creation of a Supplementary Protection Certificate for Medicinal Products [1992] OJ L182/1.

[26] Case C-350/92 *Spain v Council* [1995] ECR I-1985, paras 13–22.

was a little more extensive. Referring to past case law, he was of the opinion that the Court had made it clear that the argument of exclusive national competence for matters covered by (current) Article 345 TFEU was not correct, and he saw no reason why that conclusion would not also be valid for the exercise of Community competence.[27]

Furthermore, insofar as provisions in investment treaties protect from unlawful expropriation by providing for adequate compensation, they conform to general principles of EU law. The right to property is protected as such a general principle (as well as by Article 17 of the EU Charter of Fundamental Rights). Certain types of interference with this right may require compensation, and the Court has also recognized, in a case where Community law required the destruction of infected fish on a fish farm, that the Community could consider, in the context of its broad discretion in the field of agricultural policy, that full or partial compensation was appropriate for owners of farms on which animals had been destroyed and slaughtered.[28] If compensation can be provided for within the context of the EU's agricultural policy, it is difficult to see on what ground investment agreements concluded by the EU would be precluded from doing so.[29]

D. Existing Member States' BITs

Despite our conclusion that not all forms of investment are covered by the new EU competence, it is in any event clear that at least a number of matters traditionally regulated in BITs concluded by Member States are now within the EU's exclusive competence under Article 207 TFEU. This raises questions about the validity and fate of the close to 1,200 BITs which Member States have concluded prior to the entry into force of the Lisbon Treaty. At the time of writing, the Commission had made a proposal for a regulation establishing transitional arrangements for bilateral investment agreements between Member States and third countries. In the explanatory memorandum the Commission admits that the extent to which those existing agreements are incompatible with EU law can be the subject of discussion. However, to avoid any legal uncertainty, the Commission considers that a system for authorizing the maintenance in force of those agreements should be set up.[30] Clearly, under international law the validity of the existing agreements cannot be affected by EU law. The Lisbon Treaty cannot have the effect of modifying treaties between Member States and third countries, without the latter's consent. It is moreover doubtful whether, even under EU law, the existing agreements became invalid on 1 December 2009, when the Lisbon Treaty entered into force: there was at the time of the conclusion of those agreements no exclusive EU competence. Be that as it may, it is indeed preferable to provide for legal certainty.

---

[27] Ibid, Opinion Jacobs AG, para 28.
[28] Joined Cases C-20/00 and C-64/00 *Booker Aquaculture v The Scottish Ministers* [2003] ECR I-7411, para 85.
[29] cf Benyon, above n 1 at 101–2.
[30] Commission Proposal for a Regulation Establishing Transitional Arrangements for Bilateral Investment Agreements between Member States and Third Countries, COM(2010) 344 final, at 3.

Furthermore, the proposed regulation would enable the Commission also to authorize Member States to amend an existing agreement, or even to conclude a new one. The details of the proposed scheme need not concern us here. The principle is clearly in conformity with Article 2(1) TFEU, which provides that Member States may act in areas of exclusive EU competence 'only if so empowered by the Union'.

III. Shaping a Common EU Investment Policy: Key Challenges

As aptly noted by the Commission in its 2010 Communication, the development of a common EU investment policy 'will require more, rather then less, cooperation and coordination among the Union and the Member States'.[31] This is in part due to the limitations in the scope of the EU's exclusive competence, as examined above, and in part to the existence of well-established investment policies at the Member State level.[32]

Such cooperation and coordination will in turn imply a certain amount of flexibility in shaping the content of a common policy on investment. While the formulation of an EU model investment treaty has for the moment been ruled out, the EU will nevertheless attempt to formulate standard clauses inspired by best practices developed by Member States.[33] The challenge here is in identifying such 'best practices'. Investment treaties (including those of the Member States) have for the most part been developed through *bilateral* negotiations between a capital exporting country and a capital importing country. Through the BIT, while the latter (that is, the host country) would ensure an increased flow of much needed foreign direct investment into its economy, the former (that is, the home country) would provide its investors with certain guarantees, for example, against unfair, discriminatory or expropriatory measures by the host government. Looking at the distribution of investment disputes that have been brought against EU Member States, it is Eastern European states (such as the Czech Republic, Poland, Romania and Hungary) that have been on the receiving end of the great majority of such disputes. While these countries will be relieved when intra-EU BITs will be eventually phased out,[34] they will very likely bring to the EU policy-making table their own experiences as respondents (and particularly as losing respondents) in investment disputes. These Member States are likely to be critical of certain aspects of international investment law and arbitration.[35]

---

[31] Commission Communication, above n 4 at 11.
[32] There are approximately 1,200 BITs in force between EU Member States and third countries (roughly half of the total number).
[33] Commission Communication, above n 4 at 11.
[34] Most of the investment disputes against Eastern European countries have in fact been brought by foreign investors on the basis of BITs concluded with Western European countries like France, Germany, the United Kingdom and the Netherlands.
[35] The evolution of the United States' and Canadian investment policy in the last 15 years shows the impact of becoming a respondent in investment disputes.

Within this context, formulating a 'common' EU policy on investment is likely to raise, perhaps to a smaller scale, some of the negotiating headaches that have so far doomed most major attempts to reach a *multilateral* agreement on investment.[36] Would 'best practices' be identified from the perspective of a capital exporting country or from the perspective of a capital importing country? Moreover, depending on the third country sitting on the other side of the EU negotiating table, the scenario is likely to change.

This institutional challenge is certainly not insurmountable. Negotiations among EU Member States on the content of any future EU investment treaty will most likely permit the conclusion of future investment agreements with third countries. However, if the EU is serious about developing a 'common' policy on investment, there is an alternative path that the EU may want to explore: the formulation of model clauses (or even a model treaty) that (i) aim at a high level of investment protection; (ii) allow host states to adopt measures for legitimate public policy objectives; and (iii) promote both socially and environmentally sustainable investments. In delineating the next generation of investment treaties, the EU should certainly rely, first of all, on the multiple lessons learned by its Member States in promoting foreign investment, negotiating treaties and defending foreign investors' claims and, secondly, on the vast experience gained in building the internal market. Two critical areas will be briefly emphasized in the remainder of this section.

A. Recalibrating investment protection guarantees

Investment protection guarantees are usually worded in very general, open-ended terms and thus subject to potentially broad interpretation by arbitral tribunals. For example, a broad reading of the 'in like circumstances' or 'in like situations' component of the national treatment standard may reduce host states' ability to introduce regulatory or fiscal differentiations justified on the basis of legitimate policy objectives.[37] Equally, defining the concept of 'measures equivalent to expropriation' or 'indirect expropriation' exclusively on the basis of the measure's adverse effect on the foreign investment may lead to the imposition of a compensation requirement on the host state for legitimate regulatory measures.[38] Finally,

---

[36] Two more prominent and recent examples are the OECD-based negotiation of a Multilateral Agreement on Investment (MAI), and the WTO-based negotiation as part of the Doha Round. See Amarasinha and Kokott, 'Multilateral Investment Rules Revisited' in Muchlinski et al (eds), *Oxford Handbook of International Investment Law* (Oxford University Press, 2008) chapter 4. The Energy Charter Treaty (ECT) is, on the other hand, a successfully completed multilateral agreement covering investment issues, albeit only addressing *energy* investment. See Thomas Waelde (ed), *The Energy Charter Treaty: An East–West Gateway for Investment and Trade* (Kluwer Law International, 1996).
[37] See, eg, *Occidental v Ecuador*, Award 1 July 2004. cf Federico Ortino, 'Non-discriminatory Treatment in Investment Disputes' in P-M Dupuy, F Francioni and EU Petersmann (eds), *Human Rights in International Investment Law and Arbitration* (Oxford University Press, 2009) 344 et seq.
[38] See, eg, *Metalclad v Mexico*, Award 30 August 2000. cf Anne Hoffmann, 'Indirect Expropriation' in August Reinisch (ed), *Standards of Investment Protection* (Oxford University Press, 2008) 151 et seq.

interpreting the fair and equitable treatment standard to include a strict requirement on the host state to maintain a stable legal and business environment may
restrain the host state's ability to modify domestic legislation or to adapt it over
time.[39] While broad interpretations of the basic protection guarantees (such as the
ones just described) are not the norm, it is difficult to determine the actual or
potential adverse impact (in terms of chilling effect) of such interpretations on the
host states' willingness to adopt measures in the public interest.

As investment arbitration practice demonstrates, the fair and equitable treatment standard represents potentially the most important and most elusive obligation which is imposed on states by international investment law. The EU
recalibrating exercise should focus on this standard.[40] However, the elements
that are usually referred to by investment tribunals and legal scholars in order to
describe the meaning of the fair and equitable treatment standard are several
including, for example, due process, transparency, protection of investors' legitimate expectations, non-discrimination, arbitrariness, proportionality, reasonableness. All these principles are in themselves very broad and in turn open to differing
interpretations.

One solution would be to formulate a standard definition of what 'fair and
equitable treatment' signifies in the investment treaty context.[41] The European
integration experience provides very useful know-how. For example, the ECJ has
used the principle of proportionality as the legal instrument of choice in order to
identify whether a Member State measure adversely affecting one of the internal
market freedoms would be allowed to stand or not.[42] Equally, the ECJ has
developed certain general principles applicable within the EU legal system in
order to guarantee European citizens certain guarantees vis-à-vis public authorities
(including European ones). These include for example, legal certainty, protection
of legitimate expectations, due process and liability of public authorities.[43]

The aim of the recalibrating exercise is to go beyond the traditional approach of
looking at investment disciplines (and their interpretation) as being either pro-
investor or pro-host state. The aim is to identify certain public law disciplines that
should apply in any context (including foreign investment) as legitimate constraints
on public authority.

---

[39] See, eg, *CMS v Argentina*, Award 12 May 2005. cf Ioanna Tudor *The Fair and Equitable
Treatment Standard in the International Law of Foreign Investment* (Oxford University Press, 2008).
[40] National treatment standard and the expropriation discipline (should) function in practice as
narrower rules dealing with 'formally discriminatory' measures and 'direct' takings, respectively.
[41] The model BIT of the United States includes two annexes providing more detailed definitions of
the scope of the fair and equitable treatment standard (Annex A) and the concept of indirect
expropriation (Annex B).
[42] cf E Ellis (ed), *The Principle of Proportionality in the Laws of Europe* (Oxford University Press,
1999); N Emiliou, *The Principle of Proportionality in European Law: A Comparative Study* (Kluwer,
1996); Grainne de Búrca, 'The Principle of Proportionality and its Application in EC Law' 13 *YEL*
(1994) 105.
[43] See T Tridimas, *The General Principles of EU Law* (Oxford University Press, 2006).

B. Strengthening the link between foreign investment and sustainable development

The underlying premise of many investment agreements is to foster economic development through the promotion and protection of foreign investment. A few recent treaties have expressly referred to 'sustainable' development as one of the goals of international investment disciplines.[44] Most importantly for purposes of the present discussion, Article 205 TFEU (referring to Article 21 TEU laying down general provisions on the Union's external action) states that the Common Commercial Policy (CCP) shall be guided, inter alia, by 'human rights and fundamental freedoms' and shall pursue, inter alia, 'sustainable economic, social and environmental development'.[45]

There is scope for the EU to develop standard clauses aimed at strengthening the link between foreign investment and sustainable development focusing on three discrete areas: (1) investment promotion disciplines; (2) social and environmental provisions; and (3) corporate standards.

Although BITs are often described as 'promoting' investment, there are usually very few provisions expressly geared towards *investment promotion*. However, both host and home states normally provide, on a unilateral basis, investment promotion most notably through (i) promotion services;[46] (ii) financial and fiscal incentives;[47] and (iii) insurance mechanisms.[48]

In order to strengthen the link between foreign investment and sustainable development, the EU should develop model clauses requiring both the host and home countries to include social and environmental considerations, for example, in

---

[44] See the Preamble of the United States–Peru Trade Promotion Agreement, signed 12 April 2006, where the contracting parties resolved to 'promote sustainable development'; the Preamble of the United States–Oman Free Trade Agreement signed on 19 January 2006; the Preamble of the Canada–EFTA FTA signed on 26 January 2008; the Preamble of the Canada–Columbia FTA signed on 21 November 2008; the Preamble of the Canada–Jordan Foreign Investment Protection and Promotion Agreement (FIPA) signed in June 2007 ('Recognizing that the promotion and the protection of investments of investors of one Party in the territory of the other Party will be conducive to the stimulation of mutually beneficial business activity, to the development of economic cooperation between them and to the promotion of sustainable development'); the Preamble of the Australia–Chile FTA signed on 30 July 2008 ('to implement this Agreement in a manner consistent with sustainable development and environmental protection and conservation').

[45] Article 21.3 TEU also emphasizes that the 'Union shall respect the principles and pursue the objectives set out in paragraphs 1 and 2 in the development and implementation of the different areas of the Union's external action covered by this Title and by Part Five of the Treaty on the Functioning of the European Union, and of the external aspects of its other policies. The Union shall ensure consistency between the different areas of its external action and between these and its other policies.'

[46] Promotion services include a range of activities such as advisory services, matchmaking, business planning assistance, financial structuring advice and information about investment opportunities in order to facilitate foreign investment flows.

[47] Financial and fiscal incentives include grants, loans and equity participation as well as tax exemptions, tax deferrals and tax credits.

[48] Insurance mechanisms include mechanisms offering coverage of political and other non-commercial risk not normally included under conventional, private insurance policies. See UNCTAD *Home Country Measures* (UNCTAD, 2001).

any of the above-mentioned investment promotion activities. For example, national competent authorities should be required to prioritize (or limit) their promotion services to those investment projects that expressly address the potential impact on local communities and the environment. Equally, host and home countries should be required to include social and environmental considerations in the provision of financial and fiscal incentives, specifying what standards are to be used for purposes of social and environmental impact assessment and requiring monitoring of projects after the provision of financial incentives. Furthermore, they should condition the provision of political risk insurance to clearly defined social and environmental standards as well as subjecting political risk insurance decision-making processes to transparency requirements and independent review.

Consideration should also be given to expressly include *social and environmental provisions* in investment treaties. There are a few examples, principally in comprehensive trade agreements, of treaty provisions requiring contracting parties to enforce their domestic legislation (including particularly environmental and social legislation).[49] The Economic Partnership Agreement (EPA) between the EC and Cariforum, for example, includes a commitment not to lower labour and environmental standards in order to attract foreign investment.[50] However, the North American Free Trade Agreement (NAFTA) provides perhaps the most useful example of such a provision as well as the mechanisms envisaged in order to guarantee its enforcement (for example, the citizen submission process).[51]

A more demanding approach is to include provisions requiring Contracting Parties to ensure that their legislation provides for high levels of environmental protection and labour standards or that it conforms to relevant international standards. Again, the 2008 EC–Cariforum States EPA provides such an example as it imposes on the Contracting Parties an obligation to ensure that their own social and labour regulations and policies provide for and encourage high levels of social and labour standards consistent with internationally recognized core labour standards.[52]

---

[49] See Article 3, North American Agreement on Environmental Co-operation (NAAEC) and Article 4, North American Agreement on Labor Co-operation (NAALC).

[50] Article 73 reads as follows: 'The EC Party and the Signatory CARIFORUM States shall ensure that foreign direct investment is not encouraged by lowering domestic environmental, labour or occupational health and safety legislation and standards or by relaxing core labour standards or laws aimed at protecting and promoting cultural diversity.' Article 188 on 'Upholding levels of protection' provides in relevant part that 'the Parties agree not to encourage trade or foreign direct investment to enhance or maintain a competitive advantage by: (a) lowering the level of protection provided by domestic environmental and public health legislation; (b) derogating from, or failing to apply such legislation.'

[51] See Article 14 NAAEC. For an account of the challenges facing such mechanism, see G Garver, 'Measuring Performance through Independent Enforcement Review: Challenges and Opportunities for Independent Reviewers, the Public and the Governments and Other Institutions Subject to Review', paper presented at the *Seventh International Conference on Environmental Compliance and Enforcement* (available at <http://www.inece.org/conference/7/vol1/20_Garver.pdf>).

[52] Articles 191–192. A similar provision applies also to environmental and public health laws and policies (see Article 184). Within this approach, one should also emphasize Article 72 of the EC–CARIFORUM Agreement requiring contracting parties to take 'such measures as may be necessary, inter alia, through domestic legislation, to ensure that:...(b) Investors act in accordance with core

Within the context of foreign investment, *corporate standards* are usually found in international instruments providing voluntary principles and standards for responsible business conduct in areas such as employment and industrial relations, human rights, environment, information disclosure, combating bribery, consumer interests, science and technology, competition and taxation.[53] There are two main shortcomings of these standards: (a) they are not generally binding on investors, and (b) their coverage is rather limited as they include only general language or they focus only on certain values. For example, while providing for relatively specific standards in the labour law area (section IV), the OECD Guidelines' coverage and protection of fundamental human rights is quite limited. Among the General Policies identified in section II, the OECD Guidelines provide as follows: 'Enterprises should take fully into account established policies in the countries in which they operate, and consider the views of other stakeholders. In this regard, enterprises should:...2. Respect the human rights of those affected by their activities consistent with the host government's international obligations and commitments.'[54]

The EU should consider integrating corporate standards in investment treaties. One option would be to subject the applicability of protection guarantees (and/or investors' right to international arbitration) in investment treaties to compliance with corporate standards. While most investment protection guarantees in investment agreements (including investors' right to arbitration) are available to foreign investors that comply with host state laws, this may not ensure that investments are actually carried out in compliance with social and environmental standards as applicable to corporations. Accordingly, conditioning the availability of the protection guarantees in investment agreements to compliance with corporate standards aimed at protecting and promoting social and environmental values may indirectly strengthen the impact of such standards. Identifying the relevant corporate standards to use as benchmarks (should one refer to international labour and environmental laws and/or to industry based standards?) as well as providing for the appropriate operational mechanisms (at what stage, and by whom, should investors' compliance with relevant corporate standards be determined?) may prove challenging. In this respect, useful lessons may be learnt from the role of 'international standards' within the WTO.[55]

---

labour standards as required by the International Labour Organisation (ILO) Declaration on Fundamental Principles and Rights at Work, 1998, to which the EC Party and the Signatory CARIFORUM States are parties; (c) Investors do not manage or operate their investments in a manner that circumvents international environmental or labour obligations arising from agreements to which the EC Party and the Signatory CARIFORUM States are parties.'

[53] Eg, the OECD Guidelines for Multinational Enterprises and the UN Global Compact Principles.

[54] OECD Guidelines for Multinational Enterprises (2008) available at <http://www.oecd.org/dataoecd/56/36/1922428.pdf>.

[55] Steve Charnovitz, 'International Standards and the WTO' available at <http://ssrn.com/abstract=694346>.

IV. Concluding Remarks

The Treaty of Lisbon has, significantly, expanded the common commercial policy to foreign direct investment. It seems clear, however, that that notion does not cover all forms of investment regulated in modern BITs. As argued above, portfolio investment is not included. EU external action in this area will therefore, in all likelihood, require mixed agreements. Nevertheless, there is a risk that the new competence is turned into a legal battlefield between the Commission and the Member States. There is by now considerable experience with protracted external competence disputes in the EU, and that experience shows that such disputes are only ever resolved once the EU has managed to put together a worthwhile policy which the Member States accept. It is therefore much more important for the EU institutions to contribute to the shaping of substantive foreign investment policy, rather than getting entrenched in inter-institutional and legal warfare.

When it comes to shaping a common EU investment policy, the Union will have to straddle between continuity and innovation. Certainly in the short term, given the existence of well-established investment policies at the Member State level (including several hundreds of investment treaties in force between Member States and third countries), a certain amount of cooperation and coordination among the Union and the Member States will be unavoidable. However, in the medium/long term, the Union (and the Member States) have the possibility to design a common investment policy (whether through the formulation of model clauses or a model treaty) that, while aimed at a high level of investment protection, allows host states to adopt measures for legitimate public policy objectives and promotes both socially and environmentally sustainable investments. This will allow the Union to be at the forefront in the development of international investment law and policy. It will also fit with the overall objectives of the EU's external action.

PART IV
EU POLICIES

16

EU Competence in Criminal Law after Lisbon

Ester Herlin-Karnell

I. Introduction

The aim of this chapter is to discuss to what extent and how the Lisbon Treaty changes the legislative framework for the development of EU criminal law by analysing it in the light of the division of powers in the Union. The Lisbon Treaty has changed and shaped the constitutional framework for the rise of European criminal law, and the area of freedom, security and justice (AFSJ) more broadly by placing it at the supranational level. Gone is the awkward cross-pillar character of EU criminal law, as mainly a third pillar EU intergovernmental issue but also partly a first pillar question where the delimitation of vertical and horizontal powers has remained highly controversial.

The purpose of this chapter is twofold. First I will try to chart the constitutional changes as brought by the Lisbon Treaty in this area by setting out the basics of the new architecture of EU criminal law after the Lisbon Treaty. In doing so this chapter will look at the new and crucial criminal law provisions of Articles 82 and 83 TFEU and more specifically discuss the boundaries of these competences. Secondly, the chapter addresses the need to pay attention to subsidiarity and proportionality due to the sensitive nature of the criminal law. In doing so this chapter seeks to examine to what extent the subsidiarity and proportionality mechanisms will play any real role in this area and to what degree the national parliaments' participation in this monitoring action will control EU action in this area. This is particularly important since there is a tendency for assuming that the new role by the national parliaments in the subsidiarity monitoring process will restrain EU action in this area despite the fact that there is a general trend towards 'penal populism' both in the EU and national political arena. Accordingly, the focus of the present chapter is what it means to speak about competences in criminal law after the Lisbon Treaty. After all, it should be recalled that much of the debate pre-the Lisbon Treaty and cases such as *Commission v Council*[1] concerned the former Article 47 EU and whether any Community link could be

---

[1] Case C-176/03 *Commission v Council* [2005] ECR I-7879.

established so as to outweigh the third pillar for the safeguarding of the *acquis communautaire* (that is, the first EC pillar). Central to this case law was the principle of effectiveness when deciding on not only the delimitation of powers between the pillars but also on the need for legislation at the EU level. For this reason the present chapter will try to investigate to what extent this case law can be translated to the new framework as provided by the Lisbon Treaty.

This chapter is structured as follows. It begins by setting the scene of EU criminal law and explains briefly how criminal law got there. Subsequently, this chapter scrutinizes the provision of Article 83 TFEU. Thereafter, it looks at the impact of the protocol on subsidiary and proportionality, with particular emphasis on the relationship between subsidiarity and a minimalist approach to criminal law. The chapter concludes by discussing the future of EU criminal law and the legitimacy of it. More ambitiously, the Lisbon Treaty and its implications for competences in criminal law will be analysed against the general theme of the present book namely in the broader setting of how the EU, and EU law in particular, have been developing in recent years with particular regard to criminal law. Consequently, I seek to place my chapter in the light of the wider question of EU involvement in the AFSJ.

II. The Journey of Criminal Law in the EU

The general assumption before the entry into force of the Lisbon Treaty was that the EC—first pillar—lacked a competence in criminal law and accordingly that the criminal law was the subject for third pillar cooperation under the Amsterdam Treaty.[2] After all, criminal law was not on the, admittedly rather undefined, competence list as provided by the ex Articles 2 and 3 EC. Although some argued that this list was indicative only, the EU legislator was until recently—that is, *Commission v Council*, as aforementioned—fairly cautious with respect to criminal law, and has thus sought and found other means of remedying a lack of legislative competence. In the absence of an explicit competence the EU legislator has relied on what is now Article 4(3) TEU (ex Article 10 EC) and effective sanctions of a 'non-criminal law' nature. Accordingly, until recently the assumption was that the criminal law fell outside the legislative competence of the Community. Certainly, this remained the main opinion until the *Commission v Council*[3] judgment changed this paradigm by stating that criminal law could, nevertheless, be a matter for the EU legislator if the principle of the full effectiveness so required. This provided for a very vague and ill-defined competence in this area, which fuelled a debate concerning the exact competence contours in this area.[4]

---

[2] Articles 29–31 EU.

[3] Case C-176/03 *Commission v Council* [2005] ECR I-7879.

[4] Eg V Mitsilegas, 'The Transformation of Criminal Law in the Area of Freedom, Security and Justice' (2007) 26 *YEL* 1 and S Peers, 'EU Criminal Law and the Treaty of Lisbon' (2008) 33 *EL Rev* 507.

Nevertheless, the Lisbon Treaty solves the big theoretical question of whether there exists a competence to harmonize criminal law at the supranational level by simply asserting that it does. In other words, the Lisbon Treaty provides for a specific basis for such a crime-fighting mission by listing a whole range of crime-fighting activities as set out in Articles 82 and 83 TFEU respectively. The main question is then instead how to decide and monitor the contours of these provisions. In any case, in order to understand the constitutional significance of the Lisbon Treaty for the criminal law it is arguably necessary to place it in context.

A. The freestyle ride of criminal law in the EU from case law innovations to the rise of the Lisbon Treaty

It might appear somewhat ironic that the legislative carousel for the creation of supranational criminal law began to move in the aftermath of the failure of the Constitutional Treaty in 2005. Just as the Lisbon Treaty has now removed the former pillar structure of the EU; this was also what the Constitutional Treaty would have done. In the meantime, that is, in the absence of a constitutional document, the Court of Justice set out to create its own EU criminal law based on an extensive reading of effectiveness and the need to safeguard the former first pillar from any encroachment from the third pillar in accordance with the message given by ex Article 47 EU. As noted, in its judgment in the abovementioned *Commission v Council*[5] the Court concluded that criminal law could be subject to harmonization for the protection of the environment. After all, the protection of the environment was an EC law competence as laid down in ex Article 175 EC (now Article 192 TFEU).

In the wake of this judgment, the Commission published a communication that took for granted that almost any area in EU law could be harmonized in criminal law for the full effectiveness of EU law.[6] Most significantly, the Commission linked the outcome of *Commission v Council* with what is now Article 114 TFEU (ex Article 95 EC) and the establishment of the internal market. Subsequently, the *Ship-source pollution*[7] case confirmed that that the EU legislator would not give up on the establishment of competences in this area and once again confirmed the recurrence of such competences with regard to the criminal law. However, the Court clarified one important, although relatively straightforward, principle: it left the decision on penalties to the Member States' own discretion. After all, this was only natural as the Member States must be considered as more suited than the EU legislator to decide on whether to put someone in prison or simply impose a sanction.[8] Whatever the case, these penalties still need to comply with the principle of effectiveness and be proportionate and dissuasive.[9]

---

[5] Case C-176/03 *Commission v Council* [2005] ECR I-7879.
[6] COM(2005) 583 final/2, 24 November 2005.
[7] Case C-440/05 *Commission v Council* [2007] ECR I-9097.
[8] As cautiously pointed out before in E Herlin-Karnell, Annotation 'Ship-source Pollution Case-440/05, *Commission v. Council*, Judgment of 23 October 2007 (Grand Chamber)', (2008) 14 EPL 533.
[9] Case C-440/05 *Commission v Council* [2007] ECR I-9097 See also S Peers, *EU Justice and Home Affairs* (Oxford University Press, 2006) chapter 8.

Moreover, the judgment in *Ireland v EP and Council*[10] furthered the EC's competences in criminal law by once again stating that ex Article 47 EU dictated the game of competence delimitation between the pillars, since there only had to be a Community link established in order to decide on competence. This time it was somewhat remarkably concluded that any effect on the first pillar with the consequence of an effect on trade or disparities could result in criminalization under the internal market provision of what is now Article 114 TFEU. Hence the message of all these cases is that the question of EU criminal law has constituted a delimitation of competences question and not so much an issue of whether there is a genuine need to criminalize. What has been especially problematic with this approach has been the assumption that criminalization would increase the effectiveness of the existing framework per se.

Although much of this belongs to history by now, since the Lisbon Treaty, as noted, has merged the previous pillar and therefore supranationalized the criminal law by listing it as an EC competence, there are nonetheless some unresolved issues. In particular, it appears as if the 'effectiveness' criteria will continue to play an important role. After all, Article 83(2) stipulates that if the approximation of criminal laws and regulations of the Member States prove essential to ensure the effective implementation of a Union policy in an area which has been subject to harmonization measures.

In what follows I will try to give an account of how the question of competence allocation in EU criminal law has changed due to the entry into force of the Lisbon Treaty, in particular Article 83 TFEU, and discuss the boundaries of these competence provisions.

III. The Specific Changes Brought in by the Lisbon Treaty

The AFSJ constitutes a shared competence according to Article 4(2)(j) TFEU. Obviously, this is one of the novelties of the Lisbon Treaty that it gives guidance about the nature of the Union's competences (that is, exclusive, shared or supportive/coordinative competences). More specifically, the AFSJ is to be found in Title V of the Treaty of the Functioning of the European Union (TFEU). Title V of the Lisbon Treaty consists of five chapters, which include: general provisions (Chapter 1), policies on border checks, asylum and immigration (Chapter 2), judicial cooperation in civil matters (Chapter 3), judicial cooperation in criminal matters (Chapter 4) and police cooperation (Chapter 5). The portal provision here is Article 67 TFEU in Chapter 1 which stipulates that the Union shall constitute an area of freedom, security and justice with respect for fundamental rights and the different legal systems and traditions of the Member States. Moreover, it reads that the Union shall endeavour to ensure a high level of security through measures to prevent and combat crime, racism and xenophobia, and through measures for coordination and cooperation between police and judicial authorities and other

---

[10] Case C-301/06 *Ireland v Parliament and Council* judgment of 10 February 2009 nyr.

competent authorities, as well as through the mutual recognition of judgments in criminal matters and, if necessary, through the approximation of criminal laws.

It is fitting to begin by setting out the basic legal framework of the criminal law after Lisbon. The crucial provisions for the criminal law are Articles 82 TFEU (procedural criminal law) and 83 TFEU (substantive criminal law). These provisions need, however, to be read in the light of Chapter 1 of Title V of TFEU which sets out the general goals to be achieved in this area. These provisions provide—for the first time—rather neatly laid-down competences. Therefore, it seems appropriate to begin this section by briefly outlining the main characteristics of Article 82 TFEU and Article 83 TFEU respectively.

A. Article 82 TFEU procedural criminal law

Article 82 TFEU stipulates that judicial cooperation in criminal matters should be based on the principle of mutual recognition and should include the approximation of the laws and regulations of the Member States in the areas referred to in paragraph 2 of the same article. Paragraph 2 in turn states that the European Parliament and the Council may establish minimum rules to the extent necessary to facilitate mutual recognition of judgments and judicial decisions, and police and judicial cooperation in criminal matters having a cross-border dimension. Such rules shall take into account the differences between the legal traditions and systems of the Member States. The provision of Article 82 TFEU then sets out a list of areas within the EU's competence for legislation, such as the mutual admissibility of evidence between the Member States, the rights of individuals in criminal procedure and provisions regarding the rights of victims. Furthermore, the Article contains a 'general clause' in Article 82(2)(d) stating that any other specific aspect of criminal procedure, which the Council has identified in advance by decision (unanimity would apply here), would qualify for future approximation. Finally, this provision states that the adoption of the minimum rules referred to in this paragraph should not prevent Member States from maintaining or introducing a higher level of protection for individuals. It remains to be seen whether this constitutes a far-reaching and consistent enough solution as regards legal safeguards in criminal law proceedings.

In any case, the substantive competence provision of Article 83 TFEU is of more interest for the present chapter and concerns the interaction between EU legislation and criminalization.

B. Article 83 TFEU substantive criminal law

Article 83(1) TFEU concerns the regulation of substantive criminal law and stipulates that the European Parliament and the Council may establish minimum rules concerning the definition of criminal law offences and sanctions in the area of particularly serious crime with a cross-border dimension resulting from the nature or impact of such offences or from a special need to combat them on a common basis. Thereafter, this provision sets out a list of crimes in which the EU shall have legislative competence such as terrorism, organized crime and money laundering. It accordingly also states that the Council may identify other possible areas of crime, which meet the cross-border and seriousness criteria. Also, and interestingly, paragraph 2 of this Article reads that the possibility exists for approximation if that proves essential to ensure the effective implementation of a Union policy in an area which has already been subject to harmonization measures.

C. Enhanced cooperation and emergency brakes

A significant change as introduced by the Lisbon Treaty is the one step backwards two steps forwards mechanisms.[11] This is the so-called emergency brake and accelerator procedure. More specifically, both Articles 82(2) and 83(1) and (2) provide in their respective § 3 for the possibility of applying a so-called emergency brake if the law in question would affect fundamental aspects of a Member State's criminal justice system. More concretely, if such an emergency brake scenario occurs, a Member State may request that the measure be referred to the European Council. In that case, the ordinary legislative procedure is suspended, and after discussion and 'in case of a consensus, the European Council shall, within four months of this suspension, refer the draft back to the Council, which shall terminate the suspension of the ordinary legislative procedure'. There is, however, no such emergency possibility as regards the notion of mutual recognition, which will remain the main theme in EU criminal law cooperation. Obviously, the notion of an emergency brake looks attractive to Member States with a strong relationship between the criminal law and the nation state, and hence remedies Member State anxiety about the loss of their national sovereignty in criminal law matters.

Nevertheless, whether or not a single Member State pulls the emergency brake, the Lisbon Treaty provides for the possibility of enhanced cooperation for the remaining Member States. Although it is true that an emergency brake scenario will generate fragmentation, it is submitted that the problem is more fundamental than that. The crux is that the mere inclusion of an emergency brake does not automatically constitute a guarantee of successful European criminal law. Nevertheless, Articles 82 and 83 TFEU of Lisbon respectively state:

In case of disagreement, and if at least nine Member States wish to establish enhanced cooperation on the basis of the draft directive concerned, they shall notify the European Parliament, the Council and the Commission accordingly. In such a case, the authorization to proceed with enhanced cooperation referred to in Article 20(2) of the Treaty on European Union and Article 329 of this Treaty shall be deemed to be granted and the provisions on enhanced cooperation shall apply.

Briefly, this means that there is no obligation as set out in Article 329 TFEU of Lisbon to address a request to the Commission, specifying the scope and objectives of the enhanced cooperation in question. Neither is there an obligation (as Article

---

[11] See E Herlin-Karnell, *The Constitutional Dimension of European Criminal Law* (Hart Publishing, forthcoming 2012) chapters 2 and 4.

20(2) TFEU of Lisbon reads) that the Council as a last resort shall adopt the decision at issue. This poses two questions. First, as I have previously argued, it is possible to say that the mere fact that the Member States do not need to show the last resort requirement as stated in Article 20(2) TFEU of Lisbon can be regarded as being in disharmony with the sensitive character of criminal law as the *ultimo ratio*. Secondly, there appears to be a risk that such cooperation could result in varying degrees and notions of freedom, security and justice.[12]

D. Extended jurisdiction

Another significant change, and perhaps the most significant change as introduced by the Lisbon Treaty is the extension of the Court's jurisdiction to also cover the former third pillar area. This is one of the most important constitutional restructurings under the Lisbon Treaty. It should perhaps be recalled that prior to the entry into force of the Lisbon Treaty, such jurisdiction was based on a voluntary declaration by Member States as to whether to accept such jurisdiction in accordance with Article 35 TEU.[13] The Lisbon Treaty changes this, as it significantly extends the Court's jurisdiction within the AFSJ field.[14] The Lisbon Treaty Protocol on Transitional Provisions provides a five-year transition—or alteration—period before the existing third-pillar instruments will be treated in the same way as Community instruments.[15]

Therefore, despite the entry into force of the Lisbon Treaty and, thereby, the merging of the pillars, there will remain 'echoes' of the third pillar in terms of the

---

[12] S Carrero and F Geyer, The Reform Treaty and Justice and Home Affairs, available at <http://www.libertysecurity.org/IMG/pdf_The_Reform_Treaty_Justice_and_Home_Affairs.pdf> (last accessed 20 June 2010).

[13] Eg E Denza, *The Intergovernmental Pillars of the European Union* (Oxford University Press, 2002) chapter 9 and A Hinarejos, *Judicial Control in the European Union* (Oxford University Press, 2009).

[14] See, however, Article 10 of the Protocol on transitional provisions attached to the Lisbon Treaty, which reserves a five-year transition period as regards the Court's jurisdiction in matters formerly under the third pillar.

[15] Article 10 of this Protocol stipulates that:

1. As a transitional measure, and with respect to acts of the Union in the field of police cooperation and judicial cooperation in criminal matters which have been adopted before the entry into force of the Treaty of Lisbon, the powers of the institutions shall be following the date of entry into force of that Treaty: the powers of the Commission under Article 258 of the Treaty on the Functioning of the European Union shall not be applicable and the powers of the Court of Justice of the European Union under Title VI of the Treaty on European Union, in the version in force before the entry into force of the Treaty of Lisbon, shall remain the same, including where they have been accepted under Article 35(2) of the said Treaty on European Union.

2. The amendment of an act referred to in paragraph 1 shall entail the applicability of the powers of the institutions referred to in that paragraph as set out in the Treaties with respect to the amended act for those Member States to which that amended act shall apply.

3. In any case, the transitional measure mentioned in paragraph 1 shall cease to have effect five years after the date of entry into force of the Treaty of Lisbon.

transitional protocol and its five-year transition period. Obviously, this means that the Commission will not have the power to bring infringement procedures against Member States as regards alleged breaches of pre-existing measures during this period.[16] It also means that the complex inter-pillar structure that has characterized European criminal law will remain for some time. Moreover, as a result of the transitional rules, there will be mixed jurisdiction over different measures concerning the same subject matter, and the most feasible regime (and favourable from the perspective of the individual) should then be preferred. The crucial question seems to concern the definition of when an act is 'amended'. It has been suggested that, in the absence of any *de minimis* rule or any indication that acts are in any way severable as regards the Court's jurisdiction, any amendment— no matter how minor—would suffice. But there will obviously be less clear cases.[17] In the light of the Court's history in promoting European integration, the Court would conceivably favour the most communitarized reading of when an act is 'amended'. Moreover, this means that there can now be infringement procedures brought by the Commission in this area so there will be a further incentive for the Member States—except for the general, admittedly rather strong, message of loyalty for the Member States towards the EU. But most importantly, the Lisbon Treaty introduces the possibility of expedited procedures for persons in custody. More specifically, the Lisbon Treaty stipulates in Article 267 TFEU that, if a question is raised in a case pending before a court or tribunal of a Member State with regard to a person in custody, the Court shall act with a minimum of delay. This is obviously an extremely important change and reflects the debate on speedier justice in Europe.[18]

In what follows, this chapter will look more closely at the competence question in EU criminal law. The underlying question is as follows: to what extent has the Lisbon Treaty changed the competence web? In other words, the question arises to what extent the previous competence debate has been finally settled.

IV. The Effectiveness Criteria: No Limits to Criminalization?

It is important to discuss the constitutional scope of Article 83(2) TFEU more specifically. As explained, this provision provides for a broader competence in an area which has already been subject to the EU's harmonization programme if it would be essential for the effective implementation of a Union policy. Arguably,

---

[16] S Peers, 'EU Criminal Law and the Treaty of Lisbon' (2008) 33 *EL Rev* 507.
[17] S Peers, 'Finally "Fit for Purpose"? The Treaty of Lisbon and the End of the Third Pillar Legal Order' (2008) *YEL* 47.
[18] See, eg, C Ladenburger, 'Police and Criminal Law in the Treaty of Lisbon' (2008) 4 *EU Const* 20. However, despite the reformation of the Court of Justice's jurisdiction as provided by the Lisbon Treaty, the Court still will not have the power to review the validity or proportionality of operations carried out by the police or other law enforcement agencies of a Member State or the exercise of responsibilities incumbent upon Member States with regard to the maintenance of law and order and the safeguarding of internal security. This is likely to create interpretation problems as regards the notion of 'internal Member State security' as opposed to EU security.

this paragraph has to be seen in the light of *Commission v Council* as mentioned above. It should perhaps be recalled that in this case, the Court held that:[19]

As a general rule, neither criminal law nor the rules of criminal procedure fall within the Community's competence...however the last mentioned findings do not prevent the Community legislator, when the application of effective, proportionate and dissuasive criminal penalties by the competent national authorities is an essential measure for combating serious environmental offences, from taking measures which relate to the criminal law of the member states which it considers necessary in order to ensure that rules which it lays down on environmental protection are fully effective.

Although it is true that Article 83 TFEU constitutes *lex specialis* of criminal law in the absence of any other provisions expressly granting a competence, it is possible that Article 83(2) TFEU could prove to have significantly wide-ranging constitutional slipperiness here. As noted above, viewing Article 83(2) as a carte blanche would not only render the attribution of powers illusory but also clash with the criminal law principle that it should be the last resort as a means of control. This poses two questions: what does it mean to refer to the effectiveness of EU law and what does it mean to refer to the effectiveness of criminal law specifically? A further issue is that of legitimacy, how can effectiveness be reconciled with the principle of legality? It is not my intention to try to comprehensively answer these questions but it should be noted that the debate on effectiveness is a long-standing one in both EU law and criminal law. The point is that it is far too easy to assume that the effectiveness of EU law would automatically increase with the imposition of a criminal penalty. But there is also a constitutional problem here. It appears difficult to monitor the principle of effectiveness as it has a huge constitutional slipperiness to it. The question is whether there should be any minimum requirement imposed before reasoning based on 'effectiveness' can be considered as having passed the threshold required. Indeed, when thinking about the eager embracement of effectiveness in the context of the Court's case law it might appear somewhat surprising that by contrast most criminal lawyers and criminologists agree on the assumption that criminal law is not always effective as a means of social control.[20] Yet the fundamentals of legality/attribution of powers as discussed above may lead to complexities, or tensions, in the context of the principle of effectiveness. Although, as explained above, the delimitation of competences between the pillars now belongs to legal history, the principal question of legality and the limits of effectiveness will not go away. The reason for this is that Article 83(2) TFEU provides for a highly ambiguous competence to harmonize when necessary for the effective implementation of a Union policy that has already been subject to harmonization. This seems like a rather broadly defined competence. In conclusion, the principle of effectiveness constitutes one of the main drivers of EU integration and has played, and continues to play, a particularly important role in the development of EU criminal law.

---

[19] Case C-176/03 *Commission v Council* [2005] ECR I-7879, paras 47–48.
[20] See eg A Ashworth, *Principles of Criminal Law* (Oxford University Press, 2006) chapter 2.

A. Centre of gravity in Lisbon

The first question of interest here is the centre of gravity debate or perhaps more properly the confusion surrounding it. As indicated at the outset of this chapter, there has been a lot of discussion concerning the delimitation of powers between the pillars. Expressed in somewhat simplified terms, there have been two camps here, those who have analysed the former third pillar[21] and the AFSJ criminal law area and those who have focused on the former second pillar and the delimitation of powers in this area.[22] Both camps have been united by the importance of ex Article 47 EU and the question of the delimitation of powers between the pillars. Yet these Article 47 cases were fundamentally different from the Article 114 TFEU (ex 95 EC) as well as the classic case law on choice of the right legal basis and the *Titanium dioxide*[23] string of cases (centre of gravity). After all, in the context of Article 114 TFEU it was never about centre of gravity but about the admittedly difficult concept of market making. The question for the future is accordingly the exact contours of the new non-affect clause. It is very possible that there will be a real centre of gravity test which emerges here. After all, prior to the entry into force of this Treaty, cases such as C-301/06 confirmed that this was not really about any centre of gravity but about establishing some kind of effects on EU law that could be linked to the first pillar and then Article 47 did the rest of the job. In other words, the only thing that needed to be demonstrated was a Community link which is arguably a lot weaker than any 'centre of gravity test' could offer. Therefore, the situation changes dramatically with the Lisbon Treaty. Within the new framework, the AFSJ is incorporated into the *acquis*. The real centre of gravity questions will therefore be to demarcate the specific provision of Article 83 TFEU concerning the harmonization of substantive law from other areas where the criminal law could be brought. Article 67 TFEU (discussed below) is one candidate here, which provides for a more general legislative power for the creation of an AFSJ. Other centre of gravity disputes as regards criminal law[24] could conceivably emerge in the context of Articles 114, 325 and 352 TFEU.

Moreover, apart from the afore mentioned general competence provisions across the Treaty, Chapter 1 of Title V of the TFEU raises some interesting questions regarding the competence delimitation between Chapters 1 and 4 of Title V of the TFEU. This question is important, as there is no emergency brake as regards

---

[21] Eg the present author as well as O Lynsky and A Dawnes, 'The Ever Longer Arm of EC Law: The Extension of Community Law into the Field of Criminal Law' (2008) 45 *CML Rev* 131. Naguel Neagu, 'Entrapment between Two Pillars: The European Court of Justice Rulings in Criminal Law' (2009) *ELJ* 15, 536.

[22] Eg A Dashwood, 'Article 47 EU and the Relationship between First and Second Pillar Competences' in A Dashwood and M Marcesceau (eds), *Law and Practice of EU External Relations* (Cambridge University Press, 2008) 70.

[23] Case C-300/89 *Commission v Council* [1991] ECR I-2867.

[24] I am not discussing here security and terrorism and action taken within the TEU. Article 40 TEU stipulates a non-affect clause which means that the TEU and the TFEU are to be treated equally, but it is up to the Court of Justice to monitor this clause.

legislation adopted under Chapter 1. Indeed, it is to Article 67 TFEU that one has to turn in order to understand the broader policy mission of the EU as regards the fight against crime in this area.

B. Articles 67 and 75 setting the scene of crime prevention in the EU

Article 67 sets the scene of crime prevention at the EU level. It poses interesting questions as regards the relationship between Chapter 1 and Chapter 4 and the demarcation of powers.[25] As for competence allocation it may be argued that it is unclear to what extent criminal law could be harmonized under this Chapter. The key point though, is simply that Article 67 TFEU—the portal provision of Chapter 1—should be read in conjunction with the specific provisions on criminal law as discussed above: it sets the scene and tells us what values the Union seeks to enforce—freedom, security and justice and respect for fundamental rights. Consequently, these aspirations could be achieved by fighting crime and ensuring a high level of crime prevention and security. Moreover, Article 75 TFEU provides for the competence to adopt restrictive measures in the fight against terrorism. Therefore, a further question concerns which cases of the fight against terrorism are to be considered as falling within the scope of Article 75 TFEU as opposed to the Article 83 TFEU and the criminal law framework (which it includes in its list), or whether these Articles are intended to complement each other. It seems as if the dividing line here is administrative sanctions (freezing of funds) or criminal law, where the former is part of Article 75 TFEU and the latter forms part of Chapter 4 and Article 83 TFEU. In any case, and to further confuse matters: Article 75 TFEU stipulates, 'where necessary to achieve the objectives set out in Article 67 TFEU'. It also refers to the possible harmonization of 'related activities', which begs the question what 'related activities' actually means. Would it, for example, be possible to bring in money laundering and the financing of terrorism? In other words, although it is true that the criminal law is dealt with in Articles 82 and 83 TFEU, it is far from clear how much of the criminal law could be transferred via Articles 67 and 75 TFEU. Plainly, it confers on the Union a more general aim of fighting crime and protecting security within the Union, although it is true that the third pillar similarly emphasized the importance of creating a genuinely crime-free EU. The difference is that this crime prevention agenda will now take place at the supranational level. Accordingly, it appears fairly obvious that the abovementioned reference in Article 67 TFEU to 'measures to prevent and combat crime and, if necessary, through the approximation of criminal laws' constitutes a broadly defined outline.

---

[25] Draws on E Herlin-Karnell, 'The Lisbon Treaty and the Criminal Law: Anything New under the Sun?' (2008) 10 *EJLR* 321.

C. More harmonization outside the *lex specialis* provisions?

The following section will attempt to discuss to what extent it would be possible to harmonize the criminal law beyond the provisions of Articles 82 and 83 TFEU as discussed above. Prior to the entry into force of the Lisbon Treaty, the interesting question was to what extent the criminal law could be harmonized under Article 114 (ex Article 95 EC) and Article 352 (ex Article 308 EC) TFEU. While Advocate General Jacobs[26] was one of the first to argue that sanctions could be harmonized at the EU level even if such a competence was not one of the EU's objectives, it was not until the *Kadi* case[27] (which dramatically expanded the EU's competences to include the fight against terrorism within the first pillar) that such a possibility became viable. After all, despite the rollercoaster history of Article 308 EC (now Article 352 TFEU) as regards the degree of intervention, Opinion 2/94,[28] concerning the EU's possible accession to the ECHR, made it clear that the Union's objectives could not be extended. In this case, the Court clarified that ex Article 308 EC could not be used to widen the scope of Community powers beyond the framework created by the EC Treaty as a whole. Nor could it be used as the foundation for the adoption of provisions, which would, in substance, amend the Treaty without following the necessary amendment procedures. Furthermore, the Lisbon Treaty has not only added a sentence in Article 352 TFEU stating that the objectives cannot be extended but it also added such a reassurance in a declaration as annexed to the Treaty.[29] Even though the AFSJ and criminal law will now constitute EU objectives it appears difficult to rely on Article 352 TFEU given the specific provisions in Title V (in particular Article 83 TFEU as discussed above). Instead, Article 114 TFEU (or its predecessor Article 95 EC) appears to be the prime candidate here.

D. Article 114 TFEU (ex Article 95 EC)

As noted, in the wake of the outcome in Commission v Council, the Commission presented a communication[30] which suggested that the delimitation of power

---

[26] Case C-240/90 *Germany v Commission* [1992] ECR I-05383, AG Jacobs stated in his Opinion of 3 June 1992, 'certainly EC law in its present state does not confer on the Commission, the CFI or the ECJ the function of a criminal tribunal. It should however be noted that that would in itself not preclude the EC from harmonizing the criminal laws of the Member States if that were necessary to attain one of the objectives of the Community'.

[27] Case 402/05 *Kadi* judgment of 3 September 2008.

[28] Opinion 2/94 *Accession to the ECHR* [1996] ECR 1-1759.

[29] Declaration 42 on Article 352 TFEU reads: 'The Conference underlines that, in accordance with the settled case law of the Court of Justice of the European Union, Article 352 of the Treaty on the Functioning of the European Union, being an integral part of an institutional system based on the principle of conferred powers, cannot serve as a basis for widening the scope of Union powers beyond the general framework created by the provisions of the Treaties as a whole and, in particular, by those that define the tasks and the activities of the Union. In any event, this Article cannot be used as a basis for the adoption of provisions, whose effect would, in substance, be to amend the Treaties without following the procedure which they provide for that purpose'.

[30] COM(2005) 583 final/2, 24 November 2005.

between the first and the third pillars had been resolved once and for all by the judgment in *Commission v Council*. According to the Commission the same reasoning could therefore automatically be extended to the Article 114 TFEU doctrine on the establishment and functioning of the internal market. Although Article 83 TFEU takes away much of the need to rely on Article 114 TFEU, there are nonetheless some unresolved issues. Admittedly, money laundering, for example, which used to be the object for harmonization under Article 114 TFEU (ex Article 95 EC) through the imposition of administrative penalties, will no longer need to rely on Article 95 since the crime of money laundering is now listed in Article 83 TFEU. As noted above, one of the criteria for relying on Article 83 TFEU is that a cross-border aspect can be demonstrated. Yet there may be less clear cases where there is no cross-border element and where a market element could conceivably be identified. After all, in cases such as *Rundfunk*[31] and *Lindquist*[32] the Court stated that recourse to Article 114 TFEU as a legal basis does not presuppose the existence of an actual link with free movement between Member States in every situation referred to by the measure in question founded on that basis. Accordingly, while the Court is less explicit about what makes a market, it has ruled that a contrary interpretation could render the limits of the field of application of a certain directive particularly unsure.[33]

More importantly, it is not entirely clear to what extent Article 83 TFEU is an 'exclusive' *lex specialis*. Typically, such a dispute of conflicting legal basis has been resolved by recourse to the centre of gravity test.[34] As regards Article 114 TFEU, there is, however, as stated no real centre-of-gravity test available, the question resting rather on whether the measure at issue contributes to market creation at all. So in connection with Article 114 TFEU, 'Rather, the only question posed when examining the conferral of competences is whether a competence of the Community can be identified [in relation to market creation] or not'.[35]

Admittedly, paying attention to future obstacles is not a groundbreaking statement, but a template that has already been applied in, for example, the *Swedish Match* case.[36] After all, the Court has consistently held that while recourse to Article 114 TFEU as a legal basis is possible if the aim is to prevent future obstacles to trade resulting from the heterogeneous development of national laws, the emergence of such obstacles must be likely and the measure in question must be designed to prevent them. Thus, in *Tobacco Advertising II*,[37] the Court stipulated that reliance on Article 114 TFEU is also possible if the aim is to prevent the emergence of future obstacles to trade resulting from multifarious developments of national laws due to the enlargement, if there is an appreciable risk that such disparities would

---

[31] Joined Cases C-465/00, C-138/01 and C-139/01 *Rundfunk and others* [2003] ECR I-4989.
[32] Case C-101/01 *Lindquist* [2003] ECR I-12971.
[33] Ibid para 41.
[34] Case C-300/89 *Commission v Council* [1991] ECR I-2867.
[35] Eg M Ludwigs, Annotation C-380/03, (2007) 44 *CML Rev* 1159.
[36] Case C-210/03 *Swedish Match* [2004] ECR I-11893, §§ 30–3.
[37] *Tobacco Advertising II* Case C-380/03 *Germany v Parliament and Council* [2006] ECR I-11573.

increase, thus adding to the 'likeliness' test. This approach was more recently confirmed in the *Vodafone* case.[38] It goes without saying that if the mere fact that divergent national approaches to, for example, organized crime could create obstacles to trade capable of constituting a justification for harmonization, then this would represent a kind of carte blanche for the EU penal legislator.

E. Article 325 TFEU (ex Article 280 EC)

The same reasoning as above applies perhaps to the future possibility of harmonizing the criminal law under Article 325 TFEU (ex Article 280 EC). Indeed, it should be recalled that the old Article 280 EC stipulated that although the EC's mission was to fight fraud such an agenda could not concern the Member States' national criminal law or the national administration of justice. Although this restriction has been deleted in the Lisbon Treaty, as Mitsilegas points out though, it is not clear whether the Union would have competence under Article 325 TFEU to adopt criminal laws on fraud or whether it would need to have recourse to Article 83(2) TFEU.[39]

V. Subsidiarity and Proportionality are Especially Important in Criminal Law

As noted above, the framework as provided by the Lisbon Treaty for the criminal law includes various semi opt-outs such as emergency brakes, which could be pulled if a legislative measure would appear too sensitive to fundamental aspects of a Member State. As for EU criminalization under Articles 82 and 83 TFEU, Article 69 TFEU explicitly states that national parliaments shall ensure that proposals and legislative initiatives in this area comply with the principles of subsidiarity and proportionality (compare the current Article 5 EU noted above).

In any case, the Subsidiarity and Proportionality Protocol, as annexed to the Lisbon Treaty, imposes an obligation to consult widely before proposing legislative acts.[40] It obviously remains to be seen whether this Protocol has more teeth than the Amsterdam Protocol. It goes perhaps without saying that the emphasis on subsidiarity and proportionality is particularly important in the area of criminal law. Not only does the area of criminal law and justice throw up some big ideological questions about the right to punish and national sovereignty in these matters but this is an area where (within the framework of the third pillar) there has been a lot of hasty legislation in the aftermath of 9/11 and other terrorist attacks. Moreover, it is submitted that the subsidiarity and proportionality principles should be reflected in the criminal law as an *ultima ratio* in order to avoid excessive legislation. Indeed, though 'impact assessments' and any other evaluation exercises are steps in the right direction towards a more sophisticated attitude to EU

---

[38] Case C-58/08 *Vodafone* judgment of 8 June 2010.
[39] Mitsilegas, *EU Criminal Law* (Hart Publishing, 2009) chapter 2.
[40] Protocol on the Application of the Principles of Subsidiarity and Proportionality, Article 2.

legislation,[41] it does not help much if their outcomes are not sufficiently well explained or analysed. It is of course true that for the emergence of a European criminal legal space, the protection of the individual should be at the top of the agenda insofar as the issue concerns where such legislation is best undertaken. The point is that over-criminalization is far from effective and therefore turns the traditional efficiency test in the EU upside down.

However, this does not mean that the monitoring process in the national parliaments will automatically solve the issue of criminalization. Moreover, the national parliaments are not granted direct access to the Court in the protocol to the Lisbon Treaty which could be questioned. In any event, it has been suggested that the practical usefulness of such a monitoring system by the national parliaments is far from clear,[42] as many national parliaments are likely to adopt the position adopted by the Member State in Council.[43]

A. Will the national parliaments' participation increase penal populism?

The present subheading is intended to raise eyebrows. After all, an often stated argument by proponents for action at the EU level, in relation to justice and home affairs issues, is the fact that the citizens of Europe want the EU to be more actively involved in criminal law matters and, in particular, to fight terrorism. It is true that public support in the EU is an important component in the art of enhancing approval for the Union project. It should nevertheless be emphasized that the legitimacy of criminal law legislation requires much more than just public opinion.[44] Expressed differently, there are some fundamental rights and some crucial axioms in criminal law theory such as, in short, the imperative of legality and the right to fair trial which are absolute rights and hence not negotiable. Looking at criminal law in the national arena, history tells us that the public often tends to be in favour of a more severe criminal law system (the tough-on-crime argument) despite the fact that further legislation does not always reflect the effectiveness of a system. Sound empirical research plays an important function here. But, as is well known in criminal law policy, discussion is important in moving beyond mere opinion polling.[45] In other words, any empirical research needs to be very carefully

---

[41] The AFSJ represents a new step in this direction. See eg the Stockholm programme, 'The Stockholm Programme—An Open and Secure Europe Serving and Protecting the Citizen' (Council of the European Union Brussels, 2 December 2009). A Meuwese, *Impact Assessment in EU Lawmaking* (Kluwer Law, 2008) 126–9.

[42] G Davies, 'The Post-Laeken Division of Competences' (2003) 28 *EL Rev* 686, S Weatherill, 'Competence and Legitimacy' in C Barnard and O Odudo (eds), *The Outer Limits of EU Law* (Hart Publishing, 2009) 1.

[43] Eg K Auel, 'Democratic Accountability and National Parliaments: Redefining the Impact of Parliamentary Scrutiny in EU Affairs' (2007) 13 *ELJ* 487.

[44] I discuss this is in 'Subsidiarity in the Area of EU Justice and Home Affairs—A Lost Cause?' (2009) 15 *ELJ* 351.

[45] M Nolan, 'Law Reform, beyond Mere Opinion Polling and Penal Populism' in A Norrie et al (eds), *Regulating Device* (Hart Publishing, 2009) 165.

examined and collected, as it is equally well known that empirical data can be easily manipulated.[46]

VI. Concluding Remarks: EU Criminal Law Relocated

In this chapter, I have given an account of the competence structure of EU criminal law as provided by the Lisbon Treaty. In doing so, I have focused on the fundamental provisions of Articles 82 and 83 TFEU and discussed the scope for harmonization here. Specifically, the chapter discussed the 'effectiveness' criteria as developed in Case C-176/03, *Commission v Council* and to what extent it could be translated to the regime as provided by the Lisbon Treaty. Moreover, I looked at the emergency brake provisions and pointed out that such a brake appears ambiguous in practice since remaining Member States can move on in any case by establishing enhanced cooperation in this area.

The chapter proceeded to look at the relationship between Chapter 1 and Chapter 4 and stressed that such a demarcation is important since there is no emergency brake opportunity under Chapter 1. In this context, I also addressed to what extent Article 83 TFEU constitutes an 'exclusive' *lex specialis*. The conclusion here was that it is far from clear as to what extent the Union legislator can rely on its usual allies in this area, namely Article 114 TFEU or Article 325 TFEU. Finally, the chapter looked at the principles of subsidiarity and proportionality and stressed the importance of paying attention to these provisions, albeit adopting a realistic view and expectation as regards the function of national parliaments in this area.

In conclusion, the Lisbon Treaty provides for rather neatly laid down competences (or at least *more* neatly laid down as compared to the pre-Lisbon era) but still leaves plenty of uncertainty as regards the exact meaning of harmonization 'when necessary for the effective implementation of a Union policy' as well as the possibilities of harmonizing outside Article 83 TFEU. Yet the problem is that inadequate attention is paid to the question of just why there really should be a 'common' criminal law at the EU level at all, and how far this may damage national traditions. It is to be hoped that adequate attention and better monitoring of subsidiarity and proportionality as well as a realistic understanding of *effectiveness* as a very ambiguous concept—which should not be read as equivalent to EU legislation *for its own sake*—will provide a more sophisticated approach to the emerging phenomenon of EU criminal law and the establishment (and management) of an AFSJ.

---

[46] Ibid 165.

17

Writing Straight with Crooked Lines: Competition Policy and Services of General Economic Interest in the Treaty of Lisbon

José Luis Buendia Sierra

I. Introduction

On 13 December 2007, the representatives of the 27 Member States signed in Lisbon the Treaty amending the Treaty on European Union (the EU Treaty) and the Treaty establishing the European Community (the EC Treaty), which—following various adventures and misadventures—finally came into force on 1 December 2009.

The Treaty of Lisbon replaces the Draft Constitutional Treaty (aborted after the setback of the referendums in France and the Netherlands). Its purpose is to lay the foundations for the improved functioning of an enlarged European Union. To this end, the Treaty essentially modifies the institutional structure of the Union, which takes over from the Community as the only entity with legal personality.

The Treaty of Lisbon also contains substantial amendments to certain Community areas and policies, including competition policy and the regulation of Services of General Economic Interest (SGEIs).

This chapter will analyse the impact of the Treaty amendments as regards competition and SGEIs. While the changes in these areas may seem at first sight to have a limited scope, they have been the subject of spirited debate among specialists and even the general public.

It should not be forgotten that prior to the Treaty of Lisbon, the competition rules, unlike the other treaty provisions, had remained practically unchanged since the signature of the founding Treaties. Similarly, the SGEIs, despite being a constant subject for debate in the most recent Intergovernmental Conferences (IGCs), had not been significantly altered either, having experienced merely cosmetic changes of no legal importance. Thus, unlike those active in other areas of EU law, competition law specialists are not at all used to changes in primary law. Some of them—coming from other disciplines or other geographical areas—are not very familiar with the overall architecture of EU law, their knowledge being largely restricted to the competition rules, a fact which may explain in part some of the contradictory reactions to the changes introduced by the Treaty of Lisbon.

Given the above, the question that arises is whether the Treaty of Lisbon is more of the same or, by contrast, whether it will be a landmark in the evolution of EU law in these areas. To answer this question it is necessary to distinguish the appearance from the substance, and to separate purely legal analysis from considerations of a political nature that are capable of distorting the debate. The objective of this chapter is, therefore, to shed some light on the true legal scope, and the likely impact, of the reforms affecting competition law contained in the Treaty of Lisbon.

II. The Competition Rules in the Treaty of Lisbon

A. The substantive provisions remain substantially unchanged

The first point that must be made is that the substantive provisions of the Treaty with regard to competition policy (former Articles 81, 82, 86, 87 and 88 EC; now Articles 101, 102, 106, 107 and 108 TFEU) have remained largely unchanged.

Indeed, almost all of the limited changes to these provisions are of a purely formal or terminological nature.[1] In fact, there are only two minor substantive changes, which concern the compatibility of state aid aimed at the development of certain territories. The first is the introduction into Article 107(2)(c) TFEU of a review clause for a possible removal of the special treatment of the regions affected by the former division of Germany. The second is the addition of ultra-peripheral regions which are automatically eligible for regional aid under Article 107(3)(a) TFEU. This means that, unlike all other regions in the EU, the ultra-peripheral regions mentioned in Article 349 TFEU will automatically benefit from the particularly flexible status afforded to them by Article 107(3)(a) TFEU, irrespective of their actual level of economic development. This is great news for those regions but probably does not amount to a revolution in the EU state aid system.

The Treaty of Lisbon has also formally recognized the power of the Commission to adopt Block Exemption Regulations in both the antitrust area (Article 105(3) TFEU)[2] and as regards the application of the state aid rules (Article 108(4) TFEU).[3] However, this power only applies to the categories previously defined by the Council as eligible for block exemption. This means that these new rules are just a codification of the

---

[1] The expression 'common market' has systematically been replaced by 'internal market'; the references to 'this Treaty' in the former EC Treaty have been replaced by 'the Treaties' in order to cover both the TEU and the TFEU; and cross references to other provisions have been modified to take into account the new numbering.

[2] Article 105(3) TFEU: 'The Commission may adopt regulations relating to the categories of agreement in respect to which the Council has adopted a regulation or a directive pursuant to Article 103(2)(b).'

[3] Article 108(4) TFEU: 'The Commission may adopt regulations relating to the categories of State aid that the Council has, pursuant to Article 109, determined may be exempted from the procedure provided for by paragraph 3 of this article.'

previous institutional modus operandi for Block Exemption Regulations. The only change is that the source of the Commission's power is now directly the Treaty rather than a delegation established by a legislative act of the Council. This may have the consequence of avoiding the application of the new 'comitology' system foreseen in Article 290 TFEU. In any case, it is clear that, in essence, the Treaty of Lisbon has not changed the system for adopting such Block Exemption Regulations.

In short, there has been no meaningful change to the rules that antitrust or state aid practitioners normally applied on a day-to-day basis. If it were not for the new renumbering of the Articles, perhaps most competition practitioners would not have noticed that there had been a change of Treaty.

B. Renumbering of the Articles

Indeed, if there is a change that nobody in contact with EU law has failed to notice, it is the new name for the EC Treaty (which is now the TFEU) and, above all, the 're-renumbering' of the Articles. Thus, former Articles 81, 82, 86, 87 and 88 EC (originally Articles 85, 86, 92 and 93 of the Treaty of Rome) are now Articles 101, 102, 106, 107 and 108 TFEU.

My, purely personal, point of view is that these successive renumbering exercises were rather unnecessary from a practical point of view and have created a degree of confusion. The reasons for this change are allegedly linked to the desire to increase the transparency and accessibility of EU Treaties for the general public. It is, however, far from clear that the general public would even notice the alleged improvement. What is beyond any doubt is that this change has complicated matters for those regularly in contact with EU law. Thus, quoting a judgment or finding the case law related to an Article after so many changes has become a more complicated exercise for practitioners.

Apart from such practical inconveniences, which in the end are hardly dramatic, one has the feeling that these changes also convey a sense of instability as regards even the most important rules of the EU legal order. This seems regrettable to me at a time when most citizens look to the EU institutions for stability and solutions in an unstable world. National legislatures normally do not change the numbering of the Articles of their Constitutions or important laws like Civil Codes every time that there is a reform—for good reason. It would perhaps have been better if the High Contracting Parties had shown a similar respect for the provisions of the Treaty of Rome, in existence for more than 50 years. It can only be hoped that the next IGC does not do the same thing.

In any event, it is obvious that merely changing the Articles' numbering is unlikely to have any legal or practical impact on competition policy. As regards the substantive content of Articles 101, 102, 106, 107 and 108 TFEU, if this remains the same, at first sight it could be thought that competition law has been unaffected by the Treaty of Lisbon. However, it would be hasty—and probably wrong—to reach this conclusion.

C. Alleged changes with respect to 'principles'

Indeed, there is an allegedly important change in the part of the Treaties which sets out the 'principles' according to which the EU is supposed to operate, namely the fact that competition is not included among the objectives of the EU. Paradoxically, while this has been seen by some as a very dangerous development for competition policy,[4] others deny that there has been a change at all.[5] Such a divergence of opinion requires further examination.[6]

Most practitioners may have a tendency to underestimate the legal impact of solemn declarations of principles at the beginning of legal instruments, considering these as mere statements of good intentions with little—if any—practical relevance. For these lawyers, such principles are mere rhetorical exercises, the only important provisions being the substantive ones, the ones translating into the positive legal order the practical consequences of the former. Conversely, academics—due to the speculative nature of their work—may be more inclined to attach greater importance to declarations of principles. After all, these add another dimension to the debate about the meaning of the substantive provisions.

In my opinion, the provisions that set out objectives are more likely to have a practical impact in EU law than in other legal systems. This is due to the evolving nature of EU law, the fact that it is a relatively 'young' system, and also the influence of case law in its application. This means that, at least in theory, a change in the objectives could indirectly—through its influence on the judiciary—end up affecting the substance of EU law in the medium term.

A different question is whether the change at stake here is likely to have an impact and, if so, what kind.

(i) Objectives and means in the EC Treaty

In order to answer these questions, it is necessary to look first at the way the general provisions on the objectives of the Union interacted with the competition provisions before the entry into force of the Treaty of Lisbon.

Contrary to popular belief, competition policy was not included as one of the Community's objectives in the text of the EC Treaty, but rather as one of the means of achieving such objectives. This is crystal clear if one reads the Preamble to the EC Treaty, written in 1957 and still in force as the Preamble of the TFEU:

---

[4] Nicolas Petit, 'Traité de Lisbonne et politique de concurrence—Rupture?' *Revue de la Faculté de Droit de l'Université de Liège* 2008, 2, 265–79; A Riley, 'The EU Reform Treaty and the Competition Protocol: Undermining EC Competition Law' *CEPS Policy Briefs*, September 2007.

[5] Michel Petite, 'La place du droit de la concurrence dans le future ordre juridique communautaire' *Concurrences* I-2008. Jean-Claude Piris, *The Lisbon Treaty—A Legal and Political Analysis* (Cambridge University Press, 2010) 307–9.

[6] See also my previous article JL Buendia Sierra, 'Escribir derecho con renglones torcidos: Política de competencia y servicios de interés económico general en el Tratado de Lisboa' *Anuario de la Competencia* 2007, *Fundación ICO* 2008, 129–37.

DETERMINED to lay the foundations of an ever closer union among the peoples of Europe,

RESOLVED to ensure the economic and social progress of their States by common action to eliminate the barriers which divide Europe,

AFFIRMING as the essential objective of their efforts the constant improvements of the living and working conditions of their peoples,

RECOGNISING that the removal of existing obstacles calls for concerted action in order to guarantee steady expansion, balanced trade and fair competition.

According to the Preamble, then, the essential objective is the improvement of living and working conditions. This objective is to be achieved by eliminating the barriers which divide Europe and this in turn requires concerted action in order to guarantee fair competition. In other words, competition policy is a means of achieving the common market, which is an instrument for the improvement of people's living and working conditions.

The Articles of the EC Treaty told a similar story. Article 2 EC made clear that both the establishment of the common market and the policies and common actions listed in Articles 3 and 4 were the means of achieving the European Community's goals.[7]

Article 3(1)(g) EC referred to competition in the following terms: 'For the purposes set out in Article 2, the activities of the Community shall include...a system ensuring that competition in the internal market is not distorted'. So, this provision did not say that competition was an objective of the Community; competition was mentioned there rather as one of its 'activities'.

Another of the means that the European Community used to attain its objectives was the adoption of an economic policy based on an 'open market economy with free competition', as per Article 4 EC.

It is therefore clear, both from the context and from the text of the above provisions, that the competition rules were conceived in the European Community as a means of achieving the objectives of the common market.

It is true that the case law of the Court of Justice has been less clear as regards the status of competition; thus, various judgments have referred to competition as an 'objective' or even a 'fundamental objective' of the European Community.[8] On this basis, certain authors have claimed that, despite the literal wording of the Treaty, judicial interpretation had raised competition to the status of a 'fundamental objective' of the European Community.[9] According to this point of view, given the importance of case law among the sources of the EU legal system, one should

---

[7] The text of Article 2 EC was as follows: 'The Community shall have as its task, by establishing a common market and an economic and monetary union and by implementing common policies or activities referred to in Articles 3 and 4, to promote throughout the Community a harmonious, balanced and sustainable development of economic activities, a high level of employment and of social protection, equality between men and women, sustainable and non-inflationary growth, a high degree of competitiveness and convergence of economic performance, a high level of protection and improvement of the quality of the environment, the raising of the standard of living and quality of life, and economic and social cohesion and solidarity among Member States.'

[8] Case C-289/04 P *Showa Denko* [2006] Rec I-5859, para 55.

[9] Nicolas Petit, above n 4 at 271.

recognize that competition has in any event become a fundamental objective of the European Community.

(ii) Objectives and means in the Draft Constitutional Treaty

This point of view seemed to be confirmed when the Draft Constitutional Treaty tried to codify this interpretation of the case law by converting competition policy into an express objective, establishing in its Article I-3.2 that '[t]he Union shall offer its citizens an area of freedom, security and justice without internal frontiers, and an internal market where competition is free and undistorted' and defining 'the establishing of the competition rules necessary for the functioning of the internal market' as an exclusive competence of the Union in Article I-13.1.b.

As is well known, however, following the problems with ratification in certain Member States, the Draft Constitutional Treaty never entered into force.

(iii) Objectives and means after the Treaty of Lisbon

The alleged removal of competition from the objectives of the European Union arose at the last moment of the negotiations for the re-launching of the constitutional process that finally led to the Treaty of Lisbon.

In the European Council of June 2007, the French President asked for—and managed to obtain—the agreement of the Heads of State and Government, apparently not without certain resistance from some of them, to a proposal to eliminate the reference to the 'free and undistorted competition' objective contained in Article I-3.2 of the Draft Constitutional Treaty. In order to reach an agreement and to somehow compensate for the effects of this modification, it was finally decided to include in the Treaty of Lisbon a new Protocol on the internal market and competition.

The removal was a last-minute surprise to almost everybody, since the point had apparently not been previously raised or discussed at a technical level.

There was much talk at that time of an attempt to downgrade competition policy as a result of political interests, specifically because of the desire to placate part of the electorate in some Member States who view free competition with some suspicion. Thus, some have claimed that the negative result of the referendum to ratify the Constitutional Treaty in France was partly due to the French electorate's distrust of an alleged extreme liberalism of Anglo-Saxon origin, which places too much emphasis on free competition and that, we are told, is one of the reasons for the lack of protection from the threats that exist to the welfare state model.[10]

---

[10] The French Secretary of State for EU affairs recognized that the proposal was an attempt to placate the concerns of French citizens expressed in the referendum: 'Toutefois, nous devons réagir en France face aux inquiétudes de l'opinion publique telles qu'elles se sont exprimes en 2005 . . . Chez nous, l'inquiétude résulte d'un amalgame entre concurrence, financiarisation, règne des intérêts financiers. Le débat sur la concurrence est le réceptacle de toutes ces inquiétudes. C'est pour cette raison que nous avons souhaité, lors du conseil européen de juin, que la concurrence libre et non faussée ne figure pas dans les objectifs du traité mais soit un instrument de fonctionnement du marché

Apparently, the only practical objection to the change was the risk that removing competition from the Treaty objectives would prevent the use of Article 352 TFEU as a legal basis for future modifications of the Merger Regulation. Article 352 TFEU can only be used to adopt measures not expressly provided for in the Treaty but that are nevertheless necessary to achieve the objectives of the Treaty; it is on the assumption that competition was an essential Treaty objective that the merger control system was adopted on the basis of this Article. However, the reforms introduced by the Treaty of Lisbon suggested that, due to concerns about subsidiarity, the future use of Article 352 TFEU would be much more difficult and strictly confined to measures that were indispensable for the EU to fulfil its tasks.[11]

Their fears were allayed through the argument that competition policy was an essential element of the internal market and that the establishment of the internal market remains an essential EU objective.[12] Accordingly, Article 352 TFEU could be used in the future to adopt legislation concerning competition. This legal reasoning was included in a Protocol on the Internal Market and Competition which was then annexed to the Treaty and whose text is as follows:

> The High Contracting Parties,
> considering that the internal market as set out in Article 2 of the Treaty on European Union includes a system ensuring that competition is not distorted,
> HAVE AGREED that:
> to this end, the Union shall, if necessary, take action under the provisions of the Treaties, including under Article 308 of the Treaty on the Functioning of the European Union. This protocol shall be annexed to the Treaty on European Union and to the Treaty on the Functioning of the European Union.

It is worth remembering that, pursuant to Article 51 of the EU Treaty, the Protocols enjoy the same legal status as the Treaties themselves.

Immediately after it was agreed to remove competition from the EU objectives, European newspapers were full of headlines referring to the 'downgrading' of

---

intérieur.' Jean-Pierre Jouyet, Colloque 'La place du droit de la concurrence dans le futur ordre juridique communautaire, Bruxelles, 8 novembre 2007' *Concurrences* no 1–2008, 9. One can imagine that the other Heads of State and Government approached the issue in a pragmatic way, considering that the requested change would be a mere political gesture without any practical implications. They probably thought that if it would help persuade French citizens to support the Treaty, it was probably worthwhile. After all, 'Paris vaut bien une messe'.

[11] Declaration no 42, concerning Article 308 of the Treaty of Lisbon (Article 352 TFEU in the consolidated version of the text): 'The Conference underlines that, in accordance with the settled case law of the Court of Justice of the European Union, Article 308 of the Treaty on the Functioning of the European Union, being an integral part of an institutional system based on the principle of conferred powers, cannot serve as a basis for widening the scope of Union powers beyond the general framework created by the provisions of the Treaties as a whole and, in particular, by those that define the tasks and the activities of the Union. In any event, this Article cannot be used as a basis for the adoption of provisions whose effect would, in substance, be to amend the Treaties without following the procedure which they provide for that purpose.' Paradoxically, and despite this declaration, the fact that the list of objectives of the EU has been substantially increased should rather facilitate the future use of the mechanism of Article 352 TFEU. It seems indeed difficult to think of any measure that could not be attached to at least one of the objectives now listed in Article 3 EU.

[12] Jean-Claude Piris, above n 5 at 308.

competition policy and reporting on the concern voiced by specialists and those entrusted with its application.[13] However, once it was clear that the modification was a fait accompli and the details became known, media interest diminished considerably.

Naturally, the French authorities claimed victory once the decision was taken. It seems very clear that, from a political point of view, they got what they wanted. It is less clear whether this was instrumental in calming the fears allegedly expressed by some French citizens in the referendum. And it is even harder to judge whether such fears ever had any objective link to the existence of Article 3(1)(g) EC. One may doubt it. In any event, this is not for lawyers to decide, but rather for sociologists or even anthropologists.

What we can do here is try to understand what may be the impact—if any—of such modifications from a legal point of view. Could it be a case of 'much ado about nothing'?

In order to answer this question, we will now examine precisely what the Treaty of Lisbon specifically contributes, compared to its predecessors.

The first point that must be made is that, as previously explained, the substantive provisions of the Treaty with regard to competition policy (Articles 101, 102, 106, 107 and 108 TFEU) have remained largely unchanged.

It is true that in the wording of the Treaties, as rearranged by the Treaty of Lisbon (EU Treaty plus TFEU plus Protocols), competition policy is not expressly mentioned in the statement of objectives of the European Community that are now contained in Article 3 of the EU Treaty. However, the establishment of the internal market does come within this objective (Article 3(3) of the EU Treaty)[14] and, in accordance with the contents of the Protocol on the Internal Market and Competition annexed to the Treaty, 'the internal market as set out in Article 3 of the Treaty on European Union includes a system ensuring that competition is not distorted'.

In addition, according to new Article 3(6) of the EU Treaty '[t]he Union shall pursue its objectives by appropriate means commensurate with the competences which are conferred upon it in the Treaties', and in this regard, according to Article 3(1)(b)TFEU 'the establishing of the competition rules necessary for the functioning of the internal market' is defined as an exclusive competence of the Union.

The architecture of the Treaties has varied in such a way that considering a competence as 'exclusive' has now become particularly important. The reason is that the acts carried out in execution of exclusive EU competences would not be subject to the mechanism of control that the national parliaments now have on the basis of the principle of subsidiarity.[15] Legally speaking, then, competition policy would remain, as before, outside the scope of subsidiarity.

---

[13] See, inter alia, *International Business Times*, 23 June 2007, 'Sarkozy Toasts Competition Snip in Treaty'; *Financial Times*, 24 June 2007, 'Kroes to Hold Tough Line on Competition'.

[14] 'The Union shall establish an internal market. It shall work for the sustainable development of Europe based on balanced economic growth and price stability, a highly competitive social market economy, aiming at full employment and social progress, and a high level of protection and improvement of the quality of the environment. It shall promote scientific and technological advance.'

[15] See the Protocol on the Application of the Principles of Subsidiarity and Proportionality.

Finally, the reference to an economic policy based on the 'principle of an open market economy with free competition' remains, although it has been moved from Article 4 of the EC Treaty, in the 'principles' section, to Article 119 TFEU, which forms part of the section on Economic Policy.

(iv) A downgrading of competition?

Can we deduce from the above provisions that there has been a 'downgrading' of the status of competition within the EU legal system?

In my view, one may only speak of 'downgrading' if competition had lost a status it previously enjoyed. Yet this does not seem to be the case here.

As with political elections, the feeling of success or failure is linked to previous expectations about the results. It is true that the Draft Constitutional Treaty had created an expectation of 'competition' being given an even more important role than under the EC Treaty by its express recognition as an objective of the EU under Article I-3.2. It is obviously not pleasant for one's ego if an upgrading in status that has been announced subsequently fails to materialize. Accordingly, it is only because of the previous expectations created by the Draft Constitutional Treaty that the decision of the European Council of June 2007 felt like a downgrading (and even a humiliation) by the 'community' composed of competition policy academics and practitioners. However, from both a practical and legal point of view, not being upgraded is one thing, while being downgraded is quite another.

Given that the Draft Constitutional Treaty never came into force, the previous EC and TFEU Treaties provide the only appropriate point of comparison from a legal point of view. In this regard, as already noted, the role of competition is exactly the same in both treaties: competition is an instrument, a very important one, but—strictly speaking—not an objective in itself.

My view is that this is a perfectly logical approach and does not in any way detract from the importance of competition policy. I personally believe that competition is good for social progress and very important, but perhaps it is not the ideal absolute guiding principle for any legal system.[16] It should not be forgotten that even national constitutions of countries with market economies normally abstain from giving competition rules a specific status in their provisions about principles. It is far from obvious that the European Treaties, whose legal nature is different from (and does not go beyond that of) national constitutions, should be more ambitious in this respect.

The key issue is, however, whether or not the changes are likely to have any practical effect on the application of competition policy.

Some authors have argued that it was only because competition was considered as an essential Community objective that the Courts could interpret its substantive

---

[16] A society in which everything was subordinated to competition could perhaps be an interesting idea for an anti-utopian novel along the lines of George Orwell's *1984*, Aldous Huxley's *Brave New World* or Ray Bradbury's *Farenheit 458*.

provisions, like Articles 101 and 102 TFEU, in a fairly broad manner.[17] However, such an argument does not seem particularly convincing to me. Interpretations of the EU Courts may sometimes appear imaginative (at other times they may look rather timid), but this does not seem to be more so as regards competition than any other area of EU law. Moreover, EU case law on Articles 101 and 102 TFEU is probably not so different in its ambition from the US Supreme Court's interpretation of the Sherman Act. It is worth recalling in this context that the US Constitution does not even mention the word competition.

In fact, the most extreme example of a creative interpretation of the EU competition rules—the *effet utile* doctrine—was inspired by similar case law of the US Supreme Court. This doctrine was based on the combined application of then Articles 3(g), Article 10,[18] and Articles 81 and/or 82 EC and was established in 1977 by the *Inno/ATAB* case.[19] The basic reasoning was as follows: Article 10 prevented Member States from adopting measures depriving EC rules of their *effet utile*. Article 3(g) established undistorted competition as one of the main Community goals and then Articles 81 and 82 prohibited anti-competitive behaviour by undertakings. Taken together, all these provisions were interpreted by the Court of Justice as prohibiting Member States from depriving competition rules of their *effet utile* by adopting measures that would allow the undertakings to ignore the limits imposed by Articles 81 and 82 of the Treaty.[20] At one point this case law seemed to suggest that every state measure producing restrictive effects on competition would have *effects* similar to those of a cartel (or to those of an abuse of a dominant position). As a consequence, every state measure producing restrictive *effects* on competition would be contrary to Articles 3(g), 10 and 81 (or 82) of the EC Treaty, even in the absence of any behaviour by the undertaking. This would mean that every measure taken by the state having an impact on the price or the quantity of goods or services would be prohibited. Such an approach would have greatly reduced Member States' ability to intervene in the economy.

---

[17] Nicolas Petit, above n 4 at 274–7; A Riley, above n 4.

[18] The text of Article 10 EC was as follows: 'Member States shall take all appropriate measures, whether general or particular, to ensure fulfilment of the obligations arising out of this Treaty or resulting from action taken by the institutions of the Community. They shall facilitate the achievement of the Community's tasks. They shall abstain from any measure which could jeopardise the attainment of the objectives of this Treaty.' The current Article 4(3) EU reads as follows: 'Pursuant to the principle of sincere cooperation, the Union and the Member States shall, in full mutual respect, assist each other in carrying out tasks which flow from the Treaties. The Member States shall take any appropriate measure, general or particular, to ensure fulfilment of the obligations arising out of the Treaties or resulting from the acts of the institutions of the Union. The Member States shall facilitate the achievement of the Union's tasks and refrain from any measure which could jeopardise the attainment of the Union's objectives.'

[19] Case 13/77 *Inno vATAB* [1977] ECR 2144, paras 31–3.

[20] The leading cases of the Court of Justice were: Case 229/83 *Leclerc v Au Blé Vert* [1985] ECR 1; Case 231/83 *Cullet* [1985] ECR 305; Case 123/83 *BNIC v Clair* [1985] ECR 391; Joined Cases 209–213/84 *Nouvelles Frontières* [1986] ECR 1425; Case 311/85 *Vlaamse Reisbureaus* [1987] ECR 3801; Case 267/86 *Van Eycke* [1988] ECR 4769. For some of the literature on the subject see F Castillo de la Torre, 'State Action Doctrine in EC Antitrust Law' (2005) 28 *Word Competition* 407–31; JL Buendia Sierra, *Exclusive Rights and State Monopolies under EC Law* (Oxford University Press, 1999) 261–7.

Although the theoretical implications of this doctrine could have been far-reaching, its practical impact has been much more limited. The reasons are twofold. First of all, the Court of Justice subsequently interpreted the concept of *effet utile* in a very restrictive way. According to this more restrictive approach, which originated in 1993 with the *Meng, Reiff* and *Ohra* cases, a mere anti-competitive effect could not, in the absence of *behaviour* of undertakings, mean that the state measure was contrary to then Articles 3(g), 10 and 81 or 82 of the EC Treaty.[21] Only those state measures that impose or induce anti-competitive behaviour by undertakings, reinforce the effects of anti-competitive behaviour or delegate regulatory powers to private operators can be considered to violate these provisions. This very strict test dramatically reduced the scope of Articles 3(g), 10 and 81/82 as regards anti-competitive state measures.[22]

Moreover, in my view this case law on Articles 3(g), 10 and 81/82 of the EC Treaty never provided significant added value to EC law. The reason is that EU/EC competition law, contrary to many other competition law systems (such as US antitrust), has always had specific provisions dealing with the most significant anti-competitive state measures, such as state aid or exclusive rights. The need for 'creative' case law was therefore much less marked and its re-definition in a restrictive way has meant that, in practice, its impact has been very limited.[23]

In theory, it could be argued that the removal of Article 3(1)(g) EC by the Treaty of Lisbon has now put a definitive end to this case law (to the extent that it still exists after the 1993 judgments). I am not so sure. Indeed, according to the tables of equivalences,[24] which are legally binding, former Article 3(1) EC has not disappeared; rather it has been replaced, in substance, by Articles 3–6 TFEU. So Article 3(1)(g) EC has not vanished; it has simply been transformed. One can still see its substance in Article 3(1)(b) TFEU, which defines as an exclusive EU competence 'the establishing of the competition rules necessary for the functioning of the internal market'. Moreover, the logic of the *effet utile* rule was primarily based on the combination of Article 10 EC, whose substance still exists in the new Article 4(3) EU, with the obligations contained in Articles 101 and 102 TFEU, which have not been modified. Article 3(1)(g) EC was just a kind of *toile de fond*, reinforcing the reasoning. For this reason some of the *effet utile* judgments did not even mention it.

Accordingly, the possibility of the EU Courts applying today the *effet utile* case law does not seem to be affected by the Treaty of Lisbon. One may like or dislike the current precarious state of health of this case law and its practical irrelevance, but it is hard to say that this has caused noticeable problems for the functioning of

---

[21] Case C-2/91 *Meng* [1993] ECR I-5797, para 14; Case C-185/91 *Reiff* [1993] ECR I-5847, para 14; and Case C-245/91 *Ohra* [1993] ECR I-5878, para 10. This case law has been largely confirmed in many subsequent judgments, such as: Case C-35/99 *Arduino* [2002] ECR I-1529; Case C-309/99 *Wouters* [2002] ECR I-1577; and Case C-198/01 *CIF* [2003] ECR I-8055.

[22] N Reich, 'The "November Revolution" of the European Court of Justice: Keck, Meng and Audi revisited' (1994) 21 *CML Rev* 459–62; B Van Der Esch, 'Loyauté fédérale et subsidiarité: à propos des arrêts du 17 novembre 1993 dans les affaires Meng, Ohra et Reiff' (1994) *CDE* 536; A Bach, 'Judgments of the Court, cases Reiff, Meng and Ohra' (1994) *CML Rev* 1357–74.

[23] JL Buendia Sierra, above n 20 at 261–7.

[24] OJ C 115/361 of 9 May 2008.

EU competition law. In any event, this situation existed many years before the arrival of this Treaty and is therefore totally unrelated to the latter.

Moreover, ultimately the distinction between objective and means is not as absolute as the terms of the debate may suggest. Indeed, references to the objectives of the Treaties very often relate not to the somewhat vague objectives previously listed in Article 2 EC and now set out in Article 3 of the EU Treaty, but to the main instruments used to pursue these objectives and, above all, the establishment of the common market. We can therefore speak of 'objectives' that are strictly defined as such (*strictu sensu* or strictly speaking) that is, those mentioned in Article 3 of the EU Treaty[25] and objectives that may be interpreted as such (*latu sensu* or broadly speaking). In my view, this was the meaning of the case law which, despite the wording of the Treaties, referred to 'competition' as an important EU objective. I see no reason to consider that this case law is no longer valid after the entry into force of the Treaty of Lisbon where it is understood as referring to an objective in the second, broadly interpreted sense.

We could therefore say that, albeit indirectly—through the back door, even— competition policy has now become an objective in the wider sense as a result of its express and direct relationship with the internal market objective stated in the Protocol on the Internal Market and Competition.[26] I therefore see nothing in the Treaty of Lisbon to suggest the need to interpret Articles 101 and 102 TFEU more restrictively.

---

[25] Admittedly, the list of the said 'objectives' in Article 3 EU is quite long and its scope is not particularly strict: '1. The Union's aim is to promote peace, its values and the well-being of its peoples. 2. The Union shall offer its citizens an area of freedom, security and justice without internal frontiers, in which the free movement of persons is ensured in conjunction with appropriate measures with respect to external border controls, asylum, immigration and the prevention and combating of crime. 3. The Union shall establish an internal market. It shall work for the sustainable development of Europe based on balanced economic growth and price stability, a highly competitive social market economy, aiming at full employment and social progress, and a high level of protection and improvement of the quality of the environment. It shall promote scientific and technological advance. It shall combat social exclusion and discrimination, and shall promote social justice and protection, equality between women and men, solidarity between generations and protection of the rights of the child. It shall promote economic, social and territorial cohesion, and solidarity among Member States. It shall respect its rich cultural and linguistic diversity, and shall ensure that Europe's cultural heritage is safeguarded and enhanced. 4. The Union shall establish an economic and monetary union whose currency is the euro. 5. In its relations with the wider world, the Union shall uphold and promote its values and interests and contribute to the protection of its citizens. It shall contribute to peace, security, the sustainable development of the Earth, solidarity and mutual respect among peoples, free and fair trade, eradication of poverty and the protection of human rights, in particular the rights of the child, as well as to the strict observance and the development of international law, including respect for the principles of the United Nations Charter. 6. The Union shall pursue its objectives by appropriate means commensurate with the competences which are conferred upon it in the Treaties.'

[26] See also the opinions of Michel Waelbroeck and Michel Petite in the round table meeting, 'Quel sera l'impact du noveau traité sur le droit de la concurrence? Regards juridiques' whose content was published in 'La place du droit de la concurrence dans le futur ordre juridique communautaire, Colloque, Bruxelles, 8 novembre 2007' *Concurrences* no 1–2008, 9.

(v) A useful reminder: the close link between the internal market and competition

It follows from the above that the Treaty of Lisbon has neither downgraded the status nor amended the substance of the EU competition rules. This does not mean that it would not affect the evolution of EU competition law in other ways. The really interesting contribution of the Treaty of Lisbon to competition policy is not a change but—paradoxically—a reminder of what EU competition law was always supposed to be: a means of achieving market integration. As we will see, this return to the original sources—*resourcement*—was an unexpected but welcome surprise, since this timely restatement of the focus of EU competition law can only strengthen it.

Of course, the fact that EU competition law is a means of achieving market integration is a well-known fact. After all, from the outset the competition provisions were part of a treaty in which virtually every provision was oriented towards the establishment of a common market. It is not for nothing that for many years the Community was popularly known as 'the Common Market'. If the Treaty of Rome (and before it, the Treaty of Paris creating the ECSC) included competition rules at all it was only because they were seen as a means of integrating the markets. It is therefore not surprising that the market integration goal was for many years an essential and universally accepted element of EU competition policy.[27]

This situation has been subjected to criticism from the 1980s to the present day due to the increasing influence of American antitrust thinking, strongly influenced by the Chicago School, for whom the only acceptable objective of antitrust law is efficiency. The use of antitrust law as a market integration tool in Europe was viewed as an anomaly, hopefully a transitory one.[28] These criticisms led to a fundamental self-questioning of EU competition law and an in-depth review of policies, for example as regards vertical restraints or abuses of dominance.[29]

The situation today is that, despite these changes, the European institutions still state regularly that market integration remains an objective of EU competition policy, but the supporters of the 'more economic approach' keep insisting that

---

[27] The ECJ made this clear in Case 26/76 *Metro v Commission* [1977] ECR 1875, para 20: '[t]he requirement contained in Articles 3 and 85 of the EEC Treaty that competition shall not be distorted implies the existence on the market of workable competition, that is to say the degree of competition necessary to ensure the observance of the basic requirements and the attainment of the objectives of the Treaty, in particular the creation of a single market achieving conditions similar to those of a domestic market'. See also, among others, CD Ehlermann, 'The Contribution of EC Competition Policy to the Single Market' (1992) 29 *CMLRev* 257.

[28] See V Korah, *An Introductory Guide to EC Competition Law and Practice*, 8th edn (Hart Publishing, 2004) 12: 'Competition in the common market is also intended to further market integration, an overriding aim *considered by some* to be more important than efficiency.... *It may be surprising that many officials still give such priority to this objective 44 years after the Treaty came into force*' (emphasis added).

[29] The shift of approach is explicit in the 1999 Commission's White Paper on modernization of the rules implementing Articles 81 and 82 of the EC Treaty, OJ C132/1 (1999), which acknowledged that '[a]t the beginning the focus [of the Commission's] activity was on establishing rules on restrictions interfering directly with the goal of market integration...The Commission has now come to concentrate more on ensuring effective competition by detecting and stopping cross-border cartels and maintaining competitive market structures'.

efficiency considerations must prevail over the 'sacred cow' of market integration. The treatment of restrictions on parallel trade is one of the areas where the battle is being fought.[30]

In this context, the solemn restatement contained in the Treaty of Lisbon that free competition is part and parcel of the internal market seems enormously important. Indeed, the High Contracting Parties have just reminded us of the following:

- The Preamble of the TFEU makes a clear connection between both elements: 'the removal of existing obstacles calls for concerted action in order to guarantee ... fair competition.'
- Article 3(3) of the EU Treaty considers that the establishment of the internal market is an EU objective: 'The Union shall establish an internal market.'
- The Protocol on the Internal Market and Competition provides that 'the internal market ... includes a system ensuring that competition is not distorted.'
- Last but not least, Article 3(1)(b) TFEU states that the Union has an exclusive competence for 'the establishing of the competition rules necessary for the functioning of the internal market'.

The last point is particularly important, since in the EU legal system the European institutions only have the powers that have been attributed to them by the Treaties. It is therefore essential to note that the European institutions' competence in the area of competition is not a general one, but only relates to the competition rules that are 'necessary for the functioning of the internal market'.

In my view, this reference clearly goes beyond a mere rule for the allocation of competences between the EU and Member States. This rule not only reserves a competence but gives a basic clear indication as to how this competence must be exercised. It seems quite obvious, for instance, that an interpretation allowing a dominant undertaking to block parallel trade could hardly be construed as 'necessary for the functioning of the internal market'.[31]

Given the above, after the Treaty of Lisbon it is very difficult to claim that internal market considerations are irrelevant or subordinated to efficiency considerations, since they are clearly the basis of the EU's competence from a legal point of view. Undermining the role of market integration in EU competition law would mean undermining the EU's competence in this regard.

---

[30] See the Opinion of AG Jacobs, Case C-53/03 *Syfait* [2005] ECR I-4609 and the Opinion of AG Ruiz Jarabo, Joined Cases C-468–478/06 *Lélos* [2008] ECR I-7139. In my view, the example of parallel trade shows that the opposition between efficiency and internal market is rather artificial in many cases. The elimination of the competition provided by parallel trade not only creates an artificial barrier between the internal market, but also reduces both total welfare and consumer welfare.

[31] On parallel trade see Joined Cases C-501/06 P, C-513/06 P, C-515/06 P and C-519/06 P *Glaxo Spain* [2009] ECR I-9291; Case C-53/03 *Syfait* [2005] ECR I-4609, and Joined Cases C-468–478/06, *Lélos* [2008] ECR I-7139.

Attention will have to be paid to the possible consequences of this in the future action of the Commission and the EU Courts.[32] Nevertheless, it seems clear that everyday application of the EU competition rules must take into account the fact that market integration is not ancillary to but the *raison d'être* of the existence of these rules in the EU Treaties.

This reminder of the close links between competition and the internal market could also play an important role in the area of state aid. The original main function of EU state aid was closely related to the removal of barriers in the internal market, the basic objective being to limit competition between Member States in attracting and keeping investment in their territories. In this context, the Commission and the Member States were the actors, with undertakings playing only an ancillary role.

This situation changed (at least in theory) following the modernization of state aid policy advocated by the Commission in the state aid action plan (2005).[33] After the plan, the focus moved to competition between undertakings as the alleged main objective of state aid control. As in the antitrust area, the influence of a so-called 'refined economic approach' was also felt and 'efficiency' allegedly became the key objective of state aid policy. Internal market considerations were also discreetly relegated to a lower rank.[34]

In my opinion, the impact of the financial crisis has made clear to everybody that state aid control is, above all, an indispensable element of the internal market and that its main function is to limit subsidy races between Member States. Although the rhetoric may suggest otherwise, the truth is that competition between undertakings plays only a secondary role in this area.

In this context, the timely 'reminder' introduced by the Treaty of Lisbon is also very relevant for state aid policy. The EU competence in the area of competition, and therefore also in state aid, only exists to the extent that this control is 'necessary for the functioning of the internal market'. This means that the main role of the EU in this area is not to ensure that subsidies are aimed at efficiency-enhancing objectives (this is for each Member State to decide), but rather to prevent their negative side effects from damaging the internal market.

I am not sure whether this was the objective of those that initially planned the above modifications, but it seems clear to me that, from a legal point of view, competition policy, including both antitrust and state aid policy, has not been negatively affected by the Treaty of Lisbon: in fact, quite the reverse is true.[35]

---

[32] Nicolas Petit seems to share my view on the likely impact of this change on EU competition policy. However, contrary to me, he seems to fear this as a negative development; Nicolas Petit, above n 4 at 272–3.

[33] State Aid Action Plan—Less and better Targeted State Aid: a Roadmap for state aid reform 2005–2009 (Consultation document) {SEC(2005) 795}/COM/2005/0107 final/.

[34] For a critical analysis of these changes see: JL Buendia Sierra and B Smulders, 'The Limited Role of the "Refined Economic Approach" in Achieving the Objectives of State Aid Control: Time for Some Realism' in *EC State Aid Law: Liber Amicorum Francisco Santaolalla* (Kluwer Law International, 2008) chapter 1.

[35] Apart from the strictly legal point of view, and from a more formal perspective, not only has competition not disappeared from the Treaty of Lisbon, as some have claimed, but the word 'competition' appears in the Preamble, in Articles I-3, I-32 (twice), I-40, I-42, I-44, I-96 (twice),

III. Services of General Economic Interest in the Treaty of Lisbon

Having reached this point, we will now turn our attention to a different but closely related subject, that of Services of General Economic Interest (SGEIs).

The application of the EU rules—in particular those regarding state aid, public procurement and the freedom to provide services and establishment—to SGEIs has always been a politically sensitive matter. For instance, the debate about the legal regime for financing SGEIs is a thorny political issue among certain groups and in certain Member States. Thus, there are those who argue that EU law and practice in this area is biased against SGEIs and needs to be re-balanced.[36] For this reason, they have passionately advocated a radical reform of the treaty architecture. By contrast, others consider that the treatment of SGEIs in EU law is fair and balanced and that amending the primary law in this area would be totally unjustified.[37]

This issue could therefore be described as an area of friction between two tectonic plates, and it became a regular subject for discussion within the successive IGCs on the amendment of the Treaties, in which the position of certain Member States in this regard provided a good example of perseverance.

Thus, certain Member States expressed their concern about the alleged imbalance that they claim existed between Article 86(1) EC (now Article 106(1) TFEU), on the granting of special or exclusive rights, and the regulation of state aid contained in Article 87 EC (now Article 107 TFEU), an imbalance whose effect was allegedly the insufficient nature of the exception contained in Article 86(2) EC (now Article 106(2) TFEU) in a context in which the Commission played a central part and acted with notable independence from Member States. For this reason, these Member States sought to strengthen the protection given to those providing SGEIs with respect to the application of the state aid rules, a proposal that never found any real support from other Member States.

Initially, the Treaty of Amsterdam introduced Article 16 of the EC Treaty (corresponding to current Article 14 TFEU), a declaration of intent that did not involve any significant change, since it reiterated what was already provided for in Article 86(2) EC (now Article 106(2) TFEU). The original Article 16 stated as follows:

[W]ithout prejudice to Articles 73, 86 and 87, and given the place occupied by services of general economic interest in the shared values of the Union as well as their role in promoting social and territorial cohesion, the Community and the Member States, each within their respective powers and within the scope of application of this Treaty, shall take care that such services operate on the basis of principles and conditions which enable them to fulfil their missions.

I-101 (three times), I-102, I-106, II-107 (twice), II-113, II-116, 119 (twice), 120, 127, 173, 326, 346, 348 and in the Protocol on the Internal Market and Competition.

[36] Christian Stoffaës, *L'Europe de l'intérêt général* (ASPEurope, 1995).
[37] JL Buendia Sierra, above n 34 at chapter 10, 221–2.

The debate on the relationship between EU law and SGEIs was also affected by the evolution of the case law and in particular by the 2003 *Altmark* judgment.[38] Following this judgment, the Commission returned to the fray and in 2005 adopted the post-*Altmark* package,[39] which included a block exemption for small SGEIs on the basis of Article 86(3) of the EC Treaty (now Article 106(3) TFEU). The adoption of this package by the Commission showed that the Treaties in force provided a sufficient legal basis from which to clarify the rules concerning SGEIs.[40]

On the other side of the debate, the supporters of a treaty modification in this area, while avoiding an open debate on the issue, managed to slip in a modification of Article 16 EC, strangely tabled at the very last minute of the works on the European Convention.[41] The change was introduced in Article III-122 of the Draft Constitutional Treaty and provided an additional legal basis for establishing principles and conditions for the provision of SGEIs.[42]

This provision was one of the casualties when the Draft Constitutional Treaty was rejected by French and Dutch voters. However, after the signature of the Treaty of Lisbon, the content of Article III-122 of the Draft Constitutional Treaty (former Article 16 EC) was recycled into what is now Article 14 TFEU. Accordingly, Article 14 TFEU now goes beyond the rather rhetorical formulation of former Article 16 EC by including a new legal basis. The text of the provision is as follows (italics indicate the changes made compared to the wording of the EC Treaty):

[W]ithout prejudice to *Article 4 of the Treaty on European Union or to* Articles 93, 106 and 107 of this Treaty, and given the place occupied by services of general economic interest in the shared values of the Union as well as their role in promoting social and territorial

---

[38] This judgment clarifies the conditions under which financial compensation granted to the operator of a SGEI is not a state aid. The said conditions are rather strict. See Case C-280/00 *Altmark* [2003] ECR I-7747.

[39] Decision 2005/842/EC on the application of Article 86(2) of the EC Treaty to State aid in the form of public service compensation granted to certain undertakings entrusted with the operation of services of general economic interest, OJ L312 [2005] 67–73; Community framework for State aid in the form of public service compensation, OJ C294 [2005] 4–7; Directive 2005/81/EC amending Directive 80/723/EEC on the transparency of financial relationships between Member States and public undertakings as well as on financial transparency within certain undertakings, OJ L312 [2005] 47–8.

[40] JL Buendia Sierra, above n 34 at chapter 10, 221–2.

[41] See the minutes of the penultimate plenary session of the European Convention held in Brussels on 4 July 2003, CONV 849/03, according to which the initiative for the adoption of this provision came from the Praesidium of the Convention. In the last session, certain members of the Convention manifested their disagreement with the introduction of this amendment, on the basis that it was not of a technical nature. See the minutes of the last plenary session of the European Convention held in Brussels on 9 and 10 July 2003, CONV 853/03.

[42] 'Without prejudice to Articles I-5, III-166, III-167 and III-238, and given the place occupied by services of general economic interest as services to which all in the Union attribute value as well as their role in promoting its social and territorial cohesion, the Union and the Member States, each within their respective competences and within the scope of application of the Constitution, shall take care that such services operate on the basis of principles and conditions, in particular economic and financial conditions, which enable them to fulfil their missions. European laws shall establish these principles and set these conditions without prejudice to the competence of Member States, in compliance with the Constitution, to provide, to commission and to fund such services.'

cohesion, the Union and the Member States, each within their respective powers and within the scope of application of the Treaties, shall take care that such services operate on the basis of principles and conditions, *particularly economic and financial conditions, which enable them to fulfil their missions. The European Parliament and the Council, acting by means of regulations in accordance with the ordinary legislative procedure, shall establish these principles and set these conditions without prejudice to the competence of Member States*, in compliance with the Treaties, to provide, to commission and to fund such services.

For its part, Article 1 of the Protocol on Services of General Interest describes the common values of the Union in relation to SGEIs, insisting on the discretion enjoyed by the national, regional and local authorities to design the provision of such services:

The shared values of the Union in respect of services of general economic interest within the meaning of Article 14 of the Treaty on the Functioning of the European Union include in particular:

- the essential role and the wide discretion of national, regional and local authorities in providing, commissioning and organising services of general economic interest as closely as possible to the needs of the users;
- the diversity between various services of general economic interest and the differences in the needs and preferences of users that may result from different geographical, social or cultural situations;
- a high level of quality, safety and affordability, equal treatment and the promotion of universal access and of user rights.

In the light of Article 2 of the Protocol, the competence of Member States to provide, entrust and organize services of general interest of a non-economic nature is not affected by the Treaty.

The above texts are not at all easy to interpret. The convoluted grammar of Article 14 TFEU suggest a Herculean struggle to combine references to SGEIs with the autonomy which the Member States have in this area and with the respect for previously existing provisions of the Treaties, like Articles 106 and 107 TFEU. It is hard to predict what the outcome of such conflicting elements will be.

The regulation of SGEIs in the Treaty is, therefore, undoubtedly paradoxical. At first sight, it could be argued that the values of solidarity that underlie SGEIs should lead to strengthened integration at the European level, and not to a closing of national borders. However, the idea of a positive EU competence in this area—including solidarity elements between citizens of different Member States—is totally excluded. The concept of European public services simply does not exist; instead, the debate is entirely about protecting national public services from EU interference.

Given this context, it is paradoxical that in this area there is a Community legal basis for SGEIs but no Community competence, not even one that is shared with Member States. What purpose then does this legal basis serve, if any?

One can only imagine the kind of purpose that proponents of this legal basis had in mind. Perhaps they wanted a legal basis enabling the adoption of rules, a 'framework directive' that would establish a type of 'protective shield' around SGEI operators, in an attempt to protect them from the competition rules, and particularly the provisions of the Treaty on state aid. The key point is that such a legal instrument can be adopted by qualified majority, whereas changes to the Treaties require unanimity.

If this were the point of the proposal, it would seem very difficult to achieve from a purely legal point of view. Indeed, if one wants to restrict the scope of a treaty provision, the only legal way to do this is to amend it in accordance with the procedures for amendment of the Treaty. Secondary legislation can never modify primary law. If one cannot get the required unanimity of the Member States, the primary law simply cannot be changed.

Even if, for the sake of argument, a secondary law instrument could modify the Treaty, it is clear that a legal basis that starts with the words 'without prejudice to Articles ... 106 and 107 of this Treaty' would not be the ideal instrument to use to try to amend the scope of Articles 106 and 107 of this Treaty.

Given the accumulation of contradictory caveats in its wording, it seems much easier to identify what cannot be done with Article 14 TFEU (amend the scope of competition or state aid rules, change the allocation of competences between EU and Member States, ...) than what can be done with it.

Ultimately, it may well be that the actual impact of this new legal basis is limited. The Treaties have other provisions that have never been used thus far.[43] Indeed, in November 2007 the European Commission refused to exercise its power to initiate legislation to propose this framework directive, arguing that the new protocol would be sufficient.[44]

In view of the above, the Commission's position seems neither unexpected nor unreasonable.

IV. Conclusion

The surprising manner in which the changes affecting competition and SGEIs were introduced was far from ideal. Given the importance of both areas in EU law, one would have expected a minimum degree of transparency and a more open debate on the merits of these modifications.[45]

Although it may initially appear that competition policy has been removed from its lofty status of 'EU objective' to which it was raised in the Draft Constitutional

---

[43] Eg Articles 116 and 117 TFEU.

[44] Communication of the Commission to the European Parliament, the Council, the European Economic and Social Committee and the Committee of the Regions, accompanying the Communication on 'A single market for 21st Century Europe' Services of general interest, including social services of general interest: a new European commitment {COM(2007) 724 final} Brussels, 20 November 2007.

[45] It seems questionable whether it would have satisfied the criteria of transparency and good governance that are advocated by the TFEU itself at Article 15(1): 'In order to promote good governance and ensure the participation of civil society, the Union institutions, bodies, offices and agencies shall conduct their work as openly as possible.'

Treaty, perhaps the reality is somewhat different. While the removal of the reference to 'free and undistorted competition' is certainly not something to be proud of as far as the image of Community competition policy is concerned, an objective analysis allows more positive conclusions to be reached.

Thus, despite the fact that the objective pursued was perhaps not the strengthening of competition policy, the new Treaty of Lisbon has actually achieved this result, albeit indirectly, through its connection with the internal market. This is because the remembrance of the existence of this connection should lead to a more orthodox and stricter application of the competition and state aid rules.

With respect to SGEIs, the contribution of the Treaty of Lisbon is limited to the introduction of a legal basis—Article 14 TFEU—that allows the Parliament and the Council to establish the principles under which SGEIs should operate.

This provision is not without paradoxes. First of all, it makes it clear that it does not create an EU competence for SGEIs yet it fails to explain the need for a legal basis without an EU competence. The most likely explanation would be to see it as a possible instrument to limit the application of existing EU rules to SGEIs. However, the new provision is hedged by so many caveats (for instance, it is without prejudice to state aid and competition rules) that it would be difficult to find a viable use for it.

To sum up, if one looks at the amendments made by the Treaty of Lisbon to the competition rules and SGEIs the conclusion is that, on balance, the changes are rather limited in substance and, contrary to the initial impression, will probably strengthen EU competition policy. It therefore seems true that sometimes 'God writes straight with crooked lines'.

18

Energy Policy after Lisbon

Leigh Hancher and Francesco Maria Salerno[1]

I. Introduction

Often outsiders know us better than ourselves. In order to understand the state of affairs of EU energy policy after Lisbon, it is instructive to consider the International Energy Agency (IEA) report published in 2008.[2] For the IEA, EU energy policy was kept in check by the pre-eminence of Member States because the latter remained ultimately responsible for their national energy mix; and 'indigenous energy resources are a national, not European, resource', which meant that the Union could not impinge on how these resources should be exploited.

At the same time, the report noted that the EU had been able to achieve significant developments notwithstanding. In effect, the Commission proposed, and the Council and European Parliament adopted far-reaching packages of legislation on (i) the internal energy and gas markets and (ii) on climate change (which includes both renewable energy and emission trading legislation). These two packages, to be implemented into national law by March 2011, December 2010 (for renewable energy legislation), and December 2010 (for the emission trading legislation) respectively, will shape the further development of European energy and climate change policy over the years to come. Moreover, the Commission's competence to propose far-reaching measures on energy has seldom been contested before the European courts in the past. Inter-institutional disputes over a proposed legal basis have been resolved by way of political compromise.

On 1 December 2009 the Lisbon Treaty entered into force. It introduced a specific provision on energy. The aim of this chapter is to review what this has meant for the EU energy policy. In particular, the chapter will assess if and how the introduction of a new specific provision on energy makes it easier to adopt new legislative and policy developments, expanding the scope of the legislation already in place and/or whether it may lead to an even more ambitious policy content than the legislation adopted under the EC Treaty. It will do so by reviewing not only energy-specific

---

[1] The authors would like to thank Andrea Cilea for his invaluable assistance.
[2] See IEA, 'Policies Review—The European Union' 27 (available through the IEA's website).

legislation, but also by looking at the impact of the new title on energy in other related areas of EU law (which may be impacted by the new Treaty).

For instance, given the continued presence of state-owned or controlled companies in the energy sector, as well as the continued if not increasing penchant for state intervention in the energy sector, the amendment to the former Article 3(g) of the EC Treaty—and the removal of the establishment of 'a system ensuring that competition in the internal market is not distorted' as an objective of the Union—is not without relevance in this complex sector, even with the addition of Protocol 27 about Internal Market and Competition, which is meant to mitigate that exclusion by underlining the continued relevance of that principle.[3] Similarly, the insertion of Protocol 26 on Services of General Economic Interest constitutes an important development for energy policy, given that security of energy supply considerations are often invoked by Member States to justify national energy policy choices, sometimes in conflict with EU energy policy. Finally, the changes regarding the external relations domain are also likely to have repercussions on energy, given that one of the Commission's priorities is that the EU is able to speak with 'one voice' especially in its relation to key partners.[4]

Before turning to these issues, the chapter provides an historical background to Article 194 TFEU and an overview of its content.

II. Article 194 TFEU: The Historical Background

A. The EC Treaty

Historical reasons partially explain why the EC Treaty did not identify energy as one of the main policy areas. When the Treaty of Rome was concluded in 1957 energy was at the centre of the Member States' attention. Indeed, at that time, coal was the most important source of primary energy. The six founding Member States had pooled their interests in that area in the context of the European Coal and Steel Community (ECSC). In addition, the Euratom Treaty would also ensure cooperation in the field of nuclear energy which at that period appeared to be the other primary energy source which could give the Community its energy independence. In 1957 natural gas was not yet perceived as an important source of primary energy and mineral oil was considered to be sufficiently apprehended by the rules on the free movement of goods. As regards electricity, the state of technical development of electricity grids hardly allowed large-scale trans-frontier electricity trading. So, in 1951 the ECSC Treaty and in 1957 the Euratom Treaty offered a sufficient legal basis for a common energy policy of the day.

---

[3] For a discussion of this change, see chapter 17 above.
[4] See press release IP/10/1492, 'Energy: Commission Presents its New Strategy Towards 2020'.

B. The Union Treaty

The Treaty on the European Union of 1992 was, like the EC Treaty, a framework treaty. It integrated the Treaties which existed at that time: Title II integrated the Treaty on the European Community (EC), Title III, the Treaty of Coal and Steel (ECSC) and Title IV the Euratom Treaty. Although the Union Treaty explicitly integrated the two Treaties that essentially deal with energy-related matters, it did not further address or identify energy as a policy issue. The list of objectives laid down in Article 2 did not refer to energy at all.[5]

C. The debate during the drafting of the Constitutional Treaty

As one of the major aims of the original, failed Constitutional Treaty, was to ensure a clear division of competences between Europe and national governments, in the interests of transparency and democracy, it was hardly surprising that energy finally got the mention it deserved in that treaty.

In the draft documents produced by the Convention under the guidance of Giscard d'Estaing energy was listed in Articles 1–13 as an 'area of shared competence', along with the internal market, environment and consumer protection.[6] How that competence was to be shared was further specified in Article III-152 (later re-numbered as III-157)—the specific (draft) Article dealing with energy:

1. In establishing an internal market and with regard for the need to preserve and improve the environment, Union policy on energy shall aim to:

   (a) ensure the functioning of the energy market,
   (b) ensure security of energy supply in the Union, and
   (c) promote energy efficiency and saving and the development of new and renewable forms of energy.

---

[5] 'The Community shall have as its task, by establishing a common market and an economic and monetary union and by implementing the common policies or activities referred to in Articles 3 and 3a, to promote throughout the Community a harmonious and balanced development of economic activities, sustainable and non-inflationary growth respecting the environment, a high degree of convergence of economic performance, a high level of employment and of social protection, the raising of the standard of living and quality of life, and economic and social cohesion and solidarity among Member States.'

[6] '1. The Union shall share competence with the Member States where the Constitution confers on it a competence which does not relate to the areas referred to in Articles 12 and 16.

2. Shared competence applies in the following principal areas: internal market, area of freedom, security and justice, agriculture and fisheries, excluding the conservation of marine biological resources, transport and trans-European networks, energy, social policy, for aspects defined in Part.III, economic, social and territorial cohesion, environment, consumer protection, common safety concerns in public health matters.'

2. The measures necessary to achieve the objectives in paragraph 1 shall be enacted in European laws or framework laws. Such laws shall be adopted after consultation of the Committee of the Regions and the Economic and Social Committee. Such laws or framework laws shall not affect a Member State's choice between different energy sources and the general structure of its energy supply, without prejudice to Article III-130(2)(c).

The actual text proved contentious. It was argued by some commentators that its inclusion could have actually been interpreted as a step backwards and as a limitation upon the Commission's powers to propose new measures aimed at completing the energy market liberalization process. Other Member States feared that the text of the Article would have posed a serious threat to national control over energy resources and supply policies.

The Irish government as president of the Council in January–June 2004 had originally proposed in mid-May of 2004 to resolve the deadlock by simply deleting the offending text of the (draft) Article III-157 and removing any reference to energy in Articles 1–16. This solution, while having the virtue of simplicity, would have created something of a legal void, with the only mention of energy being relegated to the then Article III-130 on environmental policy. That Article provided that measures which significantly affect a Member State's choice between different energy sources and the general structure of its energy supply can only be adopted by unanimous vote in Council.[7]

---

[7] '1. European laws or framework laws shall establish what action is to be taken in order to achieve the objectives referred to in Article III-129. They shall be adopted after consultation of the Committee of the Regions and the Economic and Social Committee.

2. By way of derogation from paragraph 1 and without prejudice to Article III-65, the Council of Ministers shall unanimously adopt European laws or framework laws establishing:

(a) measures primarily of a fiscal nature;
(b) measures affecting:

(i) town and country planning;
(ii) quantitative management of water resources or affecting, directly or indirectly, the availability of those resources;
(iii) land use, with the exception of waste management;

(c) measures significantly affecting a Member State's choice between different energy sources and the general structure of its energy supply.

The Council of Ministers may unanimously adopt a European decision making the ordinary legislative procedure applicable to the matters referred to in the first subparagraph of this paragraph.

In all cases, the Council of Ministers shall act after consulting the European Parliament, the Committee of the Regions and the Economic and Social Committee.

3. General action programmes which set out priority objectives to be attained shall be enacted by European laws. Such laws shall be adopted after consultation of the Committee of the Regions and the Economic and Social Committee.

The measures necessary for the implementation of these programmes shall be adopted under the terms of paragraph 1 or paragraph 2, according to the case.

D. The final text in the Constitutional Treaty

Further discussion, and in particular pressure from the United Kingdom government led to the re-insertion of the energy Article on the eve of the Inter-Governmental Conference (IGC) summit, and some last minute tweaks to the final text adopted on 18 June 2004.

The final result is a clearer separation of powers. Pursuant to Article I-14, energy was thus firmly enshrined as one of the 11 areas of shared competence (together with internal market, environment, trans-European networks and consumer protection):[8]

1. The Union shall share competence with the Member States where the Constitution confers on it a competence which does not relate to the areas referred to in Articles I-13 and I-17.

2. Shared competence between the Union and the Member States applies in the following principal areas:

   (a) internal market;
   (b) social policy, for the aspects defined in Part III;
   (c) economic, social and territorial cohesion;
   (d) agriculture and fisheries, excluding the conservation of marine biological resources;
   (e) environment;
   (f) consumer protection;
   (g) transport;
   (h) trans-European networks;
   (i) **energy** [bold added];
   (j) area of freedom, security and justice;
   (k) common safety concerns in public health matters, for the aspects defined in Part III.

---

4. Without prejudice to certain measures adopted by the Union, the Member States shall finance and implement the environment policy.

5. Without prejudice to the principle that the polluter should pay, if a measure based on paragraph 1 involves costs deemed disproportionate for the public authorities of a Member State, such measure shall provide in appropriate form for:

   (a) temporary derogations, and/or
   (b) financial support from the Cohesion Fund.'

[8] Competition policy and common commercial policy remained, of course, matters of exclusive competence however, as confirmed by Article I-13:

> 1. The Union shall have exclusive competence in the following areas: (a) customs union; (b) the establishing of the competition rules necessary for the functioning of the internal market; (c) monetary policy for the Member States whose currency is the euro; (d) the conservation of marine biological resources under the common fisheries policy; (e) common commercial policy. 2. The Union shall also have exclusive competence for the conclusion of an international agreement when its conclusion is provided for in a legislative act of the Union or is necessary to enable the Union to exercise its internal competence, or insofar as its conclusion may affect common rules or alter their scope.

In the majority of cases the relevant legislative measures would be adopted by qualified majority. However, the amended text provided that such laws must not affect a Member State's rights to determine the conditions for exploiting its energy resources, its choice between different energy sources and the general structure of its energy supply, without prejudice to the (draft) Article III-130 on environmental policy. In other words, for these last two areas, unanimity is required. The same unanimity rule was to apply to taxation measures.

The final text was, as a result, a carefully crafted compromise between national sovereignty over natural resources and taxation, and a shared Union competence for the rest. It was probable that the European institutions could not adopt measures directing a Member State to use its produce from its own energy resources for the benefit of the Union, even in the interests of security of energy supply and/or solidarity throughout the Union. Nor could the Community institutions usurp the functions of national governments in the event of an energy crisis. This is further borne out by the wording of what was Declaration number 22 annexed to the Final Act to the Constitutional Treaty, which states that: 'The Conference believes that Article III-256 does not affect the right of the Member States to take the necessary measures to ensure their energy supply under the conditions provided for in Article III-131'.[9]

However, the Union would probably have been entitled to exercise its competence on security of supply to adopt a measure to build up Community-wide oil stocks for emergency purposes and require the Member States to contribute to the maintenance and financing of such stocks. Whether such a measure would have won the necessary political backing would have been quite a different matter.

III. Article 194 TFEU

Despite the considerable political opposition in the negotiations on the new Treaty, energy now receives an explicit recognition in Article 4 of Part I of the Treaty as one of the Union's shared competences. In Part III, which assembles, amends and renumbers the EC Treaty, rules affecting the energy sector are not substantially

---

[9] Article III-131 is the provision dealing with the rights of Member States to deal with internal disturbances:

> Member States shall consult each other with a view to taking together the steps needed to prevent the functioning of the internal market being affected by measures which a Member State may be called upon to take in the event of serious internal disturbances affecting the maintenance of law and order, in the event of war, serious international tension constituting a threat of war, or in order to carry out obligations it has accepted for the purpose of maintaining peace and international security.

amended. A separate energy title XXI is now included consisting of a single Article—Article 194—specifying how competence is to be shared.[10] Pursuant to this provision:

1. In the context of the establishment and functioning of the internal market and with regard for the need to preserve and improve the environment, Union policy on energy shall aim, in a spirit of solidarity between Member States, to:
   (a) ensure the functioning of the energy market;
   (b) ensure security of energy supply in the Union;
   (c) promote energy efficiency and energy saving and the development of new and renewable forms of energy; and
   (d) promote the interconnection of energy networks.

2. Without prejudice to the application of other provisions of the Treaties, the European Parliament and the Council, acting in accordance with the ordinary legislative procedure, shall establish the measures necessary to achieve the objectives in paragraph 1. Such measures shall be adopted after consultation of the Economic and Social Committee and the Committee of the Regions.

Such measures shall not affect a Member State's right to determine the conditions for exploiting its energy resources, its choice between different energy sources and the general structure of its energy supply, without prejudice to Article 192(2)(c).

3. By way of derogation from paragraph 2, the Council, acting in accordance with a special legislative procedure, shall unanimously and after consulting the European Parliament, establish the measures referred to therein when they are primarily of a fiscal nature.

Thus, Article 194 sets out the four main aims of Union policy on energy to ensure the functioning of the energy market, to ensure security of supply of the Union

---

[10] In the so-called Reform Treaty, the predecessor to the Lisbon Treaty, the Title was XX and the Article number was 176 A (see <http://www.consilium.europa.eu/uedocs/cmsUpload/cg00014.en07.pdf>). The wording reads as follows:
1. In the context of the establishment and functioning of the internal market and with regard for the need to preserve and improve the environment, Union policy on energy shall aim, in a spirit of solidarity between Member States, to: (a) ensure the functioning of the energy market; (b) ensure security of energy supply in the Union; and (c) promote energy efficiency and energy saving and the development of new and renewable forms of energy; and (d) promote the interconnection of energy networks. 2. Without prejudice to the application of other provisions of the Treaties, the European Parliament and the Council, acting in accordance with the ordinary legislative procedure, shall establish the measures necessary to achieve the objectives in paragraph 1. Such measures shall be adopted after consultation of the Economic and Social Committee and the Committee of the Regions. Such measures shall not affect a Member State's right to determine the conditions for exploiting its energy resources, its choice between different energy sources and the general structure of its energy supply, without prejudice to Article 175(2) (c). 3. By way of derogation from paragraph 2, the Council, acting in accordance with a special legislative procedure, shall unanimously and after consulting the European Parliament, establish the measures referred to therein when they are primarily of a fiscal nature.

and to promote energy efficiency and saving and the development of new and renewable forms of energy, and finally to promote the interconnection of energy networks. These aims are to be executed in a spirit of solidarity between the Member States.

Article 194(2), however, stipulates that Union legislation shall not affect a Member State's choice between different energy sources and the general structure of its supply, without prejudice to Article 192(2) (dealing with environmental policy). Legislation furthering these aims can be adopted by qualified majority but any matter falling within the scope of Article 194(2) is subject to unanimity. The same unanimity rule continues to apply to energy taxation measures—as confirmed by Article 192(3).

The final text of the energy title remains a carefully crafted compromise between national sovereignty over natural resources and energy taxation issues and a shared Union competence for the rest.[11] This is confirmed by Declaration number 22 annexed to the Final Act. Nevertheless, the new Article 194 confirms the Union's competence to adopt preventative measures to avoid security threats and may well provide a basis for political backing for more far-reaching preventative measures in the future.

IV. Article 194 TFEU: What Difference Does it Make?

In this section we will critically assess whether and how the introduction of a specific Article on energy has already had an impact on EU energy policy. In order to do so, this section will first review the state of EU energy policy before the entry into force of the Lisbon Treaty, and then describe the developments that have occurred since.

A. The situation before Article 194 TFEU: the Third Package and the climate change legislation

(i) The Third Package

The recent Third Package measures,[12] adopted in 2009 based on Article 95 EC (now Article 114 TFEU) illustrate that the European institutions had already

---

[11] Article 122 states that 'Without prejudice to any other procedures provided for in the Treaties, the Council, on a proposal from the Commission, may decide, in a spirit of solidarity between Member States, upon the measures appropriate to the economic situation, in particular if severe difficulties arise in the supply of certain products, notably in the area of energy'.

[12] See (i) Parliament and Council Directive (EC) 2009/72 concerning common rules for the internal market in electricity and repealing Directive (EC) 2003/54, [2009] OJ L211/55; (ii) Parliament and Council Directive (EC) 2009/73 concerning common rules for the internal market in natural gas and repealing Directive (EC) 2003/55, [2009] OJ L211/94; (iii) Parliament and Council Regulation (EC) 713/2009 establishing an Agency for the Cooperation of Energy Regulators, [2009] OJ L211/1; (iv) Parliament and Council Regulation (EC) 714/2009 on conditions for access to the network for cross-border exchanges in electricity and repealing Regulation (EC) 1228/2003, [2009]

enjoyed extensive competence in the matter of energy policy. Even if this package does not give the Union institutions the power to mandate a particular investment or to require Member States to promote a particular cross-border infrastructure, a closer examination of its provisions reveals that the powers of the Commission to influence national energy choices is now considerable.

Importantly, the Third Package introduces a shift in the balance of competences between the European, national and regional levels, so that, on certain issues at least, Member States have lost important powers as well as opportunities to proceed with further 'inter-governmental' and ad hoc arrangements at the regional energy market level. This is not the place to enter into an exhaustive analysis of the Third Package. Three examples suffice to illustrate the point advanced here: (a) the new unbundling regime, (b) the role and duties of national regulators and (c) the creation of the new Agency for the Cooperation of Energy regulators (ACER).

(a) The unbundling regime

A controversial element of the new legislative package is Article 9 of Directive 72/2009 (electricity) and Directive 73/2009 (gas). This Article introduces 'ownership' unbundling—also referred to as full, structural unbundling—for Transmission System Operators (TSOs). In the previous Directives, now repealed, TSOs had been required to bring their transmission activities under separate legal entities. The Commission concluded in various reports, including the Sector Enquiry Report, that mere legal unbundling was insufficient to guarantee the objectives of the internal energy market exercise. Vertically integrated companies would continue to give preferential terms of access to their related production and supply companies, to the detriment of new market entrants. Under these rules the ownership and operation of the transmission system could still be carried out by a subsidiary of a company that also had generation and/or supply interests, the European Commission had concerns regarding the independence of the transmission system and the potential barrier this could represent for competition.[13]

The Third Package as originally proposed by the European Commission only included two options: full ownership unbundling (FOU)[14] and independent system operator (ISO).[15] The European Council introduced the independent

OJ L211/15; (v) Parliament and Council Regulation (EC) 715/2009 on conditions for access to the natural gas transmission networks and repealing Regulation (EC) 1775/2005, [2009] OJ L211/36.

[13] See the DG Comp report on the energy sector inquiry (SEC(2006)1724, 10 January 2007) which found, among other things, that there was poor integration between European energy markets and barriers to entry for new entrants. The Commission considered that this was partly caused by vertical foreclosure and concluded that further unbundling would help address these problems by improving the independence of the networks.

[14] FOU requires that ownership and operation of the transmission system is carried out by a company that is independent from supply or generation.

[15] Technically a derogation from FOU, the ISO option allows the ownership of the assets to remain with a vertically integrated undertaking (VIU) but requires that an independent system operator is fully responsible for operation.

transmission operator (ITO)[16] and Article 9(9)[17] options later on in the legislative process after pressure from Member States (notably France and Germany) wishing to retain a position whereby the ownership and operation of the transmission system could remain with the vertically integrated undertaking. Article 9(9) has been referred to as the 'Scottish option', introduced following a request from the UK government to secure a possible derogation for its own unique arrangements in Scotland. Article 9(9) is open to any Member State that is able to demonstrate compliance with the requirements.

Given that Member States now have some flexibility in choosing between the various models—FOU, ISO, ITO or ITO+—a number of Member States were prepared to withdraw their objections to the Community's exercise of its powers to interfere with matters of national property law. The Commission has already been assured by its legal services that it has the competence to require FOU in any event, and that there was little chance that any Member State could rely on Article 245 EC (now Article 345 TFEU) to oppose the measure.

Even though these models are complex and their eventual implementation will give rise to some diversity in approach across the Union, it is important to note that TSOs must now also be certified by the national regulatory authority (NRA). Once the procedure has been initiated, the regulatory authority has four months to adopt a decision on the certification of the TSO. Thereafter the decision is forwarded to the European Commission, which has two months to examine the regulatory authority's decision and deliver an opinion on compliance with the directive requirements.[18] The Commission may, if it considers it appropriate, request that the new Agency for the Cooperation of Energy Regulators provide an opinion. If so, the two-month period shall be extended for a further two months.

Except in relation to Article 9(9), the European Commission's opinion is not binding, however, the NRA will be required to take the 'utmost account' of it. In practice, it is expected that an NRA will follow the opinion and therefore the NRA will require a good reason to make a divergent decision. Within two months of receiving the European Commission's opinion, the NRA must have reached its final decision on the certification of the TSO.

A novel feature of the new unbundling rules is that they are also extended to third-country companies, via the certification procedures. Article 11 of both Directives deals with this issue. Where certification is requested by a TSO which is controlled by a person or persons from a third country, the NRA shall notify the

---

[16] The ITO allows both ownership and operation to remain within a legally unbundled subsidiary of a VIU subject to strict regulation and oversight by the NRA.

[17] Article 9(9) allows the status quo to be maintained, insofar as the transmission system belonged to a VIU on 3 September 2009 and there are arrangements in place which guarantee more effective independence of the transmission system operator than the ITO option.

[18] The certification process can potentially take up to 10 months, and therefore in order for certification to be completed in time to allow designation to take place by March 2012, the candidate TSOs must initiate the certification process by around May 2011. The certification procedure can also be initiated on the regulatory authority's own initiative or by the European Commission.

Commission including a notification of any circumstances which would result in a third-country company acquiring control of a transmissions system or transmission operator. The NRA shall refuse certification if it has not been demonstrated that the entity concerned complies with the requirements of Article 9 and that the granting of certification will not put at risk the security of energy supply of the Member State and the Community. In this respect the NRA must take into account the rights and obligations of the Community with respect to that third country arising under international law including any agreement concluded with one or more third countries to which the Community is a party and which addresses the issue of security of energy supply as well as any bilateral agreements insofar as they are in compliance with Community law.

The rationale for this clause, sometimes referred to as the 'Gazprom clause', is to be found in Recital 25 of the Electricity Directive and the equivalent Recital 22 of the Gas Directive. Although an agreement with a third country authorizing reciprocal control of national TSOs is not a prerequisite for certification and thus control by an investor from a third country, this provision is still of major importance and will ensure that European transmission systems are not controlled by vertically integrated third-country suppliers.

It follows from Article 11 that even though the NRA is prepared to recognize that the company seeking to acquire a TSO complies with the unbundling rules, the national authority can effectively overrule that decision if the granting of certification would put security of supply at risk. It would appear from the wording of the provision that a Member State is entitled to put its own security of supply interests above those of the Union. This reflects continued deference to the principle of subsidiarity on security of supply issues, a subject which is returned to below at section D.

Should the Union conclude an international agreement with one or more third countries which addresses the issue of security of supply, this will take precedence over the Directives and can also derogate from their provisions. The question of the scope and nature of the Union's competences to conclude international agreements in the energy field is returned to in section F below.

Finally, it may be noted that the last word has not been said on unbundling. Article 47 of the Directive 72/2009 (electricity) and Article 52 of the Gas Directive require the Commission to adopt by 3 March 2013 a specific detailed report assessing whether the ITO option can lead to effective unbundling. In the event of a negative assessment the Commission shall submit further proposals to the European Parliament and the Council to ensure fully effective unbundling by 3 March 2014.

(b) National regulators

The new Directives impose a large list of duties and obligations on the NRAs and require that they are entrusted with sufficient resources and powers to carry out these duties. In particular, Article 37(4)(d) of Directive 72/09 (electricity) and Article 41(3)(d) of Directive 73/09 (gas) require the NRAs to impose effective, proportionate and dissuasive penalties on undertakings not complying with their obligations under the Third Package.

More importantly, a major innovation of the Third Package is that national regulators must now not only be independent from the industry which they regulate, they must also enjoy a certain amount of independence from their national governments. Thus, according to Article 35(4)–(5) of Directive 72/09 (electricity) NRAs shall 'not seek or take direct instructions from any government or other public or private entity when carrying out the regulatory tasks.... the regulatory authority can take autonomous decisions, independently from any political body' (Article 39 of Directive 73/09 (gas) has identical provisions).

In order to gauge the extent to which these provisions limit Member States' ability to influence national energy policy, suffice it to compare with analogous provisions on NRAs in the field of telecommunications. According to Article 3 of Directive 2002/21/EC on a common regulatory framework for electronic communications networks and services, NRAs 'shall act independently and shall not seek or take instructions from any other body in relation to the exercise of these tasks assigned to them under national law implementing Community law. This shall not prevent supervision in accordance with national constitutional law.' In effect, the requirement of independence from the government and, especially, from 'political bodies' is much more nuanced.

Moreover, only NRAs (and non-government officials) may participate in the new Agency for the Cooperation of Energy Regulators. This means that governments are excluded from an important forum of policy-making.

(c) ACER and comitology

ACER is essentially an advisory body which will provide both the Commission and the NRAs with opinions on various issues including, the monitoring of TSOs and their cooperation at the regional or at the community level through the new European Network of Transmission System Operators for Electricity (ENTSOs), implementation of projects to create new interconnector capacity, check the security of the network and importantly approve the compliance programme of vertically integrated TSOs cooperating within a joint undertaking covering two or more Member States for capacity allocation. ACER may only take specific decisions, subject to Commission veto, on cross-border infrastructures.

The creation of the new agency, ACER in Regulation 713/2009 was facilitated by a high level of political support and the European Council agreed in 2007 on the need to establish an independent body to cooperate on cross-border gas and electricity issues. Support for a new agency was also echoed in the European Parliament. Nevertheless, the powers eventually conferred on the ACER are somewhat minimal due to the Commission's insistence on a narrow interpretation of the so-called 'Meroni doctrine',[19] which sets limit on the Commission's ability to delegate powers to agencies.[20] In particular, the Commission firmly linked ACER's tasks and objectives to the goals of the Third Legislative Package as ACER provides a framework for the implementation of energy policy. Thus, the Commission was able to remain safely within the parameters of Article 95 EC as interpreted by the Court in setting up this new agency.[21] It can be concluded that the new agency does not challenge the Commission's preferred model of a unitary approach to the executive function.

Another distinctive characteristic of the Third Package is the extensive delegation of regulatory powers by the Council to the Commission by way of comitology procedures—and in particular the so-called regulatory procedure. The Directives and Regulations in effect delegate substantial regulatory power to the Commission and allow it to adopt guidelines and frameworks and to amend the various annexes to the Directives and the Regulations in accordance with the comitology proce-

---

[19] See Case 9/56 *Meroni v High Authority* [1958] ECR 133.

[20] First, the delegation of powers must be necessary for the performance of the tasks assigned to the delegating institution by the Treaty. This condition does not appear particularly onerous as *Meroni* does not require an express legal basis as a prerequisite for delegation. A general principle to delegate, subject to the conditions of lawful delegation, seems to have been recognized by the Courts (Case T-333/99 *X v ECB* [2001] ECR II-3021). Second, the delegating authority cannot confer powers on an agency different from those which itself possesses. Third, the exercise of the powers conferred on the agency must be subject to the same conditions as those to which it would be subject if the delegating authority was exercising them directly. One of the Court's concerns in *Meroni* had been that the powers conferred on the agency at issue in that case were not subject to the conditions to which they would have been subjected had they been exercised directly by the High Authority (see paras 149–50). Fourth, the delegation of powers cannot be presumed—it must be expressly provided—implied delegation is not valid (see Case T-311/06 *FMC Chemical v EFSA* [2008] ECR II-88, para 66). Finally, the powers delegated may only involve clearly defined executive powers the use of which must be entirely subject to the supervision of the delegating institution. The delegation of discretionary powers or a real transfer of responsibility is not permitted. This is probably the most important of the five conditions. It follows that institutions may not delegate any core functions. Nevertheless, subsequent case law has not provided any firm guidance on how to distinguish between clearly defined executive powers and powers which entail the exercise of wide discretion, and this has given rise to substantial commentary. In general, there appears to be consensus that *Meroni* precludes the delegation of rule-making powers. Nevertheless, there are sufficient arguments to suggest that *Meroni* should not necessarily be interpreted restrictively as AG Leger reflected in his Opinion in *Tralli* (Case C-301/02 P *Tralli v ECB* [2005] ECR I-4071). The *Meroni* case had involved the delegation of tasks falling within core activities in the field of economic policy. At the same time the Court of Justice had stressed that delegation could be lawful if the agency in question was subject to an effective system of supervision and control by the delegating institution (para 151).

[21] Regulation 713/2009 takes Article 95 EC as its legal basis—and is as such a harmonizing measure. As the Court of Justice had confirmed in earlier case law, Article 95 could be used as a legal basis for instruments which provided for a multi-stage model with intermediate steps which would also contribute to the approximation of laws. Moreover, in the ENISA (European Network and Information Security Agency) case (Case C-217/04 *United Kingdom v Parliament and Council* [2006] ECR I-3771), the Court of Justice further clarified the scope of Article 95 EC in relation to the creation of Community agencies. The Court of Justice recognized that Article 95 EC conferred on the Community legislature some discretion as to the selection of the most suitable method of approximation in complex, technical fields. Such measures did not have to be addressed to the Member States, but could relate to the establishment of a Community body, as long as the objectives and tasks of that body were closely linked to the subject matter of the relevant harmonization measures. Further, the body should provide a framework for the implementation of those measures. ENISA facilitated the objectives of the internal market for electronic communications.

dures. The Court of Justice seems to have taken a more liberal approach to the delegation of powers pertaining to the internal organization and management of the Community institutions. The *Vitamins* case appears to confirm that if the Community legislature wished to delegate power to amend aspects of a legislative act, it must ensure that the power is clearly defined and that the exercise of that power is subject to strict review in the light of objective criteria.[22]

In summary, the old Treaty provided considerable scope for the delegation of regulatory powers, under certain conditions, to specialized agencies, such as ACER, as well as for the delegation of regulatory powers to the Commission itself. The Third Package has made ample use of the second possibility, albeit, that an overly restrictive interpretation of the *Meroni* doctrine has limited the role of the agency.

(ii) Climate change legislation

The above is further underscored by the legislation adopted to combat climate change.

At the European Council meeting of 8 March 2007 the Heads of State agreed 'An Energy Policy for Europe', one of the pillars of which was the EU commitment to a binding target of a 20 per cent share of renewable energies in overall EU energy consumption by 2020, and saving 20 per cent of the EU's energy consumption compared to projections for 2020.[23]

Before the Treaty of Lisbon entered into force, the new Climate Package was adopted, consisting of four measures: the revised Renewable Energy Directive, the amended Directive on Emissions Trading Sytsem (ETS), an 'effort-sharing' Decision setting binding national targets for emissions from sectors not covered by the EU ETS; and a Directive creating a legal framework for the safe and environmentally sound use of carbon capture and storage technologies.[24] All

---

[22] Joined Cases C-154 and C-155/04 *The Queen ex parte Alliance for National Health* [2005] ECR I-6451, para 60.

[23] See Council Conclusions, available at <http://www.eppgroup.eu/Press/pfocus/docs/March07.pdf>.

[24] (i) Parliament and Council Directive (EC) 2009/29 amending Directive (EC) 2003/87 so as to improve and extend the greenhouse gas emission allowance trading scheme of the Community, [2009] OJ L 140/63; (ii) Parliament and Council Decision (EC) 406/2009 on the effort of Member States to reduce their greenhouse gas emissions to meet the Community's greenhouse gas emission reduction commitments up to 2020, [2009] OJ L 140/136; (iii) Parliament and Council Directive (EC) 2009/31 on the geological storage of carbon dioxide and amending Council Directive (EEC) 85/337, Parliament and Council Directives (EC) 2000/60, 2001/80, 2004/35, 2006/12, 2008/1 and Regulation (EC) 1013/2006, [2009] OJ L 140/114; (iv) Parliament and Council Directive (EC) 2009/28 on the promotion of the use of energy from renewable sources and amending and subsequently repealing Directives (EC) 2001/77 and 2003/30, [2009] OJ L 140/16.

these measures were based on Article 175(1) TEC on environment, save for the provisions on biofuels of the revised Renewable Energy Directive, which were based on Article 95 TEC on approximation of laws.

These measures are also far-reaching in scope and again illustrate that the EC Treaty already proved an adequate basis for the adoption of ambitious and also highly innovative measures in the field of climate change.

Suffice it to note that the revised Renewable Energy Directive imposes binding targets on Member States as to the share of energy from renewable sources (besides binding obligations on Member States regarding the sustainability of biofuels and other bioliquids).

It is difficult to deny that, by doing so, the revised Renewable Energy Directive impinges on Member States' rights to determine their energy policy and, specifically, their energy mix. Accordingly, Member States which might have reserves of indigenous fossil fuel will find their ability to rely on such reserves affected. Indeed, the impact on national energy policy was so strongly felt that two Member States had in fact threatened to veto the package. However, the revised Renewable Energy Directive took as a basis Article 175(1) EC (now Article 192 TFEU) (environment) which only requires qualified majority voting, hence this would have little impact.[25]

(iii) Intermediate conclusion

The EC Treaty therefore already allowed the Community to realize far-reaching structural changes in the ownership of key infrastructure and to consolidate a considerable shift of regulatory power in the Commission in order to realize and subsequently supervise the mechanics of the internal energy market.

Against this background, the remainder of this section will assess whether the new title on energy has enabled the Union to go further than before in designing and implementing European energy policy by looking at energy-specific initiatives as well as to other related areas. The considerations below are based on developments until February 2011.

B. Article 194 TFEU and its impact on EU energy policy

(i) Energy: proposed legislation

Since the entry into force of the Lisbon Treaty, the Commission has relied on Article 194 TFEU as the legal basis for a number of legislative proposals in the field

---

[25] There is, however, some doubt as to whether this in fact was the correct legal basis, as opposed to Article 175(2) EC which would have required unanimity and would have marginalized the role of the European Parliament to providing a mere opinion. However, the Commission had argued that as Member States use renewable energy and already have decided to increase renewable energy's share, the proposal would not significantly affect the Member States' choice between different energy sources or the general structure of their energy supply, and so did not fall under Article 175(2) EC (see COM (2008) 19, Proposal for a Directive of the European Parliament and of the Council on the promotion of the use of energy from renewable sources).

of energy, often replacing Article 114 TFEU on approximation of laws as the legal basis.[26] The most important pending proposals are the following:

• Proposal for a Community instrument to facilitate infrastructure investment

On 17 November 2010 the Commission published a communication on energy infrastructure priorities for 2020 and beyond.[27] The Communication envisages the adoption of an Energy Security and Infrastructure Instrument, which will be the legal framework to remove some of the obstacles to investment in new energy infrastructure. This initiative stems from the March 2009 European Council, which called for a 'thorough review of the trans-European Networks for Energy framework (TEN)' by adapting it to the challenges of the EU energy policy and 'the new responsibilities conferred to the Union by Article 194 of the Treaty of Lisbon'.

Indeed, the old approach based on Article 170 TEC on TEN suffered from a number of shortcomings as outlined by the Commission itself in the Communication on the Implementation of the Trans-European Energy Networks in the Period 2007–2009.[28] In particular, the Commission mentioned that 'the weaknesses of TEN-E have come to the fore in 2007–2009. The programme has responded too slowly to the major challenges which have emerged in recent years, and is poorly equipped to deal with the growing challenges which will arise from the 2020 and 2050 ambitions. The new policy environment creates a challenge for TEN-E, which has neither the resources nor the flexibility to make a full contribution to the delivery of the ambitious energy and climate goals'.[29]

Against this background, the Proposal at hand marks a significant policy development in the energy field and is likely to be the first measure based on Article 194 TFEU which constitutes a significant advance in the *aquis*.

On 4 February 2011 this proposal received firm endorsement by the Council, which stated in its conclusions 'No EU Member State should remain isolated from the European gas and electricity networks after 2015'.[30]

• Proposal for a regulation on energy market integrity and transparency

On 8 December 2010 the Commission unveiled a proposal for establishing a tailor-made regime for the oversight of the trading of energy products at power exchanges and in the over-the-counter (OTC) markets. The proposal is based on Article 194 (2) TFEU.[31] If adopted, this proposal will enact a tailor-made market abuse regime.

---

[26] See Commission's Communication to the European Parliament and the Council on the consequences of entry into force of the Treaty of Lisbon for ongoing inter-institutional decision-making procedures (COM(2009) 665 final of 11.12.2009).

[27] See COM(2010) 677 (available at <http://eur-lex.europa.eu/LexUriServ/LexUriServ.do?uri=S-PLIT_COM:2010:0677(01):FIN:EN:PDF>).

[28] See COM(2010)203 (available at <http://ec.europa.eu/energy/infrastructure/studies/doc/2010_0203_en.pdf>).

[29] Ibid 9.

[30] Council conclusions, 4 February 2011 (available at <http://www.consilium.europa.eu/uedocs/cms_data/docs/pressdata/en/ec/119141.pdf>).

[31] See COM(2010) 762/3 (available at <http://ec.europa.eu/energy/gas_electricity/markets/doc/com_2010_0726_en.pdf>).

Thus, it will be a sector-specific application of the general rules on market abuse, as provided by Directive 2003/6,[32] which was based on Article 95 TEC (now 114 TFEU) on approximation of laws.

Considering that this proposal would share with the general market abuse regime the internal market as its main rationale, it is difficult to argue that this proposal is linked to the entry into force of the Lisbon Treaty. In fact, it is unlikely that this proposal could not have been adopted on the basis of the old Article 95 TEC (now 114 TFEU).

Energy: adopted legislation—the Regulation on notification to the Commission of investment projects in energy infrastructure

Prior to the entry in force of the TFEU, the Commission's proposal had been based on Article 284 EC and Article 187 Euratom. Under those two identical Articles, the Commission is entitled to collect any information and carry out any checks required for the performance of the tasks entrusted to it.

The committee on legal affairs of the European Parliament reviewed the question of the correct legal basis of the Commission's original proposal in January 2010,[33] and considered whether the new Article 194 TFEU as well as Article 170 EU on trans-European networks might have been relied upon. The latter Article would allow for the full involvement of the European Parliament under the ordinary legislative procedure, while Articles 337 TFEU and Articles 187 Euratom only allow for consultation.

It may be recalled that in Case C-178/03 *Commission v Parliament and Council* the Court of Justice had held that recourse to a dual legal basis was not possible where the procedures are incompatible with each other or where it is liable to undermine the rights of the Parliament.[34] The Court further held that the choice of legal basis must be based on objective factors which are amenable to judicial review, in particular the aim and content of the measure.

The Parliament's legal affairs committee, having reviewed the aims of the proposed measure, concluded that although the new Regulation would require collection of information on infrastructure projects, the content of the proposed Regulation also clearly related to energy policy aims. The very objective of the data collection process was to evaluate in the light of energy investment projects what action the Union should take in case of any supply difficulties. Furthermore, the Commission had in its explanatory memorandum accompanying the proposal claimed that the proposed Regulation was consistent with the establishment of an internal market and with the Community's climate and energy policy. Hence Article 194 TFEU should have been the appropriate legal basis.

Although the European Parliament adopted the view of its legal affairs committee and recommended the choice of Article 194 TFEU as the correct legal basis, and a political agreement was reached in the Council on 12 March 2010 to this effect, on 24 June 2010 the Council adopted Regulation 617/2010 on notification to the

---

[32] OJ [2003], L96/16.   [33] A7-0016/20100.   [34] [2006] ECR I-207.

Commission of investment projects in energy infrastructure.[35] This measure was adopted on the basis of Article 337 TFEU and Article 187 Euratom, with the European Parliament only being empowered to provide an opinion.

On 12 October 2010 the European Parliament lodged an appeal against the Council, challenging the legal base of the Regulation.[36]

Energy: adopted legislation—the Regulation on gas security of supply

It should be noted that the Third Package Gas Directive and Regulation contain provisions with respect to the increasingly important subject of security of supply. Both measures are based on Article 95 EC, as explained above. These measures essentially require Member States to take certain measures to monitor security of supply and in particular indicators at national level (see Article 5 of Directive 73/2009).

The Gas Security of Supply Directive 67/2004, adopted on the basis of Article 100 EC, imposed a rather loose set of obligations on Member States to put in place security of supply policies, specifying roles and responsibilities of market actors and to put in place national emergency measures. All in all there was a strong emphasis on subsidiarity with respect to security of supply measures in this legislation. This is also reflected in Article 45 of the new Gas Directive 73/2009.

At the same time, however, the Third Package measures contain a number of provisions which aim at closing the regulatory and legal gap which can develop as a consequence of the subsidiarity requirements on security of supply. In particular, two new Articles aimed at the promotion of regional cooperation and solidarity as well as provisions with respect to coordinated network operation may provide a possible framework within which the 'missing links' in the Union's gas infrastructure network can be determined and dealt with.

For example, Article 6 of the Gas Directive obliges Member States to cooperate in order to promote regional and bilateral solidarity and to coordinate their national emergency plans on an *ex ante* basis. Article 8(10)(a) of the Gas Regulation, in turn, requires ENTSO-G (the network of gas transmission system operators) to adopt and publish a network development plan, which must include Union-wide aspects of network planning and must identify investment gaps, notably with regard to cross-border infrastructure.

Although the Third Package introduces a number of provisions that aim to improve the coordination of the nationally determined measures to deal with security of supply problems, neither these measures nor the 2004 Security of Supply Directive provided for a specific policy for security of gas supply to be defined at Community level. In fact, as Article 194(2) TFEU makes clear, security of supply remains in the hands of the Member States. This is also borne out by Declaration Number 35, according to which 'The Conference believes that Article 194 does not affect the right of the Member States to take the necessary measures to ensure their energy supply under the conditions provided for in Article 347'. For

---

[35] OJ L [2010] 180/7.
[36] See Case C-490/10 (information available at <http://curia.europa.eu>).

this reason, the emergence of an EU legislative competence on security of supply represents a major step forwards, which deserves to be analysed in detail.

Indeed, the Commission recognized this major gap in its Second Strategic Energy Review of 2008 and in July 2009 it proposed a new Regulation which aims to safeguard the security of Europe's gas supply. The decision to speed up the development of revised security of supply legislation is taken in the context of geo-political events, such as the recent Russian–Ukrainian gas crisis, which revealed certain inadequacies in Directive 2004/67/EC.[37] Moreover, in the wake of the most recent gas crisis in January 2009, the European Council and European Parliament called for an accelerated revision of the existing Directive.

The Commission's original proposal

The Commission's initial proposal for a Regulation on the security of gas supply, published on 16 July 2009, and based on Article 95 EC, was ambitious and was likely to test the limits of how far the Union could go in imposing a European security of supply policy.[38] The objective of the proposal was clear: that all Member States address gas security seriously so that, when the next supply crisis hits, no country within the Union is at risk of significant economic losses, or worse. However, in the Commission's proposal there were two largely conflicting approaches to achieving this:

- The first one consisted of defining security of supply 'standards' that, once applied by all Member States, would guarantee a minimum level of security of supply across the EU. The most discussed of these rules is the 'N-1' indicator.

- The second approach consisted of asking Member States to perform 'risk assessments' of their gas systems, based in part on the supply standards they have to comply with. Those assessments would be part of 'preventive action plans' that the Commission would then review.[39]

The legislative process

Not surprisingly, then, the negotiation resulted in a significant weakening of the standards. The fact that the 'N-1' rule on the capacity of the supply infrastructure is highly disputable as an indication of gas supply security made it easier for Member States to justify weaker versions, but it is fair to say that they would have weakened any rule.

There are indeed very good reasons, as discussed by Noel,[40] why Member States resist such an approach. Let us define gas supply security as the ability to meet final

---

[37] Certain flaws in the Directive—particularly the lack of coordination between Member States— were already apparent when the Commission published a Communication on the implementation of Directive (EC) 2004/67 in November 2008.

[38] COM(2009) 363.

[39] See the Addendum sent by the General Secretariat of the Council to the Delegations on 22 January 2010, on regional cooperation.

[40] See P Noël and SA Findlater, Comment on the Draft EU Regulation on Gas Supply Security: Electricity Policy Research Group, University of Cambridge; available at: <http://www.eprg.group. cam.ac.uk/tag/noel/July%202009>.

contracted energy demand in the face of a gas supply disruption. All Member States already enjoy a certain degree of security which can always be increased, at a cost. Because the cost of attaining any given level of security can differ widely between countries, the sensible level of insurance will be country-specific.

Moreover, most Member States know little about this cost. Therefore, even if one assumes that social attitudes towards energy supply insecurity are the same everywhere, Member States are bound to resist a centrally defined minimum level of security—that is, unless they are absolutely certain to be above it already. It is important to note that Member States that are already very secure have no reason to push for tougher standards because gas security is not a pan-European public good: insecurity in Sofia, Riga or Warsaw does not translate into insecurity in Paris, Berlin or Rome; reciprocally, security produced in Slovakia cannot be free-ridden upon in Slovenia.

Even if all Member States were ready to spend time and money on this problem, given the nature of the issue at hand they would resist the imposition of a centrally defined, meaningful standard. This is reminiscent of the negotiation that produced the notoriously benign Directive 2004/67, the original version of which did include a meaningful gas supply security standard.[41]

By contrast, the other proposed approach, based on national gas security assessments and the negotiation of national action plans, was from the start a more promising way to ensure that all EU Member States address this problem adequately. This is because this approach is based on an innovative bottom-up policy process, associating Member States, the Commission and independent experts working on a regional basis. The policy process would serve the following purposes:

- Reveal the gas security situation in all Member States;
- Increase and share knowledge among Member States about gas security policies and measures, including their cost;
- Incentivize national governments to make gas security policy choices that are economically sensible and politically responsible.

As one observer commented, 'to make it a European policy success it should be clarified and simplified. The bottom-up dimension should be strengthened so that the text is less politically contentious for member states and more effective at raising the ambition of national gas supply security policies'.[42]

As a matter of fact, the negotiation at Council level revealed three clear trends:

- The determination of the Member States to weaken the standards.

---

[41] See COM(2002) 488 final, 2002/0220 (COD), Article 4.

[42] See P Noël, 'Ensuring Success for the EU Regulation on Gas Supply Security'; Electricity Policy Research Group, University of Cambridge, February 2010, and ibid, *Beyond Dependence: How to deal with Russian Gas* (ECFR/09, November 2008), available at <http://ecfr.eu/content/entry/russia_gas_policy_brief/>.

- The recognition that the risk assessment process and the national action plans are among the most valuable features of the Regulation.
- The recognition that there should be more regional cooperation on gas security policy.

The first of these three trends illustrates what the negotiation over the Directive 2004/67 had already shown, namely: that the standards approach, however appealing at first glance, faces serious hurdles in an EU negotiation. Mandating an arbitrary minimum level of security contradicts the Member States' legitimate claim to define how much insurance they should buy and how and when to buy it. On the contrary, devising a set of 'standards' that all Member States should comply with amounts to mandating a uniform minimum level of security; it makes national security assessments redundant. Against this background, the second and third trends create an opportunity to make a clear choice in favour of a bottom-up approach based on security assessments, national action plans and regional cooperation.

Regulation 994/2010
The new Regulation replacing Directive 2004/57 is based on Article 194(2) and the ordinary legislative procedure. This has allowed the European Parliament to have a substantial influence on the final text. Although the Regulation stresses the need for solidarity between the Member States it is eminently clear that sovereign rights over national energy resources are not affected by the Regulation (see Recital 39). Furthermore, the shared responsibility to ensure security of supply is placed on natural gas undertakings, the Commission, advised by the Gas Coordination Group (GCG) and the competent authorities of the Member States (as defined in Article 2(2), as opposed to NRAs, and the ACER who only need to be consulted on certain matters (see Articles 3 and 4).

The ACER will, however, be represented in the GCG. At the same time, the new Regulation introduces various measures to enable and even require permanent bi-directional capacity on all cross-border interconnections between Member States. The NRAs have a role to play in these procedures although Articles 6 and 7 of the Regulation also include competent authorities in the 'authorities concerned' whose task it is to determine that new transmission infrastructure is constructed to enable reverse flows. NRAs are required to take into account efficiently incurred costs in upgrading infrastructure and enabling reverse flow shall be reflected in tariffs. Security of supply remains a sensitive matter and despite the improved coordinated response to a supply crisis that this Regulation should facilitate, this still remains a governmental and not a regulatory response.

C. Energy and competition policy

In the Guidelines on the Application of Article 81(3) EC (now Article 101 TFEU),[43] the Commission stated that 'Goals pursued by other Treaty provisions can be taken

---

[43] OJ 2004 C 101/97.

into account to the extent that they can be subsumed under the four conditions of Article 81(3)'.[44] Under this approach, energy policy considerations could become relevant in granting an exemption to an otherwise restrictive agreement only insofar as they can be 'subsumed' under efficiency consideration.[45]

An example may be illustrative. In *CECED*,[46] the Commission granted an exemption to an agreement between washing machine manufacturers to phase out machines with high electricity consumption. According to the Commission, cost savings for consumers were greater than the price increase that could derive from the fact that cheaper models would no longer be available on the market and that certain manufacturers might be at a disadvantage for lack of adequate technology, hence the reduced competition might lead to an increase in price. On this reading, the environmental benefit stemming from the agreement is 'subsumed' under efficiency considerations, which—*in casu*—offset the restrictive effects.

An argument could be made that, with the entry into force of the Lisbon Treaty, this approach could be subject to change. In particular, the combined effect of (i) the new title on energy and (ii) the provision of Article 7 TFEU, which explicitly stated that 'The Union shall ensure consistency between its policies and activities, taking all of its objectives into account', could mean that energy considerations might 'trump' competition considerations. In this respect, let us consider the following.

It has been proposed that, in order to counterbalance the negotiating power of gas suppliers, a 'gas purchasing group' could be established,[47] while noting that such a form of collaboration would need an exemption under Article 101(3) TFEU, an issue that has arisen in connection with the Commission's proposals to back a Caspian Gas Purchasing Group.[48] The key point is: what considerations should carry the day in redeeming the restrictive nature of such cooperation? On the 'efficiency' reading of Article 101(3) TFEU, only considerations that can be 'subsumed' in terms of cost-savings would be relevant to obtain an exemption. By contrast, if we accept that the introduction of Article 194 TFEU has enhanced the status of the energy policy vis-à-vis the competition policy, then it should likewise be accepted that public policy considerations also play a role. In this respect, the Commission could consider the importance of 'being able to speak with one voice' and/or other similar energy policy considerations, and balance the achievement under energy policy with the restrictive effects.

The publication in early 2011 of the Guidelines on the applicability of Article 101 of the Treaty on the Functioning of the European Union to horizontal co-operation agreements,[49] however, signals that the Commission has not embraced the public policy approach. First of all, the 2011 Guidelines do not contain a

---

[44] Ibid para 42.
[45] See G Monti, *EC Competition Law* (Cambridge University Press, 2007) 89–123.
[46] OJ 2000 L 187/47.
[47] See Notre Europe, *Towards a European Energy Community: A Policy Proposal* (2010) 115–16.
[48] See the statement by Eurogas, 'Caspian Development Corporation, Preliminary Remarks' Eurogas, 30 June 2009, O9 PP 370.
[49] OJ 2011 C 11/1.

separate chapter on 'environmental agreements' as was the case in the previous guidelines. According to the Commission, 'Standard-setting in the environment sector, which was the main focus of the former chapter on environmental agreements, is more appropriately dealt with in the standardization chapter of these guidelines'.[50]

Second, in the chapter dedicated to standard setting, the Guidelines propose an example which draws on the facts of the *CECED* case, as it involves washing machine manufacturers agreeing 'to no longer manufacture products which do not comply with certain environmental criteria (for example, energy efficiency)'.[51] The reasoning proposed by the Commission to support an exemption under Article 101(3) TFEU can be summarized as follows:

- Newer, more environmentally friendly products are more technically advanced, offering *qualitative efficiencies* in the form of more washing machine programmes which can be used by consumers.

- There are *cost efficiencies* for the purchasers of the washing machines resulting from lower running costs in the form of reduced consumption of water, electricity and soap.

- The efficiency gains outweigh the restrictive effects on competition in the form of increased costs.

Thus, the 2011 Guidelines on Horizontal Agreements seem to be based on the notion that the environmental benefits of the agreement can be 'subsumed' in efficiency considerations and that such considerations outweigh the restrictive effects. In other words, the Commission does not seem minded to consider relevant public policy considerations per se. This would mean that, in spite of the introduction of Article 194, the Commission would be unlikely to accept public policy justifications as factors that may lead to the application of Article 101(3) TFEU.

However, one must acknowledge that these are complex issues and that a lot would depend on the specificity of each case. The Commission might attempt to read economic considerations into public policy arguments, thus granting exemptions. For instance, Ikonnikova and Zwart have considered how the use of import quotas in the EU could have an 'efficiency' effect by encouraging supply diversification and strengthening the buyers' power and increase their surplus.[52] Thus, it is not impossible that the Commission may be induced by the introduction of a provision on energy to use its powers under Article 101(3) TFEU in a way that is compatible with the energy policy objectives.

---

[50] Ibid fn 1.
[51] Ibid para 329.
[52] See Ikonnikova and Zwart, 'Reinforcing Buyer Power: Trade Quotas and Supply Diversification in the EU Natural Gas Market' Tilec Discussion Paper, DP 2010-018, available at <http://ssm.com/abstract=1593546>.

D. Energy, security of supply and state sid

The European Union rules on state aid are of considerable importance to the energy sector given the traditionally high level of involvement of governments in energy production and supply.[53] Governments continue to play an important role with respect to ensuring an orderly transition from closed to open markets under competition and more importantly, with respect to designing energy policies that can ensure security of supply.

As already noted above in connection with the introduction of a directive on security of gas supply, security of supply can be a source of tension between EU and national energy policy as this domain remains a jealous precinct of Member States, as the drafting of Article 194(2) TFEU makes abundantly clear. The interface between national and EU energy aspects of security of supply (electricity and gas) is well embodied in Article 15(4) of Directive 2009/72/EC, pursuant to which, 'A Member State may, for reasons of security of supply, direct that priority be given to the dispatch of generating installations using indigenous primary energy fuel sources, to an extent not exceeding, in any calendar year, 15% of the overall primary energy necessary to produce the electricity consumed in the Member State concerned'.

This Article shows that a Member State may have a right to favour a 'national' fuel in terms of access to the grid, relative to fuel coming from other EU Member States, when reasons of security of supply are present. However, the limitation of Union trade that is inherent in this rule is acceptable, provided that it respects the 15 per cent threshold. This rule can be combined with a subsidy to the undertaking that uses the national fuel, which often is not competitive for reasons of costs. In this case, the rule mentioned above is applied in combination with the state aid rules. As a matter of fact, this provision has been used on five occasions so far in the context of the state aid rules:

- Case NN 49/99—Spain—costs of transition to competition;[54]
- Case N 6/A/2001—Ireland—Public Service Obligations imposed on the Electricity Supply Board with respect to the generation of electricity out of peat;[55]
- Case N 34/99—Austria—Stranded costs compensation;[56]
- Case C 7/2005—Slovenia—Electricity tariffs;[57]
- Case N 178/2010—Spain—Public service compensation linked to a preferential dispatch mechanism for indigenous coal power plants.[58]

---

[53] See in this respect, L Hancher and FM Salerno, *EU Energy Law* (Claeyes and Casteels, 2010) Vol II, Part 5.
[54] OJ 2001 C 268/7.
[55] OJ 2002 C 77/27.
[56] OJ 2002 C 5/2.
[57] OJ 2007 L 219/9.
[58] Available through DG COMP's website.

Each case is very fact-specific and so it is difficult to draw firm conclusions. However, the following considerations can be useful:

First of all, the intensity of the control exercised by the Commission through the years has increased.

- In Case C 7/2005, which is the last pre-Lisbon case, the Commission opened a formal investigation procedure because 'it was not in a position to assess the proportionality of the compensation' for the service of general economic interest, that is, the production of electricity from indigenous fuel.[59]

- In the final decision the Commission concluded that the measure was not aid because it had a purely compensatory nature (in accordance with the *Altmark* case law). However, in order to arrive at this conclusion it carried out a thorough assessment of the justification provided by the national authorities, including whether there were alternative choices that would have been more efficient.[60] This, one may argue, goes as far as questioning national energy policy on security of supply and imposing a high degree of control on it.

Second, in the first post-Lisbon case, that is, Case N 178/2010 on the subsidy to Spanish coal for the production of electricity, the Commission recalled the principle that:

The wide discretion enjoyed by Member states when defining what they consider as services of general economic interest has long been recognized in the case law. In the specific context of the electricity market, it is important that the public service requirements can be interpreted on a national basis, taking into account national circumstances and subject to the respect of EU law. In particular, the strategic importance of indigenous energy sources when these are scarce, and the geostrategic considerations involved in decisions concerning security of supply must be given due consideration.[61]

However, the Commission also noted that:

[T]he comments submitted by third parties in this case, as well as the current status of liberalization in the energy sector in Europe, call into question the validity of Spain's arguments related to security of supply. Therefore, in the light of these comments, the Commission considers it necessary to verify whether the Spanish authorities' conclusion that the notified scheme constitutes a service of general economic interest is manifestly erroneous.[62]

---

[59] OJ 2005 C 63/2 (decision to open formal investigation).

[60] See Decision in Case C 7/2005, OJ 2007 L 219/9, paras 112–15: 'the choice of Trbovlje was the one that led to providing the service of general economic interest at the least cost to the community, having regard to the specific factual and legal constraints prevailing in this case. In the present case the public service obligation consists in ensuring national security of supply up to 2009 by using indigenous primary energy fuel sources, to an extent not exceeding in any calendar year 15% of the overall primary energy necessary to produce the electricity consumed in Slovenia. (113) In the current situation, no more than two power plants in Slovenia could in any event have fulfilled the public service obligation in question in their current state. These are the Šoštanj plant and the Trbovlje plant.... *Slovenia has therefore used the most economically efficient way to achieve the public service obligation which consists in producing electricity with domestic fuel.*' (Emphasis added.)

[61] See Decision in Case N 178/2010, available through DG COMP's website, para 78.

[62] Ibid para 90.

This shows that the Commission is prepared to review security of supply reasons adduced by Member States before authorizing state aid measures. Indeed, in *Federutility* the Court remarked that:

> It follows from the very wording of Article 106 TFEU that the public service obligations which Article 3(2) of Directive 2003/55 allows to be imposed on undertakings must comply with the principle of proportionality and that, therefore, after 1 July 2007, those obligations may compromise the freedom to determine the price for the supply of natural gas only in so far as is necessary to achieve the objective in the general economic interest which they pursue and, consequently, for a period that is necessarily limited in time.[63]

However, the extent to which the Commission can question these justifications would have been one of the issues before the Court, as the decision in Case N 178/2010 was appealed but the applications for annulment were subsequently withdrawn.[64]

E. Energy and environment

Article 194(2) TFEU provides a legal basis for legislation needed to achieve 'the objectives in paragraph 1', which also include 'promote energy efficiency and energy saving and the development of new and renewable forms of energy'. Thus, Article 194(2) TFEU could be used as a legal basis for enacting environmental legislation. This raises the issue as to whether this provision—which envisaged the use of the normal legislative procedure—could be used to bypass the more cumbersome procedure envisaged under Article 192(2) TFEU on the environment, which foresees a unanimous decision of the Council.[65] The following considerations are in order.

First of all, as noted above, Article 194(3) TFEU requires a unanimous decision of the Council for measures that are 'primarily of a fiscal nature'. Moreover, measures adopted under Article 194(2) TFEU pursuant to the normal legislative procedure may not affect 'a Member State's right to determine the conditions for exploiting its energy resources, its choice between different energy sources and the general structure of its energy supply'. Thus, measures of this kind will also require a unanimous Council Decision.

Second, it is true, however, that, as Vedder noted, there is 'an institutional oddity' insofar as a measure in the field of eco-taxation might be subject to different procedures depending on whether it is presented as an environmental measure—for which the Article 192(2) procedure would be applicable—or an energy measure, for which the lighter Article 194(2) TFEU procedure might be invoked. Since, depending on the procedure chosen, European institutions might be excluded from consultations and thus will have standing to challenge the legal basis adopted. The case on the Regulation on notification to the Commission of investment projects in

---

[63] Case C-265/08, 24 April 2010, nyr, para 33.
[64] See cases T-484/10 *Gas Natural v Commission*; T-486/10 *Iberdrola v Commission*; T-490/10 *Endesa v Commission*; T-520/10 *Comunidad Autonoma de Galicia v Commission* removed from the Register on 13 August 2011.
[65] See H Vedder, 'The Treaty of Lisbon and European Environmental Law and Policy' (2010) *Journal of Environmental Law* 285–99.

energy infrastructure mentioned above is therefore illustrative of a possible trend towards more transparency.

F. Energy and external relations

Given the Union's growing dependency on external energy suppliers, an important aspect of its external role will be to forge a coherent external policy and where necessary, to promote the conclusion of a range of international agreements, on trade in energy, on investment in energy production facilities and on network infrastructure. Persuading the EU Member States to act together on matters of external energy security has become a major goal of the institutions. The Commission has cited developing a stronger external EU energy policy as one of its key priorities in its 2020 energy strategy as published on November 2010.[66] At the European Council meeting on 4 February, the Council confirmed the need for better coordination in the field of external relations. (See Conclusion number 11, PCE 026/11.)

The new Article 194 TFEU makes no reference to the external dimension of energy policy, but this may be remedied by the fact that the Lisbon Treaty aims to avoid past dichotomies between economic and political external policy of the Union. Hence the Treaty introduces a number of substantive amendments, such as the centralization of the objectives of external action. However, institutional modifications have also been made.

As a result, certain provisions in the Lisbon Treaty could potentially improve the coordination of the Union's external action on energy, although at first sight, the reforms now embodied in Part 5 of the new Treaty have not greatly altered the underlying principle that this is an area primarily reserved for intergovernmental decision-making.

Indeed, over the past decades the EC has already become party to important international agreements on energy and environmental matters. Moreover, in the specific energy field a large number of Strategic Partnerships with major supplier countries have been brokered. However, the EC's competence to conclude international agreements was often contested.

The Treaty now sets out and codifies the competences of the Union to conclude treaties in its Article 216 TFEU and the nature of these external competences (exclusive, shared or complementary) is made explicit in Article 3(2) TFEU. Article 261(1) TFEU 'amounts to a constitutionalisation of the doctrine of implied powers, drawing for its formulation on the Court of Justice'.[67] The new Treaty has expanded the possibilities for the use of implied powers and the flexibility clause (Article 352 TFEU) by loosening the link between internal objectives and external action.

---

[66] See above n 4.
[67] See further M Cremona, 'External Relations and External Competence of the European Union: The Emergence of an Integrated Policy' in Craig and De Búrca (eds), *The Evolution of European Law*, 2nd edn (Oxford University Press, forthcoming 2011) 371–461, 385.

Furthermore, the extension of the Common Commercial Policy (CCP) to include Foreign Direct Investment (FDI) in Article 207(1) TFEU could have important repercussions for the energy sector.

(i) Common Commercial Policy

The Union is now explicitly allowed to conclude international agreements in the field of CCP, listed in Article 3(1)(e) TEU as an exclusive competence. The scope of the CCP competence is clarified in Article 207(1) TFEU to cover foreign direct investment (FDI) and the achievement of uniformity in measures of liberalization. The inclusion of FDI is especially important for the energy sector. It would appear that the inclusion of FDI in the new Treaty could be explained in the light of attempts within the World Trade Organization (WTO) to conclude an agreement on this matter but the Treaty does not limit the scope to the commercial aspects of FDI.

The clarification of the scope of the CCP and the fact that all aspects of the CCP now fall under the exclusive competence of the EU are expected to contribute to a streamlining of the conduct as well as the coherence of EU trade policy and this may also be of relevance to external energy policy. The extension of the scope of exclusive competence could significantly reduce, but not necessarily eliminate the need of further mixed agreements in the energy sector (a prominent example being the Energy Charter Treaty).[68]

EU trade agreements will indeed replace mixed trade agreements. But energy agreements often cover more than one policy dimension and the dividing line between trade-related and other policy measures has always been rather vague. The Energy Community Treaty, for example, between the European Community and Albania, Bosnia, Croatia, the former YRM, Montenegro, Serbia and UNMIK of 2006 was entered into on the basis of Articles 133 and 175 EC[69] and made binding on the Member States by virtue of Council Decision 29 May 2006.[70]

However, in cases where agreements cover policies outside the scope of the CCP with no exclusive competence, the Member States will still be required to ratify the relevant agreement.[71] The new generation of EU free trade agreements—for

---

[68] All 27 Member States and the European Communities are Parties to the Energy Charter Treaty—see Council and Commission Decision of 23 September 1997 [1998] OJ L 69.

[69] The legal basis as stated in the Council Decision is: Articles 47(2), 55, 83, 89, 95,133 and 175, in conjunction with the first sentence of the first subparagraph of Article 300(2) and the second subparagraph of Article 300(3) thereof.

[70] [2006] OJ L 198/15.

[71] See Council and Commission Decision (EC, ECSC, Euratom) 98/181, on the conclusion, by the European Communities, of the Energy Charter Treaty and the Energy Charter Protocol on energy efficiency and related environmental aspects, OJ 1998 L 69; Opinion 2/00 *Cartagena Protocol* [2001] ECR I-9713 paras 34–47 (notably, the fact that an international trade agreement might pursue multiple objectives did not call into question the main finding of the Court, ie that the Protocol was an instrument pertaining to environmental policy; consequently, Article 175 EC was deemed to be the appropriate legal basis). In that regard, the Court stated that the practical difficulties associated with mixed agreements are not relevant when it comes to the choice of the legal basis for Community measures; but see *contra* Case C-281/01 *Commission v Council ('Energy Star Agreement')* [2002] ECR I-12049.

example, with Mercosur—will be mixed agreements due to the complexity and wide range of policies covered.

(ii) Foreign Direct Investment

The fact that foreign direct investment (FDI) is now an exclusive competence of the Union could also have important consequences for the energy sector and is not without importance for the implementation of the 'Gazprom clause' in Article 11 of the new gas and electricity directives, which—as discussed above—provides for a special procedure when the undertaking that is to be designed as a transmission system operator is controlled by 'a person or persons from a third country or third countries'. Where certification is requested by a TSO which is controlled by a person or persons from a third country the NRA shall refuse certification if it has not been demonstrated that the entity concerned complies with the requirements of Article 9 and that the granting of certification will not put at risk the security of energy supply of the Member State and the Union. In this respect, the NRA must take into account the rights and obligations of the Union with respect to that third country arising under international law including any agreement concluded with one or more third countries to which the Union is a party and which addresses the issue of security of energy supply as well as any bilateral agreements insofar as they are in compliance with Community law.

According to some commentators, Article 207 TFEU could be interpreted to the effect that Member States are no longer able to conclude so-called bilateral investment treaties (BITs) with third countries unless they are empowered by the EU to continue or conclude such agreements (see Article 218 TFEU). The opportunity and the form of such an empowerment will need to be worked out between the EU institutions and the Member State.

This provision is also relevant for the legality of inter-governmental agreements (IGAs) underpinning major gas and oil pipeline infrastructures which often incorporate measures to protect foreign investment against expropriation and to ensure fair and equitable treatment. A recent example of such an agreement is the Nabucco IGA signed on 13 July 2009 between Turkey, Bulgaria, Romania and Hungary. This agreement for which the Commission acted as a facilitator, also sets out some key terms and conditions under which the Nabucco pipeline can be operated. In particular it ensures that the regime applied in the Turkish part of the pipeline with respect to third party access is compatible with the legal requirements that apply within the Union.[72]

Although the pipeline is exempted from regulated third party access (TPA) under Article 18 of the second Gas Directive, TPA rules still apply as at least 50 per cent of the capacity of the pipeline has to be sold on the open market.[73] The IGA ensures that this capacity is also effectively available to third parties in Turkey,

---

[72] See C Jones (ed), *EU Energy Law: The Internal Energy Market: The Third Liberalisation Package* (Claeys and Casteels, 2010) vol I.

[73] The decision is available at <http://ec.europa.eu/energy/infratructure/gas/gas_exemptions>.

the only non-Member State involved. If the TPA rules had not been respected in this part of the pipeline, then parties could not have enjoyed the possibility of shipping gas from the Caspian to Austria.

While some commentators maintain that only those aspects of FDI that are linked to trade are covered by the new provisions on external competence, others argue that the Union has an exclusive competence to adopt investment policy measures enabling the investor to exercise a certain influence on an economic activity. Even those favouring a broader interpretation of Article 207 TFEU dispute whether or not measures to protect foreign investment against expropriation would fall within its scope, arguing that the EU lacks parallel internal competences.[74]

Needless to say, this interpretation is also disputed, and it is argued that the scope of the Union's external competence for FDI is not limited to those aspects where the Union has exercised this internal competence. One can therefore only agree with the general conclusion shared by many experts in this complex area that 'one thing is clear: given the uncertainties of the scope of the new Article 207 TFEU, a decisive role will be played by the ECJ. It would have been better if Member States had clarified this important issue in advance'.[75]

A further uncertain question is the impact of the new provisions on existing BITs. According to Article 351 TFEU and Article 4(3) TEU, Member States shall be obliged to adapt their BITs to EU law.[76] The Treaty of Lisbon does not provide a transitional period, however, so the possibility of 'grandfathering' such agreements is also controversial. Notably in Case C-205/06 *Commission v Austria* of March 2009, the Court directed the Commission to take any steps which might facilitate mutual assistance between the Member States, the legality of whose BITs were thrown into doubt by that ruling, and their adoption of a common attitude (paragraph 44).

The European Council, at its Energy Council meeting of 4 February 2001, offered to inform the Commission from 1 January 2012 of all their new and existing BITs with third countries and the Commission must make this information available to other Member States in an appropriate form. (See PCE 026/11, conclusion number 11.) The Commission has in turn welcomed the Council's 'groundbreaking' decisions as providing it with the essential momentum to ensure a strong European representation in future relations with external countries. (Commissioner Oettinger, Statement on the outcome of the EU Summit, Speech number 11/71 delivered on 4 February 2011.)

---

[74] For a systematic review of these different opinions and an excellent analysis of the topic, see A Dimopoulus, 'Regulation of Foreign Investment in EU External Relations Law' PhD thesis defended at the EUI, Florence, 2010.

[75] See J Wouters et al, 'The European Union's External Relations after the Lisbon Treaty' in S Griller and J Ziller (eds), *The Lisbon Treaty EU Constitutionalism without a Constitutional Treaty?* (2008, European Community Studies Association of Austria Publication Series) Vol 11, 173.

[76] The Commission had already successfully established that certain clauses in existing BITs were in breach of Article 307 EC (now Article 351 TFEU)—Case C-205/06 *Commission v Austria* 3 March 2009 and Case C-249/06 *Commission v Sweden* 3 March 2009 and Case C-118/07 *Commission v Finland* 19 November 2009. In July 2010 the Commission published a draft Regulation establishing transitional arrangements for BITs. COM(2010) C-7172/1.

(iii) Limitations on external competence

Although the Treaty includes competences that are overtly external, such as external trade and commercial policy, as well as on the protection of the environment, there is no clear external competence to act in the field of energy policy attributed to the Union in Article 194. On the contrary, it may be maintained that the Union's competence is limited to the four internal aspects listed in that Article and that the scope of the EU's energy policy is constrained to the internal market— that is to free movement of goods and undistorted competition.[77]

At the same time, it must be recalled that the former TEC had already provided an internal competence to the EC but did not explicitly grant a power to act externally. In this respect, and in order to extend the EC's competence to act externally, the Court of Justice had developed the principle of parallelism: if the Treaty grants internal competence and the EC has exercised this internal competence then there is an implied power for the EC also to act externally. The nature of the implied external competence at stake is exclusive as far as the internal competence has been exercised. Independent external action by the Member States would affect the common rules established by the EC.

The Court of Justice had also accepted in Opinion 1/94 that the EC may also have an external competence, even if this external competence is not explicitly provided for in the Treaties, but when the EC adopts an internal act (based on an internal competence) stating that from now on, the negotiation and conclusion of international agreements in a certain field of competence will be for the EC and not the Member States. With regard to implied external competences the Court of Justice also accepted that there could be an implied external competence for the EC even though the internal competence of the EC had not yet been exercised but whether the competence at stake here was an exclusive one has been a matter of continued controversy.

On the basis of the *ERTA* doctrine it was argued that the external competence could only be exclusive after it had been exercised and as long as the Union had not acted, the Member States are allowed to act externally independently. In the *Open Skies* case,[78] however, the Court of Justice stated that there was no need for the EC to exercise the external competence at the same time as the internal competence (as provided for in Opinion 1/76) since the EC could coordinate internally the external actions of the Member States. In combination with the further statement by the Court of Justice in Opinion 1/03, this seems to restrict the external competences of the Member States to a considerable extent.

---

[77] See eg, H Vedder, 'The Treaty of Lisbon and European Environmental Law and Policy' (2010) *Journal of Environmental Law* 285–99, who suggests that this could mean that an external energy policy will have to be conducted on the basis of Article 192 TFEU as it is outside the scope of the internal market. The inclusion of climate change as a regional or worldwide environmental problem that may be addressed by the EU's environmental policy in his view confirms this. Thus many climate change measures will, as a result, have to rely upon Article 192 TFEU.

[78] Case C-476/98 *Commission v Germany* [2002] ECR I-9855.

This complex case law is now codified in the new Article 216 TFEU, an Article already criticized for its vagueness by the Czech constitutional court.[79] Indeed, the latter part of Article 216 TFEU ('the conclusion of an agreement is necessary in order to achieve within the framework of the Union's policies, one of the objectives referred to in the Treaties') can be read as providing further competence to act externally, going beyond the 'parallelism' of internal and external competences. The nature of this competence does not, however, seem to be exclusive. Article 3(2) TEU does not refer to an exclusive competence. Mixity will therefore remain important in external energy policy, and as EU President Herman van Rompuy has stressed, 'the EU will not replace individual bilateral relationships with our strategic partners . . . the most important thing is not to speak with one voice but to have common messages and a shared sense of direction.'[80]

G. Nuclear energy and Lisbon

The relationship between the EC Treaty and the Euratom Treaty proved a source of controversy during the IGC leading up to the drafting of the Convention, and it is perhaps hardly surprising that the Lisbon Treaty failed to resolve this. Although Member States called for the abolition of the Treaty and the consolidation of certain of its provisions into the new Treaty, the Euratom Treaty now forms part of the new constitutional arrangements, albeit in essentially unamended form.

The relationship between the new Treaty and the Euratom Treaty is regulated by Protocol 36. Some Member States supported the idea of revising and updating the Euratom Treaty, and confirmed their willingness to do so in a Declaration to the Final Act of Lisbon Treaty.[81]

Notably, Declaration number 54, signed by Germany, Ireland, Hungary, Austria and Sweden, notes that the core provisions of the Euratom Treaty have not been substantially amended since its entry into force and need to be brought up to date. They therefore support the idea of a Conference of the Representatives of the Member States, which should be convened as soon as possible. It may also be noted that two other Declarations attached to the Final Act of the Treaty establishing a Constitution for Europe deal with certain aspects of nuclear energy in two of the new Member States, that is (i) Lithuania (Declaration number 35)[82] and (ii) Slovakia (Declaration number 37)[83] and commit the Union to financing the gradual closure of the nuclear plants involved. Ignalina was scheduled for closure in 2009 while the Slovak Bohunice VI was scheduled for closure a year earlier.

State finance for and support to the nuclear industry elsewhere in the Union in the form of subsidies will remain problematic, at least until the present Euratom Treaty is updated, if at all. The Euratom Treaty, unlike the EC and the former

---

[79] Decision 2008/11/26 Pl. ÚS 19/08: Treaty of Lisbon I, para 186.
[80] Speech delivered at the University of Warsaw, 17 January 2011 and reported in *EU Energy*, no 250, 28 January 2011, 4.
[81] OJ 2007 C 306/231–271, 268.
[82] OJ 2004 C 310/401–474, 467–8.
[83] OJ 2004 C 310/401–474, 469.

ECSC Treaty does not contain any specific provisions on state aid control. At the same time, the Euratom Treaty is a '*lex specialis*'. Nuclear energy is likely to remain a special case in that the TFEU rules on state aid at least cannot be straightforwardly and directly applied to evaluate aid to this sector. However, the relationship between the EC Treaty and the Euratom Treaty seems not to have proven problematic in the past with regard to the application of the competition rules or the rules regarding merger clearance.

H. Lisbon, energy and SGEIs

Defining and assigning competence to services of general economic interest (SGEIs) also proved controversial in the negotiations on the Treaty, leading to the insertion of Article 14 in the text as well as a separate Protocol (number 26) on SGIs. This Protocol recognizes that such services are shared values of the Union and the essential role and wide discretion of national, regional and local authorities in providing, organizing and commissioning these services is underlined, including the high level of quality, safety and affordability and the promotion of universal access and user rights.

The Protocol does not, however, deal with the financing of such services, so that the Treaty rules on state aid (now Articles 107–109) continue to apply as before. Given that at least in respect of gas and electricity the internal market legislation has now already introduced substantial harmonization, the future significance of Article 14 TFEU and the Protocol may be limited. In particular, as a result of the adoption and entry into force of the internal market Directives 96/92 and 98/30, and 54/2004 and 55/2004, followed by the 'Third Package' directives and regulations of 2009, there are now major limitations on the scope for Member States to define as public service obligations tasks which are not expressly mentioned in Article 3 of the Directives.[84]

However, it should also be borne in mind that the energy directives, unlike for example, the Directives and related measures adopted for the postal and telecommunications sectors, do not designate particular services or activities as universal services while others are treated as competitive services. In the electricity and gas sectors it is clear from the text of Article 3(2) that Member States can impose on any undertaking operating in the relevant sector a public service obligation, irrespective of the type of service, or class of customers to whom that service is provided.

Obligations with respect to environmental protection, for example, can apply to all undertakings supplying all categories of customers, whether eligible or captive

---

[84] See in this respect, C Jones, *EU Energy Law* (Claeys and Casteels, 2010) Vol I, chapter 6.10 which concludes: 'in practical terms, this means that it will be very rarely, if ever, necessary to derogate from the Directives to achieve a public service obligation, because in practice all the public service objectives mentioned in Article 3(2) can be achieved without doing so. For example, the Commission has not indicated that any such derogation was granted by a Member State under the first electricity and gas Directives. This can be more clearly seen by an analysis of the individual public service criteria listed in Article 3(2).'

customers.[85] The Electricity and Gas Directives do, however, recognize in their recitals that Member States can take appropriate measures to guarantee public services for households and small enterprises (see now Recital 42 of Directive 72/2009; Recital 47, Directive 73/2009).[86]

Secondly, the Directives already explicitly provide for specific exemptions from their rules with a view to the realization of legitimate public service obligations. It may therefore be difficult for Member States to justify the adoption of measures which go beyond these specific exemptions or derogations.

Thirdly, account must still be taken of the Community interest—the last sentence of Article 106(2) TFEU. The text of Article 3(8) of the 2003 Directives originally limited this interest to eligible customers but as from 1 July 2007 the Community interest has included compliance with full competition for all classes of consumer.

Fourthly, and as a result of the entry into force of the Directives, the Commission, and the Court are likely to scrutinize in closer detail the actual instruments and procedures for designating undertakings which are to perform the tasks listed in Article 3(2) of the Electricity and Gas Directives. This same Article 3(2) is also maintained in full in the new Directive 72/2009 (electricity) and Directive 73/2009 (gas).[87] That Article makes it clear that the obligations must be clearly defined, transparent, non-discriminatory, verifiable and should guarantee equality of access to national consumers for all EU electricity companies. The Commission will increasingly expect a Public Service Obligation (PSO) to be well defined and verifiable and put out to competitive tender insofar as possible.[88] Obviously this is not possible insofar as such obligations are entrusted to transmission system operators, as these are (usually) natural monopolies.

In the recent *Federutility* case,[89] the Court was required to establish the limits of the role of the Italian NRA in imposing PSOs on the liberalized gas market in the absence of effective competition. The Italian energy regulator had elected to fix 'reference prices' for the sale of gas to certain customers by way of *ex ante* regulation.

First, the Court noted that the price for the supply of natural gas must, as from 1 July 2007, be determined solely by market forces, a requirement that follows from the very purpose—the total liberalization of the market for national gas. However, the Court also recognized that it was apparent that the Second Gas Directive 55/2008 is also designed to guarantee that 'high standards' of public service are maintained and the final consumer is protected. Article 3(2) expressly allows Member States to impose 'public service obligations' on gas companies, which could relate to the 'price of supply'.

---

[85] See also Case C-245/08, pending.

[86] See for an assessment of similar recitals in the IEM Directives of 2003, the AG's Opinion in Case C-245/08, 20 October 2009.

[87] OJ 2009 L 211/55 and L 211/94.

[88] See further the Opinions of the AG in Case C-507/03 *Commission v Ireland* [2007] ECR I-9777 and Case C-507/03 *Commission v Ireland*, 14 September 2006.

[89] Case C-265/08, 24 April 2010, nyr.

Second, the Court also confirmed that—irrespective of harmonization—Member States are entitled to define the scope of their 'public service obligations' and to take account of their own national policy objectives and national circumstances. As a result, the Court concluded that the Gas Directive still allows Member States to assess, after 1 July 2007, whether it is necessary to impose measures to ensure that the price of the supply of natural gas to final consumers is maintained at a reasonable level. At the same time, the Court imposed several conditions in order to ensure that the national measure was also proportional. Significantly, as for the economic factors justifying intervention, the Court noted that, 'it is for the referring court to verify whether... taking account in particular of the objective of establishing a fully operational internal market for gas and of the investments necessary in order to exert effective competition in the natural gas sector... such an intervention is required'.

Thirdly, however, the Court limited Member States' ability to introduce provisions which derogate—even temporarily—from the internal energy market rules by reiterating that such provisions ought to pass a proportionality test to be valid. In this respect, the *Federutility* ruling seems to be in contrast with the recent decision in the Spanish coal case mentioned above, where the Commission adduced its obligation of deference to Member States' choices in terms of security of supply, thus imposing upon itself a limitation on its ability to review the justifications provided by a Member State. Indeed, one of the grounds of (the now withdrawn) appeal invoked the infringement of Articles 3(2) and 11(4) of the Second Electricity Market Directive (identical to Article 15(4) of the Third Electricity Directive) and Article 106(2) TFEU for failure to carry out a proportionality check.[90]

V. Conclusions

Although the inclusion of a title on energy was a hard-fought battle, one may reflect on whether it will really lead to major changes in the way in which European energy policy is formulated, implemented and enforced.

Certainly the introduction of a new legal framework will be only part of the picture: even if the new title could be interpreted as conferring enhanced competence on the Union at the expense of the Member States, the political will to use these powers is another matter. Even without these powers, the European institutions were able to adopt several key legislative packages, culminating in the Third Energy Package and the equally ambitious climate change package. The introduction of an explicit competence—albeit shared—may have the effect of enhancing consistency and transparency in the Union's legislative procedure, but as illustrated above, if the results of the first year of 'post-Lisbon' are taken as illustrative, this is not necessarily the case. Certain types of measures are still based on general treaty provisions. Moreover, the inclusion of a new title has not meant that the Commis-

---

[90] See the summary of the application published in the OJ 2010 C 328/51.

sion has an easier passage in the Council to realize its ambitions, as illustrated by the substantial watering down of its initial proposals for a new Regulation on Security of Gas Supply.

Progress towards a unified policy on external gas security and Union solidarity remains difficult. It is perhaps in the area of external competences that the future impact of the new Treaty will be the most difficult to predict. On the one hand, certain exclusive competences appear to be enhanced, particularly through the inclusion of FDI within the scope of the CCP, but on the other hand, the new treaty provisions are by no means clear, and substantial uncertainty as to the nature of that competence remains. This is regrettable, given that the realization of a coherent and effective European energy policy is increasingly an external affair.

19

EU Sports Law: The Effect of the Lisbon Treaty

Stephen Weatherill

I. Introduction

The influence of the Treaty of Lisbon on sport in Europe is both profound and trivial. It is *profound* in that for the first time sport is subject to explicit reference within the Treaties establishing and governing the European Union. Given the fundamental principle that the EU possesses only the competences conferred upon it by its Member States, the novelty achieved by this express attribution in the field of sport counts as immensely constitutionally significant. But for two reasons the Treaty's influence is also *trivial*. First, because the content of the new provisions has been drawn with conspicuous caution, so that the EU's newly acquired powers in fact represent a most modest grant made by the Member States. And second because, notwithstanding the barren text of the pre-Lisbon Treaty, the EU has in fact long exercised a significant influence over the autonomy enjoyed by sports federations operating on its territory. So the Lisbon Treaty reveals a gulf between constitutional principle—where it seems to carry great weight—and law and policymaking in practice, on which its effect is likely to be considerably less striking.

The purpose of this chapter is to reflect on the development of 'EU sports law' during the long period in which an explicit treaty mandate was lacking and to assess the extent to which the Lisbon Treaty will change the picture. Given the observations made in the opening paragraph, such changes are not likely to be dramatic, but nonetheless changes there will be, both at the level of detail and in the direction of securing a deeper legitimacy for EU intervention in the field of sport. A question which also deserves to be addressed is one that goes beyond the specific case of sport: why, in a treaty which is in many ways marked by assertion of state control over and in some respects autonomy from the pattern of EU integration, has sport found its way into the very small group of policy areas in which EU competences have been formally *increased*?

II. EU Sports Law—the Road to Lisbon

The EU possesses no general regulatory competence. It has only the competences and powers attributed to it by its treaties. In the EC Treaty this was stipulated in Article 5 (1) EC, whereas since the entry into force of the Lisbon Treaty this 'principle of conferral' is located in Article 5 TEU. Prior to the entry into force of the Lisbon Treaty on 1 December 2009 the EU was equipped with no explicit powers in the field of sport. More than that: the EC Treaty did not mention sport at all. But *ab initio* in *Walrave and Koch*[1] the Court rejected a line of reasoning that would have rigidly separated sports governance from EC law. That would have sheltered a huge range of practices with economic impact from the assumptions of EC law, damaging the achievement of the objectives of the Treaty. Instead, the Court has consistently taken the view that insofar as it constitutes an economic activity, sport falls within the scope of the Treaty and sporting practices must comply with the rules contained therein. But they *may* comply, even if apparently antagonistic to the foundational values of the Treaty. In the landmark decision in *Walrave and Koch* the Court accepted that the treaty rule forbidding discrimination on grounds of nationality does not affect the composition of national representative sides. Such 'sporting discrimination' defines the very nature of international competition, and EU law does not call it into question.

The authority of the EC, now EU, to supervise sporting practices was and is rooted on the economic impact of sport. It therefore derived from the broad functional reach of the relevant rules of the Treaty (free movement and competition law, most conspicuously, and also the basic prohibition against nationality-based discrimination), but it was denied any specific legislative competence in the field of sport. Sport's 'road to Lisbon' is paved by the decisions of the Court, and subsequently those of the Commission, which applied first the free movement provisions and later the competition rules to sport. But the Treaty was never applied to sport as if it were merely a normal industry. Instead, a more creative approach was adopted, requiring a significant investment of resources in making sense of the intersection between the demands of EC law and the aspirations of sport in circumstances where the Treaty did not spell out any guidance.

The core of the challenge is well captured by two observations made by the Court in its famous *Bosman* ruling.[2] First, the Court declared that:

In view of the considerable social importance of sporting activities and in particular football in the Community, the aims of maintaining a balance between clubs by preserving a certain degree of equality and uncertainty as to results and of encouraging the recruitment and training of young players must be accepted as legitimate.[3]

The Court, while finding that the particular practices impugned in *Bosman* fell foul of the Treaty because they did not adequately contribute to these legitimate aims,

---

[1] Case 36/74 [1974] ECR 1405.
[2] Case C-415/93 [1995] ECR I-4921.
[3] Ibid para 106.

showed itself receptive to embracing the special features of sport. So sport's distinctive concerns are *not* explicitly recognized by the Treaty but they are drawn in to the assessment of sport's compliance with the rules of the internal market (*in casu* free movement) by a Court which is visibly anxious to identify what is *legitimate* in the special circumstances of professional sport. Second, the Court added remarks in the *Bosman* ruling about 'the difficulty of severing the economic aspects from the sporting aspects of football'.[4] This hits the nail squarely on the head. The vast majority of rules in sport also exert an economic impact, and it is that economic impact which triggered the application of the rules of the Treaty. Few sporting rules will not also have economic implications. The implication is that sporting practices will commonly fall within the scope of application of the Treaty, especially in the context of professional sport, which then makes all the more important the choices made about what is treated as a *legitimate* sporting practice.

Typically, sporting bodies have sought to argue for a generous interpretation of the scope of the 'sporting rule' which is wholly untouched by the Treaty, and, if the matter is judged to fall within the scope of the Treaty, they have then aimed to defend their practices as necessary to run their sport effectively. It is for the Court (or in appropriate cases the Commission) to consider the strength of these claims, and in doing so the EU institutions are forced to reach their own conclusions on the nature of sports governance—conclusions which are frequently (though not invariably) less persuaded by the need for sporting autonomy than is urged by governing bodies.

III. The Practice of EU Sports Law

The story of the manner in which first the Court and more recently the Commission developed the law in its application to sport is a complex though intriguing one. It reflects the need to allow a *conditional* autonomy to sporting practices—an autonomy *conditional* on respect for the core norms of the Treaty. The matter has been addressed in full elsewhere.[5] The purpose of this summary is simply to set the scene in preparation for reflection on why there was a readiness in the negotiation of the Treaty of Lisbon to respond to this pattern of development by bringing sport explicitly within the Treaty for the first time, and also in order to assess the extent to which Lisbon changes the situation.

Deliège provides a good example. The litigation concerned the selection of individual athletes (*in casu* judokas) for international competition.[6] Participation was not open. One had to be chosen by the national federation. If one was not chosen,

---

[4] Ibid para 76.
[5] See eg R Parrish, *Sports Law and Policy in the European Union* (2003); S Weatherill, *European Sports Law* (Manchester University Press, 2007); E Szyszczak, 'Is Sport Special?' in B Bogusz, A Cygan and E Szyszczak (eds), *The Regulation of Sport in the European Union* (TMC Asser Press, 2007); S Van den Bogaert and A Vermeersch, 'Sport and the EC Treaty: A Tale of Uneasy Bedfellows' (Edward Elgar, 2006) 31 *ELRev* 821.
[6] Cases C-51/96 & C-191/97 *Deliège v Ligue de Judo* [2000] ECR I-2549.

one's economic interests would be damaged. This was a classic case which brought the basic organizational structure of sport into contact with the economic interests of participants. The Court stated that selection rules 'inevitably have the effect of limiting the number of participants in a tournament' but that 'such a limitation is inherent in the conduct of an international high-level sports event, which necessarily involves certain selection rules or criteria being adopted'.[7] Accordingly, the rules did not in themselves constitute a restriction on the freedom to provide services prohibited by the Treaty. So a detrimental effect felt by an individual sportsman does not mean that rules are *incompatible* with the Treaty. The *Deliège* judgment is respectful of sporting autonomy, but according to reasoning which treats EU law and 'internal' sports law as potentially overlapping.

The application of the Treaty competition rules to sport was a matter carefully avoided by the Court in *Bosman* itself. But the Commission came to adopt a functionally comparable approach to sport: that is, it did not exclude sport from supervision pursuant to the relevant treaty provisions but equally it did not rule out that sport might present some peculiar characteristics that should be taken into account in the analysis. The Commission's *ENIC/UEFA* decision offers an illustration.[8] It concluded that rules forbidding multiple ownership of football clubs suppressed demand but were indispensable to the maintenance of a credible competition marked by uncertainty as to the outcome of all matches. A competition's basic character would be shattered were consumers to suspect the clubs were not true rivals. The principal message here is that sporting practices typically have an economic effect and that accordingly they cannot be sealed off from the expectations of the Treaty. However, within the area of overlap between EU law and 'internal' sports law there is room for recognition of the features of sport which may differ from 'normal' industries.

There is a 'policy on sport' to be discerned here, albeit that its character is influenced by the eccentric development generated by the Treaty's absence of any sports-specific material and the essentially incremental nature of litigation and complaint-handling. Formally, this 'policy' involves a batch of decisions determining whether or not particular challenged practices comply with the Treaty. One can discern thematic principles binding together the decisional practice—respect for fair play, credible competition, national representative teams, and so on—but the EU is not competent to mandate by legislation the structure of sports governance in Europe.

The precise legal basis underpinning the Court's approach has long been rather murky. What is this 'sporting exception'? Does it mean that a practice falls outwith the scope of the Treaty altogether? Or is it that the rules have an economic effect and fall within the scope of the Treaty but are not condemned by it because they also have virtuous non-economic (sporting) effects?[9] In the summer of 2006 the

---

[7] Ibid para 64.
[8] COMP 37.806 ENIC/UEFA, IP/02/942, 27 June 2002.
[9] For extended analysis see R Parrish and S Miettinen, *The Sporting Exception in European Law* (TMC Asser Press, 2007); also S Weatherill, 'On Overlapping Legal Orders: What is the "Purely Sporting Rule"?' in Bogusz, Cygan, and Szyszczak, above n 5.

Court brought a welcome degree of analytical clarity to the matter. In *Meca-Medina and Majcen v Commission* the applicants, professional swimmers who had failed a drug test and been banned for two years, had complained unsuccessfully to the Commission of a violation of the Treaty competition rules. The CFI (as it then was) rejected an application for annulment of the Commission's decision.[10] So did the ECJ (as it then was).[11] But whereas the CFI attempted to insist that anti-doping rules concern exclusively non-economic aspects of sport, designed to preserve 'noble competition',[12] the ECJ instead stated that 'the mere fact that a rule is purely sporting in nature does not have the effect of removing from the scope of the Treaty the person engaging in the activity governed by that rule or the body which has laid it down'.[13] And if the sporting activity in question falls within the scope of the Treaty, the rules which govern that activity must satisfy the requirements of the Treaty 'which, in particular, seek to ensure freedom of movement for workers, freedom of establishment, freedom to provide services, or competition'.[14] A practice may be of a sporting nature—and perhaps even 'purely sporting' in *intent*—but it falls to be tested against the demands of EU trade law where it exerts economic *effects*. But, just as in *Bosman*, the Court in *Meca-Medina* did not abandon its thematically consistent readiness to ensure that sport's special concerns should be carefully and sensitively fed into the analysis. It took the view that the general objective of the rules was to combat doping in order for competitive sport to be conducted on a fair basis; and the adverse effect of penalties on athletes' freedom of action must be considered to be inherent in the anti-doping rules. The rules challenged in *Bosman* were not in the Court's view necessary to protect sport's legitimate concerns but in *Meca-Medina* the Court concluded that the sport's governing body was entitled to maintain its rules. It had not been shown that the rules concerning the definition of an offence or the severity of the penalties imposed went beyond what was necessary for the organization of the sport.

In *Meca-Medina* the Court took a broad view of the scope of the Treaty, but having brought sporting rules within its scope it shows itself readily prepared to draw on the importance of matters not explicitly described as 'justifications' in the Treaty in order to permit the continued application of challenged practices which are shown to be necessary to achieve legitimate sporting objectives and/or are inherent in the organization of sport. That, then, becomes the core of the argument when EU law overlaps with sports governance: can a sport show why prejudicial economic effects falling within the scope of the Treaty must be tolerated in a particular case? As the Court put it in *Meca-Medina*, restrictions imposed by rules adopted by sports federations 'must be limited to what is necessary to ensure the proper conduct of competitive sport'.[15] This is a statement of the *conditional autonomy* of sports federations under EU law. And in addition, and central to the

[10] Case T-313/02 [2004] ECR II-3291.
[11] Case C-519/04 P [2006] ECR I-6991.
[12] Para 49 CFI, above n 10.
[13] Para 27 ECJ, above n 11.
[14] Ibid para 28 ECJ.
[15] Ibid para 47 ECJ.

primary importance of the ruling, it is an assertion of the need for a case-by-case examination of the compatibility of sporting practices with the Treaty.[16] There is no blanket immunity: there is no zone of 'sporting autonomy' that can be treated as naturally and inevitably beyond the reach of EU law.

The Commission absorbed the Court's thematic approach in its White Paper on Sport issued in July 2007.[17] The Commission examines aspects of practice explicitly in the light of *The specificity of sport* (para 4.1). It explains that the specificity of European sport can be approached through two prisms:

- The specificity of sporting activities and of sporting rules, such as separate competitions for men and women, limitations on the number of participants in competitions, or the need to ensure uncertainty concerning outcomes and to preserve a competitive balance between clubs taking part in the same competitions;

- The specificity of the sport structure, including notably the autonomy and diversity of sport organisations, a pyramid structure of competitions from grassroots to elite level and organised solidarity mechanisms between the different levels and operators, the organisation of sport on a national basis, and the principle of a single federation per sport.

It extracts this from the decisions of the Court and it insists that future application of the rules, embracing 'specificity', must comply with the Treaty. Elaboration is provided by the supporting Staff Working Document, which identifies key features of the 'specificity of sport' to include interdependence between competing adversaries, uncertainty as to result, freedom of internal organization, and sport's educational, public health, social, cultural and recreational functions. Substantial Annexes, containing detailed legal analysis, deal with *Sport and EU Competition Rules* and *Sport and Internal Market Freedoms*.

The key point, however, is that insofar as concessions are made to sporting 'specificity' they are made on terms dictated by EU law; and, moreover, a case-by-case analysis of sporting practices is required. A general exemption is 'neither possible nor warranted', in the judgement of the Commission.[18] This legal analysis is heavily dependent on *Meca-Medina*, which is the only decision of the Court explicitly referred to in the body of the White Paper. From the perspective of governing bodies in sport there are two principal objections to this position. The first is that EU law misperceives the nature and purpose of sport and that it intervenes in an insensitive and destructive manner. The second is that a case-by-case approach generates great uncertainty for those involved in the organization of

---

[16] See S Weatherill, 'Anti-doping Revisited—The Demise of the Rule of "Purely Sporting Interest"?' (2006) *European Competition Law Review* 645; M Wathelet, 'L'arrêt Meca-Medina et Majcen: plus qu'un coup dans l'eau' 2006/41 *Revue de Jurisprudence de Liège, Mons et Bruxelles* 1799; A Rincón, 'EC Competition and Internal Market Law: On the Existence of a Sporting Exemption and its Withdrawal' (2007) 3 *Journal of Contemporary European Research* 224.

[17] COM (2007) 391. Full documentation is available at <http://ec.europa.eu/sport/white-paper/index_en.htm>.

[18] Staff Working Document, above n 17 at 69, 78.

sport. Such anxieties have been audible for many years, but *Meca-Medina* inflamed the debate and the ruling attracted pained criticism from those close to sports governing bodies.[19] Similarly, the White Paper has been greeted from this perspective with a degree of mistrust from those detecting a diminished concern on the part of the Commission to take full account of the supposed special character of sport.[20] This is the more general context within which *Meca-Medina* has been attacked for stripping away some of the autonomy to which sports governing bodies regularly lay claim as necessary and appropriate. Such rebukes may be fair, they may be unfair—but the essential *contestability* of the practice of EU intervention in sport, allied to the deficiencies and constitutional restraint embedded in the Treaty itself, is plain. So too is the magnitude of the sums of money at stake.

IV. The Politics of the 'Sporting Exception'

The result of the evolved pattern sketched above is that sports bodies need to engage with EU law. Their ideal outcome, periodically voiced with yearning, would be to immunize sport from the application of EU law. This would be in principle possible, though given that it would require the setting aside of the Court's interpretation of provisions of the Treaty by dint of unanimously agreed treaty revision, it has never seemed politically realistic. It would, moreover, involve some heroic drafting. Some aspects of sport, such as protection of intellectual property rights, are not at all 'special' but rather ferociously commercial and should surely not be immunized from legal control. So a formula would need to be drafted which would protect necessary 'sporting' rules from legal oversight. This would be extremely difficult to achieve and, in any event, its interpretation would ultimately fall for authoritative determination by the Court in Luxembourg, which would not be what those seeking 'sporting autonomy' would want at all.

The Declarations on Sport agreed at Amsterdam and Nice are revealing. They show political disinclination to agree binding rules on sport and, moreover, even in a non-binding setting, there is no evident appetite to swallow the more aggressive appeals for partial or total immunity advanced by sporting 'insiders'.

The Declaration on Sport attached to the Amsterdam Treaty merely asserts that:

The Conference emphasises the social significance of sport, in particular its role in forging identity and bringing people together. The Conference therefore calls on the bodies of the European Union to listen to sports associations when important questions affecting sport are at issue. In this connection, special consideration should be given to the particular characteristics of amateur sport.

---

[19] See eg G Infantino (Director of Legal Affairs at UEFA), 'Meca-Medina: A Step Backwards for the European Sports Model and the Specificity of Sport?' UEFA paper 02/10/06, available at <http://www.uefa.com/MultimediaFiles/Download/uefa/KeyTopics/480391_DOWNLOAD.pdf>; J Zylberstein, 'Collision entre idéaux sportifs et continges économiques dans l'arrêt *Meca-Medina*' 2007/1–2 CDE 218.
[20] J Hill, 'The European Commission's White Paper on Sport: A Step backwards for Specificity?' (2009) 1 *International Journal of Sport Policy* 253.

The Nice Declaration is rather more elaborate but reveals a similar tone. A Declaration on 'the specific characteristics of sport and its social function in Europe, of which account should be taken in implementing common policies' was annexed to the Conclusions of the Nice European Council held in December 2000. This concedes the absence of any direct powers in the area, but accepts that in their action taken under the Treaty the institutions must 'take account of the social, educational and cultural functions inherent in sport and making it special, in order that the code of ethics and the solidarity essential to the preservation of its social role may be respected and nurtured.' The European Council calls also for the preservation of 'the cohesion and ties of solidarity binding the practice of sports at every level'.

The adoption of these Declarations is important in the sense that it showed that the tension between the EU's absence of explicit competence in the field of sport and the activity of its Court and Commission in applying the rules on free movement and competition had squeezed out a political response. But the legal form and the chosen content is telling: non-binding Declarations which do little more than sketch broad aspiration and generalities was the best that sport was able to extract from the political process. These Declarations emphatically do not subvert the core of the *Bosman* ruling's firm application of the fundamental treaty rules governing free movement law to sport. Indeed this was expressly acknowledged by the Court in both *Deliège*[21] and in *Lehtonen*[22] where it treated the Amsterdam Declaration as confirming its own case law, not calling it into question. A 'sporting exception' is as far away as ever.

Underlying this narrative is the appreciation that for sport to secure protection from the EU and its legal order it must in some way engage with it, not dismiss it as irrelevant. After all, as the practice of the Court and the Commission accumulated it became increasingly plain that the EU's institutions did not merely show rhetorical acceptance of the claim that 'sport is (sometimes) special'. They put it into practice, and gave the green light to a number of challenged practices, ranging from rules against multiple club ownership[23] to selection for international competition[24] to collective selling of broadcasting rights.[25] Even in *Meca-Medina* the outcome was *not* to preclude anti-doping controls. The EU—the Court, the Commission—was something that sports bodies could do business with. UEFA, in particular, is notable for adapting its strategy towards a more cooperative model.[26] And this theme helps to explain the negotiation and likely impact of the provisions newly inserted by the Treaty of Lisbon.

---

[21] Cases C-51/96 & C-191/97, above n 6 at paras 41–2.
[22] Case C-176/96 [2000] ECR I-2681, paras 32–3.
[23] Above n 8.
[24] Above n 6.
[25] Decision 2003/778 *Champions League* [2003] OJ L291/25.
[26] B García, 'UEFA and the European Union: From Confrontation to Co-Operation' (2007) 3 *Journal of Contemporary European Research* 202.

V. The Long Haul: Negotiating the Treaty of Lisbon

The Convention on the Future of Europe opened in February 2002. The small number of documents submitted which dealt explicitly with sport tended to have in common an anxiety that the special character of sport has been undermined and a consequent ambition to craft more legally durable protection than is provided by the Amsterdam Declaration.[27] None, however, offers a detailed explanation of what is really reckoned to be wrong with the current situation. So, for example, the Report of M Lamassoure on the division of competences between the European Union and the Member States asserts that *Bosman* was 'ill-advised' but does not explain why.[28] At least at this stage, one's impression was that sport was mounting a modestly effective, if intellectually thin, case in favour of acquiring some degree of protection from EU law. But there was no clear notion of precisely what shape this might take—and, as will be explained, one never really emerged.

One of the few contributions to deal explicitly with sport was the so-called 'Freiburg draft'.[29] This is helpfully illustrative not merely for its failure to persuade mainstream thinking at the Convention but also for what it reveals about the difficulty of framing a reliable shelter for sport. In its Article 24, entitled 'Respect for the Sovereignty of the Member States', the draft provided that when exercising the competences assigned by the Treaty, the Union shall respect the sovereignty of the Member States especially in listed areas which 'are characteristic for their national identity and their fundamental constitutional legal order': 'sports policy' appears on the list. Union measures shall not 'encroach upon the core area of these sovereign rights'. But to which institutions of the Union is this direction addressed? If it is a control over the exercise of *legislative* competence then it is of little moment, because there is scarcely any such legislative activity. If it is a restraint on the application of the law of the internal market to sport then it is much more significant: but it is also horribly imprecise. How wide an exclusion is intended? It is inconceivable that all of the commercial activities undertaken in the field of sport would be immunized from EU law and so the formula simply throws up awkward boundary disputes. As a general observation, any attempt to carve out sectoral protection is difficult given the logic of the Treaty as a broadly based, functionally driven regime, and the Freiburg draft, like other similarly motivated controlling devices advanced at the Convention,[30] persuaded few of its operational viability. The provision in the Treaty post-Lisbon which comes closest to Article 24 of the Freiburg draft is Article 4(2) TEU, but its direction that the Union shall respect the national identities and essential functions of the Member States does not mention

---

[27] See especially CONV 33/02 17 April 2002 (Duhamel), CONV 337/02 10 October 2002 (Tajani), CONV 478/03 10 January 2003 (Haenel et al). Documentation is available at <http://european-convention.eu.int> (accessed 11 June 2010).

[28] At <http://european-convention.eu.int/docs/relateddoc/511.pdf>, 19.

[29] CONV 495/03 20 January 2003.

[30] For a survey see S Weatherill, 'Competence Creep and Competence Control' (2004) 23 *Yearbook of European Law* 1.

sport and is unlikely to be apt to cover it, or at least *all* of it—and in any event it envisages a process of assessing the worth of particular state features in the context of the achievement of the EU's objectives whereas by contrast the Freiburg draft sought to seal off core areas of 'sovereignty' from EU intervention.[31]

The majority view was more favourably disposed to placing sport within the explicit scope of the Treaty for the first time—or at least it was not inclined to side with such aggressive curtailment in the scope of EU activity. A 'Digest of contributions to the Forum', prepared in the summer of 2002 in advance of a plenary session on civil society, advised of a 'call for a specific legal basis for support for sport'.[32]

The Praesidium was famously influential in dictating the terms of the debate at the Convention. It presented a 'preliminary draft Constitutional Treaty' to a plenary session on 28 October 2002. There was at this stage no place for sport. However, the draft text proposed by the Praesidium and released on 6 February 2003 inserted sport into Part I of the Treaty as an area where the EU would be competent to take 'supporting action'.[33] And once the Praesidium's February 2003 text had added sport to the list of competences where supporting action could be taken little active dissent was provoked. The deal was done.

The Convention over, the Draft Treaty establishing a Constitution for Europe submitted to the President of the European Council in Rome in July 2003 duly placed sport alongside education, vocational training and youth as an area of 'supporting, coordinating or complementary action' and added detailed provisions in a new Article buried deep in Chapter V of Title III of Part III of the text, under the title *Education, Vocational Training, Youth and Sport*. This provided that 'The Union shall contribute to the promotion of European sporting issues, given the social and educational function of sport'. Union action was to be aimed at 'developing the European dimension in sport, by promoting fairness in competitions and cooperation between sporting bodies and by protecting the physical and moral integrity of sportsmen and sportswomen, especially young sportsmen and sportswomen'. There is a degree of ambiguity here: the EU's role in the field of sport is to be made legitimate but the grant of competence is limited and rather vague.

Ultimately, the Convention's text underwent adjustment as particular points, largely of an institutional nature, proved indigestible to the intergovernmental conference (IGC) later in 2003. But much of the Convention's text, and the essential pattern it had piloted, endured unaltered. For sport there was some small change beyond the cosmetic. The Treaty establishing a Constitution finally

---

[31] One might understand the concern to protect national constitutional identity in the BVerfG's *Lisbon* judgment as a version of the Freiburg draft wrapped up in national, rather than EU, constitutional dress (<http://www.bundesverfassungsgericht.de/entscheidungen/es20090630_2bve000208en.html>), but here too it would be a surprise if (all aspects of) sport were found to form part of that identity.

[32] CONV 112/02 17 June 2002.

[33] On the lobbying to achieve this change, see B García and S Weatherill, 'Engaging with the EU in Order to Minimize its Impact: Sport and the Negotiation of the Treaty of Lisbon' (2012) 19 *Journal of European Public Policy*.

agreed in late 2004 included sport alongside education, youth and vocational training as an 'area of supporting, coordinating or complementary action' while the substantive elaboration provided that 'The Union shall contribute to the promotion of European sporting issues, while taking account of the specific nature of sport, its structures based on voluntary activity and its social and educational function.' Here, then, was a potentially significant change: the reference to the 'specific nature of sport' was added between the middle of 2003 and the end of 2004.[34] Its significance is considered below. Union action was to be aimed at 'developing the European dimension in sport, by promoting fairness and openness in sporting competitions and cooperation between bodies responsible for sports and by protecting the physical and moral integrity of sportsmen and sportswomen, especially young sportsmen and sportswomen'. On this aspect of the new provisions, then, there was minimal change between 2003 and 2004. And it was added that the Union and Member States 'shall foster cooperation with third countries and the competent international organisations in the field of education and sport, in particular the Council of Europe': this provision had appeared in the Convention's finally agreed 2003 text but with reference *only* to education.

The Treaty establishing a Constitution, fatally damaged by its rejection in referendums in France and the Netherlands during 2005, was laid to rest after an introspective period of reflection in 2007. The story is told elsewhere of how the Treaty of Lisbon was prepared so as to be sufficiently different from the Treaty establishing a Constitution to justify withdrawal of the promise of a referendum (except in Ireland) but not so different that the substance of the planned institutional reforms would be lost.[35] As far as sport is concerned, however, the narrative is one of consistency. What was agreed at the end of 2004 in the Treaty establishing a Constitution was left untouched in 2007 as the Lisbon Treaty was negotiated and agreed.

VI. The Lisbon Treaty

The Lisbon Treaty brings sport within the explicit reach of the founding Treaties for the first time. In formal terms, then, it is profoundly significant. As is well known, the effect of the Lisbon reforms is formally to abolish the three pillar structure crafted for the EU at Maastricht. From 1 December 2009 the European Union has been founded on two Treaties which have the same legal value: the Treaty on European Union (TEU) and the Treaty on the Functioning of the European Union (TFEU). It is the amendments to what was the EC Treaty, and is now the TFEU, which grant sport its newly recognized formal status.

However, although the *fact* of sport's addition to the list of EU competences is undeniably important, the detailed content of this competence newly granted by the Member States to the EU is far less remarkable. The details, agreed in 2004 and

---

[34] Ibid.
[35] See chapter 1 by P Berman in this book.

reaffirmed in 2007, are found in the vast Part Three of the TFEU, which is entitled 'Union Policies and Internal Actions', specifically in Title XII of Part Three *Education, Vocational Training, Youth and Sport.* So sport is inserted into an amended version of Chapter 3 in Title XI of the old EC Treaty, which was designated 'Education, Vocational Training and Youth'. Under the post-Lisbon re-numbering the relevant Treaty Articles are Articles 165 and 166 TFEU.

Article 165 stipulates that the Union 'shall contribute to the promotion of European sporting issues, while taking account of the specific nature of sport, its structures based on voluntary activity and its social and educational function'. And, pursuant to Article 165(2), Union action shall be aimed at 'developing the European dimension in sport, by promoting fairness and openness in sporting competitions and cooperation between bodies responsible for sports, and by protecting the physical and moral integrity of sportsmen and sportswomen, especially the youngest sportsmen and sportswomen'. Article 165(3) adds that the Union and the Member States 'shall foster cooperation with third countries and the competent international organisations in the field of education and sport, in particular the Council of Europe'. Article 165(4) provides that in order to contribute to the achievement of the objectives referred to in the Article, the European Parliament and Council, acting in accordance with the ordinary legislative procedure, after consulting the Economic and Social Committee and the Committee of the Regions, shall adopt incentive measures, excluding any harmonization of the laws and regulations of the Member States; and that the Council, on a proposal from the Commission, shall adopt recommendations.

VII. Assessing the Impact of the Lisbon Treaty

The principal motivation behind the inclusion of sport in the Treaty is not to elevate the EU to a position of primary importance in the regulation of the sector. It is, instead, an attempt to make clearer the relationship between the EU and sport, under an assumption that the pre-existing state of the law, developed without any mandate granted explicitly by the Treaty, had failed to provide security.

It is in the first place important to note that there is created only a supporting competence for the EU, the weakest type of the three principal types of competence mapped in Title I of Part One of the TFEU. The basic competence descriptor is found in Article 6(e) TFEU, 'The Union shall have competence to carry out actions to support, coordinate or supplement the actions of the Member States'. The areas of such action shall, at European level, include (inter alia) 'education, vocational training, youth and sport'. Moreover the provisions are drawn carefully and narrowly, stressing that the Union shall do no more than 'contribute' to the promotion of European sporting issues. And though legislation may be adopted, it is confined to 'incentive measures, excluding any harmonisation'.

This cautiously drawn formula is designed to reassure those who fear the rise of the EU as a sports regulator. The Commission's 2007 White Paper declared that 'sporting organisations and Member States have a primary responsibility in the conduct of sporting affairs, with a central role for sports federations'. This deference to the value of sites for the regulation of sport other than the EU in general and the Commission in particular follows the Nice Declaration. The Lisbon Treaty is consistent with this theme. The EU's role, though formally recognized, is plainly designed to be limited and it lacks concrete shape. And Article 6 TFEU reinforces the impression that the EU's role in sport is strictly subsidiary to that of the Member States and governing bodies in sport. But modest though the change is, this is different from the position prior to Lisbon. Lisbon plus the 2007 White Paper provides institutional momentum. The first EU Sports Council was held in May 2010.

The EU's role in the field of sport is legitimated. Sporting bodies can no longer claim that sport is none of the EU's business. Instead one would expect them to claim that it is the EU's business but only to a very limited extent, and only insofar as respect is shown for its 'specific nature'. This is an important change, both constitutionally and strategically. The theme here is consistent: sports bodies must engage with the EU as part of a strategy to minimize its perceived detrimental effect on their practice. They cannot simply ignore it but nor are they strong enough to extract a promise of immunity. So what is left is the ambiguous middle ground—the Lisbon Treaty's inclusion of sport in the text of the Treaty but on terms which are far from clear. The risk is plainly that Lisbon will be treated as a legitimation of the EU's involvement in sport in a way which generates intervention going beyond what the Treaty in fact envisages. That is: scrupulous adherence to the limits imposed by the Treaty may be overtaken by more ambitious institutional practice. This is certainly dangerous and should be monitored.[36] Not only the constitutional competence but also the basic expertise of the EU institutions to develop a general policy on, say, anti-doping is lacking. Their primary interaction with sport should be where it touches specific rules of the Treaty: free movement and competition. Should the EU overuse its new legislative competence it will risk damaging its legitimacy.

The most immediately obvious aspect of the Lisbon reforms for those actively involved in sports governance is likely to be the creation of an EU budget stream devoted to sports projects. It may not be large, it may not be easy to access, but the current position whereby any sports-related project needed to be fitted often awkwardly into some other project where the EC did hold a competence has been brought to an end. So the designation of 2004 as the European Year of Sport was necessarily presented in the governing legal measure as the European Year of Education through Sport, based on what was then Article 149 EC on education.[37] The 2007 White Paper already provides a framework for EU action, and the entry into force of the Lisbon Treaty may prove important in facilitating a coherent and financially secure pattern of development.

---

[36] The House of Lords Select Committee on the European Union, while noting the increased profile of sport in the Treaty post-Lisbon, urges the government 'to ensure that the European institutions adhere to this provision' (Tenth Report 2007–2008, para 8.49, <http://www.parliament.the-stationery-office.co.uk/pa/ld200708/ldselect/ldeucom/62/6202.htm>).

[37] Dec 291/2003/EC [2003] OJ L43/1.

VIII. Is 'EU Sports Law' Now Different?

Hitherto the principal body of 'EU sports law' has been shaped by the subjection of sporting practices to the treaty rules on free movement and on competition. What effect will the Lisbon adjustments have on their interpretation? The formula chosen in the Lisbon Treaty does not give sports governing bodies the pure autonomy they may have desired. It is instead a cautiously phrased version of the notion that 'sport is special'. Ever since the *Walrave* ruling in 1974[38] the institutions of the EU have offered periodically inconsistent explanations of how and why sport is special, but now that sport finally enjoys explicit recognition in the Treaty, the newly intro- duced and admittedly open-ended provisions will doubtless provide the framework for future debate, policy articulation and litigation. It is true that Article 165 TFEU is not formally 'horizontal' in nature: unlike, for example, environmental protec- tion (Article 11 TFEU) and consumer protection (Article 12 TFEU) it is not embedded in all the Union's activities. However, the Court has been willing to absorb non-binding texts pertaining to sport issued at EU level in exploring the nature and scope of the relevant rules of the Treaty.[39] Article 165, introduced at Lisbon, goes further: it is binding. So even though sport's special features are not located in a horizontal treaty provision, one would have readily anticipated that the Court would be receptive to their invocation in litigation arising out of free movement and competition law, and this was confirmed in the first 'post-Lisbon' sport-related judgment, *Bernard*.[40]

Textual analysis is worthwhile, even if ultimately inconclusive. Union action shall be aimed at 'developing the European dimension in sport, by promoting fairness and openness in sporting competitions and cooperation between bodies responsible for sports, and by protecting the physical and moral integrity of sportsmen and sportswomen, especially the youngest sportsmen and sportswomen'. This is a mix of the obscure and self-evident, spiced by an unsettling imprecision about just what the EU's developmental role really is. 'Openness' could be vague window-dressing which has no legal bite or it might be employed to argue for example that EU law, interpreted in the light of Article 165(2) TFEU, does not tolerate rules that exclude non-nationals from competitions designed to crown a national champion. This was mentioned as an issue deserving attention in the Staff Working Document accompanying the White Paper[41] and in 2008, the Commis- sion, answering a question by MEP Ivo Belet, contented itself with a cautious reply setting out its basic approach to the application of EU law to sport and promising a study on access to individual sporting competition for non-national athletes.[42] Access restrictions vary state by state, sport by sport, and it is at least possible that

---

[38] Above n 1.
[39] Cases C-51/96 & 191/97, above n 6 at paras 41–2; Case C-176/96, above n 22 at paras 32–3.
[40] Case C-325/08 [2010] ECR I-2177, para 40.
[41] Above n 17 at 45.
[42] WQ P-4798/08. The contract was awarded to TMC Asser Instituut in 2010, Contract Notice 2010/S 31-043484.

recognition of the promotion of openness as a feature of the European dimension of sport will strengthen the force of a legal challenge by an excluded participant.

Probably it is the direction that the Union shall take 'account of the specific nature of sport, its structures based on voluntary activity and its social and educational function' that will become the most high-profile consequence of the Lisbon reforms. Consider, for example, rules in football requiring that squads contain a minimum number of 'home grown' players: that is, players developed and trained for a defined period in the country in which the club is based. The Commission, following *Bosman*, has not been prepared to accept that football may re-instate rules in club football based directly on nationality, but the 'home-grown' rules favoured by UEFA are *not* based directly on nationality. Young players who are nationals of Member State X count as home-grown in Member State Y as long as they have spent long enough in the early part of their career on the books of a club in Member State Y. Doubtless such rules are indirectly discriminatory on the basis of nationality, because most home-grown players in Y will also be nationals of Y, but it is orthodox in EU law that indirect discrimination may be shown to be objectively justified. The 'home-grown' rules would be defended as means to promote balance in sporting competition (because richer clubs could not simply fill their squads with expensively purchased finished products) and as a device to encourage the training of young players. Both concerns have been recognized by the Court in *Bosman* as legitimate in sport. No Court ruling exists on the compatibility of such rules with EU law but the Commission has accepted that 'home grown' rules are potentially compatible with the Treaty. The Staff Working Document accompanying the 2007 White Paper merely mentions this as one of several important outstanding issues,[43] but in May 2008 the Commission, publishing an independent (and poorly written) study on the compatibility of the scheme with EU law, announced a firmer view. It considers the home-grown rule to be compatible with EU law in the light of its contribution to promoting balance in sporting competition and encouraging the training of young players.[44]

It is an approach that may prevail, but it is far from uncontroversially correct. The argument rooted in competitive balance is thin: rich clubs will plainly still acquire the best players while poorer clubs will find that the available pool of talent in which they can fish has been artificially diminished by the requirement to hire a defined number of 'home-grown' players. And it is far from clear that creating a protected class of 'home-grown' players, who will certainly enjoy higher wages than equally skilled non-qualifying players simply because clubs need to hit their quotas, is sensible as a means to improve the quality of training. Better, one might think, to open up the market so young players have to sink or swim rather than enjoy artificial buoyancy because of where they happen to have been 'grown'. Given these objections and given that there are other and plausibly more appropriate ways to achieve the objectives pursued by the home-grown rules it is at least arguable that they are incompatible with EU law.[45]

---

[43] Above n 17 at 76.
[44] IP/08/807, 28 May 2008, <http://ec.europa.eu/sport/news/news270_en.htm>.
[45] cf S Miettinen and R Parrish, 'Nationality Discrimination in Community Law' (2008) 5 *Entertainment and Sports Law Journal*, <http://www2.warwick.ac.uk/fac/soc/law/elj/eslj>.

This is merely to scratch the surface of an intriguing debate, but the purpose of this chapter is not to offer a concluded view. Rather, it merely questions whether the adjustments made by the Lisbon Treaty make any difference. The Lisbon reforms might alter the outcome, or they might merely re-frame the analysis. Post-Lisbon, one would expect the football authorities to headline their defence by asserting the 'specific nature of sport' recognized by the Treaty as a reason for accepting rules of this type that one would not expect to find in other industries. Moreover, one might anticipate that it would be argued that the 'specific nature of sport' recognized by the Treaty dictates that the institutions of the EU should adopt a light touch in reviewing the choices made by sports bodies, who have much greater expertise in understanding what really is 'specific' about sport. It is at least possible that the Court and the Commission will be tempted to show a greater deference to sporting choices than they did prior to the entry into force of the Lisbon Treaty. But the changes are sufficiently ambiguous to rule out confident prediction. In *Bernard*[46] the Court simply used Lisbon to 'corroborate' its own case law, which suggests it is not minded to alter course. The slippery quality of the Lisbon innovation is such that one can do more than observe that sport can, at last, rely on explicit wording contained in the Treaty to structure its argument that sport is 'special' while reflecting that this may be merely a confirmation of how the Court has always treated sport since *Walrave and Koch*.

One could readily regard this as a sport-specific manifestation of a more broadly applicable tilt. The changes to substantive EU law made by the Lisbon Treaty are very few and mostly cosmetic. However, Article 3(3) TEU states that 'The Union shall establish an internal market'. The pre-Lisbon Article 3(l)(g) EC provided that the activities of the EC shall include 'a system ensuring that competition in the internal market is not distorted', and the Court on occasion relied explicitly on this provision in interpreting the competition rules.[47] It is now lost from the text of the Treaty proper. This concession was apparently extracted during the Treaty negotiations in 2007 by the French, where part of the reason for voter dissatisfaction appears to have been disquiet over a perceived hard-edged pro-competition philosophy. A Protocol on the Internal Market and Competition attached to both the EU Treaty and the TFEU states that the internal market referred to in Article 3 TEU 'includes a system ensuring that competition is not distorted'. And in formal terms Protocols carry the same legal force as the Treaty itself. So perhaps the concession extracted by the French is of no practical or constitutional significance. But it cannot be excluded that the Court might conclude that the prominence of the Union's commitment to undistorted competition has been reduced and that it accordingly carries less weight than it has done hitherto when pitched against other concerns such as social cohesion or targeted industrial policy. One could certainly expect public authorities wishing, for example, to grant aid in circumstances where there are objections rooted in consequent competitive distortion to the market to

---

[46] Case C-325/08, above n 40 at para 40.
[47] Eg Case C-67/96 *Albany International* [1999] ECR I-5751; Case C-453/99 *Courage v Crehan* [2001] ECR I-6297.

argue that the balance of priorities has been shifted away from that aim by the Lisbon Treaty. The Commission may reject any such adjustment; the Court may too. And anyway, even before the entry into force of the Lisbon Treaty, the Court declared that the EU has 'not only an economic but also a social purpose'[48] so in fact the application of the Treaty's economic law provisions has not been sealed off from considerations of a non-economic nature. As with sport, so too at a much more general level in the development of EU trade law: it is plain that Lisbon provides some fresh material for those wishing to dull the blade of EU market-driven intervention, although it is not yet clear whether outcomes will ultimately be any different from those that would have been reached before the entry into force of the Lisbon Treaty.

IX. Conclusion

The evolution of sports law in the EU represents a fascinating case study into the interaction of the orthodox rules governing the market-making project and the rules, formally sourced in private organizations, which underpin the global regime of sports governance. The EU's law does not compete with sport's own 'internal law'—it instead permits it a conditional autonomy. And in fixing the nature of those conditions, the institutions of the EU, primarily the Court and the Commission, have been forced to develop a concept of legitimate sports governance despite the absence of any directly relevant material in the Treaty itself.

Lisbon changes everything—and nothing. After Lisbon there is no longer any doubt that the EU has a legitimate, if subordinate, role in the field of sport. There will be legislation (of a supporting nature): there will be a budget. And the Treaty does at last contain material capable of nourishing the Court's interpretation of the free movement and competition rules in the particular context of sport. The specific nature of sport is now written into the Treaty. One would suppose that sporting bodies would no longer waste time claiming EU law has no application to their activities and instead seek to rely on the wording of the new provisions as a basis for minimizing the transformative effect of EU law on their practice. However, since the Court and the Commission have not in the past blindly applied EU law to sport as if it were a 'normal' industry it remains to be seen whether Lisbon really changes anything or whether instead it simply confirms existing practice. The vague nature of the new provisions delegates considerable power to the Court and Commission to make that choice, but the most likely outcome is—no change. EU law has *always* treated sport as 'special'.

---

[48] Eg Case C-438/05 *International Transport Workers' Federation v Viking Line ABP* [2007] ECR I-10779, para 79.

Index

ACER (Agency for the Cooperation of Energy
    Regulators) 375, 378–80, 387
acquis communautaire 45, 220, 269–70, 273
administrative cooperation 43, 100
Advocates General (AG)
    appointments to the courts 208–11
    Alber 172
    Fennelly 216 n 10
    Jacobs 319–20, 342, 360 n 30
    Léger 219, 379 n 20
    Maduro 172, 218, 219 n 24, 227, 317
    Mengozzi 55, 272, 276
    Ruiz Jarabo 360 n 30
    Sharpston 165 n 57, 174, 179
    Trstenjak 52 n 32
AETR doctrine 299, 305, 316–17
AFSJ, *see* Freedom, Security and Justice
agriculture and fisheries 100, 369, 371
    agricultural and forestry plots 319
    agricultural policy 86, 320
    animal slaughter 320
    Common Agricultural Policy (CAP) 78, 86
    common fisheries policy 371
    community milk quota rules 164 n 51
    fish farms 320
    see also health; marine biology
Ahern, Bertie 32 n 139
Albania 394
Algeria 143–5, 153–4
    President Ben Bella 144
Amato, Giuliano 11–13, 53 n 40
American Convention on Human Rights 176
    see also human rights; USA
Amsterdam Protocol 219, 344
animal welfare 43, 48
    see also health: animal
anthropology 354
antitrust law 359
    see also Chicago School; USA
approximation of laws 43, 379 n 21, 381–3
arbitrariness 323
archives 307 n 69
art 307 n 69
Ashton, Catherine 37, 238–9, 243
asylum 43, 105, 161, 170, 179, 203, 334,
    358 n 25
    see also border control; immigration;
        migration; refugees
Australia 324 n 44
Austria 59 n 67, 176, 319, 390, 396, 398
aviation, civil 82 n 124
    European Aviation Safety Agency 82 n 124

Badinter, Robert 147–8
Balkan States, Western 132 n 32, 134, 141
banking
    bail-outs for commercial banks 241
    transfer of banking data 250
    see also European Central Bank; financial crises
Bar European Group 3 n 1
Barnier, Michel 12 n 40
Barroso initiative 259
Barroso, Jose Manuel 237, 242–3
Basque Country 281
    see also Segi; terrorism
BBC (British Broadcasting Corporation) 30,
    32 n 138, 166 n 60, 20 n 80
    see also television; United Kingdom
Beano, The 166
Beckett, Margaret 23 n 91
Belet, Ivo 416
Belgium 143, 171
    Belgian constitution 154 n 176
    Belgian Presidency 11, 112, 244
    Eupen-Malmedy, German community
        in 154 n 176
    Flemish and Walloon communities in
        154 n 176
    Prime Ministers of:
        Jean-Luc Dehaene 11, 12 n 40, 13, 117
    see also hunting
Bella, Ben 144
Berlin 22 n 90, 386
    Berlin Declaration 22
    see also Germany
bilateral investment treaties (BITs) 89 n 17,
    312–17, 395–6
    of existing member states 320–1
    see also Foreign Direct Investment (FDI)
bilateral relations 135, 153, 236, 398
Bill of Rights, EU 178, 208
    see also Charter of Fundamental Rights;
        ECHR; USA
Blair, Tony 19, 29–30, 166
block exemption 348–9, 363
    see also competition: policy
border control/ checks 105, 203, 334, 358 n 25
    see also asylum; immigration; migration;
        refugees
Bosnia 394
bribery 326
    see also corruption; fraud
Britain, *see* United Kingdom
British Diplomatic Service 12 n 41
    see also diplomatic services

British Labour Party 149
Brown, Gordon 29–30
Bruton, John 12 n 40
budget, the EU 253–4
  budgetary procedures 12 n 43
  budgetary provisions 5 n 6, 59–60
  expenditure 45 n 16, 253, 256
  revenue 256
  see also financial crises; taxation
Bulgaria 22, 136 n 52, 137 n 56, 177, 395
  see also Sofia
business 14, 160, 313, 324 n 44, 46, 326
  see also enterprise
Buzek, Jerzy 240

Canada
  Canada-Columbia trade relations
  324 n 44
  Canada-Jordan trade relations
  324 n 44
  investment policy in 321 n 35
CAP, *see* agriculture and fisheries
capital movement 302, 314–19, 144 n 104, 108
capitalism 20 n 80
Cariforum 325–6
Caspian Gas Purchasing Group 388
Caspian Sea 396
CDDH (Steering Committee for Human
    Rights) 181–2, 192
CEECs (Central and Eastern European
    Countries) 131–3, 137 n 57
  'big bang' enlargement 134
CFI, *see* General Court
CFSP, *see* Common Foreign and Security
    Policy
Charter of Fundamental Rights
  application of the Charter rights 164–171
    Article 51 of the Charter 164–5
    UK case law on the Charter 170–1
    see also United Kingdom: UK-Ireland
      Protocol; UK-Poland Protocol
  Cologne Presidency Conclusions 156, 159
  language of the 159 n 26
  origins and evolution 155–9
  protection of rights by the 159–64
    exhaustive catalogue of rights? 163–4
    relationship with the ECHR 159, 162–3
    rights, freedoms and principles of 159,
      161–2, 168
    rights protected and their sources 159–60
  use of the Charter before the European
    Courts 172–9
    the Charter before EU courts 172–5
    the Charter and the European Court of
      Human Rights 175–8
Chicago School 359
  see also antitrust law
children
  childrens' rights 91, 172, 296 n 22, 358 n 25

New York Convention on the Rights of the
    Child 160
  see also employment: child; youth
Chile 324 n 44
Chirac, Jacques 19
Christian Democrats 255
Christopherson, Henning 12 n 40
citizenship, EU 7, 17, 42–3, 46,
    174, 179
  citizen submission process 325
  see also European Citizens Initiative
Civil Codes 349
civil justice 6, 8
civil law 203
civil protection 100–1
Civil Service Tribunal 197, 210
climate change 26, 32 n 139, 222 n 37, 367,
    375, 381, 397 n 77, 401
  see also energy; environment; sustainable
    development
Clinton, Hillary 240
cohesion 43, 230
  economic 351 n 7, 369
  social 100, 351 n 7, 358 n 25, 362–4, 369,
    371, 418
  territorial 80 n 101, 91, 100, 358 n 25,
    362–4, 371
Cohesion Fund 371
Cold War 10
collective bargaining 166, 169 n 74
College of Commissioners 243
Columbia 324 n 44
comitology 66, 74, 76–80, 83–4, 232–3,
    251–2, 349
  and ACER 378–81
commercial policy
  and development 56, 272
    see also foreign policy
  reform of the common commercial
    policy 292–312
  see also Common Commercial Policy (CCP);
    trade; external; investment
Committee on Institutional Affairs 6 n 8
Committee of Ministers 187
  see also Dooge Committee
Committee of the Regions (CoR) 21 n 83, 200,
    221–2, 227 n 54, 230, 365, 370,
    373, 414
Common Commercial Policy (CCP) 56–7, 86,
    98, 292–311, 312–15, 319, 324, 327,
    371, 394
  see also commercial policy; Foreign Direct
    Investment (FDI)
Common Foreign and Security Policy (CFSP)
  acts of the 277
  from pillar talk to constitutionalism
    265–91
  scope and nature of the competences to
    conduct a 266–8

voting rules in 279
see also Common Security and Defence Policy (CSDP)
common market 86, 103, 131, 294, 348, 351, 358–9, 369
Common Security and Defence Policy (CSDP) 42, 231, 266, 287–9
communism 8
Community Charter on the Fundamental Social Rights of Workers 160
Community Method 6 n 14, 51, 63, 80, 86, 237, 246
competition
 anti-competitive behaviour 356–7
 competitiveness 246, 351 n 19
 and energy 387–9
 law 71 n 53, 347–50, 357–60, 404, 416
 policy 347–66
  competition rules in the Treaty of Lisbon 348–61
 Protocol on the Internal Market and Competition 352–4, 358, 360, 362 n 35, 418
 see also block exemptions; Services of General Economic Interest (SGEIs)
conflict management 231
 conflict prevention 266
 post-conflict stabilization 266
 prevention of conflicts 92 n 23, 267, 275
 see also peace; terrorism; war
Constitution for Europe 13–21, 98, 108, 115, 119, 130, 181, 279, 285, 292, 312, 398, 412
constitutional symbolism 62–84
constitutionalism 67 n 30, 224, 265–91
consumer protection 43, 48, 86–7, 100, 169, 255, 326, 369, 371, 416
Convention on the Future of Europe (2002–2003) 11–12, 118, 147, 158, 279, 285, 411
convention method 11, 112, 119–20, 259
Copenhagen 131–2, 138 n 65, 145
 see also Denmark
Corbett, Richard 32
COREPER (Committee of Permanent Representatives) 244
corruption 134
 see also bribery; fraud
COSAC (Conference of European Affairs Committees) 98, 257, 260
Council of Europe 110, 155–6, 177–8, 181, 186–7, 207
Council Legal Service 15
Council for Trade in Services 295 n 19
Court of Auditors, European 200, 251, 258
Court of First Instance (CFI) 157, 172, 197, 281
Court of Justice, *see* European Court of Justice

Cowen, Brian 34
criminal justice 15 n 55, 17, 25, 27, 170, 179, 336
 crime prevention 102, 341
 criminal investigation 57
 see also police; punishment; torture; USA: death row
criminal law
 English 160
 EU competence in 331–46
 effectiveness criteria 338–44
  centre of gravity debate 340–1
  crime prevention in the EU 341
  harmonization outside *lex specialis* provisions 342
  TFEU articles 342–4
 the journey of, in the EU 332–4
 organized crime 336, 344
 principle of legality 339
 specific changes brought in by the Lisbon Treaty 334–8
  enhanced cooperation and emergency brakes 336–7
  extended jurisdiction 337–8
  procedural criminal law 335
  substantive criminal law 335–6
 subsidiarity and proportionality, role of 344–6
 see also bribery; emergency brake and accelerator procedure; fraud; money laundering; mutual recognition; national parliaments, role of; penal populism; PJCCM; police; principle: of effectiveness; terrorism
crisis management 241–2, 266
 see also financial crises; international crises
Croatia 125, 133–4, 394
culture
 cultural services 307
 Europe's cultural heritage 307, 358 n 25, 91
currency 101, 242, 358 n 25
 single common 7, 152
 see also Euro, the customs 203, 293–4
 union 98, 145, 371
Cyprus 135 n 48, 137 n 56, 57
Czech Republic 22, 35–6, 137 n 56, 159, 166, 235, 321
 Czech Constitutional Court 36, 398
 Czech Declaration, The 166 n 66
 Presidents of:
  Vaclav Klaus 36
 see also Prague
Czechoslovak Velvet Divorce 154

Dastis, Alfonso 12 n 40
data protection 43, 48–9, 53, 217
Davidson, Ian 32 n 139
de Gaulle, Charles 144 n 106

Declaration on Fundamental Principles and
    Rights at Work 326 n 52
Declaration on Worker's Rights, Social Policy
    and Other Issues 35
defence policy, *see* Common Security and
    Defence Policy (CSDP); European
    Defence Agency
Dehaene, Jean-Luc 11, 12 n 40, 13, 117
    see also Belgium
Delors, Jacques 6–7, 11 n 37, 251
    see also European Commission
democratic deficit 136, 148 n 142, 233
Denman, Daniel 167
Denmark 5–8, 15, 18, 22 n 88, 23, 26, 29,
    34–5, 110, 116–17, 121, 145–7
    Copenhagen criteria 131–2
    Folketing 23, 29
    Prime Ministers of:
        Anders Fogh Rasmussen 19
    referenda in 1972 145 May 1993 7
    see also Copenhagen
deposit guarantee schemes 222
developing countries 92 n 23, 267, 271, 296–7
    see also poverty
development cooperation 43, 102, 268–76,
    290, 294, 369, 372
    see also foreign policy
DG (Directorate-General)
    DG DEV (Directorate-General for
        Development) 238
    DG RELEX (Directorate-General for External
        Relations) 238, 245–6
    see also external relations
    DG TRADE (Directorate-General for Trade)
        238
    see also European Commission;
diplomatic service 12 n 41, 87, 235, 288–9
disarmament operations 266, 287
disaster relief 246
    natural or man-made disasters 92 n 23, 267
    see also international crises
discrimination 43, 48, 91, 93 n 25
    age 173
    disability 48, 93 n 25, 163 n 47
    ethnic 48, 93 n 25
    indirect 417
    nationality-based 43, 45, 404
    non- 48, 101–2, 130, 135, 139, 163, 173,
        302, 313, 319, 323, 358 n 25, 404
    racial 48, 93 n 25
    religious 48, 93 n 25
    sexual 48, 93 n 25, 140, 163 n 47
    sporting 404
Divisional Court 31
Dooge Committee 6
Doha Round 322 n 36
double-majority
    principle 151 n 158
    voting 18, 25–6

DSU (Dispute Settlement Understanding),
    see WTO
Dublin 29–36
    see also Ireland
Dublin Regulation 170
due process 323

EAEC (European Atomic Energy
    Community) 43, 44 n 10, 58–61,
    128 n 4, 129 nn 7, 10, 146 n
    121, 129
ECHR (European Convention for the
    Protection of Human Rights and
    Fundamental Freedoms)
    accession (EU) to the ECHR:
        agreement on 181–3
        effects of 194
    ensuring the correct interpretation of EU
        law 192–4
    and the European Court of Justice 204–8
    extent of supervision of EU conduct 187–9
    participation of the EU in the control
        bodies 186–7
    respective roles of the EU and its member
        states as respondents 189–91
    scope of rights and obligations arising for the
        EU 183–6
economic and monetary policy 43, 99, 101,
    241, 371
economic recovery 241
    stimulus packages 241
    see also banking; financial crises
ECOWAS (Economic Community of West
    African States) 51, 56–7, 88 n 10,
    270
ECSC (European Coal and Steel
    Community) 128 n 4, 129 n 7, 8, 10,
    142 n 92, 146 n 121, 129, 359,
    368–9, 394 n 71, 399
    see also energy: resources
education and training
    education 34–5, 48, 80, 100, 161, 305–7,
        412–15
    university degrees 80 n 101
    vocational training 100, 412–14
    see also children; sport; universities and
        institutions; youth
EEA (European Economic Area) 135, 153 n 170
    EEA-EFTA legal orders 153 n 170
EEAS (European External Action Service)
    231–2, 235–46, 250, 285, 287–90
effet utile doctrine 356–7
EFTA (European Free Trade Association) 141,
    153 n 170, 324 n 44
elderly rights 162
elections
    national, of EU Member States 143 n 99, 256
    US Congressional 256
    see also European Parliament elections

electricity
consumption of 368, 379, 388–9
directives 375, 377–9, 395, 399–401
Electricity Policy Research Group, Cambridge
University 385 n 40, 386 n 42
ENTSOs (European Network of
Transmission System Operators for
Electricity) 378
European networks of 382
security of supply 390–1
tariffs 390
see also energy; TSOs
emergency brake and accelerator procedure 336
employment
child 162 n 44, 169
French 20
German 173
legislation 255
provisions on 43, 45 n 16, 47–8, 80, 91, 123
n 38, 100 n 38, 101, 297, 326, 351
n 7, 354 n 14, 358 n 25, 369 n 5
in the public service 124
relations 326
unemployment 20
see also seasonal employment
empty chair policy 151
EMU (Economic and Monetary Union) 7, 152
energy
and competition policy 387–9
consumption of 75 n 75, 380
crisis, *see also* gas: crises 372, 374
efficiency and saving 370, 374
washing machine manufacturers 388–9
Energy Council meetings 4 Feb 2001 396
energy-related products 75 n 75
Energy Security and Infrastructure
Instrument 382
and environment 392–3
and external relations 393–8
infrastructure 383–4
market
abuse 382–3
integrity and transparency 382
liberalization 370
new market entrants 375
over the counter (OTC) markets 382
networks 373–4, 382
nuclear 398–9
Bohunice VI power plant 398
Ignalina power plant 398
policy
Energy Policy for Europe 380
emission trading legislation 367
after the Lisbon Treaty 367–402
power plants
coal 390
nuclear 398
Šoštan 391 n 60

Trbovlje 391 n 60
renewable 367, 380–1
resources, types of
atomic 16, *see also* EAEC
biofuels 381
bioliquids 381
coal 368, 391, *see also* ECSC
oil, mineral 368, 372, 395
peat 390
steel, *see* ECSC
see also electricity; gas; water
security of supply 390–2
and state aid 390–2
Strategic Energy Review of 2008 385
taxation measures 374
eco-taxation 392
TEN-E (trans-European Networks for Energy
framework) 382
see also ACER; climate change; environment;
ETS; IEA; sustainable development
England, *see* United Kingdom
enhanced cooperation 8, 42–3, 45–6, 336,
346
ENIC 406
see also sports law
**ENISA (European Network and Information
Security Agency)** 379 n 21
enlargement, EU 128–154
enterprise 80, 326
small enterprises 400
see also business
environment
and energy 392–3
environmental policy 394 n 71, 397 n 77,
123 n 38, 370, 372, 374
environmental protection 48, 162, 169, 226,
268, 324 n 44, 325, 339, 399, 416
greenhouse gas emissions 226, 380
pollution 333
see also climate change; energy; NAP;
sustainable development; waste
management
ERTA doctrine 397
Estonia 137 n 56, 225–6
ETS (Emissions Trading System) 380
equality 43, 48, 91–2, 130, 135, 139, 149,
160, 296–7
between men and women 48, 135, 162 n 42
351 n 7, 358 n 25
see also discrimination
Eur-lex 4 n 3, 173 n 91, 382 n 27
EURACTIV 222 n 38, 244 n 29
Euro, the 91, 101
exchange rate 243
see also currency
Euro-crisis 241–2
Eurobarometer surveys 9, 20 n 79
see also opinion polls

Eurogas 388 n 48
see also gas
Eurogroup 242–3
Eurojust 259
Europe 2020 Strategy 80
EuropeAid 238
see also European Commission
European Arrest Warrant 171
European Central Bank 42, 44, 59, 70,
    151 n 153, 198–200, 202, 241,
    243, 251
European Citizens Initiative 230, 261
European Commission
and the High Representative for Foreign
    Affairs (HR) 42, 231, 237–8,
    285–7, 237–8
and European Parliament 157, 236–7, 309
and the European External Action Service
    (EEAS) 237–8
President(s) of the 230, 237
    Jose Manuel Barroso 237, 242–3
    Jacques Delors 7, 11 n 37
see also DG (Directorate-General):
    DG DEV; DG RELEX; DG TRADE
European Convention, *see* ECHR
European Council
Commission Report to the 213 n 2
General Secretariat of the 231, 288–9, 388 n 39
meetings, list of:
    Biarritz (Oct 2000) 112
    Brussels
        June 2006 21–2, 140
        March 2007 379–80
        June 2007 352–4
        Feb 2010 393
    Cologne (June 1999) 9 n 35, 112, 155–9
    Copenhagen (June 1993) 131–2
    Edinburgh (Dec 1992) 7, 15
    Essen (Dec 1994) 132
    Laeken (Dec 2001) 8 n 27, 10, 62, 113
    Luxembourg (Nov/Dec 1997) 132–3
    Madrid (Dec 1995) 131
    Milan (June 1985) 6 n 10
    Nice (Dec 2000) 110, 410
    Rome (July 2003) 412
    President(s) of the 237
    Herman Van Rompuy 37, 242–3
European Court of Human Rights
    (ECtHR) 162 n 45, 172, 175–8, 180,
    186–94, 201, 205
European Court of Justice (ECJ)
doctrine on implied external powers 299
and fundamental rights 204–6
and the Lisbon Treaty 197–212
jurisdiction of the 28, 42–4, 50, 54, 59, 98,
    198–204
nomenclature of the 197
see also Advocates General; Judges jurisdiction
European Defence Agency 35 n 153, 102

European Economic and Social Committee
    (EESC) 21 n 83, 230, 365 n 44, 370,
    373, 414
European Economic Community (EEC) 5, 86,
    128 n 4, 269, 298
European Federation 106
see also federalism
European Framework Laws 64, 279
European Investment Bank 5 n 6
European Ombudsman 160 n 27, 251
European Parliament
constitutional development 254–6
Council of Ministers 6 n 14, 144–6, 151,
    157, 230, 255, 370
budget of the 253–4
commission's appointment and accountability
    to the 250–1
committee on Constitutional Affairs 257
composition of the 28 n 117
Elections 121, 206, 250, 256, 261
    June 1999 9
    June 2009 38
general scrutiny 253
international agreements 249–50
Legal Affairs Committee of the 146 n 123
legislative powers 248–9
Presidents of the
    Jerzy Buzek 240
rights of scrutiny over delegated
    legislation 251–3
role and function of the 308–10
see also European Commission
European Union
accession to 90, 109
    criteria for membership 131–3
    procedure for membership 133–4
see also enlargement, EU
democratic legitimacy of 261
EU Civil Service Tribunal 197
EU Fundamental Rights Agency 159 n 26
functioning of the 42–4, 273, 288 n 42
member states of, *see under individual member
    states*
philosophy underlying the EU system 105
rotating Presidency of the 239
size and composition of EU institutions 140
symbols of the 16, 26
    anthem 26
    flag 26
territory of the Union 140, 179
values and objectives of 25, 48, 59, 91, 93
withdrawal from
    continuity of relations 153
    criteria for withdrawal 148–9
    EU's disintegration capacity 152
    impact on EU institutions and
        budget 153
    procedure for withdrawal 148, 150
    threat of withdrawal 151

withdrawal after Lisbon 128–54
withdrawal mechanisms 147
unilateral withdrawal 142, 147, 149, 152
see also Charter of Fundamental Rights;
    language; treaty structure, of the EU
European Social Charter 160
European Stability Mechanism 38 n 162, 242
see also financial crises
Europol 259
Evian accords 144
excise duties 95
external relations 265–330
and energy 393–8
see also DG RELEX

Fabius, Laurent 257
family
law 123 nn 38, 39, 168 n 70, 259
life 161–2
reunification 157
favor validitatis 96
federalism
European 111
federal model 147 n 141, 148 n 142
federal systems 216, 305–6, 310
federalization 306
see also European Federation
financial crises 38 n 162, 241, 361
see also banking; crisis management; European
    Stability Mechanism; Greece: Greek
    debt crisis; Iceland
financial and fiscal incentives 324–5
see also taxation
financial provisions 5 n 6
financial services 76, 252, 284, 316–17
Finland 258
Finnish Parliament 258
flexibility clause 43, 50, 56 n 57, 57, 86–7,
    90–3, 99, 123, 255, 393
declining role of 103–6
foreign affairs
Foreign Affairs Council (EU) 230–1, 234–5,
    239, 244, 286–7, 289
Foreign Affairs and Security Policy 26, 42,
    150, 250, 285
High Representative for 250, 285–7
Foreign Office, *see* EEAS
Foreign Direct Investment (FDI)
challenges in shaping a common EU
    investment policy 321–2
free movement of capital and implied
    powers 315–18
measures under the new competences 318–20
the notion of 'foreign direct investment'
    314–15
recalibrating investment protection
    guarantees 322–3
and sustainable development 324–6

Towards an EU Policy on 312–27
see also bilateral investment treaties (BITs);
    Common Commercial Policy (CCP);
    investment; portfolio investment;
    trade
foreign policy: *see* Common Foreign and
    Security Policy (CFSP); Common
    Security and Defence Policy; foreign
    affairs
Foreign Relations Council 238
FOU (Full Ownership Unbundling) 376
France 26, 115, 138, 209, 235, 243, 321 n
    34, 376
Constitution, French 29, 144 n 107
Constitutional Treaty in 352
French National Assembly 143, 257
French Secretary of State for EU affairs 352
Presidency of
    Jacques Chirac 19
    Valéry Giscard d'Estaing 11–17, 32 n 139
    Charles de Gaulle 144 n 106
    Georges Pompidou 138
    Nicolas Sarkozy 22–3, 26, 354 n 13
referenda in 19–20, 22–3, 29, 110, 347, 413
    petit oui (Sept 1992) 7
    May 2005 352–4
see also Algeria; Paris
Franco-German Declaration of Nantes 118
fraud 344
see also bribery; corruption
free market model 20
free movement
of citizens 104–5
of goods 20 n 80, 144 n 103, 165,
    368, 397
obstacles on 223
of workers 124
see also capital movement
freedom
of assembly 186
of association 124
of expression 135 n 48, 161
to provide services 165, 362, 406–7
see also religion and belief
Freedom, Security and Justice, Area of
    (AFSJ) 331–2, 334, 337, 340, 342,
    345 n 41, 346
see also Justice and Home Affairs (JHA)
Fukushima 246
see also international crises
Fuller, Dr Thomas 199
functionalism 106
funds
freezing of 284, 317, 341
structural 254
transfer of 284

game theory 151

gas
  Caspian Gas Purchasing Group 388
  crises
    gas crisis in January 2009 385
    Russian-Ukrainian gas crisis 385
  ENTSO-G (the network of gas
      transmission system operators) 384
  Europe's gas supply 382, 385
  GCG (Gas Co-ordination Group) 387
  markets 367–8, 375, 377–9, 389, 395–6,
      399–402
  gas security of supply 384–7, 390, 392
  see also energy: policy; Eurogas
Gemerek, Bronisław 11 n 37
General Affairs Council 230
General Court, *see* Court of First Instance
Geneva Convention 160
Germany 21–2, 32–3, 37, 59 n 67, 141, 171,
      209, 243, 256, 303, 321 n 34, 348,
      376, 398
  Basic law of the Federal Republic
      (*Grundgesetz*) 32, 161
  Bundesrat 9, 33
  Chancellors of
    Angela Merkel 21, 32 n 139
  German Constitution 76, 224
  German Constitutional Court
      (*Bunderverfassungsgericht*) 7, 32–3, 67, 69,
      94, 97, 106
  German *Länder* 9, 33 n 145, 306
  Grundrechte 161
  Higher Regional Court, Stuttgart 171
  Karlsruhe 29, 94 n 26
  'laserdrome' games, banning of 224
  Lissabon Urteil 105
  Presidency of 22–3, 115, 155
  Staatenverbund 32
  West Germany 144 see *also* Berlin
Gibraltar 206
Giscard Convention 105
Giscard d'Estaing, Valéry 11–17, 32 n 139
globalization 10–11, 87, 313
Goldsmith, Lord, QC 166 n 61, 167–8
Grand Chamber 173 n 92, 175, 186, 333 n 8
Greece 5 n 5, 6 n 11, 129 n 6, 133 n 40,
      170, 242
  Greek debt crisis 243–4
Greenland 143, 145–7, 150, 154
  1982 referendum 145
  fishery issues in 146
  Greenlandic parliament and government 145
  population size in 146
Greens 255
Group of Wise Men 117

Hain, Peter 147 n 137, 304
Haiti 246
  see also international crises
Hänsch, Klaus 12 n 40

health
  animal 225
  environmental 325 n 52
  food 96
  health care 80, 166
  natural 79, 96
  occupational health and safety legislation
      325 n 50
  public 43, 47–8, 100, 298, 300, 325 n 52,
      369, 371, 408
  services 305–7
  see also tobacco; WHO
Herzog, Roman 157
hierarchy of norms 62–3, 66, 84, 118
High Contracting Party 186, 188
history 307 n 69
home affairs, *see* Justice and Home Affairs
      (JHA)
human rights
  breaches of 194
  fundamental principles of 42, 48, 156, 171,
      178–211, 267, 296–8, 324, 326,
      358 n 25
  litigation 155, 177
  policy 158 n 18
  respect for 91–2, 129–31, 133 n 35, 135, 139
  Universal Declaration of 161
  see also American Convention on Human
      Rights; ECHR; European Court of
      Human Rights
humanitarian aid/ assistance 43, 102, 245, 268,
      288, 294, 369, 372
  see also international crises; rescue services
Hungary 59 n 67, 137 n 56, 321, 395, 398
  Hungarian Constitutional Court 148 n 144
hunting 165

Iceland 135, 153 n 170
IEA (International Energy Agency) 367
IMF (International Monetary Fund) 314
immigration 6, 8, 43, 80, 105, 174, 179, 203,
      222, 334, 358
  see also border control; asylum; migration;
      refugees
implementation
  implementing powers 51, 72–3, 76–9,
      81–2, 252
  notion of 78
implied powers, doctrine of 393–4
Indian Ocean
  Réunion 143 n 100
indirect expropriation 322–3
industrial relations 326
industry 43, 100, 326, 378, 398, 404, 419
Infantino, G. 409 n 18
information disclosure 326
information society 80
institutional balance 228–47
institutional reform 229–32

driving forces behind 232–5
inter-institutional relations in practice
    239–47
and the Lisbon Treaty 229–32
new complexity of EU inter- institutional
    relations 235–9
insurance 324–5, 386–7
intellectual property 43, 299–301, 306,
    315, 409
intergovernmental conferences (IGCs)
    2003–2009 114–17
European Union IGC 30 n 125
IGC Legal Experts Group 15, 25 n 99
IGC Working Party of Legal Experts 15
see also Piris Group
intergovernmentalism 6, 229, 290
International Criminal Court 176
international crises 246
earthquake in Haiti (2010) 246
Libya conflict (2010) 246
nuclear disaster in Fukushima (2011) 246
see also crisis management; disaster relief;
    humanitarian aid/ assistance; rescue
    services; terrorism: 9/11 attacks
International Labour Organization (ILO) 16,
    110, 135 n 48, 326 n 52
international law
binding 34, 105, 180
development of 91, 296, 358 n 75, 395
International Law Commission 190
principles of 86, 92, 94, 116–17, 185, 267,
    297, 320, 377, 395
public 4, 7, 108, 142
Society of International Law 312 n 1
of treaties 109
see also principle: of conferral
international relations 52 n 31, 87, 89 n 14, 92,
    267, 286
investment
international investment law 312, 321,
    323, 327
investment arbitration practice 323
investment liberalization 295, 302–3, 318
investment promotion 324–5
see also commercial policy; Foreign Direct
    Investment (FDI); MAI; portfolio
    investment; trade
IPEX system 260
Iran 284
Ireland 5 n 5, 8 n 23, 18, 22 n 88, 27–9, 33–5,
    59 n 67, 116, 121, 125, 235, 242,
    390, 398, 413
constitutional provisions 34
defence in 35 n 153
ethical issues in 33
farming sector in 33
International Fund for Ireland 276
Irish Commissioner 33
Irish government 33–4, 116, 370

Irish neutrality 33–4
Irish referenda 9
Irish Supreme Court 18
Package for Ireland 116
Presidency of 115
taxation in 33
Taoiseachs of
    Bertie Ahern 32 n 139
    Brian Cowen 34
UK-Ireland Protocol 164, 169–70
worker's rights systems in 33
see also Dublin; hunting
ISO (Independent System Operator) 376
Israel 129 n 6
Italy 97, 143 n 101, 144, 209
Italian postal service 172
Presidency of 15, 115 n 20, 123
Prime Ministers of
    Giuliano Amato 11
see also Rome
**ITO (Independent Transmission
    Operator)** 376, 378

Jordan 324 n 44
Jouyet, Jean-Pierre 353 n 10
Judges
appointments to the courts 208–11
Bratza 175, 177 n 117
Costa 175
Fuhrmann 175
Jociené 177 n 117
Kovler 176
Lorenzen 177 n 117
Malinverni 176
Nicolaou 177 n 117
Ress 177–8
Sajó 177 n 117
Tulkens 175
Villiger 177 n 117
judicial
cooperation 43, 202–3, 273, 334–5, 337
independence 210–11
ratio decidendi 217
review 31, 52–3, 72–3, 97, 198–9, 206, 211,
    215, 221–7, 253, 383
jurisdiction
Enforcement actions by the Commission 198
of the European Court of Justice 42–3, 50,
    59, 202–3
Judicial review of Union measures 198
Justice and Home Affairs (JHA) 6, 17, 26–8,
    34–7, 137, 170, 202, 230, 257, 333,
    337, 345
2998th Council Meeting 186 n 13
see also Freedom, Security and Justice

Kerr, Sir John 12 n 41, 13
Klaus, Václav 36
Kosovo, *see* United Nations: UNMIK

Laeken Declaration 8, 10, 12–14, 18, 64, 111,
    113–14, 118, 120, 158
land use 370
language
    constitutional 62
    official languages of the EU 140
    linguistic diversity 306–7, 358 n 25
    typical of international treaty law 108
    Treaty languages 126
    see also translation
Latvia 137 n 56, 241
    see also Riga
lawmaking
    aspects of 62
    delegated 77
    powers 63, 74, 215
    procedures 63
    process 62–4, 66, 69, 77, 83–4, 98
    in the shadow of constitutional arrangements
        79–83
    state-oriented model of 84
    subordinate 62, 74
    Union 62, 79
lex generalis 60 n 71, 274
lex metior rule 176
lex specialis, doctrine of 60 n 71, 164, 187 n 15,
    272, 274, 339, 342–3, 346, 399
liberalism 26, 352
Liberals 255
Libya 246
    see also international crises
Liechtenstein 153 n 170
Lithuania 137 n 56, 398
Lloyd Jones, J. 117
London 29–36
    see also United Kingdom; universities and
        institutions
Lugano Opinion 89, 99
Luxembourg 133 n 35, 155, 171, 178, 214, 409
    Luxembourg Accords 151 n 161
    Prime Minister J-C Juncker 242
    referenda in 19
    see also European Council: meetings

MAI (Multilateral Agreement on
        Investment) 322 n 36
macro-economic coordination 241, 246
Malta 137 n 56, 57, 256
Mance, Lord 167 n 68
marine biology 98, 100, 369, 371
    see also agriculture and fisheries
marriage 176
    same-sex marriage 175–6
        see also sexuality
maternity protection 162 n 44
medicine and veterinary science
    European Medicines Agency 82 n 125
    medicinal products 82 n 125, 319
    see also pharmaceuticals

Member States, EU, *see under individual
        country*
Méndez de Vigo y Montojo, Iñigo 12 n 40, 157
Mercosur 395
Merkel, Angela 21, 32 n 139
Meroni doctrine 63, 82, 379–80
Messina Conference 3
migration 56, 203
    see also asylum; border control; immigration;
        refugees
Miliband, David 11 n 37
military, the
    advice 287
    assets 266
    funding 35
    matters 52, 245
    operations 285, 290
    see also conflict management
minority rights 132 n 29, 134–5
    see also equality
Modus Vivendi 252
money laundering 172, 336, 341, 343
Montenegro 394
morality 168 n 70, 179
movement of capital, *see* capital movement
museums 307 n 69
music 307 n 69
mutual recognition 64, 335–6
    see also criminal law

NAFTA (North American Free Trade
        Agreement) 325
NAP (National Allocation Plan) 226
    see also environment
national parliaments, role of 9, 11, 12 n 42, 26,
        32 n 139, 42, 64 n 12, 96, 158 n 16,
        214 n 3, 220, 224, 248, 256–61
    Protocol on the 73, 136 n 49
    see also European Parliament
Netherlands, the 19–20, 22–3, 26, 115, 143 n
        101, 210, 235, 321 n 34, 347, 413
    Prime Ministers of
        Jan Peter Balkenende 32 n 139
    Referenda, Dutch
        May 2005 20, 23 n 91
    State Council (Raad van State) 29
Netherlands Antilles, the 5 n 6
Neighbourhood Policy 46, 49
newspapers 353–4
    Economist, The 13 n 45, 48, 33, 149 n 149
    EU Observer 19 n 72, 159 n 26
    Financial Times 354 n 13
    Guardian, The 17 n 63, 20 n 79, 80,
        159 n 25
    International Business Times 354 n 13
    Monde, Le 20 n 79
    Sun, The 166
    Times, The 166 n 59
Nice Declaration 8–9, 36, 410, 415

Nordic countries 258
see also Denmark; Finland; Greenland;
Iceland; Norway; Sweden
Norway 135, 138, 153 n 170
NRA (National Regulatory Authority) 376–8,
387, 395, 400
nullum crimen principle 176

OCTs (Overseas Countries and
Territories) 143
OECD (Organisation for Economic
Co-operation and Development)
302 n 46, 314, 322 n 36, 326
Oettinger, Commissioner 396
Oman 324 n 44
Open Method of Co-ordination (OMC) 63
opinion polls/ polling 33, 345
TNS-Sofres 20 n 79
see also eurobarometer surveys
orange card procedure 258–9
see also yellow card procedure

Papandreou, George 12 n 40
parallel trade 360 see *also* trade
Paris 353 n 10, 386
Gare du Nord 13 n 47 *see also* France
passerelles 30, 33, 122–3, 232
Pastis principle 308
patents 319
Patten, Chris 243
peace
international 56, 91, 274, 296 n 22
peace-keeping 266
peace-making 266
preservation of 68, 92 n 23, 139 n 69, 267–8,
275, 358 n 25, 372 n 9
see also conflict management; war
penal populism 331, 345–6
Penelope Project 13
pensions 80
Peru 324 n 44
Peterle, Alojz 12 n 40
pharmaceuticals
pharmaceutical products 82, 319
see also medicine and veterinary science
pillar talk 265–91
see also three-pillar system
Piris Group 15, 28
PJCCM (Police and Judicial Cooperation in
Criminal Matters) 273
see also criminal law; police
placement services 162 n 44, 169
Poland 19, 22 n 88, 27 n 111, 35, 137 n 56,
162 n 44, 209, 226, 235, 321
Foreign Ministers of
Bronisław Gemerek 11 n 37
UK-Poland Protocol 36, 159, 162 n 44, 164,
166–71, 178
see also Warsaw

police
cooperation 25, 27, 31, 43, 202–3, 334–5,
337 n 15
matters 17, 23, 38, 186, 338 n 18
see also criminal law; PJCCM
policy-framing 50
political cartoons 19 n 74, 28
political science 111 n 9
politics
European Union 4, 228, 244, 279
global 233
high vs low 238–9
and history 60
and religion 140
portfolio investment 302, 314–18, 327
see also Foreign Direct Investment
(FDI); investment
Portugal 5 n 5, 19, 22 n 88
Presidency of 27
poverty
eradication of 91, 92 n 23, 267, 296,
358 n 25
European Platform against Poverty 80 n 103
risk of 80 n 101
see also developing countries; quality of life;
standard of living
Prague 29–36
see also Czech Republic
principle
of coherence 90
of conditionality 132
of conferral 42, 44, 48, 93, 95, 105, 227,
305, 404
of consistency 42, 46, 48, 93, 238, 279, 287,
289, 324 n 45, 388, 401
of effectiveness 332–3, 339
of enhanced cooperation 8 n 26, 45 n 14,
46, 336
of exclusivity 52, 89
of institutional balance 56
of legality 339
of parallelism 89, 306, 397
precautionary 161 n 41
of pre-emption 87–9, 100–2, 106
of primacy 26, 52–5, 102, 109, 147, 205, 283
of the rule of law 281, 283
of sincere cooperation 48, 52–3, 59, 100–1,
151, 284, 305, 356 n 18
see also discrimination; equality;institutional
balance; proportionality;subsidiarity
Prodi, Romano 13 n 47, 157 n 10
professional life 169
promotion services 324–5
property
industrial property rights 319
movable and immovable 315
national property law 376
ownership of 303, 319
real estate 314, 316

property (*cont.*)
  right to, the 161, 320
  see also intellectual property
proportionality, principle of 42, 44, 48, 51–2,
    59, 93–4, 101, 104, 106, 162, 171,
    203, 214–15, 217, 224, 298, 323,
    331–2, 338 n 18, 346, 392, 401
  Commission on Subsidiarity and
    Proportionality 221 n 36
  and criminal law 344–5
  degressive 256
  digressive 141
  and subsidiarity: a better control 95–8
  Subsidiarity and Proportionality
    Protocol 98 n 34, 220, 222 n 40, 227, 257 n
      14, 260 n 22, 344, 354 n 15
  see also subsidiarity
protectionism 313
PSC (Political and Security Committee) 285
Public Service Obligation (PSO) 400
public services 31 n 135, 298, 364, 400
  see also education; health; water;
      punishment 162
  capital 184 n 11
  see also criminal justice; torture

QMV (Qualified Majority Voting) 30 n 128,
    64 n 11, 69 n 45, 70 n 46, 47, 250,
    259, 308 n 72
quality of life 351 n 7, 369 n 5
  see also poverty; standard of living

racism 334
  see also xenophobia
Rasmussen, Anders Fogh 19
reasonableness 323
Reding, Viviane 159 n 26
referenda, *see under individual EU Member
    States*
refugees 160, 170
  see also asylum; border control; immigration;
      migration
Regulatory Procedure with Scrutiny (RPS) 252
religion and belief 48, 93 n 25, 139–40
  churches 48, 140 n 73
  Christianity 48, 140
  freedom of 135 n 48
  humanism 139–40
  Islam 139
  religious organizations 48
  see also discrimination
rescue services 203, 266, 287
  see also humanitarian aid/ assistance
research and development 80 n 101
  Center for Applied Policy Research,
    Munich 152 n 166
  Center for European, Governance and
    Economic Development research
    151 n 156

Electricity Policy Research Group, Cambridge
    University 385 n 40, 386 n 42
  freedom of the arts and sciences 160 n 36
  see also science and technology; space;
      universities and institutions
Riga 386
  see also Latvia
Romania 22, 136 n 52, 137 n 56, 140, 321, 395
Rome 386
  see also Italy
Royal Institute of International Affairs 9 n 32,
    27 n 110
rule-making 74 n 70, 379 n 20
  by private actors 83–4
  see also law making
Russia 205 n 12, 385

sanctions 43, 45 n 16, 48, 59, 123, 198,
    241, 276, 289, 291, 297, 332, 335,
    341–2
Santer Commission 9, 251, 253
Sarkozy, Nicolas 22–3, 26, 354 n 13
Schengen area 8, 28, 45 n 14, 135
Schuman Declaration 3
science and technology 326
  scientific and technological advance 91, 354
    n 14, 358 n 25
  see also medicine and veterinary science;
      pharmaceuticals; research and
      development; space
Scotland 17, 154 n 174, 376
  see also United Kingdom
seasonal employment 222 n 41
  see also third-country nationals
secession 142 n 91, 144, 146–7, 152, 154
security
  internal 57, 203, 338 n 18
  international 11, 92 n 23, 266–8, 274–5,
    372 n 9
  public 52 n 31, 317
  see also Common Foreign and Security Policy
      (CFSP); peace
Segi 53 n 41, 281
  see also Basque Country; terrorism
Serbia 394
Services of General Economic Interest
    (SGEIs) 347–66
  and energy 399–401
  in the Treaty of Lisbon 362–5
  see also competition: policy
sexuality
  homosexuality 140
  rights of transsexuals 175–6
  see also discrimination; marriage
Simplification Working Group 14
social Europe 12 n 42, 18, 20
social exclusion 91, 298, 358
social inclusion 80, 215 n 6
social progress 91, 351, 354 n 14, 355, 358 n 25

social protection 43, 48, 80, 105, 169, 215 n 6,
  315 n 7, 369 n 5
social security 23, 105, 123 n 38, 166
social services 300, 307 n 69, 365 n 44
Socialists 255
sociology 354
Sofia 386
  see also Bulgaria
Solana, Javier 239, 243, 285
solidarity rights 168
South America
  French Guiana 143 n 100
Slovak Republic (Slovakia) 137 n 56, 386, 398
Slovenia 133 n 36, 137, 210, 386, 390, 391
  n 60
Small Arms and Light Weapons (SALW)
  270–6, 290
space 43, 49, 87, 102, 104, 369, 372
  see also research and development; science and
    technology
Spain 5, 19, 38, 115, 209, 235, 319, 390–1
  Prime Ministers of
    José Zapatero 32 n 139
  Spanish Constitutional Tribunal 148 n 144
  Spanish Presidency 238, 244
Spinelli, Altiero 111
sports law, EU 403–19
  athletics 405, 407, 416
  conditional autonomy of sports
    federations 407
  Declaration on Sport 409
  EU Sports Council 415
  European Year of Sport 415
  evolution of 416–19
  football 404–6, 417–18
  Freiburg draft 411–12
  Lisbon Treaty, the 413–14
    impact of 414–15
    negotiating 411–13
    road to Lisbon 404–5
  specificity of sport, the 408–9
  sporting discrimination 404
  'sporting exception,' politics of the 409–10
  practice of 405–9
  see also education and training; ENIC; UEFA;
    youth
standardization, European 83–4
Stockholm Programme 203, 345 n 41
standard of living 351 n 7, 369 n 5
  see also poverty; quality of life state aid 99,
    223, 293, 348–9, 357, 361–6, 390,
    392, 399
  action plan (2005) 361
  and energy 390–2
Strasbourg Court 175, 177–8, 205–6
strategic leadership 229, 239, 242
Straw, Jack 12–13, 16, 167
Stuart, Gisela 12 n 40

Stuttgart Declaration 5
subsidiarity
  application of 215, 220, 222
  Commission on Subsidiarity and
    Proportionality 215 n 5, 221 n 34
  and criminal law 344–6
  and the European Court of Justice 216–20
  infringement of 260
  judicial review of 222–6
  Lisbon, subsidiarity and the Court 220–2
  and a minimalist approach to criminal
    law 332
  principle of 12 n 42, 42, 44, 48, 51, 59, 72,
    88, 93–4, 101, 104, 106, 164, 227,
    257–61, 164, 227, 257–61, 331,
    353–4, 377, 384
  and proportionality: a better control 95–8
  subsidiarity in the courtroom 213–27
  subsidiarity so far 214–16
  Subsidiarity and Proportionality Protocol 98
    n 34, 220, 222 n 40, 227, 257 n 14,
    260 n 22, 344, 354 n 15
  see also proportionality
supranationalism 236, 290
sustainable development
  of economic activity 91, 351 n 7, 354 n 14,
    358 n 25
  and Foreign Direct Investment (FDI) 324–6
  sustainable management of global natural
    resources 48, 91, 92 n 23, 92 n 23,
    267, 296–7
  see also environment
Sweden 22 n 88, 59 n 67, 398
  Swedish Parliament 222
  Swedish Presidency 203
  see also Stockholm Programme
Switzerland 153

taxation 33, 43, 326, 372
  eco-/ energy 374, 392
  indirect 95
  tax credits 324 n 47
  tax deferrals 324 n 47
  tax exemptions 324 n 47
  tax harmonization 88
  tax rates 223
  see also budget, the; financial and fiscal
    incentives; Ireland
technical assistance 284
technical cooperation 43, 274, 276, 294
telecoms 378
telephones, mobile 218 n 18
  roaming charges 218
television 307 n 69
  TF1 television 20 n 79
  see also BBC
terrorism
  9/11 attacks 344

terrorism (*cont.*)
  counter-fanaticism 10
  counter-terrorism 57, 266, 317,
    341–2, 345
  as a criminal act 284, 336, 340 n 24
  financing of 341
  war on terrorism 290
  see also Segi; war
theatre services 307 n 69
third-country nationals 102, 222, 314
  as seasonal workers 222
Third Package, the 375–81, 384, 389
three-pillar system 7, 41, 63, 202, 265, 413
  see also pillar talk
tobacco 56 n 55, 171, 217, 227
torture 162, 183–4
  see also punishment
tourism 43, 87, 100–1
town and country planning 370
TMC Asser Instituut 416 n 41
TPA (Third Party Access) 395–6
trade
  external 49, 292–7, 309–11, 397
  free and fair 91, 296, 358 n 25
  in goods 299–301, 304
  international 92 n 23, 267, 294, 296, 300–3,
    308, 313, 394 n 71
  liberalization 294–5, 297–8, 313
  policy 292–300, 308–11, 394
  sanctions 297
  in services 295 n 19, 300–1, 306, 313
  Trade Policy Committee 308
  see also Council for Trade in Services;
    commercial policy; intellectual
    property; investment; NAFTA;
    parallel trade; WTO
Trade-Related Investment Measures
  (TRIMs) 313
trade union rights 135 n 48
trans-European networks 87, 100, 369, 371,
    382–3
  see also energy: TEN-E
translation 245, 260
  see also language
transport 43, 49, 86, 100, 369, 371
  Intelligent Transport Systems 75 n 75,
    76 n 78
  International Transport Workers'
    Federation 169 n 74, 419 n 47
  modes of transport 75 n 75, 76 n 78
  road transport 75 n 75, 76 n 78
treaty, terminology of 116 n 26
treaty amendment
  adjustments to the treaties 125, 129, 130,
    136–7
  procedure 118–19, 127 n 44
  process 24, 37–8
treaty-implementing 305
treaty-making 46, 50, 305, 315

drafters of the Lisbon Treaty 51 n 28, 60, 62,
    65, 302–3
treaty reform process 23 n 96, 233, 274 n 20
treaty revision procedures 107–27, 257
  past and future of treaty revision 126–7
  treaty revision tradition (1951–2009) 107–11
  treaty revision round (2002–2009) 111–17
  reform of, by the Lisbon treaty 117–26
    debates (1999–2009) 117–19
    ordinary revision procedures 47, 59, 94,
      117, 119–22, 124–6, 254
    revision through accession or
      withdrawal 125–6
    simplified revision procedures 33, 38 n
      162, 45, 47, 94, 104–5, 117, 119,
      122–5, 254, 259
treaty simplification 158 n 16
treaty structure, of the EU 18, 36, 40–61, 242
  applying common and general provisions
    48–9
  linking the two treaties 44–8
  separating the two treaties? 54–8
  special nature of the CFSP 49–54
  two treaty solution 41–4
Trevi Group of Interior Ministers 5
TSOs (Transmission System Operators)
    375–8, 384, 395
  see also electricity; energy: gas: ENTSO-G
Turkey 129 n 6, 133–7, 140–1, 153, 395
  Negotiating Framework for
    Turkish accession 133 n 35, 135 nn 47, 48,
    137, 141

UACES Conference 229 n 3, 236 n 22, 239 n 26
UEFA 406, 409 n 18, 410, 417
  Director of Legal Affairs: G Infantino 409 n 18
  see also sports law
Ukraine 385
UNCTAD 324 n 48
Union Minister for Foreign Affairs 17, 26
United Kingdom (UK) 5 n 5, 28, 143, 149 n
    150, 167–70, 180, 203, 209–10, 321
    n 34, 371
  High Court in England 165
  Home Department
    Secretary of State for the 156 n 7, 170 n
      77, 80
    House of Commons 9 nn 30, 32, 23 n 91,
      30 n 130, 31 n 137, 32 n 139,
      33 n 147
    Coalition Government 31 n 137
    European Scrutiny Committee 30 n 125
    Foreign Affairs Committee 23 n 95, 24 n
      97, 30 n 125
    Ian Davidson, MP 32 n139
  House of Lords 19, 165 n 56, 222
    Constitution Committee 30 n 125
    European Union, Committee of the
      167, 219

Select Committee on the EU 415 n 35
Foreign and Commonwealth Office 3 n 1, 4 n
   3, 23 n 92
Foreign Secretaries of
   Margaret Beckett 23 n 91
   David Miliband 11 n 37
   Jack Straw 12–13, 16, 167
Minister for Europe
   Keith Vaz 166
   Peter Hain 147 n 137, 304
Prime Ministers of
   Tony Blair 19, 29–30, 166
   Gordon Brown 29–30
Supreme Court, the 167 n 68
UK Association of European Law 3 n 1
UK case law on the Charter of Fundamental
   Rights 170–1
UK-Ireland Protocol 164, 169–70
UK-Poland Protocol 36, 159, 162 n 44, 164,
   166–71, 178
see also BBC; British Diplomatic Service;
   British Labour Party; criminal law:
   English; hunting; London; Scotland
United Nations
   Global Compact Principles 326 n 53
   High Commissioner for Refugees 170
   Organization 110
   UN Charter 12, 92, 266–7, 296–7,
      358 n 25
   UNESCO (UN Educational, Social and
      Cultural Organization) 16
   UNMIK (UN Interim Administration
      Mission in Kosovo) 394
   UN Security Council 287
United States of America (USA)
   Bill of Rights 178
   death row 171
   historical evolution of the 16
   investment policy in 321 n 35
   model BIT of the 323 n 41
   Secretary of State
      Hillary Clinton 240
   and the transfer of banking data 240, 250
   United States-Oman Free Trade relations
      324 n 44
   United States-Peru Trade relations
      324 n 44
   US antitrust law 357
   US Constitution 356
   US Supreme Court 356
   see also American Convention on Human
      Rights; elections: US Congressional;
      NAFTA
universities and institutions
   Cambridge University 13 n 46, 386 n 42
   European University Institute 118, 301 n 44
   Robert Schuman Centre 118
   Georg-August-Universität, Göttingen 151 n 156

*Institut d'études europénnes (l'Université libre de
   Bruxelles)* 209 n 17
King's College, London 3 n 1
Milan University 89 n 16
University of Warsaw 398
University of Zagreb, Croatia 226 n 53
see also education; research and development
Uruguay Round 312

value pluralism 140
Van Rompuy, Herman 37, 237, 242–4
Vaz, Keith 166
Vienna Convention 108–9, 126, 142
visa policy 203
Vitorino, António 12 n 40, 157
VIU (Vertically Integrated Undertaking) 376 n,
   15, 16, 17
voting systems 235
   see also referenda

war
   Cold War 10
   in the event of 372 n 9
   World War II 10, 36
   see also conflict management; peace; terrorism
Warsaw 386
   see also Poland; universities and institutions:
      University of Warsaw
waste management 370
   see also environment
water 298, 370, 389
   see also energy; environment
welfare state model 352
West Indies 143 n 100
   Guadeloupe 143 n 100
   Martinique 143 n 100
Westendorp Reflection Group 7
whipping system 255
WHO (World Health Organization) 110
   see also health
women's rights 135 n 48
   see also equality
workers' rights 33, 35, 166
working conditions 162 n 44, 169, 351
world economy 92 n 23, 232 n 11,
   267, 296
WTO (World Trade Organization) 292 n 6,
   295, 297, 299 n 32, 300–1, 304,
   307, 309, 313, 316 n 15, 322 n 36,
   326, 394
   Dispute Settlement Understanding
      (DSU) 309
   see also trade

xenophobia 334
   see also racism
   yellow card procedure 220–1, 226, 258–9
   see also orange card procedure

youth 80, 100, 412–14
  young people at work 169
  Youth Convention 12
  Youth Forum 14
    see also children; education and training;
        sports law

**Yugoslav Republic of Macedonia, the former
  (FYROM)** 134, 394
**Yugoslavia, the former: International Criminal
  Tribunal for** 176

Zapatero, José 32 n 139